Part 4: Civil Procedure

The American Illness and Comparative Civil Procedure 159
Daniel Jutras

The Proportionality Principle and the Amount in Controversy 175
Peter B. Rutledge

The Allocation of Discovery Costs and the Foundations of
Modern Procedure 201
Martin H. Redish

Does Increased Litigation Increase Justice in a Second-Best World? 211
Jeremy Kidd and Todd J. Zywicki

Part 5: Tort Law

A Tamer Tort Law: The Canada-U.S. Divide 229
Michael Trebilcock and Paul-Erik Veel

The Expansion of Modern U.S. Tort Law and Its Excesses 249
George L. Priest

Regulation, Taxation, and Litigation 270
W. Kip Viscusi

Part 6: Contract Law

An English Lawyer Looks at American Contract Law 291
Michael Bridge

Text versus Context: The Failure of the Unitary Law of Contract
Interpretation 312
Robert E. Scott

Exit and the American Illness 336
Erin O'Hara O'Connor and Larry E. Ribstein

The Dramatic Rise of Consumer Protection Law 361
Joshua D. Wright and Eric Helland

CONTENTS

Acknowledgments   xi

PART 1: INTRODUCTION

The Rule of Law in America   3
F.H. Buckley

PART 2: RELATIVE DECLINE

An Exceptional Nation?   43
F.H. Buckley

PART 3: EMPIRICAL EVIDENCE

Are Americans More Litigious? Some Quantitative
Evidence   69
J. Mark Ramseyer and Eric B. Rasmusen

Lawyers as Spam: Congressional Capture Explains Why
U.S. Lawyers Exceed the Optimum   100
Stephen P. Magee

Regulation and Litigation: Complements or Substitutes?   118
Eric Helland and Jonathan Klick

Does Product Liability Law Make Us Safer?   137
W. Kip Viscusi

For Esther and Sarah

Published with assistance from the foundation established in memory of
Philip Hamilton McMillan of the Class of 1894, Yale College.

Yale University Press books may be purchased in quantity for educational, business, or promotional use. For information, please e-mail
sales.press@yale.edu (U.S. office) or sales@yaleup.co.uk (U.K. office).

Designed by James J. Johnson.
Set in Scala type by Westchester Book Group.
Printed in the United States of America.

Library of Congress Cataloging-in-Publication Data

The American illness : essays on the rule of law /
edited by F.H. Buckley.
pages cm
Includes bibliographical references and index.
ISBN 978-0-300-17521-9

1. Law—United States.   I. Buckley, F. H. (Francis H.),
1948–editor of compilation.
KF389.A44 2013
340'.11—dc23
2012037080

A catalogue record for this book is available from the British Library.

This paper meets the requirements of ANSI/NISO Z39.48-1992
(Permanence of Paper).

10 9 8 7 6 5 4 3 2 1

EDITED BY F.H. BUCKLEY

The American Illness

ESSAYS ON THE RULE OF LAW

Yale UNIVERSITY PRESS

NEW HAVEN & LONDON

THE AMERICAN ILLNESS

Part 7: Corporate and Securities Law

How American Corporate and Securities Law Drives
Business Offshore 381
Stephen M. Bainbridge

Part 8: Criminal Law

Corporate Crime, Overcriminalization, and the Failure
of American Public Morality 407
Jeffrey S. Parker

Part 9: How Nations Grow (or Don't)

The Legacy of Progressive Thought: Decline, Not Death,
by a Thousand Cuts 435
Richard A. Epstein

Overtaking 472
Robert Cooter and Aaron Edlin

The Rule of Law and China 487
Francis Fukuyama

Part 10: Changing Course

Reversing 505
F.H. Buckley

Contributors 527

Index 531

ACKNOWLEDGMENTS

These essays are the proceedings of a conference held on December 3–4, 2010, in Alexandria, Virginia, and each essay benefited from the comments of the other participants. Pam Entsminger Ryon helped organize the conference from which the book emerged, and Christopher Gardner and Robert Hopkins provided useful assistance.

My own chapters benefited greatly from comments by Al Cortese, Richard Epstein, Jacob Goldberg, Hon. Edith Jones, Jon Klick, John Lott, Bill Niskanen, Mark Ramseyer, Peter Rutledge, Hon. John Tyson, Hon. Clifford Taylor, and Mike Trebilcock. I am especially grateful to those who offered advice on cross-country constitutional law: Joe Bast, Jonathan Clark, Jeffrey Jenkins, Tom Lindsay, Harvey Mansfield, Pippa Norris, Tom Pangle, Charles Rowley, Jason Sorens, and Gordon Wood. In particular, Jane Atzenstat, Christopher Moore, and Alastair Sweeny helped me better understand the Anglo-Canadian model of self-government. Had I known more of it earlier I might not have waited so long to appreciate the discrete charm of Canadian constitutional history. I also thank George Mason University School of Law for its support.

Editors at Yale University Press, notably Michael O'Malley and Bill Frucht, gave me the benefit of their advice, and I thank them. Two anonymous referees provided very useful suggestions, and I also thank Joyce Ippolito, Jaya Chatterjee, and Ann-Marie Imbornoni for their helpful editorial advice.

Since the conference was held, two of its participants passed away. Bill Niskanen was acting chairman of President Reagan's Council of Economic Advisors and for many years chairman of the Cato Institute. He is remembered by the many friends and scholars to whom he generously gave of his time. Larry Ribstein left us too soon. He was a courageous scholar with a tough exterior that masked an inner kindness that he showed to the many younger scholars whom he mentored.

As always, my essays would have been much less readable without the invaluable editorial assistance of Esther Goldberg, to whom I owe thanks for that and much, much more.

PART 1:

INTRODUCTION

The Rule of Law in America

F.H. BUCKLEY

Fifty years ago we thought we knew how to make a country rich: self-government, good education, free markets, and loads of World Bank infrastructure grants. Nothing very complicated, in short. We know better now. The gap between rich and poor countries, which we expected to shrink, has grown larger. What we failed to recognize was the role of intangible assets: the cultural values of thrift and industry, honesty in government, and the rule of law.

What the rule of law might mean is, as we shall see, not always clear. But however one might define it, rich countries enjoy a robust rule of law, and departures from it in third-world countries have left their citizens impoverished. More recently, America itself has suffered from an economic decline, and this book asks, with the assistance of leading scholars in the legal academy, whether a decline in the rule of law has contributed to this. America sends experts to lecture people in other countries about the importance of the rule of law, but in doing so, do we fail to recognize the beam in our own eye?

America's legal system, and its reliance upon lawyers, has long made it the world's outlier. Other countries seem to depend more on informal social norms and less on legal ones. Here, however, the rule of lawyers seems almost to be coded in the country's DNA. Or so at least Edmund Burke thought, as he surveyed the men whom today we call the Founders of America. In his 1775 Speech on the Conciliation with the Colonies, Burke attributed the "untractable" spirit of the colonists to their lawyers and students of law: "This study renders men acute, inquisitive, dexterous, prompt in attack, ready in defence, full of resources. In other countries, the people, more simple, and of a less mercurial class, judge of an ill principle in government only by an actual grievance; here they anticipate the evil. . . . They augur misgovernance at a distance; and sniff the approach of tyranny in every tainted breeze."[1]

Not everyone would disapprove of the Founders' litigiousness. Moreover, America's fascination with the law has not prevented it from becoming the richest country in the world. It does not follow, however, that America's legal system has been a help and not a hindrance. Beethoven wrote the Ninth Symphony in spite of his deafness and not because of it.

The question of what the legal system has contributed is more acute today because of America's recent economic decline. Before now, the contribution of the legal system, positive or negative, had been obscured by the relative advantages the country enjoyed when compared with other nations. As we will see in my article that follows, these advantages have been largely dissipated in recent years, and America's exceptional legal system, warts and all, will now stand out in sharper focus. And that is why this book is timely.

The Rule of Law

This is the century of the rule of law. In the 20th century, economists such as Milton Friedman offered a simple prescription for economic growth. All that a country like Russia need do, he thought, was shrink the state by privatization: "Just after the Berlin Wall fell and the Soviet Union collapsed, I used to be asked a lot: 'What do these ex-communist states have to do in order to become market economies?' And I used to say: 'You can describe that in three words: privatize, privatize, privatize.' But, I was wrong. That wasn't enough. The example of Russia shows that . . . privatization is meaningless if you don't have the rule of law."[2] Friedman's prescription for growth was an important component of what came to be called the Washington Consensus, a set of classically liberal policies that dominated the literature about economic development after the fall of communism. Apart from privatization, other elements included deregulation, free trade, and low taxes. Property rights came in last in the list. As Friedman and others came to realize, however, this ignored the crucial role of social and legal institutions in promoting growth.

The recognition that the simple economic rules of the Washington Consensus could not capture the secret of growth, and that institutions mattered, came to be called neo-institutional economics.[3] Neo-institutional scholars argued that changes in growth patterns could not be explained without recourse to cultural differences. For example, Ghana and South Korea had very similar economies and per capita GDP in the 1960s. Thirty years later, the South Korean per capita GDP was 15 times that of Ghana. What explained the difference, said Samuel Huntington, was each country's culture.[4]

Culture embraces such things as the private virtues of fidelity, thrift, and industry, the social norms of promise-keeping and trust, and the practice of religion. One important component is legal culture, or the rule of law. Daniel Kauffman reports that rule of law variables are associated with significantly better development outcomes: "An improvement in the rule of law (or, say, control of corruption) from relatively poor to merely average performance would result in the long run in an estimated fourfold increase in per capita incomes, a reduction in infant mortality of a similar magnitude, and significant gains in literacy."[5]

The economist's recent discovery of the rule of law has been mirrored in the legal academy. In the 1970s and 1980s, an influential group of radical legal scholars, associated with the Critical Legal Studies Movement, rejected the goals of formal equality, certainty, and predictability, which are the hallmarks of the rule of law. For the CLSers, law was necessarily indeterminate, in failing to provide a single right answer in most or all cases. Indeterminacy was then a permission slip for socially progressive judges and lawyers to bend the law to suit their politics. Such ideas, once fashionable, now find few adherents, and most legal academics, like their peers in departments of economics, have come to recognize that departures from the rule of law are troubling.

But what is the rule of law? In what follows I distinguish between two things it might mean: the absence of government corruption and a benign set of legal norms. Let us take each in turn.

A. Corruption

Studies show that corruption has a significant negative effect on economic performance.[6] Entrepreneurs and investors cannot safely start or finance businesses in states that cannot credibly commit to respect property rights and to honor contracts.[7] As a prosperous society, then, one might expect America to rank high on measures of credible commitment and to have relatively little corruption. Surprisingly, however, the U.S. does not come out particularly well on cross-country measures of corruption. Transparency International conducts surveys of business leaders on their perceptions about bribery, kickbacks, and public sector anti-corruption efforts, and ranks the U.S. behind many of its first-world competitors.[8]

This likely understates America's corruption problem, when corruption is understood to embrace wasteful lobbying of the kind described in Steven Magee's article. What corruption is for poor countries, lobbying is for rich ones, a means of obtaining political influence through the expense of

Table 1.1   Transparency International's 2011 Corruption Perception Index

Country	Rank	Score
New Zealand	1	9.5
Denmark	2	9.4
Finland	2	9.4
Sweden	4	9.3
Norway	6	9
Australia	8	8.8
Canada	10	8.7
Germany	14	8
United Kingdom	16	7.8
United States	24	7.1

Source: Transparency International Corruption Perception Index, at cpi.transparency.org /cpi2011/results/.

money.[9] No other country has anything like the number of American lobbyists who load up legislation with interest group bargains.

This is not to suggest that lobbying is devoid of value or that it is unworthy of First Amendment protection. Lobbyists do provide useful information about the likely effect of legislation. At the same time, however, there is little reason to think that interest group pressure is invariably benign, where a concentrated rich group (e.g., an industry association) competes against a dispersed and poorly organized group (e.g., consumers).[10] When a narrowly concentrated group is able to act collectively, through lobby groups, it has an incentive to redistribute wealth to itself even if its gains are small compared with the losses it imposes on the society as a whole. In a large country such as America, the dispersed groups are relatively more spread out, and the relative clout of the concentrated groups stronger. Interest groups just might provide unbiased information—but only as an incidental by-product of their business.

B. Legal Norms

Courts might fail to adhere to the rule of law for a variety of reasons. The judges might be corrupt; they might not be independent of the government; they might shirk their duties and impose unnecessary wait times on litigants; they might be ill-trained. None of these problems beset American courts (even if American judges are greatly underpaid).[11] Instead, any departure from the rule of law in America results from the content of its legal norms, which frustrate the intentions of bargainers and permit their property to be plundered.

It is conventional to distinguish between thick and thin definitions of the rule of law.[12] A thick definition would include democratic institutions and the protection of personal and religious freedom. As I define it, a thin definition of the rule of law would include substantive private law rights: contracts are enforced and private parties are protected from looting by the state or other private parties. Countries that adhere to a thick definition are attractive places to live; countries that adhere to a thin definition are attractive places to do business.[13]

A country might have both kinds of rule of law, or one and not the other. China seems to be adopting a thin rule of law without embracing a thick version. As for the U.S., an adherence to the rule of law, thickly defined, has obscured America's relative weakness on a thin definition of the rule of law. This is a pleasant place to live, but we are shipping business and jobs offshore, often to first-world countries that adhere as closely as we do to a thick definition of the rule of law.

While I concentrate on a thin definition of the rule of law, I do not wish to minimize the importance of upholding a thick rule of law. We should want both, even if one seems at times to exclude the other. For example, Justice Roger Traynor, who eviscerated the law of contracts in California in *Pacific Gas,*[14] was also the first judge to hold that an anti-miscegenation statute was unconstitutional.[15] However, that's not to say that the choice is between a socially progressive but economically dangerous Roger Traynor and an economically sophisticated but socially illiberal judge. Other first-world countries that adhere more closely to a thin rule of law have no lessons to take from America on democracy and civil rights.

How then should we define the thin rule of law? I argue that it must have a substantive component, that its rules must permit entrepreneurs to flourish without fear of predation, that contracts should be enforced and that tort law predations should be banned. That is not what the thin rule of law is typically taken to mean. Instead, the rule of law is defined as the output of a set of formal, neutral procedural requirements. The best known such definition is that offered by Lon Fuller in his Storrs Lectures.[16]

According to Fuller, laws should be (1) general, (2) publicly promulgated, (3) prospective (i.e., not retroactive), (4) clear, (5) consistent (i.e., not contain any contradictions), (6) practicable (i.e., not demand the impossible), (7) constant over time, and (8) congruent with the actions of officials. If we accept that list as defining the rule of law, America's departures from it will be apparent to readers of this book.

Laws are general when established in the name of the whole society and applied in the same way to all parties. For the most part that is true in the U.S. However, the ability of plaintiffs to forum-shop, and the perceived tendency of some courts to stick it to out-of-state defendants, as described by Mark Ramseyer and Eric Rasmusen, suggest a troubling departure from the norm of generality.

Before laws can be said to be public, two conditions must hold. They must be publicly promulgated so that everyone can look them up, and they must not be so complicated and detailed as to be effectively unintelligible. It doesn't help to publish laws if no one can understand them. American laws are public in the first sense, but one might wonder whether they satisfy the second sense of publicity. Business regulations, promulgated in mind-numbing detail, with criminal sanctions attached, can make felons of people who are without a guilty motive or mind, a problem described in Jeffrey Parker's essay.

American private law rules are often anything but clear. Contextualist rules of contractual interpretation, described by Robert Scott and prescribed by the Uniform Commercial Code (UCC), permit courts to ignore a clearly written contract and make its meaning wholly obscure. The tort law regime discussed by George Priest makes it difficult for manufacturers to put a value on anticipated civil liability costs. Formerly, unmeritorious claims were given short shrift under the doctrine of demurrer, in which judges granted a motion for summary judgment by the defendant. The decline of demurrer in America introduces a degree of uncertainty that has little parallel in other first-world jurisdictions that dispense with juries in non-criminal matters. The loss of predictability adds a level of risk and imposes a cost on American business.

In the past, American private law rules were fairly constant over time, as George Priest and Richard Epstein note. A law student transported from 1900 to 1960 would not have found his lectures unfamiliar. However, the 1960 student transported to 1980 would be confronted with entirely new theories of law and legal rules, and would have felt like Rip Van Winkle. The changes weaken the incentives of parties to make long-term reliance investments in contracts and relationships.

Rules are congruent with the actions of officials when courts and regulators agree on standards of liability. Were that the case, federal and state regulators would "pre-empt" the courts, and a manufacturer would have a defense against a law suit if it had conformed with safety regulations. However, this pre-emption defense is not available to defendants, as Eric Helland and Jonathan Klick note in their article, and as Kip Viscusi does in his second article.

On Fuller's definition of the rule of law, then, one might not give America's private law rules high marks. But even if they scored better, is that all there is? Fuller saw the rule of law as a set of neutral procedures, where rules are established in accordance with a democratic process under a thick rule of law. What the substance of the rules might be seemed not to matter. Similar procedural and substance-free definitions of the rule of law were proposed by Dicey and Hayek,[17] the assumption being that, provided one gets the procedural inputs right, the substantive outputs will take care of themselves.

However, Fuller's procedural categories provide an inadequate definition of the rule of law. A legal regime might offer generality, publicity, clarity, consistency, constancy over time, and congruency with regulators, and still be a legal system from Hell. It might weaken property rights and impose civil liability on the flimsiest of grounds, all the while conforming to Fuller's idea of law. It might permit disappointed bargainers to walk from their contracts whenever they turn against them. It might narrow the scope of free bargaining to nothing by expanding the categories of paternalism and perfectionism.[18] It might leave an economy in ruins and still count as the rule of law.

That is a very short-sighted idea of the rule of law, if freedom matters, if wealth is better than poverty, and if one wants to fund social programs with something more substantial than pious aspirations. For this reason, I suggest that a thin rule of law must have a substantive content and must bar what Mark Ramseyer and Eric Rasmusen describe as "judicially sanctioned theft."[19] The probability that one's property will be unjustly taken from one in a tort action, that one's contracts will not be enforced, is as troubling as the depredations of a corrupt court system, if the probability of loss is the same.

We might have a sterling set of constitutional liberties, on a thick definition of the rule of law, but still see weak economic growth if the legal system imposes an excessive burden on business parties. This is well understood when it comes to excessive taxation. What is less well understood is how American private and criminal law gives business an incentive to locate abroad. A study cited by Ramseyer and Rasmusen found that multinational companies reported that they spend a disproportionate amount on litigation in the United States, relative to their expenditures in foreign jurisdictions. U.S. litigation costs were between four and nine times higher than non-U.S. costs (as a percentage of revenue).[20] These findings are echoed by the International Trade Administration at the U.S. Department of Commerce, which reports that "many foreign investors view the U.S. legal environment as a liability when investing in the United States."[21] Skeptics deride such statements as self-serving, but they are hard to ignore in the present economic environment. U.S. multinationals shed 864,000 U.S. jobs in the first decade of this century. The jobs are coming back, mind you, just not here. During the same period, U.S. multinationals increased employment overseas by 2.9 million.[22] Similarly, the U.S. share of global foreign direct investment declined from 31 percent in 1980 to 13 percent in 2006.[23]

The challenge to America is deepened by the adoption of liberal economic policies by authoritarian states, such as China. Formerly it was thought that political and economic liberty went hand in hand, and that authoritarian states that adopted liberal economic policies, as Chile did in the 1970s, would in time liberalize their political regimes. The rise of China has led some to predict that a stable authoritarian capitalism, a thin but not a thick rule of law, might prove to be a sustainable model for economic development, and threaten the economic and political dominance of the United States and the West.

Because I suggest that departures from the rule of law have harmed this country, several of the book's essays compare U.S. to foreign law. The book is thus a contribution to the nascent field of comparative-law-as-if-the-economy-mattered.[24] Distinctions between the civilian's *causa* and the common lawyer's consideration, which greatly interest comparative lawyers, never gave transactional lawyers a moment's pause. What is of greater interest, and has been largely ignored by comparitivists, is whether a country's private law regime imposes relatively high costs on businesses and gives them an incentive to relocate elsewhere—and that is the subject of this book.

Whether American judges should look to foreign precedents is deeply controversial. Liberals like the idea, conservatives hate it. But no legal system is as consistently as pro-plaintiff as that of America, and that might give both sides pause. Comparative law is a two-way street. To take but one example, discussed by Michael Trebilcock, the Canadian Supreme Court has imposed damages caps for non-pecuniary losses, but when similar rules were enacted here by state legislatures, they were often struck down by state Supreme Courts. What is mandated there is prohibited here. If we are told to look to foreign law when it comes to capital punishment, then, we might also do so for the private law questions discussed in this book.

The verdict of the world is conclusive, St. Augustine said, and when John Henry Newman read this his Anglican insularity was pulverized. The American legal academy, especially the part that defends its private law regime, is also a little insular. Unlike Newman, however, it resists the world's judgment. Where others see differences it finds convergence ("Look, class actions in France!"). And where it sees differences it ascribes them to a want of legal sophistication. There is not a little chauvinism in this, which one hopes might be tempered by a study of comparative private law.

What comparativists object to, with reason, are economists who paint with the broadest strokes and blur over critical legal differences. For example, a well-known (and much criticized) study reports that countries with a common law tradition, such as England and America, provide better investor protection than civil law countries.[25] While this usefully picks up on the differences between Kenya and Columbia, it misses the very sharp divergence between American and commonwealth law described in this book. If the comparative lawyer should seek instruction from the economist, the economist too must seek advice from the lawyer. And this book is a contribution to that literature.

The Book's Essays

A. An Exceptional Nation?

If America were still exceptionally a country of free trade, immigration, low taxes and public debt, and strong human capital, departures from the rule of law might not matter so much. Now, however, the playing field has been leveled, and differences in legal regimes assume greater importance.

- Formerly, Americans had a unique access to an enormous and very wealthy free trade zone—the United States of America—from which foreign competitors were restricted by trade walls. Lowering trade walls has benefited Americans in absolute terms, but has also resulted in a relative decline in American wealth.
- Prior to 1965, entrepreneurs from first-world countries had little difficulty emigrating to the U.S. Today, however, America competes poorly for entrepreneurs, when compared with many of its first-world rivals.
- The U.S. no longer enjoys the income tax advantage it formerly enjoyed over other countries, since the Reagan tax revolution has spread worldwide and U.S. taxes have increased. As for business taxes, the World Bank places the U.S. at 61 out of 183 economies.
- Government spending and borrowing has increased in this country relative to the rest of the Organization for Economic Co-operation and Development (OECD). While other first-world countries are shrinking the size of the state, ours is expanding and government debt has been downgraded.
- Formerly, America enjoyed human capital advantage over other countries. That is no longer the case, as K–12 education has declined and family structures have weakened in this country. While such advantages cannot power economic growth by themselves, this is not to say that they are irrelevant.

The principal obstacle to the law reforms proposed in this book is a sense of complacency. We might throw away a not-insignificant part of our GDP each year on wasteful litigation and compliance with inefficient laws—but what does that matter? The point of this essay, then, is to suggest that many of America's former advantages have been lost, and that wasteful laws are a luxury we can no longer afford.

B. Empirical Evidence

Are Americans beset with a litigation crisis? That depends, say *Mark Ramseyer and Eric Rasmusen*. For run-of-the-mill cases, the American litigation machine works about as well as the civil litigation systems of other countries.[26] Where it flies off the rails is in high-profile disputes, such as asbestos and securities law litigation. The problem is especially acute in class action litigation, which the authors describe as "rampantly abused" because of lax procedural rules.

Even for routine cases, however, Americans sue more frequently than people in countries that closely resemble the U.S. For example, per capita litigation rates are four times higher in the U.S. than in Canada. In part, this might evidence sociological differences: more than most people, Americans are thought to rely on legal as opposed to social norms.[27] As Ramseyer and Rasmusen note, the difference might also be due to the vagueness of American legal standards, which encourages litigation. One study of the effect of uncertain legal norms compared litigation rates in the U.S. and Canada on the wrongful discharge of employees. Even though employees are given more protection against wrongful discharge in Canada, in one year only 7 percent of firings there resulted in litigation, as compared with 23 percent in the U.S. The difference resulted from the greater uncertainty in U.S. standards, as well as the possibility of higher damages awards.[28]

The Ramseyer-Rasmusen thesis about American Exceptionalism in high-profile cases has been evidenced elsewhere. In a scholarly analysis of American legalism, Robert Kagan reviewed more than 34 detailed cross-country studies of litigation in specific policy areas, such as hazardous waste cleanups and exposure to harmful chemicals. All but two studies found substantially higher litigation rates in the U.S.[29] One review of cross-country litigation levels concluded that the United States is an outlier in both the quality and quantity of its litigation.[30]

The Ramseyer-Rasmusen article is valuable for its spade work in measuring cross-country differences in the number of lawsuits, judges, and lawyers. *Stephen Magee*'s article is also a useful contribution to the cross-country analysis of the role of law in society, even if his results are more suggestive than dispositive. The article reprises the author's work on the Magee curve in a series of articles 20 years ago. Those earlier articles argued, uncontroversially, that there is such a thing as too many lawyers in society (as where they reach 100 percent of the population).[31] There is also such a thing as too few lawyers, as where business parties enter into financial transactions without the benefit of legal advice for want of lawyers. The result is the upside-down U-shaped curve, now called the Magee curve.

What is controversial is where the apex of the curve might be. Magee puts it significantly to the left of the American level of 3.65 lawyers per

100,000 people. We'd be worse off economically without any lawyers, he notes, but we'd be even better off if we had a third fewer lawyers, and he reports that this works out to a cost of $1 trillion to the American economy.

Few things can make one more cynical about American politics than the way it protects trial lawyers. When health care reform was debated in 2009–10, it was generally thought that lawsuit reform was an important element in any cost containment strategy. When the Patient Protection and Affordable Care Act ("ObamaCare") was passed, however, lawsuit reform was shelved. As Howard Dean explained, the people who wrote the bill just didn't want to take on the trial lawyers.[32] What emerged instead was a pilot program to study medical malpractice reform, with $1 million allocated to each of the 50 states. That was a non-starter, but it appears that the trial lawyers didn't stop there. The states won't collect the $1 million if they propose legislation that would limit attorneys' fees or impose caps on damages. Since these are the two most popular lawsuit reforms, these restrictions amount to a poison pill.[33]

Magee's earlier work attracted a good deal of criticism, much of it unwarranted. He has been faulted for suggesting that if only a third of America's lawyers retired tomorrow, all would be well. But that's not his claim. If they retired their place would simply be taken by new entrants to the bar. The problem, as he notes, is not the number of lawyers but rather a legal system that makes it profitable for an excessive number of people to practice law. And that is no more than what other contributors to this book assert.

Magee has also been criticized for assuming that lawyers will join forces in order to advance their mutual interests.[34] To do so, they must overcome a free-rider problem: since each lawyer will find it cheaper to let other lawyers bear the costs of collaboration (financing judicial elections, supporting lobby groups, and so on), no lawyer will do so. While that is an excellent theoretical point, this is one of those cases where what works in theory doesn't work in practice. As Magee notes, lawyers have emerged as one of the most powerful lobby groups in American politics.[35] Evidently, the free-rider problem has not been a barrier.

Magee has also been faulted for assuming that the value of lawyers is to be measured only by their contribution to GDP, as if the other benefits of the rule of law—the protection of civil liberties, the prevention of crime—did not matter.[36] However, Magee nowhere says this, and he explicitly denies it in his essay. Moreover, the criticism rests on the false assumption that our level of lawyers results in a society where civil liberties are better protected in America than in other first-world countries with a smaller numbers of lawyers. Somehow, other countries—Japan, England, France—manage to be more or less civilized even if they lack America's prodigious number of lawyers.

There are, however, benign explanations for why we might expect to see more lawyers in the U.S. than in more hierarchical or close-knit societies such as Japan and Canada. In such societies post-contractual misbehavior is checked by a thicker set of norms and long-term business relationships. Reputations matter more in such countries, and lawyers matter less.[37] Explanations of this kind might explain part of the puzzle—but likely no more than a part.

It is conventional (and banal) to say of an empirical article that it suggests the need for further research. The same can be said of virtually every empirical paper. In the case of the Magee curve, one might want to see the greater number of observations that time-series data would provide. There is only so much one can infer from a data set of 33 observations, even if the results are statistically significant. For example, Magee uses lawyer density in the year 2000 to predict economic growth from 1970 to 2007. The future doesn't predict the past, but Magee is constrained to simplify because of data limitations. It would also be helpful if (magically) we knew how many of a country's lawyers were active in the practice of law, and how many of them were transactional lawyers. Finally, we would want to know whether lawyer-legislators are on average more likely to support legislation that promotes litigation.[38]

There is nevertheless reason to think that Magee is more right than his critics. American litigation rates are considerably higher than those of comparable first-world countries. And that is just what one would expect, if America's procedural and tort law tilts toward plaintiffs in the exaggerated manner described in subsequent articles in this book. It would be odd indeed if the differences in legal rules described by Dean Jutras and Professor Trebilcock had no effect whatever on litigation rates. If that were the case, why do trial lawyers resist such reforms?

Trial lawyers minded to defend America's high litigation levels sometimes argue that, were they lower, we would require a greater degree of regulation. This assumes that litigation and regulation are substitutes: more of one, less of the other. That argument would be more persuasive if the regulatory burden were higher in other countries with lower litigation levels. That's not the case, however. When first-world regulatory regimes have been compared, American regulatory law stands out as more detailed, complex, legalistic, and adversarial. Regulatory enforcement is "by the book," and severe criminal sanctions may be meted out on breach. Relative to similar countries, America has both more litigation and heavier regulation.[39]

Even within the U.S., there is no evidence of a trade-off between litigation and regulation. When they examine state litigation levels and proxies for regulatory activity, *Eric Helland and Jonathan Klick* find that regulation and litigation look more like complements: more of one, more of the other. One explanation for this is that the remarkable number of regulations with which a firm must comply, as well as the mind-numbing number of reports to be filed, gives trial lawyers more ammunition when civil remedies are appended to regulatory breaches. In sum, America has a general culture of interference with business decisions, which expresses itself through both litigation and regulation.

Might that nevertheless make us better off, with business taking a greater degree of efficient care? No, says *Kip Viscusi,* when it comes to product liability law (where consumers sue manufacturers for product defects). Product liability awards have increased at the same time that accident rates have declined. There is no evidence that higher liability awards result in safer products—just the opposite, for manufacturers are hit when they innovate and introduce new, safer products.[40] New safety technologies should be encouraged, but product liability law punishes the innovator. In addition, excessive damages are awarded, and firms that seek to provide efficient levels of care through cost-benefit analysis are pilloried and made to pay punitive damages.

C. Civil Procedure

No country more closely resembles the U.S. than Canada. Both countries have a similar inheritance of British traditions and institutions, notably the common law, and the two economies are similar in structure and
highly integrated. Each country is the other's largest trading partner, and
they share the world's largest bilateral trading relationship. Other than
Americans, no one knows more about the U.S. than Canadians. This is
true as well of Canadian lawyers, who keep a close eye on trends south of
the border. For this reason, *Daniel Jutras* correctly notes that Canadian and
American legal systems cannot be seen as two solitudes. Nevertheless, differences in civil procedure law would make conservative American lawyers
green with envy.

- Class actions are few in number in Canada (and very rare in Europe).
- Unlike American plaintiffs, Canadian plaintiffs must plead the facts to
  support their claim, which limits the scope of discovery.
- Discovery is tightly restricted in Canada; by contrast, generous U.S.
  discovery rules, which might ask defendants to bear millions of dollars
  in expenses, permit opportunistic and unmeritorious plaintiffs to hold
  up defendants with settlement offers that are less than the costs the
  defendant would incur on discovery.
- Canada (like the rest of the world) makes losers pay for a portion of the
  successful party's costs. Anomalously, that doesn't happen in the U.S.,
  and whether or not the difference increases litigation levels in America,
  it does affect the mix of cases by giving unmeritorious American plaintiffs a greater incentive to sue.
- The right to have civil cases adjudged by a jury is afforded constitutional protection in the U.S. In Canada, civil juries were abolished as
  a sensible reform measure. Since much of the blame for outrageous
  damages awards in America has been attributed to juror ignorance and
  passion,[41] the difference advantages Canadian defendants.

These differences, also discussed by Michael Trebilcock and George
Priest, increase the costs and risk of failure for Canadian plaintiffs, and
decrease their expected damages awards. If litigation rates are four times
smaller in Canada than the U.S., then, the difference should not occasion
surprise. Subsidize something and you get more of it; penalize it and you
get less of it.

One cannot appreciate the difference in civil procedure regimes without understanding the difference in norms of legal ethics. In America, much more than elsewhere, lawyers are encouraged to advance their client's interests "without regard to the interests of justice in the particular case or broader social concerns. American lawyers' professional culture is unique in permitting and implicitly encouraging them to advance unprecedented legal claims, coach witnesses, and attempt to wear down their opponents through burdensome pretrial discovery."[42]

Many of the idiosyncratic features of American civil procedure are too deeply embedded in our culture to be easily changed. The right to a civil jury responds to deeply rooted egalitarian and populist sentiments,[43] and is guaranteed by the Seventh Amendment. A loser-pay rule was proposed in Texas, but what emerged was a watered-down rule. Reform efforts have tended to focus instead on discovery rules, and *Peter Rutledge* proposes making discovery costs proportional to the amount in controversy. At present, American plaintiffs can bring an action without alleging a factual basis for the claim and then impose discovery costs in the millions of dollars that bear no relation to the expected value of the action. Unsurprisingly, many defendants prefer to settle for an amount less than they would bear in discovery costs. Rutledge would address the extortion problem by restricting the plaintiff's right to impose discovery costs when the amount of damages claimed is small. As that might simply give plaintiffs an incentive to inflate the claim, Rutledge proposes that the plaintiff be required to post a bond, which defendants could draw down on, when the size of the claim increases.

Rutledge's proposal would rely on the courts to police abusive and opportunistic plaintiffs, a task at which courts have not heretofore distinguished themselves. *Martin Redish's* proposal would remove the problem from the discretion of the courts through the simple device of allocating all discovery costs to the plaintiff. As the party who both initiates the discovery and benefits most as a result of it, the plaintiff should bear the costs, on fundamental principles of quasi-contract or quantum meruit. If I do something for you, at your request, and from which you benefit, elementary notions of justice as well as well-recognized legal principles would permit me to recover from you. The same principle, argues Redish, should permit defendants to recover the cost of discovery from the plaintiffs who request it.

A theoretical literature in the law-and-economics tradition argues for various policies that increase litigation levels. Such studies make the assumption that, in all other respects, American civil procedure and tort law are in tip-top shape. If only the few remaining barriers to lawsuits were removed, then, we might have an efficient level of litigation. Descending from Planet Trafalmadore to Planet Earth, however, American civil procedure and tort law seem excessively pro-plaintiff, at least when compared with the rest of the world. For non-Americans, the idea that American civil procedural rule should be tweaked to increase litigation levels will seem risible.

In their article, *Jeremy Kidd and Todd Zywicki* take issue with this law-and-economics literature, focusing on lawyer advertising and third-party financing of legal claims. Lawyer advertising was recognized as a constitutional right by the Supreme Court more than 30 years ago,[44] and since then lawyers have become major advertisers on radio, television, and the Internet. Some economists cheered this, since barriers to advertising tend to reduce competition and increase the prices consumers pay. Kidd and Zywicki also discuss legislative initiatives championed by the plaintiffs' bar to permit third-party financing of litigation, a change that would permit plaintiffs' lawyers who have invested in class action litigation to sell a portion of their inventory of claims to bankers. Once again, considered in isolation, the change is a benign one.

Kidd and Zywicki argue that legal policies should not be seen in isolation, however, at least where everything else seems broken. Where a car veers excessively to the left, an adjustment that worsens the problem makes no sense, even if the correction seems sensible when considered by itself alone. Changes that commend themselves in a first-best world, where everything else is copacetic, might make things worse in a second-best world if they exacerbate a pathology.

Kidd and Zywicki identify a second reason why procedural reforms should not be seen in isolation. It is no accident, they suggest, that America has the most pro-plaintiff rules of both civil procedure and tort law. Procedural and substantive rules are endogenous, they suggest. They rub

off on each other. Procedural rules that invite plaintiffs to sue tend to produce pro-plaintiff substantive law. There is nothing very novel in this
claim. Sir Henry Maine said very much the same thing, when he observed
that English substantive law looked as though it had been secreted through
the interstices of procedure.[45] This also should give one pause before ad-
vantaging plaintiffs further.

D. Tort Law

America is also an outlier in its substantive tort law, which beckons
plaintiffs to court. The substantial differences between American tort law
and that of the country it most closely resembles are described by *Michael
Trebilcock and Paul Veel.*

Unlike U.S. courts, Canadian courts do not impose strict liability on
manufacturers for product defects. Instead, a finding of negligence is required. Canadian plaintiffs are assisted by the doctrine of res ipsa loquitur,
which shifts the burden of proof to the defendant when the goods were
under its exclusive control. Nevertheless, the defendant can avoid liability
if it can show that the accident was not attributable to its negligence.[46]

Canadian courts are also a good deal more parsimonious in assessing
damages. The Canadian Supreme Court capped damages for non-pecuniary
losses (e.g., pain and suffering, wrongful death) at $100,000 in 1978 (ad-
justed subsequently for inflation). Remarkably, American courts have
struck down such caps as unconstitutional when they were enacted by state
legislatures. As for punitive damages, a Canadian court might grant an
award on the same set of facts as a U.S. court. In practice, however, Canadian punitive awards are many times smaller. A 1991 Ontario study cited by
Trebilcock and Veel found few cases in which the award exceeded $50,000.

In his article, *George Priest* describes the many ways in which America's
substantive and procedural tort law regime is the world's outlier. The expansion of liability since the 1960s places a tort law tax on the economy, in
which the losses exceed gains to the economy. It also makes America less
competitive, at a time when other countries are competing most effectively
with us.

Fifty years ago the idea took hold, among American academics and
judges, that tort law should seek to provide consumers with insurance

against product defects, and that it usefully does so by imposing strict liability on manufacturers through class action litigation. As Priest notes,
however, tort law is a very imperfect vehicle for insurance. When compared with the private insurance that consumers might buy on their own,
tort insurance is very costly because trial lawyers will take 30 to 40 percent
of the recovery as their fee. And that doesn't include the defendant's costs.
Add them in, says Vicusi in the following article, and there are legal expenses of 75 cents for every dollar of recovery.

Any insurance component of the recovery is also regressive: the poor
pay more. In private insurance, the insurer can charge a higher premium
to wealthy customers to reflect their higher anticipated claims. But that
doesn't happen when the insurance takes the form of strict liability in tort.
This is because the manufacturer will charge the same price to both rich
and poor consumers, and this price will reflect the expected greater damages award to rich plaintiffs.

Priest notes that part of the cost of American tort law comes from its
unpredictability. Robert Kagan offered one example. A Japanese chemical
company decided not to market an air freshener in the U.S. that it sells in
large volumes in Japan because of the threat of some difficult-to-anticipate
theory of liability. The product is designed to neutralize the smell of tobacco smoke. Even though the company could not see how the product
might prompt litigation, it thought that American trial lawyers might be
able to come up with some novel theory of liability.[47]

It is never clear how much academic theorists influence the shape of
legal rules. However, to the extent that they do, Priest places part of the
blame for the expansion of liability on law-and-economics scholars, notably Richard Posner. Priest's hero is Ronald Coase, who pointed out in *The
Problem of Social Cost* that rules of liability do not affect the behavior of
bargainers when they are able to contract around inefficient rules in order
to exploit bargaining gains. This is the Coase theorem, and from it Priest
makes the normative point that contracts that shift risks from one party to
another should be enforced. But American courts frequently disregard
contractual choices. Instead, they impeach free bargaining rights under
rules of paternalism that take choices away from the parties. In this, says
Priest, they were aided and abetted by Richard Posner's *positive thesis* of the

common law, which argued that courts always adopted efficient legal rules. If courts always get it right, then who cares what the parties say they want?

No one now subscribes to Posner's positive thesis. However, Posner's defense of American courts can today be heard from those who reject the claim that the tort regime is in crisis. Like Posner, they assume that American courts get it right (and, by inference, that benighted, conservative foreign courts get it wrong).

Tort law and regulation intersect in two ways. First, as Helland and Klick explain in their article, they both might deal with the same kinds of risks, so that one might be seen as a substitute for the other. That in practice they seem to overlap and duplicate each other, as the authors note, should give one pause and suggest that litigation levels are excessive. Second, litigation might serve regulatory goals when the outcome of a case is an undertaking by the defendant (or even an industry) to comply with judge-made regulations. The developing trend toward "regulation by litigation" is the subject of *Kip Viscusi*'s second article in this book.

Viscusi argues that industry-wide standards are better enunciated by regulatory agencies than by courts, since agencies have access to experts and testing procedures that courts lack, and since the loss of uniformity and predictability when matters are left to courts imposes a cost on manufacturers. This is especially the case where liability turns on a warning label, and where the manufacturer has relied on a label blessed by an agency. The excessive warnings, as manufacturers try to anticipate what courts around the country will require, can result in an informational overload that leaves consumers less informed. In addition, regulation by litigation increases the reversibility problem described in the article by Trebilcock and Veel. While wasteful regulations may be withdrawn when a new administration comes to town, wasteful court settlements are harder to reverse.[48]

Viscusi pays special attention to the Master Settlement Agreement (MSA), in which the court approved a compact among tobacco companies and state attorneys-general that heavily regulated the tobacco industry. Though the MSA imposed enormous liabilities, major tobacco firms supported it because it discourages new entrants in the market. No tears have been shed for the tobacco companies, but this was still a very poor substitute for administrative regulation. The MSA was negotiated with none of the procedural safeguards of agency rule-making, no cost-benefit analysis, and no opportunity for public input. With a reported $11 billion payout in legal fees, the MSA represents a tempting precedent for trial lawyers that, if left unchecked and applied in other industries, would weaken our economy.

E. Contract Law

Reading American contract law can give an English commercial lawyer a mild case of vertigo. The language is familiar, the signposts are the same, but peering into the dispositions of cases reveals an unfamiliar and disconcerting world. One follows a path, confident of its direction, only to find oneself in a very different place from that which one expected.

Part of the difference stems from doctrines that to English ears sound foreign (and, dare I say it, civilian): unconscionability, good faith, fair dealing. And yet these differences have the curious feature that they grow smaller as one approaches them. Courts invoke them as hortatory devices, but few cases seem explicitly to turn on them. However, this can lead to the opposite error of minimizing differences between the two countries.

The differences are there, argues *Michael Bridge,* and what they come down to are very dissimilar beliefs about the value of commercial certainty and the role of the courts in implying terms and duties in business dealings. English courts are very much aware that firms will forgo profitable investments in business relationships if they cannot assume that contracts will be enforced. More than American courts, English courts are also more likely to think globally and recognize how their law brings foreign business and finance to their country.

Among American scholars, there is a growing and belated recognition that Wetlaw—the idea that every bargain deserves its day in court, that a contract might be set aside when things turn out badly for one side after commodity prices increase,[49] and that judges know the minds of the parties better than the parties do themselves[50]—has not proved as valuable for the American economy as it has for American lawyers. There is now a turn toward the idea that courts should intervene less, to what an American lawyer would call Willistonian formalism, after Samuel Williston, the conservative treatise writer of the pre-Realist age of 100 years ago.

Robert Scott shares this turn to conservatism, at least for the individually tailored contracts commercial parties negotiate for themselves. These he distinguishes from consumer contracts, where liberal rules of interpretation might make more sense. However, American contract law is unitary in prescribing the same set of rules for both commercial and consumer contracts.

Scott then distinguishes between two theories on interpretation: a liberal contextualism and a conservative textualism. Under contextualism, courts may look beyond the written contract to import terms or meanings from background oral discussions or trade terms; under textualism courts do not stray beyond a writing to interpret what the parties meant. In contextualist jurisdictions, its rules of interpretation are mandatory: the parties cannot bargain around them. Not so in textualist jurisdictions, where the parties in their contract may invite a court to examine contemporaneous oral statements and understandings. The expansion of choice under textualism argues for its superiority.

Scott is the most eminent American contracts scholar of his generation. His concern for murky law and excessive litigation, and his conclusion that American contract law took a wrong turn in the Realist Revolution with the Restatement and UCC Article 2 it spawned, must give pause to those who defend this form of American Exceptionalism—as will his preference for the more conservative English law of contracts described by Michael Bridge.

In their article, Michael Trebilcock and Paul Veel expressed a preference for the system of federally appointed provincial judges in Canada, as opposed to the state judges in the U.S. who are appointed or elected by state politicians or voters. A federal appointment avoids the problem of interstate exploitation—of U.S. state court judges who favor in-state plaintiffs over out-of-state defendants in order to transfer money to their state. Federally appointed Canadian (and American) judges don't have the same "homer" instincts as U.S. state judges. However, federal appointments sacrifice the benefits of jurisdictional competition, in which judges seek to attract business to their state by offering a more attractive set of laws. This appears to happen in U.S. contract law. In their contracts, parties may specify the state whose law is to govern their contract. As Scott notes, when given the choice, parties prefer the textualist regime of New York law over the contextualist regime of California law, and this points to the superiority of textualism.

In their article, *Erin O'Hara O'Connor and the late Larry E. Ribstein* describe in more detail the process of jurisdictional competition under which states may tailor their laws to attract business or people. In contract law, the competition depends importantly on the freedom the parties are granted to exit inefficient legal regimes. Through a choice-of-law clause they might specify that the law of another state is to govern their contract; through a choice-of-court clause, they might choose the courts of another state as the forum for their litigation, and through an arbitration clause they might remove the proceedings from the American court system altogether.[51]

In recent years courts have become more willing to recognize the right of parties to choose the law to govern their agreements, a right given a degree of recognition by the Restatement (Second) of Conflict of Laws, and the authors conclude that the parties' ability to choose their legal regime by contract offers a partial solution to the American Illness. Party choice of law is most likely to be respected in contracts between commercial parties, less so in consumer contracts, and not at all when the action sounds in tort and a contractual nexus is lacking.

Robert Scott proposed that problems in consumer contracts be taken from the courts and dealt with through a regulatory regime, such as that offered by consumer protection laws. But are consumers really helped by such laws? *Joshua D. Wright and Eric Helland* suggest not. They point out the hidden costs of recent efforts to strengthen consumer protection, costs that are magnified by class action litigation.

F. Corporate Law

A decade ago the New York Stock Exchange launched half the world's new public companies. By 2006 it launched just one in 12, as firms moved to the London Stock Exchange and other venues. *Stephen Bainbridge* lays much of the blame on Paul Sarbanes and Mike Oxley, sponsors of the 2002 Sarbanes-Oxley corporate reform legislation (SOX), whose photographs are displayed by London brokers as their favorite Americans.[52] They know whom to thank for legislation that drives the American securities industry to Britain and other countries.

While SOX greatly (and in Bainbridge's view, inefficiently) increased the reporting duties of U.S. public firms, it is not the only thing that drives securities business offshore. The prospect of litigation based on federal securities law is another reason for the decline in the American securities market, as Ramseyer and Rasmusen also noted. Firms are less exposed to shareholder suits and pay less for directors' and officers' insurance in other countries. For smaller companies in particular, the savings are significant.

Bainbridge lays the blame for SOX on the recent economic crisis, which he says resulted in "bubble" legislation. Bubble laws are statutes that offer hasty and ill-conceived solutions to economic crises. That's only part of the story, however. To understand how something as ghastly as SOX could be passed, he argues, one must also appreciate the strength of populism in America, which pitches Main Street against Wall Street, the underdog against the "monied interest."

There is yet another side to the story. Countries like the U.K. refrain from hobbling themselves with inefficient securities laws because they have a stronger sense of the importance of global competition and a more modest view of their own country's importance. It is difficult to see how an American could support SOX unless he thought, secure in his arrogance and smugly contemptuous of other countries, that his country is on top of the world and that the insignificant provinces of the rest of the world are unworthy of his attention.

G. Criminal Law

When Russian businessman Mikhail Khodorkovsky was sentenced a second time, even Russian leaders knew that his show trial would affect how people saw the idea of doing business in their country. "I think that a significant part of the international community will have serious questions," said a senior aide to President Dmitry Medvedev. "The assessment of the risks of working in Russia will increase."[53]

America isn't Russia, of course, not by a very, very long shot. But then, one has the strong sense that it isn't England or Canada either. For business people, the risk of going to prison would appear to be higher here than in other first-world countries. Criminal prosecutions of Conrad Black, Denis Kozlowski, Michael Milken, Martha Stewart, and other Enemies Of The

People have little parallel in the rest of the first world, and may be a consequence of the populist impulses Stephen Bainbridge detects in American
securities legislation. When the stock market crashes, one doesn't hear the
English call to jail financial executives, as one does here.[54] But if an American securities firm hedges its bets, taking a position against an investment
it recommended to a client—why, that's fraud.[55] And if gas prices soar, the
Justice Department should investigate speculators.[56] For economic villains,
innocence should not be a defense. In America, it seems, criminal law is
sometimes the continuation of politics by other means.

Popular pressure matters less in other countries. Unlike American district attorneys, Canadian crown attorneys are career civil servants. They
might be appointed to the bench, but they do not court the limelight or run
for office. They don't look for headlines to advance private political or professional ends.

America appears to rely on criminal law more than other countries, to
the point that many complain of "overcriminalization" in this country. The
idea that there are too many crimes and too many people in jail enjoys
broad support on both ends of the political spectrum.[57] The number of
criminal offenses in federal statute and regulations is, literally, unknowable. One commentator described the "federal criminal code" as "simply an
incomprehensible, random and incoherent, duplicative, incomplete, and
organizationally nonsensical mass of federal legislation."[58] The result, according to a leading criminal law academic, the late William Stuntz, is that
we are moving closer to a world in which the law on the books makes every
American a felon.[59]

The subject of *Jeffrey Parker's* article is excessive corporate and white-
collar criminal prosecutions, and what this might mean for the economy.
If American overcriminalization sends business offshore, it contributes to
economic decline and the American Illness. Consider, for example, how
business people might react to the case of Krister Evertson:

> Evertson never had so much as a parking ticket prior to his arrest. . . . An
> Eagle Scout, National Honor Society member, science whiz, clean energy
> inventor, and small business entrepreneur, Krister is now a felon. The
> nightmare that took two years of his freedom and hundreds of thousands
> of dollars . . . began when he made a simple error: he failed to put a

"ground" sticker on a package that he shipped. Despite his clear intention to ship by ground—as evidenced by his selection of "ground" on the shipment form and payment for "ground" shipping—the government prosecuted him for his error anyways.

When the jury acquitted Krister, the government turned around and charged him again, this time for alleged abandonment of toxic materials. Krister had securely and safely stored his valuable research materials in stainless steel drums, at a storage facility, while he fought for his freedom in trial over the missing shipping sticker. He ultimately spent two years in a federal prison for his mistake.[60]

The structure of American criminal law proceedings very much tips the scale toward the prosecutors. In federal grand juries, prosecutors exercise enormous discretion and are virtually immune from judicial supervision. They can call witnesses (including the target of the investigation) without revealing the nature of the case, and can introduce hearsay evidence. Not surprisingly, they seldom fail to win an indictment. As a firm suffers an enormous reputational loss on indictment, the mere threat of grand jury proceedings is often enough to bring it to its knees. The Department of Justice increasingly employs its bargaining leverage through deferred or non-prosecution prosecution agreements, in which it waives or defers criminal prosecution in return for undertakings by the firm. These can involve restitutionary payments, appointing someone to the board of directors, or detailed business regulations. One U.S. attorney, now Governor Chris Christie of New Jersey, had a firm endow a chair in business ethics at Seton Hall Law School, Christie's alma mater.[61]

What Parker decries is the decline of the moral element in criminal law, in the requirement of mens rea (or intentional wrongdoing). The mens rea requirement was imported into the common law by canonists, who argued that criminal wrongdoing, like sin, assumed moral guilt. "God considers not the action, but the spirit of the action,"[62] said Peter Abelard; which meant there was no place for Anglo-Saxon strict liability criminal offenses. More recently, however, strict liability, which dispenses with the need for mens rea, has made a comeback in the form of "public welfare crimes," such as the ground sticker requirement that Krister Everton flouted. Very early on, Oliver Wendell Holmes foresaw the new direction the law would take. "While the terminology of morals is still retained . . . the law . . . , by the very necessity of its nature, is continually transmuting those moral standards into external and objective ones, from which the actual guilt of the party concerned is wholly eliminated."[63]

The adoption, many hundreds of years ago, of mens rea standards, of the idea that liberty depends on restricting criminal law to a narrow compass, was a signal achievement in the progress of civil and political liberty. Nowadays, however, these are "just a few ideas that have ceased to be modern," as Evelyn Waugh's Basil Seal remarked. Their abandonment, inspired by the most progressive political thought of the day, puts innocent people at risk of the most severe restrictions on liberty available to the state. What is worse, the American system of criminal procedure gives ambitious prosecutors enormous powers with virtually no accountability. In this way, corporate criminal and white-collar crime penalties weaken our economy and contribute to the American Illness.

H. How Nations Grow (or Don't)

This book has been long on description and short on diagnosis. What *Richard Epstein* offers is diagnosis. Most of what ails America, he argues, can be attributed to the Progressive ideology of state planning and restrictions on choice, which informed the New Deal and which has been revived by the Obama administration. From health care legislation to the expansion of tort liability, Epstein sees a common threat: a reliance on experts and planners to get it right, a desire to see the power of the state expanded, and a rejection of individual bargaining rights.

Epstein attributes the increased threat of tort law liability in the past 50 years to the expansionist tendencies that were part of Progressive thought. The public realm expanded, the private realm shrunk, and private parties lost the right to write enforceable bargains to correct mistakes made by judges. The enormous increase in the number of lawyers over that period evidences the dramatic changes in legal rules. From 1870 to 1970, the number of lawyers per capita in the U.S. remained about the same. Over the next 28 years, however, the number increased almost threefold, from 1.2 to 3.3 lawyers per 1,000 people.[64]

If Progressivism was the problem, the prior question is why it took hold in America. We had been told that it wouldn't, indeed that *It Didn't Happen Here,* Seymour Martin Lipset's book that explained why socialism was rejected in the U.S. Of all countries, we were to be immune from the policies Epstein decries. It seems, however, that we are not so exceptional after all.

Robert Cooter and Aaron Edlin ask for private law rules that promote innovation and entrepreneurship as the engines of economic growth. Sadly, many of the rules described in this book appear disproportionately to penalize innovators and entrepreneurs. Kip Viscusi discusses the bias against innovation in tort law, where it's better to stick to unsafe old ways than to innovate with safer new ways. As an example, the Ramseyer-Rasmusen and Bainbridge articles discuss the way in which "stock drop" securities litigation penalized Silicon Valley innovators. In stock drop litigation, a clever trial lawyer files a class action law suit immediately after a stock price decline, alleging that the firm failed to disclose a risk to investors. Then there's contract law. As entrepreneurs are often "new men," they more than members of the club rely on strict contractual enforcement, of the kind that appears to be better provided in England, according to Michael Bridge. Finally, as a risk-taker and innovator, an entrepreneur is more likely to contravene one of the numberless and unknowable criminal law rules described by Jeffrey Parker.

The unstated but controversial assumption that underlies the Cooter and Edlin article is that future generations matter, that government policies that benefit those alive today might nevertheless be unjust if they impoverish those who come after us. Of course, we know that future generations matter when it comes to preserving the environment, to curbing greenhouse gases, and to addressing global warming. What is controversial is the idea that no-growth economic policies that impoverish future generations are related to questions of social justice. Journalistic debates about social justice are generally framed in terms of payoffs to people around today, not those who will come after us, and yet the question of intergenerational justice, of what is owed future generations, for all its uncertainties and confusion is perhaps the principal moral and political issue of our time.

In theory, it would seem, social policies should be *time-consistent*. That is, the welfare needs of one who lives 100 years from now should count as much as a similarly placed person today. "Everyone counts as one," said Jeremy Bentham, "and no one counts as more than one." If so, the value of consumption 100 years from now should not be discounted when compared with consumption today. That is, what economists label the "social discount rate," which measures the extent to which future consumption is devalued, should be set at zero.

In practice, no country does set its social discount rate at zero. In part, this is because of fears that to do so, today's generation would have to invest everything for the happiness of future generations (so many of them, so few of us . . .).[65] More to the point, one wouldn't expect that today's voters will be indifferent between wealth transfers to themselves and to those who will live 100 years from now. One simply wouldn't expect that degree of altruism from anyone.

That said, the social discount rate is not infinite either. We can't ignore the way in which the public debt overhang described in the article by Ramseyer and Rasmusen places a tax burden on future generations[66] or the impact that declining growth will have on them. Since our economy is in the doldrums, the Cooter and Edlin thesis has a particular bite. The OECD reports that the average U.S. GDP growth from 2001 to 2010 was 1.69 percent a year.[67] For some emerging economies, notably China, the growth rate was on average 10 percent a year over that period. Were these trends to continue, the United States would be quickly overtaken, not only as an economic power but also as a provider of social welfare. What Cooter and Edlin argue, therefore, is that social justice argues for rejecting economically harmful policies, such as those identified elsewhere in this book. In particular, they take aim at state capitalism, the 17th-century Colbertian *étatisme* in which politicians as venture capitalists are thought better able than the market to pick economic winners—high speed trains, clean energy, green jobs, and the like.

The case of China confounds conventional thinking on state capitalism, among other things. A despotic, communist country that within living memory killed many millions of its own people has emerged from poverty into an enormous economic power. Over the past 30 years, 400 million

Chinese emerged from poverty, an expansion of wealth unmatched in history.[68]

It had hitherto been thought that democracy and economic wealth necessarily go hand in hand, that prosperity creates a middle class that demands democracy, and that democracy in turn engenders the legal structures that foster economic growth. However, China has growing prosperity without democracy. From this, some have even concluded that, *pace* Cooter and Edlin, state capitalism can outperform market capitalism.[69]

It is, of course, too early to say what the future might bring, but several distinct possibilities suggest themselves. The first is the Chilean model, in which economic prosperity turns a dictatorship into a democracy. As the Chinese economy expands, it will grow a middle class that demands personal freedoms and democracy.[70] China's experiment with a thin rule of law might thus lead to a thick rule of law. Nearly every country with a per capita income above $10,500 is democratic. (The exceptions are some oil sheikdoms and a few Asian tigers such as Hong Kong.) China is now at $4,300. We'll see what happens if several hundred million more Chinese are brought into the middle class.

The second possibility is a reversal of growth. As a Chinese middle class develops, the same pressures for democracy might result in a Tien-an-Mien Square crackdown and a repression that kills the economy, leaving China with neither a thin nor a thick rule of law. At present, the Chinese Communist Party spends an enormous amount of time and energy worrying about social stability. Those worries are going to increase, and then what?

The third possibility has been labeled the Beijing Consensus,[71] with a thin but not a thick rule of law persisting over time. The bargain offered the Chinese people ("we'll make you rich, just don't bother asking for democracy") might prove to be stable, especially since the Communist Party's threats of murderous repression are wholly credible. Similarly, the bargain offered foreign investors that their contracts and property rights will be respected might prove credible over time, as China distinguishes itself from untrustworthy kleptocracies.

Frank Fukuyama suggests a fourth possibility, one of a quiet return to earth. China's remarkable economic growth will not prove sustainable, argues Fukuyama, because of its inherent weaknesses. What China lacks are the religious and ethical underpinnings of the rule of law in the West, and as such its commitment to a thin rule of law will likely not prove sustainable. In addition, China's embrace of capitalism is very recent, and it is entirely possible that a new generation of leaders ("bad emperors") will prefer to maximize something other than economic growth, such as military expansion. Moreover, the success of the country's economic policies requires a necessarily imperfect top-down policing of corruption at lower levels of the bureaucracy. Finally, as Cooter and Edlin point out, state capitalism, if that is what Chinese capitalism amounts to, cannot be expected to outperform market capitalism.[72]

This is not to say that America's economic system, with its recent intervention on behalf of failing firms, its increased level of dirigisme, and its enormous defense industry, can be described as market capitalism. Moreover, the religious and ethical traditions of the West, which Fukuyama regards as crucially important in explaining the rule of law, seem to have weakened. Trust in institutions and in other citizens has declined, and social ties have become less binding and more ephemeral—a process that Fukuyama himself described in *The Great Disruption*.[73] In the 50 years between 1957 and 2007, the U.S. population increased 75 percent, while violent crime increased by 720 percent, divorces by 287 percent, and births to unwed mothers by 850 percent.[74] This is social decay on a massive scale. If what distinguishes the rule of law in China from that of America is our religious and moral heritage, then we seem to have eaten into our social capital.

As Fukuyama notes, it is unlikely that China will be able to maintain a 10 percent GDP growth rate. Like emerging nations generally, China had a very high growth rate as it emerged from a pre-capitalist economy. "Follower" countries find it easy to free-ride on the successful innovations of more advanced nations that have led the way,[75] and China has been quick to copy the intellectual property of the West. As follower countries achieve higher levels of development, however, their growth rate slows unless they can compete with advanced countries in the production of new technologies and innovation. While China is now seeking to do just that, projections that it will surpass the U.S. may or may not pan out.

However, the current fixation with China obscures a broader point, which is that America faces competition not from one country only but from the entire world. It is arrogant to assume that it's us versus them, two giants only in the ring. The reality is that there are a host of countries eager to compete with the U.S., and that are effectively doing so now.

How then will America fare in the future? Will it successfully reverse course and meet the new challenges of international competition? That subject I leave to the last essay in the book.

The American legal system and the country's economy are moving targets. For example, the articles in this book were written before the Supreme Court upheld the Patient Protection and Affordable Care Act ("Obamacare"). As I write, we await to see whether America will fall off the "fiscal cliff" or whether Congress can find its way to achieve a compromise and avoid sequestration and the expiry of the Bush tax cuts. Whatever will happen, one does not expect that the problems described in this book will be quickly resolved, or that the need to address them will be less pressing in the future. America's exceptionally costly legal regime seems destined to remain in place, so long as the unsightly mix of inertia and chauvinism in this least attractive form of American Exceptionalism remains unchallenged.

Notes

1. Edmund Burke, "Speech on Conciliation with the Colonies," in I The Founders' Constitution 4–5 (Philip B. Kurland and Ralph Lerner, eds., 1987).

2. Milton Friedman, Economic Freedom behind the Scenes, Preface to Economic Freedom of the World Report: 2002 Annual Report (2002), at http://www.cato.org/special/friedman/friedman/friedman4.html.

3. See Douglass North, Institutions, Institutional Change, and Economic Performance (1990).

4. Samuel Huntington, Culture Matters: How Values Shape Human Progress xiii (2000).

5. Daniel Kaufmann, Rethinking Governance: Empirical Lessons Challenge Orthodoxy 17 (World Bank, 2003). For an example of how firms react to government corruption by moving to other countries, see Amol Sharma, India's Tata Finds Home Hostile, Wall Street Journal, April 13, 2011.

6. Andrei Shleifer and Robert W. Vishny, Corruption, 108 Q. J. Econ. 599 (1993); Stephen Knack and Philip Keefer, Institutions and Economic Performance: Cross-

country Tests Using Alternative Institutional Measures, 7 Econ. & Politics 207 (1995); Rafael L. Porta, Florencio López-de-Silanes, Cristian Pop-Eleches, and Andrei Shleifer, Judicial Checks and Balances, 112 J. Pol. Econ. 445 (2004); see generally Pranab Bardhan, Corruption and Development: A Review of Issues, 35 J. Econ. Lit. 1320 (1997).

7. See Douglass North and Barry Weingast, Constitutions and Commitment: The Evolutions of Institutions Governing Public Choice in Seventeenth Century England, 49 J. Econ. Hist. 803 (1989).

8. The Transparency International corruption rankings are quite similar to those of the World Bank. See http://info.worldbank.org/governance/wgi/pdf_country.asp. On the World Economic Forum's measure of bribery and the extent to which government officials show favoritism to well-connected firms and individuals when deciding upon policies and contracts, the U.S. ranks 42nd and 50th, respectively, out of 142 countries, and 42nd in bribery. See http://www3.weforum.org/docs/WEF _GCR_Report_2011–12.pdf, at Table 1.05 and 1.07.

9. Nauro F. Campos and Francesco Giovannoni, Lobbying, Corruption and Political Influence, 131 Public Choice 1 (2007).

10. Mancur Olson, The Logic of Collective Action (1965).

11. American federal judges make about a quarter less than their Canadian brethren, and often less than their clerks make in their first year of practice, leading the chief justice to complain of the difficulty in attracting and retaining competent judges. Several things have been thought to account for the problem. Judicial salaries are set by Congress, and conservative politicians might wish to punish the bench for its perceived liberal views on civil liberties and national defense. Similarly, liberals might think that judges who emerge from the less well-paid branches of the legal profession will be more sympathetic to their views. Judicial salaries are linked to congressional salaries, and politicians of all stripes might wish to preserve the linkage as a means to bootstrap congressional salaries. Finally, trial lawyers might welcome a decline in the quality of the bench, since better-paid and more sophisticated judges would on average rely less on counsel to take them through complicated financial transactions. Each of these views has been forcefully expressed to me by federal judges.

12. See Michael J. Trebilcock and Ronald J. Daniels, Rule of Law Reform and Development: Charting the Fragile Path of Progress ch. 1 (2008), for a useful discussion of these issues.

13. The difference resembles Roberto Unger's distinction, from The Merchant of Venice, between Venice (where we do business) and Belmont (where we want to live); see Roberto Unger, The Critical Legal Studies Movement, 96 Harv. L. Rev. 561, 622–23 (1983), with the notable difference that there is no reason why one society might not feature both cities. The nastiest places in the world generally have neither. In Brian Tamanaha's typology, I am distinguishing between a thin substantive and a thick formal version of the rule of law. Brian Z. Tamanaha, On the Rule of Law 91 (2004). There is no end to the number of ways in which to skin a cat.

14. Pacific Gas & Elec. Co. v. G. W. Thomas Drayage Co., 69 Cal. 2d 33 (1968).

15. Perez v. Sharp, 32 Cal. 2d 711 (1948).

16. Lon Fuller, The Morality of Law 44–91 (1969).

17. A. V. Dicey, Introduction to the Study of the Law of the Constitution 110–15 (1982). F. A. Hayek, The Road to Serfdom 80 (1994). Hayek assumed that, with suitable procedural rules, the substantive rules would take care of themselves in benign spontaneous order. This was bolstered with the belief that one could safely repose confidence in common law judges. See F. A. Hayek, The Constitution of Liberty 131–249 (1960); I Law, Legislation and Liberty (1973). George Priest's essay in this volume takes Richard Posner to task for making the same second assumption.

18. See F.H. Buckley, Fair Governance: Paternalism and Perfectionism (2009).

19. The two forms of rule of law, thick and thin, may thus be in tension, where adherence to socially liberal reforms enacted by governments that adhere to a thick rule of law require a departure from the thin rule of law I describe here, a point noted by Brian Tamanaha in The Dark Side of the Relationship between the Rule of Law and Liberalism, 33 NYU J. Law & Liberty 516 (2008).

20. Lawyers for Civil Justice, Civil Justice Reform Group, U.S. Chamber Institute for Legal Reform, Litigation Cost Survey of Major Companies 3 (2010).

21. International Trade Administration, U.S. Department of Commerce, Assessing Trends and Policies of Foreign Direct Investment in the United States 7 (2008), available at http://www.trade.gov/publications/abstracts/trends-policies-fdi-2008.asp.

22. B. Barefoot and Raymond J. Mataloni Jr., Operations of U.S. Multinational Companies in the United States and Abroad: Preliminary Results from the 2009 Benchmark Survey Table 6, Bureau of Economic Affairs (November 2011).

23. Id. at 6.

24. See Ralf Michaels, Comparative Law by the Numbers? Legal Origins Thesis, Doing Business Reports, and the Silence of Traditional Comparative Law, 57 Am. J. Comp. L. 765 (2009).

25. Rafael La Porta, Florencio López-de-Silanes, Andrei Shleifer, and Robert Vishny, Law and Finance, 106 J. Pol. Econ. 1112 (1998); see also Rafael La Porta et al., Judicial Checks and Balances, 112 J. Pol. Econ. 445 (2004). On the "legal origins" thesis, see generally Kenneth W. Dam, The Law-Growth Nexis: The Rule of Law and Economic Development 31–35 (2006).

26. The World Bank data on the difficulty of enforcing contracts, seen in Table 2 of Ramseyer-Rasmussen, might paint too favorable a picture of U.S. contract law. The World Economic Forum ranks the U.S. as 36th out of 132 countries in the efficiency of the legal framework in settling disputes, behind Canada (10th), the U.K. (13th), and France (22nd). See http://www3.weforum.org/docs/WEF_GCR_Report_2011–12.pdf, at Table 1.10.

27. The differences between the U.S. and Canada are discussed in Seymour Martin Lipset, Continental Divide: The Values and Institutions of the United States and Canada (1990).

28. Laura Beth Nielsen, Paying Workers or Paying Lawyers: Employee Termination in the United States and Canada, 21 Law & Policy 247 (1999).

29. Robert A. Kagan, Adversarial Legalism and American Government: The American Way of Life (2003). See also Robert A. Kagan, On Surveying the Whole Legal Forest, 28 Law & Soc. Inquiry 833 (2003).

30. W. A. Bogert, Consequences: The Impact of Law and Its Complexity 114 (2002).

31. Washington, D.C., is making progress toward that number. The city's population is about 600,000. Subtracting from that the 255,000 people who are under 21 leaves 345,000. Subtracting again the 115,000 who are thought to be functionally illiterate leaves 230,000 people. The estimated 80,000 lawyers in the District constitute 35 percent of the remaining adult population. Erin Delmore and Marisa M. Kashino, How Many Lawyers Are There?, Washingtonian, December 1, 2009.

32. Mark Tapscott, Dean Says Obamacare Authors Don't Want to Challenge Trial Lawyers, Wash. Examiner, Aug. 26, 2009.

33. Editorial, Chloroform for Tort Reform, Wash. Times, Nov. 6, 2009.

34. Charles R. Epp, Do Lawyers Impede Economic Growth?, 17 Law & Soc. Inquiry 585 (1992).

35. See further Thomas F. Burke, Lawyers, Lawsuits, and Legal Rights 45–51, 56, 185–87 (2002).

36. See Frank B. Cross, The First Thing We Do, Let's Kill All the Economists: An Empirical Examination of the Effect of Lawyers on the United States Economy and Political System, 70 Texas L. Rev. 645, 676–78 (1992).

37. See Ronald J. Gilson, How Many Lawyers Does It Take to Change an Economy?, 17 Law & Soc. Inquiry 635 (1992).

38. One study of lawyers in Congress found a significant but small pro-litigation effect. Thomas F. Burke, Lawyers, Lawsuits, and Legal Rights 188–89 (2002).

39. Robert A. Kagan, Adversarial Legalism: The American Way of Law 186–94 (2001). On the World Bank's 2009 Regulatory Quality Index, the U.S. ranks 22nd, behind most first-world countries. See http://info.worldbank.org/governance/wgi /index.asp.

40. A vivid example of this is provided by ongoing litigation against Yamaha. After it introduced an improved and safer version of its Rhino recreational vehicle, it was sued on the theory that the innovation was an admission that the older product was unsafe. For a report on the company's success in one such case, see Editorial, Yamaha Takes on the Tort Bar and Wins, Wall Street Journal, March 28, 2011.

41. See David A. Schkade, Cass R. Sunstein and Daniel Kahneman, "Deliberating about Dollars: The Severity Shift," in Cass R. Sunstein et al., Punitive Damages: How Juries Decide 43 (2002).

42. Robert A. Kagan, Adversarial Legalism: The American Way of Law 55 (2001).

43. See Oscar G. Chase, Law, Culture and Ritual: Disputing Systems in Cross-Cultural Context 55–58 (2005).

44. Bates v. State Bar of Arizona, 433 U.S. 350 (1977).

45. Sir Henry Maine, Early Law and Custom 389 (1891).

46. The cross-border difference in liability regimes might not matter so much, if American courts got the standard of liability and the quantum of damages right—but then, as the other essays in this book point out, there isn't much reason to think that they do so.

47. Robert A. Kagan, "The Consequences of Adversarial Legalism," in Regulatory Encounters: Multinational Corporations and American Adversarial Legalism 372, 384 (Robert A. Kagan and Lee Axelrad, eds., 2000).

48. A point noted by Andrew P. Morriss, Bruce Yandle, and Andrew Dorchak, Regulation by Litigation 162 (2009).

49. See, e.g., Aluminum Co. v. Essex Group, Inc., 499 F. Supp. 53 (W.D. Pa., 1980).

50. On the limits of this form of paternalism, see F.H. Buckley, Fair Governance (2010).

51. Of arbitration, the recent tendency to "lawyer-up" the proceedings with costly procedural devices that mimic court proceedings has made that a less attractive exit option.

52. L. Gordon Crovitz, Exporting Wall Street, Wall Street Journal, Feb. 28, 2011, at A17.

53. Davos Man and Khodorkovsky, Wall Street Journal, January 24, 2011, at A16.

54. William Greider, How Wall Street Crooks Get Out of Jail Free, The Nation, March 23, 2011.

55. Halal Touryalai, Criminal Charges Loom for Goldman Sachs after Scathing Senate Report, Forbes, April 14, 2011.

56. Jeremy Pelofsky and James Vicini, As Gas Prices Soar, Task Force to Explore Energy Fraud, Wash. Post, April 21, 2011.

57. Adam Liptak, Right and Left Join Forces on Criminal Justice, N.Y. Times, Nov. 23, 2009, at A1.

58. Julie R. O'Sullivan, The Federal Criminal "Code" Is a Disgrace: Obstruction Statutes as a Case Study, 96 J. Crim. L. & Criminology 643 (2006).

59. William Stuntz, The Pathological Politics of Criminal Law, 100 Mich. L. Rev. 506, 511 (2001). See also Harvey A. Silverglate, Three Felonies a Day: How the Feds Target the Innocent (2009).

60. Statement of Jim E. Lavine before the House Committee on the Judiciary Subcommittee on Crime, Terrorism, and Homeland Security, September 28, 2010, at http://judiciary.house.gov/hearings/pdf/Lavine100928.pdf. U.S. v. Evertson, 320 Fed. Appx. 509; 2009 U.S. App. LEXIS 5936 (9th Cir. 2009, cert. den., 130 Sup. Ct. 460 (2009).

61. Richard A. Epsetin, The Deferred Prosecution Racquet, Wall Street Journal, Nov. 28, 2006.

62. Abelard, "Intention and Sin," in Freedom and Responsibility: Readings in Philosophy and Law 170 (Herbert Morris, ed., 1964). See also Francis Sayre, Mens Rea, 45 Harv. L. Rev. 974 (1932).

63. Holmes, The Common Law 38 (1881).

64. See Ronald H. Sander and B. Douglas Williams, Why Are There So Many Lawyers? Perspectives on a Turbulent Market, 14 Law & Social Inquiry 431 (1989).

65. This seems to me to be an example of a broader and mistaken criticism of utilitarianism, that it demands too much from us and thus is self-defeating. Utilitarianism, it is said, requires each of us to sacrifice ourselves for the benefit of others, and in doing so to reduce our happiness, and a philosophy whose idea of the good is to maximize happiness would therefore make us all miserable. Applied to the problem of intergenerational justice, each generation would be called on to immiserate itself for the benefit of subsequent generations. In Reasons and Persons 27–28 (1984), Derek Parfit offered a short answer to this paradox: An ethical theory that would promote well-being may stop short of making everyone miserable without being inconsistent.

66. This assumes that today's taxpayers are not indifferent as between public debt and taxation—that is, when the people who do the borrowing won't be around to pay back the debt through their taxes. The contrary view, much disputed, is called "Ricardian Equivalence." See Robert J. Barro, On the Determinants of the Public Debt, 87 J. Pol. Econ. 940 (1979).

67. OECD.StatExtracts, at http://stats.oecd.org/Index.aspx?DatasetCode=SNA _TABLE1.

68. Fareed Zakaria, The Post-American World 89 (2009).

69. For an unsympathetic view, see Ian Bremmer, The End of the Free Market: Who Wins the War between States and Corporations 52 (2010) ("State capitalism is not an ideology. It is simply communism by another name or an updated form of central planning").

70. Gary S. Becker, China's Next Leap Forward, Wall Street Journal, Sept. 29, 2010, at A21.

71. Stefan Halper, The Beijing Consensus: How China's Model Will Dominate the Twenty-first Century (2010).

72. "Rather than demonstrating the advantages of centrally planned long-term investment, as its foreign admirers sometimes suggested, China's bullet-train experience shows what can go wrong when an unelected elite, influenced by corrupt opportunists, gives orders that all must follow—without the robust public discussion we would have in the States." Charles Lane, China's train wreck, Wash. Post, April 24, 2011, at A17.

73. The Great Disruption: Human Nature and the Reconstitution of Social Order (2000).

74. Source: Statistical Abstract (various years).

75. On the growth spurts of "follower" nations, see Alexander Gerschenkron, Economic Backwardness in Historical Perspective: A Book of Essays (1962).

PART 2:

RELATIVE DECLINE

An Exceptional Nation?

F.H. BUCKLEY

> If something can't go on forever, it won't.
> —HERBERT STEIN

M ost Americans subscribe to the idea of "American Exceptionalism." When polled, 80 percent of respondents report that, because of its history and Constitution, America "has a unique character that makes it the greatest country in the world."[1] A belief in American Exceptionalism is also a badge of faith in the country's future. Whatever problems the country might have, it will surmount them, as it always has done in the past. For some, the label also means a belief in the special destiny of John Winthrop's (and President Reagan's) "city upon a hill," an example to the world of a virtuous, democratic self-government that secures the blessings of liberty for its citizens. More controversially, others might think that, as an exceptional nation, America has a *mission civilisatrice* to bring democratic self-government to backward countries— although that view has taken some hits of late.[2]

Notwithstanding the polls, Americans' faith in their country has recently been shaken, through an unpopular war, political gridlock, and (more than anything) economic decline. President Obama has observed that he sees America as exceptional only in the banal sense that every country is exceptional. "I believe in American exceptionalism, just as I suspect that the Brits believe in British exceptionalism and the Greeks believe in

Greek exceptionalism."[3] To say that every country is exceptional (*Greek* exceptionalism?) is of course to say that no country is exceptional.

In time, Americans might come to share President Obama's cheerless view of his country. For the moment, we see ourselves as comfortably on top of the world, resting upon our economic capital, not a little contemptuous of other countries. Yet nagging doubts intrude. We are in an economic crisis, with slow growth and shrinking job levels. We owned the 20th century—but since then new rivals, such as China, have emerged, and we are less than confident that we will have a proprietary claim over the 21st century.

We have a growing sense that America is in decline, and that in time it might become a country like the others. We have had many economic downturns in the past, but what is different this time is the fear that we will not bounce back, that something is structurally wrong and that we must adjust to diminished expectations. For the first time, we no longer believe that our children will be better off than we were.[4]

Few things are more central to the idea of American Exceptionalism than the sense that, more than anywhere else, this is a country where talent is rewarded and people can get ahead. We can accept income inequality so long as we have income mobility. However, it turns out that we don't have that either, when compared with other first-world countries. Table 2.1, taken from the Pew Economic Mobility Project 2011, measures "intergenerational elasticity" (the relationship between a child's and his or her parent's rank on the income ladder) and reveals that the U.S. is one of the least mobile societies in the first world. Nearly half in the earnings advantage is passed on across the generations in the U.S., compared with less than one-fifth in Canada.

We have all been led to believe that in America, anyone can move up the ranks with the proper amount of industry and discipline. What we don't want are permanent classes of peasants and aristocrats. That's our idea of what Europe is or was, and we've always seen the U.S. to be different from that. We see America, not Denmark, as the land of opportunity. If it turns out that we are more class-ridden than the Europeans, then a core understanding of what American Exceptionalism means will have been lost.

Table 2.1   Comparable Estimates of the Intergenerational
Elasticity of Earnings between Fathers and Sons

Country	Elasticity
U.K.	0.5
Italy	0.48
U.S.	0.47
France	0.41
Spain	0.4
Germany	0.32
Sweden	0.27
Australia	0.26
Canada	0.19
Finland	0.18
Norway	0.17
Denmark	0.15

Source: http://www.economicmobility.org/assets/pdfs/PEW_EMP
_US-CANADA.pdf.

What about economic freedom? Where America once prided itself on being "the land of the free," it now faces competition from other countries, and in the Heritage Foundation's 2011 Index of Economic Freedom it is listed as "mostly free," behind a group of "free" countries.

To some extent, the decline reflects the "rise of the rest," the catch-up of other countries that were devastated by World War II and hobbled by growth-killing ideologies. In 1945 America produced half of the world's Gross Domestic Product. Europe was emerging from war, and Far Eastern countries remained undeveloped. In succeeding decades, many Asian and African countries achieved independence but immediately crippled their economies through socialist policies and departures from the rule of law. The same self-inflicted wounds hampered economic growth in Latin America during the period.[5] It is hardly surprising that, relative to the rest of the world, America was so prosperous.

Since then America's share of world GDP has fallen to less than 20 percent. While much of the decline occurred in the 1970s, America has

Table 2.2   Heritage Index of Economic Freedom, 2012

Country	Rank	Score	Category
Hong Kong	1	89.9	Free
Singapore	2	87.5	Free
Australia	3	83.1	Free
New Zealand	4	82.1	Free
Switzerland	5	81.1	Free
Canada	6	79.9	Mostly Free
Chile	7	78.3	Mostly Free
Mauritius	8	77.0	Mostly Free
Ireland	9	76.9	Mostly Free
United States	10	76.3	Mostly Free

Source: http://www.heritage.org/index/.

continued to decline in recent years, relative to other first-world countries. Between 2000 and 2010, America's GDP fell from 61 to 42 percent of the combined GDPs of the other G-20 countries.[6] And the relative decline is expected to continue. The IMF (International Monetary Fund) projects that in 2016 America's share of world GDP will fall to 17.7 percent, less than China's share.[7]

Were this to happen, Americans might lose their sense of their country as exceptional, and that would be regrettable. American Exceptionalism is benign, to the extent that it promotes a healthy optimism and a willingness to court economic risks, to gamble on new ideas, to pick oneself up after a fall. Should Americans lose their optimism, they will be the poorer for it. At the same time, exceptionalism is a two-edged sword (as I grow older, everything begins to seem a two-edged sword), for it can breed a dangerous complacency about the country's problems. In the 1950s, the British, who had yet to come to terms with their country's decline, called this an "I'm all right, Jack" attitude, and there are echoes of a similar smugness among some in America today. As in postwar Britain, the sense of decline and the need for reform is repressed by an overpowering sense of national superiority.

Why Relative Decline Matters

Should we worry about relative decline? In absolute terms, Americans are far wealthier than they were in 1945, or even 1975. Apart from their increased purchasing power, technological changes have given us consumer products—home computers, cell phones, life-saving drugs—that were unavailable in the very recent past. Nor is that about to change. No one will take away our iPads. Moreover, many would find a world in which wealth is more equally distributed to be morally preferable to one in which half the world's wealth is concentrated in 5 percent of its population. About a sixth of the world's population—a billion people—live on less than a dollar a day, and we should want to see them share in global prosperity even if this results in a further decline in the U.S. share of world GDP.

Even so, the relative decline of American wealth must give one pause, for several reasons. First, relative preferences—how we rate compared with our neighbors—do matter to all of us. Were America's share of world wealth to drop precipitously, Americans would have to come around to their president's view of their country as unexceptional, and that would be emotionally painful. No one likes to come in second. Or 10th, or 30th.

Second, the relative change in the country's wealth would upset the military balance of power, and while many have decried an America that acts as the world's policeman, the alternative might easily prove far worse. In 2009, the United States incurred 43 percent of global military spending. For a country in economic decline, that would not be sustainable, and the withdrawal of America from the world's stage might lead to the Wars of American Succession, as regional powers—some of them very nasty indeed—assert their new relative strength. Former close allies would find themselves obliged to seek alliances with a very different and unpleasant set of friends.

Third, a decline in relative wealth would be personally unsettling for many Americans. The United States remains the preferred destination country for immigrants, and little more than 1 percent of Americans now live abroad. With a significant economic decline, all this would change. Parents would become used to seeing their children less often, on their trips home from China or Europe. In the past, foreigners bore these emotional costs; now Americans would do so as well.

All of these are real costs, and none of them is pleasant to contemplate. What concerns me, however, is the fourth reason why relative decline matters. To the extent that the decline is a consequence of avoidable, wasteful policies, a failure to address them represents a pure deadweight loss. The prospect of American decline should therefore focus attention on the ways in which the country can become more competitive. This book focuses on inefficiencies in its legal system. Before going there, however, we should ask why America's litigation culture is more of a problem today than formerly.

One reason is that the burden of bad law is simply greater today than it was in the past. The American legal system circa 1960 was not greatly different from that of other first-world nations. Since then, however, American civil procedure, tort, contract, corporate, and criminal law has diverged from that of other countries, and the other essays in this book describe how the difference has harmed the U.S.

The other reason is that the burden of bad law weighs more heavily against us now because many of the advantages we formerly enjoyed have been dissipated. When compared with other countries in the past, America had democratic institutions, free land, low taxes, small government, an immunity from European wars, and an open-door policy for immigrants. These were low-lying fruit—but now the fruit have mostly been eaten.[8] Other countries have caught up with us, and what advantages we have they now have too. Indeed, what were advantages are sometimes now disadvantages, as other countries compete better than we do in such areas as immigration and taxes. In sum, we've lost the luxury of complacency that permits us to ignore any deficiencies.

The inefficiencies of our legal system are a luxury good. We might kick a few hundred billion dollars into our tort system, much of that wasteful, but for a country as rich as ours, what does that matter? In today's more straightened economic circumstances, however, it becomes a little harder to dismiss this as chump change.

Free Trade

In 1945 American manufacturers had privileged access to the world's greatest consumer market: that of the United States. Other countries seeking to export to the U.S. faced high tariff walls or import restrictions. Within the United States, however, manufacturers in one state could ship goods to consumers in another state without facing interstate trade barriers. The Commerce Clause of the U.S. Constitution gives Congress the right to regulate commerce "among the several states," and by implication the "Dormant" Commerce Clause vests Congress with the sole power to do so and forbids states from improperly burdening interstate commerce.

The trade advantages U.S. manufacturers enjoyed in 1945 have been substantially dissipated. As we noted, our share of world GDP has been halved, and as Americans consume less of the world's goods, and people in other countries consume more, access to American markets is less important for foreign producers. For their part, American producers have opened up plants in other countries to service the growing consumer markets there. Apart from this, foreign producers enjoy greater access to U.S. markets because of the lowering of U.S. trade barriers under the GATT/WTO multilateral system and bilateral free trade agreements America has signed with major trading partners. In the past, the choice between Seattle and Vancouver as the site of a business plant would have seemed a no-brainer. Seattle would have given a manufacturer much better access to American markets. The choice isn't so clear today, after the North American Free Trade Agreement gives Canadian manufacturers ready access to American markets.[9]

If there is one proposition to which virtually every economist would subscribe, it is that free trade is economically efficient.[10] On average, it makes people better off in the country that adopts free trade. There are winners and losers, but gains to winners exceed losses to losers. Free trade provides consumers with cheaper goods and permits manufacturers to specialize in what they do best and take advantage of scale economies in production. Protectionism also encourages wasteful rent-seeking in which domestic manufacturers court politicians for subsidies and special tariffs against foreign competitors. Free trade between countries therefore commends itself for the same reason that free trade within the United States does, under the Dormant Commerce Clause.

Lowering trade walls has benefited Americans in absolute terms, but might also have resulted in a relative decline in American wealth by strengthening foreign manufacturers and enriching other countries.[11] That is not to say that we would want to go back to high tariff walls. Just the opposite. In a global economy, the countries that will fare best in the future are those that embrace free trade, not protectionism. In recent years America has backed away from free trade, a goal that other countries continue to pursue. As Richard Epstein notes in his article, the current administration appears to have embraced the mercantilist view that trade is a zero-sum game, that foreign prosperity comes off the back of American workers. Unless reversed, the turn to protectionism may be expected to hasten American decline, in both relative and absolute terms.

Immigration

Everything begins in mysticism, said Charles Péguy, and ends in politics. For Americans, the mysticism of immigration, the idea that we are a country of immigrants, has a powerful hold over the imagination. It reinforces the idea of American Exceptionalism, since a country must be exceptionally attractive if immigrants want to come here. To attract immigrants, a country must offer benign, democratic, and liberal institutions.[12] It must be rich and permit entrepreneurs to flourish. High immigration levels are thus a badge of public virtue.

There is nevertheless a bit of puffery in the label of a "country of immigrants" when applied to America. To claim that title, a large percentage of a country's people should be foreign-born. However, only about 13 percent of American residents (legal and illegal) were born in another country, as compared with 20 percent in Canada and 26 percent in Australia—the true nation of immigrants. At 13 percent, America is only a little ahead of Great Britain (11 percent).[13]

Behind the mysticism are the politics of U.S. immigration policies, and these are not always pretty. From the time of the Founders, there was never a time when immigration was not debated in political terms, with an eye to how the new arrivals would vote.[14] Federalists such as John Adams welcomed conservative immigrants from Great Britain and feared radical immigrants from republican France. For Jeffersonian Republicans it was just the opposite. After the potato famine, the arrival of the Democratic

Irish Catholics prompted the creation of the conservative and anti-immigrant Know-Nothing party. Subsequently, immigrants split their votes, as reliably Republican Protestant immigrants arrived from Germany and the Scandinavian countries, and immigration became less politically contentious. By the 1890s, however, the advantage began to swing in one direction again as Democratic voters arrived from southern and eastern Europe, and the Republican party finally curtailed immigration in 1924, imposing national origin quotas that favored more-conservative immigrants from western Europe. For political parties, especially those threatened at the polls, the temptation was always to prorogue the electorate and put a new electorate in its place.[15]

U.S. immigration policies were radically changed in 1965, when national origins quotas were replaced with preferences for family reunification. People from countries that had recently supplied immigrants were given a leg up, while those from countries that had supplied immigrants centuries before found it much harder to get in. In the 1950s, two-thirds of legal immigrants came from Europe or Canada. By the 1990s that figure had fallen to 16 percent. During the same period, the percentage of legal immigrants from Latin America and Asia rose from 31 to 81 percent.[16]

Family reunification policies have two things going for them. Unlike national origins quotas, they appear racially neutral (even if it didn't quite work out that way).[17] They also strengthen family bonds—and who's against that? Indeed, no one is suggesting a return to racist immigration policies of the past. Instead, the debate over legal immigration concerns the qualifications of immigrants and their spillover effects on natives. The question is whether immigrants create more new jobs for natives through business startups than they take away from them by competing for existing jobs. The findings are mixed, and immigration is one of the most contentious and politicized of research topics.

What is uncontroversial is that the United States could do a better job of competing for the highly qualified immigrants who are more likely to confer economic benefits on natives.[18] America is exceptional in the way in which, more than any other first-world OECD country, it favors family-based immigration and admits relatively few employment-based immigrants.

Table 2.3   Legal Immigration, 2006

Country	Total (thousands)	Immigration/ Pop. (%)	Employment (%)	Family (%)	Refugee/ Asylee (%)	Other (%)
Australia	191.9	0.97	40.7	51.1	7.4	0.9
Austria	46.4	0.57	47.7	41.0	11.1	0.3
Belgium	36.1	0.34	58	35.4	6.6	0.0
Canada	251.6	0.80	22.1	60.8	17.0	0.1
Denmark	21.7	0.40	65.7	23.8	5.0	5.5
France	169.0	0.28	26.1	59.0	4.4	10.5
Germany	216.0	0.26	70.3	23.3	2.8	3.6
Italy	204.3	0.35	53.2	41.7	3.1	2.0
Japan	96.1	0.08	29.8	31.3	0.1	38.8
Neth.	59.4	0.36	29.0	46.6	24.3	0.0
New Zeal.	54.8	1.32	32.6	57.9	9.6	0.0
Sweden	74.0	0.89	35.0	37.1	27.9	0.0
U.K.	343.2	0.57	53.2	31.8	8.9	6.0
U.S.	1,266.3	0.42	5.6	70.3	17.1	7.0

Source: OECD International Migration Outlook 2008, at www.oecd-ilibrary.org/social-issues
-migration-health/data/oecd-international-migration-statistics/international-migration-database
_data-00342-en?isPartOf=/content/datacollection/mig-data-en.

In addition to restricting the number of economic immigrants, the U.S. also burdens them with additional costs. Economic immigrants often enter the U.S. under a temporary visa and thereafter apply for permanent alien (green card) status. The procedure is time consuming and (for those who wisely retain an immigration lawyer) costly. Immigrants must show, under labor certification standards, that they are not taking a job away from a native American, and this process can take as long as two years. During all this time, an immigrant, who will typically have given up a job in his or her exit country, will not know whether he or she will be permitted to remain in the U.S. That's not how professionals like to be hired.

By contrast, Canada, the U.K., Australia, and New Zealand eliminate most of the risk and cost through its points system. Potential immigrants can quickly check online to see if they qualify for admission, based on the number of points they accumulate on a calculator that asks questions about age, education, language ability, arranged employment, and wealth. It's not rocket science, if politics and projected voting patterns are kept out of it.[19]

America's reluctance to compete for qualified immigrants likely imposes enormous, if hidden, costs. Immigrants added hundreds of thousands of jobs and powered the high-tech boom of the 1990s. One study found that a quarter of all technology and engineering businesses, and more than half of Silicon Valley startups, created between 1995 and 2005 had a foreign-born founder. And a quarter of international patents filed in the U.S. in 2006 were based on the work of foreign-borns.[20] Just the sort of people we want to keep out, in short. We admit about 150,000 economic immigrants a year, but the queue of applicants is over 500,000.[21] For more immigrant-friendly countries, America's policies are a pure gift.

A move to a more entrepreneurial immigration system would likely offer non-economic spillover benefits. Economic immigrants are less likely to commit crimes or to rely on the welfare system, and for countries that favor them, immigration is less contentious. The natives are more likely to welcome immigrants, who in turn are more likely to assimilate to the natives.[22]

Taxes

The U.S. no longer enjoys a tax advantage over other countries. In part, this is because the Reagan tax revolution of the 1980s has spread worldwide. In addition, U.S. taxes have increased since then, as have the complexity of America's tax laws and the cost of navigating around them.

The World Bank ranks the U.S. favorably in the "ease of doing business," where it comes in at number 4, internationally.[23] That's great, but in one important area the U.S. lags behind: it ranks 69th out of 183 countries in "paying taxes": the number of hours it takes to prepare, file, and pay taxes and the total tax rate borne by the standard business. Table 2.4 lists the rankings. Unsurprisingly, the U.S. ranks behind several major competitors; surprisingly, it ranks no better than Nordic countries.

Table 2.4   Corporate Taxes

Country	Rank	Hours per Year to Prepare Taxes	Total Tax Rate (federal and provincial)[a]
Hong Kong	3	80	23.0
Singapore	4	231	27.1
Canada	8	131	28.8
Denmark	14	135	27.5
Switzerland	12	63	30.1
United Kingdom	24	110	37.3
Norway	27	62	41.6
Finland	28	93	39.0
Netherlands	43	127	40.5
Sweden	50	122	52.8
France	58	132	65.7
United States	72	187	46.7

[a] Includes social contributions and labor taxes paid by the employer, property and property transfer taxes, dividend, capital gains and financial transactions taxes, waste collection, vehicle, road, and other taxes, and excludes employee withholding taxes. See Paying Taxes 2012: The Global Picture, Appendix 4, Table 1, at http://www.doingbusiness.org/~/media /FPDKM/Doing%20Business/Documents/Special-Reports/Paying-Taxes-2012.pdf
Source: Doing Business 2012: Doing Business in a More Transparent World, International Bank for Reconstruction and Development/The World Bank, at www.doingbusiness.org /~/media/fpdkm/doing%20business/documents/annual-reports/english/db12-fullreport.pdf.

The relatively high U.S. corporate tax rate discourages multinationals and foreign firms from producing in the U.S., and this increases U.S. unemployment and lowers real wages. The tax code also places U.S. firms at a comparative disadvantage when doing business abroad. For the most part, foreign firms that invest in other countries pay taxes only on earnings that they bring back to their country. Anomalously, U.S. firms are taxed on worldwide income and must pay the difference between the U.S. tax rate and the lower foreign corporate tax rate, even if they leave the earnings in the foreign country. Martin Feldstein explains how this advantages foreign firms: "French and American firms that invest in Ireland pay a corporate tax of only 12.5% to the Irish government. The French firm can then bring its after-tax profit back to France by paying less than 5% on those repatriated profits while an American firm would have to pay the 22.5% difference between our 35% corporate tax and the 12.5% Irish tax."[24] As Feldstein notes, this encourages U.S. firms to leave the foreign earnings abroad, rather than bringing them back and investing in America. Foreign firms also have a leg up in acquiring foreign firms, since they pay lower taxes on the acquired firm's profits. This is especially harmful in the high-tech world, where a business acquisition gives the acquirer access to new technology.

As seen in Table 2.4, the number of hours it takes to prepare and file tax returns in the U.S. is considerably higher than in comparable countries. Added to this are the costs of lawyers and accountants, which are multiplied by the Sarbanes-Oxley corporate governance requirements described by Stephen Bainbridge in this book. Then there are the wasteful efforts at social engineering, such as the costly home mortgage interest deduction (about $80 billion a year). By driving housing prices up, the tax break was one of the hidden causes of the housing bubble and the subsequent market meltdown in home prices. And for all of that, it didn't even give us home ownership rates any higher than Britain or Canada.

Worse still is America's form of state capitalism, in which the government tries to pick winners through special tax breaks ("tax expenditures") for business. As Robert Cooter and Aaron Edlin explain in their article, we would not expect politicians to outperform investors in identifying profitable opportunities. Moreover, the tax breaks divert firms from what they should be doing—finding business investments—to rent-seeking effort to cajole politicians for favors. In addition to rent seeking is the "rent extraction" by politicians who squeeze campaign contributions from firms in return for a special little tax break. Fareed Zakaria minces no words about the American culture of corruption: "The American tax code is a monstrosity, cumbersome and inefficient. It is 16,000 pages long and riddled with exemptions and loopholes, specific favors to special interests. As such, it represents the deep, institutionalized corruption at the heart of the American political process, in which it is now considered routine to buy a member of Congress's support for a particular, narrow provision that will be advantageous for your business."[25] An object lesson in the utility of investing in lobbyists and tax lawyers is provided by General Electric, whose CEO is President Obama's liaison to the business community and chairman of the President's Council on Jobs and Competitiveness. General Electric, the country's largest company, earned profits of $14.2 billion in 2010. Nevertheless, it paid no taxes: "Its extraordinary success is based on an aggressive strategy that mixes fierce lobbying for tax breaks and innovative accounting that enables it to concentrate its profits offshore."[26] What a recipe for competitiveness!

Public Debt and Government Spending

Issuing public debt, in the form of bonds and other debt obligations, usefully permits a government to pay for valuable services such as national defense. Failed states have *really* low public debt to GDP ratios. There comes a point, however, when the debt load excessively burdens a country and its citizens. For example, Portugal's 2011 gross public debt is 111 percent of that country's GDP, and the country is in a debt crisis. As for America, we're at 101 percent, 5 percent more than the 15 countries of Europe.[27] Some people think that *net* public debt (all financial liabilities less financial assets) is a better measure of a country's solvency, and if that's the criterion, America looks shakier still. At 75 percent of GDP, the U.S. is tied with Portugal and 15 percent higher than the Euro area.[28]

A study of the relationship between public debt and GDP found only a weak correlation between the two below a threshold of 90 percent. Below that figure, it's not clear whether debt levels harm the economy. Above 90 percent, however, high debt levels are correlated with a declining growth rate, with a 10 percent increase in the debt-to-GDP ratio associated with an annual 0.15 slowdown in GDP growth for advanced economies.[29] Even before the recent recession, the annual growth rate of the U.S. economy was an anemic 2 percent, while that of China was 10 percent. A further decline in the growth of the American economy might well be transformational—and not in a good way. We've not seen this yet, but it would be foolish to dismiss such concerns.

What did we get from the expansion of public debt? The recent increase in federal spending was supposed to lift us from a recession and kick-start the economy. Since 2009, stimulus spending, timely and targeted, has aimed to promote new industries that the private sector had inefficiently passed over ("green jobs"). Though we have experimented with every gadget in the Keynesian toolbox, from auto bailouts, cash for clunkers, home-buyer tax credits, to near-zero interest rates, all we have reaped is increased unemployment and a stalled economy.

At present, the burden of America's debt load is cushioned by low interest rates. As the debt load increases, U.S. debt may be downgraded further and interest rates may rise. The deficit can also be expected to increase substantially, as baby boomers retire and the Social Security bill comes due. The President's Commission Report of Fiscal Responsibility warned of a coming debt crisis that would force the government to implement the most stringent of austerity measures.

> By 2025 revenue will be able to finance only interest payments, Medicare, Medicaid, and Social Security. Every other federal government activity—from national defense and homeland security to transportation and energy—will have to be paid for with borrowed money. Debt held by the public will outstrip the entire American economy, growing to as much as 185 percent of GDP by 2035. Interest on the debt could rise to nearly $1 trillion by 2020. These mandatory payments—which buy absolutely no goods or services—will squeeze out funding for all other priorities.
>
> Federal debt this high is unsustainable. It will drive up interest rates for all borrowers—businesses and individuals—and curtail economic growth by crowding out private investment. By making it more expensive for entrepreneurs and businesses to raise capital, innovate, and create jobs, rising debt could reduce per-capita GDP, each American's share of the nation's economy, by as much as 15 percent by 2035.[30]

In sum, there is a growing sense that something *must* be done. But *will* enough be done to avert a crisis?

Formerly, American economic conservatives could take heart in the relatively smaller size of government in this country. In 1960, American government spending was roughly the same as that of comparable first-world countries, expressed as a percentage of GDP. By 1990, after several decades of Keynesian spending in other countries, the American government was 13 percent smaller than the governments of its first-world rivals. Since then

Table 2.5   Size of Government: Government Spending as a Percentage
of GDP

Country	1960	1990	2010
Australia	21.2	34.9	36.3
Canada	28.6	46	43.8
France	34.6	49.8	56.2
Germany	32.4	45.1	46.7
Italy	30.1	53.4	50.6
Japan	17.5	31.3	40.7
New Zealand	26.9	41.3	43.0
Norway	29.9	54.9	46.0
Sweden	31	59.1	53.1
U.K.	32.2	39.9	51.0
Average	28.4	45.6	46.7
U.S.	27.0	32.8	42.3

Source: Vito Tanzi and Ludger Schuknecht, Public Spending in the 20th Century 6, at
Table 1.1 (2000), OECD Economic Outlook no. 89 367 (2011), General Government Outlay as a
Percentage of GDP, Annex Table 25 (federal, state, and local expenditures plus Social
Security).

the gap has narrowed considerably. The size of the U.S. government is now
about the same as that of Australia, Canada, and New Zealand—and this
is before the bill for health care reform ("Obamacare") comes due.

However measured, the size of government in the U.S. and other countries would appear to be a drag on the economy. The empirical literature
on economic growth suggests that the growth-maximizing size of government is not more than 30 percent of GDP.[31] Beyond that level, government
spending would appear to reduce the size of the pie.

Human Capital

For most individuals, and for everyone who is young, the greatest source
of wealth is anticipated future earnings. What these will be depends upon
what economists call human capital: the intelligence, education, work hab-

its, and personal virtues that correlate with a person's economic success. National wealth in turn is a function of the human capital of its citizens, as well as the spillover benefits (which economists call social capital) of living in a country where other people have high human capital. I am worse off if I live in a country whose citizens are ill educated, untrustworthy, or otherwise have low human capital.[32]

Formerly, America enjoyed a significant human capital advantage over other countries. That is no longer the case, as K–12 education has declined and family structures have weakened in this country. While such advantages cannot power economic growth by themselves, this is not to say that they are irrelevant.

In the not so distant past, an American high school diploma was a badge of quality and signaled that one was sufficiently educated for most of the available jobs. Students were equipped with basic math skills and knew how to use the English language. That's no longer the case. Math skills have declined and the job of teaching students how to construct a sentence has been passed on to college instructors. In moving away from rustbelt, factory jobs to an information economy, we've required a stronger skill set from students, which high school cannot hope to provide.

Other countries have not seen the same decline in student performance. In the most recent OECD Program for International Student Assessment (PISA) rankings, which provide a snapshot of a 15-year-old's knowledge and skills in math, science, and reading in 65 countries, the United States placed 30th in math and 23rd in science. In reading it placed 15th, well below Canada and Australia.

The poor performance of U.S. students would not seem attributable to teacher salaries, since American teachers are the best paid in the world.[33] Immigrant children represent a special challenge for teachers, but Australia and Canada have higher immigrant populations. Some have offered demographic explanations for the poor U.S. performance. When African Americans and Latinos are taken out of the mix, the remaining two-thirds of U.S. students are reported to perform at Canadian levels. Of course, it's not fair to compare two-thirds of American children with 100 percent of Canadian children (especially given higher immigration figures for Canada), but the greater problem is that one can't pretend that

Table 2.6   Human Capital

Country	Student Performance: Math (2009)	Student Performance: Science (2009)	Student Performance: Reading (2009)	Divorce per 1,000 (2000)	Single Parent Families	Prison Population per 100,000
Australia	514	527	515	2.7 (1998)	16.8	129
Canada	527	529	524	2.46	22.1	117
Norway	498	500	503	2.0	—	73
Netherlands	526	522	508	3.2	11.1	87
Germany	513	520	497	3.5	15.0	83
Japan	529	539	520	3.1	12.3	55
Sweden	494	495	497	3.8	17.6	70
U.K.	492	514	494	4.0	21.5	155 (England and Wales)
Singapore	562	542	526	—	—	249
Italy	483	489	486	1.0	10.2	109
France	497	498	496	3.0	21.0	315
U.S.	487	502	500	6.2	25.8	730

Source: OECD Program for International Student Assessment; U.S. Statistical Abstract, Doing Better for Families, OECD 2011; International Centre for Prison Studies (University of Essex), at http://www.prisonstudies.org/info/worldbrief.

one-third of American students simply don't count, when evaluating American social capital in general. ("Them? Never mind about *them!* They're not *us!*")

Americans who express optimism about their country's future often point to its higher education system, where the country remains the world's leader. Its elite institutions are the best anywhere, and American research and development leads the world. A country's ability to attract star scientists has substantial spillover benefits for its economy, and in the past America has been the net winner in the competition for them.[34] That's not about to change quickly, but who is to say that America will maintain its intellectual edge throughout the 21st century? Elite institutions are a luxury good of a rich economy, and economic decline can result in a brain drain to richer countries. There is a global competition for talent,[35] and as the rest of the world becomes wealthier we should expect America's intellectual advantage to be dissipated. Our immigration policies, which ask foreign postgraduate students to return home, don't help.

There is a further reason why intellectual assets will become more dispersed in the future. In the past, location was all-important: a researcher needed to work closely with colleagues on the cutting edge of his or her discipline. Papers were shared slowly, and often long after the intellectual breakthrough. Publishing might come years later. Scholars worked in "clusters," geographically related networks of universities, research institutions, think tanks, and companies.[36] High-tech development was centered in Silicon Valley, and great universities such as Stanford and MIT spun off research firms in Palo Alto and Cambridge.

In the future, however, that is likely to change. Travel is cheaper, of course, but more importantly, papers are accessible worldwide and immediately though Internet publishing sites such as Social Science Research Network (SSRN). As of the end of 2010, there were 50 percent more Internet users in China—457 million—than the total U.S. population.[37] The world total of Internet users approaches two billion people.[38] Distance learning, where students are in different cities or countries, has been with us for some time, and distance scholarship is already a reality. Scholars can collaborate in real time on papers, and three-dimensional virtual reality conferences can be expected to replace the faculty workshop. We'll still want to bounce ideas off a colleague down the hall, but we'll also become accustomed to virtual visits with our peers in India and China.

A recent Royal Society study describes the trend toward globalization and predicts a relative decline for American science. Today more than 35 percent of scientific articles published in international journals are written by cross-border collaborators, up from 25 percent 15 years ago. China has already overtaken the U.K. in research publications, and some time before 2020 it is expected to surpass the U.S.[39]

In other measures of human capital, Americans fare poorly. Its divorce rate is the highest in the world, and the percentage of children raised by single parents and the prison incarceration rate are the highest in the first world. In his article, Jeffrey Parker lays the blame for the high prison rate on excessive American criminal penalties, which were levered up in the 1990s when federal sentencing guidelines were adopted. But that can't be the whole story. Prior to the adoption of the guidelines and get-tough-on-crime measures at the state level, America had the highest level of violent crime in the first world.[40] After tougher anti-crime measures were adopted, American violent crime levels fell to first-world levels (homicide apart, where America still leads the first world). One might plausibly conclude that other countries simply do not require the high level of sanctions needed to deter American criminals.

As we have seen, America isn't very exceptional when it comes to taxes and public debt. It is exceptional, however, in its family structure and crime rates. Exceptional doesn't always mean better. That's not to say that high divorce and crime rates tell us much about economic decline. In the past, criminality and prosperity went hand in hand. The most astute observer of American society reminded conservatives who worried about social pathologies that these were closely linked to libertarian values of which they presumably approved, and which make for independence, entrepreneurship, personal advancement, and a distrust of authority. "In a country that stresses success above all," said Seymour Martin Lipset, "people are led to feel that the most important thing is to win the game, regardless of the methods employed in doing so."[41]

In one respect, America does have a human capital advantage. Its fertility rate of 2.06 is just below the replacement level of 2.09, and is one of the highest in the first world. Add to that the influx of immigrants to the country, and America's population can be expected to continue to expand. By contrast, Japan's low fertility rate of 1.21, combined with that country's hostility to immigration, has been likened to a demographic time bomb. However, one can make too much of the benefits of an expanding population. Otherwise, Niger, with its fertility rate of 7.6, would clean up. The addition of one more worker will increase a country's GDP—but not its GDP per capita unless the employee contributes more than the average native. Thus an expanding population will not increase American GDP per capita unless succeeding generations and the cohort of new immigrants have greater human capital than the average American native does today. Given America's record on education and other measures of social capital, and our immigration policies, it is less than clear that this will happen.[42]

Conclusion

Standard & Poor's downgraded America's public debt on August 5, 2011, and life went on. The stock market fluctuated widely, then returned to prior levels. Bond yields remained low. The dollar dropped in value, until investors realized that it remained the only game in town. As much as America might seem in decline, Europe seems in competition with us on the downward slopes. There are also signs that China's boom years are behind it.

These are snapshots of a world in change in the fall of 2011. Nevertheless, there is reason to think that the structural problems that I have described will continue to affect the United States for years to come. In that case, America's rule of law disadvantage, described in the following chapters, will stand out in sharper relief. If so, we can no longer pretend that we can safely ignore the costs of inefficient legal rules.

We turn, therefore, to an examination of the American legal system, where the country is decidedly exceptional.

Notes

1. Byron York, Poll: Americans Believe in American Exceptionalism, Not as sure about Obama, Washington Examiner, Dec. 22, 2010. The best study on what the

term might mean remains Seymour Martin Lipset, American Exceptionalism: A Double-Edged Sword (1996).

2. On the way in which America's self-image as a progressive country powered an expansionary colonial and foreign policy, see Robert Kagan, Dangerous Nation: America's Place in the World, from Its Earliest Days to the Dawn of the 20th Century (2006).

3. James Kirchick, Squanderer in chief, Los Angeles Times, April 28, 2009.

4. http://www.rasmussenreports.com/public_content/business/general_business /december_2010/only_17_say_today<#213>s_children_will_be_better_off_than _their_parents.

5. See Sebastian Edwards, Left Behind: Latin America and the False Promise of Populism (2010).

6. Charles Wolf, The Facts about American 'Decline,' Wall Street Journal, April 13, 2011.

7. IMF Bombshell: Age of America Nears End, in http://www.marketwatch.com /story/imf-bombshell-age-of-america-about-to-end-2011−04−25?link=MW_home _latest_news. In the recent scholarly literature, American Declinism is very much a growth industry. See, e.g., Niall Ferguson, Colossus: The Rise and Fall of the American Empire (2005); Martin Jacques, When China Rules the World: The End of the Western World and the Birth of a New Global Order (2009).

8. The metaphor is Tyler Cowen's. The Great Stagnation: How America Ate All the Low-Hanging Fruit of Modern History, Got Sick, and Will (Eventually) Feel Better (2011).

9. Forgetting, for the moment, the American tendency to cheat on its NAFTA obligations, when pressured to do so by American interest groups, through legal fictions such as "anti-dumping."

10. See Douglas A. Irwin, Free Trade under Fire (3d ed., 2009); Douglas A. Irwin, Against the Tide: An Intellectual History of Free Trade (1996). For a review of free trade's effect in alleviating a country's poverty, see Jagdish Bhagwati, In Defense of Globalization ch. 5 (2004); David Dollar and Art Kraay, Growth Is Good for the Poor, 1 J. Econ. Growth 195 (2002).

11. For example, Canada seems to have been the relative winner from the cross-border expansion of trade between the two countries that resulted from NAFTA. While increased trade benefited both countries in absolute terms, it had a far greater impact on Canada, for the simple reason that the U.S. accounts for about 80 percent of Canadian exports, while Canada accounts for only 20 percent of U.S. exports.

12. The idea that states compete for immigrants through their political institutions was the core of Turner's Frontier Thesis. Frederick Jackson Turner, The Frontier in American History ch. 1 (1921).

13. For the United States, see http://www.census.gov/prod/2010pubs/acs-11.pdf and http://www.cis.org/immigrants_profile_2007. For Canada, see http://www4 .hrsdc.gc.ca/.3ndic.1t.4r@-eng.jsp?iid=38. For Australia, see http://www.immi.gov

.au/media/fact-sheets/15population.htm. For Great Britain, see Table 1.1: Estimated population resident in the United Kingdom, by country of birth, April 2009 to March 2010. Office for National Statistics. http://www.statistics.gov.uk/downloads/theme _population/population-by-birthcountrynationality-apr09-mar10.zip (Great Britain).

14. On the history of U.S. immigration policies, see Maldwyn Jones, American Immigration (2d ed. 1992).

15. That was Bertolt Brecht's satirical suggestion in his poem "The Solution."

16. George J. Borjas, Heaven's Door: Immigration Policy and the American Economy 41 (1999).

17. The number of legal immigrants from Mexico in 2009 was 40 percent higher than that for all of Europe combined. 2009 Yearbook of Immigration Statistics Table 2 (Dept. of Homeland Security 2010), http://www.dhs.gov/xlibrary/assets /statistics/yearbook/2009/ois_yb_2009.pdf.

18. See F.H. Buckley, "The Market for Migrants," in Economic Dimensions of International Law (Jagdeep Bhandari and Alan Sykes, eds., 1997); Ayelet Shachar, The Race for Talent: Highly Skilled Migrants and Competitive Immigration Regimes, 81 N.Y.U. L. Rev. 148 (2005).

19. For proposals that the U.S. mimic the points system, see Darrel M. West, Brain Gain: Rethinking U.S. Immigration Policy 132–34 (2010); Tim Kane and Robert E. Litan, Knowledge Economy Immigration: A Priority for U.S. Growth Policy (2009); Borjas, supra note 9, at 58–61, 192–93. For the points test itself, see http://www.visabureau.com/canada/points-test.aspx.

20. Vivek Wadhwa, Ben Rissing, AnnaLee Saxenian, and Gary Gereffi, Intellectual Property, the Immigration Backlog, and a Reverse Brain-Drain: America's New Immigrant Entrepreneurs: Part I, Duke Science, Technology & Innovation Paper No. 23 (2007).

21. Vivek Wadhwa, Guillermina Jasso, Ben Rissing, Gary Gereffi, and Richard B. Freeman, Intellectual Property, the Immigration Backlog, and a Reverse Brain-Drain: America's New Immigrant Entrepreneurs: Part III (August 2007).

22. Jacob L. Vigdor, Comparing Immigrant Assimilation in North America and Europe, Figure 13 (Manhattan Institute Civic Report 64, May 2011) (Canada scores 82 and the United States 58 on an assimilation index).

23. Doing Business 2012: Doing Business in a More Transparent World, at http:// www.doingbusiness.org/rankings.

24. Martin Feldstein, Want to Boost the Economy? Lower Corporate Tax Rates, Wall Street Journal, February 15, 2011.

25. Fareed Zakaria, How to Restore the American Dream, Time Magazine, Oct. 21, 2010.

26. David Kocieniewski, G.E.'s Strategies Let It Avoid Taxes Altogether, New York Times, March 24, 2011.

27. Gross public debt is a consolidation of accounts for the central, state, and local government. See OECD Economic Outlook no. 89 (June 2011), at http://stats.oecd .org/Index.aspx?QueryId=29868.

28. OECD Economic Outlook No. 89 Annex Tables, Annex Table 33, at http://www.oecd.org/document/3/0,3343,en_2649_34573_2483901_1_1_1_1,00.html.

29. Navigating the Fiscal Challenges Ahead, Appendix 3 (IMF, 2010); Carmen M. Reinhart and Kenneth S. Rogoff, Growth in a Time of Debt, 100 Am. Econ. Rev. 573 (2010).

30. The Moment of Truth, Report of the National Commission on Fiscal Responsibility and Reform 11 (December 2010), http://www.fiscalcommission.gov/sites/fiscalcommission.gov/files/documents/TheMomentofTruth12_1_2010.pdf.

31. Vito Tanzi and Ludger Schuknecht, Public Spending in the 20th Century (2000); Johannah Branson and C. A. Knox Lovell, A Growth Maximising Tax Structure for New Zealand, 8 Int. Tax ∫ Pub. Fin. 129 (2001).

32. A 2006 World Bank study asserted that intangible capital (meaning human and social capital and social institutions) is the largest share of total wealth in most countries. Kirk Hamilton et al., Where Is the Wealth of Nations? Measuring Capital for the 21st Century 87 (2006).

33. On how spending more money on schools doesn't improve student performance, see Eric A. Hanushek and Alfred A. Lindseth, Schoolhouses, Courthouses, and Statehouses: Solving the Funding-Achievement Puzzle in America's Public Schools (2009).

34. Lynne G. Zucker and Michael R. Darby, "Star Scientists, Innovation and Regional and National Immigration," in David B. Audretsch, Robert E. Litan, and Robert J. Strom (eds.), Entrepreneurship and Openness: Theory and Evidence 181 (2009).

35. See Ben Wildavsky, The Great Brain Race: How Global Universities Are Reshaping the World ch. 1 (2010).

36. Michael E. Porter, Location, Competition, and Economic Development: Local Clusters in a Global Economy, 14 Econ. Dev. Q. 15 (2000).

37. http://designative.info/2011/04/02/internet-in-china-number-of-chinese-internet-users-reaches-457-million/.

38. http://www.internetworldstats.com/stats26.htm.

39. Knowledge, Networks and Nations: Global Scientific Collaboration in the 21st Century, RS Policy Document 03/11 6, 43 (2011).

40. Lipset, supra note 1, at 46–49.

41. Id. at 47.

42. An expanding population will make it easier for a state to fund its Medicare and Social Security benefits. However, that goes to wealth transfers between people in an economy and not to the creation of wealth. In the case of countries such as Japan—and perhaps the U.S.—what one anticipates is simply a form of bankruptcy in which unsustainable promises are broken, which is what the current Republican budget plan envisages. When the time comes, we'll stiff the elderly. After all, we always knew that Social Security was a tax paid to support a social welfare scheme.

PART 3:

EMPIRICAL EVIDENCE

Are Americans More Litigious?
SOME QUANTITATIVE EVIDENCE

J. MARK RAMSEYER AND ERIC B. RASMUSEN

M any observers suggest that American citizens sue more readily than citizens elsewhere, and that American judges shape society more powerfully than judges elsewhere. We examine the problems involved in exploring these questions quantitatively. The data themselves indicate that American law's notoriety does not result from how we handle routine disputes. Instead, it results from the peculiar and dysfunctional way American courts handle particular legal doctrines such as class actions.

Let's begin with some stories.

McDonald's coffee. Stella Liebeck ordered coffee at a McDonald's drive-through and promptly spilled it on her lap. Because of her absorbent sweat pants, she suffered severe burns. She sued, and a jury awarded her $2.86 million, cut by the judge to $650,000. Eventually, Liebeck and McDonald's settled out of court.[1]

Spill, sue, go home with $2.86 million. The courts-as-demented-slot-machines story shocked most readers, and the case's eventual settlement got buried in the newspapers' back pages. As odd as the bizarre verdict, however, was the positive press it earned among legal professionals.

Predictably, the trade association for the plaintiffs' bar (formerly the Association of Trial Lawyers of America; now pleasantly renamed the American Association for Justice) celebrated the award as a victory for justice. More curiously, even prominent law professors found good things to say about $2.86 million for a coffee spill.[2]

Chipotle's wheelchair. Maurizio Antoninetti wheeled himself into a Chipotle Mexican Grill and complained about the service-line counters. Set at a height convenient for those who could walk, they were too high for Antoninetti. The restaurant said it would happily show him the food in cups or at a private table, but Antoninetti would have none of that. He sued. The Americans with Disabilities Act (ADA) entitled him to "reasonable accommodation," he argued, and a special viewing at a special table was inferior. He wanted the full "Chipotle experience." For that, the franchise needed to install lower counters.

The Ninth Circuit found for Antoninetti, and granted injunctive relief. The chain was required to install lower counters—counters convenient for wheel-chaired customers and inconvenient for everyone else. And because the District Court had awarded Antoninetti only $136,537 in attorney's fees, the Circuit Court remanded the case to give him more.

Since immigrating to the United States in 1990, Antoninetti had sued more than twenty businesses over service quality. Only once had he ever returned to an establishment, the Court acknowledged, but it declared that point irrelevant. The restaurant owed wheelchair customers lower counters whether Antoninetti would ever eat there again or not.[3]

Cigarettes. In the 1990s, Mississippi plaintiffs' lawyer Richard "Dickie" Scruggs sued cigarette companies on behalf of 46 states. By convincing consumers that smoking was safe, he argued, the companies had increased the Medicaid bills that state governments had to pay. That anyone in the past half-century really thought smoking safe was unclear. What was clearer was that, by killing its victims quickly and early, smoking reduces—rather than increases—government health care and pension costs.[4]

But never mind such questions. Under the 1998 Tobacco Master Settlement Agreement, the companies agreed to restrict their marketing and lobbying and to pay $246 billion over 25 years ($900 million to Scruggs's law firm).[5] And the intellectual class cheered. The *New York Times* applauded the settlement and lamented that the regulatory strictures were not harsher still.[6]

A reader might think Americans use litigation in place of legislation and regulation. He might think judges wield enormous and capricious power. He might think litigants unpredictably manipulate the power of the state by using (or abusing) a judicial branch immune from any democratic checks. He might also think that for American businesses, law is as important as commerce. Making a good product at low cost is all well and good, of course. But retaining a top-flight law firm to protect the firm's assets against those who would judicially expropriate them would seem a sensible first priority.

If true, the need to protect one's firm from judicially sanctioned theft is a distinctively American exigency. It is not a story one hears about other wealthy democracies, common though it is in poorer countries. What is more, the intellectual impulse to defend these outcomes instinctively also seems uniquely American. Courts in other countries do issue bizarre opinions from time to time, for idiocy knows no boundaries. But "tort reform" as a major policy issue is a peculiarly American debate.

We undertook this project to quantify the use of courts across countries. Quickly, however, we realized that we could not reliably measure what really matters. The theoretical problems lay in identifying measurable phenomena that accurately reflect the impact of courts. The empirical problems stemmed from the high aggregation level of the data available.

That data does indicate, however, that for routine contract, tort, and property disputes, courts in America perform about as well as in other wealthy countries. The notoriety of the U.S. legal system does not stem from these routine disputes. It stems instead from the abysmal performance of U.S. courts when they encounter certain high-profile disputes. Aggregate numbers are not informative about this kind of dysfunction, though much can be said about it, as we will do in the last part of this chapter.

Table 3.1   Measures of Litigation

Essay section for sources and definitions	Suits filed per 100,000 people	Judges per 100,000 people	Lawyers per 100,000 people	Motor Insurance (% GDP)	Motor Insurance ($US/car)	Cost of Contract Action (% of value)
	B, C	D	E	G	G	F
Australia	1,542	4	259	0.81	664	20.7
Canada	1,450	3.3	292	1.35	1,574	22.3
France	2,416	12.47	70	0.93	786	17.4
Japan	1,768	2.83	12	0.72	754	22.7
England,*=U.K.	3,681	2.22	277	*0.93	*927	*23.4
U.S.	5,806	10.81	380	1.45	1,464	14.4

Notes: The various national definitions are important and are explained in the essay. The star (*) indicates "United Kingdom" since Scotland and Northern Ireland have legal systems distinct from England.

Comparative Litigation Statistics

A. Conclusion as Introduction

The results. Table 3.1 shows a number of proxies for the use of the courts across six wealthy democracies. We will discuss them as a group first, and then review the proxies individually.

Note first that although each of the proxies plausibly measures court usage, the proxies do not correlate with each other very closely. The U.S. has about a quarter more suits per capita than does the U.K., but four times as many as Canada. It has fewer judges per capita than France, but four times as many as the U.K. It has 17 times as many lawyers per capita as Japan, but the same number as Australia. It has twice the motor vehicle insurance costs of Australia, but lower costs than Canada.

Note second that America is not special. From the stories that dominate the newspapers, our courts seem crazed. Yet most litigation involves nothing like those bizarre disputes and so they only lightly affect measures such as suits filed or the number of judges. Ordinary litigation involves car crashes and broken contracts. These disputes dominate the courts. All six countries use courts to resolve this kind of dispute, and the courts resolve them similarly, maintaining stable property rights and facilitating efficient investment. Indeed, a central reason these countries are wealthy is that their courts handle these routine disputes well.

Their significance. Table 3.1's level of aggregation tells us about what we might call "first-order law": the typical disputes over automobile accidents and contract claims. Countries differ in how well their courts handle these mundane disputes. Even among wealthy democracies some courts handle them more efficiently than others. But compared with developing economies even the least efficient does reasonably well. Despite a bewildering array of organizations and procedures, the end results are similar.[7]

American notoriety stems instead from what we might call "second-order law": coffee spills, ADA suits, and tobacco settlements. These cases generate controversy, make a few trial lawyers rich, and provoke relentless calls for reform. This law can profoundly affect social relations and the economy, but not because the cases are common or even because they transfer large amounts of money. Rather, the measurable, litigated cases cause households and firms to take expensive precautions of little social value.

The U.S. is exceptional not in how it handles first-order law, but in how it handles second-order law. In the typical accident or contract claim, U.S. courts do reasonably well. They may face somewhat more litigation than other rich democracies, but not much. In the second-order cases, however, the U.S. courts entertain claims that courts in other well-functioning economies would dismiss in short order. In the process, they necessarily create a drag on American business. As was said some time ago: "Increasingly, the civil justice system seems to be two different systems. One is a stable system that provides modest compensation for plaintiffs who claimed slight or moderate injuries in automobile and other accidents that have been the major source of litigation for 50 years. The second is an unstable system that provides continually increasing awards for claims for serious injuries in any type of lawsuit, and for all injuries, serious or not, in product liability, malpractice, street hazards and workplace accidents."[8]

B. Suits per Capita

When someone claims that the U.S. is exceptionally "litigious," what evidence might be cited to support the claim? What might someone else cite to dispute it? What does such a claim even mean? To explore these questions, turn first to the number of civil suits filed.

The United States. Although most litigation in the U.S. occurs in state (not federal) courts, data on state court litigation are maddeningly elusive. The court systems themselves differ widely. Some states use small-claims courts, while others do not. Some states use subject-specific courts, while others route all suits to a single court. Those states that do use small-claims courts employ widely varying jurisdictional cut-offs. Faced with such disparate systems, the National Center for State Courts (the NCSC) does the best it can, but about 10 percent of the states return its surveys with incomplete data. Another 10 percent report the wrong data.

Doing what it can with those surveys, the NCSC finds that plaintiffs filed 7.9 million suits in state courts of unified and general jurisdiction in 2006 and another 10.2 million suits in limited jurisdiction courts (e.g., small-claims courts), a total caseload of 18 million.[9]

Additionally, plaintiffs filed 272,000 new civil suits in federal District Courts, including 34,000 contract claims, 4,000 real property claims, and 77,000 tort claims (15,000 of them relating to asbestos). The rest of the claims were statutory: 53,000 prisoner petitions, 32,000 civil rights cases, 19,000 labor law cases, 13,000 social security claims, and 11,000 intellectual property disputes.[10]

Within the state courts, case composition varies widely. In Kansas, 89 percent were contract disputes and 5 percent small claims, while in Wisconsin 16 percent were contracts disputes and 64 percent small claims. Among seven states reporting detailed composition data, tort cases ranged from 1.5 to 8.0 percent of the total.[11] Small claims comprised 44 percent of incoming civil cases. General civil cases—tort, contract, and real property cases not filed as small claims—were 37 percent, most of them contract cases (Civil Caseloads, at 21).

The federal government surveyed state filings that went to trial (Langton and Cohen). The parties settled or abandoned 97 percent of cases in courts of general jurisdiction, though of the cases that did go to trial, 61 percent were torts. Consistent with the phenomenon of the "vanishing trial,"[12] in the nation's 75 most populous counties the number of general civil cases disposed of by trial declined 50 percent from 1992 to 2005.

Japan. In 2008, disputants filed 2.3 million civil cases in the Japanese courts at all levels,[13] a majority of them (1.4 million) in summary courts with jurisdiction over claims of less than 1.4 million yen (Courts Act, Sec. 32; in Aug. 2010, $1.00 = 85 yen).

Many of these "cases" involved petitions for various orders in insolvency or other specialized proceedings. Of the 2.3 million newly filed cases, Japanese courts catalogued only 828,000 as "litigation suits." And within the district (as opposed to summary) courts, only 222,000 involved "litigation suits."

Recent court statistics do not break down litigation by subject, but in 1994 the district courts heard 146,392 "litigation suit" claims: 35,220 involved loans and credit transactions, 33,447 real estate, and 6,360 traffic accidents (Tab. 23, Shiho tokei, 1994). In the summary courts, 195,240 of the 244,131 suits involved loans and credit transactions, 4,623 real estate, and 1,215 traffic accidents (id., at tab. 10). Besides the 2.3 million new "civil" cases in 2008, Japanese filed 766,000 domestic relations suits in family courts.

England and Wales. In England and Wales, plaintiffs filed 2.01 million civil suits in county courts in 2007. They also filed 127,664 family law cases.[14] As in the U.S. and Japan, most suits involved "money claims." Of two million filings in 2007, 1.6 million were money claims, 284,000 were for recovery of land, 8,000 for return of goods, and 67,000 for insolvency.[15]

Canada. In the year ending 2009, plaintiffs filed 324,015 general civil cases (including small claims) in the Canadian provinces and territories of Nova Scotia, Ontario, Alberta, British Columbia, the Yukon, the Northwest Territories, and Nunavut. They filed another 175,628 family law cases. A former English colony, a common-law legal system, a North American neighbor—yet Canada has but a quarter of the litigation in the U.S. Indeed, it has less litigation per capita even than the famously "nonlitigious" Japanese.

Australia. Like the U.S. and Canada, Australia maintains a federal structure for its courts. It couples one federal (i.e., national) court system, with separate court systems in each of its nine states and territories. We were able to obtain data on court filings for six of the nine, an area with about 90 percent of the Australian population. Plaintiffs in these states filed 302,000 suits (allocating the federal filings by population).[16]

France. France has four kinds of specialized trial courts. In 2006 plaintiffs filed 943,597 new cases in the Tribunaux de grande instance (general law, large suits), 614,480 in the Tribunaux d'instance (general law, small suits), 3,294 in the Tribunaux paritaires des baux ruraux (rural areas), 198,455 in the Conseils de prud'hommes (employment disputes), and 193,534 in the Tribunaux de commerce (commerce). This yields a total of 1,953,360 suits, of which 422,790 were family law cases. Adding the remaining 1,530,570 non-family civil suits yields a litigation rate of 2,416 per 100,000 people.

C. Qualifications

We enter these calculations in the first column of Table 3.1. The numbers reflect with reasonable accuracy what they purport to measure: the number of times people file non-family civil suits in court. They only haphazardly proxy for the role courts play in society. Although the number of filings might seem to measure that role, consider the following three complications.

Small-claims courts. If one were interested in the extent to which people use the courts to resolve economically substantial disputes, one might want to exclude the very smallest claims. And if one wanted to measure the role courts played in society, a small suit obviously should count for less than a large one. Since states and countries differ in their cutoffs, however, omitting small-claims courts could be highly misleading; one country's figure might still include mostly petty disputes while another's does not.

The definition of "case." The same category of disputes does not generate the same number of cases in every country. Take divorce, which in the U.S. will almost always lead to a measured case, since the divorcing couple generally must file a suit in court. By contrast, in Japan most divorces never enter court records. To part ways, a couple simply goes to city hall and enters a divorce on the "family registry." Only when they can't agree on the divorce terms will they appear in family court. Only 12 percent of divorces end up in court, and only 1 percent actually go to trial.[17] Naturally, American couples would thus appear to be more litigious.

Predictability. How often plaintiffs sue also turns on how predictable courts are.[18] Litigation is more expensive than settlement. If the disputants know that the court will award amount $X, they can just transfer the $X by themselves and pocket the fees they would otherwise have paid their lawyers. If you know what a judge will do anyway, why pay to have a trial in two years and ask him?

Disputants litigate rather than settle only if they each hold optimistic estimates of their prospects in court. Because they face higher expenses if they litigate than if they settle, that cost difference creates a "settlement window." So long as the difference in their estimates of the litigated outcome is smaller than the settlement window, they both gain by settling. Only if they disagree enough about what the judge will do will they pay their lawyers and take their chances.

If we want to measure court activity, then we do want the number of filings and trials rather than the amount of claims asserted in the shadow of the law. A country with more erratic courts (e.g., the United States with its civil juries) will have more litigation than a country with predictable courts (e.g., Japan with its bureaucratic judges). On the other hand, if we want to measure the amount of wealth transferred according to legal rules, then we would instead like to include settlements. For example, we might define "litigious" citizens to include disputants who extract damages by asserting their legally protected rights even if they rationally and self-interestedly settle their claims. Under that definition, a country might be "litigious" even with few suits or judges per capita.

Traffic accidents in Japan. The course of traffic accident disputes in Japan illustrates this dynamic. As Japan emerged from the devastation of World War II, very few people owned cars. By the 1960s, the economy was growing at double-digit rates each year. Increasingly, Japanese chose to spend what they earned on automobiles. As they did, they increasingly killed each other on the roads. Accidents boomed, and so did litigation (even without a change in the court system, to recall our earlier point).

After traffic accident cases began to increase rapidly, the Tokyo District Court established a special traffic section in 1962. As Dan Foote recounts, the new panel immediately found itself swamped. Quickly, the traffic section realized it had to routinize its treatment of cases. At first, it kept its formulas internal to the courts. It published handbooks for judges detailing its "rules of thumb for damages" and standards on comparative negligence. In time, however, the Tokyo traffic section took its dissemination efforts beyond the courts. It began announcing its rules to the bar and the public. The culmination came with what Foote describes as "a special 161-page issue of [one of the principal legal journals] in 1975 consisting entirely of explanations of the compensation and comparative fault standard used by the courts."[19]

From 1964 to 1968, the number of suits filed in district courts over traffic accidents more than doubled, from 2,378 to 5,514,[20] rising from 3 to 7 percent of civil suits. After 1971, the number of suits began to fall. Plaintiffs filed 11,118 traffic claims that year (14 percent of all suits). By 1975, they filed only 5,808 (8 percent of all suits), and by 1980 only 3,484 (3 percent of all suits). Indeed, writes Foote, by the end of the decade the judges in the Tokyo traffic section found themselves "at loose ends due to lack of work. Beginning in 1978, [they] began handling workers' compensation cases, as well as automobile cases, since there was no longer enough traffic accident litigation to keep [them] busy."[21]

With better highways, automatic stoplights, additional sidewalks, and safer cars, the number of deaths due to traffic accidents plummeted from

21,535 in 1970 to 11,752 in 1980. Yet the number of cases filed fell faster still, from 11,620 to 3,484—a 70 percent drop. Civil litigation in general did not fall. In 1970, plaintiffs filed 74,733 non-traffic suits; by 1980, they filed 102,075.

Although they increasingly took their disputes out of the courts during the 1970s, Japanese traffic-accident disputants still settled by the expected court outcome. Ramseyer and Nakazato compared the amounts paid by automobile insurers in wrongful death claims with the amounts awarded the heirs to accident victims in court.[22] In virtually all cases where heirs would have had legal claims against drivers, they obtained compensation from the drivers' insurers. Out of court, they collected mean amounts that closely tracked the mean amounts courts would have awarded.

Thus cases filed per capita do not provide a good measure even of first-order law, if by that we mean the extent to which the courts are influential in resolving first-order disputes. They provide a somewhat better measure of how much the courts decide directly rather than indirectly, but even then they do not provide a good measure of the importance of the wealth transfers.

D. Judges per Capita

The numbers. As an alternative index for the role courts play in society, take the number of judges. This would address to some extent the problem of suits varying in importance, since more important suits require more time from judges.

In the U.S., state courts employed 29,379 judges in 2004.[23] In 2009 the federal government employs 875 "Article III" judges (with life tenure),[24] another 352 Bankruptcy Judges, 567 Magistrate Judges[25] and 1,422 Administrative Law Judges.[26] Add it all up and we have 32,595 judges, or 10.81 per 100,000.

In 2010 Japanese courts employed 15 Supreme Court Justices, eight High Court Presidents (chief judges), 1,782 Judges (trial and intermediate appellate), 1,000 Assistant Judges (judges in their first 10 years of employment), and 806 Summary Court Judges (not all of them legally trained), for a total of 3,611 judges,[27] or 2.83 per 100,000 population.

In 2008 England and Wales employed 110 High Court judges, 653 Circuit Judges and 438 District Judges, a total of 1,201 judges,[28] or 2.22 per 100,000. The High Court judges hear criminal appeals and difficult civil cases.

Circuit Judges and District Judges staff the County Courts and hear family and most civil cases. The Crown Courts do not hear civil cases, but they do use Circuit Judges. In addition, there were 1,305 Recorders and 29,419 Justices of the Peace. Recorders are part-time judges. Justices of the Peace are lay magistrates who handle minor criminal cases. Although not full judges, they do handle cases that judges would handle in the United States.

Given its federal structure, Canada employs judges in both its federal (national) and provincial courts. It had about 80 federal judges and 1,100 provincial judges, or 3.3 judges per 100,000 population.[29]

Australia similarly employs judges and magistrates in both federal and state courts. It has about 100 federal judges and about 740 state judges, or 4.00 judges per 100,000 population.[30]

French courts employ 7,896 Magistrats de l'ordre judiciaire.[31] Per 100,000 population, that's 12.47.

Qualifications. Our discussion of the English courts shows that measuring the number of judges is not as simple as it seems, since "judge" is an ambiguous term when several different levels of adjudicators exist. Moreover, we lightly passed over the problem that judges deal with criminal as well as civil cases, and the ratio between the two cases differs between countries. As with the number of suits filed, however, the problem with the number of judges lies less in the numbers themselves than in their significance. From time to time, observers use the number of judges to proxy for the demand for judicial services. Implicitly, they suggest that governments appoint the judges they do because people file the lawsuits they do. In fact, however, causation just as plausibly runs the other way. People may file the suits that they do because of the number of judges the government has appointed. With more judges, trial dates will come sooner, and plaintiffs will sue more and have less time to settle.[32]

E. Lawyers per Capita

The numbers. We measure the number of lawyers per 100,000 population to be 380 in the United States, 12 in Japan, 277 in England, 292 in Canada, 259 in Australia, and 70 in France.[33]

Qualifications. As often discussed,[34] the number of lawyers captures the social importance of law only imperfectly at best. In many societies, lawyers sell services only tangentially related to the law and unrelated entirely to courts. In other societies, a wide variety of non-lawyers sell law- and court-related services. Some lawyers do litigate, of course. In Japan, until recently they seldom did anything else. Because the government recognized their monopoly only on litigation-related services, they focused on litigation. In the U.S., only a minority of lawyers actually litigate. And in the U.K., all barristers litigate, while no solicitor does. In some countries, lawyers counsel. Although in Japan traditionally lawyers rarely gave business or personal advice, in the U.S. most lawyers do routinely. In the U.K., solicitors give business advice, while barristers do not. Some lawyers do nothing legal at all. Many American lawyers abandon their legal practice within a few years. Elsewhere, lawyers stay with their profession their entire life.

Some countries may have few licensed lawyers, while a wide variety of non-lawyers sell legal services. Again, take Japan. Among the countries in Table 3.1, it has the fewest lawyers: less than a tenth as many as the U.S., England, Canada, or Australia, and less than half as many as France. The reason is simple: for most of the postwar period, the government set the pass rate on the bar exam below 3 percent. Even when they could not afford (or even find) a lawyer, however, Japanese citizens could buy legal services. They could turn to licensed tax agents for tax advice. They could consult licensed patent agents on intellectual property. They could obtain wills and corporate charters from notary publics. And firms could obtain their corporate and contract advice by hiring unlicensed graduates of the many college law departments.

Given these objections, some scholars look not at licensed legal practitioners, but at university graduates with legal training. By this metric, Japan has more legal experts even than the U.S. Using this approach, Kevin Murphy, Andrei Shleifer, and Robert Vishny index the amount of rent-seeking in a society by the size of university law departments.[35] Averaging across a large number of countries, both developed and developing, they find that the more law graduates in a society, the slower its GDP will grow. Conversely, the more engineering students it graduates, the faster that GDP will grow. The example of Japan versus the United States shows that this approach is fraught with peril: not everyone with an undergraduate law degree works in the business of law, just as not all those with history degrees work in the field of history.

F. Ease of Doing Business

In its well-known "Doing Business" studies, the World Bank measures the difficulty of performing various small business tasks in different countries. The specificity of the tasks measured is an attractive feature of the approach. Table 3.2 shows the results the Bank obtained for the difficulty of enforcing a contract.[36] According to the Bank, firms in our six wealthy democracies require similar numbers of procedures to enforce a deal. They will spend 300 to 400 days in all of the countries except Canada, and consume 14 to 24 percent of the money at stake.

We include sub-Saharan Africa in Table 3.2 to show how first-order measures differ between developed and developing countries. The region includes primarily dysfunctional economies, and the legal framework in the area reflects (and contributes to) the dysfunction. A sub-Saharan firm that tried to enforce a contract in court would file nearly 40 procedures, spend over 600 days, and consume nearly half of its claim.

G. Auto Insurance Rates

A high level of auto accidents is an inevitable sign of an advanced economy. With accidents come injuries, and with injuries come lawsuits— except in Quebec, with its no-fault system. As shown in Table 3.1, insurance

Table 3.2   Difficulty of Enforcing Contracts

Country	Procedures (number)	Time (Days)	Cost (% of Claim)
Australia	28	395	20.7
Canada	36	570	22.3
France	29	331	17.4
Japan	30	360	22.7
United Kingdom	30	399	23.4
Sub-Saharan Africa	39	644	49.3
United States	32	300	14.4

costs per car are highest in Canada and the United States ($US 1,574 and $US 1,474) and are between $US 664 and $US 927 in the other four countries (OECD, *Insurance Statistics Yearbook 1998–2007*, 2007 data; World Bank, *WorldDataBank*, http://databank.worldbank.org/ddp/home.do).

Americans and Canadians, however, crash more. Their rates of annual fatalities per 10,000 cars in 2009 were 1.3 and 1.0, compared with 0.6 and 0.7 for the United Kingdom and Japan (OECD, Road Safety Annual Report 2011, http://internationaltransportforum.org/irtadpublic/pdf/11IrtadReport .pdf.) Thus, American costs for this, the most common serious tort, are by no means out of line.

H. The Towers Perrin–Tillinghast Estimates

As a final measure of litigation, we mention the analysis of tort costs by the consulting firm Towers Perrin–Tillinghast (now part of Towers Watson), well known for its measurements of tort costs over time in the United States. Its annual U.S. estimates, still coming out each year, use the extensive data on insurance premiums collected by A.M. Best for sale primarily to businesses, with adjustments for such things as self-insurance. Those reports describe methodology clearly and break down the data into categories that allow its construction to be understood. Its international studies, however, which ended in 2006, do not describe their methodology or data sources.[37] We are not aware of suitable international data sources that would be available, so we are skeptical of the numbers in Table 3.3. Nonetheless, because they are so well known, we reproduce them here. In addition, we note that another survey of the large U.S. companies found that litigation costs increased 73 percent from 2000 to 2008, and that these costs constituted a much more substantial burden for the firms than they are for companies outside the U.S.[38]

American Dysfunction

Most of the measures we examined above suggest that America is not that unusual. In suits per capita, the ratio between the U.S. and the U.K. is less than between the U.K. and Canada. Americans do have more judges per capita, but fewer than the French, and "judge" is hard to define anyway.

Table 3.3 TTP Estimates of Litigation Costs

Country	2000	2001	2002	2003
Belgium	1.00%	1.08%	1.01%	0.96%
Denmark	N/A	0.44	0.48	0.58
France	0.75	0.75	0.76	0.74
Germany	1.25	1.25	1.19	1.14
Italy	1.75	1.72	1.70	1.70
Japan	0.79	0.80	0.81	0.80
Poland	N/A	N/A	0.60	0.59
Spain	1.04	1.03	1.01	1.04
Switzerland	0.63	0.69	0.81	0.75
U.K.	0.53	0.64	0.66	0.69
U.S.	1.82	2.03	2.22	2.23

Source: Towers Perrin–Tillinghast, U.S. Tort Costs and Cross Border Perspectives: 2005 Update 12 (2006).

Americans have the most lawyers per capita, but not many more than Australians. And Americans seem not to find contracts especially hard to enforce or to face unusually high automobile insurance premia.

Why, then, the American notoriety? It does not result from the way the legal system handles routine disputes. Instead, it derives from more special areas of law. We will look at two as examples: securities class actions and asbestos torts. Although aggregate quantitative measures suggest that litigation in the U.S. does not differ substantially from litigation elsewhere, aggregation over myriad categories can easily hide a myriad of sins. In several discrete areas, American courts function in a manner one can only describe as disastrous.

A. The Mechanism

Within the U.S. legal system, class actions are a particular scourge. Though a small fraction of suits, they wreak havoc out of proportion to their numbers.

As a form of group litigation, they have antecedents in colonial times. As "class actions," they date to Rule 23 of the 1938 Federal Rules of Civil

Procedure. But in their modern, rampantly abused form, they date to the 1967 revisions of Rule 23.

The drafters of the modern class action tried to design a mechanism that would let victims cost-effectively prosecute claims for wrongs that impose large losses on the community as a whole but trivial damages to any one victim. Suppose a firm negligently pollutes and causes damages of $1 million to nearby land. If one person owns that land, he will sue for the $1 million. For damages that large, it is worth hiring a lawyer. With a credible threat to sue, he can demand $1 million in settlement out of court.

Suppose the firm had not one but 1,000 neighbors, each owning a small piece of the damaged land. The firm has caused the same aggregate injury, but no one of the victims could hire a lawyer for less than the amount he could win in court. Since none of the 1,000 would sue, none could credibly threaten to sue. Unable to threaten credibly, none would recover anything out of court.

Suboptimal precautions will result. If the firm faced one neighbor, it would pay for any negligence, and therefore would adopt efficient precautions against pollution. Facing 1,000 neighbors, it escapes liability for its negligence and so neglects precautions. The class-action suit eliminates that misincentive by imposing the same incentives the firm would face if just one person owned the land.

So far, so good. But there is a hitch. Someone has to initiate the suit. Under the U.S. system, a lawyer with an eye for an opportunity masterminds the class-action suit. He identifies a legal wrong and locates several victims. He suggests that they retain him to sue on behalf of them and all others "similarly situated." They and the others have the right to "opt out" of the litigation and pursue their claims independently. Should they not opt out, they will find themselves bound by whatever outcome the lawyer obtains: the suit has "claim preclusive" effect. The clients are too scattered to control the lawsuit, so the lawyer does that. As an incentive, he collects a contingency fee.

The class action mechanism is a creature almost exclusively of the American legal system. Although some European countries have considered adopting the class action, the main venues that have done so are a few

Canadian provinces, Australia, and Brazil.[39] Why not adopt, if the incentive effect is so desirable?

Problems. Agency problems plague the attorney-client relationship in the best of situations, but class actions reach the ultimate in agency slack. Because each plaintiff has only a small stake in the litigation, no one of them even tries to monitor the lawyer. He operates as an autonomous actor: independent, unmonitored, and free to pursue his own interests. As the preeminent class-action lawyer William Lerach once infamously bragged (now, for his litigation tactics, a convicted felon): "I have the best practice in the world. I have no clients."

The class-action attorney's misaligned incentives particularly skew settlements. Given the trivial size of their claims, few victims pay attention to settlement bargaining. The defendant can take advantage of that by negotiating a settlement that is generous to the lawyers and stingy to his clients. The attorney agrees to take a generous fee, always in cash, and a much smaller recovery for his clients, often "in-kind" as free samples of the defendant's product.

The class-action rules do require the judge to approve any settlement, precisely to avoid this problem. Because the attorneys for both sides favor the settlement, however, nobody will criticize it in court. Accustomed to an adversarial system in which they seldom take initiative, judges defer. They are busy people. They like to please at least some of the people in front of them. And they are linked by social interactions, gratitude for appointment (if by "merit panel"), old school ties, or campaign contributions to attorneys, defense and plaintiff, and not to non-lawyers. Too often, the important conflict is not between the plaintiff and the defense with the judge staying neutral, but between the lawyers and the non-professionals.

B. Securities Class Actions

Even within class actions, securities claims are notorious. Attorneys locate firms whose share price has fallen. They then argue that the firms (or the firms' officers, whom the firms will typically indemnify) caused the fall through misconduct—mismanagement, conflicts of interest, or misrepresentations. To recover the loss in the firm's market capitalization, the attorneys sue on behalf of the shareholders.

Until the mid-1990s, judges named a firm to the lucrative "lead attorney" role if it filed the first claim. Filing first, asking questions later, attorneys raced to the courthouse when share prices fell, and looked for misconduct later. The 1995 Private Securities Litigation Reform Act (PSLRA) was supposed to change that. The act asked judges to pick as lead plaintiffs those with the largest financial claims rather than those who file first. According to Stephen Choi and Adam Pritchard, however, the problem remained.[40] The trial lawyers simply switched their effort from racing to the courthouse to courting institutional investors. Commercial mutual funds generally rejected being plaintiffs, so attorneys mostly recruited the more politicized government-sponsored funds and labor union pension plans.

Any financial gain to investors from even a successful suit is minimal. Suppose a firm settles for $30 million: a third to the attorneys and two-thirds to the plaintiffs. Because the firm pays the settlement, its market value falls even more. In effect, the firm's current shareholders pay the damages. Because the settlement goes to the shareholders at the time of the alleged misconduct (many of whom still own their shares in the firm), those former shareholders receive cash. The settlement reduces the value of the stock held by one group of investors, increases the cash held by an overlapping group of investors (but by one-third less, subtracting the lawyers' fees) and enriches the law firm that engineers the transfer.

Magnitudes. From 1996 to 2009, the number of securities class action suits exceeded 300 only once (514 in 2001), and in 2006 it was only 131. Recall that in a typical year, plaintiffs in the U.S. file 272,000 federal suits and 18 million state suits. Securities class actions are a wart on a whale.

Yet to settle these few suits firms pay dearly. In 2009, there were 221 new filings. The mean settlement value that year was $13 million, the total was $2.8 billion, and the total attorney fees plus expenses were $0.963 billion.[41] The problem is not that firms lose in court. Of 238 suits filed in 2000, by mid-2010 the parties had settled 146 and judges had thrown out 85. Of the remaining seven, only four had gone to trial—and the parties settled all four before the verdict. More generally, since the 1995 PSLRA, plaintiffs have filed over 3,400 securities class actions in federal courts, and only 27 went to trial, about one in 100. Of those, plaintiffs won six and obtained a mixed verdict in five. Thus, of the 3,400 suits since 1995, plaintiffs won anything at all in court in only 11.[42]

Nonetheless, firms have paid out massive amounts. In 60 percent of cases, the defendants settle, most for $20 million to $60 million, but some for more. The largest 10 settlements up to July 2010 transferred over $1 billion each, the largest being Enron's $7.2 billion in 2010 and WorldCom's $6.2 billion in 2005.[43]

The few other countries with class action provisions manage to avoid these large transfers. Australia introduced class actions in 1992. In no year since have attorneys filed more than six securities class actions.[44] Some Canadian provinces have offered class actions since 1978. Attorneys did not file the first securities class action until 1997, however, and in no year have attorneys filed more than nine.[45]

American securities class actions are not simple transfers from one group of investors to another. The plaintiffs' bar imposes a massive toll charge on the transfer. For engineering the transfers from one set of investors to another, they charge over $400 million a year. In each of the years 2005, 2006, and 2007 they took over $1 billion.

Politics. Why do Congress and the courts let securities class actions continue? The answer lies in the politics of the bar. Attorneys in all sectors give heavily to the Democratic Party. In 2008, attorneys with Chicago's Sidley and Austin gave $1.4 million to politicians, 81 percent to Democrats. Sidley was, to be sure, the scene of the 1980s romance between Barack and Michelle Obama, but other large firms gave heavily to Democrats too. Sidley's Chicago rival, Kirkland and Ellis, gave $1.3 million, 76 percent to Democrats. New York's Skadden Arps gave $1.7 million, 82 percent to Democrats, and even the more traditional Sullivan and Cromwell—the quintessential "Wall Street establishment" firm—gave $1.2 million, 75 percent to Democrats.[46] The trade association for the plaintiff's bar gives even more, and more overwhelmingly to Democrats. That group in 2008 gave over $3 million to politicians, 95 percent to Democrats.[47] It lobbies hard against tort reform of all kinds and particularly hard against reform of the securities class action. By all odds, it was because of trial lawyer pressure that Bill Clinton vetoed the 1995 PSLRA, only to find himself overridden by the heavily Republican Senate.[48]

For a sense of the color involved, consider a phone call one of us received in the mid 1990s. At the time, Ramseyer taught at the University of Chicago Law School. The call came from an associate at a well-known law firm specializing in securities class actions. The associate explained that they wanted to retain Ramseyer in connection with a suit against a certain large Japanese corporation. The law firm had filed suit in an American state court, alleging misstatements in the firm's Japanese securities filings. "What did the firm misstate?" Ramseyer asked. "We don't know," the associate answered. "That's why we want to retain you." It was enough that the stock price had fallen; the excuse to sue could always be found if they hired the right expert.

C. Asbestos

Mississippi plaintiffs' attorney Richard F. "Dickie" Scruggs called them "magic" jurisdictions: "The trial lawyers have established relationships with the judges that are elected; they're State Court judges; they're populists. They've got large populations of voters who are in on the deal, they're getting their piece in many cases. And so, it's a political force in their jurisdiction, and it's almost impossible to get a fair trial if you're a defendant in some of these places. . . . The cases are not won in the courtroom. They're won on the back roads long before the case goes to trial. Any lawyer fresh out of law school can walk in there and win the case, so it doesn't matter what the evidence or law is."[49]

Scruggs made his first millions suing the asbestos companies in "magic" courtrooms. He made his first hundreds of millions suing the tobacco companies in the same places. He made millions more suing State Farm over its Katrina payments. After the harm was done, he went to prison in 2008 for bribing two of the "magic" judges in the asbestos and Katrina litigation.

Few fields of tort litigation cut a broader swath through the American economy than asbestos. The Towers Perrin consulting firm estimates the total cost (compensation, attorney fees, and administrative expenses) of the U.S. tort system in 2003 at $246 billion. Of that, $9 billion was from asbestos.[50]

Asbestos was a miracle insulator. It did not conduct electricity. It did not burn. It absorbed sound. It was nonreactive with chemicals. Yet asbestos, if breathed, could injure, and even kill, particularly in combination with tobacco smoke. After a 20- to 40-year latency period, it could cause diseases ranging from asbestosis to mesothelioma to lung cancer. Asbestos is a necessary but not sufficient condition for mesothelioma and asbestosis, and a contributing factor for lung cancer. Estimates of the number of people asbestos killed range widely, from 40,000 to over 300,000 between 1965 and 2009.[51]

Tort law is an odd vehicle for asbestos harm remediation, and in some ways profoundly inappropriate. The people clearly hurt were those who encountered asbestos at work. Yet employers and employees negotiate contracts with each other in competitive markets. Employers choose to hire an employee who offers the right combination of attributes (talent, effort, experience) at the lowest price (wages, insurance, and other benefits). Employees choose to work for a given firm if it offers the best mix of pay, environment, location, and other amenities. If an employer imposes a health risk, employees will agree to work there only if the firm promises a pay-and-amenity package that compensates for the risk.

Employers and employees do not always understand all the risks involved. As in any other contract, the optimal legal rule is the one that induces them to invest cost-justified (but only cost-justified) resources in studying potential harms. The rule that does best is the rule that holds them to their promises, that bans intentional false statements, and that lets residual harms lie where they fall.

It has long been known that asbestos injures health. It is commonly written that Pliny the Elder suggested the use of respirators and noted that purchasers of slaves who had worked in asbestos mines should be mindful of their reduced lifespan.[52] At least as early as 1918, insurance companies were declining life insurance coverage to asbestos workers.[53] Henry Johns, founder of the largest asbestos company, Johns-Manville, died in 1898 of "dust phthisis pneumonitis."[54] The very name of the ailment "asbestosis," coined in 1925, suggests that the danger was known.[55] Workers may not have read Pliny, but surely they realized that breathing rock fibers was not healthful. The court concluded in the 1973 leading case that the plaintiff worker knew that his breathing of asbestos was bad for him, that workers frequently discussed the danger, and that the danger was well known in the medical literature.[56]

History. Asbestos litigation began with that 1973 case. The plaintiff had installed asbestos insulation for three decades. When he found himself with asbestosis and mesothelioma, he sued the manufacturers of the material his employers had told him to install. He knew the dust was bad for him, but not how bad, he argued, and the manufacturers had a duty to find out, track him down, and warn him of the dangers. The court agreed.[57] The manufacturers were liable, under the doctrine of "strict liability," even though the plaintiff was guilty of contributory negligence.

Asbestos litigation exploded. As of 2002, 730,000 plaintiffs had filed asbestos-related claims. They sued 8,400 firms, 80 of which have now filed for bankruptcy (including Johns-Manville). Through the course of the litigation, the defendants paid (the Rand Corporation calculates) $70 billion. They paid $21 billion to their own lawyers, $19 billion to the plaintiffs' lawyers, and $30 billion to the plaintiffs themselves.[58]

Seventy billion dollars paid to deliver $30 billion in compensation—compensation for which the plaintiffs negotiated off-setting pay packages ex ante anyway. What went wrong? Part of the cause lies in the legal doctrine itself. Asbestos users could have insisted that the sellers insure them against injury, but they chose to bear the risk of loss themselves. Declaring tort to have supplanted the essentially contractual character of the relationship, courts held the manufacturers liable anyway.[59]

Another problem was Scruggs's "magic" jurisdictions. Often the plaintiff can choose the forum in which to litigate. Because large corporations operate over the entire U.S., they have close enough contact with each state to subject them constitutionally to jurisdiction anywhere. Federalism plus product liability plus class actions makes for a poisonous mixture.

A sensible legal system would limit venue shopping. U.S. state and federal law does not. Instead, Mississippi can enforce a joinder rule under which an attorney can "file a single case that involves a Mississippi resident suing an out-of-state defendant and then join thousands of out-of-state claims to the original case."[60]

Attorneys for asbestos plaintiffs migrated to the jurisdictions offering the most magic. As of the mid-1990s, three counties in Texas accounted for a quarter of all new state-court suits. Within a few years, two Mississippi counties joined them. From 1998 to 2000, plaintiffs filed nearly 20,000 asbestos cases (10 percent of the total) in those two Mississippi counties.[61] In Jefferson County, Mississippi (pop. 9,740), 73 mass-action lawsuits representing more than 3,000 plaintiffs were filed in 2000.[62] As of 1995, just 10 law firms represented three-quarters of all new asbestos suits.[63] Economist Michelle White estimates that by trying a case in one of the magic jurisdictions a plaintiff increased his judgment by $1.7 to 2.6 million.[64]

The stakes. In part, Scruggs won the settlements he did by raising the stakes against the defendants. As in securities class actions, the asbestos bar extracted settlements by threatening overwhelming liability. The RAND Corporation estimates that from 1993 to 2001, 730,000 plaintiffs litigated only 526 trials. The lawyers selected cases they could win to go to trial to provide public examples they could point to for private settlements. Of the cases that went to trial, they won 64 percent with mean damages of $812,000 in the wins, and punitive damages averaging $1.4 million in the 17 percent of cases that awarded them.[65]

The plaintiff's bar pushed clients with mesothelioma and other serious injuries to trial and used the threat of that litigation to settle the rest of their cases. In 2002, for instance, plaintiffs asserted 1,856 mesothelioma claims and 50,112 claims involving no malignancy, many of which involved no impairment at all.[66]

On behalf of his asbestos clients, Scruggs recovered $300 million. For himself, he collected another $25 million.[67] Recalling our earlier figures, note that he indeed was the most efficient processor of asbestos litigation, a very good deal for his clients.

Expert witnesses. In 2008, the *Wall Street Journal* reported that one doctor had diagnosed over 7,300 individual claimants with asbestos-related diseases: "Defendants presented evidence that Dr. Kelly was neither a radiologist nor a pulmonologist and had failed the test that certifies doctors to read X-rays for lung disease. They also showed that the overwhelming majority of hospital radiologists who had reviewed Dr. Kelly's patients found no evidence of disease. An outside panel of radiologists who looked at Dr. Kelley's work found abnormalities in only 6 of 68 patients; Dr. Kelley had found abnormalities in 60 of those 68."[68] For each diagnosis, the plaintiffs' lawyers paid Kelly $500.

In 2005 Texas federal judge Janis Jack uncovered a bigger scam still. Presiding over silicosis suits,[69] she noticed a sudden and massive increase in silicosis claims, but diagnosed by a remarkably small number of doctors: "Twelve doctors diagnosed all 9,083 Plaintiffs. This small cadre of non-treating physicians, financially beholden to lawyers and screening companies rather than to patients, managed to notice a disease missed by approximately 8,000 other physicians—most of whom had the significant advantage of speaking to, examining, and treating the Plaintiffs."[70] The increase coincided with the shift in focus at several law firms from asbestosis to silicosis. Silicosis and asbestosis look very different in an X-ray, and a patient almost never has both diseases.[71] Curiously, Judge Jack's plaintiffs arrived with both diseases.

When Dr. Harron first examined 1,807 plaintiffs' X-rays for asbestos litigation (virtually all done prior to 2000, when mass silica litigation was just a gleam in a lawyer's eye), he found them all to be consistent only with asbestosis and not with silicosis. But upon reexamining these 1,807 MDL plaintiffs' X-rays for silica litigation, Dr. Harron found evidence of silicosis in every case.[72]

Judge Jack concluded that all but one of the 10,000 or so cases were fraudulent. Were the attorneys foolish to have brought them to court? She did impose a $8,250 fine on the worst-offending law firm, saying, "The Court trusts that this relatively minor sanction will nonetheless be sufficient to serve notice to counsel that truth matters in a courtroom no less than in a doctor's office." Perhaps the shame of it overwhelmed the reprimanded lawyers, but most of us would draw the exact opposite conclusion about truth in courtrooms. In any case, despite Judge Jack's contempt for the claims, she remanded all but the lone meritorious one to state courts—in Texas and Mississippi.[73]

D. Katrina

After Hurricane Katrina became news, Scruggs turned to State Farm Insurance. The insurer had unfairly denied claims brought by Gulf Coast residents, he argued. On behalf of 640 clients, he negotiated $80 million in settlements for 640 clients and $26.5 million for the attorneys.

How Scruggs induced State Farm to pay illustrates the tie between litigation and politics. In this case, the method was to buy an attorney general, use him to threaten criminal charges against the civil defendant, and get the charge dropped if the defendant paid up. Scruggs was a major benefactor of Mississippi Attorney General Jim Hood. In the 40 days before one election, Scruggs, a close associate, and two lawyers gave $472,000 to the Democratic Attorneys General Association, which then gave $550,000 to Hood's campaign.[74] State Farm faced a simultaneous civil suit from Scruggs and criminal investigation from Hood. Hood's deputy insurance commissioner recalled Hood saying, "[If] they don't settle with us, I'm going to indict them all, from [State Farm CEO] Ed Rust down." But State Farm settled and the criminal investigation was closed.[75]

Of course, American law is not infinitely malleable, and Scruggs did go one step too far. With the enormous fees at stake, Scruggs and his fellow attorneys fell into bitter disputes. To obtain a ruling in his favor against a co-counsel in the Katrina litigation, Scruggs offered a judge a mere $50,000. The judge went to the FBI, the U.S. Attorney prosecuted Scruggs, and in 2008 Scruggs was sentenced to five years in prison.

Implications

From coffee spills to securities class actions to asbestos experts to tobacco settlements, American courts have made a name for themselves as a wild lottery with a big payout for a lucky few specialist lawyers. At least in part, however, the reputation is unfounded. American judges seem to handle routine contract and tort disputes as well as their peers in other wealthy countries. Americans do not file an unusually high number of law suits. They do not employ large numbers of judges or lawyers. They do not pay more to enforce contracts. And they do not pay unusually high prices for insurance against routine torts.

Rather, American courts have ruined their good name by mishandling a few special aspects of law. In this article we used securities actions and mass torts as illustrations, but anyone who reads a newspaper could suggest alternatives. The implications for reform are straightforward: focus not on litigation as a whole, but on areas of law where America is unique.

Notes

1. Liebeck v. McDonald's Restaurants, P.T.S., Inc., 1995 WL 360309 (N.M.D.C. 1994).

2. See Galanter, Oil Strike in Hell: Contemporary Legends about the Civil Justice System, 40 Ariz. L. Rev. 717, 731 (1998); Lempert, Why Do Juries Get a Bum Rap: Reflections on the Work of Valerie Hans, 48 DePaul L. Rev. 453, 459 (1998–1999); Miller, The Pretrial Rush to Judgment: Are the 'Litigation Explosion,' 'Liability Cases,' and Efficiency Clichés Eroding Our Day in Court and Jury Trial Commitments?, 78 N.Y.U. L. Rev. 982, 987 (2003); Haltom and McCann, Java Jive; Genealogy of a Juridical Icon, in Distorting the Law: Politics, Media, and the Litigation Crisis 183 (2004).

3. Antoninetti v. Chipotle Mex. Grill, Inc., 08–55867, http://www.ca9.uscourts .gov/opinions/view_subpage.php?pk_id=0000010681 (9th Cir. 2010).

4. Viscusi, The Governmental Composition of the Insurance Costs of Smoking, 42 J. Law & Econ. 575 (1999).

5. Master Settlement Agreement, http://www.naag.org/backpages/naag/tobacco /msa/msa-pdf/MSA%20with%20Sig%20Pages%20and%20Exhibits.pdf/file_view. For the history, see Wikipedia, "Tobacco Master Settlement Agreement," http://en .wikipedia.org/wiki/Tobacco_Master_Settlement_Agreement (May 31, 2010).

6. Holes in the Tobacco Settlement, N.Y. Times, June 27, 1997.

7. In this regard, the data has not improved. Galanter, supra note 2, and Markesinis, Litigation-Mania in England, Germany and the USA: Are We So Very Different?, 49 Cambridge L. J. 233 (1990).

8. M. A. Peterson, as quoted in Markesinis, supra note 7.

9. S. Strickland et al., State Court Caseload Statistics, 2007: Supplement to Examining the Work of State Courts tabs. 1, 2 (2007).

10. 2007 data from U.S. Dept. Commerce, Statistical Abstract of the United States, 2010 Tab. 323 (2010).

11. Court Statistics Project 2, National Center for State Courts, Examining the Work of State Courts: An Analysis of 2007 State Court Caseloads [hereafter "CSP"], available at www.ncsconline.org/D_research/CSP/2007B_files/EWSC-2007-v21 -online.pdf, www.courtstatistics.org.

12. See Galanter, The Vanishing Trial: An Examination of Trials and Related Matters in Federal and State Courts, 1 J. Empirical Legal Stud. 459 (2004).

13. Japanese court filing data from the Shiho tokei nempo website at http://www .courts.go.jp/search/jtspo010.

14. U.K. Min. of Justice, Judicial and Court Statistics 2007 tabs. 4.1, 5.1 (2007).

15. U.K. Min. of Justice, Judicial and Court Statistics 2007 tab. 4.1 (2007).

16. Based on annual reports filed by the various courts, and available from their websites.

17. Kosei rodo sho, Rikon ni kansuru tokei [Divorce Statistics] 21 (2009).

18. The classic explanations are Landes, An Economic Analysis of the Courts, 14 J. Law & Econ. 61 (1971); Posner, An Economic Approach to Legal Procedure and Judicial Administration, 2 J. Legal Stud. 399 (1973).

19. Foote, Resolution of Traffic Accident Disputes and Judicial Activism in Japan, 25 L. Japan 19, 27, 29 (1995).

20. Ramseyer and Nakazato, The Rational Litigant: Settlement Amounts and Verdict Rates in Japan, 18 J. Legal Stud. 263 (1989); Shiho tokei nempo website, supra note 13; traffic deaths from Japanese Ministry of Health and Welfare.

21. Foote, supra note 19, at 30.

22. Ramseyer and Nakazato, supra note 20.

23. See CSP, supra note 11.

24. Office of U.S. Courts, Federal Judgeships, available at www.uscourts.gov /JudgesAndJudgeships/FederalJudgeships.aspx.

25. Office of U.S. Courts. 2009 Annual Report of the Director: Judicial Business of the United States Courts 36 (2010).

26. Burrows, Administrative Law Judges: An Overview 2 Congressional Research Service, April 13, 2010, available at towmasters.files.wordpress.com/ . . . /administrative-law-judges-an-overview.pdf.

27. Saiban sho shokuin teiin ho [Act Authorizing the Number of Employees in the Courts], Law No. 53 of 1951, as amended March 31, 2010.

28. Min. of Justice, Judicial and Court Statistics 2007, tab. 9.1.; see also Wikipedia: http://en.wikipedia.org/wiki/Courts_of_England_and_Wales, http://en.wiki pedia.org/wiki/Judiciary_of_England_and_Wales).

29. www.fja.gc.ca/appointments-nominations/judges-juges-eng.html.

30. Compiled from annual reports for the various courts, available on the official websites.

31. INSEE, Moyens en personnel de la Justice, available at www.insee.fr/fr /themes/tableau.asp?ref_id=NATnon05317&reg_id=0.

32. See Priest, Private Litigants and the Court Congestion Problem, 69 B.U. L. Rev. 527 (1989).

33. ABA, National Lawyer Population by State, available at new.abanet.org/mar ketresearch/PublicDocuments/2009_NATL_LAWYER_by_State.pdf; Membership JFBA, available at www.nichibenren.or.jp/ja/jfba_info/membership/index.html; Number of lawyers in CCBE Member Bars, available at www.ccbe.eu/fileadmin /user_upload/NTCdocument/table_number_lawyers1_1179905628.pdf; Federation of Law Societies of Canada, available at www.flsc.ca/en/about/about.asp. Considerable variation exists by state in Australia, in the regulation of the bar. Questioned by the Japan Federation of Bar Associations, the Law Council of Australia estimated

the number of lawyers in Australia in 2006 at 58,000. See www.nichibenren.or.jp/en/directory/data/Australia.pdf. However, the Australian Bureau of Statistics found that in 2008 the legal services industry "employed" (apparently including non-lawyers) 99,696 persons. See Australian Bureau of Statistics, 8667.0—Legal Services, Australia, 2007–08, available at www.abs.gov.au/AUSSTATS/abs@.nsf/Latestproducts/8667.0Main%20Features32007-08?opendocument&tabname=Summary&prodno=8667.0&issue=2007-08&num=&view=.

34. Including by us; see Nakazato, Ramseyer, and Rasmusen, The Industrial Organization of the Japanese Bar: Levels and Determinants of Attorney Income, 7 J. Empirical Legal Studies 460 (2010).

35. Murphy, Shleifer, and Vishny, The Allocation of Talent: Implications for Growth, 106 Q.J. Econ. 503 (1991).

36. World Bank Doing Business Project, Enforcing Contracts, available at www.doingbusiness.org/ExploreTopics/EnforcingContracts/.

37. The report says: "To estimate tort costs in 10 other countries, we used a methodology similar to the one we used to estimate U.S. tort costs. . . . The data available in the analyses of non-U.S. tort costs, particularly the self-insurance component, are limited." See Towers Perrin–Tillinghast, U.S. Tort Costs and Cross Border Perspectives: 2005 Update 12 (2006).

38. Lawyers for Civil Justice, Litigation Cost Survey of Major Companies (2010).

39. Thomas D. Rowe, Jr., Foreword: Debates over Group Litigation in Comparative Perspective: What Can We Learn from Each Other, 11 Duke J. Comp. Int'l L. 157, 157–59 (2001).

40. S. J. Choi and A. C. Pritchard, Securities Regulation 113–15 (2008).

41. Milev, Patton, Pnacich, and Starykh, Trends 2010 Mid-Year Study: Filings Decline as the Wave of Credit Crisis Cases Subsides, Median Settlement at Record High Figs. 1, 18, 19, 20 (2010).

42. Milev et al., id. at 16, 19, Fig. 13.

43. Milev et al., id at Tab. 2.

44. Houston, Starykh, Dahl, and Anderson, Trends in Australian Securities Class Actions: 1 January 1993–31 December 2009 (2010).

45. Berenblut, Heys, and Starykh, Trends in Canadian Securities Class Actions: 1997–2008 (2009).

46. See www.opensecrets.org/industries/contrib.php?ind=k01&cycle=2008.

47. Id.

48. Choi and Pritchard, supra note 40, at 107.

49. Boyer, The Bribe, New Yorker, May 19, 2008.

50. Towers Perrin–Tillinghast, U.S. Tort Costs: 2004 Update 2–3 (2004).

51. S. J. Carroll, D. Hensler, J. Gross, E. M. Sloss, M. Schonlau, A. Abrahams, and J. S. Ashwood, Asbestos Litigation xix, 15–18 (2005).

52. We repeat the Pliny story here, but it actually seems to be mythical, if ubiquitous. Nobody gives a specific citation to Pliny's work. See Browne and Murray,

Letter: Asbestos and the Romans, 336 Lancet 445 (1990); Ross and Nolan, History of Asbestos Discovery and Use and Asbestos-Related Disease in Context with the Occurrence of Asbestos within Ophiolite Complexes (Geological Society of America, Special paper 373, 2003), available at specialpapers.gsapubs.org/content/373/447 .abstract.

53. In re Joint Eastern & Southern Dist. Asbestos Lit., 129 BR 710—Dist. Court 1991, at 737.

54. Asbestos.com, New York Mesothelioma and Asbestos Exposure Risks, Sept. 30, 2009, available at www.asbestos.com/states/new-york/.

55. It seems the term was coined by Oliver in 1925, not Cooke in 1927, contrary to the common belief. See Bartrip, Review: History of Asbestos Related Disease, 80 Postgraduate Med. J. 72 (2004).

56. Borel v. Fibreboard, 493 F.2d 1076 (5th Cir. 1973).

57. Borel, 493 F.2d at 1086.

58. S. J. Carroll et al., Asbestos Litigation xxv–xxvii, 6, 70–71, 79, 109, ch. 5 (2005) (73 bankrupt firms); White, Understanding the Asbestos Crisis, unpub'd, May 2003, at 2, available at www.law.yale.edu/documents/pdf/white.pdf (600,000 claimants).

59. See Prosser, The Assault upon the Citadel (Strict Liability to the Consumer), 69 Yale L.J. 1099 (1960); Prosser, The Fall of the Citadel (Strict Liability to the Consumer), 50 Minn. L. Rev. 791 (1966). Although only in the U.S. has asbestos litigation become a major business, the possibility has existed in other countries too. In Japan, the Osaka District Court let plaintiffs recover against the national government, on the theory that the government caused the injury by not regulating asbestos more expeditiously. See Sekimen higai de kuni ni baisho meirei [Compensation Order to Country for Asbestos Damages], 47 News, May 19, 2010. For a comparison of various countries, see Roenneberg, Asbestos: Anatomy of a Mass Tort, Munich Re, available at http://www.munichre.com/publications/302–06142_en.pdf.

60. White, supra note 58.

61. Carroll et al., supra note 58, at 63.

62. Boyer, supra note 49.

63. Carroll et al., supra note 58, at 24.

64. White, supra note 58, at 3.

65. Carroll et al., supra note 58, at xxii, 35, 49–53; White, supra note 58, at 13.

66. Carroll et al., supra note 58, at 49–53, 72, 76.

67. Who's Afraid of Dickie Scruggs?, Newsweek, Dec. 5, 1999.

68. Colombo the Asbestos Sleuth, Wall St. J., Dec. 23, 2008; Michigan Malpractice, Wall St. J., Nov. 10, 2008.

69. In re Silica Products Liability Litigation, 398 F. Supp. 2d 563 (S.D. Tex. 2005); see The Silicosis Abdication, Wall St. J., Apr. 7, 2009. .

70. In re Silica, 398 F. Supp. 2d at 633.

71. Id. at 595.

72. Id. at 607.

73. Behrens and Schaecher, RAND Issues Report on Abuse of Medical Diagnostic Practices in Mass Litigation, Engage, Oct. 2009, at 108–111, available at www.shb.com/attorneys/Behrens/RANDReport_2010.pdf.

74. Parloff, The Siege of State Farm (2008), available at money.cnn.com/2008/04/09/news/newsmakers/parloff_scruggs.fortune/index/htm.

75. Id. Lange, Anatomy of a Shakedown: Dickie Scruggs' Mighty Fall, Y'all, Politics, Dec. 24, 2008, available at www.yallpolitics.com/index.php/yp/post/13431/.

Lawyers as Spam

CONGRESSIONAL CAPTURE EXPLAINS WHY U.S. LAWYERS EXCEED THE OPTIMUM

STEPHEN P. MAGEE

The lawyers of the United States form a party ... which adapts itself with greater flexibility to the exigencies of the time and accommodates itself without resistance to all of the movements of the social body. But this party extends over the whole community and penetrates into all of the classes which compose it; it acts upon the country imperceptibly, but finally fashions it so suit its own purposes.

—Alexis de Tocqueville (1832)

Among the numerous advantages promised by a well-constructed Union, none deserves to be more accurately developed than its tendency to break and control the violence of factions. . . . A pure democracy, can admit no cure for the mischiefs of faction. . . . Such democracies have ever been spectacles of turbulence and contention; have ever been found incompatible with personal security or the rights of property; and have in general been as short in their lives as violent in their deaths.

—James Madison, Federalist Papers 10

The dean of the Harvard Law School once joked that by the year 2023 there would be more lawyers in the United States than people. I address the problem of too many lawyers by examining the number of lawyers in 33 countries, including the U.S. The international data reveals the surprising result that lawyers can be compared to Spam: not the unwanted email, but the cheap composite meat product. Using economic language, Spam is a normal good at low income levels (people buy more as their per capita income rises), but becomes an inferior good at middle to high income levels (people buy less as their per capita income rises).

Lawyers are like that. Across emerging economies, they are normal goods (lawyers per capita rise as country income and wealth increases), but for wealthier economies they are inferior goods (the number of lawyers per capita decreases as country income rises). The data shows that lawyers are like Spam for virtually all higher-income countries except the United States. The U.S. has a higher lawyer ratio than all advanced countries and all emerging economies except one: Uruguay.

This article extends my earlier research on the optimum number of lawyers,[1] and concludes that the American Illness can be attributed in part to a legal system that employs an excessive number of lawyers, which in turn is a consequence of excessive lawyer representation in the U.S. Congress.

Comparing lawyers to Spam is not meant to be pejorative. It just means that the income elasticity of demand for them becomes negative after some point. Lawyers are economically necessary for nation-building in developing countries. Once the legal system has been constructed, however, these legal construction workers become less necessary, and beyond a certain level, more lawyers mean a weaker economy. For the U.S., I find that that our economy would be stronger if our legal system were reformed so that the U.S. required a third fewer lawyers and lawyers had much less influence over the U.S. Congress.

I do not say that the American economy would be stronger if a third of its lawyers retired tomorrow. They are just a symptom of the problem. Economics predicts that their places would simply be taken by another group of freshly minted lawyers. The problem is with the entire legal system itself, which the lawyers have molded for their own purposes. The result is substantial inefficiencies in American law and procedures that create an excessive demand for lawyers.

Explaining Lawyer Density

The data in Figures 1a and 1b show lawyer densities (lawyers per capita) measured against income and wealth per capita for 27 countries. Notice that, like Spam, lawyer densities increase and are normal goods for per capita incomes of about $18,000 per year and per capita wealth of about

$180,000.[2] Thereafter, they become inferior goods and decline in numbers as income and wealth increase.

As economies develop, the need for lawyers to serve emerging business opportunities and litigation expands. Once a legal system is in place, however, there are economies of scale in its use and lawyers decline relative to the population as incomes grow. More lawyers are required to create a legal system but fewer are needed to maintain it—at least for efficient legal systems under non-lawyer control.

This brings us to the case of the United States. Notice how exceptional the U.S. appears in both parts of Figure 1. The large number of U.S. lawyers per capita cannot be explained by either income or wealth.

Lawyer Capture of the U.S. Political System

The quotes from Alexis de Tocqueville and James Madison at the beginning of this article suggest an explanation for American Exceptionalism, in its large number of lawyers. If lawyers partially capture the political system and the legal system, they can alter both laws and legal procedures to enrich themselves at public expense.

One consequence of lawyer capture of the political process is a temporary increase in the rates of return to lawyers. These gains will be short-lived as the high returns will stimulate entry and increases in the number of lawyers. But this higher lawyer supply will lower income per lawyer, building up pressure within the profession to increase lawyer demand even further. This is a lawyer version of Say's Law: increased supply creates its own demand.[3] The influx of new lawyers causes increased lobby pressure for increasingly inefficient laws and legal procedures to maintain demand.[4] Unfortunately, activities that stimulate excessive litigation and spurious legal complexity have negative consequences for the economy.

The most direct test of this lawyer capture theory is to see whether countries with undue lawyer influence over politics also have higher numbers of lawyers per capita. A statistical proxy for lawyer influence over politics is the percentage of lawyers in national congresses.

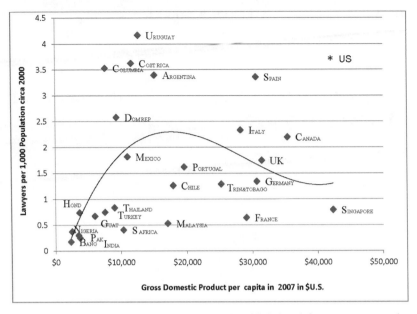

Figure 1a. Lawyers are economically normal goods below $18,000 per capita (they rise with income) but are inferior goods above that (they decline as income rises)

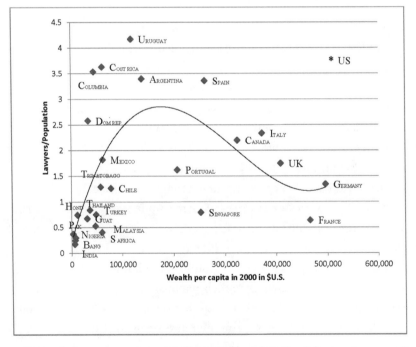

Figure 1b. Lawyers are economically normal goods below $180,000 in per capita wealth but are inferior goods above that (they decline as wealth rises)

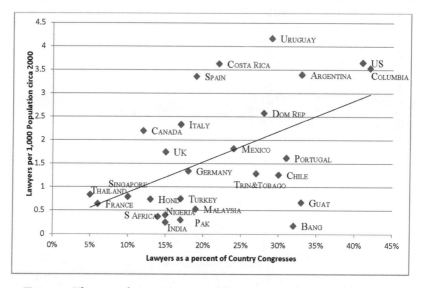

Figure 2. The more lawyers in a country's congress, the more lawyers in the economy

The data in Figure 2 do not establish but are consistent with the lawyer capture theory. Countries with higher percentages of lawyers in national congresses do tend to have more lawyers per capita. The positive and statistically significant effect of lawyers in national congresses on lawyers in economies is shown in Table 3.5. The next question is, are lawyers in the United States over-represented in the U.S. Congress?

Figures 3a and 3b report the relation between the percentage of lawyers in national congresses and national GDP per capita and wealth per capita. Notice that, as before, lawyers in national congresses also display the Spam effect for all countries except the U.S. America is exceptional among advanced countries with its high and statistically abnormal percentage of lawyers in Congress.

An alternative explanation is that countries with more lawyers would be expected to elect more lawyers to their national congress, just as countries with more doctors would be expected to elect more doctors. One would generally expect countries with more professionals to elect more of them to the national congress, as is the case with Argentina, Costa Rica, and Uruguay. In contrast, there are eight times more lawyers in the U.S. Con-

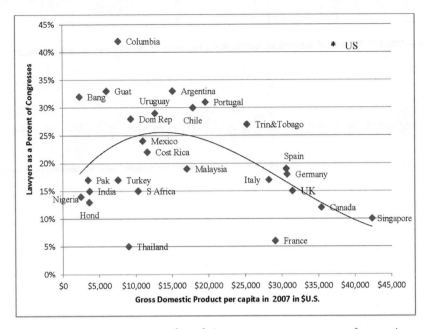

Figure 3a. Lawyers are normal goods in country congresses up to $13,000 in per capita income but are inferior goods above that

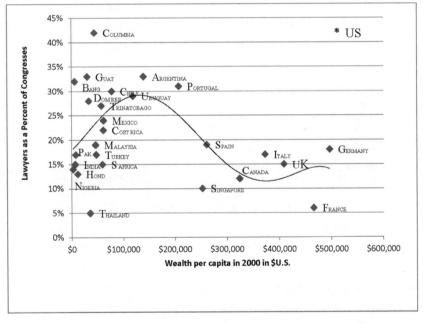

Figure 3b. Lawyers are normal goods in country congresses up to $130,000 in per capita wealth but are inferior goods up to the high-income countries

Table 3.4   Ratios of Lawyers

Country	Lawyers % of Professionals	Lawyers % of National Congresses
Argentina	27	33
Costa Rica	32	22
Uruguay	45	29
United States	5	41

gress than there are in the American professional labor force. The more than one million U.S. lawyers were only 5 percent of the 20.5 million American professional workers, but lawyers were 41 percent of the U.S. Congress in 2003.

In sum, Figures 3a and 3b indicate that neither the high level of income nor wealth accounts for the abnormally high percentage of lawyers in the U.S. Congress. The following discussion explains qualitatively how that high percentage of lawyers is correlated with other forms of lawyer influence over political control of the American legal system.

In recent decades, lawyers have constituted about 40 percent of the U.S. House of Representatives[5] and at times have reached 60 percent of the U.S. Senate. The Senate is thus the forum in which one would expect to see the greater exercise of lawyer capture. As an example, liability reforms in the 1990s that would have reduced spurious product liability suits were passed in the House but stalled in the Senate. Controls on lawyer tobacco fees also largely went down to narrow defeats in the Senate.

Lawyer votes are reinforced by powerful lawyer lobbies. Early in the 2000s, *Fortune* magazine ranked trial lawyers among the top half-dozen most powerful lobbies in Washington, ahead of the AFL-CIO, the Chamber of Commerce, government employees, bankers, doctors, real estate agents, teachers, and the entertainment industry.[6] In the 1999–2000 campaign cycle, lawyers topped the list of all industries contributing to the 107th Congress.[7]

The Republicans captured both houses of Congress in 1994, and Newt Gingrich and others proposed their famed "Contract with America." As part of that, the House of Representatives passed a number of measures reforming torts and litigation. However, the Republican-controlled Senate, despite heavy pressure from trial lawyers, did not even schedule hearings on most of the proposals.

Trial lawyers have been especially active in running for the Senate and for state attorney generalships, which Walter Olson calls "the two great power bases in American politics that allow their occupants to stay more or less indefinitely in crusade or attack mode." He points out that in recent years, lawyers have held more than half of all cabinet posts and state governorships. The most successful lawyer-politicians are trial lawyers who are wealthy enough to finance their own campaigns. The American Bar Association, consisting mostly of defense and transaction lawyers, has also fought hard through the years through its membership and as a lobbying organization against measures that would curb excessive litigation.[8]

Some wag once said that wars and lawyers are the two most effective ways of converting durable goods into nondurable goods. The lack of public concern over the wasteful costs of redistributive legal activity may come from the invisibility of wealth effects, an issue addressed in an early article by W. A. Brock and myself.[9]

Too Many Lawyers Hurts the U.S. Economy

Figures 1 and 3 provide visual evidence that the United States has too many lawyers. This section quantifies, through a statistical model, how many lawyers are too many. We saw in Figures 3a and 3b a potential explanation for why the U.S. may have too many lawyers: the U.S. Congress has succumbed to lawyer capture. What this would predict is legislation that inefficiently increases the demand for lawyers at a cost to the economy. Lawyers create private income for themselves and the spillover benefits of property rights and social order. But they also impose serious transaction costs.

I now seek to estimate the economic optimum number of lawyers, which permits an estimate of the benefits of the optimum number of lawyers and

Table 3.5   Lawyers and Economic Growth

Dependent Variable	Regression 1 GROWTH compound annual growth in GDP/pop. 1970–2007	Regression 2 LAWYERS number of lawyers per 1,000 pop.	AVERAGE average of each variable for the 33 countries
LAWYER lawyers per thousand population	1.330 (0.052)		1.45
LAWYER^2 lawyer variable squared	−0.270 (0.085)		3.50
OPENNESS exports plus imports as % GDP	0.007 (0.016)		80%
GDP 1970 natural log of GDP per capita	−1.118 (0.001)		8.55
EDUCATION % of males with secondary education or more	0.035 (0.000)	−0.008 (0.439)	54%
ASIA equals 1 for Asian countries	1.203 (0.031)	−0.356 (0.449)	0.21
INTERCEPT constant	8.393 (0.000)	−0.387 (0.625)	

(continued)

Table 3.5   (*continued*)

LAWYERS IN CONGRESS % of lawyers in congresses		0.054 (0.034)	21%
GDP/POP 2000 gross domestic product/capita ($000)		0.391 (0.030)	9.0
GDP/POP^2 2000 gross domestic product/capita squared		−0.023 (0.076)	$175
GDP/POP^3 2000 gross domestic product/capita trebled		0.0004 (0.128)	$4,325
Number of Observations	33	33	
R^2 (Adjusted)	0.61	0.44	
World Optimum Lawyer Ratio	2.45 (note 13)	2.55	
Percent Excessive U.S. Lawyers	33	30	

Notes: Statistical significance in parentheses. Most variables came from World Development Indicators, at http://data.worldbank.org/indicator. The male educational variable in the growth equation is from the Barro and Lee data set, at http://barrolee.com/. Nigeria's SIZE variable is taken from the Central Bank of Nigeria, at http://www.cbn.gov.ng/.

the costs of too many lawyers. The model first estimates the optimum number of lawyers with respect to average annual GDP growth rates. I then derive the number of U.S. lawyers from zero up to the economic optimum and the number of lawyers that exceeds the world optimum level of lawyers. The last step is to calculate the benefits of U.S. lawyers (those U.S. lawyers up to the optimum amount) and the costs of excessive U.S. lawyers (those from the optimum up to the actual number of U.S. lawyers) on U.S. GDP in 2007.

To make these calculations, I here extend my earlier work[10] and examine the relationship between lawyer density (a proxy for overall legal system activity) and economic growth in a data set of 33 countries, using an ordinary least squares estimation procedure. In column 1 of Table 3.5, the compound annual growth rate in GDP per capita over the period 1970 through 2007 (GROWTH) is regressed on the number of lawyers per 1,000 population around the year 2000 and four other drivers of economic growth. This permits an estimate of the optimum number of lawyers.

Three of the explanatory variables for these regressions came from Robert Barro's study of economic growth.[11] Barro had a data set for 84 countries, while I have data on lawyers per capita and lawyers in national congresses for only 33 countries. For this reason I employ three of Barro's explanatory variables, and not all of them. These three variables are OPENNESS (exports plus imports as a percentage of GDP), GDP 1970 (the log of initial GDP per capita in 1970), and EDUCATION (the percentage of males in the country with education at the secondary level or higher). In addition, I employed a variable for ASIA (taking the value of 1 for Asian countries and 0 otherwise) since such countries had significantly higher growth rates over the 37 years that I studied.

I also employed two lawyer variables. LAWYER is the number of lawyers per 1,000 population around the year 2000, and LAWYER^2 is the same number squared. I employed LAWYER^2 because the relationship between the economic growth and the number of lawyers is nonlinear.

Using these explanatory variables, the first regression of Table 3.5 explains 61 percent of the variability in GROWTH. The coefficients of the explanatory variables have the expected signs, and the lawyer variables are significant at the 10 percent level. The coefficients of LAWYERS and LAWYERS^2 indicate that growth rises with lawyers at low lawyer densities but falls at higher lawyer densities. This suggests that there is an economically optimum ratio of lawyers to population across countries, and that a third of U.S. lawyers are above the world economic optimum.[12] I separately tested the endogeneity (or causation question) of lawyers affecting growth and growth affecting lawyers, and found that growth does not affect the number of lawyers.[13] This justifies my use of ordinary least squares regressions in Table 3.5.

To calculate the costs of the lawyers is straightforward. As explained in note 13, the optimum number of lawyers can be derived from Table 3.5, employing the following equation: Growth $= 1.33*L - .27*L^2$. This gives one a figure for the optimum number of lawyers of 2.45 per 1,000 people, with a growth rate of 1.64 percent a year.[14] However, the U.S. has 3.65 lawyers per 1,000 people, which implies a growth rate of 1.26 percent.[15] This implies a decrease in U.S. growth of (1.64 percent − 1.26 percent =) 0.38 percent per annum between 1970 to 2007 below the optimum growth rate as a consequence of an excessive number of lawyers. On this model, for each year during this period, U.S. economic growth was 0.996 of what it might have been. This slower growth reduced U.S. GDP over the 37 years (through compounding) by .996 Thus, by 2007, U.S. per capita income was 89 percent of what it might have been with an optimum number of lawyers. For 2007, this was 11 percent of the then GDP of $14 trillion, or $1.5 trillion, a permanent and ongoing economic loss.[16]

Figure 4's optimal lawyer curve provides an intuitive visual representation of these results. To arrive at the adjusted residual growth, I subtract from actual growth the growth predicted by these non-lawyer explanatory variables. Here the per capita number of lawyers on the horizontal axis is plotted against residual growth on the vertical axis, with residual growth defined as the economic growth less the growth explained by the non-lawyer explanatory variables (OPENNESS, GDP 1970, EDUCATION, and ASIA) of the first regression of Table 3.5. For each of the 33 countries shown, there is a single dot.

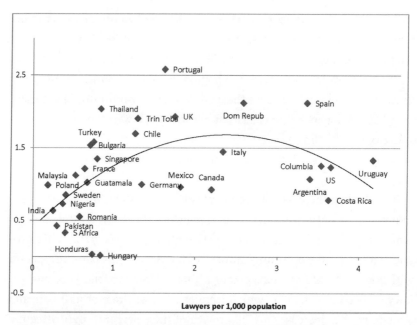

Figure 4. The optimum lawyer curve: GDP growth residuals on lawyers per 1,000 population: 33 percent of U.S. lawyers are above the optimum of 2.45 lawyers/1,000

The left side of the figure indicates that as lawyers increase per capita, the positive facilitative and spillover effects of legal activity dominate the negative redistributive effects. Among other things, this includes a legal system's institution-building and the value of the rule of law in emerging market countries. On the right side of the curve, however, the negative effects of too many lawyers and legal system sclerosis dominate their positive effects, so that growth rates decline as the numbers of lawyers per capita increase.

Why does the U.S. have so many lawyers? One reason is that the country is wealthy. A larger economy requires a larger number of lawyers. The question I have posed, however, is whether the U.S. has an excessive number of lawyers as a consequence of lawyer capture of law-making bodies. As we saw in Figure 2, the U.S. has an exceptionally high percentage of lawyers in Congress (which is a proxy for lawyers in U.S. legislatures generally). To see whether this might explain the number of U.S. lawyers, the second column of Table 3.5 regresses the per capita number of lawyers (LAWYERS/1,000) on the percentage of LAWYERS IN CONGRESS and six other explanatory variables. In these six variables I included an EDUCATION variable because a more educated population would be likely to have more lawyers, and ASIA because Asian countries make less use of lawyers than other countries. The coefficients of these two variables were not significant, however. What was significant were the nonlinear GDP/POP variables shown in Figure 1a and the LAWYERS IN CONGRESS variable.

The LAWYERS IN CONGRESS variable reflects the capture theory discussed at the beginning of the article, and is a proxy for the lobbying activity by which lawyers obtain favorable legislation. It permits us to show the relationship between the large percentage of lawyers in the U.S. Congress and the number of lawyers in the economy. In the U.S., 41 percent of the members of Congress are lawyers. That is roughly double the 33-country sample average of 21 percent of lawyers in national congresses. The relevant coefficient in the LAWYER equation in Table 3.5 is .054, meaning that a rise of one percentage point of lawyers in national congresses would be associated with a rise of .054 in a country's lawyer density. Thus the fact that that the U.S. has 20 percentage points more lawyers (0.41–0.21) than the 33 countries in this study means that the U.S. has (20*.054 =) 1.10 more lawyers than the average country. Thus, if the U.S. had the world average of lawyers, it would have 2.55 lawyers per 1,000 instead of 3.65, which is quite close to the economic optimum derived earlier (2.45 lawyers per 1,000).

In sum, lawyers are normal economic goods at low levels of both income and wealth but they become inferior goods at higher income and wealth, both in the national economies. W. C. Fields once joked that some lawyers are good and some are bad, but we don't need any of them. Well, he was wrong: the United States does need about two-thirds of them. My subject has been the other third.

A Proposed Solution to Lawyer Capture and Congressional Corruption

The problem of lawyer capture is just a small piece of the larger American problem of special-interest lobbying. Lobby groups in Washington get special-interest legislation passed that transfers wealth away from disorganized voters, taxpayers, and future generations. These transfers dwarf criminal activity in the economy. The problem is that the public purse is a commons that invites a feeding frenzy by organized lobbies. The result is collective irresponsibility manifested by federal budget deficits for 53 out of the past 60 years.

The problem is that political and legal corruption is caused by an absence of property rights at the group level. It is a legal failure in that the rule of law does not apply to organized lobbying groups. Academic experts on political economy have struggled to solve Madison's factions problem of lobbying corruption for the past 200 years. However, few realize that it is simply a property rights problem. The American legal system does not protect voters and disorganized citizens from organized redistributive lobbies. The $700 billion subprime lending fiasco that unraveled in 2008 was heavily driven by Wall Street and other lobbies watering down Washington oversight of the financial system. Sadly, reform is impossible because our political system requires that the change required would have to be endorsed by the very groups who would lose from reform.

To borrow Ted Turner's words, the lobbies causing the problems won't lead, follow, or get out of the way. Madison's admonition is more apt today than it was in the 1780s: we must "break and control the violence of factions" so that America will not be "short in our remaining life and violent in our death." Americans can only fantasize about an idealized French-type revolution, one in which nobody would get killed.

This article has measured the loss of American gross domestic product attributable to political and legal problems. The one-dimensional focus of America on money is also a partial cause of these problems. As a professor of economics also teaching MBA students, I too have contributed to this mess. Robert Kennedy made a speech about the Gross National Product that has helped temper my preoccupation with economic solutions to broader questions. He said that national income measures many things of negative value, including the transactions cost of redistributive waste. He concluded:

> However, the gross national product does not [measure] the health of our children, the quality of their education, or the joy of their play. It does not

include the beauty of our poetry or our marriages or our public debate or the integrity of our public officials or the value of healing by our physicians. It measures neither our wit nor our courage; neither our wisdom nor our learning; neither our compassion nor our devotion to our country; it measures everything, in short, except that which makes life worthwhile. And it tells us everything about America except why we are proud to be Americans.[17]

Notes

The author is indebted to Devrim Ikizler and Theodore Magee for their diligent research assistance in the preparation of this article. The data for Table 3.5 are available at http://www.mccombs.utexas.edu/faculty/stephen.magee/. A longer version of this article will be forthcoming as a book by Stephen P. Magee, The Optimum Number of Lawyers.

1. Stephen P. Magee, The Optimum Number of Lawyers: A Reply to Epp, 17 Law and Social Inquiry 667–93 (1992).

2. For clarity, most of the figures in this article are based on a 27-country sample. The regressions in Figure 4 and Table 3.5 are based on a larger sample of 33 countries. The data for wealth are in 2000 and for lawyers are around 2000; the data for income are from 2007. The source of the wealth data is World Bank, Wealth of Nations, 2000, http://siteresources.worldbank.org/INTEEI/Home/20666132/WealthofNations conferenceFINAL.pdf. The lawyer data comes from individual country information and a European survey of lawyer numbers. The results are statistically significant in both. The U.S. was excluded in estimating the curves because it is such an outlier.

3. Classic labor economics says that increases in supply lowers both the wages received and the average hours worked for existing workers. However, what I shall call "Say's U.S. Lawyer Law" states that increases in the supply of lawyers creates artificial demand for lawyers and can raise average hours worked per lawyer. An intuitive understanding of this law is captured in the old aphorism that only one lawyer in a town will starve, but if the town has two lawyers, they will both prosper.

4. Another explanation for large numbers of lawyers is the tragedy of the commons. The tragedy exists when public services are largely free: national defense, roads, highways, public schools, libraries, the federal budget, and the right to sue others. When laymen and lawyers do not have to pay the full costs that they impose on the legal system and the economy, the system is overutilized.

5. The average job tenure for the principal leaders of the U.S. House of Representatives (the committee chairmen, speaker, majority leader, and whip) was 27 years, per Dan Greenberg, Term Limits: The Only Way to Clean Up Congress, Heritage Foundation Reports, August 10, 1994. That is five years longer than the average

tenure of 22 years for the five kings and queens of England for the 110 years from 1901 through 2011.

6. Walter Olson, The Rule of Lawyers 265–66 (2003).

7. Catherine Crier, The Case against Lawyers 182 (2002).

8. Olson, supra note 6, at 268, 276, 280, 290.

9. William A. Brock and Stephen P. Magee, "The Invisible Foot and the Waste of Nations," in Neoclassical Political Economy: The Economics of Rent Seeking and DUP Activities 170–85 (David Colander ed., 1984) examined how tort litigation converts wealth into income. To illustrate, consider the case of purely redistributive legal activity that has no positive efficiency or justice-related effects. If purely redistributive plaintiffs receive $1 billion in wealth from defendants and have to pay their attorneys a 30 percent contingency fee, then $300 million of wealth is converted into income. The irony is that this $300 million loss in national wealth is effectively unmeasured and seldom discussed publicly, while the $300 million increase in national income might be recognized and heavily discussed in the financial press. Our point was that there is an asymmetry in society's recognition of the wealth losses that are associated with redistributive income gains.

10. Supra note 2.

11. Robert J. Barro, Human Capital and Growth, 91 Am. Econ. Rev. 12 (2001).

12. The optimum is calculated as follows. Ignoring other variables, we can write growth as $G = aL + bL2$, where L is lawyer density, a is the coefficient on L, and b is the coefficient on $L2$. The optimum lawyer level, L^*, is the lawyer density where the derivative of growth with respect to lawyers equals zero (at the highest point of the curve in Figure 4). That derivative set to zero is $dG/dL = a + 2bL = 0$. Solving for L yields the optimum number of lawyer per 1,000, $L^* = -a/2b = 1.33 \, / \, (2^*.27) = 2.45$. This result is robust to variable specifications and estimation techniques.

13. I employed a two-stage least squares procedure to estimate GROWTH. Regression 1 of 3.5 assumes that lawyers affect economic growth. However, economic growth might also be expected to affect the number of lawyers. A 2SLS regression, in which the number of lawyers is estimated with instrumental variables, tests for the endogeneity problem. The instrumental variables, predicting LAWYER and LAWYER[2], were the number of lawyers in Congress, as well as variables based on GDP in 2000, which was uncorrelated with GDP growth. (Some but not all of the countries that had high values of GDP in 1970 also had poor growth over the 1970–2007 period, and vice versa.) In the 2SLS equation, the instrumented lawyers and lawyers-squared variables were both significant in explaining growth at the .10 level. In the other structural equation, I found that instrumented growth was very insignificant in explaining lawyers. Thus the 2SLS experiment tells us that growth does not explain lawyers but lawyers do explain growth, which justifies the use of an OLS procedure to estimate growth and lawyers in Table 3.5.

14. Optimal Growth rate $= 1.33(2.45) - .27(2.45)^2 = 1.64$ percent.

15. U.S. Growth rate $= 1.33(3.65) - .27(3.65)^2 = 1.26$ percent.

16. While this estimate is robust, estimates of the positive effects of U.S. lawyers were not (37 percent of GDP or $5.2 trillion).

17. Excerpt from a speech by Robert F. Kennedy at the University of Kansas, March 18, 1968, three months before he was assassinated.

Regulation and Litigation

COMPLEMENTS OR SUBSTITUTES?

ERIC HELLAND AND JONATHAN KLICK

Michael Avery, Mark Covington, Sam DeFrank, Carly Vickers, and Todd Shadle were all involved in separate relatively minor traffic accidents in the early 1990s. Each of their accidents required minimal repairs to their vehicles. Their insurer, State Farm, had a policy of repairing damaged cars with parts that were not made by the original equipment manufacturer (OEM). The use of non-OEM parts would have reduced each individual's bill between $45 and $155. Avery and Shadle opted for OEM parts and paid the cost difference themselves. The others had their vehicles repaired using non-OEM parts.

In 1997 these five drivers, along with almost all other State Farm customers who had non-OEM parts installed on their vehicles or who paid the difference between OEM and non-OEM parts, were included in a class of about 4.5 million people.[1] The plaintiff class alleged that State Farm's policy of using non-OEM parts was a breach of contract because the insurer promised to restore their cars to their pre-loss conditions. They further alleged that State Farm had committed fraud by violating Illinois consumer protection statutes. The alleged violation resulted, according to the plaintiffs, from the inferiority of non-OEM parts. The alleged damages to each individual plaintiff in the case were so small that the action would not have been brought without the class action procedural mechanism. The question at issue was whether non-OEM parts were really inferior to OEM parts.

In this class action, State Farm faced litigation on behalf of anyone in 48 states[2] who had had his or her car repaired with non-OEM parts. The aggregated damage judgment in the initial cases was $1.2 billion, a sum representing a third of State Farm's net income in 2007. Faced with the possibility of such large damages, most defendants would have settled and discontinued the use of non-OEM parts. State Farm did the latter, but it did not settle. The judgment against State Farm was overturned, but not before the case had altered company policy toward non-OEM parts.[3] While the State Farm case is atypical in its size, the cumulative effects of several class actions against a company can have a similar effect on a firm's practices.

This change in policy would not be surprising if virtually every state had not previously regulated the issue of whether insurers could use non-OEM parts. Non-OEM parts were allowed in Illinois if their use was disclosed on the consumer's estimates, the parts were of like kind and quality, the manufacturer was identified on the part, and a warranty was provided. Illinois already had regulations designed to balance the competing goals of lower costs versus higher quality repairs. In effect, the litigation created a parallel system of regulation.

On one level, operating a system of state regulation and a parallel system of regulation through the courts is redundant and potentially contradictory. Further, the system generates its own administrative costs. In the 27 cases in the RAND Insurance Class Action database that reported attorneys' fees, the average fee award constituted 29 percent of the gross common fund.[4] The median award was 30 percent, and the largest award was 41 percent.[5] This is slightly higher than the Eisenberg and Miller estimate of 22 percent,[6] but it is consistent with some other findings in the literature. Further, this does not include defense costs or the cost of administering the case by the courts.

Despite the cost, the operation of potentially redundant and expensive regulatory systems might perhaps be justified on two grounds:

1. Administrative regulation and class actions can both be used in the process of controlling behavior with states alternating in their use

depending on which one can be operated more cheaply on the margin. That is, the two systems serve as substitutes in the regulatory production function in the same way that manufacturers use both labor and capital in producing goods but, on the margin, more labor implies less capital and vice versa;

2. Class actions allow consumers to influence regulatory policy when administrative regulators are captured by industry.

The first hypothesis is that regulation by an administrative office and regulation by the courts using class actions are simply substitutes. The choice is not either administrative regulation or class actions: administrative regulation represents the minimum standard that courts can go beyond if the agency in question has not protected consumers at the relevant legal standard. Regulation represents a minimal level of deterrence that does not require litigation, but if that level is insufficient, then litigation will provide an additional backstop.

To take a prominent example, the Securities and Exchange Commission (SEC) has long argued that private securities litigation is a substitute for SEC fines. This division of labor supposedly frees up enforcement resources and allows the SEC to target firms that private attorneys would not.

The second justification for operating a dual system is the possibility of regulatory capture. Economists, starting with Stigler,[7] have argued that regulators are likely to be captured by the industry they regulate. The source of this capture is a collective action problem. The cost to an industry resulting from regulation is concentrated, while the benefits to consumers from the regulation are diffuse. For example, in the case of price regulation, no consumer has an incentive to lobby the regulator to control prices, as the individual gains are too small to warrant the effort of lobbying. Regulated industries, in contrast, have incentives to lobby for more generous rate increases.

Some observers argue that since courts are less likely to be captured by industry than a regulatory agency with a single jurisdiction, class actions can represent a check on the ability of industry to determine regulatory policy. The point extends beyond regulated prices. In the case of breast implants, Hersch argues that the initial motivation of the consumer class actions was a perception that regulation was lax because the Food and Drug Administration (FDA) was unwilling to actively monitor medical devices.[8] In cases such as lawsuits against handgun manufacturers, the argument goes even one step further. The political process, according to proponents, is deadlocked and unable to produce meaningful safety regulation. The courts offer an avenue for a "more rational" standard for consumer protection.

In this article, we examine the substitution hypothesis.[9] Insurance regulation in the United States is largely in the hands of the states. Although regulatory agencies are similar in many respects, it is not an overstatement to say that the U.S. has 51 separate regulatory regimes for insurance. State regulation generally focuses on two areas: solvency regulation and market regulation. Solvency regulation, which requires insurers to maintain adequate reserves and guaranty funds and meet financial disclosure requirements, is relatively homogenous across states. But market regulation, which regulates insurance products, practices, and prices, varies dramatically. We use this variation to evaluate the link between insurance regulation and class action litigation.

We test whether regulation and litigation are substitutes on the margin. Specifically, if regulation has some deterrent value, the probability that a company commits a wrongful act is a function of the level of regulation. This implies that more active regulators should be associated with less harm in their jurisdictions. Once a harm or perceived harm occurs, the case enters the civil justice system if the plaintiff's attorney expects that the case is likely to be successful and financially viable.[10]

We use data from the National Association of Insurance Commissioners concerning the regulatory environment in each state.[11] We link these data to a unique dataset, the RAND Insurance Class Action database. The data on class actions contain information on class actions against firms in the insurance industry for 748 distinct cases that were open at least once during the period of 1992 to 2002. Because the data are reasonably comprehensive for the companies responding to the survey, we are able to link the frequency of class action litigation to the states' insurance regulation data.

We examine multiple facets of the regulation litigation tradeoff. First, we examine whether a regulator's interest in a particular cause of action reduces the likelihood that class actions covering this cause of action will be filed in the regulator's home state.

Second, we examine several measures of regulatory stringency in the state to determine whether there is a substitution effect between regulatory action and litigation. For example, we use state regulatory budgets as a proxy for regulatory stringency, a factor that varies enormously from state to state, examining the relationship between levels of stringency and the incidence of class actions.

Third, we examine whether class actions are less frequent if regulators had previously issued an administrative decision on a particular issue, or if there are no existing state laws on the particular issue. In a system where regulation and litigation are substitutes, if regulators are silent, then the private attorneys are more likely to step in. Using OEM parts cases, we examine whether states that have not issued rulings on the use of non-OEM parts have more OEM class actions. Since the issue is unsettled, the theory goes, class actions fill the regulatory void.

Understanding the relationship between litigation and regulation, especially as it relates to the insurance industry, takes on special importance given the current financial crisis. The uproar over the government's $170 billion commitment to bail out American International Group (AIG), along with similar (though less dramatic) problems among other insurers, may be a harbinger of sweeping changes in how we regulate the insurance industry in the U.S.

The next section discusses the nature of insurance regulations and provides some background on class action litigation necessary to motivate our empirical investigation. We then discuss the data and examine the evidence for a substitution between administrative regulation and class actions.

The Substitution Thesis

There are several theoretical reasons why we might observe a tradeoff between regulation and class actions. The seminal Shavell model of the relationship between regulation and litigation provides a useful starting point.[12] Shavell's model provides conditions for the efficient use of both regulation and litigation in a system geared toward incentivizing individuals to take the socially optimal level of care.

Shavell posits that liability and regulation serve as substitutes on the margin. All other things equal, as the regulatory standard (or enforcement level in the real-world setting where not all violations are discovered by the regulator)[13] is raised, there is less need for liability in generating socially optimal behavior. In fact, in the limit, if the regulatory standard is set above the social value of the harm avoided, we will have too much care taken, in which case any additional care induced by liability will be pure social waste. Further, as a positive matter, the higher the regulatory standard, the less harm that will occur, leaving a smaller domain for litigation, all other things being equal.

In Shavell's model, regulation is most useful where harm across parties is similar, whereas litigation is most useful where there is a high degree of variability across parties. In class actions, where by definition the harms are similar across parties, the case for regulation is strongest and that for litigation is weakest, on the Shavell model.

The Data

To investigate the relationship between litigation and regulation, we use a unique data source covering the experience of insurance companies with class action litigation. The dataset contains information on class actions against firms in the insurance industry derived from 988 case-level surveys from 130 insurance companies, describing 748 distinct cases that were open at least once during the period of 1992 to 2002. The information was gathered through a survey that concentrated on larger insurance companies in the property-casualty, life, and health markets. The complete dataset contains information on cases filed between 1984 and 2002.

The survey asked the responding companies to describe, for each such case in which they were a named defendant, the courts of filing and disposition, the names of other defendants in the case, whether there were also similar cases filed earlier or in other jurisdictions, the lines of insurance involved, the key allegations of the plaintiffs, key statutes involved, whether the issue of regulatory jurisdiction was raised by any of the parties, the description of the actual or putative class, the geographical scope of the actual or putative class, the outcome of any certification process, the manner in which the case was resolved, and the details of any settlement or trial verdict for the plaintiffs. Table 3.6 contains the distribution of cases by insurance line. The vast majority of cases in the data concern automobile insurance.

Examining data for the 12 companies that were able to provide complete information about their experience with class actions between 1992 and 2002, we find a strong upward trend in the amount of class action litigation involving these insurers. While the actual numbers of cases remains small throughout the period, 14 cases in 1994 rising to 68 in 2002, the percentage increase is dramatic. This represents growth by a factor of five throughout the period.

Focusing on a subset of these cases, the growth in cases alleging harm to nationwide or multi-state classes of plaintiffs grew at an even more dramatic rate in this period. At the beginning of the period, there were only two such cases (one nationwide and one multi-state) in 1992 up to highs of

Table 3.6   Lines of Insurance Involved in the Case

Lines	Percentage of All Cases
Automobile	67.5
Homeowners	12.8
Life	7.1
Workers' Compensation	6.3
Health	2.4
Multiple Lines	1.2
Annuities	1.2
Earthquake	1.2
Mobile Home	0.9

Source: Nicholas Pace, Stephen J. Carroll, Ingo Vogelsang, and Laura Zakaras, Insurance Class Actions in the United States (2007).

19 multi-state and 16 nationwide classes in 1999, a percentage increase of more than 1,600 percent.

Unless underlying behavior or social damages worsened during this period, the substitution model suggests that we should have seen an off-setting reduction in regulation during this period. This is not the case. Although litigation appears to have become a more important force in the regulatory setting, there is no evidence of a dramatic decrease in regulation. In fact, as measured by budget resources and staffing levels, regulatory action increased during this time period.

Two important caveats are required. Respondents are more likely to have reported newer cases. A number of responding insurers indicated that older class actions litigated near the start of our study period were not tracked in a way that would allow them to be as identifiable. For this reason the growth may be less dramatic than it appears. The second limitation is that we do not generally know the size of the class. A simple explanation of the growth of class actions may well be that earlier cases represented more individuals than later cases, such that the overall impact of class actions litigation during this period is unchanged.

The cases also concern a number of different allegations. About half of the cases involved claims related to health care providers as assignees of medical benefits in automobile policies (either as part of personal injury protection plans in "no-fault" states or as first party medical payments coverage in "add-on" states), various property coverage claims, claims by policyholders or beneficiaries under automobile uninsured/underinsured motorist coverage, diminished value claims related to first-party automobile coverage, and various workers' compensation issues. Diminished value allegations were the most frequently cited in our data.

Self-Reported Regulatory Interest and Litigation

To draw any inference about the substitution thesis, we had to confirm that our regulators and class actions were operating in the same domains. That is, we had to ensure that the regulators saw the issues being litigated as falling within their purview. If they do, the substitution thesis would predict lower levels of litigation. However, that seems not to have happened. A survey of state regulators reports that the incidence of class action litigation is unrelated to the regulators' self-reported assertions of interest in the matter.

To determine the relationship between regulator interest and class actions, the RAND Institute for Civil Justice conducted a survey in 2005 of staff members of state departments of insurance.[14] Seventeen states completed the survey. The survey asked the regulators to rank the 260 key allegations made by the plaintiffs in our cases according to their relationship with the traditional activities of the regulator.

The substitution thesis would predict that class actions alleging a particular cause of action should be more frequent when surveyed regulators respond that the cause of action is outside their regulatory mandate. For example, most regulators responded to the survey saying that "vanishing premium" cases were within their regulatory mandate.[15] Given the level of interest in the harm generated by vanishing premiums, we would expect them to be rare in the data. In fact, however, our analysis shows that class action frequency has no relationship to regulatory interest. In sum, regulators and class actions appear to be concerned with similar issues.

Regulatory Resources

The substitution thesis might not hold if state regulators lack the resources to take action in cases that concern them. To test this, we selected three measures of regulatory stringency: the regulatory budget per insurance firm, the number of market conduct exams per insurance firm regulated by the state, and the number of market conduct examiners per insurance firm regulated by the state.

Our data on regulatory activity come from insurance regulators, as seen in the National Association of Insurance Commissioners (NAIC) "Insurance Department Resources Report." According to the NAIC website, this "provides an in-depth look at the resources of the 55 insurance departments." Ideally, we would like information on regulatory activity specific to the line or allegation, but the data provided by the NAIC are not this specific.

Figure 5 shows the relationship between budgets and the number of class actions filed in the state. The insurance regulator's budget is the

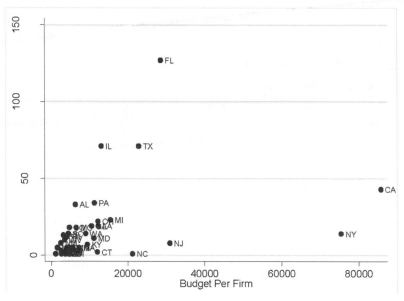

Figure 5. Number of cases and budget per firm

broadest measure of the resources devoted to insurance regulation in the state. As in the case of the survey data, a substitution between regulation and class actions would predict that class actions are more frequent when budgets are tighter. The results suggest that the relationship between regulatory stringency and class actions is either flat or weakly positive. When states provide more resources to regulators we see more, not fewer, class actions.

One concern is that the states' budgets might mask important differences in the scope of a state agency's regulatory activity. Our other measures of regulatory stringency are more specific. Market conduct exams are broad investigations into the business practices of insurers in the state. For example, according to the Maryland Insurance Commissioner, its Compliance Unit reviews insurance company operations to determine how the company operates in the market place. The examiners' review includes, but is not limited to, sales practices, advertising materials, underwriting practices, and claims handling practices. Examinations often help alert companies to problems and serve as a form of consumer protection. The resulting examination report presents a detailed analysis of a company's general business practice.

Although some level of investigation is regularly conducted by state regulators, there is wide variation in the frequency of these inspections. The New Jersey Department of Banking and Insurance explains that inspections may be based on an increase in complaint volume, an increase in the frequency of complaints on a particular issue, the findings of a prior exam, a change in the company's market presence, or the length of time since the last exam.

The frequency with which a firm can expect to have its business practices reviewed in the state as well as the number of inspectors the state retains to conduct these exams are useful proxies for regulatory resources.

In Figures 6 and 7, we present a plot of these measures of regulatory stringency against the number of class actions filed in the state. A few states, such as New York, stand out in the frequency with which they inspect the firms under their jurisdiction, while several other states, such as Florida, stand out for the frequency with which class actions are filed in their borders. Overall, we find no evidence for the hypothesis that class actions will be more common in states with relatively weak regulatory environments.

One concern may be that we miss interesting variation by treating all states equally. That is, perhaps substitution emerges if we weight states by their population since an effect in California might be masked by non-effects in states where very few people live anyway, limiting their practical importance in drawing general conclusions. If we scale the number of class actions filed by the population of the state under the assumption that class actions may be more likely in states with larger population, the pictures change slightly, but the broad interpretation remains the same. There is no evidence of a substitution effect between insurance class actions and the stringency of regulation.

One possible reason for this divergence is that class actions can be filed in places other than where the harm originated. A case in New York, for example, might actually cover harms in other states but is filed in New York because an insurer is headquartered there or for other idiosyncratic reasons. Examining the number of cases filed on behalf of residents of a state regardless of where the case was filed generates the same qualitative

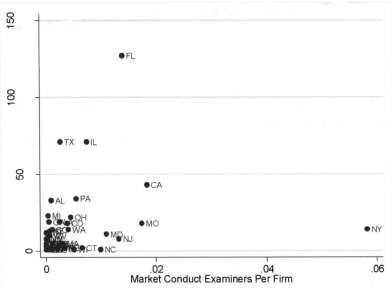

Figure 6. Number of cases and market conduct examiners per firm

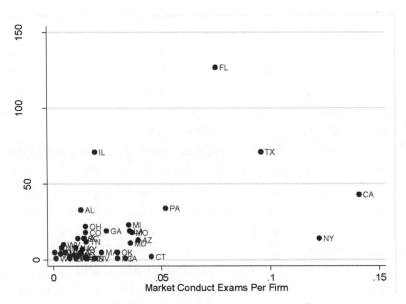

Figure 7. Number of cases and market conduct exams per firm

results for all of our indicators of regulatory stringency. Again, states that devote more resources to enforcement appear to also be more likely to feature their citizens as class members.

Graphical representations of data have the potential to obscure underlying relationships, especially if there are idiosyncratic differences across states. This "unobserved heterogeneity" makes it difficult to sort out the causal relationship between regulation and litigation. For example, if a given state demands a higher level of consumer protection, it may exhibit both more regulation and litigation, even if on the margin the state substitutes between the two mechanisms.

To address this worry, in a 2007 article in the *Journal of Tort Law*, we examined these relationships in a regression framework. By using this methodology, we could control for some of the other differences across states that may confound isolating the relationship between litigation and regulation. Specifically, we included constant state fixed effects to account for baseline differences in the level of consumer protection demanded by state residents. These baseline differences may arise due to wealth and income effects or from other sources of differential preferences.

Wealth and income effects may be particularly important in this context as consumer protection may be a normal good and high-income states are likely to provide more funding for their regulators. Thus, even with a high degree of regulation, residents of richer states may be more apt to litigate because they expect more protection. Failure to account for this effect would lead an analyst to examine the average relationship between regulation and litigation, as is done in the graphs above, when the theoretical hypothesis concerns the marginal relationship. The regression framework allows us to net out any constant preference-induced differences in the relationship between regulation and litigation, focusing attention on what happens to litigation when a given state changes its regulatory activities.[16]

The regression framework also allows us to account for national litigation trends that occur independently of any regulatory changes. For example, if federal procedural rules make it more difficult to bring a class action, we would expect the number of class actions to decline everywhere to some extent. It is important to net out these effects by including year effects in the regression equation. The regression methodology also allows us to account for differences in other attributes of the litigation to ensure that a simple count of cases is meaningful. For example, if the number of cases declines but there is a shift toward allegations that generally generate larger judgments and settlements, we would not want to count that as a decline in litigation activity. By controlling for differences in case attributes, we can mitigate the importance of these kinds of issues.

The regression results we present in the 2007 article are very consistent with the graphical results presented above. We do not find a statistically significant negative relationship between the likelihood an insurer faces a class action in a given state litigation and the regulation metrics we examine. In fact, any statistically significant relationships we find are positive relationships. For example, we find that when the number of market conduct exams per insurer increases by 10 percent, the likelihood an insurer will face a class action in that state goes up by about 2 percent. This result is statistically significant at the 10 percent level. If we instead focus on the number of market examiners per insurer in the state, when that metric rises by 10 percent, the likelihood of an insurer facing a class action in that state increases by almost 8 percent. This effect is statistically significant at the 1 percent level.

When we examine the likelihood of facing a class action filed on behalf of state residents in another jurisdiction, we find less evidence of a positive relationship between litigation and regulation. The coefficients generally still suggest a positive relationship, but they are much smaller in magnitude, leading to a lack of statistical significance. However, we still find zero evidence of substitution on the margin.

These regression results provide confidence that the graphical analysis presented above is not obscuring some true substitutability between litigation and regulation on the margin. If anything, the more systematic examination of the data through regression techniques is suggestive of complementarity, not substitutability. In further research, it would be interesting to examine whether this complementarity is driven by litigants filing in the wake of some regulatory discovery, regulators piggy-backing on the discoveries of litigants, or some combination of these.

The Evidence from Non-OEM Parts Litigation

To get a more precise view of how litigation and regulation interact, we examine the controversy surrounding the use of OEM parts in accident repairs. While our aggregate data does not support the substitution thesis, it may be that a more narrow focus might reveal that litigation results from gaps in rules.

According to the United States Government Accountability Office (GAO), 40 states have enacted some form of legislation governing the use of OEM parts.[17] Of these states, 36 require companies to identify if aftermarket parts are used in the repair. A warranty is required by 27 states, and 23 states require a manufacturer's ID for tracking purposes on any non-OEM parts. Although the use of OEM parts is regulated, every state insurance commission and consumer product safety commission in the U.S. allowed it, and two states, Massachusetts and Hawaii, required it.

There have been many studies of the safety of non-OEM parts, much of it at the behest of regulators. Generally, such studies report that non-OEM parts differ only cosmetically from OEM parts and create little or no safety risk. Whether or not one agrees with the regulators' decisions on OEM parts, it is hard to argue that the issue had not been evaluated and that regulators and legislators had not reached a consensus favoring the regulated use of non-OEM parts.

The fact that 40 states regulated the use of non-OEM parts provides a basis for an evaluation of class actions as a substitute for regulation. If the 10 states that did not have rules or disallowed certain practices had more class actions, this would support the substitution thesis. When regulation is vague or nonexistent, private attorneys would then fill the void. However, this is not what we observe. Remarkably, all of the states with above average litigation filings in the RAND Class Action dataset had previously issued regulations on non-OEM parts.

The results are similar when we break down the filing rates by specific regulation. The regulations we examined include requirements about: (1) disclosure, (2) consent, (3) a duty to identify whether non-OEM parts will be used (4) or whether the aftermarket part is of like quality, (5) warranties, (6) disclosure as to warranties, (7) a ban on requiring non-OEM parts, and (8) disclosure of the non-OEM manufacturer. We also examined the case in which no regulations existed.

We find that the number of class actions filed in a state is either indistinguishable in states that regulated certain practices or that class actions are more common in states that had explicit regulations. For four of the regulations, these differences are statistically significant: (1) states that required disclosure had almost one additional OEM parts case relative to those that did not require disclosure; (2) states that required estimates to identify non-OEM parts had an average of .93 more class actions during the sample period; (3) states requiring a warranty on non-OEM parts also had an average of one additional class action over those states that did not require warranties; and (4) states that had no regulation in place had .8 fewer cases than those with some regulation of non-OEM parts during the sample period. The existence of prior regulations on the allegation under litigation has essentially no negative effect on the filing rate of class actions. This is inconsistent with the substitution thesis.

The same conclusion arises if we adjust for population. There is no statistically significant difference in states with and without a particular regulation, or any regulation. The implication of this is that more populous states are both more likely to be the filing location of a class action lawsuit covering OEM parts, and that these states are also more likely to have issued rulings on the use of non-OEM parts.

However, we did find evidence consistent with the substitution thesis when we examined cases filed on behalf of individuals not residing in the state of filing (e.g., a case filed in Illinois that includes class members who are residents of Missouri). The majority of states with an above average number of suits on behalf of residents outside the filing state are states that had not issued a ruling on non-OEM parts. States without regulation of OEM parts are more likely to have cases brought on behalf of their residents, but these cases are more likely to be decided in other states.

Although the facts of these cases are complex and remain controversial, the important feature of the cases for our purposes is the plaintiffs' allegation that non-OEM parts were in fact unsafe and that insurance companies breached their contracts with policy holders by using non-OEM parts. Specifically, the effect of the *Avery* case mentioned above, at least until it was overturned, was to cause a number of insurance companies to switch to OEM parts even though regulators in many of those states had specifically permitted non-OEM parts.[18]

Conclusion

We find that class action filing location is not determined by a lack of interest on the part of local regulators. Nor are filings more likely in states with fewer regulatory enforcement resources. We do find, however, that class actions are more frequently brought on behalf of residents of states whose regulatory authority has not issued rules in a particular area, but these cases are filed in states that are more likely to have regulations in place. Thus, in all but one of our tests, we find no evidence to support the substitution thesis. Moreover, the one instance where we do find evidence of the thesis has the unusual feature that cases are brought on behalf of those who live in states with ambiguous regulations in states that have regulations specifically allowing the conduct.

Finding little support for the standard law-and-economics explanation for the dual regulatory and litigation system, we are left seeking other models of the relationship between regulation and litigation. Elsewhere, we present evidence that litigation does not generally serve to undo regulatory capture. Thus the two primary economic justifications for dual regulatory and litigation systems appear to be inconsistent with the data. Although it is possible that economic theorists have simply missed a strong justification for the dual system during the 30 years since this topic first garnered interest in the law-and-economics literature, efficiency concerns seem to support calls for regulatory preemption of litigation.[19]

Notes

1. Avery v. State Farm Mut. Auto. Ins. Co., WL 955543 and WL 1022134 (Ill. Cir., 1999). See State Farm Media Backgrounder for estimate of class size available at http://www.statefarm.com/about/media/backgrounder/avery_sf.asp (last accessed on March 12, 2009).

2. Residents from Arkansas and Tennessee were not included.

3. The class was certified on July 1997 in Williamson County, Ill. On October 4, 1999, a jury awarded $456 million to the plaintiffs for breach of contract. This award was followed four days later by an additional award of $730 million for consumer fraud made by Judge John Speroni. The award included $600 million in punitive damages. On April 5, 2001, the Appellate Court reduced the verdict by $130 million but let stand $1.05 billion of the award. In 2005, the Illinois Supreme Court overturned the judgment against State Farm. The Court unanimously ruled that class should not have been certified because it was too broad and that the plaintiffs failed to demonstrate either a breach of contract or consumer fraud.

4. More information on this database is available at http://www.rand.org/pubs/monographs/MG587–1.html.

5. Nicholas Pace, Stephen J. Carroll, Ingo Vogelsang, and Laura Zakaras, Insurance Class Actions in the United States (2007).

6. See T. Eisenberg and G. Miller, Attorney Fees in Class Action Settlements: An Empirical Study, 1 J. Emp. Legal Stud. 27, 51–52 (2004).

7. George Stigler, The Theory of Economic Regulation, 2 Bell J. Econ. Mgmt. Sci. 3 (1971).

8. Hersch, Breast Implants: Regulation, Litigation and Science. Regulation through Litigation, AEI-Brookings Joint Center for Regulatory Studies, Washington, D.C. (2002).

9. We examine the regulatory capture hypothesis, as well as some other ad hoc rationales, in Helland and Klick, To Regulate, Litigate, or Both, available at SSRN: http://ssrn.com/abstract=1375522.

10. We examine the relationship between harm generation while controlling for the likelihood of litigation in Helland and Klick, The Tradeoffs between Regulation and Litigation: Evidence from Insurance Class Actions, 1 J. Tort. L. Article 2 (2006).

11. These data are published in the NAIC's Insurance Department Research Report. The most recent report is available at http://www.naic.org/store_pub_naic_state.htm#dept_resources.

12. Shavell, A Model of the Optimal Use of Liability and Safety Regulation, 15 Rand J. Econ. 271 (1984); Shavell, Liability for Harm versus Regulation of Safety, 13 J. Legal Stud. 357 (1984).

13. Although the Shavell model does not distinguish between the standard and its enforcement (i.e., Shavell assumes that any standard can be enforced perfectly), in the real world, standards are not self-enforcing. This implies that, for any given standard, the care achieved will be a function of enforcement. For simplicity, we will assume that regulators adopt optimal enforcement levels.

14. See Pace, supra note 5.

15. Vanishing premium cases are generated by an insurer's claim that premiums will vanish over time, without a lifetime of payments, where premiums failed to disappear because the financial assumptions were unrealistic.

16. Heterogeneity in preferences can work through a number of different channels in addition to the income and wealth one discussed above. Other issues could

involve differential risk aversion leading to a higher desired consumer protection level.

17. Motor Vehicle Safety: NHTSA's Ability to Detect and Recall Defective Replacement Crash Parts Is Limited, GAO-01–215 (2001).

18. This point is made in Schwartz and Lorber, State Farm v. Avery: State Court Regulation through Litigation Has Gone Too Far, 33 Conn. L. Rev. 1215 (2001).

19. While there are many arguments offered in favor of preemption by practitioners, economics scholarship has also offered support for this position. See, e.g., Schwartzstein and Shleifer, Litigation and Regulation (2009), working paper available at http://papers.ssrn.com/sol3/papers.cfm?abstract_id=1344505.

Does Product Liability Law
Make Us Safer?

W. KIP VISCUSI

Tort liability for personal injuries and property damage caused by products is known as product liability. Among the most prominent products associated with product liability claims are pharmaceutical products, medical devices, private aircraft, automobiles, and cigarettes. Damages awarded to injured parties raise the costs of providing the product, thus increasing the costs to the firm of selling unsafe products. Where the damages equal the value of the harm, the damages payment leads the firm to internalize the costs of the harm and creates incentives for the firm to produce safer products. In this article I focus primarily on whether American product liability law does in fact enhance product safety.

Posing the question of whether product liability law is safety-enhancing does not, however, imply that this framing of the mission of product liability is appropriate. Higher levels of safety may not be desirable. For almost all products, it does not make economic sense to ensure that products are risk-free. Rather, from the standpoint of economic efficiency, for continuous safety choices the penalties established through tort liability should provide financial incentives for firms to provide the products that achieve a level of risk that equates the incremental benefits of greater safety with the incremental costs.[1] Thus, if the safety level of the product falls short of the efficient level, product liability can potentially play a productive role by pe-nalizing firms for a shortfall between the level of product safety provided and the efficient level of safety, thus pushing the level of safety closer to its efficient level.

This task of establishing efficient incentives for product safety is not limited to a point in time. As technological change evolves over time, firms should continue to improve their products to maintain this benefit-cost balance. Technological change generally will lead to enhanced safety levels in any given product if the changes involve innovations that decrease the costs of providing safer products. If the cost of providing a given level of safety decreases, then the firm will find it efficient to improve the safety of the product.

However, technological change also may lead to the introduction of new products posing novel risks. Whether product liability will make products safer is a question that should be framed more broadly in terms of whether product liability also fosters the introduction of welfare-enhancing new products. The court's task of assessing innovative products often entails more problematic judgments than with assessments of existing technolo-gies, so that the concern for safety with respect to innovations may in fact stymie such innovations. Novel products may be safer than existing prod-ucts but may pose new kinds of risks. If there is a bias of product liability against novel risks, then there will be a disincentive with respect to prod-uct innovations.

A review of the empirical evidence and case studies on the role of prod-uct liability demonstrates that the idealized world in which the tort liability system is supposed to produce efficient levels of safety is not how product liability law actually performs. As I will demonstrate, the report card on the performance of product liability law is mixed. In some instances tort liability does serve a potentially risk-reducing role by fostering new safety measures. However, the safety-enhancing role of liability fails to be real-ized in general because of fundamental deficiencies in product liability law and the way such cases are handled by the courts. In particular, courts make excessive and unpredictable awards, and stumble when faced with uncertainties. New products posing uncertain risks are especially hard hit so that product liability often serves as a barrier to innovations that would reduce accidents.

The Efficient Safety Reference Point

In a simple economic framework in which firms have constant unit costs of production, providing products with a higher level of safety will result in a higher level of unit costs for the product. In the case of competitive markets, the additional costs associated with safer products will raise unit cost levels, which in turn will raise the price of the product purchased by consumers by an amount equal to the cost of greater safety.[2] Thus consumers are in effect purchasing a product liability insurance policy as part of a bundled product. Whether consumer welfare is enhanced by greater safety or whether the additional safety is excessive from consumers' standpoint depends on whether consumers value the safety improvements more than the increased product price.

The role of product liability law in the economy should be quite selective, since market forces will foster safer products so that safety levels are not generally awry. Indeed, there is no useful function of product liability law if markets function perfectly. In a well-functioning market, firms will deliver products that have an efficient level of safety even in the absence of product liability law. This assumes that consumers are fully informed of the risks and consequences of their product choices, in which case consumer preferences as expressed in the marketplace will generate the desired mix of products and levels of safety that reflect consumers' valuation of the risk and consequently the associated benefits of safety. If safer products are desirable, consumers will be willing to pay more for these products, and companies will produce them.

For product liability law to serve a constructive role from the standpoint of setting the efficient level of product risk, there must be some form of market failure, such as inadequate consumer knowledge of the risks. The presence of product-related injuries is not sufficient for concluding that there is an inadequate level of safety. In a typical personal injury case with an identifiable victim, the probability of harm may appear to be 1.0 ex post since the consumer was in fact injured, but what matters is the level of the risk ex ante across the entire population of consumers of the product. In judging whether there is a shortcoming in risk beliefs, the task is to ascertain what a reasonable consumer would have anticipated as the probability of harm, not whether the injured consumer was clairvoyant and anticipated that there would definitely be an injury.

Whether risk beliefs are accurate depends on both the level of the risk and the degree to which people have information about the risk. Certainly it is rarely the case that people know the exact probabilities of harm from different products. Products often pose multiple risks, and understanding all these hazards may require detailed technical expertise. However, the appropriate task for consumers is to have a sufficient understanding of the multiple risks of the product so that they would assess the expected cost imposed by the harms as being as severe as they would in a situation of perfect information.

That consumers do not have perfect risk beliefs does not necessarily imply that there is a market failure. Errors in risk beliefs are not random. Many systematic patterns have been identified in the empirical literature on risk beliefs. A pertinent empirical phenomenon is that people tend to overestimate small mortality risks, such as the risk of dying of botulism, and underestimate very large risks, such as the lifetime risk of heart disease from all causes.[3] For the most part, product risks tend to involve small probabilities of serious adverse outcomes, and people will consequently exhibit a tendency toward risk overestimation of product-related risks.

Problems of risk underestimation will be more pronounced for hidden risks. The presence of benzene in Perrier that was discovered in 1990 is a well-known example of a risk that had formerly been hidden, but this is not a unique situation. Medical patients may not be aware of adverse drug interactions that are not disclosed to the patient and cannot be determined by the patient based on personal experience or other information sources. The locus of areas in which government regulation or product liability can play a constructive role will depend on the nature of the risk and what consumers know about the risk. In particular, if there is asymmetric information in which the manufacturer is informed but consumers are not, then government regulation such as required disclosure of information may be warranted.

Liability Criteria

The first question is when liability should be imposed,[4] and this will depend on the context of the product's use. For concreteness, I will concentrate on products purchased by a consumer in a market context, where the potential injury is to the consumer. Whether consumers understand the risk to themselves is a pivotal concern. Consumers will be willing to pay less for products that may cause them harm. Products may also injure third parties who are not involved in a business relationship with the producer. Thus defective brakes or acceleration problems with a car could lead to harm to pedestrians or other drivers' vehicles. To the extent that these harms are subsequently internalized by the product purchaser through tort liability, the consumer in turn will incorporate the cost of such harms in the purchase decision. There can, of course, be exceptional cases that are not adequately addressed by either the market or tort liability, as when firms scale back tort liability claims through bankruptcy proceedings.

The structure of standard liability rules can potentially lead to efficient levels of safety. Under a negligence standard, firms will be liable for product-related injury costs only if the level of safety that they provide is below the legal standard. If that standard is set at the economically efficient level of safety for the product, the failure to meet the standard will lead firms to pay injured parties for the cost of the accident, leading the firm to internalize these costs, which in turn will provide subsequent incentives for the firm to provide products with levels of safety that meet the standard.

The economic analysis for strict liability is simpler as there is no need to set the standard at an efficient level. Since firms will pay for all accident costs, the firm internalizes all safety losses associated with the product and will consequently provide an efficient level of safety. However, consumers will not have any incentive to exercise care, to choose safe products, or to match their product choices with their own safety-related productivity if all accident costs are borne by the firm. Standard law-and-economics prescriptions generally couple strict liability with a contributory negligence standard.

Liability and Risk Trends

The rise of product liability costs and, in particular, the emergence of occasional product liability "crises" would be consistent with an underlying soundly functioning liability regime if an increase in product risks accounted for the high liability costs.[5] However, by almost every measure the United States has become safer over the past century, and accident rate trends bear no apparent relation to liability costs surges.[6] Total unintentional injury death rates have declined for over a century. Data going back almost a century are available for individual component risks such work-related deaths, home-related deaths, accidental deaths from firearms, and other risks, and these hazards also have declined from their levels 80 years ago. The principal exception is that the number of motor-vehicle deaths and motor-vehicle death rates are higher than they were a century ago. However, the number of cars in use and the usage of these cars have risen dramatically over time. Adjusting for intensity of use, motor-vehicle risks have plummeted from 33.38 deaths per 10,000 vehicles in 1913 to 1.51 deaths per 10,000 vehicles in 2008. Similarly, the death rate per 100 million miles has decreased from 21.65 in 1923 to 1.33 in 2008.

Despite the high levels of safety and continued improvements in safety, product-related insurance costs remain high. The value of net premiums in 2008 was $1.3 billion for aircraft liability, $2.8 billion for product liability, and $38.6 billion for other liability, including industry coverages for negligence, carelessness, or failure to act.[7] Many large firms also self-insure so that examination of insurance premiums understates the cost of product liability to firms throughout the economy.

Longer-term trends in liability reflect factors other than safety levels alone. As society has become wealthier, we have become less willing to accept risk. Advances in technology also can increase liability levels if the standards for what constitutes reasonable care have changed.[8]

These long-run trends do not, however, account for very abrupt shifts in the level of liability. A puzzle noted by Priest is that within specific time periods in which product liability premiums have exhibited sharp increases, there is no apparent increase in product risk levels to account for the increase.[9] There is therefore a mismatch between the surges in liability costs associated with the tort liability crisis in the mid-1980s and the level of product-related risks. The periodic upward shifts in liability costs bear no apparent relation to increased levels of product riskiness.

The problems posed by product liability insurance are related to both the level of liability insurance costs and their variability, which creates substantial uncertainty for the firm. The absence of predictable liability costs will make it difficult for firms to distinguish which safety investments are worthwhile and which are not. This problem is much more acute for bodily injury losses than property losses. The main index of insurer profitability is the loss ratio, which is the ratio of losses to premiums. Ignoring the role of interest earned on premiums that are invested, a loss ratio above 1.0 implies that the insurer is losing money, and a loss ratio below 1.0 implies that the insurer is making money on the policies it has written. Thus the loss ratio is an inverse measure of insurer profitability. The bodily injury component of liability exhibited much higher loss ratios and more variable loss ratios than did the property damages component throughout the liability crisis period.

In a competitive market that has reached long-run equilibrium, one would expect insurer profitability as measured by the insurance loss ratios to be equalized across industries and for different kinds of insurance coverage, assuming other reasonable conditions are met, including a similar distribution over time in the occurrence of the losses. However, there is evidence of substantial variation in terms of the level of the loss ratios as well as the variability across industries and within industries. The profitability problems of insurance are more pronounced for bodily injury coverage, as is the variability in loss ratios, which in turn will create more highly variable premiums and uncertainty for the affected industries.

The high loss ratios and substantial variability of loss ratios for bodily injury coverage in the 1980s contributed to the tort liability crisis in that era. Insurers responded by raising insurance rates and, in some extreme instances, by denying coverage. In addition, to the extent that the fluctuation in insured losses reflects loss trends more generally, the uninsured costs will exhibit similar fluctuations.

After the passage of a series of tort liability reforms in the mid-1980s to contain damage awards, insurance loss ratios stabilized.[10] For general liability, there were widespread reform efforts as 12 states enacted reforms to control liability costs in 1985, 22 states enacted reforms in 1986, and 12 states enacted reforms in 1987. Whereas general liability loss ratios formerly had exceeded 1.0, in 1986 and subsequent years loss ratios decreased to levels that stabilized around 0.8.

The costs of liability imposed on insurers are but one manifestation of the costs borne by firms. To assess the liability costs for firms, Viscusi and Hersch undertook a stock market event study of 29 product liability lawsuits.[11] Such studies seek to determine statistically the effect of different events, such as major court decisions, on the firm's stock price after taking into account longer-run trends and other factors. The awards against companies were associated with a significant decline in stock market price relative to similar firms. It is also noteworthy that newspaper reports of pending lawsuits also led to negative returns as investors began to anticipate the adverse effects of product liability.

Innovation and New Product Development

The costs imposed by product liability law might serve a useful deterrence function if they provide incentives for firms to change their products to make them safer or for firms to discontinue products that are so unsafe that they should not be marketed. These effects flow from the basic economic theory and the structure of product liability law. However, the presence of substantial uncertainty in liability costs will tend to mute these effects, and there is no assurance that jury decisions will provide the right signals to firms.

Determining whether and how product liability affects product design are empirical issues, and the results are not encouraging. A useful proxy for assessing whether product liability law enhances product safety is to see if it stimulates the development of new, possibly safer products. There have been two regression analysis studies at the firm level of the overall relationship between product liability and product innovation, neither of which found effects that supported the textbook paradigm of higher liability costs fostering the introduction of safer products. Similarly, there has been one regression analysis study of decreases in the role of product liability, which showed that such changes did not undermine safety but may have had the opposite effect.

Novel risks have been found to be harder hit by liability costs than more familiar hazards.[12] A study by Viscusi and Moore examined the effect of product characteristics on liability costs as well as the effect of liability costs on research and development. Industries that have a high rate of technological change, or which have a high patent rate, have high shares of liability costs relative to sales for the firm.[13] In contrast, industries where the firms have made no new product introductions have lower bodily injury liability costs. These relationships are consistent with the view that the courts dislike novel technologies.

The study also found that increased product liability has a nonlinear effect on innovation: low levels of liability boost investments in novel technologies, but this effect tapers off and eventually becomes reversed and turns negative at very high levels of bodily injury costs relative to sales.[14] Thus, at very high levels of liability costs, product liability has a counterproductive effect.

A subsequent study by the same authors, using a different measure of effects on innovation, found that liability costs initially boost product R & D but then subsequently decrease R & D at very high levels of liability costs.[15] The liability costs/sales variable is associated with higher product R & D investments at low levels of costs but eventually becomes reversed for high liability costs.[16] Sorting out causality remains difficult, but the evidence is suggestive of a positive relation between liability costs and safety that holds only for low levels of costs.

These results suggest that product liability's aversion to new technologies has been harmful. At substantial levels of liability costs, the net effect of liability is to shut down innovation and discourage new product introductions. This is not the case at low and moderate levels of liability costs, where product liability promotes R & D for new products and leads to new product introductions. However, even here new product introductions may not be warranted on benefit-cost grounds. This is because it is not clear whether consumers would be willing to pay the extra cost for the safety improvements. We lack data to permit such judgments on an overall basis. What we do know is that extremely high liability costs appear to have counterproductive effects as they impose substantial costs but discourage changes in products and new product research. Withdrawing products from the market or choosing not to introduce new products often becomes the most desirable course in the presence of substantial expected liability costs.

New safety technologies should of course be encouraged, and these results are therefore troubling. If product liability was meant to reduce risk, it seems to have failed in its mission. Strikingly, one study found that *reducing* tort liability makes us safer. An empirical analysis by Rubin and Shepherd found that the enactment of noneconomic damages caps and product liability reform were among the measures associated with a decrease in the non-motor-vehicle accidental death rate over the 1981–2000 period for states that implemented these measures as compared with states that did not.[17] On balance, tort reform led to a reduction of 24,000 deaths over the two-decade period. Reductions in liability costs enhance safety.

Punitive Damages

Punitive damages often combine two elements that tend to reduce the efficacy of product liability as a safety incentive promotion device. The awards often tend to be very large. As we saw, very large damages amounts tend to have a counterproductive effect in that they serve to reduce R & D on new products, diminish new product introductions, and lead to withdrawal of more novel or risky products from the market. The second difficulty with punitive damages is their tremendous uncertainty and unpredictability. If firms cannot anticipate what financial sanctions they will incur for various product designs, there will not be the clear-cut incentive guidance needed to foster efficient risk levels.

The enormous scale and financial uncertainty associated with punitive damages is borne out in "blockbuster punitive damages awards," or punitive damages awards of at least $100 million. As of 2008 there had been 100 such punitive damages awards that reached or exceeded the $100 million threshold. Even within the blockbuster punitive damages award grouping there is tremendous variability in the award amounts, which reach as high as $145 billion in *Engle v. R. J. Reynolds,* a cigarette class action case in Florida.[18]

These awards do not reflect any sense of what is appropriate from the standpoint of establishing efficient levels of safety. Although law-and-economics models generally envision a deterrence role for punitive damages only in cases with a probability of detection below 1.0 (where compensatory damages might not adequately deter because some harms are undetected), punitive awards bear little relation to any meaningful principles for establishing safety incentives. To the extent that the awards are designed by jurors to punish the company or "send it a message," there will be associated fixed costs incurred by the company, but these awards tend not to impose the kinds of costs that can be reflected in the expected costs of production and hence will not serve as a safety incentive mechanism.

Table 3.7 provides a breakdown of the distribution of the blockbuster punitive damages awards. With the exception of seven awards for violent crimes, the defendant in these blockbuster cases is a firm in one of the designated industry groups. Most of the industry cases are product-related. There are of course some notable exceptions, such as awards for fraud against the finance, investment, and insurance industry group, and the award for the Exxon Valdez oil spill that affects the energy and chemical industry tally. However, most of the industry group awards can be traced to product-related risks.

The automobile, cigarette, and pharmaceutical awards all involve products. While one automobile case (*BMW of N. Am., Inc. v. Gore*) involved repainting of car doors, the other cases involved deaths and serious injuries associated with motor vehicles. Because these cases tended to involve claims of design defects for which the risks were not apparent at the time of sale, the liability costs associated with these punitive damages could not be internalized. Moreover, there is no reason to believe that firms would anticipate punitive damages awards in excess of $100 million.

Table 3.7 Blockbuster Punitive Damages and the Ratio of Punitive Damages to Compensatory Damages by Industry Type[a]

Industry Involved	Number of Punitive Damages Awards	Mean Punitive Damages	Mean Compensatory Damages	Mean Ratio of Punitive to Compensatory Damages
Automobile Industry	9	900.71	160.89	19.12
Cigarette Industry[b]	5	10,240.92	2,078.87	11,125.31
Energy, Chemical Industry	25	1,531.59	701.61	90.09
Finance, Investment, Insurance Industry[c]	23	546.33	222.45	59.20
Pharmaceuticals, Health Care Industry	16	503.69	109.29	40.98
Violent Crime	7	350.05	114.49	19.87
Other Industry	15	273.63	103.00	13.82

[a] Damages are calculated as millions of 2008 dollars.
[b] For the cigarette industry, all columns exclude the *Engle* award.
[c] For the finance, investment, insurance industry, the mean ratio excludes *Garamendi v. Altus Finance, S.A.*, which has zero compensatory damages.
Source: A. F. Del Rossi and W. K. Viscusi. The Changing Landscape of Blockbuster Punitive Damages Awards. 12 Am. L. Econ. Rev. 116 (2010). Table 2.

The five blockbuster awards against the cigarette industry that are shown in Table 3.7 are all for individual smoker harms. The class action case in the outlier *Engle* award is the sixth blockbuster case affecting the cigarette industry, and is not included in Table 3.7 since it is such a large award that it would distort the mean award levels. Because there is a latency period of decades before smoking risks become apparent, the cigarettes involved in these cases were marketed long before there were any such blockbuster punitive damages awards, as the first such blockbuster punitive damages award in any context was in 1985. Moreover, since the cigarette industry had never paid damages in any smoking case until after the 1998 Master Settlement Agreement, firms would not have incorporated the subsequent liability costs into the product price at the time of sale since the costs presumably were not anticipated at the time of sale. Thus, from the standpoint of safety incentives, there is a mismatch between the imposition of the blockbuster punitive damages award and the formation of corporate expectations and product safety decisions that could ultimately affect the likelihood and level of such awards.

The tremendous uncertainty posed by large and unpredictable punitive damages awards has attracted the attention of the U.S. Supreme Court. The Court's decision in *State Farm v. Campbell* suggested that there be a single-digit upper bound on the ratio of punitive damages to compensatory damages, and for maritime cases the Court subsequently suggested a usual upper bound ratio of 1:1 in *Exxon Shipping Co. et al. v. Baker*.[19] These guidelines are not necessarily binding, and they do not serve to put punitive damages on fully rational footing. As with all such soft or binding caps, the proposal that there be some kind of rigid mathematical structure that is not informed by a sound basis for setting punitive damages does not address the more fundamental problem that juries do not have guidelines for mapping their concerns into dollar damages amounts.[20]

A series of experimental studies summarized in Sunstein et al. has documented numerous shortcomings in jury behavior, some of which will be discussed below with respect to specific problems that arise with respect to product liability cases.[21] But the fundamental problem is that juries are being asked to determine whether punitive damages are warranted and, if so, to set the magnitude of these awards without any specific guidance as to how their assessment of the defendant's behavior should relate to the dollar value of the award.

As with product liability generally, whether punitive damages do have a deterrent effect is ultimately an empirical question. In an examination of differences in risk levels between states that permit punitive damages awards and those that do not, I found no evidence of such a deterrent influence.[22] The risk categories examined included toxic chemical accidents, toxic chemical accidents involving injury or death, toxic chemical releases, surface water discharges of chemicals, total chemical releases in surface water, medical misadventure deaths, total accidental deaths, total insurance premiums, medical malpractice insurance premiums, product liability premiums, and other liability premiums. The examination of an extensive set of risks that could potentially be influenced by punitive damages reveals no statistically significant deterrent effect.

Uncertainty, Hindsight Bias, and New Products

As we saw, product liability costs are particularly likely to affect new products and to discourage new product introductions when liability costs are high. This differential burden on new products can be traced to a series of contributing factors in terms of how people perceive uncertain risks, such as the hazards posed by new products, as compared with comparable risks from existing products for which the risks are better known.

One source of bias can be traced to ambiguity aversion. In the classic Ellsberg paradox, people would prefer a known probability of winning a prize to an uncertain probability of the same magnitude. Subsequent work has shown that in the case of people facing losses, precisely understood probabilities of the loss are viewed as less harmful than less well understood probabilities of the same magnitude. While there are some exceptions to this pattern, particularly when probabilities are extremely close to zero or one, there is a well-established aversion to facing imprecisely understood chances of a loss.

How this bias affects judgments is illustrated by experimental results in Viscusi for a sample of state court judges.[23] The judges were asked, on behalf of a pharmaceutical company, to decide between two different drugs that could be used as contrast agents in a CAT scan. Old Drug had well-known properties and offered a 1/100,000 chance that the patient would suffer a fatal adverse reaction. New Drug served the same function, and based on clinical trials the best estimate of the expected magnitude of the risk was 1/150,000. However, the risk posed by New Drug was uncertain, as it could have been zero or as high as 1/50,000. Even though New Drug was safer based on the expected level of risk, 57% of the respondents preferred to market the Old Drug. In discussions with the judges regarding their preference for the riskier, but well-known hazards of Old Drug, the judges indicated that there is less blame accorded to companies that market risky products with well-known hazards than for newly emerging risks.

Another perceptional factor that influences people's assessments of new products with uncertain properties is hindsight bias, which is the courtroom counterpart of Monday-morning quarterbacking. Product liability claims by their very nature are filed after there has been an injury. At the time the product is marketed the risk may be an uncertain prospect, but eventually the hazard becomes well known. Ideally, jurors should assess risks at the time the product is marketed. However, doing so is difficult from a psychological standpoint. Once the adverse event occurs, people tend to believe that the risk should have been anticipated.

The tendency of people to overestimate the ex ante risk levels in legal contexts where there are identifiable victims was noted by Judge Frank Easterbrook in a case involving injury suffered on a department store escalator:

> The ex post perspective of litigation exerts a hydraulic force that distorts judgment. Engineers design escalators to minimize the sum of construction, operation, and injury costs. Department stores, which have nothing to gain from maiming their customers and employees, willingly pay for cost-effective precautions. . . . Come the lawsuit, however, the passenger injured by a stop presents himself as a person, not a probability. Jurors see today's injury; persons who would be injured if buttons were harder to find and use are invisible. Although witnesses may talk about them, they are spectral figures, insubstantial compared to the injured plaintiff, who appears in the flesh.[24]

Unfortunately, despite the well-established problems associated with hindsight bias, it is difficult for people to overcome such biases when judging risky behaviors. To test the influence of hindsight bias, I examined the performance of judges and jurors in a rail accident case in which different groups of respondents were asked either to make the corporate risk-taking decision ex ante or to judge the corporation's decision after an accident had occurred.[25] Judges performed better than jurors in terms of aligning their ex ante risk decisions and their judgments after an accident had occurred. However, in the jury sample, participants favored the risk-taking behavior before the accident occurred, but after an accident occurred levied punitive damages because the initial decision to take the risk was regarded as reckless.

Corporate Risk Analysis for Risky Products

Ideally, companies marketing potentially risky products should make some assessment of the risk posed by the product, the costs associated with improving product safety, and consumers' likely valuations of products with different levels of safety to determine the efficient safety level for the product. At the most formal level, such an assessment would entail a benefit-cost analysis to determine the appropriate level of the risk. While such assessments may be desirable in theory, in practice they make the company very vulnerable. Having done a risk analysis and concluded that some risk-free or lower-risk variant of the product is not desirable, the company will appear to have knowingly made a reckless decision to expose consumers to risk if it turns out that there are product-related injuries. Thus, such analyses could serve as a trigger for the award of punitive damages instead of being treated as a component of responsible corporate risk decisions.

Such fears of harsh judgments against corporate risk analyses have been borne out in a variety of major product liability cases. The Ford Pinto cases involved drivers and passengers who suffered burn injuries while in the car.[26] In response to a government regulatory initiative from the U.S. Department of Transportation, Ford had done a risk analysis with respect to moving the gas tank location, which would affect the likelihood of burn injuries. Moving the tank to a safer location would have raised the product price, which Ford concluded would not pass a benefit-cost test. After the injuries occur, jurors tend to compare the identifiable victims with the minor cost of relocating the tank, whereas the more appropriate comparison is the expected benefits and costs before the product is marketed.

Ford Motor Company is not the only automobile company that has been pilloried for undertaking corporate risk analyses.[27] In a blockbuster punitive damages award case against the Chrysler Corporation, jurors awarded punitive damages of $250 million because the company had done a risk analysis of an allegedly defective door latch in the Chrysler minivan.[28] Chrysler maintained that the door latch did not increase the risk significantly and that altering the design was not worthwhile as it would have imposed a $100,000 fixed retooling cost and a $0.50 per vehicle parts cost.

The plaintiff's attorneys portrayed Chrysler as a corporate villain simply for undertaking a risk analysis: "Chrysler officials at the highest level cold bloodedly calculated that acknowledging the problem and fixing it would be more expensive, in terms of bad publicity and lost sales, than concealing the defect and litigating the wrongful death suits that inevitably would result."[29]

Experimental evidence indicates that undertaking a benefit-cost analysis increases judgments against the corporation.[30] In this study, jurors were told that the company followed the same procedures used by the National Highway Traffic Safety Administration in assessing safety devices and that the company also used the same value of statistical life (VSL) that the agency uses to value the safety improvements of alternative designs. The VSL amount is greater than the usual compensatory damages award for wrongful death, and so one would expect a finding of no liability. However, the mock juries levied punitive damages against the company. Thus, responsible corporate risk analysis has the perverse effect of boosting damages awards rather than reducing them.

Conclusion

Rather than creating an environment to foster safer products, product liability law often has adverse consequences. Some of the problems stem from the inherent nature of product risk decisions and the function of tort liability, while others may derive from individuals' cognitive limitations and inability to think properly about balancing risk and cost. Thus it would be both incorrect and an oversimplification to blame all the ills on the tort liability system. That system functions reasonably well for many types of accidents, such as personal motor-vehicle accidents. However, tort liability falls short with respect to products.

The first class of problems stems from the judgment biases of jurors. Because of loss aversion biases, jurors will impose excessive penalties on novel risks. Because of hindsight biases, jurors will believe incorrectly that the risk could have been anticipated.

The second class of problems arises from excessive levels of damages. Although jurors tend to agree about what behavior is blameworthy, they are all over the map in assessing damages. Compensatory damages for economic loss are reasonably well defined. However, assessments of pain and suffering awards and punitive damages awards are fraught with error, no doubt in part because jurors are not given firm guidance with respect to how they should go about setting the level of these damages. The result is that there may be multi-billion-dollar blockbuster punitive damages awards, but these awards do not enhance safety because they are random, rare events. More generally, for large levels of punitive damages costs there is in fact a counterproductive effect of punitive damages that discourages product improvements and new product introductions. Exiting the market altogether is often the desired course.

Third, firms are hampered in their efforts to reduce risks in an efficient manner by juror aversion to the measurement of risk. Companies that conduct risk analyses are vilified for intentionally endangering the public. When confronted with particular injury cases, the jury's balancing abstracts from the ex ante expectations that necessarily guide corporate decisions and instead compare the identifiable victim with the product-specific cost of greater safety.

Other articles in this book make the point that American firms are much more likely to incur tort liability than firms in other countries. To the extent that product liability law in this country deters innovation and drives up product costs beyond what consumers would want to pay, it contributes to the American Illness.

Notes

1. This standard result assumes that firms are making a continuous choice of the level of safety where safety levels are increasingly costly to provide and the marginal valuations of greater safety decline as the safety level increases.

2. There also may be an allowance for normal profit margins and retailer markup.

3. For a review of this evidence, see W. K. Viscusi, Reforming Products Liability (1991).

4. S. Shavell, Foundations of Economic Analysis of Law (2004), provides a general review of liability criteria.

5. There may, of course, be other causes of increases in insurance premiums, such as a decrease in interest rates, which decreases the return that insurance com-

panies can earn on their invested premiums. These influences fall under the general heading of what are termed "underwriting cycles."

6. National Safety Council, Injury Facts: 2010 40–41, 48–49, and 120–121 (2010).

7. Insurance Information Institute, Insurance Industry Fact Book, 51 (2010). Firms that self-insure are excluded from these tallies.

8. Evolving information about product risks that have a long latency period, as in the case of asbestos, also may contribute to long-term liability trends. By 1983 asbestos cases accounted for a quarter of all federal liability cases, and by 1987 the asbestos share was over 50%. See W. K. Viscusi, The Dimensions of the Liability Crisis, 20 J. Legal Stud. 147 (1991) for supporting data.

9. G. Priest, Products Liability Law and the Accident Rate, In Liability: Perspectives and Policy 184–222 (R. E. Litan & C. Winston, eds., 1988).

10. The data discussed here are from W. K. Viscusi & P. Born, The National Implications of Liability Reforms for General Liability and Medical Malpractice Insurance, 24 Seton Hall L. Rev. 1743 (1994).

11. W. K. Viscusi & J. Hersch, The Market Response to Product Safety Litigation, 2 J. Reg. Econ. 215 (1990).

12. W. K. Viscusi & M. J. Moore, "An Industrial Profile of the Links between Product Liability and Innovation," in The Liability Maze: The Impact of Liability Law on Safety and Innovation 81 (P. W. Huber & R. E. Litan, eds., 1991).

13. More specifically, the authors analyzed the log of this value.

14. The measure used for product innovation in Viscusi and Moore, supra note 12, is the rate of product R & D divided by industry sales.

15. W. K. Viscusi & M. J. Moore, Product Liability, Research and Development, and Innovation, 101 J. Pol. Econ. 161 (1993).

16. This result holds true whether the liability cost measure is bodily injury losses, bodily injury premiums, property damage losses, or property damage premiums.

17. The only reforms associated with an increase in the death rate were reforms to the collateral source rule. P. H. Rubin & J. Shepherd, Tort Reform and Accidental Deaths, 50 J. L. & Econ. 221 (2007).

18. Howard A. Engle, Md., v. R. J. Reynolds Tobacco, Florida Cir. Ct., No. 94–08273 CA-22 (Nov. 6, 2000).

19. 554 U.S. 471 (2008).

20. C. Sunstein, R. Hastie, J. Payne, D. Schkade, & W. K. Viscusi, Punitive Damages: How Juries Decide (2002).

21. Id.

22. W. K. Viscusi, The Social Costs of Punitive Damages against Corporations in Environmental and Safety Torts, 87 Geo. L. J. 285 (1998).

23. W. K. Viscusi, How Do Judges Think about Risk?, 1 Am. L. Econ. Rev. 26 (1999).

24. Carrol v. Otis Elevator, 896 F.2d 210, 215 (7th Cir. 1990) (Easterbrook, concurring).

25. Samples of judges and jury-eligible citizens were each divided into two groups. One group considered the ex ante decision to repair the train track to avert an accident, while a second group considered the same scenario in an ex post variant in which no repair was undertaken and an accident occurred. See Viscusi, supra note 22, for further description.

26. G. Schwartz, The Myth of the Ford Pinto Case, 43 Rutgers L. Rev. 1013 (1991), provides a detailed review of the Ford Pinto case and the mythology surrounding it.

27. Undertaking risk analyses is consequently viewed as a transgression rather than a laudable aspect of responsible product design.

28. Jimenez v. Chrysler Corp., No. 2-96-269-11 (D.S.C. Oct. 8, 1997).

29. Donald C. Dillworth, Fourteen Jurors Punish Chrysler for Hiding Deadly Defect, 34 Trial 14 (February 1998).

30. W. K. Viscusi, Corporate Risk Analysis: A Reckless Act?, 52 Stan. L. Rev. 547 (2000).

PART 4:

CIVIL PROCEDURE

The American Illness and Comparative Civil Procedure

DANIEL JUTRAS

ost comparative legal scholarship lines up along three different
axes, each emphasizing a distinct relationship between two legal systems, cultures, or traditions. The first axis highlights
similarities, shared traits, common assumptions, and, ultimately, convergence. It is most often connected to a reformist agenda, underlining the
positive outcomes of a particular set of rules or practices that has emerged
in a sister jurisdiction. The second axis highlights difference, distinctive-
ness, cultural specificity, and, ultimately, divergence. It is most often
connected to a conservative or traditionalist agenda, underlining the in-
commensurability of rules and practices lying deep below the surface of
superficial comparison. The third axis calls into question the idea that the
legal systems of different first-world countries are autonomous from each
other, and highlights their mutual interpenetration and ongoing dialogue.
It is most often connected to a thick, descriptive agenda, underlining the
complexity of the interaction of legal systems, cultures, and traditions in a
dynamic global setting.

This article briefly compares civil procedure in the United States with
that of other countries, with an emphasis on Canada, as the country that
most closely resembles the U.S. Similarities between the two systems of
civil procedure are greater, and differences stand out in sharp relief. In the

first part, I review the similarities, with the idea that some of the reforms introduced in Canada could be viewed as possible cures for what this book describes as the American Illness. The second part turns this assumption on its head, and identifies key differences between the two legal systems that arguably stand in the way of a reconfiguration of American civil justice along more conservative, Canadian lines. The third part tracks the flow of cross-border litigation (and litigation models) as an antidote to simplistic accounts of convergence and divergence in matters of civil procedure.

It is standard fare, in comparative legal scholarship, to announce that comparison is a dangerous exercise, and that no comparison can be fully effective without an exhaustive picture of the system as a whole—each part is said to be intricately connected to every other part, and never to be considered in isolation. I should be taken to have uttered all the necessary caveats and cautionary notes: by definition, the comparison between Canada and the United States can only be partial in this short article.[1]

Inside Looking Out—Canadian Civil Justice Considered

Twenty-five years ago, John H. Langbein set the standard for comparative civil procedure in the United States with a detailed account of how U.S. and German civil justice differed.[2] Langbein identified several irritants in the American civil justice system—the pursuit of wasteful pretrial examinations and discovery, the coaching of witnesses, the reliance on biased experts, the excesses of cross-examination—and drew on German civil procedure to propose a different equilibrium between judges and lawyers in the resolution of disputes. His essay sparked a spirited debate on the limits of comparative civil procedure. Some said Langbein presented a partial representation of both systems of civil justice, at once unduly favorable to the German side, and unduly critical of the American side.[3] Others said that Langbein failed to give proper weight to the significant institutional and cultural differences that existed between Germany and the United States, which rendered unrealistic his proposals for reform of American civil justice.[4] Langbein pulled no punches in his replies.[5]

Canada provides a better model for comparison than Germany, since Canada stands closer to the United States in its conception of the role of the judge, the adversarial process, and the autonomy of litigating parties. Civil justice in Canada rests on an adversarial system culminating in a concentrated, temporally continuous trial. Subject to the overall managerial role of the judge, the parties and their lawyers are the masters of their case. They identify the relevant facts; select, examine, and cross-examine witnesses before the judge; and make legal arguments in support of the position they advocate. The Canadian judge, much like her American counterpart, does not make evidentiary orders determining which witnesses will be heard on which facts, does not conduct examination of witnesses, and does not normally appoint independent experts to assist the Court. The trial and pre-trial periods are distinct in Canada as they are in the United States, and parties conduct pre-trial examinations and documentary discovery on both sides of the border. In Canada as in the U.S., the vast majority of cases settle before reaching trial. Every Canadian province now has a class action regime supporting aggregate litigation in the law of securities, products liability, consumer law, and the like. Contingent fee agreements are now valid in Canada. Overall, the affinities are obvious.

To be sure, the systems are not identical. Federal courts play a much less significant role in Canada than they do in the United States. Trial and appellate courts in the provinces deal with the vast majority of civil cases, subject to the ultimate oversight of the Supreme Court of Canada. One Canadian province is a mixed jurisdiction with a codified regime of civil procedure: in Quebec, substantive private law is drawn from the civil law tradition, while public law and the administration of justice in the province have their roots in the common law tradition. Judges in Canada are appointed by the Executive, and never elected. Jury trials have all but disappeared in civil matters. As for attorneys' fee shifting, the winner can generally expect to recover fees from the loser, in whole or (more often) in part. Those differences are not trivial, especially the latter three. Nonetheless, the two systems of civil justice remain fairly close in their configuration.

There is, however, no "Canadian Illness." Leaving aside the considerable problem of access to justice, Canadian scholars, judges, and lawyers do not describe their civil justice system as broken, unhealthy, or feverish. By contrast, in one of his replies to his critics, Langbein stated that "Americans operate a system of civil procedure whose excesses make it a laughing stock to the rest of the civilized world. Our system is truth-defeating, expensive, and capricious—a lawyers' tax on the productive sector."[6] I take this to be an appropriate, albeit provisional, statement of something that ails America, at least in matters of civil procedure. Can a cure be found in Canada?

Richard Marcus defines American procedural exceptionalism—a neutral spin on the American Illness?—as a set of distinguishing characteristics including, most prominently, "relaxed pleading, broad discovery, jury trial, limited cost shifting, potentially remarkable awards for pain and suffering or punitive damages, and heavy reliance on private lawyers to enforce public norms."[7] On these and related matters, Canadian civil procedure is somewhat different from its American counterpart.

First, fact-pleading is the norm in Canada. The American idea of notice-pleading, which allows claims to be introduced on the thinnest of factual foundations, is unheard of in Canada. Under the rules in force in Canada, a statement of claim or originating process must contain at least a summary statement of all the material facts giving rise to each element of the claim.[8] Greater specificity in pleadings enables parties to join issue on what is truly contentious, stands as an obstacle to frivolous claims, and circumscribes discovery—or so the theory goes.

Oral and documentary discovery are also increasingly regulated in Canada following significant civil justice reform initiatives in many provinces. Under new rules of procedure in British Columbia and Ontario, no party may exceed a total of seven hours of oral examinations for discovery, unless the court orders otherwise or parties consent.[9] In litigation where the amount in dispute is relatively small, oral examinations for discovery are even more severely restricted: British Columbia and Ontario limit them to two hours per party where the amount in dispute is $100,000 or less,[10] whereas Quebec simply prohibits oral examinations where the claim is worth less than $25,000.[11] Furthermore, documentary disclosure and discovery are more constrained in Quebec, where parties still rely on the adversarial pre-trial process to trigger the production of relevant information.

Parties may seek from their opponent the production of documents of which they are aware, or the existence of which is disclosed in the context of oral discovery, but no affidavit of documents need be filed, and no party is required to disclose all documents in its possession that may be relevant to its opponent's case. Quebec judges can also wield extensive powers to stop or circumscribe discovery if it is abusive, vexatious, or useless.[12] In Ontario, discovery is closely managed by judges under a new rule that requires parties to file a discovery plan that determines in advance the timing, duration, and scope of both oral and documentary discovery.[13] Canadian jurisdictions have restricted the scope of discovery to what is "relevant to any matter in issue" in an action, moving away from open-ended discovery of all matters "related" to the dispute.[14] Finally, Canadians recognize and seek to limit the burdensome costs of electronic discovery.[15]

These measures go hand in hand with other efforts to reduce the costs and delays of civil justice, both seen as obstacles to genuine access to justice. Canadian jurisdictions followed the lead of some American state and federal courts and the direction of recent reforms in the U.K. to give judges managerial responsibilities and increase the efficiency and responsiveness of the civil justice system: early case planning conferences, judicial conciliation and settlement conferences, compulsory mediation, strict timelines and scheduling orders, summary judgment opportunities, and channeling of cases through standard and fast-tracks, all subsumed under a general principle of proportionality.[16] Parties are encouraged to match the effort and expenditure invested in a case to the value of the dispute, and judges are given powers to ensure that the civil justice system does not use up resources that are out of proportion with the stakes of the dispute.

Most or all of these measures are consistent with the current configuration of the American civil justice system. Indeed, several of them have their origin in American reform efforts and migrated to Canada over the past two decades. Within this set of measures, the scope and effect of rules on pleadings and discovery is a perennial topic of discussion on both sides of the border, and multiple amendments to these rules have been introduced in the recent past.[17] Results are difficult to measure, and the most recent constraints on time, duration, and scope of discovery in Canada have yet to be evaluated. It is fair to say that both Canadian and American courts now confront the limits of rule-making in addressing the costs and delays of civil justice. Existing rules and judicial powers may not be enforced and invoked as often as they should, and controlling the costs and length of litigation will likely require deeper, continuing shifts in the culture of judges and in the conception of zealous advocacy espoused by lawyers.

In short, many of the rules in force in Canada that could address the "truth-defeating, expensive and capricious" characteristics of American civil procedure have already been identified, discussed, and assessed in the United States. Possible cures are known, but do not seem to get much traction.[18] The benefits of firm constraints on the duration and number of oral examinations on discovery are viewed with skepticism. Nor can relief be found in narrower definitions of the scope of discovery and the relevance standard, which do not provide clear and enforceable ex ante boundaries. The same can be said of an overarching principle of proportionality—it is too vague to be of any use. Heightened fact-pleading is known but seems unpopular in America, where plaintiffs without access to key information supporting their claim are deemed to deserve a chance to build their case through discovery.[19] With a similar logic, fee-shifting rules in force in Canada might be viewed as a barrier to litigation in many American jurisdictions.[20] Limiting access to jury trials in civil matters raises constitutional issues in the United States that are not relevant in the Canadian context.

In other words, despite the similar configuration of the systems of civil justice in Canada and the United States, it appears that different accounts of the optimal trade-off between the cost of procedure and the cost of error in fact-finding are at play in these reform initiatives.[21] In Canada, efforts to address the unnecessary costs and delays of justice are intrinsically tied to the hope that effective reform will *increase* the number of claims that can realistically be brought to court. The initiative for these reforms has come from judges, law societies, bar associations, and governments. All begin from the premise that the rate of litigation is low, and that greater access to justice—that is, enhanced opportunities for ordinary citizens to resolve their disputes in court—can and must be achieved through tighter judicial controls and cost-effective processes or short-cuts.

In the United States, by contrast, civil justice reforms are also assessed in relation to the inherent value of litigation, and there appears to be greater tolerance for processes that are more costly if they ultimately support the weaker plaintiff's right to be heard and facilitate his or her access to the courthouse.

Outside Looking In—The Discourse of American Exceptionalism

"Few polities are as self-consciously exceptional as the Americans."[22] Indeed one might say that the one thing that is truly exceptional about American civil justice is its own discourse about how exceptional it is. No other legal system or tradition speaks of its litigation rates as pathological, unique, or quirky. While deep concern with the costs and delays of justice is shared widely within the industrialized world, the American preoccupation with excessive litigation is unmatched anywhere in the world.

For the past 30 years, the idea that Americans are uniquely litigious and that frivolous claims are clogging the courts has been a dominant theme of civil justice and tort reform movements in the United States.[23] The argument that this phenomenon has damaged American competitiveness, interfered with prosperity, and affected the U.S. trade balance is part and parcel of representations of the American Illness. The American Tort Reform Association's website claims:

> Today, America's $246 billion civil justice system is the most expensive in the industrialized world. Aggressive personal injury lawyers target certain professions, industries, and individual companies as profit centers. . . . These lawsuits are bad for business; they are also bad for society. They compromise access to affordable health care, punish consumers by raising the cost of goods and services, chill innovation, and undermine the notion of personal responsibility. The personal injury lawyers who benefit from the status quo use their fees to perpetuate the cycle of lawsuit abuse. They have reinvested millions of dollars into the political process and in more litigation that acts as a drag on our economy.[24]

Surveys of CEOs and ordinary citizens confirm that the belief in this (permanent) state of crisis is widespread.[25] Fundamental reforms to address this excessive litigiousness and the unhealthy entrepreneurial spirit of plaintiff lawyers continue to be publicly advocated at the state and federal levels, and are strongly supported by conservative politicians and media. As stated by John Nockleby, "The rhetorical frame is so well established that it is no longer even necessary to cite authority for the propositions that litigation is skyrocketing or that people file frivolous law suits."[26] The claim that American civil justice is out of control and hurting the economy has been challenged and undermined by a group of equally vocal legal scholars, who criticize the use of "meta-anecdotes and voodoo figures."[27]

For my purposes, it is not important to determine who is closest to the truth in this debate, although I confess my sympathy for the skeptics and deniers whose claims find better support in the empirical evidence. Compelling and objective data are not readily available, and in the end, perceptions may matter more than reality.[28]

The situation is quite different in Canada, where litigation rates do not resemble a "litigation crisis." The limited empirical evidence that is available suggests that Canadians need not worry about excessive litigation. In the three most populous provinces of Canada, the number of new civil filings (excluding family matters, but including small claims) is less than 1,400 per 100,000 people.[29] The equivalent rate in the United States is almost four times higher.[30] Most civil claims filed in these three provinces are fairly small: In Quebec, 82 percent of the new claims are worth $70,000 or less, and one-quarter of these are small claims where the amount in dispute is less than $7,000. In Ontario, 43 percent of the new civil claims are small claims, valued at less than $25,000.[31] Beyond that, it is difficult to ascertain the characteristics of these civil claims, because reporting tends to vary from province to province. Nonetheless, it is clear that automobile accidents, which generate a very significant proportion of new filings in the state courts in the United States, do not represent a large proportion of civil claims in Canada. Indeed, in Quebec, automobile accidents generate almost no civil litigation, and claims for bodily injury arising from such accidents are compensated through a provincial administrative scheme and are not litigated before ordinary courts. Landlord-tenant disputes, labor disputes, and work-related injuries are also litigated outside of the courts of general jurisdiction.

Whatever the numbers tell us, from a comparative perspective what is most significant is the absence in Canada of any debate over an alleged litigation crisis. The representations of civil justice within political culture in Canada reflect neither of the twin characteristics that define American (procedural) exceptionalism: neither the long-standing and deep faith in the courts as a primary site of private and public ordering—what Robert Kagan defines as "adversarial legalism,"[32] nor the more recent, but no less powerful, "legal hypochondria" that colors all discussions of civil justice reform.[33]

Whether or not American citizens are measurably more litigious than Canadians, public discourse does matter. The absence of these fundamental themes in Canada is significant, and underlines a key cultural difference that must serve to contextualize all comparisons between Canadian and American civil procedure. Indeed other crucial differences between the political contexts of both countries must be taken into account in any comparisons of civil justice systems, including the wider reach of social welfare and public health care in Canada, the greater faith in government as the locus of redistribution of wealth, the different political economy—in the sense of the different conception "of the role that the state is expected to and does play in determining the general welfare of its citizens,"[34] and the relative Canadian indifference to populist and anti-statist politics.

All in all, comparative civil procedure—or rather, a comparison of the *discourse* on civil procedure on either side of the border—does reveal a deep divergence of political cultures in Canada and in the United States. The similarities and affinities identified in the first part of this text seem to lose their significance when placed in this larger context. And yet, the examination of similarities and differences assumes the existence of autonomous legal systems and cultures, neatly packaged, self-contained, and ready to be compared. Reality is more complex.

The View from Nowhere: Litigation without Borders

The flow of ideas and practices across borders is such, nowadays, that comparative civil procedure can no longer posit autonomous civil justice systems as its basic unit of analysis. In this respect, the international influence of the American model is considerable. As stated by Marc Galanter: "Notwithstanding the deficiencies of our legal system, it is worth recalling that one realm in which the United States has remained the leading exporter is what we may call the technology of doing law— constitutionalism, judicial enforcement of rights, the organization of law firms, alternative dispute resolution and public interest law. For all their admitted flaws, American institutions provide influential models for the governance of business relations, the processing of disputes, and the protection of citizens."[35]

Writing 20 years ago, Galanter could not have anticipated the formidable consequences of globalization of litigation, so his remarks were directed at the circulation of the American model around the world. Over the past decade, however, there have been signs that cross-border movement affects not just the "technology of doing law" but litigants themselves, who are tempted by the exceptional context of American litigation. In the most extreme examples, as recently as 2007, the United States witnessed the filing of securities fraud class actions brought by foreign purchasers who had bought a foreign issuer's securities on a foreign exchange. The phenomenon became known as "foreign-foreign-foreign plaintiffs" or "f-cubed classes."

Some courts in the United States quickly created procedural and substantive barriers to these claims.[36] With the doors of U.S. courthouses increasingly closed to f-cubed plaintiffs, other jurisdictions began to entertain global class actions. The Netherlands, in particular, offers a vehicle for the approval and enforcement of universal class action settlements,[37] and in Canada, Ontario Courts have now approved the certification of global securities class actions.[38]

Whatever the fate of this emerging phenomenon of transnational litigation, there is no question that the American institution of class actions is penetrating non-U.S. domestic civil justice systems.[39] Whether this will alter the political culture of those other jurisdictions and "contaminate" them with the American Illness is an open question. Indeed, the United States version of class actions encapsulates three key features that are at odds with the culture of litigation in other jurisdictions. First, American class actions rest on a unique combination of individual initiative and large-scale effects—private parties are given the power to launch, without an explicit mandate, litigation that eventually binds thousands of people who may not even be aware that their personal rights are being litigated. In the United States, aggregate litigation is neither altruistic nor institutional, as would be the case if class actions could be initiated only by associations or disinterested representatives. Rather, it is driven by the representative's self-interest and is nonetheless binding on all. Second, American class actions rely to a significant degree on entrepreneurial lawyering and on the conception of litigation as a profit activity. The financing of class actions explicitly depends on the eventual gains that can be drawn by lawyers (or third-party financial backers) from their investment in the uncertain rights of others. Third, American class actions manifest the belief that public policy can be developed, enacted, and implemented through civil litigation; or, stated differently, that effective large-scale regulation of economic activity can be achieved through the adversarial consideration of private disputes.

These three features of American class actions are at odds with the political and legal cultures of many countries, and this explains the frosty reception of this procedural device in Europe over the past decade or so. In Europe, generally speaking, the bureaucratic state is viewed as the primary site for enforcement of economic norms, and regulation by litigation is an oxymoron. Contingent fee arrangements are highly controversial, and viewed by many as a source of intractable conflicts of interest. And the idea that one's right of action may be exercised by another, without a proper mandate, is regarded as a violation of basic tenets of civil procedure. As a result, while it is true that class action regimes are being introduced or considered in many countries around the world, the transplant yields different species of aggregate litigation in these various locations.[40] Most regimes contain restrictions that are foreign to the American model: representative litigation may exclude claims for damages and be limited to injunctions or declaratory relief, or it may be restricted to certain types of claims (such as consumer litigation); class actions may require opting-in for class members, as opposed to the standard opt-out mechanism known in the United States; and cost-shifting, loser-pays rules as well as prohibitions on contingent fee arrangements may make these claims less attractive to the plaintiff bar.[41]

In Canada, in contrast, it is quite likely that the introduction of U.S.-style class actions will have—or have already had—an impact on political and legal culture. All provinces now have a class actions regime, and contrary to European regimes, no Canadian province limits class actions to specific areas of litigation, or to organizational standing. Individuals may initiate class actions as representatives, and all regimes now constitute the group on an opt-out basis (at least for in-province claimants). Judges in Canada routinely agree to certify settlement classes. Financing of class actions is also moving in the direction of entrepreneurial lawyering: contingency fees are allowed, and third-party financing is in development.

Nonetheless, the overall number of class actions in Canada remains fairly low in comparison with the number in the United States.[42] In Ontario, for instance, only 12 new applications for certification of a class action were filed in 2010, down from 37 in 2007. In this respect, the situation in the Province of Quebec remains unique. With a little over half of the population of Ontario, Quebec witnessed four times the number of new class actions introduced in 2010—that is, 40 new class actions were initiated in that year. The regime of class actions in Quebec tends to favor plaintiffs: it is not necessary to show (as plaintiffs must do in other provinces) that class action proceedings are preferable to other means of resolving the dispute, with common questions predominating over individual questions; no evidence need be presented at the certification stage; appeal rights are asymmetrical, with no appeals from decisions to authorize the class action; and the province provides (partial) public funding to support the pursuit of class actions.[43] A class of entrepreneurial plaintiff lawyers is clearly emerging in Quebec, and seems to be well connected to recent developments in the United States: well over a third of all new class actions introduced in Quebec last year are copied from claims currently being litigated or settled in the States. Arguably, the conditions are now present in Quebec for a perfect (litigation) storm.

In the end, the current trends in relation to class actions in Canada suggest that there is no perfect separation between the cultures of civil justice on either side of the border. Canada is not necessarily a kinder, gentler place. There may not be a "Canadian Illness," but there is no obvious Canadian advantage. While full convergence of civil procedure and litigation practices in Canada and the United States is still off in the distance, if at all, the globalization and heightened commodification of legal services have made American exceptionalism much less exceptional.

Notes

1. On the cultural dimensions of civil procedure in the United States, see O. Chase, American "Exceptionalism" and Comparative Procedure, 50 Am. J. Comp. L. 277 (2002); O. Chase, Some Observations on the Cultural Dimension in Civil Procedure Reform, 45 Am. J. Comp. L. 861 (1997).

2. J. H. Langbein, The German Advantage in Civil Procedure, 52 U. Chi. L. Rev. 823 (1985). See also H. Kötz, Civil Justice Systems in Europe and the United States, 13 Duke J. Comp. & Int'l L. 61 (2003).

3. See R. J. Allen, S. Köck, K. Riechenberg, and D. T. Rosen, The German Advantage in Civil Procedure: A Plea for More Details and Fewer Generalities in Comparative Scholarship, 82 N.W.U. L. Rev. 705 (1987–88).

4. See O. Chase, Legal Processes and National Culture, 5 Cardozo J. Int'l & Comp. L. 1 (1997); J. C. Reitz, Why We Probably Cannot Adopt the German Advantage, 75 Iowa L. Rev. 987 (1990).

5. See, e.g., J. H. Langbein, Cultural Chauvinism in Comparative Law, 5 Cardozo J. Int'l & Comp. L. 41 (1997). See also J. D. Jackson, Playing the Culture Card in Resisting Cross-Jurisdictional Transplants: A Comment on Legal Processes and National Culture, 5 Cardozo J. Int'l & Comp. L. 51 (1997).

6. Langbein, id. at 48.

7. R. L. Marcus, Putting American Procedural Exceptionalism into a Globalized Context, 53 Am. J. Comp. L. 709 (2005).

8. See, e.g., British Columbia Supreme Court Civil Rules, B.C. Reg. 168/2009, rule 3-1.

9. Ontario Rules of Civil Procedure, R.R.O. 1990, Reg. 194 (Courts of Justice Act), Rule 31.05.1; British Columbia Supreme Court Civil Rules, id., Rule 7-2 (2).

10. Ontario Rules of Civil Procedure, id. at Rule 76.04 (2); B.C. Supreme Court Civil Rules, id., at Rule 15-1 (11).

11. Quebec Code of Civil Procedure, Revised Statutes of Quebec. c. C-25, art. 396.1.

12. Id. at art. 396.4.

13. Supra note 9, at Rule 29.1.

14. Id. at Rules 30.02 (1) and 31.06 (1).

15. Rule 29.1.03 (4) of the Rules of Civil Procedure in Ontario, supra note 9, requires civil litigants to have regard to the Sedona Canada Principles in the preparation of their discovery plan. See http://www.lexum.umontreal.ca/e-discovery /documents/SedonaCanadaPrinciples01–08.pdf.

16. See, for example, Rule 1-3 of the British Columbia Supreme Court Civil Rules, supra note 10; see also article 4.2 of the Quebec Code of Civil Procedure, supra note 11.

17. For a comparative assessment of pleading rules, see S. Dodson, Comparative Convergences in Pleading Standards, 158 U. Pa. L. Rev. 441 (2009–2010). For a comparative assessment of rules on discovery, see G. C. Hazard Jr., From Whom No Secrets Are Hid, 76 Tex. L. Rev. 1665 (1997–1998).

18. In another article in this book, Peter Rutledge nonetheless argues in support of a stricter principle of proportionality, connecting the costs of discovery to the amount in controversy.

19. See Dodson, supra note 17; A. N. Steinman, The Pleading Problem, 62 Stan. L. Rev. 1293 (2009–2010).

20. D. L. Rhode, Frivolous Litigation and Civil Justice Reform: Miscasting the Problem, Recasting the Solution, 54 Duke L. J. 447, 474–475 (2004–2005).

21. G. P. Miller, The Legal-Economic Analysis of Comparative Civil Procedure, 45 Am. J. Comp. L. 905 (1997).

22. Marcus, supra note 7, at 710.

23. For a recent overview of the conservative civil justice reform movement of the past decades, see L. S. Mullenix, American Exceptionalism and Convergence Theory: Are We There Yet?, 49 Supreme Court L. Rev. 41 (2010).

24. http://www.atra.org/. See also the legal blog site at http://overlawyered.com/.

25. See J. K. Robbennolt and C. A. Studebaker, News Media Reporting on Civil Litigation and Its Influence on Civil Justice Decision Making, 27 Law and Human Beh. 5 (2003); IALS 2010 Civil Litigation Survey of Chief Legal Officers and General Counsel, at http://www.du.edu/legalinstitute/pubs/GeneralCounselSurvey.pdf. Compare with the results of the survey conducted in 2008 by the Oxford Institute of European and Comparative Law, available at http://www.competition- law.ox.ac.uk /iecl/pdfs/Oxford%20Civil%20Justice%20Survey%20-%20Summary%20of%20 Results,%20Final.pdf .

26. J. T. Nockleby, How to Manufacture a Crisis: Evaluating Empirical Claims Behind "Tort Reform," 85 Or. L. Rev. 533, 535 (2007).

27. M. Galanter, News from Nowhere: The Debased Debate on Civil Justice, 71 Denv. U. L. Rev. 77, 100 (1993–1994).

28. In the aftermath of The World Bank's project on Doing Business, there is now quite a bit of (controversial) quantitative scholarship assessing the effectiveness of different legal systems in relation to economic development. See the most recent data at http://www.doingbusiness.org/. For a recent overview and evaluation of this quantitative scholarship, see J. Reitz, Legal Origins, Comparative Law and Political Economy, 57 Am. J. Comp. L. 847 (2009); R. Michaels, Comparative Law by Numbers?, Legal Origins Thesis, Doing Business Reports, and the Silence of Traditional Comparative Law, 57 Am. J. Comp. L. 765 (2009).

29. Statistics on the civil justice system are sketchy and scattered across each jurisdiction in Canada. For 2008–2009, Quebec courts report a total of 109,338

new civil filings, for a population of 7.8 million, yielding a rate of 1,402 claims per 100,000 people. See (for the Court of Québec only), http://www.tribunaux.qc.ca/c -quebec/CommuniquesDocumentation/RapPublic2009.pdf . The Superior Court of Quebec does publish statistics—current statistics are on file with the author. For 2007–2008 (the latest available data), Ontario courts report 147,687 new civil filings, for a population of 12.8 million, yielding a rate of 1,153 claims per 100,000 people. See http://www.ontariocourts.on.ca/scj/en/reports/annualreport/07–08 .pdf. For 2008–2009, the British Columbia Supreme Court reports 65,674 new civil filings, for a population of 4.35 million, yielding a rate of 1,509 claims per 100,000 people. See http://www.courts.gov.bc.ca/supreme_court/about_the_supreme _court/annual_reports/2009%20Annual%20Report%20%28May%2021,%20 2010%29.pdf .

30. See Eric Rasmussen and Mark Ramseyer, elsewhere in this book, who report a litigation rate of 5,800 new civil filings per 100,000 people in the United States.

31. See the 2007–2008 Annual Report of the Ontario Superior Court at http:// www.ontariocourts.on.ca/scj/en/reports/annualreport/07–08.pdf.

32. R. A. Kagan, Adversarial Legalism: The American Way of Law (2001).

33. D. L. Rhode, Frivolous Litigation and Civil Justice Reform: Miscasting the Problem, Recasting the Solution, 54 Duke L. J. 447, 449 (2004–2005).

34. J. Reitz, Political Economy and Separation of Powers, 15 Transnat'l L. & Contemp. Probs. 579, 584 (2006).

35. Galanter, supra note 27, at 102.

36. See, e.g., In re Royal Dutch/Shell Transp. Sec. Litig., 522 F.Supp.712 (D.N.J. 2007); In Re Vivendi Universal S.A. Sec. Littig., 241 F.R.D. 213 (S.D.N.Y.2007); Morrison v. National Australian Bank, 130 S. Ct. 2869, 2888 (2010).

37. See W. H. van Boom, Collective Settlement of Mass Claims in the Netherlands, available at SSRN: http://ssrn.com/abstract=1456819.

38. See Silver and Cohen v. Imax Corporation, 2011 ONSC 1035 (CanLII) at par. 59–63.

39. See S. Issacharoff and G. P. Miller, Will Aggregate Litigation Come to Europe, 62 Vand. L. Rev. 179 (2009); R. A. Nagareda, Aggregate Litigation across the Atlantic and the Future of American Exceptionalism, 62 Vand. L. Rev. 1 (2009).

40. "American-style" class actions regimes are still quite rare in Europe, and it is only by taking into account other forms of collective litigation, such as complaints by association or interest groups, that one can claim an expansion of aggregate litigation in Europe. More or less restrictive regimes for class actions have been introduced in Sweden, Italy, Spain, and the Netherlands, among others, but the American model is effectively rejected in France, Switzerland, and, most recently, in the U.K. as well. See country reports on the Global Class Actions Exchange, http://globalcl assactions.stanford.edu/category/categories/country-reports.

41. It should, however, be noted that third-party litigation funding is permitted in Germany, the U.K., Belgium, and the Netherlands. See C. Hodges, Developments in Collective Redress in the European Union and United Kingdom 2010, at

http://globalclassactions.stanford.edu/sites/default/files/documents/1010%20Class
%20Actions%20UK%202010%20Report.pdf.

42. All data here are drawn from the national database of class actions established by the Canadian Bar Association. See http://www.cba.org/ClassActions/main/gate/index/. While the data are not fully reliable for all provinces, practices rules in Quebec and Ontario include reporting requirements that make this database fairly accurate.

43. See Quebec Code of Civil Procedure, supra note 11, articles 999 to 1051.

The Proportionality Principle and the Amount in Controversy

PETER B. RUTLEDGE

A s chapter 1 of this book suggests, the American legal system is unique in countless ways. Its system of civil procedure is no exception. Practices such as pleading rules and discovery norms set America apart from many foreign countries, including our common-law cousins. Over a decade ago, these differences prompted John Langbein to observe:

> Americans operate a system of civil procedure whose excesses make it a laughing stock to the rest of the civilized world. Our system is truth-defeating, expensive, and capricious—a lawyers' tax on the productive sector. Some Americans do not want to admit the dimensions of our failure in civil justice. Powerful vested interests, especially at the trial bar, thrive from this dysfunctional system. They do not want it subjected to the searching critique that results from comparative study. Cultural chauvinism—the claim that cultural differences prevent us from adopting and adapting the superior procedural devices of other legal systems—is an effort to switch off the searchlight of comparative law. In truth, the cultural differences that touch on the basic choices in civil procedure are trivial. The real explanation for the tenacity of our deeply deficient system of civil justice is not culture, but a combination of inertia and the vested interests of those who profit from the status quo.[1]

Langbein did not mince words, and those words added fuel to the fire of criticism already directed at the American system of civil procedure.

Yet, as Langbein appreciated better than most critics, diatribes about any system of rules (civil procedure or otherwise) do little to advance academic understanding unless they first articulate a coherent theory of what normative principles should underlie that system and then acknowledge the costs of jettisoning it. Sometimes, comparisons may cause us to conclude that the most familiar is, indeed, the most optimal, as the Swiss did when they recently reformed their system of civil procedure and imported almost nothing from foreign practice.[2] Like the Swiss, proud defenders of the American system are quick to point out its virtues: that notice pleading lowers barriers to entry in the courthouse and liberal discovery has ensured greater accuracy in fact-finding than an inquisitorial system that does not guarantee one party access to relevant documents in its adversary's possession.

Against that background, this article, which focuses on matters of pleading and discovery, offers a frank assessment of some of the problems with the American system of civil procedure and an original solution to those problems. My thesis may be summarized as follows: the system of pleading and discovery is in need of repair but not along the lines that most observers think. Rather than parsing the fine distinctions between notice and plausibility pleading or tweaking a party's initial disclosure obligations, we should instead ensure that the process costs of our system of dispute resolution are proportional to the amount in controversy. In the jargon of civil procedure, we need to reinvigorate the proportionality principle. We should do so by explicitly linking the parties' discovery entitlements to the amount in controversy (as established in the complaint and any counterclaim). Moreover, in order to give the parties adequate incentives to plead accurately the amount in controversies, parties seeking relief should be required to post a bond. The proceeds of this bond would be available to shift the costs of discovery compliance when a plaintiff propounds discovery requests that are not proportionate to the value of the controversy.

This article develops that thesis in four parts. It first articulates a normative vision of the goals toward which any system of civil dispute resolution should aspire. It then surveys the empirical landscape and measures

the extent to which our civil justice system achieves—or fails to achieve—
these goals. It also examines some of the current proposals for civil justice
reform and identifies their weaknesses. Next, it lays out both wings of the
proposal—(1) tying the discovery rights to the amount in controversy and
(2) the bond requirement. Finally, it anticipates and responds to the major
criticism that the proposal will invite.

To What Ends Should Our System of Civil Procedure Aspire?

Far too frequently, our system of civil procedure is criticized (or defended) in an acontextual manner. That is to say that its apologists (and
detractors) describe the system without formally considering the underlying values that it espouses (or should espouse). In order to avoid that trap,
I make explicit here such a normative vision at the outset. My goal is not
to resolve the debate definitively but rather simply to establish a common
ground for discussion, and thereby avoid the sorts of acontextual critiques
that plague the civil procedure literature.

The vision articulated here finds its roots in two streams of literature:
(1) dispute resolution and (2) law-and-economics. The dispute resolution
literature, especially the work of Lon Fuller, teaches us to think of the civil
justice system as one of several "forms" of dispute resolution.[3] In other
words, despite the salience of reported opinions in civil litigation, many
disputes never reach the courts.[4] They may be arbitrated; they may be mediated; they may be settled; or they may be resolved over a handshake and
a beer. These forms of dispute resolution are socially desirable in two respects. First, they reduce social costs because the disputants do not need to
call upon the resources of the state to resolve their dispute. Second, these
alternative forms of dispute resolution also shorten the queue for litigants
who are in the civil justice system and, thereby, enable those litigants to
obtain results from the system more quickly.

As essential insight follows from the foregoing—namely, that the civil
litigation system serves as a default system when one of these other forms
fails to resolve the dispute. This may be because the parties are not in priv-
ity of contract (and thus have not agreed to arbitrate). It may be because the

parties' anticipated outcomes are too distant from each other (thereby precluding settlement). It may be because one of the parties possesses information bearing on the merits that it is reluctant to disclose to the other party (thereby precluding a mediated solution). It may be because the parties' incentives are so askew (think of a bet-the-company case) that the conditions for mutually agreement resolution are not possible. Or it may be because one (or both) of the parties believes that forcing the dispute into civil litigation will enhance its bargaining position. Whatever the cause, we need to be mindful of the types of disputes that end up in our civil litigation system rather than being resolved by some other form.

The law-and-economics literature teaches us that the goal of the civil litigation system should be to promote lawsuits when such suits are socially desirable.[5] Social desirability can be measured by comparing the social benefits and costs of litigation, when it is prohibited and when it occurs.[6] Here, scholars teach us that any system of civil litigation must be vigilant about three potential social costs—false acquittals, false convictions, and litigation costs.[7] Any system of civil litigation that seeks to minimize these costs encounters an inescapable tension—namely, that it is not possible to minimize all three costs simultaneously.[8] A system that seeks to avoid false acquittals likely will entail higher litigation costs (as the cost of truth-seeking will necessitate more intrusive discovery into information in the defendant's possession).[9] By contrast, a system that seeks to minimize false convictions may lead to lower litigation costs but also enhances the risk of false acquittals (as plaintiffs lack access to the information needed to prove their case).[10]

This normative backdrop helps to identify the exceptional features of the American system. Since the adoption of the Federal Rules of Civil Procedure, the American system generally has tolerated higher litigation costs in order to reduce the risk of an erroneous outcome (whether a false acquittal or a false conviction). Liberal notice-pleading rules and generous discovery rules reflect this approach. Under that system, the purpose of a complaint is merely to put one's adversary on notice about the topic of the lawsuit; it does not have to set forth the factual basis for the claim. Unless the complaint is dismissed based on some obvious defect, the plaintiff then is entitled to receive copies of the defendant's relevant documents and to depose the defendant, his or her employees, and other relevant witnesses (which may then provide or reinforce the factual basis). By contrast, continental European and Asian systems have trended in the opposite direction—placing greater emphasis on reducing litigation costs (but thereby increasing the risk of an erroneous outcome). Consequently, these systems tend to impose stricter fact-based pleading requirements and are miserly in their approach to discovery.[11] Under these systems, plaintiffs must set forth the factual basis for their claims already in their complaints; failure to do so will result in dismissal. Moreover, even where the factual showing is sufficient, the plaintiff in most European and Asian systems does not have the same entitlement to receive copies of relevant documents from the defendant or to depose the defendant, his or her employees, or other relevant witnesses before trial (meaning that the case often rises or falls on the facts that the plaintiff is able to adduce).

Has Our System of Civil Procedure Achieved Those Ends?

This section does two things. First, it tries to identify the precise failings of our current system of civil litigation. Second, it discusses the incompleteness of pleading reform as a solution to these problems.

A. What Precisely Is Wrong with Our System of Civil Litigation?

Criticism of our system of civil litigation is nothing new. As Roscoe Pound famously observed over a century ago: "Dissatisfaction with the administration of justice is as old as law."[12] Our experience under the Federal Rules of Civil Procedure has been no exception to Pound's general observation. After a brief "golden age" following the Rules adoption, some participants and observers began to complain that the new Rules had made the barrier to entry too low and exposed defendants to costly and unjustified fishing expeditions.[13]

In the 1970s and 1980s, the Rules architects sought to respond to these criticisms. These responses took two main forms.[14] First, the Rules were modified several times to impose marginal limits on discovery (such as limits on the number of interrogatories and time limits on depositions).

Second, the Rules were revised to encourage active case management by district judges, on the theory that early intervention by the judge could overcome protracted pretrial disputes.

Our current system of civil litigation must be addressed against this history of criticism and reform. The current consensus, according to one report at a major conference on the topic at Duke Law School, is that the current system was too expensive and takes too long to bring cases to resolution.[15] Most data confirm this consensus. According to one recent survey of Fortune 200 companies, total litigation costs between 2000 and 2008 were approximately $4.1 billion and average $115 million per company, a 112% increase over the reporting period.[16] The same study revealed that, measured as a percentage of corporate revenue, litigation expenses for these corporations had increased 78% over the same period.[17] (The time frame captured by the study is noteworthy, for the increases postdate many of the above-described efforts to rein in costs in the civil litigation system.)[18] This steady increase in costs affects not simply the parties but the United States' long-run competitiveness.[19]

The advent of electronic discovery has exacerbated these problems.[20] This avenue of information gathering has grown increasingly popular as more corporate documents are generated electronically.[21] Nightmarish anecdotes abound, including one where a non-party government agency incurred over $6 million (approximately 9% of its annual budget) complying with an electronic discovery order.[22] More recent research has sought to assess this phenomenon systematically and suggests that these nightmarish anecdotes are not entirely unrepresentative.[23] While 2006 amendments to the Federal Rules have sought to temper the financially crippling effects of electronic discovery,[24] their efficacy is questionable.[25] A recent report of the Institute for the Advancement of the American Legal System found that the average costs of complying with electronic discovery obligations in a mid-size case were approximately $3.5 million.[26]

Of course, an expensive system is not a priori undesirable. If the social value of the litigation is sufficiently high, then the high dispute resolution costs may be entirely justified. Moreover, empirical research suggests that some cases in federal court involve little to no discovery.[27] Nonetheless, the

cost data should alert us to the possibility that, in cases that do involve discovery, the excessive costs of resolving disputes can force parties to settle
even where they may have a meritorious defense.[28]

So is this expense socially undesirable? Though more empirical research in this area is desperately needed, the available literature suggests
the answer may be yes. Twenty years ago, the President's Council on Competitiveness found that discovery accounted for 80% of litigation costs in
the United States, a figure supported by the reports of corporate in-house
counsel.[29] A more recent study found that discovery composes half of all
litigation costs and, in the most expensive cases, equals 90% of litigation
costs and 32% of the amount in controversy.[30] Most recently, research into
the civil litigation system revealed strong correlations between litigation
costs and factors such as the size of the controversy, longer processing
times, and electronic discovery.[31] These results remain, however, quite
preliminary.

Survey evidence supports the idea that our civil litigation system is too
expensive relative to the amount in controversy. A recent survey by the
ABA Section on Litigation typifies the survey data: 78% of plaintiffs' lawyers, 91% of defense attorneys, and 94% of attorneys with mixed plaintiff/
defense practices believe that litigation costs are not proportional to the
value at least in small-stakes cases (smaller percentages concur with the
proposition in large-stakes cases).[32] To be sure, such survey evidence is not
the ideal thermometer by which to measure the ills of our civil justice system. Nonetheless, in addition to supporting the general idea that our system of civil litigation is out of whack, survey evidence is valuable for a
second, independent reason. It can capture users' *perception* of how the
system operates. That perception is important, for it can influence a party's behavior on matters such as whether to initiate litigation (in the hope
of exploiting expensive discovery to extract settlement) and whether to
settle it (even if a party's position is meritorious).

The American litigation system is unquestionably expensive. Moreover,
both empirical and survey evidence suggests that these expenses are disproportionate to the value of a suit. Just as importantly, this state of affairs
has fostered a broader perception about the disproportionate expense of

the American litigation system, one that can affect party behavior and American competitiveness.

B. The Incompleteness of the Pleading Reform Project

The prescription du jour for these maladies has been pleading reform.[33] While the original Federal Rules were modeled largely on a system of notice pleading, recent changes have moved us closer toward (though certainly not to) a system of fact-based pleading. For example, specific statutes such as the Y2K Act and the Private Securities Litigation Reform Act require plaintiffs to plead certain claims with an exceptional degree of factual specificity.[34] More generally (and more significantly), several recent Supreme Court decisions have required proof that the allegations in the case were at least "plausible."[35]

These reforms have had some effect on disproportionately expensive litigation (despite criticism in the academic literature).[36] By raising the bar before a plaintiff has access to discovery, they reduce the risk that cases will enter the stage where discovery is entirely out of proportion to the value of the dispute. Very preliminary empirical data indicate that heightened pleading standards can filter out cases lacking any substantive basis.[37] This evidence accords with comparative research showing that countries that require more detailed pleadings are better able to control the costs of their civil litigation system.[38]

Nonetheless, pleading reform is a rather blunt tool for addressing the proportionality problem and cannot represent a complete answer to the difficulties that trouble current civil litigation practice. Even if the Supreme Court sorts out what it means by the "plausibility standard," pleading reform does not address the underlying problem of what happens to a lawsuit that satisfies the plausibility (or other) standard. In other words, once a complaint surmounts the motion to dismiss, the parties are off to the races in discovery, at which point all of the above-described perils of the discovery process kick in. Given the extensive literature demonstrating how discovery costs (compared with, say, pleading practice) drive the costs of civil litigation, it is only when we directly link pleading reform with discovery reform that we can begin to get at the core difficulties ailing our system of civil litigation. The next section takes up that task.

A Proposal Premised on the Proportionality Principle

An obvious solution to the proportionality problem would be to eliminate the system of party-controlled discovery entirely and replace it with an inquisitorial system where the judge controls the production and exchange of information. That solution, however, is not unproblematic. As a normative matter, this would elevate the risk of false acquittals in meritorious cases. Even if that cost were acceptable, as a practical matter, such an approach has not attracted a groundswell of support.

Instead, I offer an original proposal designed to address the imbalance in our current system of civil litigation and more compatible with the existing Rules framework. That proposal expressly ties a party's entitlement to discovery to the amount in controversy (and nothing else). In order to ensure that parties do not exaggerate the amount in controversy, I defend a requirement that the plaintiff post a bond tied to the amount in controversy.

A. Proportionality: A Primer

Under the proportionality principle, the degree of pretrial process would be proportional to the value of the controversy.[39] The principle links pleading practice and discovery practice.[40] A party's entitlement to discovery is directly correlated with what it pleads.[41] At a high level of abstraction and at its extreme poles, the principle is relatively easy to apply. High-stakes, complex cases such as antitrust disputes involving allegations of world-wide price fixing likely would necessitate extensive discovery. By contrast, low-stakes, simple cases like a garden-variety unpaid bill would not.

Like any good principle, though, the devil lies in the details. How does one measure the value of a case? How does one measure its complexity? How much discovery does a complex antitrust case require? How little discovery does a case about an unpaid bill really need?

The Federal Rules of Civil Procedure provide one approach. Rule 26(b)(2)(C)(iii) provides that a federal court must limit discovery when it determines that "the burden or expense of the proposed discovery outweighs its likely benefit, considering the needs of the case, the amount in controversy, the parties' resources, the importance of the issues at stake in the action, and the importance of the discovery in resolving the issues."

In theory, the Rule is unassailable. It requires judges to undertake a sort of cost-benefit analysis—weighing the value of the information against the cost of obtaining it. In practice, however, this Rule has not lived up to its expectations, and its operation has been substantially criticized in the academic literature.

Criticism comes from two corners. First, the Rule is structurally flawed. It requires the judge to make an assessment about the case with incomplete information.[42] That is, the Rule forces the judge to determine the value of a particular category of information to the case before the judge fully understands what the case is about. Given that one party is seeking the information and knows the case better than the judge, the judge will be reluctant to second-guess that party's assessment about the importance of that information to the case.

Second, the Rule has not been efficacious. It has largely failed to cabin runaway discovery disputes.[43] The basic problem is the multi-factor quality of Rule 26(b). Like most multi-factor tests, it is far too malleable and fails to provide sufficient guidance to judges on when they should refuse discovery on the ground that it's disproportionate to the value of the information.[44]

This assessment of the proportionality principle teaches us several important lessons. First, to overcome these difficulties, we need a version of the Rule that allows the judge to apply the proportionality principle based on information easily available to him. Second, whatever standard the judge applies, it should be relatively simple and straightforward, not a squishy multi-factor balancing test that leaves parties and judges directionless.

B. Dusting off Rule 8(a)(3)

Here I propose replacing the multi-factored approach embodied in Rule 26(b)(2)(C)(iii) with a simpler approach tied more directly to the amount in controversy. That is, the parties' entitlement to engage in discovery should be directly and exclusively correlated with the value of the dispute—and not any of the other factors currently set forth in Rule 26(b)(2)(C)(iii).

The idea of linking discovery entitlements to the amount in controversy finds support in both state practice and international practice.[45] The most familiar example, perhaps, is small-claims court, where parties in small-stakes disputes forgo many of the formalities of a trial (including discovery) in return for an expedited decision. Their entitlement to that simplified system of processes is explicitly linked to the amount in controversy. As an example of more general civil practice, Colorado Rule 16.1 peremptorily prohibits discovery in cases where the amount in controversy is under $100,000.[46] On the international stage, several foreign courts, including those in England, Scotland, certain provinces in Canada, and Spain, all tailor the extent of discovery and disclosure to the amount in controversy.[47] For example, under the Expedited Litigation Pilot Program in British Columbia, where the amount in controversy is less than $100,000, the parties are required to engage in expedited exchange of information, may take depositions only with the court's permission, must limit their depositions to two hours, and may use only one expert witness.[48]

So how would we begin to adopt these models to practice under the Federal Rules? Rule 8(a)(3) provides a ready-made platform for this approach. Under Rule 8(a)(3), a plaintiff is asked to set forth the "demand for the relief sought."[49] This is typically overlooked in the academic literature and, with the exception of cases premised on diversity jurisdiction, plays virtually no role in practice. This is hardly surprising. Once the dispute has begun, the value of the controversy set forth in the pleadings is wholly irrelevant to the proceeding.

How would discovery be tied to the amount in controversy? One might begin by drawing on Professor Edward Cooper's proposed simplified rules of civil procedure.[50] While Cooper's proposal contains a good deal of nuance, its essential features may be briefly summarized: the simplified rules would fall into three different categories: (1) for all disputes under $50,000; (2) for all disputes under $250,000 if plaintiffs elect to opt in to the rules and no defendant objects; (3) in all cases where all plaintiffs offer and all defendants accept the option to proceed under the simplified rules.[51] Parties would have broad disclosure obligations tailored to their knowledge of documents relevant to a fact disputed in the parties' pleadings. Discovery would be presumptively limited to three depositions per side (not to exceed three hours), ten interrogatories, and ten requests for admission. Document requests would have to specify the precise documents sought unless a party obtained leave of the court to request a category of documents.

Cooper's proposal does not explicitly address the issue of electronic discovery, which, as noted above, has taken center stage in the complaints about the system of civil litigation. To take into account that development, I would modify Cooper's proposal so that a party would be able to propound an electronic discovery request only in two circumstances: (1) where the party specified the particular piece of electronic discovery sought (such as an email account or a particular party's or employee's electronic information), or (2) where the amount in controversy is sufficiently high as to justify the expense typically associated with searching for electronic information.[52]

Initially, then, the discovery schedule proposed here would consist of three fields: (1) low-stakes (or voluntarily selected) cases that qualify for the above-described simplified rules, (2) higher-stakes cases that qualify for the traditional array of discovery tools (but with limited electronic discovery), and (3) highest-stake cases that qualify for this traditional array of tools and also qualify for electronic discovery. As courts and parties become acquainted with the rules (and empirical legal scholars study its operation), the schedule can be expanded and modified.

C. Discouraging Exaggerated Claims

If the parties' discovery entitlements are a function of the amount in controversy (and nothing else), this raises an obvious concern: how do we control the risk that a plaintiff will simply exaggerate the amount in controversy in an effort to invoke more generous discovery entitlements than the case really warrants? At least three alternatives are possible—a sanctions regime, a cost-shifting regime, and a bond requirement.[53]

A sanctions regime presents one method for controlling exaggerated pleading of the amount in controversy requirement (in an effort to opt into a more favorable discovery regime). This approach would function in a manner not unlike current Rule 11, which sets forth certain obligations for counsel signing pleadings (like complaints). Adapted to this context, a sanctions regime would specify that, by signing the complaint, the plaintiff's counsel certifies that the alleged amount in controversy both is not designed to "needlessly increase the cost of litigation" and has "evidentiary support."[54] A failure to abide by these obligations would result in a monetary sanction.[55]

A sanctions-based approach to the problem suffers from two main flaws. First, it distracts the court from the guts of the litigation. Defendants skeptical of the alleged amount in controversy would be encouraged to challenge the amount through a Rule 11 motion, which would then tie up the court in satellite litigation over the evidentiary basis for the alleged amount in controversy. Second, and more importantly, empirical evidence indicates that Rule 11 has not been a particularly effective vehicle to police pleading abuse.[56] Judges are reluctant to use it (perhaps because of the above distraction), and the penalties have not served as a particularly effective deterrent. For these reasons, we need to look elsewhere to identify an effective mechanism by which to control exaggerated valuations of the amount in dispute.

Cost-shifting presents a more promising alternative.[57] Under cost-shifting principles, each party would pay the costs of the other party's compliance with discovery requests and orders. Until recently, the Federal Rules were silent on the matter of cost-shifting. With the advent of electronic discovery, the idea gained some favor,[58] and the 2006 amendments to Rule 26, discussed above, have given courts a firmer footing to consider the option. Nonetheless, "the use of cost-shifting remains extremely limited—if not all but non-existent."[59]

Cost-shifting avoids many of the problems of the Rule 11 approach. It does not require the court to become tangled up in satellite concerns over the evidentiary basis for a party's allegations. Indeed, it should not require the court's involvement at all (unless disputes arise between the parties over whether the compliance costs incurred with a particular discovery request are themselves excessive—perhaps in an effort to pressure the party seeking discovery to settle).[60]

More significantly, cost-shifting offers the potential to address some of the problems identified above—namely, the concern that the costs of resolving the dispute will be disproportionate to the value of the dispute. By placing the burden of paying for discovery squarely on the part seeking it, it encourages each party to calculate carefully the value of the information that it is seeking, and thereby to limit its requests to those sources of information of core importance to its case. In a dispute involving only $250,000, it would be irrational for a party to propound a discovery request requiring its adversary to conduct a massive search of electronic information if the costs of that search (and the consequent price to be paid by the requesting party) far outstrip the value of the relief sought.

Nonetheless, cost-shifting does entail some problems. First, the effectiveness of cost-shifting depends not on the quality of the dispute but instead on the depth of a party's pockets. A party with substantial resources aligned against a party with relatively few resources may not greatly care about having to bear the costs of the other party's discovery compliance if it can afford it. This might happen, for example, when a major industry player sues a start-up competitor in an effort to drive it out of the industry. The proposal here avoids this problem because it expressly links a party's discovery right to the value of the dispute; even a deep-pocketed plaintiff (or defendant) that is prepared to absorb its adversary's significant discovery-related costs could not abuse the discovery system.

Second, cost-shifting enhances the risk that plaintiffs with meritorious claims either will be less likely to bring suit or less able to ferret out the information necessary to prove its case due to the cost that a plaintiff must bear in order to unearth that information.[61] By placing the full burden on the party seeking the information, a cost-shifting rule increases the cost of litigation to that party. In some cases, this will result in the true negative costs of false acquittals when meritorious claims are not pursued (even as imposing discovery costs on the defendant will in some cases result in false positive costs when innocent defendants settle unmeritorious claims). Perhaps for this reason, most cost-shifting requests are denied (according to the available empirical research).[62] The challenge, then, becomes to find a solution that captures the benefits of cost-shifting while minimizing this risk.

A bond requirement might fit the bill. Though perhaps more familiar in the criminal justice system, bonds can and do perform important functions in our civil litigation system as well. Parties seeking to obtain preliminary injunctions can be required to post bonds.[63] Similarly, parties appealing adverse judgments can be required to post bonds.[64] In both circumstances, the bond serves an important function—namely, it helps to ensure that the other party (the target of the injunction or the judgment creditor) has an opportunity to be made whole if the party seeking relief (the movant for the preliminary injunction, the appellant) fails in its effort. There is no principled reason why the bond cannot serve similar functions in other spheres of civil procedure.[65]

A bond requirement could operate as part of the proposal discussed here. The size of the bond would vary with the amount in controversy (and consequently the applicable discovery schedule). For example, in a relatively low-stakes case, the discovery schedule would authorize only a limited degree of discovery, and the plaintiff's bond would be correspondingly low. Depending on the percentage of the bond that would be cash-collateralized, the plaintiff's immediate out-of-pocket expense would be only a fraction of that amount. By contrast, in a larger-stakes case, the discovery schedule might entail much higher discovery costs, and the plaintiffs would be required to post a relatively larger bond, and its up-front cash obligation would be concomitantly higher.[66]

A bond holds the potential to control exaggerated claims about the amount in controversy (in an effort to obtain more generous discovery rights) while avoiding some of the drawbacks of a pure cost-shifting regime. Like the cost-shifting regime, it requires the plaintiff to assume some financial responsibility for the defendant's costs of compliance with the process costs of the dispute. Thereby, it helps to ensure that the defendant is made whole for the discovery costs that it incurs (much like the bond in the preliminary injunction and appeal contexts). However, it bears two significant differences from traditional cost-shifting proposals. First, the immediate financial burden on the plaintiff is relatively lower (posting only the collateralized portion of the bond). Second, the ultimate financial burden on the plaintiff may likewise be lower (in the event that the bond proceeds are never paid to the defendant). As such, this approach reallocates a portion of the litigation costs while reducing the risk of false acquittals.

If one accepts the general idea of a bond as a means of controlling exaggerated claims about the amount in controversy, then it becomes important to flush out three details: (1) the trigger for when the bond requirement kicks in, (2) the standards for when the bond proceeds will be paid to the defendant, and (3) the size of the bond.

As to the trigger, the plaintiff should be required to post the bond at the time he or she propounds the first round of discovery. That is the moment when the plaintiff's actions are causing the defendant to incur search costs either to respond to or to contest the discovery requests. In order to standardize operation of the bond requirement, it may be advisable eventually to bar discovery entirely until the judge has ruled on any dispositive motions, as some statutes currently provide.[67]

As to the criteria, several options are theoretically possible. One would automatically entitle the defendant to draw down the bond as he or she incurs discovery costs (subject to any litigation over the reasonableness of the defendant's cost estimate). Another would allow the defendant to draw down the bond when he or she prevails in the litigation (subject to elaboration on what it means to "prevail"). A third standard would permit the defendant to draw on the bond when it can be demonstrated that the costs of complying with a particular discovery request are disproportionate to the value of the suit.

The third approach most faithfully advances the proportionality principle. The first approach is not really calibrated to proportionality so much as it is to cost-control and burden allocation, and the proper means of addressing that concern is through a cost-shifting rule. The second approach has some appeal but is also not calibrated to the proportionality principle. It goes to some length to make the prevailing defendant whole by providing compensation for the costs of discovery, but, as the experience with fee-shifting statutes demonstrates, it can be a complicated exercise to determine when a defendant prevails.[68] For example, how should a court decide whether to allow the defendant to draw on the bond when it dismisses some claims at summary judgment, but the jury returns a verdict for the plaintiff on claims that survive summary judgment?

The third approach, in contrast to the other two, expressly links the defendant's entitlement to costs with the proportionality principle. It limits the defendant's recovery to situations where the discovery schedule does not adequately capture the search costs. This may be due to the plaintiff's design of the discovery requests. It might also be due to the defendant's structure (e.g., an interrogatory requesting detailed financial information may entail far higher costs for a multinational company like General Electric than for a private individual or a small business). This approach also encourages moderation by plaintiffs (and communication between the parties). When a particular discovery request prompts a defendant to request payment under the bond, the plaintiff can decide whether to stick with the request (and incur a financial obligation) or modify the request in order to reduce the financial impact that the defendant must bear.

Finally, as to price, the amount of the bond should bear some relationship to the expectation that the discovery requests will entail disproportionate costs. For example, suppose that the underlying research into the discovery schedule suggested that disputes of a particular value (say $100,000) entailed average discovery costs of $5,000. Suppose further that the *range* of discovery costs in disputes around this amount had a lower end of $0 and an upper end of $20,000. The bond might then be priced some standard deviation above the average cost (without forcing the plaintiff to insure against the full cost of the extreme case). A plaintiff in such a case might thus be required to post a bond of $5,000 to $6,000 (and, depending on the structure of the bond market, the plaintiff's actual out-of-pocket costs would be only a fraction of the total bond amount). While we do not yet have the empirical data to calculate that figure precisely, the theory suggests that the pricing would occur along these lines.

In sum, this part has introduced an original solution to the proportionality problem in civil litigation. First, the parties' discovery entitlements should be calibrated directly (and exclusively) with the amount in controversy. Second, the plaintiff should be required to post a bond, the amount of which would be tied to the discovery schedule. The proceeds of the bond could be allocated to the defendant when the discovery requests are disproportionate to the value of the suit. This approach harnesses some of the benefits of cost-shifting proposals (while avoiding some of its drawbacks) and taps into the benefits of bond requirements used elsewhere. Admittedly, though, the proposal is not immune from controversy or criticism.

The next and final section of this article anticipates and responds to some of those criticisms.

Criticisms and Responses

The preceding section has set forth a proposal that expressly linked the party's entitlement to discovery with the amount in controversy in the dispute. This represented a more sure-footed way to embed the proportionality principle in the civil Rules, to overcome the shortcomings of Rule 26(b) and to address some of the failings (actual and perceived) in the civil litigation system, especially the concern that the costs of discovery, rather than the merits, would drive the resolution of the case. In this final section, I anticipate and respond to several potential criticisms of this proposal.

One criticism of the proposal might be that it will be too difficult for plaintiffs to measure the amount in controversy at the start of the suit. According to this argument, the plaintiff cannot accurately know the amount of the damages at the suit's commencement. In some cases, the amount of the damages will depend on information in discovery; in other cases, it will be necessary to retain experts, which may occur only after the case has commenced. Consequently, plaintiffs may either understate their damages (thereby depriving themselves of needed discovery) or overstate their damages (thereby incurring needless costs in terms of the bond).

Two responses to this criticism are possible. First, it overlooks the importance of pleading standards at the start of the case. Even under plausibility pleading, a court still assumes the plaintiff's version of the events to be true. Consequently, the plaintiff should be able to construct a relatively accurate assessment of the value of the case on the assumption that his or her account of events is correct.[69] Second, and more importantly, this criticism takes an unrealistic view of the work that plaintiffs' lawyers undertake before they take on a case. In arbitration, claimants must carefully calculate the amount in controversy, as the arbitrators' and arbitral institution's fees often depend on that amount.[70] Numerous reports have documented how plaintiffs' attorneys estimate the value of the case in order to decide whether to take the case and the likely financial investment necessary to pursue it.[71] Those accounts necessarily imply that plaintiffs' attorneys have both the tools to ferret out the information necessary to assess a case's value and the ability to calculate that value.[72] The proposal suggested here simply requires them to make explicit a calculation that they already are undertaking.[73]

Second, one might object that the amount in controversy does not adequately capture the complexity of the case. Relatively low-stakes disputes (like an injury claim with affirmative defenses) may entail relatively fact-intensive and complex questions of fault and causation. By contrast, relatively high-stakes disputes (like a breach of contract action in a large-scale investment project) may turn on relatively few factual propositions. According to this criticism, measures of complexity, rather than value, should drive the scope of discovery.[74]

This is a formidable objection but is not insurmountable. For one thing, tying discovery to the complexity of the case creates its own difficulties. It requires judges to figure out the meaning of complexity and then map it onto the discovery needs of the case. Moreover, while it certainly is true that the value of the controversy is not a perfect proxy for complexity, this argument ignores the essence of the proportionality principle. It is precisely the point of the proportionality principle that low-stakes disputes should not entail excessive complex discovery, particularly where the costs of that discovery begin to butt up against the value of the case. Under those circumstances, litigation may well not be socially optimal, and the case may be a poor candidate for the civil litigation system. Admittedly, the current proportionality principle of Rule 26(b)(2) captures complexity more explicitly than the proposal I offer here, as part of the Rule's multi-factor test. Yet the problem, as already explained, is that the multi-factor test becomes so unworkable that the Rule fails to perform its necessary filtering function in terms of shaving out excessive discovery requests. The clearer rule offered here, while perhaps not capturing all of the nuance, is far easier to apply.

If it were shown that the amount in controversy measure was ineffective in capturing the value and corresponding discovery needs, modifications of the proposal are possible.[75] For example, one might make presumptions about values rebuttable. If a plaintiff believed that it had a low-stakes but discovery-intensive dispute, it might petition the court for an adjustment to the case's classification in the discovery schedule (with a corresponding shift in the bond). This might compromise the workability of the proposal but could calibrate it slightly better to the difficulty flagged by this criticism.

A final criticism is that the bond requirement will discourage lawsuits. Since the bond requirement increases the up-front costs of plaintiffs (or their lawyers), this will discourage some otherwise meritorious claims. This is especially so in higher-stakes disputes, where the bond requirement would be concomitantly higher.

At a theoretical level, it certainly is true that the bond requirement raises the short-term costs of a party. To the extent this discourages nuisance suits, the outcome is not entirely undesirable.[76] To the extent it discourages suits more broadly, it should be emphasized that the effect is one more of degree rather than of kind. Under any system of dispute resolution, a party must carry a degree of up-front costs (filing fees, attorney time, case preparation costs). While this certainly adds to them, existing means can absorb that cost (just as it absorbs other costs). For example, an attorney operating on a contingency fee might simply factor those costs into the assessment of the case (as the attorney factors in other case-preparation and case-maintenance costs). Moreover, to the extent other up-front costs that plaintiffs must bear can be reduced, the aggregate costs to the plaintiff might well be no different. Finally, if the bond requirement were found to systematically deter categories of plaintiffs from maintaining particular categories of cases, one could imagine a system where a party could petition in a particular case for waiver of the bond requirement. Relaxation of the bond requirement would address the cost and access issues but might thereby eliminate one of the principal tools for avoiding excessive claims of the amount in controversy.

Notes

I should like to thank Frank Buckley, Justice Kurt Heller of the Austrian Constitutional Court, Hillel Levin, Judge Paul V. Niemeyer, and Judge Gerald Tjoflat for their thoughts on the ideas discussed in this article. Professor Adrian Zuckerman and participants in his graduate Civil Procedure Seminar at Oxford University Law

School provided invaluable feedback. Special thanks also go to Judge Rebecca Kourlis and her colleagues at the Institute for the Advancement of the American Legal System for their input and access to their fantastic resources. Dean Rebecca White provided financial support for this research, and the University of Vienna Law School's Institute fuer Zivilverfahrensrecht provided excellent facilities and support during my residence there.

1. John Langbein, Cultural Chauvinism in Comparative Law, 5 Cardozo J. Int'l Comp. L. 41, 48 (1997). See also John H. Langbein, The German Advantage in Civil Procedure, 52 U. Chi. L. Rev. 823 (1985).

2. See Samuel P. Baumgartner, Civil Procedure Reform in Switzerland and the Role of Legal Transplants ("Legal Transplants"), in Common Law, Civil Law and the Future of Categories 18–26 (Janet Walker and Oscar G. Chase, eds., forthcoming).

3. Lon L. Fuller, The Forms and Limits of Adjudication, 92 Harv. L. Rev. 353 (1978).

4. Not all see this development as salutary. See Owen Fiss, Against Settlement, 93 Yale L. J. 1073 (1984).

5. Hylton, When Should a Case Be Dismissed?, 16 Sup. Ct. Econ. Rev. 39, 44 (2008).

6. Steven M. Shavell, The Social versus the Private Incentive to Bring Suit in a Costly Legal System, 11 J. Legal Stud. 333 (1982).

7. Hylton, 16 Sup. Ct. Econ. Rev. at 45; Epstein, Bell Atlantic v. Twombly: How Motions to Dismiss Become (Disguised) Summary Judgments, 25 Wash U. J. L. Policy 61 (2007); Bone, Economics of Civil Procedure at 146–48; Bone, The Process of Making Process: Court Rulemaking, Democratic Legitimacy and Procedural Efficiency, 87 Geo. Wash. L. Rev. 887, 911 (1999).

8. Bone, Economics of Civil Procedure at 2.

9. Id. at 128–32.

10. Id.

11. Geoffrey P. Miller, The Legal-Economic Analysis of Comparative Civil Procedure, 45 Am. J. Comp. L. 905 (1997); IAALS Report (2009); Scott Dodson, The Challenge of Comparative Civil Procedure: Civil Litigation in Comparative Context, 60 Ala. L. Rev. 133 (2008); Geoffrey C. Hazard, From Whom No Secrets Are Hid, 76 Tex. L. Rev. 1165, 1671 (1998); Scott Dodson, Comparative Convergences in Pleading Standards, 158 U. Pa. L. Rev. 441 (2010); American College of Trial Lawyers Task Force on Discovery and the Institute for the Advancement of the American Legal System, Final Report ("ACTL Report") App. A at 1 (Mar. 11, 2009).

12. Pound, The Causes of Dissatisfaction with the Administration of Justice, 40 Am. L. Rev. 729 (1906).

13. See, e.g., E. Barrett Prettyman, Procedure in Anti-Trust and Other Protracted Cases, 13 F.R.D. 41, 62. For a useful synopsis of the history of criticisms following the adoption of the Federal Rules of Civil Procedure, see Lawyers for Civil Justice et al., Reshaping the Rules of Civil Procedure for the 21st Century: The Need for Clear, Concise, and Meaningful Amendments to Key Rules of Civil Procedure (white paper

delivered at the 2010 Conference on Civil Litigation at Duke Law School); Rebecca L. Kourlis et al., Reinvigorating Pleadings, 87 Denv. U. L. Rev. 245, 251 (2010).

14. Stephen B. Burbank and Linda J. Silberman, Civil Procedure Reform in Comparative Context: The United States of America, 45 Am. J. Comp. L. 675 (1997). See also Edward D. Cavanagh, Twombly, The Federal Rules of Civil Procedure and the Courts, 82 St. John's L. Rev. 877, 884–89 (2008); Richard L. Marcus, Discovery Containment Redux, 39 B.C. L. Rev. 747 (1998); Linda Mullenix, Discovery in Disarray: the Pervasive Myth of Pervasive Discovery Abuse and the Consequences for Unfounded Rulemaking, 46 Stan. L. Rev. 1393 (1994).

15. Institute for the Advancement of the American Legal System, Preserving Access and Identifying Excess: Areas of Convergence and Consensus in the 2010 Conference Materials ("Preserving Access").

16. See generally Robert E. Litan, Through Their Eyes: How Foreign Investors View and React to the U.S. Legal System (Aug. 2007)

17. Id.

18. For a good overview of the economic impact of the civil litigation system at the time these reforms were being implemented, see Walpin, America's Failing Civil Justice System: Can We Learn from Other Countries?, 41 N.Y. L. Sch. L. Rev. 648 (1996–97).

19. U.S. Dep't of Commerce, The U.S. Litigation Environment and Foreign Direct Investment: Supporting U.S. Competitiveness by Reducing Legal Costs and Uncertainty ("Litigation Environment") (Oct. 2008). This gels with earlier research from the American Tort Reform Association finding that the civil justice system generates direct and indirect costs of more than $200 billion annually. See Walpin, 41 N.Y. L. Sch. L. Rev. at 648.

20. See generally Rand Institute for Civil Justice, The Legal and Economic Implications of Economic Discovery: Options for Future Research (2008); Institute for the Advancement of the American Legal System, Electronic Discovery: A View from the Front Lines (2008) ("Front Lines") (discussing prevalence of electronically stored information and massive costs of compliance with electronic discovery orders).

21. Victor E. Schwarz and Christopher E. Appel, Rational Pleading in the Modern World of Civil Litigation: The Lessons and Public Policy Benefits of Twombly and Iqbal, 33 Harv. J. L. Pub. Policy 1107, 1143 (2010) (large organizations generate 250–300 million emails per month); Kourlis, 87 Denv. U. L. Rev. at 253 (claiming that 99% of information generated today by firms is electronic); Scott A. Moss, Litigation Discovery Cannot Be Optimal, but Could Be Better: The Economics of Improving Discovery Timing in a Digital Age, 58 Duke L. J. 889, 893–94 (2009) (noting that 90% of corporate communications are electronic and that businesses exchange approximately 2.5 trillion emails annually); Lawyers for Civil Justice et al., Reshaping the Rules of Civil Procedure for the 21st Century: The Need for Clear, Concise, and Meaningful Amendments to Key Rules of Civil Procedure ("Reshaping the Rules") at 46 nn. 199–200 (2010) (collecting research on electronic document production by companies).

22. In re Fannie Mae (discussed in ILR Report). For a collection of anecdotes, see Martin A. Redish, Back to the Future: Discovery Cost Allocation and Modern Procedural Theory ("Back to the Future") (2010) (manuscript on file with author).

23. Emery G. Lee and Thomas E. Willging, Litigation Costs in Civil Cases: Multivariate Analysis ("Multivariate Analysis") (Mar. 2010). See also Federal Judicial Center, National Case-Based Civil Rules Survey Results (2009).

24. Under Federal Rule of Civil Procedure 26(b)(2)(B), "a party need not provide discovery of electronically stored information from sources that the party identifies as not reasonably accessible because of undue burden or cost." If the requesting party shows good cause, the court may order discovery, taking into account the proportionality principle and subject to conditions (such as cost-shifting).

25. Lawyers for Civil Justice et al., Litigation Cost Survey of Major Companies 25–55 (May 2010).

26. Front Lines at 5.

27. See Thomas E. Willging et al., Discovery and Disclosure Practice, Problems, and Proposals for Change (1997).

28. See also Frank Easterbrook, Discovery as Abuse, 69 B.U. L. Rev. 635, 636–37 (1989).

29. President's Council on Competitiveness, Agenda for Civil Justice Reform in America 1–3 (1991).

30. Willging et al., An Empirical Study of Discovery and Disclosure Practice under the 193 Federal Rule Amendments, 39 B.C. L. Rev. 525, 544–46, 548–49 (1998).

31. Multivariate Analysis, supra note 23, at 11–14.

32. ABA Section of Litigation, Member Survey on Civil Practice: Summary ("ABA Survey") (Dec. 2009). See also Institute for the Advancement of the American Legal System, Civil Litigation Survey of Chief Legal Officers and General Counsel Belonging to the Association of Corporation Counsel ("IAALS Survey") 19 (2010); ACTL Report. Easterbrook, Discovery as Abuse, 69 B.U. L. Rev. at 637.

33. For a thorough recent survey of the literature, see Steinman, The Pleading Problem, 62 Stan. L. Rev. 1293, 1296–97 nn. 10, 12 (2010).

34. 15 U.S.C. § 6601 et seq.; 15 U.S.C. §78u-4(b).

35. Bell Atlantic Corp. v. Twombly, 550 U.S. 544 (2007); Ashcroft v. Iqbal, 129 S. Ct. 1937 (2009).

36. See, e.g., A. Benjamin Spencer, Understanding Pleading Doctrine, 108 Mich. L. Rev. 1 (2009); A. Benjamin Spencer, Plausibility Pleading, 49 B.C. L. Rev. 411 (2008).

37. See, e.g., Patricia W. Hatamyar, The Tao of Pleading: Do Twombly and Iqbal Matter Empirically?, 59 Am. U. L. Rev. 553, 556 (2010) (presenting data to support the proposition that the post-Iqbal dismissal rate is significantly higher than the comparable pre-Twombly rate).

38. Institute for the Advancement of the American Legal System, A Summary of Comparative Approaches to Civil Procedure ("Comparative Approaches").

39. See Bone, The Economics of Civil Procedure at 217–24.

40. In Twombly, the Supreme Court recognized this essential relationship: "it is only by taking care to require allegations that reach the level suggesting conspiracy that we can hope to avoid the potentially enormous expense of discovery in cases with no reasonably founded hope that the discovery process will reveal relevant evidence." 550 U.S. at 559. See also Steinmann, 62 Stan. L. Rev. at 1351 ("Discovery costs are, however, a crucial part of the debate over how strict or lenient federal pleading standards ought to be").

41. In its recent report on revisions to the federal rules, the American College of Trial Lawyers wrote, "Proportionality should be the most important principle applied to all discovery." ACTL Report at 7.

42. Moss, 58 Duke L. J. at 920, 924.

43. See Twombly, 550 U.S. at 559; 8 Wright and Miller Section 2008.1 at 121. See also Easterbrook, 69 B.U. L. Rev. at 638–39 ("The portions of the Rules of Civil Procedure that call on judges to trim back excessive demands have been . . . and are doomed to be hollow"); Richard A. Epstein, The Risks of Risk/Utility, 48 Ohio St. L. J. 469, 476 (1987) (blaming "malleable discovery tests for inexorable expansion of tort liability"); Ronald J. Hedges, A View from the Bench and the Trenches: A Critical Appraisal of Some Proposed Amendments to the Federal Rules of Civil Procedure, 227 F.R.D. 123, 127 (2005).

44. Back to the Future at 10–14; Easterbrook, 69 B.U. L. Rev. at 640.

45. The nexus between proportionality and discovery recently formed a core principle of the IAALS/ACTL Final Report on Discovery. See ACTL Report at 9.

46. Colo. R. Civ. P. 16.1. For a recent report on the experience of bench and bar under the rule, see Corina Gerety, IAALS Surveys of the Colorado Bench and Bar on Colorado's Simplified Pretrial Procedure for Civil Actions (2010).

47. Comparative Approaches at 22, 35–37, 54.

48. British Columbia Sup. Ct. R. Civ. P. 68, discussed in Comparative Approaches at 36.

49. Fed. R. Civ. P. 8(a)(3).

50. See Edward H. Cooper, Simplified Rules of Federal Procedure, 100 Mich. L. Rev. 794 (2002).

51. Cooper did not pluck these figures out of thin air. Instead, they reflect detailed empirical research by the Federal Judicial Center about the value of disputes in federal court. Id. at 1797. Moreover, the opportunity for parties to "opt in" to the simplified schedule reflects the reality that some cases involve little to no discovery at all.

52. Admittedly, there may be instances in which the search for electronically stored information is cheaper and faster than searching paper files. Here, one might need to distinguish between readily searchable electronic databases and backup tapes where the extraction costs are higher. As e-discovery practices become more settled, it may become advisable further to modify these thresholds. For now, however, the simplicity and workability of the model proposed here outweigh the values of incorporating that nuance. I am especially grateful to Judge Kourlis and her colleagues at the IAALS for the comments on this point.

53. Another possibility, not explored here due to page constraints, would be a loser-pays rule as to costs.

54. Fed. R. Civ. P. 11(b)(1), (3).

55. Fed. R. Civ. P. 11(c).

56. For articles collecting criticism of Rule 11's efficacy, see Peter A. Joy, The Relationship between Civil Rule 11 and Lawyer Discipline: An Empirical Analysis Suggesting Institutional Choices in the Regulation of Lawyers, 37 Loyola L.A. L. Rev. 765 (2004); Gerald F. Hess, Rule 11 Practice in Federal and State Court: An Empirical, Comparative Study, 75 Marq. L. Rev. 313 (1992).

57. See Robert D. Cooter and Daniel L. Rubinfeld, An Economic Model of Legal Discovery, 23 J. Legal Stud. 435 (1994); Edward H. Cooper, Discovery Cost Allocation: A Reply to Cooter and Rubinfeld, 23 J. Legal Stud. 465 (2004); Back to the Future at 13 note 37 (collecting literature).

58. See, e.g., Zubulake v. UBS Warburg LLC, 217 F.R.D. 309, 324 (S.D.N.Y. 2003).

59. Back to the Future at 12.

60. See Bone, Economics of Civil Procedure at 230.

61. Id. at 204–15.

62. See Corince L. Giacobbe, Note, Allocating Discovery Costs in the Digital Age: Deciding Who Should Bear the Costs of Electronically Stored Data, 57 Wash & Lee L. Rev. 257, 290 (2000).

63. Paul Stancil, Balancing the Pleading Equation, 61 Baylor L. Rev. 90, 195–96 (2009).

64. Id. at 195–96.

65. Id. Stancil explains how a bond requirement could be used to relax pleading requirements so that plaintiffs are not required to satisfy the plausibility standard of Twombly and Iqbal.

66. Though space constraints prevent a complete elaboration of this idea, the principle would also operate in the case of counterclaims and cross-claims. In both instances, the counterclaimant/cross-claimant would be required to post a bond in order to trigger additional discovery rights.

67. See, e.g., Private Securities Litigation Reform Act, 15 U.S.C. § 78u-4(b)(3).

68. Cost-shifting may, however, supply an appropriate remedy in cases where the defendant is employing disproportionate discovery as a tactic designed to undermine a plaintiff's effort to bring a meritorious claim.

69. Hylton, 16 Sup. Ct. Econ. Rev. at 47.

70. See, e.g., International Chamber of Commerce, Rules of Arbitration 26.

71. ABA Survey at 5; Thomas A. Eaton and Harold S. Lewis, Rule 68 Offers of Judgment: The Practices and Opinions of Experienced Civil Rights and Employment Discrimination Attorneys, 241 F.R.D. 332 (2007).

72. Indeed, in a few cases, federal statutes already require plaintiffs to make this sort of calculation. For example, the Y2K Act required a complaint to contain "a statement of specific information as to the nature and amount of each element of damages and the factual basis for the damages calculation." 15 U.S.C. § 6607(b).

Similarly, judges sometimes have to make this calculation when, for example, deciding whether a case satisfies the amount-in-controversy requirement. See 28 U.S.C. § 1332.

73. One might, of course, turn this argument on its head. Supposing that plaintiffs know the actual value of their lawsuit, it might harm their settlement position to require them to disclose it. I personally do not find such a requirement objectionable, particularly if it results in settlements that approximate the actual value of the claim rather than ones based on an exaggerated claim.

74. For such a proposal, see Schwartz and Appel, 33 Harv. J. L. Pub. Policy at 1107.

75. Such modifications might be especially appropriate where, for example, nonmonetary factors better capture the public importance of the case (for example, a major constitutional challenge to a legislative enactment). See The Sedona Conference, Commentary on Proportionality (Oct. 2010).

76. See Rosenberg and Shavell, A Model in Which Suits Are Brought for Their Nuisance Value, 5 Int'l Rev. L. Econ. 3, 4–5 (1985).

The Allocation of Discovery Costs and the Foundations of Modern Procedure

MARTIN H. REDISH

The Federal Rules of Civil Procedure are rapidly approaching their 75th birthday, which will come in the year 2013. Seventy-five years is a long time, and while the Rules have of course been amended significantly at various points over the years, their basic structure remains largely the same as in their original formulation. When first promulgated in 1938, the Rules had an immediate and dramatic impact on civil adjudication by replacing long accepted procedural practices with very different methods of resolving disputes. There can be little question that the new system, spearheaded by the genius of Advisory Committee Reporter Charles Clark,[1] radically altered not only the actual procedures themselves, but also the underlying set of values that had previously rationalized our procedural system.

In place of the draconian requirements of the demanding fact-pleading standard, which required a plaintiff to know all of the circumstances surrounding his or her injury in detail at the time of the pleading, the new Federal Rules demanded considerably less at the pleading stage. The information that was unavailable at the pleading stage could now be gathered through a complex system of court-enforced discovery.[2] This dramatic change was premised in some sense on the notion that "mutual knowledge of all the relevant facts gathered by both parties is essential to proper litigation."[3]

Despite the admiration that those who shaped the Federal Rules no doubt deserve, serious problems have remained. For the most part, those problems have revolved around the significant burdens that the Rules' elaborate discovery process has imposed on litigants and the judicial system. In many ways, discovery is reminiscent of the invention of fire. Like fire, if used properly the discovery system can dramatically improve our situation. If abused, however, discovery can cause immeasurable damage. This point is underscored by the Supreme Court's lingering concern over the serious burdens caused by the elaborate discovery process that represented the original Federal Rules' most significant innovation. Designed to enable litigants to gather the information necessary to facilitate accurate decision-making and the effective vindication of substantive rights, the discovery process has a dark side that seems to have been largely undervalued at the time of the Rules' framing. At least in an important category of litigation—those cases in which significant amounts of discovery are likely to take place—the costs and burdens inherent in the discovery process threaten to give rise both to serious inefficiencies in the adjudicatory process and to a potentially pathological and coercive skewing of the applicable substantive law being enforced.

The Court clearly reasoned in its recent pleading decisions that unless the pleading standards effectively perform some form of meaningful gatekeeping function, the harms caused by excessive and burdensome discovery could easily overwhelm the adjudication in much of modern high-stakes litigation.[4] Yet even with the pleadings standard performing this filtering function, the fact remains that in cases that are allowed to proceed beyond the pleading stage, the burdens and costs of discovery are likely to continue to be substantial. The problems of excessive discovery, then, remain a significant concern.

Revisers of the Federal Rules have, over the years, sought to remedy the harms of discovery. As the Supreme Court itself has recognized, however, at least in the "mega-litigation" context, serious problems remain.[5] Yet there do exist hitherto untapped alternatives. It is my position that foundational precepts of economic, moral, and political theory dictate a dramatic alteration in the structural operation of the discovery process. If implemented, this change would undoubtedly reduce the costs and burdens of the process while preserving the bulk of its beneficial functions. This alteration would recognize that the costs of discovery are, from the outset, properly attributed to the requesting party, rather than the responding party. Indeed, classic notions of quantum meruit—long recognized as an indisputable moral and legal dictate in the law of contracts—permit no other conclusion. Were this alteration in the nature of the discovery process to be implemented, an immediate economic externality—one that currently plagues all discovery requests—would immediately be removed. As a result, the discovery system would be relieved of most forms of even non-abusive "excessive" discovery requests—discovery that is simply not justified on the basis of a rational cost-benefit analysis.

Discovery and the Substantive-Procedural Balance

It was quite clear, when the Federal Rules were first promulgated, that by simultaneously reducing the barriers imposed by the fact-pleading requirement and establishing a complex set of court-enforced information-gathering devices, Judge Clark and the Advisory Committee were attempting to both increase procedural fairness to plaintiffs and employ procedure as a more effective means of implementing substantive law. Because of the potential burdens of discovery, however, an unduly lax pleading standard cannot be imposed without seriously skewing the substantive-procedural balance toward pathological over-enforcement of the substantive law. To be sure, discovery is designed to play—and does play—an important role in the effective procedural implementation of substantive law by providing deserving plaintiffs with a viable means of acquiring the information necessary to enforce their rights through resort to the adjudicatory process. Nevertheless, the very same danger of pathological over-enforcement exists with regard to discovery.

The Problem of Discovery Costs

If left wholly unregulated, discovery can give rise to numerous procedural and substantive pathologies. In its most extreme form, intentionally abusive discovery effectively transforms the adjudicatory system into a means of facilitating legalized blackmail and extortion. The very threat of costly discovery likely induces rationally self-interested defendants to settle even non-meritorious suits for an amount smaller than the projected costs of discovery. Requests for wholly unnecessary discovery could thus function in an extortionate manner, financially coercing a defendant into settling unjustified claims. It is fundamentally unfair to a defendant to allow the adjudicatory system to be employed against him as a weapon of extortion.

No one, presumably, would openly sanction discovery that is unambiguously abusive. The problem, of course, is to find ways to control such pathological discovery without either effectively destroying the beneficial effects of the discovery process or establishing control methods that are as economically inefficient as the abusive discovery itself. This has proven to be far more difficult than one might have hoped. It is to consideration of this difficult issue that my analysis turns.

The "Cost Allocation" Model and the Control of "Excessive" Discovery

Although the revisers of the Federal Rules have, over the years, diligently sought to control the abuses of the discovery process, few would argue that they have been successful in that effort. Puzzlingly, despite all of these efforts the revisers have never even considered, much less adopted, the system that would remedy the problems of discovery most effectively. Such a system would, simply, allocate discovery costs to the party who both initiates the discovery and benefits most as a result of it.

From the outset, it is important to understand that what is advocated here is not a process of cost shifting. Indeed, the very use of that term necessarily concedes that the inertia of cost allocation appropriately belongs on the responding party, and must be *shifted* in order to have discovery costs attributed to the requesting party. Yet at no point has anyone— including those who drafted the Federal Rules in the first place—even attempted to rationalize the respondent-centric model of cost allocation that has dominated federal court practice since the Rules' original promulgation. Were one actually to consider the issue afresh, it would be difficult to understand the assumptions inherent in a respondent-based allocation model. It is true, of course, that in the crudest, most concrete sense the cost is immediately incurred by the responding party, not the requesting party. But that fact, standing alone, in no way necessarily implies that even at that point is the cost appropriately to be attributed to the responding party.

One may best understand the point by consideration of a simple analogy. Assume a worker asks his co-worker to do him a favor and pick up lunch for him. The co-worker does so, paying the $15 that the lunch costs. He then brings the lunch to the requesting worker; unless he was raised by wolves, the requesting worker will immediately thank the co-worker and reimburse him for his $15 expenditure on his behalf. Is such reimbursement appropriately characterized as "cost shifting" in anything but the most concrete, technical, and immediate sense? At any point in this hypothetical transaction, was the cost of that lunch appropriately viewed, morally or conceptually, as the co-worker's cost, rather than the requesting worker's cost? Long-established principles of quantum meruit readily answer that question in the negative.[6] The co-worker performed work on behalf of another, who was aware both that the co-worker was performing the work on his behalf and, as a result, incurring costs on his behalf. The law of quasi-contract unambiguously dictates that in such a situation the cost is deemed that of the party on behalf of whom the work was done, not of the party who performed the work.[7]

In fundamental ways, the discovery process is identical to this hypothetical situation. The only differences are that in the case of discovery, the performing party is usually performing the work not out of the goodness of his or her heart but rather due to the coercive threat of court sanction if he or she fails to do so. Moreover, the work performed by the responding party will not only help the requesting party but often actually harm the interests of the responding party him- or herself. These differences, however, make even more bizarre the seemingly universal but wholly unsupported assumption that discovery costs are appropriately attributed to the responding party, rather than to the requesting party.

It should be clear that as both a legal and moral matter, the costs of discovery are properly attributable, in the first instance, to the requesting party. By imposing the costs of discovery on the responding party, then, our system has effectively required the responding party to provide a subsidy to the requesting party. To be sure, assuming no constitutional problems, the system may choose to order such a subsidy. But because those who created the system implicitly—and inaccurately—assumed that the cost of discovery was properly seen as a cost to be borne by the responding party, our system has provided for a hidden subsidy, recognized by no one. At the very least, democracy demands that the decisions of those who make fundamental choices of social policy make clear what those choices actually are, so a transparent debate of whether it is fair to impose such a subsidy may finally take place. This has never been done in the case of discovery costs.

Cost Allocation and the Externalities of the Discovery Process

Wholly apart from this complete lack of transparency, the implicit assumption that the costs of discovery are to be attributed to the responding party makes little sense, from any theoretical or practical perspective. This is particularly true when coupled with the broad scope of discovery in the age of informational technology. In addition to its moral and legal bases, attribution of the costs of discovery to the discovering party, rather than the responding party, is likely to have significant instrumental benefits, because it would cure what has long been a fundamental economic pathology plaguing the discovery process: the externality inherent in the choice to invoke discovery. Simply put, under the prevailing practice the cost-benefit decision whether or not to invoke the discovery process is made by a party who risks incurring no cost, only benefit, even though it is quite conceivable that the choice will impose a significant cost on others.

This lack of economic disincentive underscores what may well be a far greater harm to the system than intentionally abusive discovery: what can be most appropriately labeled "excessive" discovery. This concept includes discovery that, while not consciously interposed for purposes of delay or harassment, nevertheless gives rise to costs greater than its benefits in finding truth. It is widely recognized that the value of finding truth cannot be considered in a vacuum, wholly divorced from the costs to which the

effort gives rise.[8] A rough judgment must always be made by some decision maker whether the likely benefit to come from the effort justifies the
effort's costs. Yet when the responding party, rather than the requesting
party, bears the costs of the process, the requesting party has absolutely no
economic disincentive not to make the request, regardless of its costs. Indeed, given that it is the requesting party's opponent who will bear that
cost, one might even suggest that in a perverse sense, the higher the cost
the greater the incentive to invoke the discovery process.

This focus on the subtle but important differences between "abusive"
and "excessive" discovery underscores the manner in which a reversal in
the ex ante presumption of discovery cost attribution can function in a
symbiotic manner with both the direct and prophylactic methods of discovery control. While those more judicially driven practices are more likely
to punish or deter *abusive* discovery, the self-executing shift in discovery
cost allocation is far more likely to deter the practice of *excessive* discovery.

The key social problem to which imposition of discovery costs on the
requesting party might give rise derives from its inherently regressive nature: the poor will be more immediately and seriously impacted by such
costs than will the rich. To be sure, this is also true of all litigation costs,
though this fact has never caused us to shift all of the poor's litigation
costs to the wealthier party. Moreover, particularly in the case of complex
class action lawsuits, the real party in interest will not be the individual
plaintiff but rather the plaintiff's attorneys, for whom the funding of such
suits is simply a cost of doing business. In these cases, it would be wrong
to see this alteration in discovery cost allocation as an inherently regressive
practice. In any event, if there are particular substantive rights that the
governmental body decides require procedural subsidization, that body
may say so at the time it creates those rights. Therefore, even if one were to
find the regressive impact of this reversal in cost allocation to be a matter
of concern, a wholesale rejection of the cost allocation model would not be
justified.

Even if society were to decide to subsidize a poorer litigant's discovery
in particular suits, it hardly makes sense to impose that cost on the opponent, rather than on society as a whole. Indeed, to allow a private individual's

unilateral filing of a lawsuit to justify imposition of discovery costs on the defendant gives rise to serious constitutional concerns of due process. The Supreme Court has long held that due process prohibits the deprivation of a defendant's property absent meaningful judicial involvement in the determination of that defendant's culpability.[9]

A conceivable objection to the reversal of the current cost allocation model might be that such a practice would simply shift the externality, for under the new model the responding party will have no incentive to keep costs down. But it is the discovering party who sets the contours of the response by the scope of its inquiries or production requests. In an important sense, then, the outer limits of the costs that the responding party will incur are set out by the requesting party. In any event, there always exists the possibility of judicial intervention to determine that the submitted costs are excessive. While it might be responded that such intervention would significantly increase the systemic burdens of the discovery process, it is highly unlikely that judicial intervention would be required in many instances. If the responding party knows that any excessive costs it incurs may well not be reimbursed, it is unlikely to risk incurring them in the first place.

Proposing Amendments to the Discovery Rules

While formal amendment of the pleading rules may not be essential, the same is not true of the discovery process. As explained earlier, the key to taming the discovery process is to understand that, in the first instance, the costs of discovery are appropriately seen as costs attributable to the requesting party, rather than the responding party. While in its current form, Rule 26(c), authorizing the issuance of protective orders, is framed in a manner that vests broad discretion in the district court's hands to "shift" costs, such a power is only rarely employed. In any event, the point of the amendment would not be merely to *authorize* the court to *shift* costs, but rather expressly to attribute the costs, in the first instance, to the requesting party. Rule 26 should therefore be amended to state unambiguously that discovery costs are attributable to the requesting party, unless applicable substantive law provides to the contrary or the court finds that a compelling reason for shifting the costs to the responding party exists.[10]

Conclusion

First-year law students have long been taught that law is not simple; there are invariably conceptual and practical complexities that must be carefully balanced. Though it is perhaps difficult for us now to see it, the genius of the drafters of the original Federal Rules was their ability to recognize those complexities and to seek carefully to balance the competing needs as a means of achieving a solution that takes all of those complexities into account.

The drafters of the Rules, of course, were only human, and humans make mistakes—especially in the process of revolutionizing an entire system. In the discovery process, their first mistake was their failure even to consider the question of to whom discovery costs were to be appropriately attributed in the first instance. Their second mistake was their flawed implicit assumption that the costs were properly to be attributed not to the party who is best able to economically internalize the costs and benefits of discovery, but to the party who has little or no control over those decisions. It is now time to correct their errors—and get ready to wish them a happy birthday.

Notes

1. See generally Michael E. Smith, Judge Charles E. Clark and the Federal Rules of Civil Procedure, 85 Yale L. J. 914 (1976).

2. See Hickman v. Taylor, 329 U.S. 495, 500–501 (1947).

3. Id. at 507.

4. See Bell Atlantic Corp. v. Twombly, 550 U.S. 544, 559 (2007):

It is no answer to say that a claim just shy of a plausible entitlement to relief can, if groundless, be weeded out early in the discovery process through "careful case management" . . . given the common lament that the success of judicial supervision in checking discovery abuse has been on the modest side. See, e.g., Easterbrook, Discovery as Abuse, 69 B. U. L. Rev. 635, 638 (1989) ("Judges can do little about impositional discovery when parties control the legal claims to be presented and conduct the discovery themselves"). And it is self-evident that the problem of discovery abuse cannot be solved by "careful scrutiny of evidence at the summary judgment stage," much less "lucid instructions to juries," post, at 1975; the threat of discovery expense will push cost-conscious defendants to settle even anemic cases before reaching those proceedings. Probably, then, it is only by taking care to require allegations that reach the level suggesting conspiracy that we can hope to avoid the potentially enormous expense of discovery in cases with no " 'reasonably founded hope that the [discovery] process will reveal relevant evidence' " to support a [Sherman Act] § 1 claim.

5. Id. at 558–559.

6. Martin H. Redish and Colleen McNamara, Back to the Future: Discovery Cost Allocation and Modern Procedural Theory, 79 Geo. Wash. L. Rev. 14–18 (forthcoming), available at http://ssrn.com/abstract=1621944.

7. Id.

8. See Mathews v. Eldridge, 424 U.S. 319 (1976) (adopting a test that balances systemic costs against goal of accuracy in determining procedural due process).

9. See, e.g., Fuentes v. Shevin, 407 U.S. 67 (1972).

10. Beyond this amendment, it would also make sense for the Advisory Committee to consider possible alternative methods of directly controlling discovery. One such method that has been suggested is restriction of the scope of available discovery. For example, respected organizations have suggested: "Discovery in general and document discovery in particular should be limited to documents or information that would enable a party to prove or disprove a claim or defense or enable a party to impeach a witness." See, e.g., Am. College of Trial Lawyers & Inst. for the Advancement of the Am. Legal Syst., Final Report 7 (2009), Final Report on the Joint Project of the American College of Trial Lawyers Task Force on Discovery and the Institute for the Advancement of the American Legal System 14 (2009) at 8. That question, however, is an issue on which this article takes no position.

Does Increased Litigation Increase Justice in a Second-Best World?

JEREMY KIDD AND TODD J. ZYWICKI

T he other articles in this book contain a wealth of evidence—both empirical and anecdotal—that something is amiss with America's legal system.[1] The exact diagnoses, as well as the prescribed remedies, are varied, as one might expect when economists and lawyers have been tasked with diagnosis and treatment, but there is significant agreement that, as it pertains to our legal system, American "exceptionalism" has dramatically increased costs with minimal corresponding benefits. In blazing new trails to legal liability, America certainly remains exceptional, but not in a way that will engender the envy of the rest of the world.

The view that something is amiss in the American legal system is not limited to proponents of tort reform. Trial lawyers seem to agree that reforms are needed, but they are much more likely to argue that the American legal system is broken because access to the courts is too limited. This argument is often made in economic terms, that greater access to the courts would be largely beneficial as a means of forcing parties to internalize externalities and provide optimal levels of deterrence. This argument favors reforms such as loosening restrictions on third-party financing of lawsuits in order to alleviate the financial burden on victims and on lawyer advertising in order to inform victims of the available options for legal recourse. There are very good reasons to believe that, in an ideal world, allowing third-party financing of lawsuits and greater lawyer advertising might yield the benefits argued by pro-access reformers.[2] Taking the arguments contained in this book as given, however, it is evident that we do not live in an ideal world when it comes to the modern American legal system.

Assuming that American litigation levels are excessive, we then ask whether procedural reforms that would increase litigation are benign. Our critique is targeted—we acknowledge the obvious benefits of litigation in many areas of the private law. But we also note that there are categories of cases where those benign conclusions do not hold—perhaps a minority of cases, to be sure, but an identifiable minority of cases that arguably exert an oversized influence over the evolution of the law and the perception of the American legal system's efficiency and fairness. In such cases, procedural reforms that commend themselves in a first-best world are not suitable for the second-best world in which we live.

The Second-Best World of U.S. Tort Law

Although most pro-access reformers phrase their arguments in moral, non-measurable terms, such as "improving access to justice," there are in theory more substantial benefits from allowing access to the courts. Tort law punishes those who impose harms through wrongful behavior, with costs to the individual victim and (where the victim is removed from productive activity) society at large. Without tort law requiring the tortfeasor to compensate the victims for the harm, the tortfeasor avoids bearing all the costs of his wrongful behavior and will engage in an inefficiently high level of tortious behavior. In an ideal world, the tort system promotes economic efficiency by enabling victims of tortious conduct to obtain redress, forcing tortfeasors to internalize their dangerous actions and thereby deterring future wrongful and wasteful behavior. Reducing barriers to access—cost, informational, or otherwise—can lead to improvements in individual and societal welfare and can improve efficiency in an ideal world. Because the consequences of any pro-access reforms can be far-reaching, it is necessary to ask how close our world is to the ideal.

Economists are often criticized for relying too heavily on the assumption of an ideal world where efficient outcomes are easily achieved. To many people, economists look like they are stacking the deck in favor of their conclusions.[3] The theory of the second-best[4] arose to address these concerns, and applying the theory allows us to consider how the optimal choice changes when we are dealing with a less-than-ideal, or "second-best," world.

In the theory of the second-best, the "optimal" solution may no longer be efficient, and the second-best solution might be preferable. As one example of this phenomenon, societies regularly face a choice between establishing bright-line rules or less precise standards to govern the conduct of individuals. In dealing with the problem of highway accidents, for example, the state might enact a rule that prohibits driving over 65 miles per hour (mph). Alternatively, it might adopt a standard that penalizes "dangerous driving." In an ideal world where information is costless and resultant errors rare, a dangerous driving standard would identify every such case. In the real world, however, information is costly and errors occur. A dangerous driving standard might then permit some unsafe drivers to escape detection, and it will then be optimal to adopt a bright-line 65-mph rule. Such a rule is a second-best solution, since it will often be overinclusive (and catch drivers who can drive safely at higher speeds) and underinclusive (and excuse drivers who can drive safely only at speeds less than 65 mph).[5] Thus, while standards might be optimal in an ideal world, in the world of the second-best we often turn to rules as the least-costly alternative—even though we know that those rules inevitably will result in errors at times.

The theory of the second-best urges caution in deciding questions of increased access to the courts. Procedural rules that increase litigation levels, even if efficient in a hypothetical first-best world, might not be desirable for two reasons. First, procedural rules that increase litigation will magnify the effects of the substantive legal rules, and if these inefficiently penalize valuable behavior, then the magnification effect will result in greater inefficiency. When in a hole, one should stop digging. And if the evidence presented by other contributors to this volume is correct, we are in a hole.

Second, procedural and substantive rules are plausibly endogenous, in the sense that a more pro-plaintiff set of procedural rules will result in a more pro-plaintiff set of substantive rules. The underlying substantive law is shaped by procedural law, and that substantive law in turn impacts the evolution of procedural rules. For example, procedural rules in many jurisdictions facilitate inefficient forum-shopping that can be used to initiate or accelerate trends in substantive liability by making it easier to bring and win dubious cases. An efficient set of substantive legal rules might thus exist in equipoise with a less than efficient set of procedural rules, with the result that a more generous set of procedural rules will tip the substantive rules in an inefficiently pro-plaintiff direction.

The endogeneity of procedural and substantive rules is in part a consequence of litigation designed to manipulate the path of legal precedent toward more expansive liability and damages, a strategy that has been described as "path manipulation."[6] As new avenues open for litigation, the self-interest of lawyers and financiers will trigger a new wave of frivolous lawsuits, pushing the boundaries of liability even further. This danger is more than merely theoretical; plaintiffs' lawyers have financial incentives to bring claims they know to be non-meritorious, knowing that all they need is a single favorable case to create a precedent that instantly opens the door to new avenues for recovery.[7] Thus a lawyer can suffer several losses, risking only the lawyers' fees and costs at stake in each case. For mass tort defendants, by contrast, every case is a "bet the company" case holding the potential for bankruptcy from an adverse judgment. Tobacco and asbestos claims, for example, were repeatedly rejected by the courts prior to their eventual acceptance, but the size of the payout more than compensated those attorneys who pursued the long-term strategy.[8] In other words, the plaintiffs' bar has strong monetary incentives to *create* liability through repeated litigation of non-meritorious claims.[9]

The same incentives that encourage plaintiffs' lawyers to push the boundaries of liability also encourage expansion of the monetary value of claims for which liability is already established. Plaintiffs' lawyers are likely to compete for clients in both price and quantity. Price competition occurs in the size of the contingency fee demanded by the lawyer. Quantity competition occurs, at least in part, in the size of damages award promised. It is essentially costless to claim higher damages, especially in the difficult-to-measure areas of non-pecuniary and punitive damages, where pleading requirements typically do not require particularity in the amount of damages, and expert testimony on damages can be modified at essentially zero cost.

External Costs of Excessive Litigation

Increased access to the courts might usefully force tortfeasors to internalize the costs of their harm and thereby deter wrongdoing. However, litigants and their lawyers also externalize some of the costs of their lawsuits.[10] First, because the court system is subsidized by the public, lawyers and litigants do not bear the full cost of congestion that they impose upon the court or the full cost associated with distinguishing valid from invalid claims, and thus impose the cost of "weeding out meritless claims" on defendants and judges.[11]

Second, the increased litigiousness imposes additional costs on defendants. They must worry not only about their out-of-pocket costs for defending the case and liability for baseless claims, but also about the costs of harm to their reputation (even from false claims if such claims are imperfectly verifiable) and the opportunity costs from time taken by senior executives and others to participate in litigation.[12]

Third, as Judge Jack observed in the silica litigation,[13] plaintiffs might themselves be harmed. Plaintiffs with meritorious claims are prejudiced when the court is congested with thousands of meritless claims that divert scarce judicial resources and attention from their claims and reduce the amount of defendants' resources available to them. These costs seem especially large in the context of high-profile nationwide class action cases that may drag on for years and involve countless hours of highly intrusive discovery proceedings.

Finally, litigation also imposes costs on society at large. The plaintiffs' bar equates increased litigation with increased access to justice, but neglects to mention the cost of that justice. It is estimated that the direct costs of the tort system make up almost 2% of GDP,[14] and half of those costs are merely the administrative costs to run the system.[15] The indirect costs are even greater. As discussed in other articles in this book, although litigation might improve products safety (although even that is unclear), the litigation system is exceedingly inefficient in doing so. Moreover, increased safety also increases the price of the goods, and to the extent that the legal system imposes excessive costs, consumers are made worse off by the higher prices that result. Producers might also design products in an unduly risk-averse fashion in order to avoid the risk, cost, adverse publicity, and uncertainty of litigation, even if they expect to prevail in the end. Other beneficial products are even kept off the markets due to the uncertainty regarding potential product liability claims, depriving consumers of these products entirely.[16] New, innovative products are particularly susceptible to this form of strategic litigation, and consumers are hurt as they are denied the benefits of technological and other innovation. U.S. businesses suffer billions of dollars in lost sales each year,[17] not to mention the jobs those lost sales represent. Litigation diverts numerous non-legal personnel from productive work, costing businesses thousands of hours in foregone productive work,[18] and the riches transferred through the litigation system draw talented youth into law schools to become lawyers, thereby drawing them away from alternative employment.[19] The fear of lawsuits also results in wasteful defensive actions, such as "defensive medicine," making medical judgments on the basis of avoiding malpractice suits rather than in the best medical interests of the patient.[20]

When all direct or indirect costs are totaled, it is estimated that the U.S. tort system costs between $600 billion and $900 billion per year, or between 4.3% and 6.5% of GDP.[21] These costs will only increase as pro-access reforms generate even more claims.

Third-Party Financing

Where third-party financing is permitted, the financier pays the plaintiff's portion of the costs of the litigation, in return for a portion of the payout awarded by the court. The loan is non-recourse, which means that the plaintiff does not have to repay the loan if the action is unsuccessful. In this respect, third-party financing is simply an extension of contingency fee arrangements, with the difference that the plaintiff's lawyers pass on the risk to the financiers.[22]

In the economic downturn of the past few years, third-party financing has proved highly attractive to the plaintiffs bar. It permits lawyers to pass on the risk of non-success in a case to the financier, and amounts to a form of inventory financing.

Third-party financing can be expected to increase the level of litigation for two reasons. First, the practice reduces the risk exposure of the plaintiff's lawyers and permits them to pursue more claims. Second, the financier will likely be permitted to take a greater stake in the outcome than a law firm might, and become in effect a purchaser of the claim.[23]

In a first-best world, third-party financing might usefully increase access to justice by impecunious plaintiffs who cannot afford to bear the costs of pursuing a claim, or who (being risk-averse) will find it efficient to sell the claim to a risk-neutral financier qua insurer.[24] However, third-party financing would also magnify the inefficiencies of the American tort system. If litigation is excessive today, it will become more excessive still when barriers to litigation are relaxed, and all of the problems outlined above will come back in spades.

Third-party financing was formerly banned as "champerty," and it remains prohibited in most states. One reason given for the ban is that, while lawyer misbehavior is constrained by codes of professional responsibility, financiers are not subject to any such duties. Thus, it is thought, financiers will call the shots and finance unmeritorious claims that lawyers would hesitate to bring on their own.[25] However, a casual look at the cases brought without third-party financing suggests that codes of ethics have done little to deter unmeritorious claims. In addition, the financier might plausibly reduce certain kinds of lawyer misbehavior, since the financier will have a greater stake in the outcome and will be well positioned to police erring lawyers. This will be particularly true of a prominent kind of misbehavior, where lawyers on both sides work out a settlement in which the plaintiff's lawyer receives virtually all of the payout. That's not something third-party financiers are likely to permit.

Attorney Advertising

Historically, attorney advertising was strictly regulated by state bar associations, and these restrictions were later codified by the American Bar Associations Code of Professional Responsibility. In 1977, however, the

United States Supreme Court struck down many of these restrictions in
Bates v. State Bar of Arizona.[26] *Bates* held that to the extent that such restrictions prohibited the provision of truthful advertising to consumers,
they advanced no economic or professionalism purpose and ran afoul of
the First Amendment. Subsequent cases have extended the holding of
Bates to protect a wide variety of lawyer (and other professional) advertising in a variety of media, often with the resistance of organized bar associations.

Economists have long recognized that advertising can, and usually
does, play a valuable role in improving economic welfare and consumer
welfare, and this in general might be true of lawyer advertising. First, advertising can alert tort victims of possible legal remedies and the benefits
of choosing a particular law firm that may have experience in the type of
harm suffered by the tort victim.[27] Without this information, a tort victim
may be unaware that legal remedies exist, and simply not bring a claim, or
else the search costs will cause the tort victim to make a suboptimal choice
of attorney, unnecessarily reducing the likelihood of obtaining redress.
Second, advertising can identify a legal firm in the minds of consumers,
and the heightened reputational concerns will give it stronger incentives to
provide good services.[28] This is especially valuable for law firms, as tort
victims would otherwise find it very difficult to measure lawyer quality.
Third, advertising can promote price competition and efficient scale economies, which can lead, in turn, to lower prices. Empirical studies of the
impact of advertising of professional services, including lawyers, generally
have found that advertising produces lower prices without any discernible
decline in quality.[29]

Today lawyer advertising is ubiquitous and sophisticated and sweeps in
all types of media: television, newspapers, Yellow Pages, television, radio,
direct mail, and the Internet, often providing "800" telephone numbers
for potential clients to contact lawyers. Stone reports that from 2000 to
2009, television advertising by attorneys (in constant dollars) rose from
$236 million in 2000 to $394 million in 2009.[30] Advertising in print media rose from $47 million to $81 million, and radio and Internet advertising doubled from $5 million in 2001 to $10 million in 2009. Overall, in
2009 attorneys spent over $485 million on advertising outlays. Attorneys

have also become proficient at garnering free news coverage about harms caused by a product, an effort often facilitated by consumer advocacy groups "closely aligned with mass tort lawyers."[31]

Although attorney advertising can be economically beneficial in many cases, these benefits are less clear in mass tort cases, where there are also substantial costs that may not be present in other contexts. As in the traditional case, advertising might be useful to help an injured person learn about his or her potential claim and locate a lawyer who will bring it. But there is good reason to believe that the benefits of attorney advertising are smaller in mass liability cases.

This is because of the way mass tort claims are structured and pursued. In a traditional tort case, an individual who is harmed seeks out an attorney who then assists in seeking redress for the harm. In mass tort actions, however, this dynamic is turned on its head. Attorney advertising dramatically expands the potential for litigation because it permits lawyers to take the initiative in recruiting legal claimants, especially for class actions. Advertising therefore enables plaintiffs' lawyers to act entrepreneurially in creating lawsuits. Rather than awaiting injured plaintiffs to come to them with actual claims, advertising allows lawyers to identify *potential claims* first, and then recruit clients to bring these claims. When combined with the power of class action lawsuits, this allows lawyers to initiate suit with little in the way of real clients and then to recruit clients after devising novel claims to pursue.[32] The advertisements are often nakedly mercenary rather than medical—one direct marketing company recruited potential claimants with the sales pitch "Find out if you have Million Dollar Lungs."[33]

Many of the possible benefits of attorney advertising, found in general litigation, are attenuated or absent in mass tort cases. First, there is no indication that advertising leads to lower prices for legal services for contingency fee cases in general or mass torts specifically. In theory, amassing tens of thousands of claimants into one class action could create economies of scale in production that could be passed on to class members in the forms of lower prices. However, there is little evidence that lawyers compete on price in contingency fee cases or that their advertisements even disclose the contingency fee percentage at all.[34] In mass tort claims, the retainer contingency fee is almost always between 33% and 40% of the recovery.[35] According to RAND's analysis of asbestos litigation, claimants' total legal expenses, including lawyers' fees and other expenses, averaged 39% of gross compensation in 1984 and in 2002. As RAND notes, "Although plaintiff lawyers may have recognized savings from routinization of the litigation (e.g. the widespread use of administrative payment schedules) . . . none of those we interviewed suggested that any of the savings have been passed on to claimants."[36]

Second, advertising in the mass tort context also may be of less value in providing a reputational bond for lawyers to consumers and less valuable in enabling entry of new lawyers into the market. Instead, the market for these cases today appears to be concentrated among a relatively small and discrete group of lawyers who effectively work together and divide the relevant product markets. As noted, price competition seems to be largely absent from these arrangements, eliminating the ability of new firms to enter by undercutting price. Similarly, the massive up-front funding cost of these cases, as well as the start-up costs of advertising to recruit plaintiffs, suggests that the need to advertise might act more as a barrier to, rather than a vehicle for, entry by law firms.

Third, attorney advertising might tend to promote bogus claims. Once potential plaintiffs begin to respond to the advertising, they must be "screened," a process that has been found to be rife with fraud.[37] Often the harms claimed by plaintiffs are difficult to verify objectively, such as shortness of breath, headaches, or insomnia. Moreover, plaintiff recruitment advertising often "helpfully" informs plaintiffs of the symptoms that they must manifest upon examination in order to be included in the class. In addition, the costs of litigation are especially large in the context of high-profile nationwide class-action cases that may drag on for years and involve countless hours of highly intrusive discovery proceedings, and this gives plaintiffs a powerful threat advantage. Amassing tens of thousands of claims, often for little more than minor injuries, lawyers can use the sheer volume of the claims as a vehicle to steamroll defendants into settlement.

Attorney advertising in the mass tort context can also facilitate improper forum-shopping by plaintiffs.[38] Mass media advertising, such as television or Internet advertising, makes it possible to recruit class members from across the country. Thus, rather than being constrained to file a case in the plaintiff's place of residence, attorneys can select the court with the most favorable likely result and then recruit class members from around the country to join the class. Brickman observes that improper forum-shopping was made easier by the very liberal joinder rules in Mississippi and West Virginia, two states with unusually pro-plaintiff courts.[39] Lawyers often found at least one properly venued plaintiff who had an especially compelling case, and joined that case to hundreds or thousands of more dubious cases recruited by litigation screenings. This ability to put forth an attractive local plaintiff at the front of the mass led defendants to fear that a local jury would award compensatory and punitive damages that could bankrupt the company. In light of this risk, and the inability to weed out the weak claims from the strong, defendants have been driven to settle frivolous claims.

Fourth, attorney advertising in mass tort cases does not appear to provide the informational benefits that other types of advertising do. For example, drug company advertising can inform consumers about untreated health problems and potential treatments. By contrast, lawyer advertising about health claims simply directs website visitors to law firms.[40] And they move quickly. A study in *CMAJ,* the journal of the Canadian Medical Association, examined the growth in Internet websites following the publication of a study in the *New England Journal of Medicine* and found that within a week of the online pre-release of an article on the dangers of a particular antibiotic (gatifloxacin) there were almost 100 Internet websites providing information on personal injury lawsuits.[41]

Under Google Adwords, advertisers can bid to have their advertisements appear first on the list of advertisers that arise when a consumer inserts a specific search term. Google charges the advertiser a price based on the number of times the sponsoring website is clicked. In 2009, the price for the search term "mesothelioma" reached $99.44 per click.[42] A 2006 review of Google Adwords found that the list of highest-priced keywords was dominated by lawyer advertisements for keywords related to mass torts.[43] For example, the top four health-related keywords were variations on searches for "mesothelioma": "peritoneal mesothelioma" ($48.38 per click), "mesothelioma" ($33.83), "mesothelioma symptoms" ($31.41), and "mesothelioma info" ($25.79). The remainder of the top ten highest-priced keywords were dominated by terms related to "mesothelioma" and "asbestos." As these extremely high prices for Internet keyword search terms indicates, the ability of lawyers to reach consumers directly by highly targeted Internet advertising is extremely lucrative. The Web domains mesothelioma.com and asbestos.com are both owned by law firms, and are designed to recruit litigation plaintiffs rather than to provide health information.

What to Do?

If the evidence presented by other contributors to this volume is correct, we have moved well beyond the efficient level of litigation, and society suffers because of it. We live in a second-best world, and this must affect how one regards procedural reforms that might commend themselves in a first-best world. We are not opposed to third-party financing and lawyer advertising, in principle. However, in the brave new world created for us by plaintiffs' lawyers and their allies, the alluring promises of increased efficiency through increased access to the court must be resisted as illusory.

Notes

1. See particularly George Priest's discussion of the expansion of liability at tort law.

2. See, e.g., Peter C. Coharis, A Comprehensive Market Solution for Tort Reform, 12 Yale J. Reg. 435 (1995); Robert Cooter, Towards a Market in Unmatured Tort Claims, 75 Va. L. Rev. 383 (1989); Mark J. Shukaitis, A Market in Personal Injury Tort Claims, 16 J. Legal Stud. 329 (1985).

3. As the criticism is usually stated, arguments about efficiency and the "optimal" outcome rely on unreasonable assumptions, rendering any predictions based on those assumptions inherently unreliable. In fairness, it should be noted that, in many cases, whether or not the optimality conditions are perfectly realistic is not central to the research being conducted, and, as such, it is unnecessary to engage in a lengthy defense of the optimality conditions.

4. Richard G. Lipsey and Kelvin Lancaster, The General Theory of Second Best, 24 Rev. Econ. Stud. 11 (1956).

5. Isaac Ehrlich and Richard A. Posner, An Economic Analysis of Legal Rule-making, 3 J. Legal Stud. 257 (1974).

6. Maxwell L. Stearns, Standing back from the Forest: Justiciability and Social Choice, 83 Cal. L. Rev. 1309 (1995).

7. Martin J. Bailey and Paul H. Rubin, A Positive Theory of Legal Change, 14 Int'l Rev. L. & Econ. 467 (1994); Paul H. Rubin and Martin J. Bailey, The Role of Lawyers in Changing the Law, 23 J. Legal Stud. 807 (1994). Zywicki details how this form of path manipulation was impossible before the evolution of the doctrine of stare decisis in the nineteenth century. Todd J. Zywicki, The Rise and Fall of Efficiency in the Common Law: A Supply-Side Analysis, 97 Nw. U. L. Rev. 1551 (2003).

8. Walter K. Olson, The Rule of Lawyers: How the New Litigation Elite Threatens America's Rule of Law (2003).

9. It can be very difficult and expensive for defendants to examine each plaintiff in order to determine the veracity of the plaintiff's claim. Lester Brickman, The Use of Litigation Screenings in Mass Torts: A Formula for Fraud?, 61 S.M.U. L. Rev. 1221 (2008).

10. Michael P. Stone, Optimal Attorney Advertising. Working paper, University of Connecticut Department of Economics, July 2010, available at http://www.econ.uconn.edu/working/2010–14.pdf.

11. In re Silica Products Liability Litigation, 398 F. Supp. 2d 563, 636 (S.D. Tex. 2005).

12. Todd J. Zywicki, Spontaneous Order and the Common Law: Gordon Tullock's Critique, 135 Pub. Choice 35 (2008).

13. In re Silica, 398 F. Supp. 2d at 636.

14. Tillinghast–Towers Perrin, 2008 Updates on U.S. Tort Cost Trends (2008), available at http://www.towersperrin.com/tp/getwebcachedoc?webc=USA/2008/200811/2008_tort_costs_trends.pdf.

15. Id.

16. Theodore H. Frank, Riverboat Poker & Paradoxes: The Vioxx Mass Tort Settlement, Legal Backgrounder 23, no. 12 (2008).

17. Lawrence J. McQuillan, Hovannes Abramyan and Anthony P. Archie, Jackpot Justice: The True Cost of America's Tort System (2007).

18. Laurence H. Silberman, Will Lawyering Strangle Democratic Capitalism?, 15 Regulation, March/April 1978.

19. Theodore H. Frank, Protecting Main Street from Lawsuit Abuse. Testimony before the Senate Republican Conference, March 16, 2009, available at http://www.aei.org/docLib/Frank%20testimony.pdf.

20. The U.S. Department of Health and Human Services reported that 79% of all physicians report ordering more tests than they believe are medically necessary because of litigation fears. The same survey indicated that 74% report referring more patients to specialists, 51% report recommending greater numbers of invasive procedures, and 41% report prescribing more medications than they believe medically necessary. U.S. Department of Health and Human Services, Confronting the New Health Care Crisis: Improving Health Care Quality and Lowering Costs by Fixing Our Medical Liability System, July 24, 2002. Doctors expended $124 billion in unnecessary health care costs in response to the threat of medical malpractice lawsuits. McQuillan, Jackpot Justice, supra note 17.

21. Frank, supra note 19.

22. Similarly, the common law doctrine known as the collateral source rule allows victims to receive help with living and medical expenses, without reducing the amount they are entitled to recover from the tortfeasor. See Michael Krauss and Jeremy Kidd, Collateral Source and Tort's Soul, 48 U. Louisville L. Rev. 1 (2010).

23. In class action litigation, however, the reality is that the entire payout might effectively end up in the pockets of the plaintiffs' lawyers.

24. Contingency fees will have alleviated both such concerns, of course.

25. See John Beisner, Jessica Miller, and Gary Rubin, Selling Lawsuits, Buying Trouble: Third-Party Litigation Funding in the United States (U.S. Chamber Institute for Legal Reform, 2009).

26. Bates v. State Bar of Arizona, 433 U.S. 350 (1977).

27. For more detailed discussions of how advertising can alert consumers to important product attributes in other areas, see Pauline M. Ippolito and Alan D. Mathios, Information, Advertising, and Health Choices: A Study of the Cereal Market, 21 RAND J. Econ. 459 (1990); Pat Kelly, Perspective: DTC Advertising's Benefits Far Outweigh Its Imperfections, Health Affairs, April 28, 2004, at W4; Dominick Frosch, David Grande, Derjung M. Tam, and Richard L. Kravitz, A Decade of Controversy: Balancing Policy with Evidence in the Regulation of Prescription Drug Advertising, 100 Am. J. Pub. Health 24 (2010).

28. Benjamin Klein and Keith B. Leffler, The Role of Market Forces in Assuring Contractual Performance, 89 J. Pol. Econ. 615 (1981). See also Richard J. Cebula, Does Lawyer Advertising Adversely Influence the Image of Lawyers in the United States? An Alternative Perspective and New Empirical Evidence, 27 J. Legal Stud. 503 (1998); Robert E. Hite and Joseph A. Bellizzi, Consumers Attitudes Toward Accountants, Lawyers, and Physicians with Respect to Advertising Professional Services, 26 J. Advert. Res. 45 (1986).

29. See James H. Love and Frank H. Stephen, Advertising, Price and Quality in Self-Regulating Professions: A Survey, 3 Int'l J. Econ. Bus. 227 (1996); Timothy J. Muris, California Dental Association v. Federal Trade Commission: The Revenge of Footnote 1.7, 8 Sup. Ct. Econ. Rev. 265 (2000); Timothy J. Muris and Fred S. McChesney, Advertising and the Price and Quality of Legal Services: The Case for Legal Clinics, 4 Am. B. Found. Res. J. 179 (1979).

30. Stone, supra note 10.

31. Brickman, supra note 9, at 226. For example, the silicone breast implant litigation was given a major boost by a widely viewed but completely unsupported television news broadcast by reporter Connie Chung.

32. See Robert A. Kagan, Do Lawyers Cause Adversarial Legalism? A Preliminary Inquiry, 19 L. & Soc. Inquiry 1 (1994); Jack B. Weinstein, Ethical Dilemmas in Mass Tort Litigation, 88 Nw. U. L. Rev. 469 (1994).

33. Judyth Pendell, Regulating Attorney-Funded Mass Medical Screenings: A Public Health Imperative? Working paper, AEI-Brookings Joint Center for Regula-

tory Studies, September 2005, available at http://regulation2point0.org/wp-content/uploads/downloads/2010/04/phpZI3.pdf.

34. Jeffrey O'Connell, Carlos M. Brown, and Michael D. Smith, Yellow Page Ads as Evidence of Widespread Overcharging by the Plaintiff's Personal Injury Bar—and a Proposed Solution, 6 Conn. Ins. L.J. 423 (2000).

35. Judyth Pendell, Regulating Attorney-Funded Mass Medical Screenings: A Public Health Imperative?, AEI-Brookings Joint Center for Regulatory Studies 05-22 (Sept. 2005).

36. Stephen J. Carroll, Deborah Hensler, Jennifer Gross, Elizabeth M. Sloss, Matthias Schonlau, Allan Abrahamse, and J. Scott Ashwood, Asbestos Litigation 103 (RAND Institute for Civil Justice, May 2005).

37. Brickman estimates, for example, that in the average litigation screening for occupational exposure to asbestos, 50% to 60% will be diagnosed with asbestosis, compared with only 3% to 4% who would be diagnosed in a clinical setting. Brickman, supra note 9. Pendell reports that between 1986 and 2004 there were "at least four impartial panels of scientists who . . . evaluated the accuracy of litigation-related asbestos diagnoses, and they have found the rate of false positives from the screening companies to range from 66% to 97%. Pendell, Medical Screenings, supra note 35. See also Joseph N. Gitlin, Leroy L. Cook, Otha W. Linton, and Elizabeth Garrett-Mayer, Comparison of "B" Readers' Interpretations of Chest Radiographs for Asbestos Related Changes, 11 Acad. Radiology 843 (2004). In the class action cases involving 10,000 silicosis claims generated by litigation screenings, United States District Court Judge Janis Jack concluded that the doctors who rendered the diagnoses on which the claims were brought and the lawyers who ordered the screenings were willing participants in a scheme to manufacture diagnoses for money. In re Silica, 398 F. Supp. 2d 563.

38. It should be emphasized that not all forum-shopping is necessarily bad. Ex ante forum-shopping, such as by contractual choice of law, likely conduces to economic efficiency. One-sided ex post forum-shopping in the tort class action context, however, is likely to create suboptimal outcomes. Todd J. Zywicki, Is Forum Shopping Corrupting America's Bankruptcy Courts?, 83 Geo. L. J. 1309 (1995).

39. Brickman, supra note 9, at 1230.

40. Id. at 1226.

41. David N. Juurlink, Laura Y. Park-Wyllie, and Moira K. Kapral, The Effect of Publication on Internet-Based Solicitation of Personal-Injury Litigants, 177 Canadian Medical Ass'n J. 1369 (2007).

42. Laurie Sullivan, Top Keyword Price Nears $100 Per Click, Online Media Daily, Oct. 14, 2009, http://www.mediapost.com/publications/?fa=Articles.showArticle&art_aid=115431.

43. Top Paying Keywords, Impact Lab, January 22, 2006, http://www.impactlab.net/2006/01/22/top-paying-keywords/.

PART 5:

TORT LAW

A Tamer Tort Law

THE CANADA-U.S. DIVIDE

MICHAEL TREBILCOCK AND PAUL-ERIK VEEL

Tort law in its traditional forms has been under attack from a variety of perspectives for several decades. On the one hand, enormous damage awards are said to drive up the costs of engaging in certain socially useful activities—such as providing certain types of medical care or innovative products—to the point that those activities are driven out the market. On the other hand, critics charge that the tort system does a poor job of providing compensation to the vast majority of people who have suffered injuries. As such, the tort system is often characterized as an unjust lottery: a small number of plaintiffs receive unjustifiably large awards for non-pecuniary losses and punitive damages, while many others are denied even a modicum of compensation to pay for necessary medical care.

Our purpose in this article is not to contribute to the expansive empirical literature on whether or to what extent there is truly a "crisis" in tort law,[1] nor is it to argue in favor of or against the replacement of the tort system in whole or in part with various no-fault compensation schemes.[2] Rather, starting from the assumption that the social cost of contemporary American tort law is higher than is desirable, our intention here is to provide a comparison between the reasonably similar tort regimes of the United States and Canada, with the goal of suggesting more modest reforms to lower the direct costs of the tort system.

While both American and Canadian tort regimes share broad substantive and procedural similarities, Canadian tort law has historically been more conservative in a variety of respects, where by conservative we simply mean that Canadian tort law is relatively less favorable to plaintiffs. Perhaps for this reason, there has been much less of a public debate over a tort law "crisis" in Canada than in the United States.[3] Thus an understanding of the Canadian tort system and how it differs from its American counterpart is useful, as it provides a potential model for a somewhat more conservative tort law regime that nonetheless is broadly similar to the current structure of American tort law.

Canada and America Compared: Is There Less of a Tort Crisis in Canada?

The conventional wisdom is that Canada suffers from less of a "crisis" in tort law than does the United States. Without attempting to define precisely what it means for there to be a "crisis" in tort law, there does seem to be some, albeit limited, empirical support that the direct costs of the tort system are lower in Canada than in the United States.

First, there appears to be some empirical support that there is less tort litigation in Canada than in the United States. A variety of empirical findings suggest that while the number of medical malpractice claims and the severity of the claims have increased over time in both Canada and the United States, proportionate numbers of such claims are still lower in Canada than in the United States.[4] Moreover, it appears that insurance premiums for doctors are lower in Canada than in the United States.[5] Similarly, the amount of products liability litigation in the United States has historically dwarfed such litigation in other jurisdictions.[6] Consistent with these findings, Kritzer, Bogart, and Vidmar find that, in the aftermath of injury, Americans are more likely to bring legal claims than are residents of Ontario.[7] In their article on comparative litigation rates in this volume, Ramseyer and Rasmusen report that for the year ending 2009, 1,450 general civil cases were filed in Canada per 100,000 people, compared with 5,806 in the U.S.

Second, there also appears to be empirical support for the proposition, which depends in part on but is broader than the first proposition, that the direct cost of tort litigation is higher in the United States than it is in Canada. The empirical evidence suggests, for example, that the size of damages awards and various insurance premiums both increased more quickly and reached a higher level in the United States than in Canada between the 1960s and 1980s.[8] Thus, if the crisis in tort law is that direct costs of the tort system are too high, it seems reasonable to conclude that there is less of a tort law crisis in Canada than in the United States.

Canada and America Compared: Liability Standards

In most domains, liability standards are similar in Canada and the United States. For the most part, both tort regimes require a finding of negligence by the defendant, in the sense that he or she has fallen below an expected standard of care, before he or she will be found liable for damages.[9] Both regimes also impose liability without any finding of fault for certain classes of wrongs. For example, both regimes impose strict liability for damages caused by inherently dangerous goods.[10]

However, Canadian and American tort regimes diverge in the area of products liability law. The dominant rule among American jurisdictions is that liability for damages caused by defective products is strict.[11] By contrast, in most Canadian provinces, manufacturer's product liability is still predicated on proof of negligence.[12]

Like American law, Canadian law recognizes the difficulty plaintiffs face in such cases of actually proving that the manufacturer was negligent. However, rather than responding to this problem by adopting a standard of strict liability in the domain of products liability, Canadian courts apply a reformed version of the doctrine of *res ipsa loquitor*.[13] Under this doctrine, the defendant is subject to a tactical burden to demonstrate that it acted in accordance with the requisite standard of care once the plaintiff demonstrates that the object that caused the harm was under the exclusive control of the defendant. Thus it remains open to a manufacturer to avoid liability by demonstrating that reasonable care was used in the manufacture or design of the product and in warning of risks associated with its use. Canadian law thereby recognizes the evidentiary difficulties faced by plaintiffs in products liability cases, yet responds to this difficulty through an evidentiary rather than a substantive solution.

Canadian and American product liability laws also differ in terms of the interaction between product liability and workers' compensation schemes. In both Canada and the United States, in systems where workers' compensation schemes are present, tort claims against workers' employers are generally barred. However, American workers' compensation schemes do not preclude injured workers from suing third parties, such as manufacturers of defective products that injure them in the workplace. By contrast, Canadian schemes often foreclose tort claims by injured workers against not only their employers but also against many third parties in return for no-fault workers' compensation benefits.[14] The Canadian model may be preferable to the American model in this respect, as many product liability claims are removed from the court system, but workers are still compensated for their injuries.

Canada and America Compared: Quantum Rules

A. Non-Pecuniary Losses

Reform-minded academics and policy-makers have paid significant attention to damages for non-pecuniary losses, such as pain and suffering and wrongful death. Such damages are necessarily difficult to translate into pecuniary terms in a just and consistent manner, and have often been extremely large. While both Canada and the United States have sought to cap non-pecuniary damages, the route traveled has been very different.

The Canadian experience with caps on non-pecuniary damages is largely a function of judicial innovation. In a trilogy of cases in the late 1970s, the Supreme Court of Canada limited claims for non-pecuniary losses for personal injuries to $100,000, indexed to inflation, largely out of a concern for the social cost of high non-pecuniary damages awards.[15] As of 2007, this cap sat at roughly $310,000.[16] While the Supreme Court of Canada referred to this cap as a "rough upper limit," this amount has functioned in practice as an absolute cap on the quantum of non-pecuniary damage awards. While individual provinces remain free to modify or abrogate this cap, no province has in fact done so.

The American experience with caps on non-pecuniary damages has been radically different. First, rather than being products of judicial creation, caps on non-pecuniary damages in the United States have been the exclusive creation of state legislatures.[17] Indeed, far from supporting the creation of caps on non-pecuniary damages, courts in a number of states have found them to be unconstitutional.[18] Second, rather than extending to all tort claims, as in Canada, many of the caps on non-pecuniary damages enacted by state legislatures have been confined to certain types of claims, such as medical malpractice claims.[19] Third, while the Canadian caps are nation-wide, the American caps have all been enacted at the state level. While Congress has considered imposing a federal cap on non-pecuniary claims in medical malpractice cases,[20] none of these efforts have thus far resulted in legislation.

The empirical research on the effects of caps on damages has yielded mixed conclusions. While some have found that caps lower payouts,[21] others have suggested that such caps actually increase economic damages, such that there is no significant overall difference in damages with or without caps.[22] Moreover, some authors have theorized that because caps on non-pecuniary damages weaken the deterrent function of tort law, such caps may actually lead to increases in claims.[23]

There has also been some controversy about whether caps reduce the "defensive medicine" of wasteful medical tests and procedures ordered by doctors who are overly concerned about litigation. Intuitively, one would expect this, and some research has confirmed this view.[24] However, Sloan and Shadle find that the enactment of caps on damages did not significantly affect Medicare payouts for various procedures.[25] Unfortunately, there does not appear to be any similar empirical research on the effect of the Supreme Court of Canada's judicially imposed cap in the late 1970s.

B. Punitive Damages

Tort reformers have also sought to limit punitive damages, because of concerns about both the quantum and the inconsistency of such damages.

While there has been some degree of convergence between the two countries, punitive damages awards in the United States still tend to be much larger than those in Canada.[26]

American rules regarding punitive damages vary sharply across states. In some states, punitive damages are prohibited except where explicitly allowed by statute, while in others they are legislatively capped, either at an absolute maximum or at a particular multiple of compensatory damages.[27] However, in most jurisdictions, punitive damages can properly be awarded to further the goals of retribution and deterrence where a defendant's conduct has been "outrageous" or "deplorable." In such cases, the quantum of punitive damages is generally determined by a jury, with appellate courts reviewing jury awards on a fairly deferential standard, sometimes characterized as reasonableness[28] and sometimes as an abuse of discretion.[29]

Beyond simply reviewing juries' punitive damages awards for reasonableness, the U.S. Supreme Court has held that the Eighth Amendment to the Constitution of the United States, which is incorporated against the states via the Fourteenth Amendment, places a constitutional limit on the magnitude of punitive damages. Specifically, the Supreme Court has held that the Eighth Amendment prohibits awards of punitive damages that are "grossly excessive." This in turn will depend on (1) the degree of the defendant's reprehensibility or culpability; (2) the relationship between the penalty and the harm to the victim caused by the defendant's actions; and (3) the sanctions imposed in other cases for comparable misconduct. On this basis, the U.S. Supreme Court held in *BMW v. Gore* that a jury award of $2,000,000 in punitive damages for a plaintiff who found out that a new car he bought had been repainted and for which he received $4,000 in compensatory damages was grossly excessive.[30] However, in other cases, sizeable punitive damages awards have been found to withstand constitutional scrutiny on the "grossly excessive" standard. For example, in *TXO Production,* the Supreme Court upheld as constitutional a punitive damages award for $10,000,000 where actual damages were only $19,000.[31]

Leaving aside constitutional considerations, the Supreme Court has recently signaled a desire to curb what it views as excessive punitive damages awards. In *Exxon Shipping Co.,* an admiralty case, the majority of the Supreme Court found that a jury award of $5 billion in punitive damages was inappropriate.[32] Rather, it held that a one-to-one ratio of compensatory to punitive damages was appropriate, and therefore lowered the punitive damages award to roughly $500 million. While this result was not reached as a matter of constitutional law and is therefore not directly binding on state courts as such, it does signal the U.S. Supreme Court's preference for restraint in the size of punitive damages awards.

The contemporary Canadian law of punitive damages shares a similar normative foundation. As in most jurisdictions in the United States, but unlike in England, punitive damages are not reserved for restricted classes of cases.[33] Punitive damages can be awarded in Canada in order to further deterrence, retribution, and denunciation, and can be awarded only where there has been "high-handed, malicious, arbitrary or highly reprehensible misconduct that departs to a marked degree from ordinary standards of decent behavior."[34]

However, beyond these conceptual similarities, punitive damages are in general much less widely awarded in Canada than they are in the United States. Unlike in the United States, in Canada punitive damages are typically awarded in cases of intentional torts, and rarely awarded in negligence or products liability cases.[35] In addition, the Supreme Court of Canada has held that in cases tried by a jury, the trial judge's charge should inform the jury that "punitive damages are very much the exception rather than the rule."[36] Moreover, "punitive damages are awarded *only* where compensatory damages, which to some extent are punitive, are insufficient to accomplish" the objectives of retribution, deterrence, and denunciation.[37]

Additionally, appellate review of punitive damages is much stricter in Canada than it is in the United States. The Supreme Court of Canada has held that appellate courts have much greater scope and discretion in reviewing punitive damages than they do with respect to other types of general damages.[38] Under Canadian law, the test to be applied by appellate courts in reviewing punitive damages awards is to ask "whether a reasonable jury, properly instructed, could have concluded that an award in that amount, and no less, was rationally required to punish the defendant's misconduct."[39]

Whether for these reasons or for others, punitive damages awards are generally much smaller in Canada than in the United States. A 1991

Ontario Law Commission Study of punitive damages awards found few awards greater than $50,000. While the quantum of punitive damages awards has risen since that time, even today there have been only a handful of Canadian awards exceeding $1,000,000 at any level of court. While the Supreme Court of Canada upheld a punitive damages award of $1,000,000 in *Whiten*[40] and $800,000 in *Hill*,[41] such awards have been rare and have been awarded only in exceptionally egregious circumstances.

While public attention in America focuses on the enormous punitive damages awards of the type seen in the *Exxon Valdez* litigation, many have argued that such awards are relatively rare. One empirical study found that juries rarely award punitive damages, especially in cases that have arguably attracted the most public attention and debate, such as medical malpractice and products liability.[42]

Canada and America Compared: Procedural Rules

Beyond the substantive rules discussed above, procedural rules also play a significant role in the relatively lower prevalence and social costs of tort litigation in Canada.

A. Civil Juries

One noteworthy procedural difference between tort suits in Canada and the United States is the availability and prevalence of jury trials in civil cases. Because civil juries are perceived to have a predilection for excessive damage awards, jury trials are sometimes thought to contribute to the tort crisis in the United States.

In the United States, the right to a jury trial in a large range of civil cases is afforded constitutional protection. Under the Seventh Amendment to the United States Constitution, plaintiffs claiming damages are guaranteed a right to a jury trial. While the Seventh Amendment applies only to federal claims and is not incorporated against the states, a number of state constitutions also contain a right to trial by jury in civil cases.

By contrast, there is no constitutional right to a trial by jury in civil cases in Canada. In Ontario, tort claims for damages can be tried by a jury at the request of either party,[43] but the trial judge retains the discretion to order that an action proceed without a jury.[44] Jury trials are also generally not permissible where equitable relief is claimed[45] or where a claim is brought against the government.[46] Even in situations where a claim could be tried by a jury, jury trials are still relatively rare.

If juries make larger damages awards than do judges sitting alone, the relatively restricted use of jury trials in Canada may help explain the relative absence of a tort crisis in Canada. However, whether juries do systematically award higher damages than do judges sitting alone is not clear. One study found little difference in the way juries and judges award punitive damages.[47] However, Hersch and Viscusi reach the opposite conclusion, finding instead that juries are more likely than judges sitting alone to award punitive damages, and that they also do so at higher levels than judges.[48]

B. Costs

Another area of divergence between the two countries is in the rules relating to the payment of the costs of legal proceedings.[49] Such rules have received significant attention as a possible source of the perceived difference in litigiousness between the United States and the rest of the world. However, as discussed below, the actual impact of these rules remains unclear.

The standard American rule for most proceedings and most jurisdictions is that each party bears its own costs (the so-called no-way cost rule).[50] By contrast, the default costs rule under Anglo-Canadian law is the two-way cost rule, under which the losing party is required to pay a substantial fraction of the winning party's legal costs.[51] While this general principle is the starting point, Ontario law provides judges with significant flexibility as to the quantum of cost awards and even whether such awards should be made at all.[52]

Ontario's cost rules are designed to encourage parties to settle lawsuits before trial. Under a mechanism commonly known as "Rule 49 offers to settle," parties who refuse certain settlement offers may be saddled with higher cost awards. Rule 49.10 of the Ontario Rules of Civil Procedure provides that where a party rejects an offer to settle made at least seven days before trial that is not withdrawn before the trial begins, the party making the offer is entitled to partial indemnity costs to the date of the offer and substantial indemnity costs thereafter.[53] This provides the parties with incentives to make early offers to settle and to accept such offers. While certain American jurisdictions do have similar rules in place,[54] these rules have generally been so weak as to prove largely ineffective.[55]

While the law of costs differs significantly between Canada and the United States, it remains somewhat unclear whether costs rules have a significant impact in practice on litigation costs and the cost of litigation overall. It is commonly argued that the Anglo-Canadian rule discourages high-risk litigation, because of the prospect of having to pay the other side's costs, while the U.S. rule may encourage more speculative tort claims. Indeed, in a 1984 study, Kritzer found that Canadians viewed fee-shifting provisions as a major reason for their perception that they are generally less litigious than Americans.[56] Similarly, it has also been argued that fee-shifting rules increase the likelihood of settlement prior to trial.

However, despite both the conventional wisdom as well as significant theorizing as to the effects that cost awards ought to have,[57] the empirical evidence finding such effects is limited. In an empirical analysis of the effect of a fee-shifting statute in constitutional litigation in the United States, Schwab and Eisenberg find that the fee-shifting statute has had very little effect on constitutional tort litigation.[58] Although the empirical research is not entirely unequivocal, there seems to be little conclusive evidence that fee-shifting regimes increase the likelihood of settlement.[59] Additionally, as Kritzer notes, many countries that do require losing parties to pay the winning parties' legal costs, such as Germany and Sweden, actually have higher litigation rates than does the United States.[60] At the very least, this latter fact suggests that any popular perception that fee-shifting rules play an overwhelming rule in determining rates of litigation is unwarranted.

C. Class Actions

One set of procedural rules that has a significant impact on the ability of plaintiffs to bring tort claims is the rules governing the availability of class actions. This is an area in which Canada and America have historically differed significantly but have increasingly converged in recent years.

Class actions in Canada are of a relatively recent vintage. The first jurisdiction in Canada to allow U.S.-type class proceedings was Quebec, which enacted legislation permitting class proceedings in 1978. In 1992, Ontario became the next province to provide for class actions. Class actions are now permitted in all jurisdictions in Canada.

While the rules governing the availability of class actions are substantially similar to those rules under American law, there are some minor differences. For example, while the requirement under rule 23(b)(3) that common issues predominate among class members applies to many American class actions,[61] this is not a strict requirement for maintaining a class action in Canada. Under most Canadian statutes, the question of whether common issues predominate over individual issues is merely a factor for the court to consider in determining whether a class proceeding would be a preferable form of proceeding.[62] Thus, in certain respects, it is actually easier to have a class action certified in Canada than in the United States, although in general the rules governing certification are substantially quite similar.

Notwithstanding these similarities, class actions are much less common in Canada than they are in the United States. This may be a function of the relatively recent origins of class actions in Canada, of the other differences in legal rules described in this article, or of some other factor entirely.

D. Discovery

Discovery rules permit a party to request information from an opposing party. While broad discovery rules may not systematically favor one party over another, they almost certainly raise the costs of litigation for both parties in the United States.

In the United States, a party's right to engage in discovery is quite broad. Under the Federal Rules of Civil Procedure, parties must provide the opposing side with all documents "regarding any nonprivileged matter that is relevant to any party's claim or defence."[63] Additionally, the Rules give parties the opportunity to depose a number of individuals in an oral examination. Under Rule 30, subject to certain exceptions, a party is entitled to take 10 depositions without having to seek leave of the court to take additional depositions.[64]

Canadian discovery rules are more limited in scope. With respect to documentary discovery, Canadian rules are relatively similar, though not identical, to American rules. For example, the Ontario *Rules of Civil Procedure* provide that parties must produce for inspection every document that is not privileged and that is relevant to any matter in issue in an action.[65] However, Ontario rules relating to oral discovery are much more limited than are corresponding American rules. As a general matter, the only individuals who may be examined orally are parties to the suit who are adverse in interest.[66] Where a corporation may be examined for discovery, the examining party has the right to examine one director, officer, or employee of the corporation.[67] Additional individuals may be examined under certain circumstances, but the circumstances when additional oral examinations are permitted are tightly circumscribed.[68] Moreover, as of January 1, 2010, parties are limited to a total of seven hours of examination for discovery, regardless of the number of parties or other persons to be examined, except in cases where the parties consent or with the leave of the court.[69]

Additionally, Ontario has recently taken steps to further limit the scope and expense of all forms of discovery. On January 1, 2010, a proportionality requirement in discovery came into effect that empowers a court to consider a variety of factors: the time and cost of answering the question or producing the document; whether answering the question or producing the document would cause the person undue prejudice or interfere with the orderly progress of the action; whether the information is available from another source; and whether an order would require an excessive volume of documents to be produced.[70] This represents an attempt to further limit the scope of discovery, but the practical impact of the rule remains to be seen.

E. Notice Pleading

Differences in pleading rules between the United States and Canada also have significant implications for the scope of discovery. While the United States employs, for the most part, a system of notice pleading that does not require that plaintiffs in their statement of claim provide the facts that support the action,[71] Canada relies on a system of fact pleading. Under Canadian rules, the plaintiff must plead sufficient facts that, if true, would be sufficient to sustain a cause of action.[72] This means that while discovery in the United States is a broad and open-ended exercise to learn the facts that could sustain a particular cause of action, discovery in Canada is generally limited to obtaining evidentiary support for facts already pleaded. Fact pleading also discourages fishing expeditions in which plaintiffs commence an action without any evidence of wrongdoing to back it up.

F. Judicial Appointments

Finally, it is worth noting that all superior court judges in Canada—the judges who deal with all tort claims above a very minor amount—are federally appointed. No Canadian judges are elected or subject to appointments with a subsequent reelection, as is the case with most state-court judges in the U.S., nor are any superior court judges appointed by provincial legislatures or executives. This imposes a degree of consistency among judges in all jurisdictions and obviates any meaningful ability for plaintiffs to forum-shop for sympathetic judges. This may be another distinguishing factor in judicial determinations of liability or the quantum of damages in tort cases.

Conclusion

For the reasons discussed above, it seems reasonable to conclude that the differences in substance and procedure between Canadian and American tort law constitute part of the explanation why the direct costs of tort law are lower in Canada than in the United States. To the extent that the crisis in American tort law is an overabundance of frivolous or vexation litigation or unreasonably high damages awards, Canadian tort law can serve as an example of a broadly similar system that has tamed many of the excesses that are apparent in American tort law. The less plaintiff-friendly Canadian tort system demonstrates that, rather than rejecting the tort system entirely in favor of one or more no-fault compensation systems, America should curb the excesses of its tort law by incremental reforms that nonetheless preserve the essential features of the tort system.

However, we posit this conclusion with several caveats. First, as we suggested above, the prescription than American tort law should look to the relatively less plaintiff-friendly Canadian tort law in order to ameliorate the "crisis" in American tort law is tenable only if the crisis in American tort law is really a crisis of too much rather than too little litigation.[73]

Second, even assuming that the crisis in tort law is that too many frivolous claims are being litigated and that damages awards are too large and too random, it is by no means apparent that the optimal system is a reformed, less plaintiff-friendly tort system along the lines of the Canadian model. Indeed, it may be that no-fault systems would be preferable in a variety of respects to both the Canadian and American tort systems, at least in the domain of certain classes of accidents, and we make no claims about the relative performance of no-fault systems as compared with the tort system here.[74] Our suggestion that American scholars and tort reformers could look to the Canadian model of tort law will have appeal only for those who believe that the essential features of the tort system should be preserved.

Third, while we have outlined the Canadian system as a system that has lower direct costs, we are reluctant to reach conclusions about the relative social welfare effects of each of the tort systems. While the Canadian system may entail fewer direct social costs, it may be that the increased direct costs of the American tort regime actually achieve a preferable outcome in terms of social welfare by achieving a more socially optimal level of deterrence. Moreover, while we have no reason now to believe that a suboptimal level of deterrence is achieved by Canadian law, it is entirely possible that a proper level of deterrence is achieved in Canada either (a) because the Canadian system is free-riding on the deterrence effects of the U.S. tort system, given the integrated nature of the two economies, or (b) because Canada is willing to rely more on direct regulatory interventions to reduce the incidence of accidents, while the United States relies more heavily on the tort system. For these reasons, it is exceptionally difficult to ascertain the welfare effects that would be occasioned by the United States adopting a more "Canadian" tort system. While the theoretical bases for making such a judgment are reasonably well developed, additional empirical research is necessary to reach a determinate conclusion.

Notwithstanding these caveats, there are compelling reasons for supposing that the passive judicial role and undisciplined adversarial process often found in the United States are neither an efficient nor a fair method of adjudicating disputes.[75] In these contexts, a more pro-active, inquisitional judicial role and a more disciplined adversarial process have many social virtues. In this respect, Gordon Tullock's book, *Trials on Trial*,[76] deserves more sympathetic attention than it has hitherto received.

Notes

1. Many commentators have questioned whether there really is a "crisis" in tort law. See, e.g., Deborah Jones Merritt and Kathryn Ann Barry, Is the Tort System in Crisis? New Empirical Evidence, 60 Ohio St. L. J. 315 (1999) (finding low recovery rates and damages in medical malpractice and products liability cases); David A. Hyman and Charles Silver, Medical Malpractice Litigation and Tort Reform: It's the Incentives, Stupid, 59 Vand. L. Rev. 1085 (2006) (meta-analysis of other empirical work on medical malpractice suits, strongly contesting, inter alia, the claims that Americans are exceptionally litigious, that frivolous lawsuits are extremely common, and that damages are random and typically overcompensate plaintiffs); John T. Nockelby, How to Manufacture a Crisis: Evaluating Empirical Claims behind "Tort Reform," 86 Or. L. Rev. 533 (2007) (finding that there is no evidence for the existence of a litigation crisis, in that filing rates in tort cases are dropping, and taking inflation into account, median damage awards are declining).

2. For a more detailed overview of no-fault systems than the current article permits, see Michael Trebilcock and Paul-Erik Veel, No Fault Accident Compensation Systems, in Research Handbook on the Economics of Torts (Jennifer Arlen, ed., forthcoming).

3. Indeed, Canadians have historically seen themselves as being less litigious than their American counterparts. See, e.g., Herbert M. Kritzer, Fee Arrangements and Fee Shifting: Lessons from the Experience in Ontario, 47 Law & Contemp. Probs. 125, 129 (1984).

4. See Patricia M. Danzon, The "Crisis" in Medical Malpractice: A Comparison of Trends in the United States, Canada, the United Kingdom and Australia, 18 L. Med & Health Care 48 (1990); Michael Trebilcock, Donald N. Dewees, and David G. Duff, The Medical Malpractice Explosion: An Empirical Assessment of Trends, Determinants and Impacts, 17 Melbourne University L. Rev. 539 (1990).

5. Janelle Guirguis-Blake et al., The US Medical Liability System: Evidence for Legislative Reform, 4 Annals of Family Medicine 240 (2006); Canadian Medical Protective Association, Fee Schedule for 2011, available at http://www.cmpa-acpm.ca/cmpapd04/docs/membership/fees/2011cal-e.pdf.

6. Gary Schwartz, "Product Liability and Medical Malpractice in a Comparative Context," in The Liability Maze: The Impact of Liability Law on Safety and Innovation 28–80 at 46–51 (Peter Huber and Robert Litan, eds., 1991).

7. Herbert M. Kritzer, W. A. Bogart, and Neil Vidmar, The Aftermath of Injury: Cultural Factors in Compensation Seeking in Canada and the United States, 25 Law & Soc. Rev. 499 (1991).

8. See the discussions of the empirical evidence in Michael Trebilcock, The Social Insurance-Deterrence Dilemma, 24 San Diego L. Rev. 929, 933–936, 942–948 (1987); Trebilcock et al., supra note 4, at 542–543.

9. Importantly, regulatory pre-emption or compliance in Canada is not absolute. Non-compliance with regulatory requirements is probative of but not determinative of a finding of negligence. See The Queen (Can.) v. Saskatchewan Wheat Board, [1983] 1 S.C.R. 205.

10. Rylands v. Fletcher, [1868] L.R. 3 H.L. 1.

11. Restatement (Second) of Torts § 402A. See also the discussion in Stuart M. Speiser, Charles F. Krause, and Alfred W. Gans, The American Law of Torts, 18.27 (2003). Over 40 jurisdictions have explicitly adopted strict liability. See Spieser, id. at 18.28.

12. Allen M. Linden, Canadian Tort Law 585 (2001). However, Saskatchewan, New Brunswick, and Quebec have adopted some form of strict liability for injuries caused by defective products. See Consumer Protection Act, S.S. 1996 c. C-30, s. 64; Consumer Product Warranty and Liability Act, S.N.B. 1978, c. C-18.1, s. 27(1); Consumer Protection Act, R.S.Q. c. P-40.1, s. 53.

13. Fontaine v. British Columbia (Official Administrator), [1998] 1 S.C.R. 424.

14. For example, in Ontario, a worker employed by a "Schedule 1" employer (in certain designated industries) is not entitled to commence an action against his or her own employer and also against any other Schedule 1 employers. See Workplace Safety and Insurance Act, 1997, S.O. 1997, c. 16, Sched. A, s. 28.

15. Andrews v. Grand & Toy Alberta Ltd., [1978] 2 S.C.R. 229; Thornton v. Prince George School District No. 57, [1978] 2 S.C.R. 267; Arnold v. Teno, [1978] 2 S.C.R. 287.

16. Jamie Cassels and Elizabeth Adjin-Tetty, Remedies: The Law of Damages 170 (2d ed. 2008).

17. See, e.g., Cal. Civ. Code. § 3333.2 (non-pecuniary damages in medical malpractice cases capped at $250,000); Idaho Code § 6-1603 ($250,000 cap, adjusted to inflation, on non-pecuniary damages in personal injury and wrongful death cases).

18. A majority of courts have upheld caps on non-pecuniary damages as constitutional. See, e.g., Prendergast v. Nelson, N.W.2d 657 (Neb. 1977); Johnson v. St. Vincent Hospital, Inc., 404 N.E.2d 585 (Ind. 1980); Fein v. Permanente Medical Group, 695 P.2d 665 (Cal. 1985). However, some courts have held such caps to be unconstitutional on the basis of provisions in state constitutions. See, e.g., Arneson v. Olson, 270 N.W.2d 125 (N.D. 1978); Morris v. Savoy, 576 N.E.2d 765 (Ohio 1991); Best v. Taylor Machine Works, Inc., 689 N.E.2d 1057 (Ill. 1997). By contrast, Canadian courts have upheld as constitutional even extremely low caps for non-pecuniary damages. For example, in Morrow v. Zhang, 2009 ABCA 215, the Alberta

Court of Appeal upheld as constitutional a cap of $4,000 on non-pecuniary damages for minor injuries arising from motor vehicle accidents.

19. Carly N. Kelly and Michelle N. Mello, Are Medical Malpractice Damages Caps Constitutional? An Overview of State Litigation, 33 J. Law, Medicine & Ethics 515 (2005).

20. In the early 2000s, the House of Representatives passed a number of bills that would have imposed limits on non-pecuniary damages in medical malpractice cases, but those legislative efforts never passed the Senate. See, e.g., Help Efficient, Accessible, Low-Cost Timely Healthcare (HEALTH) Act of 2003, H.R. 5; Patients First Act of 2003, S. 11; Help Efficient, Accessible, Low-Cost Timely Healthcare (HEALTH) Act of 2004, H.R. 4280, 108th Cong.

21. David A. Hyman, Bernard Black, Charles Silver, and William M. Sage, Estimating the Effect of Damages Caps in Medical Malpractice Cases: Evidence from Texas, 1 J. Legal Analysis 355 (2009).

22. Catherine M. Sharkey, Unintended Consequences of Medical Malpractice Damages Caps, 80 NYU L. Rev. 391 (2005).

23. Claudia M. Landeo, Maxim Nikitin, and Scott Baker, Deterrence, Lawsuits, and Litigation Outcomes under Court Errors, 23 J. Law, Econ. & Org. 57 (2010).

24. Daniel Kessler and Mark McClellan, Do Doctors Practice Defensive Medicine?, 111 Q. J. Econ. 353 (1996).

25. Frank A. Sloan and John H. Shadle, Is There Empirical Evidence for "Defensive Medicine"? A Reassessment, 28 J. Health Econ. 481 (2009)

26. For a more detailed discussion of the differences in the treatment of punitive damages in Canada, England, and the United States, see Bruce Chapman and Michael Trebilcock, Punitive Damages: Divergence in Search of a Rationale, 40 Alabama L. Rev. 741 (1989).

27. See the discussion in Exxon Shipping Co. v. Baker, 554 U.S. 471 (2008). There have been occasional cases where state courts have struck down certain forms of state legislation to limit punitive damages. See, e.g., Kirk v. Denver Pub. Co., 818 P.2d 262 (Colo. 1991) (holding unconstitutional a Colorado statute that required one-third of exemplary damages awards to be paid to the state); Henderson By and Through Hartsfield v. Alabama Power Co., 627 So. 2d 878 (Ala. 1993).

28. Exxon Shipping Co. v. Baker, supra note 27.

29. Cooperman Industries Inc. v. Leatherman Tool Group Inc., 532 U.S. 424 (2001).

30. BMW of North America, Inc. v. Gore, 517 U.S. 559 (1996); Cooperman Industries Inc. v. Leatherman Tool Group Inc., 532 U.S. 424 (2001).

31. TXO Production Corp. v. Alliance Resources Corp., 509 U.S. 443 (1993).

32. Exxon Shipping Co. v. Baker, supra note 27.

33. The dominant American and Canadian approach to punitive damages can be contrasted with that employed in England. There, the House of Lords held in Rookes v. Barnard [1964] A.C. 1129 that punitive damages can only properly be awarded in three classes of cases: (1) where there was oppressive, arbitrary, or unconstitutional

action taken by servants of the government; (2) where the defendant's conduct was calculated to make a profit for himself; and (3) where a statute expressly authorizes the awarding of punitive damages.

34. Whiten v. Pilot Insurance Co., 2002 S.C.C. 18, [2002] 1 S.C.R. 595 at para. 94.

35. Cassels and Adjin-Tetty, supra note 16, at 288–290.

36. Whiten, supra note 34, at para. 94.

37. Id. (emphasis in the original).

38. Hill v. Church of Scientology of Toronto, [1995] 2 S.C.R. 1130, at para. 197.

39. Whiten, supra note 34, at para. 107.

40. Id.

41. Hill, supra note 38.

42. Theodore Eisenberg, John Geordt, Brian Ostrom, David Rottman, and Martin T. Wells, The Predictability of Punitive Damages, 26 J. Legal Stud. 623 (1997).

43. Courts of Justice Act, R.S.O. 1990, c. C.43, at s. 108(1); Rules of Civil Procedure, R.R.O. 1990, Reg. 194, r. 47.

44. Courts of Justice Act, id. at s. 108(3).

45. Id. at s. 108(2).

46. Crown Liability and Proceedings Act, R.S.C. 1985, c. C-50 at s. 26; Proceedings against the Crown Act, R.S.O. 1990 c. P.27, s. 11.

47. Theodore Eisenberg, Neil LaFountain, Brian Ostrom, David Rottman, and Martin T. Wells, Juries, Judges, and Punitive Damages: An Empirical Study, 87 Cornell L. Rev. 743 (2001–2002).

48. Joni Hersch and Kip Viscusi, Punitive Damages: How Judges and Juries Perform, 33 J. Legal Stud. 1 (2004).

49. In this article, we focus exclusively on the rules governing when parties are required to bear opposing parties' costs. There are, of course, other differences, both historic and current, in the ways in which lawsuits are funded between Canada and the United States. Perhaps most notable among these differences is that contingency fees, long permissible in the United States and even in many other Canadian provinces, were prohibited until late 2002 in Ontario. Contingency fees were permitted with the enactment of the Justice Statute Law Amendment Act, 2002, S.O. 2002, c. 24—Bill 213, Schedule A (Amendment to the Solicitor's Act).

50. There are certain notable exceptions to this rule even in the United States. For example, the standard rule in Alaska is that the loser pays the winner's costs (the so-called two-way cost rule). See Alaska Rules of Civil Procedure, Rule 82. Additionally, there are a variety of statutes that allow courts to order losing parties to pay the winning parties' costs. See, e.g., 42 U.S.C. 1988 (providing for the payment of attorney's fees for successful litigants under federal civil rights law). However, for most claims, the default rule in the United States remains that each party bears its own costs.

51. The general principle that losing parties should pay the winning parties' costs is not limited to Anglo-Canadian law, but rather is a feature of most similar legal systems. The general American rule that each party bears its own legal fees is quite

exceptional. See W. Kent Davis, The International View of Attorney Fees in Civil Suits: Why Is the United States the "Odd Man Out" in How It Pays Its Lawyers?, 16 Ariz. J. Int'l & Comp. L. 361 (1999).

52. See the factors listed in Rules of Civil Procedure, R.R.O. 1990, Reg. 194, r. 57.01.

53. Id. at r. 49.10.

54. See, e.g., Federal Rules of Civil Procedure (FRCP) Rule 68.

55. For a recent analysis of the empirical effects of the relatively robust offer-of-judgment rule in New Jersey, see Albert Yoon and Thomas Baker, A Market Solution to Civil Litigation?: An Empirical Study of Offer-of-Judgment Rules, 59 Vand. L. Rev. 155 (2006).

56. Herbert M. Kritzer, Fee Arrangements and Fee Shifting: Lessons from the Experience in Ontario, 47 Law & Contemp. Probs. 125 (1984).

57. Thomas D. Rowe, Jr., Predicting the Effects of Attorney Fee Shifting, 47 Law and Contemp. Probs. 139 (1984); Jennifer F. Reinganum and Louis L. Wilde, Settlement, Litigation, and the Allocation of Litigation Costs, 17 RAND J. Econ. 557 (1986); Robert D. Cooter and Daniel L. Rubinfeld, Economic Analysis of Legal Disputes and Their Resolution, 27 J. Econ. Lit. 1067 (1989).

58. Stewart J. Schwab and Theodore Eisenberg, Explaining Constitutional Tort Litigation: The Influence of the Attorney Fees Statute and the Government as Defendant, 73 Cornell L. Rev. 719 (1987–1988).

59. For studies finding no evidence that fee-shifting encourages settlement, see Gary M. Fournier & Thomas W. Zuehlke, Litigation and Settlement: An Empirical Approach, 71 Rev. Econ. & Stat. 189 (1989). However, for evidence to the contrary, see Don L. Coursey & Linda R. Stanley, Pretrial Bargaining Behavior within the Shadow of the Law: Theory and Experimental Evidence, 8 Int'l Rev. L. & Econ. 161 (1988) (experimental laboratory evidence finding that the Anglo-Canadian rules make individuals more likely to settle than does the American rule).

60. Herbert M. Kritzer, Lawyer Fees and Lawyer Behavior in Litigation: What Does the Empirical Literature Really Say?, 80 Tex. L. Rev. 1943 (2001–2002).

61. FRCP, Rule 23(b).

62. Class Proceedings Act, 1992, S.O. 1992, c. 6, s. 5; Class Proceedings Act, R.S.B.C. 1996, c. 50, s.4.

63. FRCP, Rule 26(b)(1).

64. FRCP, Rule 30.

65. Rules of Civil Procedure, R.R.O. 1990, Reg. 194, r. 30.02.

66. Id. at r. 31.03(1).

67. Id. at r. 31.03(2).

68. Id. at r. 31.03.

69. Id. at r. 31.05.1.

70. Id. at r. 29.2.

71. FRCP, Rule 8(a)(2). See also Bell Atlantic Corp. v. Twombly, 550 U.S. 544 (2007).

72. Rules of Civil Procedure, R.R.O. 1990, Reg. 194, r. 21.01(1)(b).

73. To the extent that the problem in tort law is actually that too few claims are being litigated, as some claim, see Richard L. Abel, The Real Tort Crisis—Too Few Claims, 48 Ohio St. L. J. 443 (1987), many (though not necessarily all) of the possible reforms suggested by this article would be counterproductive.

74. For such an evaluation, see Michael Trebilcock and Paul-Erik Veel, No Fault Accident Compensation Systems, in Research Handbook on the Economics of Torts (Jennifer Arlen, ed., forthcoming); Don Dewees, David Duff, and Michael Trebilcock, Exploring the Domain of Accident Law: Taking the Facts Seriously ch. 7 (1996).

75. Michael Trebilcock and Lisa Austin, The Limit of Full Court Press: Of Blood and Mergers, 48 U. Toronto L. J. 1 (1998).

76. Gordon Tullock, Trials on Trial (1980).

The Expansion of Modern U.S. Tort Law and Its Excesses

GEORGE L. PRIEST

Tort law in the United States was radically reformed over the past 50 years from a relatively minor mechanism for dealing with a small subset of accidents into, today, an institution that conceptually aspires to regulate all industries and social activities, making it the most significant regulatory body in American society.

Other chapters in this book document empirically the extraordinary rise of the field. This essay attempts to provide an explanation of these developments. It will show that, in theory, the expansion of tort law was well intentioned and may have served a constructive purpose over some range. The essay will also attempt to show, however, that, because of the peculiar definition of the field—in particular, legal standards that are based upon vague and undeveloped economic analysis—modern tort law today exhibits vast excesses in liability that have transformed it into a significant instrument of redistribution that harms economic welfare in the U.S. and places it at a substantial competitive disadvantage compared with other nations. In recent years, other major nations, not appreciating the harms caused by the expansion of tort liability in the U.S., have begun to expand their internal tort law on the American model. The expansion of tort liability by competitor nations will reduce the U.S. competitive disadvantage (though will not affect the competitive disadvantage against less-developed nations), but will contribute to the general diminution of world economic welfare, as has happened in the U.S., by substituting chiefly redistributionist for productive investment.

The article first presents a brief history of conceptions of tort law that preceded the modern era. It next demonstrates how these conceptions were transformed following the mid-1960s. The article then attempts to place these developments in the context of the then-emerging field of law-and-economics—in particular, the triumph of the approach of Richard Posner over that of Ronald Coase, where Posner's views were importantly influential in encouraging the expansion of the law. The article separately addresses the rise of the class action, a significant adjunct of modern tort law, which vastly increases the deleterious effects of the law by allowing modern tort litigation to gain an extraordinary economy of scale. Finally, the article discusses the economic effects of these developments.

Tort Law in the Pre-Modern Era

For the first centuries of the common law, private law—tort, contract, and property law—was seen to serve a minor role in the organization of Anglo-American life. The purpose of tort law was to compel redistribution from an injurer to a victim in a relatively small set of contexts, chiefly where the injurer had caused harm by acting in a way that deviated from normal activities. To describe this role of the law as a "system" incorrectly imports a modern sensibility. Tort law sought no more than to compel redistribution where one person harmed another through an action that substantially departed from the status quo. The standards for assigning liability—that the injurer acted "unreasonably" or failed to comply with "due care"—show the commitment of the law to upholding the status quo. A damages payment served only a compensatory—that is, redistributive—purpose. From this light, compensation, as reflected in the dominant legal remedy of compensatory damages, sought no more than to restore some victims to their pre-loss position.

In modern discussion, this view of private law has been supported by philosophical theories of corrective justice that attempt to justify this form of redistribution. These theories do not ignore the effects of legal decisions and rules on future behavior, but the role of private law viewed as a system of corrective justice, at best, is to prevent the need for future redistributive decisions. More typically, it seeks simply to restore the injured party (as much as can be done through money damages) to its pre-injury position, thus reinstating, except for the injury, the earlier status quo. Even modern theories of corrective justice view private law as serving a relatively modest role in societal affairs.

By protecting the status quo, private law, including tort law, had a limited role in the organization of a society's activities. As Holmes explained, "The cumbrous and expensive machinery [of the legal system] ought not to be set in motion unless some clear benefit is to be derived."[1] By definition, departures from the status quo, including actionable departures, are rarities. If such actions were more frequent, they would form a part of the status quo, suggesting the fluid—not principled—nature of the standard (which will be shown to have significance) and the fact that such a legal standard is not likely to affect social organization importantly.

The Rise of the Instrumental Conception of Tort Law

The modern—quasi-economic and instrumental—approach to the role of tort law was initiated in the 1940s, but became widely embraced in the 1960s and expanded thereafter.[2] An earlier academic literature sought to define a set of tort law principles that would improve societal welfare, beyond merely protecting the status quo. Building on this work, the first iteration of what would become the modern view was the concurring opinion of Justice Roger Traynor of the California Supreme Court in the now-famous case *Escola v. Coca-Cola Bottling Co.*[3] The case was simple: A waitress in a restaurant was cut when a Coca-Cola bottle exploded. The Court's majority opinion resolved the case on *res ipsa loquitur* grounds, a doctrine that presumes negligence—a departure from normal standards of behavior—from the facts of the case alone.[4] Justice Traynor, however, in a concurring opinion, argued that the manufacturer should be held absolutely liable for the injury, without regard to a showing of fault or negligence or even of a presumption of negligence through the *res ipsa loquitur* doctrine. He justified the position giving two reasons, both of which have something of an economic cast. First, the manufacturer is in a superior position to reduce the risk of injury: "Even if there is no negligence, . . . public policy demands that responsibility be fixed wherever it will most effectively reduce the hazards to life and health inherent in defective products that reach the market. It is evident that the manufacturer can anticipate some hazards and guard against the recurrence of others, as the public cannot." Second, even if the accident cannot be effectively prevented, the manufacturer can provide a form of insurance, passed on to the product's consumers in the product price: "The cost of an injury and the loss of time or health may be an overwhelming misfortune to the person injured, and a needless one, for the risk of injury can be insured by the manufacturer and distributed among the public as a cost of doing business."[5]

These two instrumental and quasi-economic goals—reducing the incidence of loss (improving safety) and, for losses that cannot be prevented, providing insurance through tort law damages—constitute the cornerstone of modern tort law. These goals were adopted as central to products liability law during the mid-1960s with the general adoption of the doctrine of strict products liability, first by the California Supreme Court,[6] then by the American Law Institute's Second Restatement of Torts,[7] and ultimately by courts or legislatures in all states.[8] The goals have been extended to other areas of tort law, beyond products, over the succeeding years.

More recently, these goals of employing the law to improve safety and provide insurance have been subsumed in the more general economic concept of "internalizing" the costs of injury to the injury-causing entity. The concept of internalizing costs is more centrally economic. The idea is to affect the productive decisions of all entities in the society by compelling them—through private law—to take accident costs into account in each of their productive decisions by directly imposing accident costs on them. Thus, the law serves to perfect the pricing system by requiring risk-generating entities to include in decision-making the price of accidents that result from their production.

At a very general level, the cost internalization concept is plausible. It becomes problematic, however, when the issue of causation is carefully addressed. As Ronald Coase showed many years ago, in the context of an interaction between a person injured and the entity whose production was involved in the injury, unless it is clear that one of the parties could have cost-effectively prevented the accident at a cost less than the other, one cannot from an economic standpoint attribute causation of the accident to either single party.[9]

Nevertheless, the goal of internalizing costs in order to create incentives to reduce the accident rate and to provide accident insurance is the dominant theory of tort law today. This goal has provided the justification for courts to expand substantive tort liability standards as well as to restrict legal defenses in a broad range of areas, from occupational safety to job-site discrimination. The goal—in particular, the internalizing costs concept—has also provided the basis for the expansion of recovery of non-economic damages, such as pain and suffering and loss of the value of life, on the argument that, if costs are to be internalized, damages should equal the full costs of the accident, measured as completely as possible.

Together, these concepts have led to a vast expansion of tort liability over the past 50 years. Whether measured in terms of litigation levels (addressed in the article by Ramseyer and Rasmusen in this volume), or in terms of tort law judgments, or more fully, judgments plus settlements, or more fully yet, judgments plus settlements plus attorneys' costs and fees, the amount of money transferred through the legal system has increased by many multiples and perhaps exponentially since the mid-1960s.[10]

In essence, the modern view has converted tort law into a regulatory institution that possesses authority over all activities in the society. From a political standpoint, direct economic regulation of industry has been relatively modest in the U.S. in comparison with other advanced nations, chiefly addressing natural monopoly industries. Modern tort law, in contrast, extends regulation through the concept of internalizing costs to all industries, indeed to all individual actions. There is no activity in the society that can escape the regulatory logic of the internalizing costs idea. Even activities that in other contexts are provided immunity from regulation—such as most governmental activities—fall under the regulatory purview of the theory of internalizing costs.

The Peculiar Role of Law-and-Economics in the Expansion of Tort Liability

As mentioned, there is an economic or quasi-economic cast to the concept of internalizing costs in order to establish incentives to promote safety and to provide insurance. Modern tort law in the U.S. was importantly affected, however, by the circumstance that the analysis and interpretation of these quasi-economic ideas was presented to the courts not by economists, nor even by lawyers with substantial understanding of economics, but by law professors who had only a vague idea of the economic principles that they were invoking, though ultimately supported by law-and-economics scholars who ignored the operation of markets as well as all empirical evidence of the effects of modern law.

In the field of products liability, which served as the most important template for the adoption of these ideas, leading to their expansion into all other areas of tort law, the principal interpreter of the new approach was Professor John Wade. In an otherwise obscure article in the *Mississippi Law Journal*,[11] Wade set forth a seven-element test to define when a product should be determined to be defective under the then newly adopted Second Restatement of Torts § 402(A), a test that came to be known as the "risk-utility" test.[12] Wade's seven-element test was adopted widely by courts in their expansion of strict products liability.[13]

From the standpoint of economic analysis, Wade's seven-element test is basically incoherent. It confuses entirely the question of whether the allegedly defective product should be banned from the market altogether—that is, whether its aggregate "risk" is greater than its aggregate "utility," the purported subject of the "risk-utility" test—with the more relevant economic issue of whether there were marginal changes that might have been made in production or design that would have cost-effectively reduced the risk of product use for the particular consumer-claimant. Wade's risk-utility test—as well as the general conception of strict manufacturer liability—mentions the role of the consumer in preventing loss, but, by focusing on the risk-utility of the product, minimizes it. The Wade test also refers to insurance, but without any careful analysis of how insurance for product-related losses may most economically be provided. Nevertheless, Wade's analysis of the issue commanded, and (almost unbelievably) still commands, wide adherence.[14]

The academic field of law-and-economics began to expand at roughly the same time as the shift in the analysis of modern tort law. Ronald Coase's famous article *The Problem of Social Cost* was published in 1962.[15] The California Supreme Court's opinion in *Greenman v. Yuba Power Prods., Inc.,* adopting the standard of strict products liability, was delivered in 1963.[16] Coase's article was far too conceptually advanced to have influenced the Court and perhaps too obscure, as it was published in an economics journal. It was not cited by the Court.

Coase's analysis in *The Problem of Social Cost* is acknowledged generally as the seminal source of the application of economic analysis to legal problems. Richard Posner's important book *Economic Analysis of Law,* published a decade later, in 1972, is commonly viewed as extending the economic approach beyond Coase and other pioneers of the field, such as Guido Calabresi,[17] to a wide range of other fields, indeed across the law in its entirety. Though often unrecognized, however, there are deep differences between Coase's and Posner's analyses of legal issues. With respect to the field of modern tort law, Posner's approach triumphed in ways that have led to the excesses that currently dominate the law.

The central point of Coase's paper—that the assignment of liability will have no effect on the allocation of resources—is essentially a proposition that private law rules will not determine outcomes so long as parties are permitted to bargain around them. Through market transactions, the interests of interacting parties in maximizing joint welfare will overcome any non-market, such as judicial, conclusion as to how resources should be allocated. I have separately described the intellectual origins of Coase's insight.[18]

Coase, however, did not anticipate the direction of modern tort law. If courts had defined modern tort law in a way that allowed for subsequent market correction, the deleterious effects of the advance of the law, described below, would never have occurred. Market corrections would have overcome the law, as described in Coase's article.

To the contrary, in the expansion of tort liability, U.S. courts framed the expansive doctrines as what would now be called "inalienability" rules, following the terminology of a famous article by Calabresi and Melamed:[19] rules that cannot be contracted around. In adopting the standard of strict products liability and associated standards serving the quasi-economic objective of internalizing costs, courts in the U.S. prohibited a manufacturer or seller from limiting its liability by contract, such as through a product warranty. Where personal injury is involved—but not, for undefined reasons, with respect to other product-related losses—a contractual limit of liability is regarded as a contract of adhesion, and consequently unenforceable.[20] In this way, Coase's analysis of the welfare-correcting function of market transactions became irrelevant in the field of products liability.

Coase's insight in *The Problem of Social Cost* was so astounding that it took many years of subsequent discussion to fully understand it. Harold Demsetz was an important figure in this respect, writing several significant articles explaining the implications of Coase's idea.[21] Reflective of the importance of the idea, many scholars felt the need to define their earlier work in contrast to it. My colleague Guido Calabresi, an important law-and-economics theorist himself, initially claimed to refute Coase's idea,[22] subsequently recanted the refutation,[23] and later claimed to have developed the idea himself, simultaneously with Coase.[24]

Important to the subsequent development of the field of law-and-economics, and in my view to the ultimate expansion of tort law in the U.S., was the publication in 1972 of Richard A. Posner's *Economic Analysis of Law*. Posner, though not an economist (important, as I will explain, because Posner has never been interested in the corrective results of market processes), but with full mastery of economic analysis, applied that analysis in an extraordinary, encyclopedic manner to all areas of the law. Some years earlier, in his first article in this vein, Posner had surveyed 19th-century U.S. tort law. This article, equally extraordinarily, analyzed *every* tort law decision by American courts in the 19th century.[25] Posner's article claimed that every 19th-century tort decision adopted a rule that achieved economic efficiency. Posner's 1972 book reinforced the conclusion of his early article on tort law, but expanded it, both over time—all tort law decisions in the 20th century were equally efficient—and over the remaining private law fields: all contract and property law decisions over all eras achieved efficiency as well.

Posner's claims in this book had a revolutionary effect on the field of law-and-economics, beyond that of Coase.[26] Posner's analysis—in particular, the focus on the effect of legal rules on the allocation of resources—appeared to derive from Coase. But Posner went substantially beyond Coase. *The Problem of Social Cost* discusses legal cases, but they are quaint decisions from England,[27] raising conceptually interesting economic issues, but of no general importance to an understanding of the broader law. Posner, in contrast, addressed all common law cases and the rules emanating from them, with apparently equal economic acumen.

The deep difference in approach between Coase and Posner has not been fully appreciated, however, perhaps concealed because both were colleagues at the University of Chicago Law School. In addition, in the early years, when the relevance of law-and-economics as a discipline was heavily disputed, Coase and Posner were allies in the trenches, defending the application of economic analysis to law against startled and poorly equipped opponents. Within law-and-economics, however, their approaches could not be more different. Posner is the anti-Coase. Coase's analysis shows that market transactions will correct any less effective allocation of resources directed by governments, including courts. Posner's efficiency-of-the-law theory, in sharp contrast, eliminates markets. According to Posner, courts (through some unexplained process called "the implicit logic of the common law")[28] adopt uniformly efficient rules. Where courts uniformly achieve efficiency, markets have no role. Coase views judges as imperfect decision-makers, though of little (save for distributive) consequence, given the ability of parties to negotiate around the rules they promulgate. Posner views judges as social engineers, always achieving efficient results. Markets are unnecessary to achieve efficiency.

The difference in these conceptual approaches defined the careers of these two great scholars, but also affected the direction and expansion of tort law in the United States. Coase, largely uninterested in common law rules, most probably because his interests were in the operation of markets, perhaps because he thought that the market could overcome any flaw in judicial decisions,[29] never focused on the common law. Following his seminal article showing the ineffectiveness of governmental—judicial—regulation of common law subjects, at least where private contracting was allowed, he studied other vestiges of socialist interference in the market. The academic project he chose following *The Problem of Social Cost* addressed the governmental monopoly of postal delivery.[30]

Posner, in contrast, through his emphasis on the uniform efficiency of all common law decisions, endorsed the expansion of tort liability in the product defect field and in other tort law fields. An important article with his gifted co-author William Landes presented a model that demonstrated that the tort law standards of negligence, strict liability, comparative negligence, and contributory negligence were, from an economic standpoint, identical in effect. All of these rules achieved efficiency.[31] This result was surprising and incredible. Roger Traynor would not have expected it; otherwise, what was the purpose of absolute manufacturer liability? John Wade would not have expected it. The Landes-Posner result was obtained, first, because it derived solely from a model; second, because the model assumed that, under strict liability, negligence, or any of their variations, courts applied optimal standards of contributory negligence with respect to victim activities. This assumption has no empirical support, though it is buttressed by the belief that all common law rules are efficient.

Other modelers in the field of law-and-economics contributed support. In an article that has been given great attention, Steven Shavell added to the foundation of the expansion of liability by showing—again, in a model—that the effects of the standards of negligence and strict liability were essentially identical, except that strict liability was advantageous in the context of what Shavell described as "unilateral accidents"—accidents in which only the activities of the injurer affect the accident rate.[32] The Shavell article remains widely cited even though, on Coase's analysis in *The Problem of Social Cost*, unilateral accidents do not exist.[33]

These various contributions of economic analysis to the understanding of the expansion of tort liability probably cannot be shown to have directly influenced courts. It is an interesting, but unanswered, question as to the extent to which the Landes-Posner or Shavell articles, or their progeny, were relied upon by courts expanding modern tort law, irrespective of citation. But those articles and the many articles that derived from them had the effect of giving an economic imprimatur to the expansion of tort liability. Their prominence diminished economic opposition to the expansion of liability.

Some scholars criticized the expansion of liability. Richard Epstein was an early opponent,[34] though understanding his views was complicated since he had written earlier articles endorsing the strict liability standard on libertarian grounds.[35] I attempted to criticize the progression of the law.[36] Popular authors, such as Peter Huber, also opposed expanded tort liability.[37] Paul Rubin attempted to resurrect a contractual approach to the problem.[38] And there were others. All of these efforts had no effect. Modern tort law continued and continues to expand.

The Rise of the Class Action in Modern Tort Law

The introduction of modern class action procedures occurred roughly simultaneously with the substantive expansion of tort liability. The Federal Rules of Civil Procedure were amended in 1966 to adopt, in Rule 23, the class action as a means of aggregating private law claims that raised similar issues of law and fact. Aggregation of claims had been possible under earlier iterations of civil procedure, through the joinder of claims or parties. The adoption of the class action mechanism formalized and simplified the procedure, especially with respect to potentially large numbers of claimants. It also endorsed the idea that benefits could be achieved from aggregating claims.

The adoption of the class action mechanism was not without an economic justification, nor was it particularly controversial at the time given the success of the internalizing costs idea. Where, in our modern society of mass production and distribution, a group of individuals claimed common harm from a single source and where the economic harm to each individual might not be sufficiently substantial to justify the costs of litigation, but where the aggregated interests of the group would do so, consolidation of the claims through the class action device would serve the economic goal of appropriately internalizing costs to the harm-causing entity. The defining justification of the procedure was to achieve the quasi-economic ambition of internalizing costs. An opponent might have argued that, if each individual claim were not worth bringing, none should be brought.[39] The dominant view, however, again from the internalizing costs conception, was that, unless some means of aggregating these less-than-litigation-worth claims were available, costs would be imposed on potential claimants that were not appropriately internalized.

A central question in the definition of the class action procedure was how to impose upon the new class action the same controls that exist in the prototypical, single-plaintiff-versus-defendant litigation. In the basic view of the adversarial litigation process, control over the litigation is placed in the hands of the plaintiff—the alleged victim of some harm—with decisions made and directions given to the attorney by the plaintiff to best control the direction of the lawsuit. In this view, the plaintiff controls the lawsuit in the same manner as a property owner decides how best to develop the property.

By definition, class actions are different. Any single plaintiff (or putative class member) will have suffered only partially—in comparison to the aggregate—from the allegedly harm-causing behavior. As a consequence, no single member of the class can personally make decisions appropriate on the basis of the full harm suffered by the class as a whole. The drafters of the class action device dealt with this problem by turning to political decision-making methods. A class would be "represented" by a class member or class members whose position was "representative" of the interests of the class and who was willing to serve a representative role. These putative class representatives would control the litigation, just as individual plaintiffs control individual litigation. Note that the conception of "representation" in class action litigation is quite muted. There is no election of representatives by the full class membership. A class member is chosen as a "representative" by putative class attorneys, though upon approval of a court, because her or his circumstances are alleged to be similar to those of other presumed members of the class.[40]

This conception of class action litigation, controlled through a weakly representative process for the advance of the action, would prove to be unrealistic. By definition, each class member possesses only a small stake—

often a trivial stake—in the litigation as a whole. Class members are not the equivalent of political representatives whose current jobs and reputation depend upon their faithful representation. Representative plaintiffs still have no serious stake in the litigation; the time commitment required of a class representative is measured in hours: some discussions with attorneys, perhaps a deposition. The parties that possess a substantial stake in the litigation—often 30 to 40 percent of a settlement—are the attorneys selected to represent the class. A representative class member will typically possess a fraction of a percent of the outcome; class attorneys, 30 to 40 percent. As a consequence, in virtually all class action litigation, effective control over the litigation is possessed by class attorneys.

At base, this device converts tort litigation into a form of bounty system where the bounty hunters—the class action attorneys—are empowered to define the grounds upon which and the defendants from whom the bounty is to be extracted.[41] This has the effect of vastly expanding the reach of modern tort law. Attorneys can develop claims of harm, find individuals allegedly subject to those harms who will agree to serve as representative class members (there typically is little cost—time only, no direct cost—to serving as a representative class member and sometimes a small gain), and bring an action, purportedly on the basis of hundreds or thousands of individuals similarly suffering from such harms. The notion that a class action is a mechanism through which a number of individuals suffering harms can band together to bring an action for redress is an artifice. The modern class action is an avenue for attorneys to create claims based upon expanded conceptions of modern tort law with the benefit of the mass aggregation of claims made possible through the class mechanism to threaten huge economic loss upon any defendant.

It is a measure of the in terrorem redistributionist effect of the modern tort class action that virtually *no* class actions, once certified, are litigated to judgment. As has been shown elsewhere, in typical civil cases that proceed to judgment, plaintiffs win as often as defendants.[42] In class action litigation, in sharp contrast, but indicative of the in terrorem feature of the process, once a class is certified, plaintiffs succeed in nearly 100 percent of cases. The class action procedure, obviously, vastly expands the effects of the expansion of tort liability.

In recent years, some modest constraints have been imposed upon class action litigation. Rule 23 of the Civil Rules has been amended to allow appellate review of class action certification. The Class Action Fairness Act moves many class actions to federal courts.[43] These are modest reforms. The potentially overwhelming economic effect of class action certification in the context of expanded tort liability standards remains a serious source of redistribution.

The Economic Effects of the Expansion of Tort Liability

What have been the effects of the extraordinary expansion of tort liability since the mid-1960s? Measuring the effects of tort law is particularly difficult since no adequate statistics exist recording either the benefits of tort judgments and settlements or their costs at any particular point or over time.

There exists, however, less systematic evidence from which inferences can be drawn as to the effects of the expansion of tort liability. As examples, at various points in time where the continuous increase in liability judgments has appeared to spike, various products and services have been withdrawn from the market. In the mid-1980s, for example, many pharmaceutical products were withdrawn, day care centers closed, many doctors shifted from obstetric and specialized surgery to less litigation-prone practices, manufacturers of private aircraft went out of business—all allegedly attributable to the increase in liability judgments.[44] There were similar withdrawals of service—especially of medical services such as obstetrics—during periods of the 1990s and early 2000s.

Certainly, one of the ambitions of the expansion of tort liability is to create incentives for the withdrawal of products or services that are excessively dangerous in the sense that their costs of production, including resulting injury costs, exceed the benefits from use of the product. In some cases, the law may have had that effect. It is difficult to believe, however, that medical services such as obstetrics or specialized surgery, or products such as general aviation, are too dangerous to provide in any form. Moreover, there is evidence that, where legislatures have adopted measures limiting the expansion of liability, previously withdrawn products and services have been restored, such as general aviation manufacture after the enactment of federal tort reform and obstetric and specialized surgery services after state tort reform, as an example, most recently in Texas.

Why would products that are not inherently excessively dangerous be withdrawn from markets with the expansion of tort liability? The quasi-economic goals of increasing safety and providing insurance, themselves, provide no obvious answer. It is well established as an economic proposition that enhanced liability will lead manufacturers and service providers to make investments in increasing safety up to the point at which the marginal benefit and marginal cost of further investments are equated.[45] Additional liability will not increase investments in precaution beyond the point of maximum cost effectiveness; it will only shift the burden of insuring losses that cannot be prevented from the victim to the injurer.

If the insurance provided through the tort system levied on manufacturers were superior to the insurance that could be obtained by potential victims—which Justice Traynor presumed—then the expansion of liability would increase the availability of risk-related products by reducing total product costs (manufacturing costs plus insurance). If the insurance provided through the tort system were the equivalent of private victim insurance, there would be no general effect on production. In contrast, where the insurance provided by the injurer through tort law, in the form of damages, is more costly than the insurance that could be obtained by potential victims and the difference in insurance costs exceeds the net benefit of the product to consumers, products and services that are not excessively dangerous will be withdrawn from markets on account of the expansion of liability because consumers are not willing to pay the increased insurance costs.

There are strong reasons to believe that tort law insurance is substantially more costly than private insurance available to consumers. Damages as measured by tort law differ dramatically from accident insurance benefits, typically purchased directly by consumers or indirectly by their employers. Third-party tort law insurance provides full recovery of medical expenses and lost income; private first-party insurance never provides full recovery, but is uniformly attended by deductibles and forms of coinsurance to control moral hazard. Tort law insurance, in addition, provides full recovery of pain and suffering loss; in contrast, there is no private first-party market for pain and suffering insurance because pain and suffering is largely unmeasurable (making it difficult to insure) and, more importantly, because it does not implicate financial well-being, the equalization of which over time is the economic function of insurance.[46] Moreover, private first-party insurance is structured in order to constrain loss in ways impossible for third-party tort insurance.[47] Finally, the costs of providing third-party tort law insurance—including attorneys' costs and fees in the judgment and settlement process—are vastly greater than the administrative costs of providing and delivering first-party accident insurance.

These systematic differences between the magnitude and structure of third-party tort law insurance and first-party insurance explain why the expansion of tort liability is not universally beneficial to consumers or other potential victims. Products and services that are not excessively dangerous will be withdrawn from markets where the differential insurance costs are greater than the net benefits of the product or service to the dominant set of users.

The criticism of modern tort law, however, can be made more sharply. The compulsion of manufacturers and service providers to include an insurance component in the sale of products and services was thought to repair a distributive failure in American society: the fact that many in the society, especially the lower-income, did not possess insurance. That was why Roger Traynor endorsed absolute manufacturer liability. There are two important problems with this conception. First, the insurance provided through tort law is generally regressive: the insurance costs added to the price of the product or service will reflect the expected liability to all consumers, high-income and low-income alike. Since those costs—expected liability judgments or settlements—are determined by the measure of damages in tort law: lost income, medical expenses, and pain and suffering (highly correlated with lost income), the insurance cost component will be higher than average for low-income claimants and lower than average for high-income claimants. As a consequence, low-income consumers pay more for product- and service-related insurance than actuarially appropriate.[48]

Second, in our modern society, perhaps unlike that of 1944 when Justice Traynor first developed the strict liability idea, or even of 1963, in

Greenman, when the idea was adopted by the California Supreme Court, Americans possess many other sources of insurance to address losses suffered from product or service use. U.S. citizens have largely first-party health insurance,[49] and also have other insurance resources that provide coverage of product-related losses: auto, homeowners, and life insurance. As discussed earlier, first-party insurance is more economical in many dimensions than insurance provided through the tort system.

This analysis also suggests the broader effect of the expansion of tort liability on innovation and economic growth. The prospect of having to include expected liability costs in the product or service price will affect the introduction of new products and services. Products and services never introduced because of a decision that expected liability costs would make them unmarketable constitute losses to innovation and economic growth that can never be observed.

The economic effects of the expansion of tort liability in the U.S. are evident. The expansion of liability has placed what is essentially a tax, a redistributionist tax, on U.S. productive investment. The tort liability tax, as explained, does not provide commensurate gain to those who benefit from it. As a consequence, it constitutes a deadweight loss on American output.

Deadweight losses will impair the competitive position of any economic actor. The deadweight loss of the U.S. tort liability tax impairs the competitive position of the U.S. in comparison to all countries not imposing such a tax. Though many European countries are moving in the direction of adopting U.S. tort law concepts—note that there is now growing asbestos litigation in Europe—none has adopted principles equivalent to those of the U.S. today. Nor certainly have lesser-developed nations, with less developed legal cultures. To the extent that they do, the competitive disadvantage of the U.S. will decline, but the economic welfare of the world will decline by substituting redistributive for productive investments.

Conclusion

There are strong reasons to believe that the expansion of tort liability since the mid-1960s has hampered innovation and economic growth. The effect of the expansion has been to shift an insurance burden to manufacturers and service providers. The provision of third-party tort law insurance is substantially more costly in many dimensions than the provision of first-party accident insurance. This shift in the insurance burden provides no benefit to consumers; indeed, it imposes greater costs on all consumers, and it imposes a regressive harm on lower-income consumers. The prospect of paying damages on account of the expansion of liability impairs innovation and economic growth because the increased insurance burden acts as a deadweight tax on innovation. The development in the U.S. of the class action mechanism accelerates these effects. Economic growth could be enhanced if tort liability were shorn of its insurance features and liability attached only where a party failed to make a cost-effective investment in prevention of the loss.

Notes

I am grateful for comments on an earlier draft to Frank Buckley, Eric Rasmusen, and participants at the conference at which the articles in this volume were first presented.

1. O. W. Holmes, The Common Law 96 (1881).

2. For a more detailed discussion of this history, see Priest, The Invention of Enterprise Liability: A Critical History of the Intellectual Foundations of Modern Tort Law, 14 J. Legal Studies 461 (1985).

3. 24 Cal. 2d 453, 461, 150 P.2d 436, 440 (1944).

4. The case appears so simple to the modern eye that one wonders why the jury verdict in favor of the waitress was appealed to the California Supreme Court. In historical context, the case raised an interesting issue regarding the res ipsa doctrine since the manufacturer had dropped off the bottle at the restaurant some substantial time (36 hours) prior to the accident. At the time, a defense to a res ipsa claim was that the manufacturer had relinquished control of the product and thus should not be responsible for any subsequent event, which was attributed to the user or consumer, again suggesting the limited reach of tort liability.

5. Escola, 150 P.2d at 440–441.

6. Greenman v. Yuba Power Prods., Inc., 59 Cal 2d 57, 377 P.2d 897, 27 Cal. Rptr. 697 (1963) (Traynor, C.J.).

7. Restatement (Second) of Torts, § 402(A) (1964).

8. For a fuller discussion of these events, see Priest, supra note 2.

9. Ronald H. Coase, The Problem of Social Cost, 3 J. Law & Econ. 1 (1960).

10. For some mid-term evidence of this trend, see Priest, Products Liability and the Accident Rate, in Liability: Perspectives and Policy at 184 (Litan and Winston, eds., 1988); Priest, How to Control Liability Costs, Fortune, April 24, 1989 at 323.

11. John W. Wade, On the Nature of Strict Tort Liability for Products, 44 Miss. L. J. 825 (1973).

12. Wade argued that courts in determining whether a product had been defectively designed should consider these factors: (a) The usefulness and desirability of the product—its utility to the user and to the public as a whole. (b) The safety aspects of the product—the likelihood that it will cause injury, and the probable seriousness of the injury. (c) The availability of a substitute product that would meet the same need and not be as unsafe. (d) The manufacturer's ability to eliminate the unsafe character of the product without impairing its usefulness or making it too expensive to maintain its utility. (e) The user's ability to avoid danger by the exercise of care in the use of the product. (f) The user's anticipated awareness of the dangers inherent in the product and their avoidability, because of general public knowledge of the obvious condition of the product, or of the existence of suitable warnings or instructions. (g) The feasibility, on the part of the manufacturer, of spreading the loss by setting the price of the product or carrying liability insurance.

13. See David G. Owen, Products Liability Law 499–504 (2005).

14. Cf. id. at 503–504. But see Owen's description of a recent Georgia Supreme Court case, Banks v. ICI Americas, Inc., 450 S.E.2d 671 (Ga. 1994), id. at 499, adopting an approach and a standard very similar to Wade's.

15. Ronald H. Coase, The Problem of Social Cost, 3 J. Law & Econ. 1 (1960) (The years do not correspond because, as is well known, the Journal of Law & Economics was years behind in its publications).

16. Supra note 6.

17. Guido Calabresi, The Costs of Accidents: A Legal and Economic Analysis (1970).

18. Priest, The Limits of Antitrust and the Chicago School Tradition, 6 J. Competition Law & Econ. 1 (2010). See also Priest, The Rise of Law-and-Economics: A Memoir of the Early Years, in The Origins of Law-and-Economics: Essays by the Founding Fathers 350 (Parisi and Rowley, eds., 2005). Coase understood that market agreements were entered subject to transaction costs. Some analysts used the existence of transaction costs to justify the expansion of liability, chiefly in property law areas though also, as will be discussed, to justify the modern class action. This argument is unavailable in the products field and in other areas where transaction costs are low.

19. Guido Calabresi and A. Douglas Melamed, Property Rules, Liability Rules and Inalienability: One View of the Cathedral, 85 Harv. L. Rev. 1089 (1972).

20. See Priest, supra note 2, for a further discussion. See also Priest, A Theory of the Consumer Product Warranty, 90 Yale L. J. 1297 (1981), for a description of the operation of the market for product warranties.

21. Harold Demsetz, When Does the Rule of Liability Matter?, 1 J. Legal Stud. 13 (1972); Demsetz, Wealth Distribution and the Ownership of Rights, 1 J. Legal Stud. 223 (1972).

22. Guido Calabresi, The Decision for Accidents: An Approach to Nonfault Allocation of Costs, 78 Harv. L. Rev. 713, 730 n. 28, 731 n. 30 (1965); Calabresi, Fault, Accidents and the Wonderful World of Blum and Kalven, 75 Yale L. J. 216, 231–232 (1965).

23. Guido Calabresi, Transaction Costs, Resource Allocation and Liability Rules—A Comment, 11 J. Law & Econ. 67 (1968).

24. See, e.g., Guido Calabresi, The Pointlessness of Pareto: Carrying Coase Further, 100 Yale L. J. 1211 (1991).

25. Richard A. Posner, A Theory of Negligence, 1 J. Legal Stud. 29 (1972). For good reason, much of the attention and respect given to Posner's conclusions derived from his prodigious energy.

26. Priest, The Rise of Law-and-Economics, supra note 18.

27. Coase studied law as an undergraduate.

28. Richard A. Posner, Economic Analysis of Law §8.1 (8th ed. 2010).

29. As editor of the Journal of Law & Economics, Coase was interested in legal rules dealing with industrial organization because he saw that regulatory policies or antitrust decisions could influence output. Regulatory commands and antitrust prohibitions cannot be contracted around. Coase did not apply the same critical approach to common law rules, perhaps because he thought contracting around was generally possible; thus, the market would correct legal rules. As mentioned, this is not true of the rules of modern tort law.

30. Ronald H. Coase, The British Post Office and the Messenger Companies, 4 J. Law & Econ. 12 (1961).

31. William M. Landes and Richard A. Posner, Joint and Multiple Tortfeasors: An Economic Analysis, 9 J. Legal Stud. 517 (1980). The point had been made earlier, though less comprehensively, in John Prather Brown, Toward an Economic Theory of Liability, 2 J. Legal Stud. 323 (1973).

32. Steven Shavell, Strict Liability versus Negligence, 9 J. Legal Stud. 1 (1980).

33. Because both parties to any accident can adjust their activity levels.

34. See, e.g., Richard A. Epstein, Modern Products Liability Law: A Legal Revolution (1980).

35. Richard A. Epstein, A Theory of Strict Liability, 2 J. Legal Stud. 151 (1979).

36. See, e.g., Priest, The Current Insurance Crisis and Modern Tort Law, 96 Yale L. J. 1521 (1987).

37. Peter W. Huber, Liability: The Legal Revolution and Its Consequences (1989).

38. Paul H. Rubin, Tort Reform by Contract (1993).

39. See Holmes's view on litigation, supra note 1. Holmes's view was more divergent from the modern approach and, if adopted, would have prevented the expansion of liability. In the passage cited at note 1, supra, Holmes wrote:

> The state might conceivably make itself a mutual insurance company against accidents, and distribute the burden of its citizens' mishaps among all its members. There might be a pension for paralytics, and state aid for those who suffered in person or estate from tempest or wild beasts. As between individ-

uals it might adopt the mutual insurance principle pro tanto, and divide damages when both were at fault, as in the rusticum judicium of the admiralty, or it might throw all loss upon the actor irrespective of fault. The state does none of these things . . .

State interference is an evil, where it cannot be shown to be a good. Universal insurance, if desired, can be better and more cheaply accomplished by private enterprise. The undertaking to redistribute losses simply on the ground that they resulted from the defendant's act would not only be open to these objections, but, as it is hoped the preceding discussion has shown, to the still graver offense of offending the sense of justice. The Common Law at 96.

Obviously, Justice Traynor, and modern tort law, rejected Holmes's judgment.

40. Other prerequisites for class certification are defined to give the representative class members individual plaintiff-like control over the class litigation. See Priest, Procedural versus Substantive Controls of Mass Tort Class Actions, 26 J. Legal Stud. 521 (1997).

41. How they do so is described in other chapters of this book, notably those in Part 3.

42. Priest and Klein, The Selection of Disputes for Litigation, 13 J. Legal Stud. 1 (1984). Put quite briefly, this result occurs because defendants are unwilling to offer a settlement equal to a plaintiff's demand where the defendant believes (more than the plaintiff) that the defendant will win the case.

43. Class Action Fairness Act of 2005, 28 U.S.C. §§ 1453, 1711–1715 (2006).

44. For a discussion of this period, see Priest, supra note 36.

45. See, e.g., William M. Landes and Richard A. Posner, The Economic Structure of Tort Law 54–80 (1987).

46. For a further discussion of these points, see Priest, supra note 36.

47. See Priest, How Insurance Reduces Risk, mimeo (1996). Briefly, insurance policies are drafted to include definitions of coverage, conditions, and exclusions that create incentives for the policyholder to constrain losses that allow reduced insurance premiums.

48. See Priest, A Theory of the Consumer Product Warranty, 90 Yale L. J. 1297 (1981); Priest, supra note 36.

49. First-party health insurers routinely pursue claims against product and service providers through subrogation provisions in their plans. A separate, but unpublished, study (Priest and Kathleen Cleaver), shows that, in modern products liability litigation, only 4 percent of litigated cases are brought by low-income claimants.

Regulation, Taxation, and Litigation

W. KIP VISCUSI

R egulation, taxation, and litigation are three policy mechanisms
that can be employed to influence individual and corporate behavior in order to advance societal objectives. These mechanisms often interact with each other, and not always in a favorable manner. As I
will demonstrate, litigation by government entities may lead to settlements
that impose excessive regulations and tax penalties. Notwithstanding the
presence of strong regulatory requirements, weak regulatory compliance
defenses offer inadequate shields against potential litigation liability. For
concreteness I focus on how different social institutions address health
and safety risks, but the principles involved apply to many other situations
as well.

My discussion takes as the policy objective the promotion of economic
efficiency, or the maximization of the net benefits to the citizenry. In many
contexts the efficient outcome will emerge from decentralized economic
decisions. With respect to health and safety risks, there is substantial evidence that markets play a constructive role, as consumers and workers are
often aware of the risks associated with products and jobs and receive
either a price cut for dangerous products or a wage premium for risky jobs.
The value of these money-risk tradeoffs is on the order of $9 million per

expected death.[1] Even in situations where real risks may be present, markets have much to recommend them, by matching people to activities and products that they prefer and that are in line with their personal attitudes toward risk.

State interference with market decisions is typically said to be justified on claims of one of four types of market failure. First, consumers and workers might be thought to underestimate the risk, leading to excessive risk-taking behavior. Second, people might act irrationally—for example, by placing insufficient weight on the effect of current decisions on their future welfare. Third, there may be informational problems, particularly with respect to informational asymmetries in which the producer knows more about the risk than does the consumer. Finally, there might be third-party harms or externalities, such as pollution resulting from industrial activity and auto accident costs inflicted by careless drivers. These externalities would not pose an efficiency problem if the third parties could bargain with the injurer to lead to an efficient level of harm prevention. If the conditions of the Coase Theorem are satisfied,[2] and there are no barriers to bargaining, then private bargains can reduce externalities such as pollution to an economically efficient level. However, as Coase recognized, there are often important practical barriers to such negotiations.

Forms of State Intervention

Establishing a rationale for intervention does not imply that every form of intervention is warranted, as the modes of intervention have different characteristics. Government regulation attempts to control behavior or technologies directly, as with the requirement that cars have airbags. Alternatively, state intervention might take the form of financial incentives to alter behavior, such as gasoline taxes designed to reduce gasoline usage. In other respects, regulation and taxation have many similar characteristics. Both policies result from a deliberative governmental process. Legislation to impose taxes is the result of legislative action, and excise taxes are often imposed with advice and input from regulatory agencies. Similarly, government regulations are subject to a formal rulemaking process. Neither regulation nor tax policies involve transfers of monetary payments to compensate injured parties. Both regulation and taxation are designed to foster prevention of risks. Regulations generally involve broad rules, such as specification standards for permissible risks. Similarly, financial mechanisms such as alcoholic beverage taxes are not tailored to the specific characteristics of the affected firm. The design and implementation of regulations are based on the technical expertise of government agencies, and in the case of tax or financial penalty policies, this expertise is augmented by legislative review. The process by which regulatory and tax policies emerge is subject to the influence of competing interest groups. Finally, tax and regulatory policies are enforced by public agencies.

The way in which the civil justice system addresses risk and environmental harms through litigation is quite different from regulation and taxation. Litigation occurs on an ex post basis, after the damage has occurred. The judgment of liability is based on facts of the specific case and not on industry-wide averages or some other aggregative approach used in setting regulatory policies. Unlike governmental intervention that draws on the technical expertise of government agencies, the courts rely on juries that in turn may be informed by experts who testify in these cases. Governmental actions are open to a wide variety of forms of public input and political influence that do not affect the functioning of the courts, which instead reflect the public through the preferences and possible biases of the jury pool and the judge.

The role of the courts differs from regulation and taxation not only in the determination of liability but also in the compensation for the harms that tort law provides. While compensation to accident victims serves an insurance function for tort victims, this is a very costly form of insurance in terms of the transaction costs associated with litigation and legal fees. Using data on a comprehensive set of tort cases from Texas, Hersch and Viscusi found that for every dollar paid to plaintiffs, there were legal expenses of 75 cents.[3] Tort liability is consequently much more costly than social insurance plans such as workers' compensation, for which the administrative costs are much less. In addition, the very high levels of sanc-

tions that may be required to establish incentives for safety may provide
too much compensation from an insurance standpoint.[4] Regulatory and
tax policies often have greater leeway in that respect.

The Regulatory Compliance Defense

A rational scheme of government regulation would not subject companies and individuals to overlapping and duplicative mechanisms for promoting safety. Thus a principal way in which tort liability and regulation
could potentially interact is through regulatory compliance defenses that
absolve defendants from the threat of litigation if they comply with government regulations. Regulatory standards are generally higher than the efficient level of safety, given the restrictive legislative mandates of regulatory
agencies. Compliance with such regulations should therefore provide evidence that the firm has struck a reasonable balance between cost and risk.
As a result, companies in compliance with regulations should not be subject to negligence claims for matters addressed by these regulations, and
certainly should not be subject to punitive damages.[5]

A review of federal regulatory policies indicates why regulatory compliance should function as a safe harbor. U.S. Department of Transportation
regulations must meet a test that the benefits of the regulation exceed the
costs, which is the standard economic version of a legal negligence test.
Regulations from the U.S. Occupational Safety and Health Administration and the U.S. Environmental Protection Agency go even further, usually mandating regulations for which the cost per life saved is well beyond
any economic efficiency reference point, such as the value of statistical life.
Similarly, in its approval process for drugs, the U.S. Food and Drug Administration (FDA) requires that drugs be shown to be both safe and effective. This approval process is quite thorough, involving a Phase I trial on
small groups, a Phase II trial on 200–300 patients with the condition, and
Phase III trials on 1,000–3,000 patients with the condition. New information may become available over time, and companies should provide the
agencies with pertinent information that might lead them to alter the regulations or the approval status of a drug. However, from the standpoint of

economic efficiency, there is no basis for the courts to second-guess the expert judgments of regulatory agencies in situations in which agencies have established pertinent regulations.

Compliance with regulatory warning label standards should also provide a safe harbor against litigation. Here the issue is not the appropriate standards of care along a continuum of possible intensity, but rather the form and content of the warning. For warnings, it is highly desirable that firms be able to provide warnings using established, uniform vocabularies. Standardizing the use of human hazard signal words such as "Danger," and restricting the use of warnings formats such as black-box warnings to particular kinds of risk situations, maintain a degree of commonality that enables consumers to interpret the relative risk being conveyed by the message and to distinguish situations in which particular care is warranted. The FDA is perhaps the most prominent example of an agency that can promote such uniformity in that it reviews and approves all warnings for drugs and medical devices.

In contrast, warnings cases that end up in courts are decided by jurors and do not adhere to a standardized warnings vocabulary. A satisfactory warning in one state, before one jury, might be unsatisfactory before another jury, in that or another state. The result will be excessive warnings, as firms try to anticipate the different standards that might be imposed. In addition, juries will be affected by hindsight bias—the kind of Monday-morning quarterbacking that leads jurors to think that a one-in-a-million accident was inevitable and foreseen by the defendant ("If only this particular warning had been included on the product, the accident would not have occurred"). Minor hazards are thus elevated to the same level as truly serious risks, leading to a warning label that, by warning of every conceivable accident, becomes so cluttered that it warns no one. If everything is labeled hazardous, then those exposed to risk will not be able to draw distinctions as to which risks merit attention.[6]

Unfortunately, regulatory compliance defenses have been rejected by the courts. Although there is a legislative provision for regulatory compliance defenses for medical devices, these defenses are not generally accepted and were recently rejected for pharmaceutical products in *Wyeth v. Levine* by the U.S. Supreme Court.[7] If meaningful regulatory compliance defenses are to emerge, they must be provided through legislatively enacted safe harbors.

State Tobacco Litigation

The linkage between regulation and litigation can also take the form of litigation that generates regulations as part of the settlement. This is most likely to happen when the plaintiff is a governmental entity that views the settlement negotiations as a mechanism for achieving policy outcomes that could not be accomplished by conventional means. To illustrate this phenomenon, this article focuses on the state tobacco litigation against the cigarette industry as a case study of how litigation can result in tax and regulatory outcomes.[8] It is also noteworthy that state tobacco litigation rejected regulatory compliance safe harbors, in that the U.S. Congress mandated warnings for cigarettes beginning in 1966, and industry compliance with these warnings has not absolved firms from liability even for failure-to-warn claims. The cigarette experience is of substantial interest in that the stakes involved in the litigation and the ultimate settlement are greater than the outcomes in any previous case. Other cases that might involve similar issues include litigation involving guns and lead paint.[9]

Although cigarettes are associated with substantial health risks, the focus of the state litigation was not on the health losses to the smokers but on the financial costs of smoking to the states. In particular, the cases were based on the gross financial externalities affecting Medicaid, and not on wrongful death or personal injury claims. There were no claims for any losses to individual smokers, whether for their financial costs or nonpecuniary losses such as pain and suffering.

State attorneys-general began filing these cases in 1995. The basis for the claims was that the cigarette industry was guilty of wrongful conduct in the manufacture and marketing of cigarettes. This conduct in turn allegedly led to smoking behavior that people would not have chosen had they been better informed or had available a different product mix including safer cigarettes. Thus, had it not been for the wrongful conduct, there would have been no financial costs associated with smoking.

At the time the litigation was filed, the prospects for success were not great as the cigarette industry had not made any payout to date in an individual smoker case, where the claims of wrongful conduct were usually similar to the claims made in the state cases. There are many consumer products associated with injuries, such as cars and sports equipment, but manufacturers are not generally liable for the financial costs associated with all product-related injuries.

Not all states filed lawsuits against the tobacco industry. For example, the state of Alabama refused to file a lawsuit, based on the premise that the risks of smoking were well known and that therefore these claims lacked a sound basis.[10] Nevertheless, all states, including Alabama, were involved in the settlement of the litigation in 1998. Four states—Mississippi, Minnesota, Florida, and Texas—settled separately. These were the states where the litigation was most advanced. At the time of the settlement, a tobacco trial for the state's claims was in progress in Minnesota. The other 46 states settled in a joint arrangement known as the Master Settlement Agreement (MSA).

The MSA imposed regulations and financial penalties that are the equivalent of a tax. The extensive regulatory components imposed a wide variety of limitations on tobacco marketing, and the tax payments and other financial sanctions total about $250 million over the first 25 years of the MSA, which runs in perpetuity. Thus, the MSA can correctly be viewed as a large-scale intervention on both the tax and regulatory dimensions.

The process by which the MSA emerged was not unlike other negotiated settlements in that it was the outcome of bargaining between the parties that was not open to the public. The states were represented by their attorneys-general, although not all of them were actively involved in the negotiations. The lead negotiator for the states was then attorney-general and now governor of the state of Washington, Christine Gregoire. The other parties to the negotiations consisted of representatives of the major tobacco companies, which were the defendants in these cases. No public interest or consumer group representatives were included in the negotiations, nor were there representatives of other tobacco companies not named in the lawsuits. Once the parties to the negotiations reached a settlement, the attorneys-general from each state had to sign off on the arrangement. There was no requirement that the state legislatures approve the deal, and in the case of Massachusetts the governor publicly opposed the settlement. Several of the state attorneys-general were running for office in 1998, and most but not all of them signed on to the agreement before the election.

The MSA as a Tobacco Tax

How the settlement should be structured was a matter of considerable debate. In a typical personal injury case, the settlement usually takes the form of a lump-sum damages payment from the defendant to the plaintiff. One might then have expected that, if successful, states might have sought a money payment based on the increased Medicaid costs attributable to smoking. Another frequent form of compensation in personal injury cases is that of structured settlements, in which payments are made over time in a manner that corresponds to the changing financial burdens over time. However, all the damages claimed in the cases were prior financial costs incurred by the states so that there was no comparable rationale for a structured settlement.

The negotiators of the MSA considered two quite different payment options. The first option was that of a lump-sum penalty, analogous to a conventional damages award. This, however, was thought unsatisfactory for several reasons. A damages award on the order of $250 billion would have pushed the tobacco companies to reorganize under bankruptcy law, with the result that, as unsecured creditors, the states would receive less than this amount. Further, since the damages payment would have been a fixed cost, it would not have affected the price of cigarettes. Firms would not have been able to pass the costs on to consumers because they would be undercut by new entrants if they attempted to do so.

The second payment option, adopted by the MSA, was to structure the damages payment in a form equivalent to an excise tax on every pack that is sold in perpetuity. This will not trigger the bankruptcy option, so that ultimately the states will be able to reap a greater financial reward from the settlement. In addition to generating a higher payout to the states than they would obtain under a lump-sum damages payment, a tax equivalent per pack will raise the price of cigarettes.[11] The effect of this increase will be to discourage smoking because, as with other products, cigarettes have a demand curve that is downward sloping. In terms of policy objectives, the per-pack damages payment serves to discourage smoking, while the lump sum payment approach does not.

The per-pack payment approach was clearly preferable for the defendants. To the extent that there is a reduction in smoking, that decrease in turn would adversely affect cigarette industry profits, but not to the same extent as would a lump-sum damages payment. The magnitude of these MSA settlement payments linked to sales is the equivalent of 40 cents per pack. Such a tax increase reflected an 18.4% increase in the price of cigarettes. With a cigarette demand elasticity in the range of -0.4 to -0.7, this price increase led to a 7–13% decrease in cigarette demand.

These calculations and the lack of a severe effect on company profits assume that all firms are subject to the same penalty. In theory, new entrants not covered by the agreement could enter the industry, undercut existing firms' prices, and gain market share. Since new entrants were not involved in the litigation and had no past wrongful conduct, they should not have been subject to the damages payments, however construed. To avoid placing the defendant firms in an adverse competitive position, the MSA also provided for payments to be made by all companies selling cigarettes, not just those companies that were parties to the original agreement.

The financial structure of the MSA settlement is consequently quite unconventional. Rather than a lump-sum damages payment, the settlement is in the form of a tax per pack of 40 cents. Moreover, this tax is not limited to defendant companies, but extends to new entrants or companies marketing new brands of cigarettes. The damages being sought in the cases were for financial costs to the states based on alleged patterns of wrongful conduct. However, the payment requirements are divorced from any past behavior but instead are levied on all firms in the industry, whether or not they caused any previous damages. Thus, the MSA in effect included a de facto excise tax arrangement that was made possible by the litigation but that was not directly linked to the harms allegedly caused by the particular companies.

One might view the payment as penalizing risks and financial costs associated with cigarette consumption in the future. Thus, even if there is no damages-based rationale linked to wrongful conduct, perhaps the tax can be viewed as a mechanism for recouping financial externalities associated with cigarettes. However, there are three principal problems with this argument—the lack of any link of the tax to any financial externalities, the failure to consider net financial externalities, and the role of political factors rather than costs in determining the MSA share amounts.

First, the penalty amount is independent of the riskiness of particular cigarettes. Even if companies developed a risk-free cigarette associated with no increase in medical costs, this product would be subject to the same tax per pack. Thus, the excise tax structure is not related to any future financial externalities caused by the cigarettes. Moreover, there is clearly no link to previous externalities: companies that did not market cigarettes and are innocent of wrongful conduct are required to pay the fee even if the cigarettes they market are risk free.

Second, if the objective of the tax penalty is to internalize the financial externalities of cigarettes, the tax should encompass all net financial externalities. The state litigation isolated one financial externality, the increased Medicaid costs associated with cigarettes. However, the adverse health consequences of cigarettes have other financial ramifications as well, including a reduction in pension costs, social security costs, and nursing home costs. My calculations of these financial consequences demonstrate that on balance cigarettes do not impose a net financial externality on society. Indeed, there is a net cost reduction of 32 cents per pack due to smoking.[12] Similarly, even excluding the role of state excise taxes, there is no net financial externality to any state. Smoking does impose costs, but these costs consist largely of the internal health losses to smokers and not financial harm to the rest of society.

Third, the MSA payments to the particular states were based on the negotiations among the attorneys-general, and were not strictly linked to tobacco-related costs. Thus, political and strategic considerations determined payouts. The State of Washington fared very well in terms of its MSA share relative to cigarette financial costs, reflecting the influence of the lead attorney-general in the litigation. All the four major tobacco-producing states fared poorly in terms of receiving a smaller share of the MSA payments than would be appropriate based on their smoking-related health care costs. A particularly striking example of the role of salient bargaining points is that New York and California, the two largest states, received almost identical shares of the settlement—12.995% and 12.997%. However, California's share of the smoking health care costs was only 8.551%, as compared with New York's 15.170% share, so that New York was shortchanged and California was substantially overpaid for smoking-related costs.

Because the payments will continue into perpetuity, the MSA payment structure will lead to long-term financial gains for the states. Given the political pressures for balancing budgets in the short term when current officials would be in office rather than the long term when future officials would have to address budgetary shortfalls, there is an incentive to reap the financial gains from the payments sooner rather than later. Several states followed this course by securitizing the proceeds whereby states were able to reap payments now in view of the discounted expected value of the future payment stream. Whether the payments are securitized or not does not influence the incentive effects of the payments.

MSA as Regulation

The MSA included a remarkable number of provisions that were regulatory in character. These restrictions resembled the kinds of policies that one would expect to emerge from either legislation or a formal rulemaking process rather than the private negotiations involved in the MSA. Notably, the regulatory components do not address specific aspects of alleged wrongful conduct, such as misrepresenting the riskiness of cigarettes, but instead consisted of a list of policy initiatives designed to reduce smoking rates.

The main cluster of regulatory initiatives pertained to cigarette industry marketing and advertising. The MSA banned the targeting of youths in advertising and the use of cartoons in advertising. Since the most well-known cartoon character used in advertising, Joe Camel, had already been permanently retired by R. J. Reynolds, this provision was not as influential as it would have been earlier. The MSA also banned the use of free samples, outdoor cigarette advertising, tobacco brand name merchandise, and payments for cigarette product placements in movies and television shows.

Although one can properly treat these measures as anti-smoking initiatives, more generally they can be viewed as advertising restrictions. In effect, the MSA provided a mechanism by which firms could establish a legal arrangement to restrict advertising. Interestingly, such an effort is the paradigmatic example of collusion by firms in an industry to deter new entrants in the market and reap anti-competitive profits.[13] Although collusion to restrict advertising in an industry is generally profit-enhancing for the firms, such collusion is illegal. The MSA, however, provided a legal mechanism by which the firms could overcome these restrictions.

A potential puzzle is why the attorneys-general would support an MSA structure that, in effect, fosters the cartelization of the cigarette industry. One possible explanation is that, driven by their myopic anti-tobacco agenda, any measure that decreased the number of cigarette companies or cigarette advertising was viewed as being in the public interest. There was no apparent recognition of the desirable aspects of market competition with respect to both product prices and product characteristics, including cigarette safety.

There is no evidence of changes in market concentration since the MSA. Instead, stability is the norm, as one would expect given the decreased potential role of market competition. In particular, the standard measure of market concentration (the HHI index) remained stable from 1997 to 2005.[14] Philip Morris, now known as Altria, has maintained its dominant market position with a market share that appears to be locked in at 49–51%.

The MSA also required the elimination of two industry trade associations, the Tobacco Institute and the Council for Tobacco Research. The Tobacco Institute is perhaps best known for producing the annual compilation of tax and sales information, *The Tax Burden on Tobacco*, which is now privately produced by consultants. As a result of the MSA, joint efforts for lobbying or funded research through these trade associations consequently would need to be replaced by separate company efforts.[15]

An even more striking regulatory outcome was the possible use of MSA fees to fund anti-smoking efforts. The potential use of the funds for either anti-smoking policies or smoking-related health care costs fell far short of the avowed purposes of the funds. Before the MSA was finalized, there were common public pronouncements that the funds were needed for anti-tobacco efforts, particularly to discourage youth smoking. However, very little of the funding was used for that purpose.[16] Many states used the funds to balance their state budgets or to fund public works projects such as road and sidewalk repair.

The MSA settlement also may have altered the political landscape in a way that ultimately led to additional regulation through the enactment of the federal 2009 Family Smoking Prevention and Tobacco Control Act. Before the MSA was reached, there were attempts to end the state cases legislatively. Although the proposed legislative resolution of the cigarette litigation was never enacted, many of the regulatory components of the proposal surfaced in the MSA and in the Family Smoking Prevention and Tobacco Control Act. That act gave the Food and Drug Administration (FDA) authority to regulate cigarettes, banned the use of descriptors such as "light" and "low tar," and introduced more extensive warnings on cigarettes, including a graphic warnings proposal by the FDA in 2010.[17] Since the MSA there have also been cigarette excise tax increases at the local, state, and federal levels, and these too may reflect a shift in the political environment.

Effects of the MSA on Litigation

The tobacco industry supported the MSA for two reasons. First, it sought to avoid all adverse competitive effects of the MSA by deterring competition. Second, it sought to reduce the uncertainty and expenses associated with tobacco litigation. However, this second objective was realized only with respect to state Medicaid cases. Three factors contributed to the continuing wave of tobacco litigation: the release of tobacco industry documents, the anchoring effect of the MSA payment, and the funding of attorneys who also engage in other tobacco-related cases.

The MSA provided for the release and posting of the tobacco industry documents and expert reports from the Minnesota case. While publicly archiving this information may appear to be innocuous, the release of these documents on the Web reduced the discovery costs associated with future litigation. The MSA marked the closure of the state liability claims so that there would not be comparable future claims, but there could potentially be future individual claims and class actions that could utilize this information in subsequent cases. After the conclusion of the MSA, there have been successful individual claims filed against the industry as well as class actions with very large verdicts.

The second way in which the MSA affected subsequent litigation is through the payout of a settlement with a value over 25 years of about $250 billion. The exact tally varied depending on what components of the costs were counted. This startling settlement amount likely had effects on both the assessment of liability and damages level in future litigation. If the tobacco industry was willing to pay out hundreds of billions in smoking-related cases, one might infer that it was guilty of major transgressions. This settlement was not a secret deal but a highly publicized event. The payout of such an enormous amount might imply wrongful conduct, which in turn would affect juror attitudes toward assessment of liability in future cases. Whereas the industry had never paid off a claim in any previous tobacco case, that record of unblemished success was tarnished.

In addition, a settlement in the billions established a new anchor for jury awards. In the entire period through 1998 there had been only three punitive damages awards of at least $1 billion.[18] However, cigarette firms have subsequently lost individual cases, with punitive damages awards of $150 million, $3 billion, and $28 billion, as well as class actions with punitive damages awards of $3.1 billion and $145 billion. Although these awards have been overturned or reduced, the $145 billion award in the *Engle* class action case in Florida has generated thousands of *Engle* progeny cases for which the industry has thus far had a mixed record of success.[19]

The third way in which the MSA affects subsequent litigation is through the substantial funding of plaintiff attorneys who represented the states in these matters. Rather than staffing the litigation in house, states retained outside attorneys who were retained on a contingency fee basis. Although the amount of these fees is not generally public, for the states for which the amounts are known the fees are quite large. In particular, the fee amounts were $1.43 billion for Mississippi, $3.43 billion for Florida, $3.3 billion for

Texas, $111 million for Missouri, and $265 million for Ohio. The Chamber of Commerce tally of tobacco case legal fees in the states for which it could obtain information was $11 billion. Because there was no competitive bidding, these huge payments generated major windfall gains.

These payments may stimulate additional tort litigation, as many plaintiff attorneys will now have the resources to launch other cases. In addition, to the extent that such windfalls establish the prospect for similar gains in tobacco class actions and other large-scale cases, the financial incentive to bring such suits will also be enhanced.

The Political Economy of Regulation and Taxation by Litigation

Before examining the process by which the MSA established regulations and tax policies, it is worthwhile to review the operation of the rule-making process generally. To initiate a rule, the agency must first obtain the approval of the U.S. Office of Management and Budget (OMB), which ensures that the rule is consistent with the agency's legislative mandate. The agency then prepares the proposed rule and an associated regulatory impact analysis that evaluates the economic consequences of the regulation. OMB has 60 days to review the proposal and determine that the rule is consistent with administrative objectives and the agency's legal authority. A key test applied by OMB is whether the benefits of the regulation are shown to exceed the costs. If OMB approval is obtained, the agency issues a notice of proposed rulemaking in the *Federal Register,* which is followed by a 30- to 90-day public comment period. The agency then prepares the final rule and must obtain OMB approval before publishing it in the *Federal Register.* Even after the final rule is published, there is the opportunity for both congressional review before the rule takes effect, and judicial rule after the rule goes into effect.

By comparison, the process by which the MSA was devised is cavalier. There was no regulatory impact analysis of the costs and benefits of the regulations, the effect on market structure, or other usual components of a regulatory impact analysis. There was no requirement that the benefits of the regulation exceed the costs. Nor was there any opportunity for public input. The process by which the MSA was developed was not open to the public or subject to any public comment period and review. The ad hoc nature of the process creates opportunities for inordinate rewards to the deal makers.

The absence of any consumer or public interest representation may have influenced the ultimate structure of the bargain. The damages payment in terms of a financial penalty per pack serves to shift the brunt of the cost of the settlement to an unpopular class of smokers, who were not represented in the bargaining process. Coupling these penalties with requirements that new entrants also pay that fee serves to protect the competitive position of existing firms. Similarly, the advertising restrictions may appear to serve a public policy purpose, but they also amount to a barrier to entry for new firms and compose a standard textbook case of collusion that firms will find to be desirable.

To the extent that the cigarette litigation experience is replicated by similar uses of litigation to impose regulatory and tax policies, the outcomes that emerge are likely to be far more harmful to society than policies that government agencies promulgate. The use of litigation settlements to impose policy outcomes falls short on two principal dimensions. First, the private interests of the parties involved in the negotiations are not synonymous with the public interest. There will be incentives to maximize private financial gains by shifting costs to parties outside the negotiations and to use the settlements for anti-competitive purposes. Smokers and potential new entrants to the cigarette market were most adversely affected by the structure of the deal. Second, the private negotiation process lacks all the substantive inputs and reviews associated with regulatory and tax policies. The input of agency experts and a wide array of business and consumer groups potentially make policies much more effective and reflective of the diverse impacts that they have across society. The participation of interest groups in the usual governmental processes is not a flaw in democratic society but a mechanism by which the preferences of these groups can be expressed.

The use of litigation by government entities to force regulatory and tax-type policies is a recent development that should be discouraged. The proper forum for developing regulatory and tax policies remains the established governmental institutions. Failure to work through the requisite political process may appear to be politically expedient for advocates of particular policy interventions, but may lead to policies that both are not well founded and are more in the private interest of the parties to the negotiation than in the broader societal interest.

The 2011 U.S. Supreme Court decision in *American Electric Power Co. v. Connecticut* will likely rein in some of the more extreme attempts at regulation by litigation. A group consisting of eight states, New York City, and three nonprofit land trusts had sought to use Environmental Protection Agency regulations to cap greenhouse gas emissions from electric utilities. In rejecting their claim, the Court recognized that the division of labor between the courts and regulatory agencies had a strong practical rationale, given the comparative advantage of different social institutions: "The expert agency is surely better equipped to do the job than individual district judges issuing ad hoc, case-by-case injunctions. Federal judges lack the scientific, economic, and technological resources an agency can utilize in coping with issues of this order."[20]

While the use of litigation to generate regulation is a practice that should be discouraged, there is good reason to foster the linkage in the opposite direction. Compliance with government regulations for safety and government-approved warnings should address concerns about whether the company was negligent or guilty of reckless behavior. For the most part, these regulations specify a level of stringency that goes beyond what is efficient from a benefit-cost standpoint. To the extent that juries nevertheless choose to find companies liable even when they are in compliance with such regulations, it is usually because of some failure of jury rationality such as hindsight bias. In contrast, regulatory agencies can make judgments of the costs and benefits across the entire class of consumers of a product, which is the appropriate vantage point.

Why do these problems of overlap and failure to consider appropriate interactions persist? In part, the courts may suffer from a tort-centric perspective. If the courts represent the sole societal mechanism for addressing inadequacies in safety and warnings, then the role of other social institutions need not be considered. But given the emergence of substantial government regulations beginning particularly in the 1970s, the legal system should adapt to the presence of other social institutions. As the decision in *Wyeth v. Levine* made clear, however, such a recognition of the proper role of the courts is likely to require legislative action specifying the nature of any regulatory compliance defense.

The developing American system of regulation by litigation will, if left unchecked, weaken our economy and undermine the legitimate role of governmental institutions. The perverse bargains cut between ambitious politicians and industries, which offer the former the political support of trial lawyers and the latter the promise of an anti-competitive market structure, are yet additional symptoms of the American Illness.

Notes

1. This $9 million value is based on the median estimate in the literature for the value of statistical life based on labor market studies, which is $7 million in year 2000 dollars, or $8.9 million in 2010 dollars. See W. K. Viscusi and J. Aldy, The Value of a Statistical Life: A Critical Review of Market Estimates throughout the World, 27 J. Risk & Uncertainty 5 (2003).

2. R. Coase, The Problem of Social Cost, 3 J. L. Econ. 1 (1960).

3. See J. Hersch and W. K. Viscusi, Tort Liability Litigation Costs for Commercial Claims, 9 Am. L. Econ. Rev. 330 (2007).

4. This is a well-known, long-standing limitation of tort liability. See, e.g., M. Spence, Consumer Misperceptions, Product Failure, and Producer Liability, 44 Rev. Econ. Stud. 561 (1977). Addressing two different policy objectives—deterrence and insurance—with a single policy instrument of a damages payment will often involve compromising one of the two objectives.

5. An American Law Institute group advocated such a defense against punitive damages. See American Law Institute, Enterprise Responsibility for Personal Injury—Reporters Study (1991).

6. Similarly, if every day at the airport merits a Department of Homeland Security Orange alert, then there will never be a motivation to exercise particular caution.

7. Wyeth, Petitioner v. Diana Levine, 129 S. Ct. 1187 (2009).

8. Much of the discussion below is documented in W. K. Viscusi, Smoke-Filled Rooms: A Postmortem on the Tobacco Deal (2002).

9. For a series of such case studies, see Regulation through Litigation (W. K. Viscusi, ed., 2002), and Regulation versus Litigation: Perspectives from Economics and Law (D. Kessler, ed., 2011).

10. The reasons for this decision are discussed in Report of the Task Force on Tobacco Litigation Submitted to Governor James and Attorney General Sessions by the Task Force on Tobacco Litigation Chaired by William Pryor, Jr., Deputy Attorney General, Oct. 2, 1996, reprinted in 27 Cumb. L. Rev. 557 (1996–1997).

11. This result is a consequence of the relatively flat supply curves for cigarettes.

12. W. K. Viscusi, Smoke-Filled Rooms: A Postmortem on the Tobacco Deal (2002).

13. W. K. Viscusi, J. Harrington, and J. Vernon, Economics of Regulation and Antitrust (4th ed. 2005).

14. W. K. Viscusi and J. Hersch, Tobacco Regulation through Litigation: The Master Settlement Agreement, in Regulation Versus Litigation: Perspectives from Economics and Law (D. Kessler, ed., 2011).

15. Given the substantial market concentration in the cigarette industry, this change was less drastic than it would have been for an industry consisting of hundreds of small businesses.

16. Only 3.5% of the funds from fiscal year 2000 to fiscal year 2005 were allocated to tobacco control. See the U.S. General Accountability Office, Tobacco Settlement: States' Allocations of Payments from Tobacco Companies from Fiscal Year 2000 through 2005, GAO-07-534T (2007).

17. In 2010 New York City also required the display of graphic cigarette warning posters at points of purchase, but that policy was overturned.

18. A. F. Del Rossi and W. K. Viscusi, The Changing Landscape of Blockbuster Punitive Damages Awards, 12 Am. L. Econ. Rev. 116 (2010), provides a listing of all punitive damages awards of at least $100 million.

19. Engle v. Liggett Group, Inc., 945 So. 2d 1246 (Fla. Sup. Ct., 2006)

20. American Elec. Power Co., Inc. v. Connecticut, 131 S. Ct. 2527, 2531 (2011).

PART 6:

CONTRACT LAW

An English Lawyer Looks at
American Contract Law

MICHAEL BRIDGE

When dealing with contract cases, English courts make much of their commitment to contractual certainty.[1] This is likely a consequence of the fact that contract law has been shaped by major commercial transactions and not by small-scale retail transactions. The paradigmatic contract, indeed, might be said to be a voyage or time charter-party or a sale of commodities. English courts tend to be acutely aware that their decisions will have an impact on sensitive, market-driven contract activity. Moreover, they are very much alive to the importance of finance in the city of London, as well as its satellite activities in insurance and dispute settlement, and so are keen not to undermine the attractions of London and English law.[2] This degree of concern is not one that I have detected in American judicial activity.

Referring to good faith, Lord Steyn once observed: "Since English law serves the international market place it cannot remain impervious to ideas of good faith, or of fair dealing . . . [yet] English lawyers remain resolutely hostile to any incorporation of good faith principles into English law. The hostility . . . is intense."[3] Lord Steyn's note of regret might reflect his training in Roman-Dutch law and not the common law. English contract and commercial lawyers lack a high moral tone. The absence of a written constitution with a bill of rights might have something to do with this, and if so the habituation of modern courts with human rights arising out of the "patriation" of the European Convention on Human Rights[4] might eventually come to provide the conditions for good faith norms to seep generally into English law. Subject to this, "the Nightmare vision of the judicial process as a legally uncontrolled act of lawmaking"[5] is one from which the English judiciary recoils. This commitment to the rule of law is evident in other ways too. Even when the law is changed, as where mistakes of law were held to be eligible for relief, English courts cling to the fiction that they are merely declaring what was always the law.[6]

Codes and Codification

To an English common lawyer, U.S. law appears at times to have mutated into a hybrid system, part common law and part civilian in character. This is the appearance presented by the Uniform Commercial Code, particularly Article 2, which seems to have acquired the character of a general contract statute. The ancestry of Article 2 can be traced back though the Uniform Sales Act 1906 to the U.K. Sale of Goods Act 1893. Both the 1893 Act (and its U.K. successor of 1979) and Article 2 contain a provision that allows access to the underlying common law, which is not a characteristic of civilian codes, but there are at least two features of Article 2 that strike an English common lawyer as civilian in character. The first is the rule of construction in UCC § 1-102(1) that the Uniform Commercial Code (UCC) be "liberally construed and applied to promote its underlying purposes and policies." The second is the emphasis placed on general principles— namely, the principles of unconscionability in § 2-302 and good faith in § 2-103(1)(j).

The first feature strikes me as licensing in extreme cases a type of interpretation that treats the text as a mere springboard for judicial flights of fancy. Does the text have to be ambiguous for this process to be open to a judge, or may the judge disregard the plain meaning of the text? Is the text itself just a historical document, to be updated by a court, or is it a continuing and constant point of reference? Is a "dynamic" interpretation of a text permissible?

My principal concern in this article, however, is the second feature, the emphasis placed on general principles. I propose to state my misgivings about both unconscionability and good faith, drawing appropriate comparisons with English law. In focusing on unconscionability and good faith, I shall try so far as possible to take appropriate account of the difference between the way the law appears on the page and the way it is applied in action. Judicial restraint, when exercised, can be a powerful inhibiting factor. Moreover, it is hard to resist the conclusion that some written law exists to make a moral demonstration—law as rhetoric rather than law in action. It may be that features of the UCC imparting to it an almost civilian flourish do not alter its true character as a mirror of the common law. It should not be forgotten, too, that English case law, with one Court of Appeal and one Supreme Court, is inherently more "manageable" than the case law of fifty jurisdictions,[7] and that the UCC and the Restatements should be viewed with this in mind.

In this short article, I shall not make any claim about the general superiority of English law, about which I have some misgivings. In England, contracts are interpreted in a contextual way that downplays the written word and opens up interpretation to a torrent of extrinsic evidence, at the same time eradicating the distinction between interpretation and implied terms.[8] In part, no doubt, because of the absence of a civil jury, the parol evidence rule, which in its classical form was to exclude extrinsic evidence that adds to, varies, or contradicts the terms of a written contact, has for many years been more or less a dead letter, and this has rendered English law particularly vulnerable to this modern interpretative approach. Nevertheless, the controls placed upon implied terms over the past 100 years[9] have been no small bulwark against excessive judicial intervention in contracts. The new dispensation of contractual interpretation is a Trojan horse carrying within it the threat of such interference.

Before turning to unconscionability and good faith, I wish to add one reservation about the codal pretensions of Article 2. This concerns draftsman Karl Llewellyn's commitment to commercial usage, which has been shown to be anchored in 19th-century German notions of a commercial zeitgeist. Article 2 is replete with references to "reasonable," "seasonable," and "usage," and at one time the merchant jury was seen as a conduit for giving practical expression to these notions. There is something of the antithesis of a code in such a legal philosophy. So far as the law tracks evolving mercantile usage, it throws off the shackles of a code.

The reality, however, is that the connection between Article 2 and mercantile usage, as intended by Llewellyn, never really took root. Judicial interpretation of (and judicial discretion relating to) particular expressions such as seasonable and reasonable by no means amounts to the same thing. There are times when, looking at Article 2, one wonders at its capacity to absorb almost indifferently commercial and consumer contracts. Just how "commercial" is Article 2 of the Uniform Commercial Code? Article 2 has been influential in filling out the content of the United Nations Convention on the International Sale of Goods 1980 (CISG), which does not apply to consumer sale transactions. Yet, with one exception,[10] nothing in the Convention suggests a difference in the content of commercial and consumer sales. Some of its provisions and philosophy, indeed, have been fed into the consumer sales laws of European Union jurisdictions by means of an EU Directive.[11]

Unconscionability

UCC § 2-302, one of the most celebrated provisions in the Code, was extravagantly described by its architect, Llewellyn, as "perhaps the most valuable section in the entire Code."[12] At first blush, it gives new life to a line of Chancery cases featuring an exotic cast of spendthrift heirs, feckless seamen, and vulnerable, income-starved people with capital assets. In England, the case law has lingered on, unreplenished, for over a century, despite Lord Denning's attempt in modern times to fashion a broad principle of unconscionability, drawing upon these and a motley collection of other case law streams.

There is a preference in English contract law for narrower and less abstract categories—in particular, for the rules dealing with undue influence. This preference for the specific is as true for unconscionability as it is for good faith, and specificity commends itself under the modern value of transparency. An outsider must wonder what UCC § 2-302 can possibly mean and will find a particular resonance in Leff's reminder that "it is easy to say nothing with words."[13] And Leff himself, protesting against the vacuity of UCC § 2-302, turned against Llewellyn his own famous dictum that "covert tools are never reliable tools."[14]

I propose to look briefly at the main features of UCC § 2-302 before turning to an assessment of its practical impact. According to paragraph (1): "If the court as a matter of law finds that the contract or any clause of the contract to have been unconscionable at the time it was made the court may refuse to enforce the contract, or it may enforce the remainder of the contract without the unconscionable clause, or may so limit the application of any unconscionable clause so as to avoid any unconscionable result." The pre-Code case of *Campbell Soup Co. v. Wentz*,[15] cited in the Official Comments, concerned the exercise of the court's equitable discretion to grant specific performance and not a claim for general or liquidated damages. The court came down heavily in favor of the defendant sellers contracting to supply goods at a forward delivery price that proved to be substantially below the market price prevailing on the day. Yet had the market gone the other way because of a glut, the sellers would have benefited from a contract price exceeding the market price at delivery. In addition to *Campbell Soup*, the Official Comments cite 10 illustrative decisions, all concerned with the interpretation of exclusion clauses (warranty disclaimers) or related matters. The Comments precede them by stating that the underlying principle of UCC § 2-302 "is one of the prevention of oppression and unfair surprise . . . and not of disturbance of allocation of risks because of superior bargaining power."[16]

None of this comes remotely close to communicating what is meant by unconscionability itself. The text of the provision appears to be directed at substantive unfairness, where the bargain is not tainted by fraud, force, undue influence, or any of the circumstances in which the parties arrived at their contract, but where the terms are excessively one-sided. However, the above comment, by referring to surprise, intimates that procedural unfairness, or the means by which the contract was concluded, may be material.[17] The distinction between procedural and substantive unfairness is crucial, since the potential scope of the provision for eroding contractual autonomy lies not so much in the former as in the latter.

Richard Epstein once referred to the doctrine of unconscionability as "one of the major conceptual tools used by courts in their assault upon private agreements,"[18] but unconscionability seems subsequently to have gone to sleep, having not had the judicial impact for which its proponents hoped and its opponents feared. Apart from an early showing in consumer transactions, unconscionability has proved to be a damp squib in commercial contracts.[19] Its continuing existence as a sacred text and its excessive generality,[20] nevertheless, threaten the finality of commercial contracts. Like the first Mrs. Rochester, there is a risk it will escape from the attic and wreak havoc downstairs.

Though UCC § 2-302 is not referred to in Lord Denning's judgment in *Lloyds Bank Ltd. v. Bundy*,[21] it is more than a coincidence that his attempt therein to fashion a general principle of unconscionability is so similar to it. The case concerned an elderly farmer who in his home was prevailed upon by his son, with the bank manager in close attendance, to guarantee the son's trading debts and give the bank a charge over the farmhouse. Both father and son had accounts at the same bank branch. The son's business was foundering and the guarantee brought only the briefest of respites. The father was under intense family pressure to bail out his son's business, as the bank manager was perfectly well aware. Lord Denning gathered together five disparate groups of cases dealing with duress of goods, the exploitation of expectant heirs and similar vulnerable people, undue influence, undue pressure, and salvage agreements, and fashioned from them the "single thread" of "inequality of bargaining power." Relief would be granted where a contracting party with "grievously impaired" bargaining power received in such circumstances a consideration that was "grossly inadequate."[22]

Lord Denning did not label this synthesis as unconscionability,[23] but that is what it amounts to. This approach was in a later case rejected by the House of Lords as unnecessary and unsuited to intervention in an area straddling gift and contract,[24] where undue influence was a more suitable "tool."[25] This rejection of the excessively high pitch of unconscionability puts one in mind of Peter Birks's dictum that unconscionability is to a lawyer as "small brown bird" is to an ornithologist.[26]

The preference shown by the House of Lords for undue influence matches the majority approach in *Lloyds Bank Ltd. v. Bundy*, leading to the same conclusion that the guarantee and charge should be set aside. In the ordinary case, the doctrine of undue influence is not engaged at all in the relationship of bank and customer. But the majority, after a scrupulous paring of the evidence, concluded that the bank manager, in his dealings over time with the father, had crossed the line that separated bank manager and confidential adviser.[27] The bank therefore owed the father a "fiduciary duty of care" to advise him to obtain independent advice in circumstances that "cried aloud [his] need for careful independent advice."[28] Banks following this clear judicial advice may still benefit from an unequal exchange and harvest a secured guarantee given for a brief respite.[29]

Substantive unfairness or inequality of contractual outcome is not per se objectionable in English law.[30] This is entirely consistent with the way that equity has settled down to provide a body of supplementary rules and not an open-ended discretion for dispensing with legal rules. The maxim "equity follows the law" is invested with real meaning. Lord Radcliffe, in a case involving penalty clauses, once remarked that courts of equity did not take it upon themselves to be "a general adjuster of men's bargains." He added: " 'Unconscionable' must not be taken to be a panacea for adjusting any contract between competent persons when it shows a rough edge to one side or the other, and equity lawyers are, I notice, sometimes both surprised and discomfited by the plenitude of jurisdiction, and the imprecision of rules that are attributed to 'equity' by their more enthusiastic colleagues."[31]

An outright rejection of unconscionability because of the way it undermines contractual certainty is also present in a famous Privy Council decision[32] where a purchaser, 10 minutes late in completing a contract for the purchase of land in Hong Kong, was granted no relief when the vendor terminated the contract and forfeited the purchaser's deposit. The contract had made clear provision for this. The following words of Lord Hoffmann are particularly pertinent: "The existence of an undefined discretion to refuse to enforce the contract on the ground that this would be 'unconscionable' is sufficient to create uncertainty. Even if it is most unlikely that a discretion to grant relief will be exercised, its mere existence enables litigation to be employed as a negotiating tactic."[33] There could hardly be a firmer statement of the need for commercial certainty.

Good Faith and Fair Dealing

A. Formation

An expansive doctrine of good faith and fair dealing[34] was written into the Restatement Second on Contracts in Alan Farnsworth's time as Reporter,[35] where it applied in the performance and enforcement of contracts. Despite an important article by Kessler and Fine,[36] which covered at some length the recognition of good faith in the formation of contracts, the principle was not expressed to apply in that area of contract law.

There had earlier been incorporated in UCC Article 2 a rule of good faith, but this rule was limited in at least two respects. First, it was not expressed as a general principle of universal application in sales law but applied only where it was expressly incorporated in a particular provision in Article 2. Second, good faith, so far as it exceeded honesty in fact and took in fair dealing, was expressed as a duty applicable only to merchants.[37] The general definition of good faith in Article 1 was initially restricted to honesty in fact[38] but now incorporates "reasonable commercial standards of fair dealing."[39] It is not entirely clear how far this new standard extends in Article 2 to non-merchants.[40]

The difference between English law and American law regarding good faith and fair dealing goes to both how such norms are presented and how cases are decided. As for presentation, Bingham L.J. once remarked that "English law has, characteristically, committed itself to no such overriding principle [viz., of 'fair and open dealing'] but has developed piecemeal solutions in response to demonstrated problems of unfairness." In the case where he uttered these remarks, a clause in the terms and conditions of a photographic library imposed very substantial holding fees on a borrower who was late in redelivering transparencies. The defendant was presented with an enormous bill for a two-week delay. Because the plaintiff had not "fairly and reasonably" brought to the defendant's attention "this unreasonable and extortionate clause," he had not secured the defendant's agreement to it when the transparencies were delivered with the terms and conditions after the parties had corresponded by telephone.[41] The clause was not struck down for being unfair. Nor was the plaintiff "penalized" for its use of the clause. Instead, as a matter of procedure, the plaintiff had failed to take the necessary steps to have the clause incorporated in the contract.

In outcomes, too, English and American law diverge when it comes to good faith and fair dealing norms. Now, it may be perfectly possible to gather a number of English cases and compare them against broadly similar cases decided in the United States under the broad banner of good faith and conclude there is little practical difference between the two systems. There are certainly shared values. For example, both systems reject a rule that a buyer must offer a fair price.[42] However, focusing for the moment on contractual formation, the clear rejection by English courts of an imposed[43] duty of good faith illustrates the existence of substantial differences in the two national systems of contract law. I shall demonstrate this by reference to two cases, *Teachers Insurance and Annuity Ass'n of America v. Tribune Co.*,[44] in a U.S. District Court, and *Walford v. Miles*,[45] in the House of Lords.

In *Tribune*, Judge Pierre Leval famously distinguished between two different kinds of preliminary contractual obligations. Type I agreements contain all the terms necessary to constitute a complete contract and are binding according to their terms. Type II agreements leave open certain major terms but impose upon the parties a duty to negotiate the remaining issues in good faith. Here the parties had concluded a "binding agreement," subject to the preparation and execution of documents satisfactory to both sides,[46] for a loan by plaintiff to defendant as part of a three-sided arrangement. The defendant was to sell the New York Daily News building on deferred payment terms to a third party and assign its payment rights to the plaintiff to pay down the loan. The reason for this structure was to provide the defendant with installment tax deferral of its gain on the sale of the building. Before the final agreement was prepared, the defendant halted the process until the plaintiff agreed that that the defendant might report the loan on its financial statement as an off-balance-sheet offset.[47]

The plaintiff objected to this and claimed that the defendant was motivated by a drop in interest rates, which would have permitted it to refinance
at cheaper rates if it backed out of the deal. Judge Leval held that, even if
the agreement was incomplete, this was a Type II agreement and the parties had bound themselves to negotiate a final agreement in good faith.
This the defendant had failed to do, by raising the matter of the offset. The
court's finding that the defendant was in part actuated by the fall in interest rates appears to provide some sort of moralistic cover for its conclusion
that the defendant was no longer free to rely upon the offset.

Turn next to the English case. *Walford v. Miles* is famous, even notorious, for Lord Ackner's assertion that "the concept of a duty to carry on negotiations is inherently repugnant to the adversarial position of the parties
when involved in negotiations." Short of contractual commitment, either
party, therefore, is entitled to pursue its own interests without consideration for the interests of the other party.

In *Walford,* the vendor walked away from the sale of a company because
of concerns about the purchaser's ability to manage it. The vendor was
asked to provide a post-completion warranty of performance by the target
company, and might be on the hook if the purchaser ran it poorly. The parties had agreed on a "lock-out" clause providing that, during the negotiation
process, the vendor would terminate negotiations with and not entertain
bids from third parties. The purchaser further claimed that the agreement
contained an implied term to negotiate in good faith as long as the vendor
desired to sell the target. It was this claim that attracted Lord Ackner's assertion. Presented as an implied term of a negotiation agreement, the claim
failed to clear the long-standing barrier erected against judicial intervention
in contracts—namely, that it be necessary to give business efficacy to the
contract.[48] The plaintiff's claim was therefore never a strong one. Any attempt to reopen the position would be liable to rebuttal on two fronts: first,
a negotiating party can substantially protect its interests by agreeing to a
"break fees" clause to cover professional fees incurred in the negotiation
process; second, the incipient recognition of express agreements to negotiate in good faith puts the onus on plaintiffs to reach such an agreement.

The question whether good faith should be accorded a role in the negotiating process is akin to the question whether prior negotiations should be

scrutinized in aid of interpreting a written contract, even at the expense of overriding the plain meaning of the written agreement. Despite substantial assaults on the plain meaning rule,[49] it appears to have held up in the majority of American jurisdictions.[50] English law is less committed to the parol evidence rule than is the case in the United States, but it has so far held the line against admitting evidence of prior negotiations so far as that evidence goes beyond the meaning of obscure expressions.[51] By somewhat different means, the two legal systems may have arrived broadly at the same position.

Nevertheless, there is a significant point of difference between English and American law in the area of formation, and that is the resistance of English law to the use of promissory estoppel to ground a cause of action based on a promisee's detrimental reliance on a promise, short of the existence of a binding contract.[52] In section 205 of the Restatement Second, the duty of good faith and fair dealing is limited to the performance and enforcement of contracts. Section 90 might be seen as a specific example of the good faith provision in the formation of contracts that did not emerge in the drafting process. The absence in English law of anything like section 90 indicates that, whilst committed to principles of waiver and promissory estoppel, English law allows their use in only a defensive way. It therefore does not have to confront the contradiction highlighted by Grant Gilmore of a promissory estoppel rule and a consideration rule sharply at variance.[53] In writing about formalities, Lon Fuller once pointed to the cautionary and signaling functions of formalities, which allowed a potential contractant to know that there was a gateway through which one had to pass to incur contractual liability and which also warned the contractant about the seriousness of the matter.[54] The same kind of arguments might be made about consideration.

The ability of a contracting party in English law to steer firmly away from contractual commitment, as a result of limitations on the use of estoppel principles and restrictions on the implication of terms in contracts, is displayed in a Court of Appeal decision, *Baird Textile Holdings Ltd. v. Marks & Spencer plc,*[55] which is a world away from the relational contract philosophy of Ian Macneil.[56] The appellants had supplied garments to the defendant retail store over a period of 30 years. As they did with their other suppliers, who were few in number, the defendants exercised stringent controls over the manufacturing processes of the plaintiffs against a background of a "special partner relationship" and a factual expectation of "once a major supplier [to the defendants], always a supplier."[57] Yet the supply contract was repeatedly entered into on yearly terms. When, as a result of major trading reverses, the defendants decided not to renew their contractual relation with the plaintiffs, the latter sought to re-characterize the contractual relationship so as to treat it as a contract of indefinite duration, terminable only upon reasonable notice, the length of which would of course depend on the length of the pre-existing relationship. Without even proceeding to trial, the court declined to imply the existence of an umbrella contract of indefinite duration, since this was not necessary as a matter of business efficacy. It also declined to find any binding representation that the defendants would continue to order garments into the future, partly on the ground of uncertainty—which garments in which styles and in which quantities?—and partly because a representation could not be used to found a cause of action. The defendants had set out deliberately *not* to create a long-term relationship recognized in law and they had succeeded. And who is to say the decision is wrong, when the defendants were suffering major and entrenched trading reverses and had commitments to their own employees and shareholders? English law does not recognize factual expectations in contract, and this case was to be no exception.

It is not merely the case that English law does not allow waiver or promissory estoppel to ground a cause of action, in the way of section 90. Rather, so firmly is the doctrine of consideration still upheld that even a clear and specific promise to hold a contractual offer open will not be binding,[58] still less an offer upon which the other party might reasonably rely upon to remain open for a period.[59] English law stands by the rule that a binding offer has to be purchased by means of an option contract. Even in a system that maintains the need for consideration, there will always be a place for artificial contracts, especially of the unilateral kind, though it should not be imagined that their existence will freely be inferred. Such a contract might, for example, be found where a potential franchisee is encouraged to incur significant expense prior to the grant of the franchise on terms broadly agreed.[60] The inference of a contract of this kind should not be expected to arise as a routine matter, and it should not be supposed that one party's pre-contract reliance costs will be re-characterized as benefit conferred on the other and thus subject to a restitutionary action.[61]

B. Performance and Enforcement

Section 205 of the Restatement Second imposes a duty of good faith and fair dealing in the enforcement of contracts. When I looked at the scope of this duty some time ago,[62] I was struck by the way that reported cases invoking the good faith principle could readily be classified under the heads of interpretation and implied terms. One case in particular, cited in the Reporter's note, laid out for me the limitations of good faith. It held that a contracting party could consent by contract to behavior of the other party that would otherwise breach the good faith standard.[63] The terms of the contract thus limited the range of that party's legitimate contractual expectations. Considerations extrinsic to contractual expectations did nevertheless emerge in some of the enforcement cases, notably where issues concerning contempt of court[64] and competition[65] came to the fore. So far as they engaged community standards, these could just as easily be expressed in terms of public policy or illegality, and all legal systems give a role more or less to such considerations.

Measuring the impact of good faith in American law by results, therefore, it was hardly a case of the New World, in a bout of prelapsarian nostalgia for its lost idealistic soul, meeting the cynical Old World in an encounter scripted by Henry James. Moreover, the same concern about the vacuity of unconscionability could be repeated for good faith. The suspicion that good faith in section 205 might amount to little more than a moral flourish was also bolstered by the way that no sanction was stipulated for breach of the good faith standard. Even the unconscionability rule in UCC § 2-302 provides for a remedial outcome. As for the literature, the most substantial contributions came from Robert Summers, whose views of good faith may be summarized as "It's what the courts do anyway" and "You know bad faith when you see it,"[66] and from Steven Burton, who in a sober piece found a rational underpinning for the existing rule of good faith in the prevention of attempts to recapture forgone contractual opportunities.[67] The two approaches could hardly have been more different. The one seemed intent on finding the presence of good faith behind formal legal reasoning, and the latter intent on minimizing its potential disruptive impact.

Has good faith made any headway in the past quarter of a century? Good faith still surfaces when contracts are interpreted and terms are implied.[68] The acid test for determining whether good faith does more than serve a rhetorical purpose is to see whether it is actually used to prevent one contracting party from rendering a type of performance or otherwise behaving in a way that would otherwise be permitted under the contract, or would restrict a party from enforcing contractual rights otherwise available. When the UCC Permanent Editorial Board issued its Commentary No. 10 on 1-203, the answer, if one treated that document as a summative statement of the role of good faith, was that good faith operated in only a subsidiary way since it did not "support an independent cause of action"; rather, it merely "directs a court towards interpreting contracts within the commercial context in which they are created, performed and enforced, and does not create a separate duty of fairness and reasonableness which can be independently breached."[69] This appears to be consistent with the mass of case law on good faith.[70]

Despite this, it has been asserted that the duty of good faith is tantamount to a tortious duty and is therefore one that overrides the provisions of the contract. The Supreme Court of Vermont, in a case where a fuel supplier was prevented from invoking an automatic termination clause triggered by the death of a key employee of the distributor, stated that "an action for its breach is really no different from a tort action, because the duty of good faith is imposed by law and is not a contractual term that the parties are free to bargain in or out as they see fit."[71] Thus the widow of the key employee had an expectation that the fuel company might negotiate a new agreement with her or buy her out at a fair price or allow her sufficient time to sell the business to a third party. This seems to be a minority approach,[72] because other courts have not allowed good faith to override the contract.[73]

Furthermore, apart from Commentary 10 and the general confinement of good faith to matters that can be dealt with by other means, there are other refreshing signs of judicial efforts to prevent good faith from getting out of hand. Judge Richard Posner has most aptly said: "The particular confusion to which the vaguely moralistic overtones of 'good faith' give rise is the belief that every contract establishes a fiduciary relationship."[74] In a case where, after the termination by the principal of a distribution agency, the agent unsuccessfully sought a period of notice and commission entitlement in excess of what was explicitly agreed in the contract, Judge Frank Easterbrook firmly stated: "Parties to contracts are entitled to seek, and retain, personal advantage. . . . Contract law does not require parties to be fair, or kind, or reasonable, or to share gains or losses equitably."[75] It is not the function of the law to fashion a contract that a more equal balance of bargaining power might have produced.

It is comforting to be told that U.S. courts "generally utilize the good faith duty as an interpretive tool to determine 'the parties' justifiable expectations,' and do not enforce an independent duty divorced from the specific clause."[76] Thus the court in the case in question declined to recognise a 40-year warranty period for steam generators conjured up from a contract that made no mention of it.

So what, then, is the harm in having an expansive duty of good faith in Article 2 and in the general law of contract? It may not be great if litigation occurs in the right court before the right judge. Yet there is always the risk that the duty might be extensively applied regardless of the terms of the contract. Even if a duty of good faith did not exist, a court disposed to solutions of this kind might well manufacture them by other means. If good faith is kept within bounds, the criticism is that it is a redundancy. Like a mannequin in a shop window, it is making a demonstration that does not match the human transactions taking place within. Judge Posner has written: "We could of course do without the term 'good faith,' and maybe even without the doctrine. We could . . . speak instead of implied conditions necessitated by the unpredictability of the future at the time the contract was made."[77] The danger remains, nevertheless, that good faith could be released from its straitjacket by well-meaning courts handling hard cases. That means that contractual certainty cannot be taken for granted.

The Unidroit Principles of International Commercial Contracts lay down a principle of good faith and fair dealing[78] and provide, moreover, as though they were a free-standing law or statute, that the parties are not at liberty to exclude or limit it.[79] If they are not free to exclude good faith expressly, it follows *a fortiori* that they may not do so impliedly by agreeing to terms that are inconsistent with it. Express duties of good faith bear the seeds of that kind of development. The more rhetorical freight that good faith carries, the more benighted contracting parties will seem when they seek to exclude it.

There is of course no express duty of good and fair dealing in the performance and enforcement of contracts in English law. A system of law uncodified by Restatement or statute cannot manufacture such a duty. Even if such a duty were treated as an implied term of the contract, it could be repelled by an inconsistent express term. Such controls as exist on exemption and similar clauses do not safeguard terms of the contract implied at common law, with the exception of the duty not to act negligently.[80] The courts at the highest level have also refused to sanction implied terms in the contract on the ground that it would be reasonable to do so.[81] It will take some time to consider whether the more relaxed approach to contractual interpretation that has prevailed in very recent times will lead in time to an understated good faith standard of performance, though not expressed in so many words.[82]

Apart from this, it is useful to highlight a few key English cases whose outcome can only be described as repelling any duty of good faith and fair dealing. The clearest examples are to be found in the commodities trade. English courts have declined to prevent a buyer from terminating a contract for early shipment when the only reason for this has been that the rice market is in decline.[83] They have also prevented a buyer from substituting a ship nominated to lift a cargo when the original ship turned out to be unavailable, but a suitable and timely replacement could be found. The seller wished to quit the contract so as to take advantage of a rising market.[84] English courts have also allowed a short seller to insist upon a near-impossible requirement that a ship nominated to lift a cargo from a wide range of potential Australian ports be fit to enter every single port in the range, even though the Australian agency with a monopoly over barley exports[85] was prepared to find a cargo for the ship in question from some of those ports.[86] The view apparently taken by the English courts is that the avoidance of an undesirable outcome in a given case is no reason to imperil commercial certainty when the contract, or contract standard form, is clear. If the trade does not like the result, then the form should be amended for the future.

Meanwhile, the loser licks its wounds. The consequence of the interplay between courts and trade associations is a sophisticated standard form that reveals in its contents the history of contract law in the trade concerned and that guarantees a fair measure of commercial certainty. This is especially important in string trading conditions, where the line between a derivative future contract and a physical forward delivery contract may be more notional than real. Those who argue passionately for the substitution in international commodity sales of the UN Convention on the International Sale of Goods 1980 for English law seem not to understand this point. The modern tendency towards relaxation in the interpretation of contracts, which so far has made no real impact on the commodities trade, has destructive potential.[87]

Conclusion

Unconscionability and good faith have the capacity to undermine commercial certainty, though American courts on the whole have so far succeeded in reining in their destructive possibilities. Subject to well-defined exceptions, business parties should be left to their own devices. Legislation dealing with commercial contracts should be practical, direct, and economical, and should not seek to make a moral demonstration. A commitment to the rule of law is thwarted if important legislative texts are deprived of meaning. A country's law of contract should be what it says it is. This is the clearest direction that can be given to ensure orderly legal development and encourage investment in the future through the contracting process.

Notes

1. For a recent example, see Golden Strait Corp. v. Nippon Yusen Kubishika Kaisha (The Golden Victory), [2007] 2 A.C. 353.

2. A striking example of this is the decision of the House of Lords in Transfield Shipping Inc. v. Mercator Shipping Inc. (The Achilleas), [2009] 1 A.C. 61.

3. Steyn, Contract Law: Fulfilling the Reasonable Expectations of Honest Men, 113 L.Q.R. 433, 438 (1997).

4. Human Rights Act 1998.

5. Hart, American Jurisprudence through English Eyes: The Nightmare and the Noble Dream, 11 Geo. L Rev 969, 974 (1977).

6. Kleinwort Benson Ltd. v. Lincoln City Council, [1999] 2 A.C. 349.

7. See G. Gilmore, The Death of Contract 62 (1974).

8. See in particular Investors Compensation Scheme Ltd. v. West Bromwich Building Soc., [1998] 1 W.L.R. 896 and Chartbrook Ltd. v. Persimmon Homes Ltd., [2009] 1 A.C. 1101.

9. Notably, The Moorcock, 14 P.D. 64 (1889). Just how seriously the courts have taken the restrictions on implied terms can be seen in modern times in Concord Trust v. Law Debenture Trust Corp., [2005] 1 W.L.R. 1591.

10. Article 6, which allows freedom of exclusion and modification with regard to the contents of the Convention.

11. EC Directive 1999/44 on certain aspects of the sale of consumer goods and associated guarantees, [1999] O.J. L171/12, transposed into English Law as Part 5A of the Sale of Goods Act 1979.

12. 1 NYL Revision Comm'n, Hearings on the Uniform Commercial Code 121 (1954), as quoted by A. Farnsworth, Contracts §4.28 (3d ed. 1999).

13. Leff, Unconscionability and the Code—the Emperor's New Clause, 115 U. Pa. L. Rev. 485, 559 (1967). The introduction of exuberant words like "wholly," "disproportionately," "strikingly," and "grossly" does not assist.

14. Id. However, another commentator saw the direct appeal to unconscionability, instead of to indirect routes of judicial attack, as demonstrative of that same dictum. A. Farnsworth, Contracts §4.28 (3d ed. 1999).

15. 172 F.2d 80 (3d Cir., 1948).

16. Citing Campbell Soup Co. v. Wentz, 172 F.2d 80 (3d Cir., 1948).

17. This is of course the celebrated distinction between substantive and procedural unconscionability.

18. Epstein, Unconscionability: A Critical Reappraisal, 18 J. Law & Econ. 293 (1975).

19. Williams v. Walker-Thomas Furniture Co., 350 F.2d 445 (D.C. Cir., 1965). The facts predated the enactment in D.C. of UCC Article 2, but the court applied the same rule as either a restatement of existing or of newly coined (!) common law.

20. In the words of one leading scholar, the impossibility of defining unconscionability with precision "is a source of both strength and weakness." A. Farnsworth, Contracts §4.28 (3d ed. 1999). This sounds good but what does it mean?

21. [1975] Q.B. 326.

22. [1975] Q.B. 326, 337–39.

23. He reserved that expression for his second group of cases involving expectant heirs and the like.

24. National Westminster Bank plc v. Morgan, [1985] A.C. 686, 708: "I question whether there is any need in the modern law to erect a general principle of relief against inequality of bargaining power."

25. Id.

26. Birks, Equity in the Modern Law: An Exercise in Taxonomy, 26 U. W. A. L. Rev. 1, 16–17 (1996).

27. [1975] Q.B. 326, 344.

28. [1975] Q.B. 326, 345.

29. See Alliance Bank v. Broom, 2 Drew & Sm. 289 (1864).

30. For a criticism of English law, see Capper, The Unconscionable Bargain in the Common Law World, 126 L.Q.R. 403 (2010), with an extraordinary reference at 416 to "the insistence by English courts that harsh terms must be imposed on the weaker party by the stronger party in a morally reprehensible manner."

31. Bridge v. Campbell Discount Co. Ltd., [1962] A.C. 600, 626.

32. Union Eagle Ltd. v. Golden Achievement Ltd., [1997] A.C. 514.

33. Id. at 519.

34. References below to good faith are to good faith and fair dealing unless otherwise stated.

35. After he took over as Reporter from Braucher.

36. *Culpa in Contrahendo,* Bargaining in Good Faith and Freedom of Contract: A Comparative Study, 77 Harv. L. Rev. 401 (1964).

37. UCC § 2-103(1)(b).

38. UCC § 1-201(19).

39. UCC § 1-201(b)(20) (excepting Article 5).

40. Moses, The New Definition of Good Faith in Article 1, 35 Uniform Commercial Code L.J. 47 (2002).

41. The reasoning in the court inclines towards putting a duty on the plaintiff to bring the clause to the attention of the defendant, but this is inexact. Rather, he could not fairly interpret the defendant's conduct as agreeing to be bound by the clause.

42. See, e.g., Market Street Associates v. Frey, 941 F.2d 588, 594 (11th Cir., 1991) ("The duty of honesty, of good faith even expansively conceived, is not a duty of candor. You can make a binding contract to purchase something you know your seller undervalues.")

43. English law is moving towards the recognition of an enforceable *express* duty to negotiate in good faith: see, e.g., Petromec Inc. v. Petroleo Brasileiro SA (No 3), [2006] 1 Lloyd's Rep. 121. If that is what contracting parties want, they should be allowed to have it even if there are some difficulties in determining what in fact is meant by good faith negotiating. Was Andrei Gromyko negotiating in bad faith for the USSR when he delivered an unending series of nyets?

44. 670 F.Supp. 491 (SDNY, 1987). See also Brown v. Cara, 420 F.3d 148 (2d Cir., 2005).

45. [1992] 2 A.C. 128.

46. In English law, this is known as a "subject to contract" agreement, the usual means of concluding a contract for the sale of land, where, even after months of negotiations, title searches, and so on, either party can freely walk away from commitment.

47. The defendant was contemplating a public offering.

48. The Moorcock, 14 P.D. 64 (1889).

49. See, e.g., Pacific Gas & Electric Co. v. GW Thomas Drayage & Rigging Co., 442 P.2d 641 (Cal. 1968).

50. See the Robert Scott article that follows this article; Trident Center v. Connecticut General Life Assurance Co., 847 F.2d 564 (9th Cir., 1988).

51. Prenn v. Simmonds, [1971] 1 W.L.R. 1381; Rugby Group Ltd. v. ProForce Recruit Ltd., [2006] EWCA Civ. 69.

52. Cf. Restatement Second § 90.

53. G. Gilmore, The Death of Contract ch. 3 (1974).

54. Fuller, Consideration and Form, 41 Colum. L. Rev. 799 (1941).

55. [2001] CLC 999.

56. I. Macneil, The New Social Contract (1980).

57. The witness statement of a former chairman of the defendants supplied to the plaintiffs.

58. Routledge v. Grant, 4 Bing. 653 (1828).

59. Cf. UCC § 2-205.

60. Cf. Hoffman v. Red Owl Stores, 133 N.W.2d 267 (Wis., 1965).

61. Regalian Properties plc v. London Dockland Development Corp., [1995] 1 W.L.R. 212.

62. Bridge, Does Anglo-Canadian Contract Law Need a Doctrine of Good Faith?, 9 Canadian Business L.J. 385 (1984).

63. VTR Inc. v. Goodyear Tire & Rubber Co., 303 F.Supp. 773 (SDNY, 1969).

64. L'Orange v. Medical Protection Co., 394 F.2d 57 (6th Cir., 1968).

65. Shell Oil Co. v. Marinello, 307 A.2d 598 (N.J., 1973).

66. Summers, "Good Faith" in General Contract Law and the Sales Provisions of the Uniform Commercial Code, 54 Va. L. Rev. 195 (1968); Summers, The General Duty of Good Faith: Its Recognition and Conceptualization, 67 Cornell L. Rev. 810 (1982).

67. Burton, Good Faith Performance of a Contract within Article 2 of the Uniform Commercial Code, 67 Iowa L. Rev. 1 (1981).

68. Market Street Associates v. Frey, 941 F.2d 588, 595 (11th Cir., 1991): "It would be quixotic as well as presumptuous for judges to undertake through contract law to raise the ethical standards of the nation's business people. The concept of the duty of good faith like the concept of fiduciary duty is a stab at approximating the terms the parties would have negotiated had they foreseen the circumstances that have given rise to their dispute."

69. Farnsworth observes that this is inconsistent with Comment 8 to UCC § 2-309(3) which, dealing with reasonable notice of termination and the striking down as unconscionable of any contractual clause dispensing with reasonable notice, refers to good faith: Contracts §7.17 note 14 (3rd ed. 1999).

70. See, e.g., Dalton v. Educational Testing Service, 663 N.E.2d 289 (N.Y., 1985); Duquesne Light Co. v. Westinghouse Electric Corp., 66 F.3d 604 (3d Cir., 1995).

71. Carmichael v. Adirondack Bottled Gas Co., 635 A.2d 1211, 1216 (Vt., 1993).

72. But see also Re Vylene Enterprises Inc., 30 F.3d 1472 (9th Cir., 1996), where the opening by the franchisor of a competing restaurant less than a mile and a half away was a breach of the duty of good faith, despite the fact that the franchisee had not been granted an exclusive territory.

73. Riggs National Bank of Washington DC v. Linch, 36 F.3d 370 (4th Cir., 1994); General Aviation Inc. v. Cessna Aircraft Co, 915 F.2d 1038 (1990); Grand Light & Supply Co. v. Honeywell Inc., 771 F.2d 672, 679 (2d Cir., 1985).

74. Market Street Associates v. Frey, 941 F.2d 588, 593 (11th Cir., 1991).

75. Industrial Representatives v. CP Clare Corp., 74 F.3d 128 (7th Cir., 1996), citing Original Great American Chocolate Chip Cookie Co. v. River Valley Cookies Ltd., 970 F.2d 273, 282 (7th Cir., 1992).

76. Duquesne Light Co. v. Westinghouse Electric Corp, 66 F.3d 604 (3d Cir., 1995).

77. Market Street Associates v. Frey, 941 F.2d 588, 595 (11th Cir., 1991).

78. (2004), Article 1.7(1).

79. Article 1.7(2).

80. Unfair Contract Terms Act 1977, s.2.

81. Liverpool City Council v. Irwin, [1977] A.C. 239.

82. Chartbrook Ltd. v. Persimmon Homes Ltd., [2009] 1 A.C. 1101.

83. Bowes v. Shand, 2 App. Cas. 455 (1877).

84. Cargill Ltd. v. Continental UK Ltd., [1989] 2 Lloyds Rep. 290.

85. And therefore at the head of the notional string that would have attached to the seller had it not been short.

86. Richco International Ltd. v. Bunge & Co. (The New Prosper), [1991] 2 Lloyd's Rep. 93.

87. Reardon Smith Line Ltd. v. Yngvar Hansen-Tangen, [1976] 1 W.L.R. 989.

Text versus Context

THE FAILURE OF THE UNITARY LAW
OF CONTRACT INTERPRETATION

ROBERT E. SCOTT

Modern contract law is nominally unitary; that is, a single set of legal rules (and presumably governing policies) applies to all enforceable promises regardless of the status of the contracting parties. Unfortunately, there are significant inefficiencies in a system that interprets the contracts between sophisticated parties who negotiate multimillion-dollar agreements with the aid of competent counsel in precisely the same way as it regulates "click-wrap" contracts between individual consumers and merchant sellers over the purchase of $50 of products on the Internet. Prominent among those inefficiencies is the confusion that results from the fractious debate between textualist and contextualist theories of interpretation. In broad brush, the differences between the two approaches are apparent: textualist theories look principally to the written agreement between the parties for the terms of the contract and the meaning of those terms; contextualist theories look beyond the writing, to pre- and post-contractual oral and written evidence of what the parties intended.

Textualist theories undergird the formal common law doctrines of contractual interpretation, such as the parol evidence and plain meaning rules. Both of these rules are designed to give parties some control over the process courts will use to interpret their contracts. The parol evidence rule, which excludes oral testimony that varies or contradicts a written contract, enables parties to narrow the evidence in disputes over their agreement: when parties provide that their writing is "fully integrated" and reflects all the terms of the contract, they forfeit the right in subsequent litigation to prove understandings they declined to include in their integrated writing. Similarly, the best understanding of the plain meaning rule treats it as a device for preserving a reservoir of terms with clear meanings that cannot be contradicted in adjudication by contextual evidence supporting a different meaning. On this account, the plain meaning rule makes available a public fund of terms with judicially protected meanings on which contractual parties can rely to communicate their definitive commitments to each other and to courts. From the textualist perspective, therefore, the parol evidence and plain meaning rules can be viewed as tools for parties to use, respectively, to restrict and provide the evidence courts will use to interpret that portion of their agreement that they intend to make legally enforceable.

This straightforward account of the interpretation doctrines as tools for parties to use in expressing their contractual intent is relatively uncontroversial. But courts sometimes perceive a conflict between the formal rules governing contractual interpretation and the principle of honoring the expressed intention of the parties as revealed by contextual evidence that otherwise would be excluded by the governing rules. Contextualist courts confronted with this apparent conflict are predisposed to deploy their equitable powers to avoid the application of formal contract doctrines that appear to achieve an unfair or unjust result. Thus, in jurisdictions following the lead of the Second Restatement of Contracts[1] and in all contracts governed by the Uniform Commercial Code (UCC),[2] contextualist theories of interpretation advocate a two-stage interpretive regime. Under this regime, written contractual language is treated merely as establishing prima facie terms, which courts can (and should) override by considering evidence of the context of the transaction if they believe that doing so is necessary to "correct" the parties' written contract by realigning it with its "true" meaning. This ex post judicial determination of the contractual obligation serves as a fallback mechanism whenever a court determines that interpreting written contract terms according to the formal rules of interpretation will fall seriously short of achieving the parties' purposes. In short, under the contextualist view every contract by default should come with a judicial insurance policy against written contract terms that, viewed in proper context, have turned out to have ill-served the parties' objectives.

This contextualist regime of contract interpretation rests on the powerful intuition that most parties, both individual consumers as well as commercially sophisticated firms, would prefer courts to take advantage of hindsight in assisting the parties to achieve their contractual objectives. Indeed, had the parties known at the time of formation what the court knows at the time of adjudication, the parties themselves would likely have written different terms. It seems perverse for a court to insist on holding parties to the plain meaning of terms that it knows the parties themselves would have rejected had they known what the court knows. Holding parties to their formally specified contract terms when those terms no longer (or never did) constitute a reasonable interpretation of the parties' shared intent would exalt formal doctrine over substance.

As compelling as it seems, however, the contextualist justification for contract interpretation rests on an unsupported premise: it presumes that all parties want courts to reinterpret the formal terms of a written contract in light of the surrounding context of the transaction so as to better achieve their shared contractual purposes. But there is good reason to doubt that commercially sophisticated parties typically, let alone always, prefer this method of interpreting their contracts. Rather than an interpretive rule that subordinates written contract terms to ex post judicial revision, both theory and available evidence suggest that sophisticated parties would prefer a regime that excludes contextual evidence unless the parties have expressly indicated their intent to delegate authority to a court to consider surrounding context evidence. By eliminating the risk that courts will erroneously infer the parties' preference for contextual interpretation, such a regime reduces the costs of contract enforcement and enhances the parties' control over the content of their contract. That control, in turn, permits sophisticated commercial parties to implement the most efficient strategies for contract design available to them.

Those who argue for mandatory contextualist interpretations often justify the abandonment of textualism as a necessary prophylactic against the exploitation of unsophisticated individuals who enter into contracts with

sophisticated parties who supply written contract terms that alter previously settled understandings. As Justice Roger Traynor famously wrote:
"The party urging the spoken as against the written word is most often the
economic underdog, threatened by severe hardship if the writing is enforced."[3] And herein lies the dilemma of a unitary contract law: assuming
that these concerns are valid reasons for imposing a mandatory contextualist regime in contracts between individual consumers and firms, they do
not apply to the firm-to-firm negotiated contracts that are the bread and
butter of commercial contracting practice.

In Part I of this article, I describe the conundrum that results from the
historical anomaly of the integration of the common law and equity into a
unitary contract law, and I show how and why the current debate came to
be framed in such peculiar ways. I then turn in Part II to offer plausible
ways in which the Gordian knot of contract interpretation can be untied.

I. The Interpretation Conundrum

A. *The Divide between Text and Context*

Legal enforcement of incomplete contracts necessarily requires the state
to interpret the terms contracting parties use to allocate contractual risk.
Interpreting disputed contracts presents the state with the opportunity to
protect (and even improve) the efficacy of those terms for future parties.
Since interpretation disputes are the largest single source of commercial
contract litigation,[4] if the courts perform the interpretation function incon-
sistently, the costs of contracting will rise. Interpretive questions thus are
both significant and complex. But despite the importance of having consistent, predictable rules of interpretation, contract interpretation is the least
settled question in contemporary contract doctrine and scholarship. Instead, contemporary courts and scholars debate vigorously the relative
merits of two polar and dichotomous approaches to the interpretation of
contracts.

At one pole is the textualist argument that defends the traditional
common-law approach to interpretation, an approach that a large majority
of common-law courts continue to follow.[5] This interpretive approach

privileges integrated written contracts over context evidence that purports to show that the agreement contained additional or different terms.[6] In addition, it bars context evidence designed to show that parties intended facially clear and unambiguous language to be understood in non-standard ways.[7]

Textualist courts, such as New York, use a hard parol evidence rule that gives presumptively conclusive effect to "merger" clauses that expressly exclude contextual evidence as to the intention of the parties. In the absence of a merger clause, New York courts determine whether contextual evidence is admissible by applying a "four corners" presumption in favor of textualism if the contract is fully integrated and appears final and complete on its face.[8] Scholars who defend textualist arguments ground their analysis on a particular contracting paradigm: the negotiated contract between sophisticated commercial parties.[9] Textualist arguments thus focus on the importance of contract design and the insight that for these parties context is endogenous; the parties can embed as much or as little context into an agreement as they wish. In this way, sophisticated parties can economize on contracting costs by shifting costs between the front end (or drafting stage) and the back end (or enforcement stage) of the contracting process.[10]

At the other pole is the contextualist approach to interpretation. Contextualist courts and commentators are reluctant to endorse formal rules for determining either the terms of a contract or the presumed meaning of those terms once they have been identified.[11] They argue that formal interpretive rules that exclude certain categories of extrinsic evidence deprive the fact finder of potentially relevant information and thus distort the court's assessment of what the parties meant by their agreement. Contextualist courts, such as California, therefore favor a soft parol evidence rule. Here the test for integration admits extrinsic evidence notwithstanding an unambiguous merger clause or, absent such a clause, notwithstanding the fact that the writing otherwise appears final and complete on its face.[12] These courts regard a merger clause as raising only a rebuttable presumption of integration, one that is subject to being overridden by extrinsic evidence that the parties lacked such intent. The contextualist approach is framed by a very different paradigm from the one that justifies textualism:

here the argument focuses on contracts between parties to standardized transactions (the consumer context) or contracts embedded in customary norms and terms of trade (the sales context). Both of these transactional prototypes undermine the assumptions of individualized contract design that animates the textualist view.

This brief description of the arguments and their key assumptions exposes a deep puzzle: since the central paradigms that support each approach to interpretation are not overlapping, what explains a debate in which each side wishes to gain primacy over the other? The answer lies in the unitary nature of contract law and doctrine. Contract interpretation rules are both unitary and mandatory—that is, when a court (or legislature) chooses either a textualist or a contextualist approach to interpretation, that choice applies to all transactional prototypes, and particular parties cannot choose ex ante to have their contract interpreted according to the disfavored approach. Thus the ongoing interpretation debate is binary—either text or context—and a victory in any state is total for one approach or the other.

Viewed in this light, the effects of the choice between text and context are clear: the textualist plain meaning rule operates in tandem with a hard parol evidence rule to reduce expected adjudication costs, but at the cost of truncating the context evidence available to the court. If the contract is fully integrated, and if contractual terms are facially clear, then the dispute will be resolved at summary judgment. Parties who want the court to see additional evidence, but avoid trials, can (and must) embed the evidence in the contract itself. A contextual interpretive rule, in contrast, shifts costs from the drafting or front end of the contracting process to the back-end litigation stage. Parties who write simple contracts in rich context environments can thus economize on front-end costs and delegate discretion to courts to interpret the express terms in light of the context evidence revealed in a full trial.[13]

B. The Sources of a Unitary Law of Contract Interpretation

The current regime of American contract interpretation applies two different sets of doctrines to resolve a contract dispute.[14] The first set consists largely of those doctrines that originated in the English courts that produced the corpus of the English common law from the twelfth to the nineteenth centuries.[15] These doctrines consist of rules—such as the parol evidence and plain meaning rules—that were administered strictly, without exceptions, to provide for cases in which the application of a rule appeared to defeat its purpose. The second set of doctrines consists largely of equitable principles that originated in the English Court of Chancery, which exercised overlapping jurisdiction with the common-law courts.[16] These principles often required judges to exercise discretion on a case-by-case basis. The result was two competing systems, often with incompatible procedural and substantive doctrines, yet overlapping in jurisdiction.[17] Conflicts among these doctrines were inevitable.

The American common law of contracts is thus suffused with legal doctrines, providing relatively clear and objective rules, combined with equitable doctrines directing courts to circumvent or override these rules whenever a judge believes that application of the legal doctrine would produce a result that is contrary to the doctrine's own purpose or is otherwise unjust. The rules governing the interpretation of contracts are prime exemplars of this structure: along with the historically legal contract doctrines, such as the plain meaning rule[18] and the parol evidence rule,[19] American contract law also absorbed equitable doctrines specifically designed to vitiate the common-law rules of interpretation.[20] As a consequence, contract interpretation law is torn between the prospective regulatory perspective of the common law and the retrospective dispute-resolution perspective of equity.

The tension between the common-law rules of interpretation and the equitable exceptions to those rules was rationalized by Samuel Williston, one of the great twentieth-century treatise writers, into a more or less coherent set of general rules that could be applied predictably by common-law courts.[21] Willistonian formalism rested on several basic claims: that contract terms could be interpreted according to their plain meaning, and that written terms have priority over unwritten expressions of agreement.[22] Williston viewed merger clauses as presumptively establishing a total integration of the agreement sufficient to exclude extrinsic evidence.[23] In the absence of a merger clause, he argued that if the writing appeared to be a complete instrument, contextual evidence should be excluded apart from the exceptional case where the additional terms might naturally be considered to form a separate agreement.[24] These views on parol evidence had a significant influence on many state courts as they decided interpretation disputes, and Williston's formalist approach to interpretation was subsequently enshrined in the First Restatement of Contracts.[25]

The underlying tensions between law and equity were just beneath the surface and were elevated to prominence by the legal realists, whose leaders included Arthur Corbin and Karl Llewellyn. Corbin advanced the view that the Willistonian rules governing interpretation were empty formalizations and that interpretation issues were context specific. In his view, courts applied the rules tactically in order to pursue overarching policy principles of fairness and natural justice. Instead, argued Corbin, courts should determine the actual intention of the parties, and all relevant evidence should be considered on the issue of intent.[26] Thus, the very evidence whose admissibility was being challenged would be admissible on the issue of whether or not the writing alone was to govern.[27] Quite clearly, Corbin's approach severely undercut the application of the traditional parol evidence rule. In order for the court to reach a just result, the context of the transaction was a necessary, indeed an essential, feature of any adjudication.[28]

Llewellyn's contextualism was rooted in his idea that courts should seek the "situation sense" of a bargain by locating it in the practices of commercial parties.[29] He believed that courts can and should determine the nature of any transaction by first adverting to the standard practices of the relevant trade. Moreover, because the signals provided by these practices were uncertain, legal incorporation through the common-law process was necessary in order to resolve the troublesome cases where the relevant norms were in dispute. Llewellyn addressed the incorporation objective in drafting those portions of the UCC governing contracts for the sale of goods by reversing the Willistonian presumption that the parties' writings were the definitive elements of the agreement.[30] Rather, Article 2 of the UCC explicitly invites an examination of context by defining the content of an agreement to include trade usage, prior dealings, and the parties' experience in forming the contract.[31] The parol evidence rule under the Code thus admits inferences from trade usage even if the express terms of the contract seem perfectly clear and are apparently integrated.[32]

And so, the battle between text and context was fully joined. As time has passed, the common-law courts have proved remarkably faithful to the Willistonian accommodation to interpretation. A large majority of courts retain "hard" parol evidence and plain meaning rules even while recognizing equitable exceptions for fraud, misrepresentation, and the like. A minority of courts has adopted Corbin's commitment to context, and in the domain of sales law, the UCC remains fully committed to Llewellyn's incorporation project.

C. Dueling Normative Justifications

The path dependence that led to the development of the unitary American law of contract explains, if not justifies, the lack of consensus on how courts should interpret contracts. But the debate between contextualism and textualism is intense precisely because, given certain premises, each approach can be normatively justified. To fully understand the current dilemma, therefore, one must first appreciate the arguments that support both interpretive methodologies.

The Justification for Contextualism. Under autonomy theories of contract, the parties' agreement has normative force because the parties actually agreed to it.[33] Thus the law's task is to enforce the parties' will the better to permit parties to realize their goals. These theories of contract require courts to find out, as far as is possible, what the parties actually meant by the words they used.[34] A contextualist approach to interpretation appears to follow logically from this freedom of contract premise: it invites courts first to learn about the commercial context and then to interpret express contract terms in light of that context.

Implicit in a contextual approach are two key assumptions: (1) that courts have the capability of learning about the commercial context, and (2) that the parties could and would have completed the contract as the court did had they been able to do so. This second assumption requires one to accept the empirical claim that the parties did not complete the contract in question because the costs of specifying the missing terms (including the cost of uncertainty) exceeded the benefits to the parties.

These two assumptions derive from quite separate concerns about the common law of contract. The assumption that courts can accurately recover the context undergirds the contextualist approach to commercial sales contracts championed by Karl Llewellyn and enshrined in Article 2 of the UCC.[35] A separate concern about the risk of fraud and exploitation in consumer transactions animates the second contextualist assumption. Those who argue for mandatory contextualist interpretations often justify such rules as necessary to prevent exploitation of unsophisticated individuals who enter into contracts with sophisticated parties who supply the written contract terms.[36] By examining the context ex post, courts are thought to be able to monitor the process by which certain terms were reduced to writing, thereby protecting unsophisticated parties from difficult-to-detect forms of exploitation.

In sum, the contextualist approach is framed by a very different paradigm from the one that justifies textualism: here the argument focuses on contracts between parties to mass-market, standardized transactions (the consumer context) or contracts embedded in customary norms and terms of trade (the sales context). Both of these transactional prototypes undermine the assumptions of individualized contract design that animate the textualist view. The contextualist regime of contract interpretation therefore rests on the intuition that contracting parties would prefer courts to take advantage of hindsight in assisting the parties to achieve their contractual objectives.

Despite the fact that common-law courts have traditionally followed a textualist approach, the UCC and the Second Restatement continue to encourage courts to be contextual.[37] Conventional scholarly wisdom has long held that the Code's interpretive approach represents a significant improvement over the formalism of the common law.[38] This is because contextualism is assumed to ascertain the parties' intentions more accurately. More evidence is usually better than less. Particular parties may have intended apparently clear language to be read in a nonstandard way, or acted under the contract in surprising ways given the contractual language. Excluding evidence of these parties' prior negotiations or practices under their contract risks interpreting the contracts in opposition to the parties' actual intentions.[39]

The Justification for Textualism. As compelling as it seems, however, the contextualist justification of a two-stage regime of contract interpretation rests on the premise that *all* parties want courts to reinterpret the formal terms of a contract in light of the surrounding context of the transaction so as to better achieve their shared contractual purposes. But there is good reason to believe that commercially sophisticated parties would prefer a regime that follows the parties' instructions specifying when to enforce formal contract terms strictly and when to delegate authority to a court to consider surrounding context evidence. By eliminating the risk that courts will erroneously infer the parties' preference for contextual interpretation, such a regime reduces the costs of contract enforcement and enhances the parties' control over the content of their contract. That control, in turn, permits sophisticated commercial parties to implement the most efficient design strategies available to them.

Given the two assumptions that support the contextualist claims, the argument against using a contextualist approach for all contracts requires evidence that (1) courts do not, in fact, learn about the relevant commercial context, and (2) sophisticated commercial parties are not readily susceptible to exploitation by a counterparty, and they would prefer to limit the back-end cost of interpretation that contextualism requires.

Adherents of textualism offer several justifications to support their claims. First, courts usefully create standard vocabularies for the conduct of commercial transactions.[40] When a phrase has a set, easily discoverable meaning, parties who use it will know what the phrase requires of them and what courts will say the phrase requires. By insulating the standard meaning of terms from deviant interpretations, this strategy preserves a valuable collective good—namely, a set of terms with a clear, unambiguous meaning that is already understood by the vast majority of commercial parties.[41]

Second, a textualist theory of interpretation creates an incentive to draft carefully. Under a contextualist theory, a party for whom a deal has turned out badly has an incentive to claim that the parties meant their contract to have a different meaning than the obvious or standard one. Such a party can often find in the parties' negotiations, in their past practices, and in trade customs enough evidence to ground a full, costly trial, and thus to force a settlement on terms more favorable than those that the contract, as facially interpreted, would direct. If a party can impeach careful contract drafting with evidence of this type, the rewards to careful contract drafting will fall relative to the costs of such efforts. In consequence, parties will write precise, directive contracts less frequently.

Finally, as suggested above, textualist interpretation permits sophisticated commercial parties to economize on contracting costs by shifting costs from the back end of the contracting process (the enforcement function) to the front end of the contracting process (the negotiating and drafting function). Parties can do this by drafting a merger clause that integrates their entire understanding, including relevant context, into the written contract and then asking the court to apply a plain meaning interpretation to facially unambiguous contract terms. When parties use a merger clause to exclude contextual evidence, an interpretation dispute over contract terms may be resolved on summary judgment. If a court decides to consider additional context evidence, it must necessarily deny a motion for summary judgment and set the case for full trial on the merits. Thus, if litigation cost is considered, there is a strong argument that many commercial parties prefer textualist interpretation so that disputes can be resolved on summary judgment rather than after a full trial. This is particularly true when commercially sophisticated parties have invested resources in extensively drafting the contract (thereby shifting costs to the front end). Such parties will rationally invest in sufficient drafting costs to ensure that a court interpreting the written document together with the pleadings and briefs will be able to arrive at the "correct interpretation" more often than not.[42]

There is some empirical evidence that supports the textualist claim. Recent work by Ted Eisenberg and Geoff Miller studying choice of law and choice of forum clauses in a data set of 2,865 contracts is consistent with a preference for textualism. Their study shows that parties chose New York law in 46% of the contracts and New York as the forum state in 41% of the contracts. California was chosen for its contract law in less than 8% of the contracts, though its commercial activity, as measured by the place of business of the contracting parties, was second only to that of New York.[43] Geoff Miller attributes this to differences in contract law between New York and California: New York strictly enforces bargains, retains a hard parol evidence and a plain meaning rule, and frequently declines to consider context evidence in resolving interpretive disputes. California, in contrast, has a contextualist interpretive regime and is predisposed to consider all material context evidence that litigating parties seek to introduce. Miller concludes that "the revealed preferences of sophisticated parties support arguments by Schwartz, Scott and others that formalistic rules offer superior value for the interpretation and enforcement of commercial contracts."[44]

II. Redrawing the Boundaries of Contract Interpretation

The preceding discussion underscores the dilemma of a unitary approach to interpretation. So long as the rules of interpretation are regarded as mandatory background procedural rules that apply to all contracts within the relevant domain, and so long as the courts continue to adopt a unitary perspective that demands that these background rules apply to all disputed contracts, the clash of perspectives between textualist and contextualist interpretation will continue unabated. The effects of this conflict are felt both in the confusion faced by transactional lawyers trying to design efficient contracts for sophisticated parties as well as in the risk that consumers may be barred from proving context evidence that rebuts false claims of contractual obligation. In this part, I outline a straightforward solution to the problem: tailor contract law to fit the very different questions that are raised when interpreting individually designed and standard form contracts.

A. Interpretive Rules for Contract Design

The law's objective should be to identify the empirical conditions under which one interpretive theory is generally superior to the other. A plausible criterion with which to judge the relative efficacy of any interpretive strategy is to select that set of rules which, all else equal, minimizes the sum of interpretive error costs and the costs of contracting. The latter costs include the ex ante costs of specifying the terms of the contract and the ex post costs of enforcement. This criterion argues for granting sophisticated parties the maximum flexibility to shift costs between the front-end specification process and the back-end enforcement process.

However, the preceding discussion vividly illustrates why contract interpretation remains so bitterly contested. Under the current doctrine, rules of interpretation are understood as mandatory and not subject to party choice. Thus, textualist and contextualist theories are posed in opposition, each one claiming the right to govern diverse transactional paradigms. It is inevitable, therefore, that, whichever rule is selected, a substantial number of contracting parties will be disadvantaged in order to advance the interests of others. A necessary corollary of the tradeoff between text and context is that parties will have preferences over interpretative rules. Some parties will prefer a hard parol evidence rule that relies on a narrow interpretive base centered on the parties' writings; others may prefer a soft rule that admits evidence of prior understandings and surrounding context evidence.

Given this heterogeneity, it would seem to follow that whatever interpretive rule a court adopts should be a default. But most commentators and courts believe (at least implicitly) that interpretive rules should be mandatory.[45] And, in fact, the rules *are* mandatory in the sense that parties cannot contract directly for textualist or contextualist interpretive rules. Textualist and contextualist courts differ, however, in the degree to which they permit parties indirectly to control how disputes over their contract are adjudicated. For example, the hard parol evidence rule that textualist courts apply permits the parties to "contract out" either by not integrating their writing fully or by including context evidence in the integrated contract. In contrast, contextualist courts apply an invariant soft parol evidence rule, so that parties cannot narrow the evidentiary base. In contextualist jurisdictions, therefore, contextualism is the only option. The fact that under current law textualism works effectively as a default rule, while contextualism is effectively mandatory, argues for textualism as the governing interpretive rule for contracts between sophisticated parties capable of rational contract planning and design.

Two canonical cases illustrate how a textualist regime can function to satisfy sophisticated party preferences for *both* text and context. The first case involves the interpretation of the meaning of express, written contract terms. A dispute over the meaning of express terms arises where written contract language has an apparently clear and unambiguous meaning but may be understood in a different way once context evidence is introduced.

This issue arises when a term in the written agreement has a plain, un-ambiguous meaning in the standard language, but one party claims that context evidence will show that the parties attributed a different meaning to the term.[46] As noted above, courts that follow a hard parol evidence rule also tend to follow the plain meaning rule (which does not look beyond the writing to understand what the parties meant), and thus exclude extrinsic evidence to resolve such disputes. Nevertheless, sophisticated parties who prefer to have context evidence considered are not disadvantaged by this rule, as they may so draft the contract, incorporating what context they wish in its express terms.

A variety of contract clauses perform this function. These include (a) "whereas" or "purpose" clauses that describe the parties' business plan and the transaction,[47] (b) definition clauses that ascribe particular mean-ings to words and terms that may vary from their plain meaning, and (c) appendices that provide more precise specifications governing perfor-mance as well as any memoranda the parties want an interpreting court to use. Alternatively, parties can elect not to incorporate a merger clause into the agreement so that any and all context evidence will be admissible. Parties can also specify in the integrated agreement that the meaning of terms should be interpreted according to the customs and usages of a particular trade or industry. Casual empiricism suggests that all of these strategies are pursued in one degree or another by commercial parties writing contracts in textualist jurisdictions.

Contrast the flexibility sophisticated parties enjoy in designing contracts that will be reviewed by textualist courts with the alternative of contract design in contextualist jurisdictions. Under the UCC, trade usage is always relevant and the text of the parol evidence rule appears to exclude context evidence from the operation of a merger clause.[48] Moreover, the Code's re-jection of the plain meaning rule means that regardless of the "terms" the court finds to be part of the agreement, the meaning of those terms will always be subject to evidence of contextual understandings that vary from any standard dictionary meaning. In short, in contextualist jurisdictions, contextualism is mandatory. This means that context evidence will in-crease accuracy for those cases in which parties intended that apparently standard language should be read in a nonstandard way in light of the underlying commercial context. But if contextualism is the only interpretive style, it necessarily increases contracting costs for some parties: giving the commercial context interpretive priority (in fact, if not formally) makes much more costly the efforts of those who wish to exclude the relevant commercial context.

The second canonical case, which illustrates the superiority of textualism, is its ability to balance text and context in a way that economizes on contracting costs. Under textualism, the parties may adopt a mixed regime, where some terms are narrowly defined, leaving little room for context; while other terms import imprecise standards, where the courts may fill in the gaps with the benefit of ex post information. This offers a flexibility absent from contextualism, and has not been well recognized by courts or commentators.

Commercial contracts commonly include both precise and vague terms, and the courts actively interpret and enforce vague terms by reference to context evidence. For example, contracts may condition one party's performance on "commercially reasonable efforts," "reasonable efforts," or "reasonable best efforts."[49] The conventional explanation is that these vague terms act as "catch-alls" that compensate for the under-inclusiveness of precise terms. To the contrary, however, the evidence shows that parties choose their mix of rules and standards to optimize the admissibility of context evidence over two dimensions: *when* the context is incorporated and *who* decides what context matters. The practical choice is between the parties at the time of the contract and the court at the later time of litigation. The parties have the comparative advantages at the time of contracting since they share in the benefits of efficient contracting. But the court does have the benefit of hindsight. In this case, uncertainty has been resolved and the court sees realized facts rather than probability distributions. The parties can't foresee all contingencies, so they can delegate to the court the task of completing the contract ex post by considering relevant context. They indicate this intention by adopting a vague contract term (or standard). The combination of vague and specific terms thus allows the parties to exploit the information advantages of both the court and the parties.[50]

In contrast, a court intent on admitting context evidence to determine the parties' actual intent will violate freedom of contract norms if it completes the contract in a way that the parties themselves would never have agreed to. To appreciate how this might occur, it is important to understand how a court's interpretive approach can affect initial contracting costs. Parties that function under a contextualist theory of interpretation may succumb to post-contractual opportunism, strategically urging interpretations that favor their ex post position. This temptation is greater as the complexity of a contract increases. The more complex the contract, the more opportunities it presents for a party to raise an ambiguity in the language. When parties consider which contract form to choose initially, they will anticipate the costs of enforcing the contract they chose. Contextual interpretation thus raises the costs of using complex contracts by impeding the ability of parties to shift costs to the front end of the contracting process when uncertainty is low.

B. Interpretive Rules for Standardized Contracts

Assuming, consistent with current law, that textualism and contextualism are regarded as mandatory background rules within their prescribed domains, I next consider the case for a mandatory contextualist rule for standardized contracts—the paradigmatic sales transaction contemplated by Article 2 of the UCC. I argued above that when levels of uncertainty are high, contract designers will shift more costs from the front end of the contracting process to the back end so as to capture the courts' hindsight advantage. Standardized contracts present yet another opportunity to evaluate this tradeoff. Casual observation as well as theory suggests that when parties contract in well-developed markets, they write simple, "modular" contracts that rely on well-established trade customs and understandings. These pre-existing patterns reduce the costs of ex ante specification but do not significantly increase ex post enforcement costs so long as the court has reliable access to the relevant trade standards. Under these conditions, contextual interpretation will reduce the costs of specifying all of the terms in the written contract because parties can rely on courts to recover ex post the understandings that are not explicitly included in the written agreement ex ante. These costs include both the costs of committing to writing the customary understandings in a particular trade or practice as well as the social costs of holding unsophisticated parties to written terms that depart from previously settled understandings.

If these conditions obtain for all (or almost all) sales contracts governed by the UCC, then contextualism could be justified as the preferred interpretive style for resolving such disputes. In fact, however, the domain of sales law under Article 2 is overbroad. It includes both standardized transactions as well as complex sales contracts susceptible to ex ante contract design. Moreover, the argument for incorporation of context rests on the questionable assumption that generalist courts are equipped accurately to incorporate context in the course of litigating disputes over the terms and meaning of written agreements. In Llewellyn's mind, the mechanism for incorporation was to have been the merchant tribunal. The merchant jury was to be a panel of experts that would find specific facts—such as whether the behavior of a contracting party was "commercially reasonable." Unfortunately, the idea of the merchant tribunal was too radical for the commercial lawyers who dominated the drafting process. Thus, Llewellyn abandoned this key device for discovering the relevant context, while still retaining the architecture of incorporation.

To be sure, courts subsequently have interpreted contracts in which context evidence has been evaluated together with the written terms of the contract.[51] But the fact-specific nature of such disputes leaves little opportunity for the context evidence introduced in a given case to serve as useful standardized terms for future parties. Moreover, the court, ignorant of the contracting environment and unaided by experts, may err in evaluating contested context evidence that is introduced by only one of the disputants. As a consequence, neither enhanced accuracy nor positive externalities will reliably result from a court's consideration of context evidence in any given sales contract dispute: to this extent, therefore, the incorporation project appears to have failed in implementation.

Conclusion

The justification for a mandatory contextualist regime rests on the assumption that all contractual transactions are homogeneous. But, to the contrary, contract law applies to a wide range of contexts and parties. Parties are heterogeneous in modern economies; contracts sometimes have to be complex, and parties often must take into account many relevant future states of the world. The greater the heterogeneity of the parties and the greater the variety of contexts to which a particular transaction applies, the more freedom parties must have to draft a written contract that addresses ex ante the particular contracting costs that they anticipate. Because the context in which parties contract is itself heterogeneous, a mandatory contextualist regime, such as that currently adopted by Article 2 of the UCC, is seriously overbroad. In failing to recognize the heterogeneity of commercial contracting, the drafters of Article 2 and the reporters of the Second Restatement as well as the state courts that follow California's lead have contributed to a decline in the quality of American contract law.[52] The merits of flexibility in shifting costs between the two stages of the contracting process override any value in automatically incorporating context in every case. Contextualism for everyone denies too many commercial parties the ability to design contracts efficiently.

The argument for contextualism as a mandatory interpretive rule in a world of mandatory interpretive rules thus reduces to the regulatory imperative of protecting unsophisticated parties—mostly individual consumers—against the risk of exploitation through deceit and other difficult-to-detect forms of fraud or manipulation of cognitive biases. But if the objective is to regulate consumer transactions in mass market settings, the notion that those interests are best protected through the common law of contract, or that protecting those interests has much to do with the rules of contract interpretation, is simply fanciful. Consumer transactions, and the equitable issues they present, can be better resolved within a regulatory regime separate from the common-law rules of contract that govern commercial parties.

Notes

1. See generally Restatement (Second) of Contracts §§210 Comment b; 212, Comment b; 214 (1979).

2. Article 2 of the UCC governs contracts for the sale of goods. See generally Uniform Commercial Code (hereinafter UCC) §§2-202(a), Comment 1(b), and Comment 2; 1–303, Comment 1.

3. Masterson v. Sine, 436 P. 2d 561 (1968).

4. An early empirical study found that 26% of a sample of 500 cases raised interpretation and parol evidence issues. Harold Shepherd, Contracts in a Prosperity Year, 6 Stan. L. Rev. 208, 223 (1954); see also David A. Dilts, Of Words and Contracts: Arbitration and Lexicology, Disp. Resol. J., May–July 2005, at 41, 43 ("The construction of contract language is the controversy most evident in contract disputes"); John P. Tomaszewski, The Pandora's Box of Cyberspace: State Regulation of Digital Signatures and the Dormant Commerce Clause, 33 Gonz. L. Rev. 417, 432 (1997–1998) ("most contract litigation involves disputes over construction of the terms in a contract").

5. A strong majority of U.S. courts continue to follow the traditional, textualist, or "formalist" approach to contract interpretation. A state-by-state survey of recent court decisions shows that 38 states follow the textualist approach to interpretation. Nine states, joined by the UCC for sales cases and the Restatement (Second) of Contracts, have adopted a contextualist or anti-formalist interpretive regime. The remaining states' doctrines are indeterminate.

6. This issue is addressed by the parol evidence rule. The rule holds that when parties choose to fully integrate a final written agreement, they forfeit the right in subsequent litigation to prove understandings they declined to include in their integrated writing.

7. The plain meaning rule addresses the question of what legal meaning should be attributed to the contract terms that the parol evidence rule has identified. Under a plain meaning interpretation, when words or phrases appear to be unambiguous, extrinsic evidence of a possible contrary meaning is inadmissible.

8. See, e.g., Morgan Stanley High Yield Sec., Inc. v. Seven Circle Gaming Corp., 269 F. Supp. 2d 206 (S.D.N.Y. 2003) (holding that the prior agreement is excluded where the writing appears in view of thoroughness and specificity to embody a final agreement). In addition, merger clauses are given virtually conclusive effect in New York. See Tempo Shain Corp. v. Bertek, Inc., 120 F.3d 16, 21 (2d Cir. 1997) ("Ordinarily, a merger clause provision indicates that the subject agreement is completely integrated, and parol evidence is precluded from altering or interpreting the agreement").

9. See Alan Schwartz and Robert E. Scott, Contract Theory and the Limits of Contract Law, 113 Yale L. J. 541 (2003).

10. For a discussion of how contracting parties can economize on total contracting costs by shifting costs between the drafting or front end of the contracting process and the adjudication or back end of the process, see Robert E. Scott and George G. Triantis, Anticipating Litigation in Contract Design, 115 Yale L. J. 814 (2006).

11. Contextualist interpretive principles are exemplified by the Uniform Commercial Code and the Second Restatement of Contracts. California is the most significant contextualist jurisdiction.

12. Pac. Gas & Elec. Co. v. G. W. Thomas Drayage & Rigging Co., 442 P.2d 641, 645 (1968) ("Rational interpretation requires at least a preliminary consideration of

all credible evidence offered to proved the intention of the parties"); see also Int'l Milling Co. v. Hachmeister, Inc., 110 A.2d 186 (1955) (extrinsic evidence of negotiations and antecedent agreements admissible to show buyer had not assented to the contract as a complete integration of the contract despite the presence of an express merger clause).

13. See Scott and Triantis, supra note 10.

14. The discussion in this part draws on Jody S. Kraus and Robert E. Scott, Contract Design and the Structure of Contractual Intent, 84 N.Y.U. L. Rev. 1023 (2009).

15. J. H. Baker, An Introduction to English Legal History 12 (4th ed. 2002).

16. Id. at 12, 100–101.

17. Id. at 111.

18. The common law applied "to documents a rule of construction that the words had to be given their ordinary meaning." Id. at 226.

19. Baker, supra note 15, at 324–325.

20. See, e.g., William Story, Commentaries on Equity Jurisprudence, §§ 153–157 (W. E. Grigsby, ed., 1884) (describing the equitable exceptions to the parol evidence rule).

21. See, e.g., Samuel Williston, Contracts 631 (3d ed. 1961) ("The parol evidence rule requires, in the absence of fraud, duress, mutual mistake or something of the kind, the exclusion of extrinsic evidence, oral or written, where the parties have reduced their agreement to an integrated writing"). For discussion, see Dennis M. Patterson, Good Faith, Lender Liability, and Discretionary Acceleration: Of Wittgenstein, and the Uniform Commercial Code, 68 Tex. L. Rev. 169, 187–188 (1989).

22. Patterson, id. at 187–188.

23. 11 Williston on Contracts § 33:2. For discussion, see Joseph M. Perillo, Calamari and Perillo on Contracts 115–116 (6th ed. 2009).

24. 11 Williston on Contracts §32:25.

25. Restatement of the Law of Contracts §240 (1932).

26. 6 Corbin on Contracts §577 (1951).

27. Id. at § 582.

28. Corbin's view was that even if the contract was an unambiguous integration, all relevant extrinsic evidence should be admissible on the issue of the meaning of the agreement. 5 Corbin on Contracts §24.7–24.9.

29. Robert E. Scott, The Rise and Fall of Article 2, 62 La. L. Rev. 1009, 1023–1024 (2002).

30. Id. at 1037–1038.

31. UCC § 1-201(3) (2010) defines "agreement" as the "bargain of the parties in fact as found in their language or by implication from other circumstances, including course of dealing or usage of trade or course of performance as provided in this act."

32. UCC § 2-202, cmt 1,2 (2003).

33. Most autonomy-based theories are premised either on a notion of consent or the exercise of will, such as the making of a promise. For discussion, see Robert E. Scott and Jody S. Kraus, Contract Law and Theory 23–26 (4th ed. 2007).

34. It is universally understood that a court's role in interpreting a contract is to determine the intentions of the parties. Intent, in turn, is determined objectively and prospectively. In other words, a court is directed to recover the parties' objectively manifested intentions concerning both the objectives or "ends" of their agreement and the "means" they may have chosen to determine those ends should they later dispute the meaning of the agreement.

35. This notion of incorporation of custom and practice is deeply imbedded in the Code. UCC §1-303, cmt 3, provides that "[Usages and customs] furnish the background and give particular meaning to the language used [in the contract] and are the framework of common understanding controlling any general rules of law which hold only when there is no such understanding." For discussion, see Robert E. Scott, The Rise and Fall of Article 2, 62 La. L. Rev. 1009 (2002).

36. See, e.g., Masterson v. Sine, supra note 3.

37. See UCC §§ 1-205, 2-202 and comments. For discussion, see Robert E. Scott, "The Uniformity Norm in Commercial Law: A Comparative Analysis of Common Law and Code Methodologies," in The Jurisprudential Foundations of Corporate and Commercial Law 149–192 (J. S. Kraus and S. D. Walt, eds., 2000).

38. See, e.g., Perillo, supra note 23.

39. Of course, the reverse could be true. The Code directs courts to construe express terms and extrinsic evidence from practices or usages as consistent with each other. But sometimes the parties may actually have intended that their clear language should be read in the standard (plain meaning) way despite the fact that the language itself conflicts with the prior practices and negotiations of the parties. In such a case, a court that relies too heavily on context risks misinterpreting the parties' actual intentions.

40. See Robert E. Scott, The Case for Formalism in Relational Contract, 94 Nw. U. L. Rev. 847, 853–856 (2000); Scott, The Uniformity Norm, supra note 37, at 157–158; Alan Schwartz, Contract Theory and Theories of Contract Regulation, 92 Revue d'Économie Industrielle 101 (2000).

41. What does it mean, then, to interpret contracts according to their "plain meaning"? Proponents of a contextual approach to interpretation have argued that meaning is necessarily contextual. To be sure, at one level, the debate over plain meaning raises deep philosophical questions about the nature and knowledge of meaning. In its purely philosophical form, the debate turns on whether any terms have on their face a unique, contextual plain meaning. But in commercial litigation the pressing question is not this deep philosophical one, but whether courts should seek to vindicate the meaning the parties actually intended or instead to assign terms a more objective meaning. Even if terms do not, strictly speaking, have a unique, plain meaning, the meanings any terms can be given range along a continuum from purely subjective to largely objective. Thus, while parties might attach purely subjective meanings to ordinary words, this does not demonstrate that the same terms do not admit of relatively more objective meanings. For discussion, see Robert E. Scott and Jody S. Kraus, supra note 33.

42. This argument is premised on the claim that firms behave as if they are risk neutral. Risk-neutral firms prefer to limit enforcement costs—say by resolving interpretation disputes by summary judgment—so long as the courts' interpretations are correct on average. It follows that sophisticated parties (i.e., firms) are more reluctant to expend resources to shrink the variance around the correct mean. See Alan Schwartz and Robert E. Scott, Contract Interpretation Redux, 119 Yale L. J. 926 (2010).

43. Theodore Eisenberg and Geoffrey P. Miller, The Flight to New York: An Empirical Study of Choice of Law and Choice of Forum Clauses in Publicly-Held Companies' Contracts (N.Y.U. Law & Econ. Res. Paper Series, Working Paper No. 08–13, 2008), available at http://ssrn.com/abstract=1114808.

44. Geoffrey P. Miller, Bargaining on the Red-Eye: New Light on Contract Theory (N.Y.U. Law & Econ. Working Papers No. 131, 2008), available at http://lsr.nellco .org/nyu/lewp/papers/131.

45. See, e.g., Steven J. Burton, Elements of Contract Interpretation 193–202 (2009). For an argument that interpretive rules should be defaults, see Alan Schwartz and Robert E. Scott, Contract Interpretation Redux, 119 Yale L. J. 926 (2010).

46. This claim could be based on the argument that other sources of evidence— such as the parties' prior negotiations—show that the written term is ambiguous, or that those other sources show that the parties attached a specialized or private meaning to the term in question. See, e.g., Pacific Gas & Electric Co. v. G. W. Thomas Drayage & Rigging Co., 442 P. 2d 641 (Cal. 1968).

47. See, e.g., the "purpose" clause from the Fountain Manufacturing Agreement between Apple Computer, Inc., and SCI Systems, Inc., available at http://contracts .onecle.com/apple/scis.mfg.1996.05.31.shtml http://cori.missour.edu.

48. UCC § 2-202(b) provides that "consistent additional terms" are excluded where the writing was "intended . . . as a complete and exclusive statement of the terms of the agreement," but no such exclusion applies to trade usage, course of performance, or course of dealing evidence under §2-202(a).

49. See University of Missouri-Columbia, Contracting and Organizations Research Institute, CORI Contracts Library, at http//cori.missouri.edu (last visited Feb. 25, 2005). Total contracts in CORI database: 24,965. Contracts with "best efforts" terms: 4,328 (17.34%). Contracts with "reasonable expenses" terms: 2,584 (10.35%). Contracts with "reasonably withheld" terms: 38 (0.0015%). Contracts with "unreasonably withheld" terms: 3,525 (14.12%). Contracts with "reasonable" terms: 13,281 (53.20%).

50. The options available to the parties are even broader than the stark choice between a rule and a standard. With the aid of interpretation maxims, parties can design combinations of specific and vague terms that more precisely define the "space" within which the court has discretion in proxy choice. For discussion, see Scott and Triantis, Anticipating Litigation, supra note 10.

51. The invitation to contextualize the contract in this manner is explicitly embodied in the Code's definition of "agreement" in § 1-201(3) and is amplified by § 1-303,

which specifies that courses of dealing, courses of performance, and usages of trade give particular meaning to, and qualify terms of, an agreement.

52. It is worth noting that in England, as well as most other common-law countries that have not experienced the "Realist Revolution," the courts continue to incline more closely to textualism. See Michael Bridge's article in this volume. The conclusion in this article is that American contract law would be better for following that example.

Exit and the American Illness

ERIN O'HARA O'CONNOR AND LARRY E. RIBSTEIN

Other chapters of this book extensively document problems created by regulatory, liability, and litigation inefficiencies in American law. Some of those inefficiencies are found in federal law, others in state law. Indeed, one who locates or conducts business in the U.S. could be exposed to the maladies of many jurisdictions within the U.S., compounding the problems of American law. Moreover, state laws that regulate business activities located elsewhere may not be subject to the same disciplinary pressures as are state laws whose ill effects are experienced only locally.

Multiple jurisdictions could mitigate inefficient regulation, however, if they enabled firms to avoid excessively high liability states and select states with more efficient laws. In other words, adopting Albert O. Hirschman's framework, the U.S. offers the potential of "exit" to offset the excesses of "voice," or the political system.[1] Permitting the parties to choose the state whose laws govern their contract, and to exit unfavorable states, would allow them to select a set of laws better matched to their needs. By contrast, legal reforms are less likely to provide an optimal set of laws, since governments lack the knowledge of the parties about their individual needs. Moreover, if parties can choose their governing laws, they can better predict the legal consequences of their conduct, and firms conducting business in multiple jurisdictions can formulate a single corporate policy to comply with a single governing law.

Party choice serves another purpose, in disciplining states with inefficient laws. A state that finds that people within it routinely exit from its laws, choosing instead to be governed by the laws of another state, will have an incentive to amend its laws to mimic the laws of the favored state.[2]

Exit from undesirable laws could occur in at least three ways. First, the firm might avoid doing business in problematic states and choose another, more benign jurisdiction to govern its activities. It might incorporate in the other jurisdiction; it might decide not to locate assets, advertise, or conduct business in problematic states; and it might through a choice-of-law clause in its contracts specify that the law of another state is to apply. Second, parties might by contract, through a choice-of-court clause, choose a court in another U.S. state to hear disputes, at least regarding legal issues that arise out of private contract. Third, parties can opt out of litigation within U.S. courts altogether by choosing either private arbitration or courts outside of the U.S. The second and third forms of exit both enable firms to avoid problematic litigation rules and enhance the likelihood that courts will apply the parties' chosen law in resolving disputes.

Exit from the U.S. jurisdictions most plagued by legal maladies can help at least partially to restore U.S. competitiveness. U.S. law does help facilitate exit. Although states may resist exit efforts by national firms, the U.S. Constitution, Congress, and the federal courts can limit state efforts to impose their laws on firms. The dormant Commerce Clause directly restrains the states from discriminating against interstate and in favor of intrastate commerce, while the positive Commerce Clause and the Supremacy Clause enable the federal government to override state legislation that burdens national and international firms. The U.S. system potentially enables firms and individuals to choose to be governed under any legal regime while maintaining the ability to conduct business (or not) anywhere else. This allows parties to pressure states to maintain reasonable laws in order to retain franchise fees, taxes, jobs, litigation, arbitration, and other opportunities.

Party choice-of-law in the U.S. is imperfect, however. To some extent, this is not unreasonable. Unlimited party choice can result in a race to the bottom in which third parties are harmed. It might also be abused by a party with oppressive bargaining power. To address these problems, exit options could be limited by the states in sensible ways.[3] Even taking such objections into account, however, the current limitations on party choice are excessive and vague. The problematic political forces that make a state inhospitable to business might carry over to the state's choice-of-law regime, and block the possibility of exit. These restrictions on party choice plausibly make interstate and international contracting parties wary of engaging in cross-border trade in the United States.

Choice-of-Law in the U.S.

Jurisdictional choice begins with physical mobility. Unless a state can compel a party to enter its courts, those courts cannot enter judgments that affect it. Personal jurisdiction rules therefore provide a basis for jurisdictional choice in the U.S., albeit a narrow one. Under the Due Process Clause of the U.S. Constitution, courts may assert jurisdiction over defendants who have had only "minimum contacts" with the state, so long as the defendant directs enough action toward the forum to make it fair that the defendant be sued in that state.[4] Thus, for example, due process is satisfied where the defendant knows it is making sales in or otherwise directing sales activity into a state.[5] Although the test ensures that a defendant has fair notice that it will be subject to the state's law, firms that depend on national advertising and distribution systems have difficulty avoiding burdensome state laws. Nevertheless, firms have some ability to avoid burdensome state laws by avoiding even minimum contacts with the state, and this possibility helps to constrain a state's ability to impose its laws on firms based in other states.

It is not clear, however, how actively firms must avoid contacts with states or what constraints are imposed on a firm's ability to structure itself and its activities in order to avoid personal jurisdiction in a particular state. In two cases recently decided by the U.S. Supreme Court, state courts have interpreted their jurisdictional authority quite expansively by asserting personal jurisdiction over companies whose products ended up in the forum even though the defendant entity did not choose to sell any of its goods in the state. In *Nicastro v. McIntyre Machinery America, Ltd.,*[6] New Jersey state courts asserted personal jurisdiction over a British manufacturer of a recycling machine that injured a scrap metal worker in New Jersey. The manufacturer commissioned another company with the same name but otherwise independent to act as its exclusive U.S. distributor. The distributor sold the machine to the plaintiff's employer in New Jersey. The New Jersey Supreme Court held that the manufacturer could be sued in New Jersey even if it did not purposely avail itself of a New Jersey market or was, as it claimed, unaware that its product was sold in the state. Instead, it was sufficient that the defendant commissioned a distributor to market the product throughout the United States. The defendant either "knew or reasonably should have known that its distribution scheme would make its products available to New Jersey consumers," and this availability created a strong presumption in favor of the exercise of personal jurisdiction over the defendant.[7] The New Jersey court's conclusion would prevent a company from attempting to shield itself from liability by simply outsourcing its distribution, but it does so in a way that makes it impossible for firms to avoid personal jurisdiction everywhere without strong control over all product distribution and steadfast avoidance of undesirable states.

The second recent case dealing with personal jurisdiction is *Brown v. Meter,*[8] a personal jurisdiction case originating from the state courts of North Carolina. Here, subsidiaries of defendant Goodyear Tire Co. manufactured tires that were sold in North Carolina. As in *Nicastro,* the manufacturers did not handle tire distribution in the United States. Instead, they "used their Goodyear parent and affiliated companies to distribute the tires they manufactured to the United States and North Carolina."[9] According to the North Carolina court, personal jurisdiction could be based on defendants' purposefully injecting their product into the stream of commerce without attempting to exclude North Carolina as a potential product market.[10] This decision would prevent companies from strategically organizing their manufacturing and distribution systems in order to avoid liability for injuries caused by the use of their products in a particular jurisdiction. Even if this goal makes sense, the North Carolina court achieved it in a way that sharply inhibits firms from controlling where they might be sued. The tire that allegedly caused the plaintiffs' injuries never entered the forum state of North Carolina, but was instead manufactured in Turkey and sold in France, where the fatal injury occurred. The North Carolina courts used the fact that *some* tires manufactured by the defendant made their way into North Carolina in order to exercise general jurisdiction over the Turkish defendant. Under this ruling, the Turkish defendant must defend any lawsuit based on any claim in North Carolina courts. A court's ability to reach a defendant's conduct based on local distribution by a separate, albeit affiliated, entity, broadly extends its reach. Combined with a court's broad power, discussed below, to apply local law, this frustrates a firm's jurisdictional choice.

The U.S. Supreme Court reversed in both cases. In *Nicastro,* a plurality opined that a state can exercise "specific" jurisdiction (that is, based on the forum's connection with the specific controversy) only if defendant engaged in conduct deliberately directed toward the forum. In *Goodyear,* the Court unanimously held that the defendant lacked the sort of "continuous and systematic general business contacts" in the forum that support "general" jurisdiction (that is, not based on the forum's connection with the specific controversy).

These decisions may tend to discipline exercises of state jurisdictional authority. They may not, however, fully allay firms' concerns about the potential reach of state court jurisdiction. In *Nicastro,* the four-member plurality was joined by concurring Justices Stephen Breyer and Samuel Alito, who refused to exclude the possibility of personal jurisdiction when companies sell to the world or target a forum from a website or through an intermediary such as Amazon. *Goodyear* dealt only with the more stringent test for general jurisdiction and expressly did not opine on the standards for piercing the veil for jurisdictional purposes between a U.S. parent corporation and its foreign subsidiary. Thus, the states' potential jurisdictional reach may continue to trouble firms contemplating selling in the United States.

A. Jurisdictional Choice and Conflict of Laws

Because states can broadly exercise personal jurisdiction over firms, parties often have no choice but to comply with a state's procedural litigation rules. At least in theory, however, parties might be able to avoid state substantive regulatory and liability rules because state conflict of law rules sometimes direct a court to apply foreign substantive law. If conflict of law rules are clear (i.e., the law of the place of sale, manufacture, or injury applies to product liability claims), parties may be able to fashion their conduct to avoid the application of undesirable laws.

Under the principle of party choice, discussed above, contracting parties could avoid undesirable laws by choosing the laws of more favorable states in their contracts. Effective exit from undesirable laws requires that parties be permitted to determine which law will apply to their actions at *formation* of the contract. If instead jurisdictional choice is effectively made by plaintiffs at the time of suit by choosing the court, manufacturers and other potential defendants must comply with the laws of all states that could exercise jurisdiction over them. We therefore distinguish consensual *party choice* (where parties specify the law to govern the contract ex ante at formation) from non-consensual *state conflicts law* (where the governing law is specified ex post at the time of trial).

U.S. courts have used several different approaches to resolve conflict of law issues. Under each approach, courts focus on the state authority to regulate rather than on facilitating party choice or predictability. Unfortunately, U.S. law reflects a distinct trend away from relatively clear rules toward vague standards. This makes it much more difficult for parties to predict the governing law at the time they engage in the relevant conduct or transactions and, therefore, to choose where to locate their assets and activities based on this law. In addition, because the vague standards enhance a court's ability to apply the law of the forum state, they diminish the parties' ability to exit from undesirable state laws.

B. The Traditional Approach

Early U.S. conflicts decisions roughly reflect the vested rights or territorial approach that is embodied in the First Restatement of Conflict of Laws. Under the territorial principle, the laws of sovereign states could control only parties present and events occurring within their borders.[11] For cases involving people and events spanning multiple states, choice-of-law turned on "vested rights," the idea that rights vest, if at all, only at one point and place in time.[12] Specifically, the First Restatement listed rules for where rights vested based primarily on the cause of action creating a right. For example, the law of the situs of property controlled real property rights,[13] the law of the place of injury dictated the rules governing most tort actions,[14] the law of the place of contract determined the validity of and obligations in a contract,[15] and the law of the place of performance determined both the legality and sufficiency of the parties' contractual performance.[16] As long as the rules were well specified and courts everywhere agreed to follow the same rules, any party could determine what law would apply to an activity or contract at the time of engaging in or making it. Under uniform rules, parties wishing to avoid the property law of Utah could purchase property elsewhere, firms could locate their commercial activities outside of states whose tort laws imposed excessive liability, and parties could form or perform contracts outside of states where contract enforcement or regulation seemed problematic.

Unfortunately, courts did not apply the traditional approach clearly and uniformly. The underlying rationale for creating rules for vesting rights was murky under the traditional approach,[17] which created problems in situations where rules were left unspecified or their application was unclear. Although simple rules always create difficulties in a world where parties and activities are increasingly mobile, the traditional rules often seemed to allocate sovereign authority arbitrarily, and the absence of a clear policy framework left courts free to fill gaps and uncertainties in particular rules however they wanted. For example, since it was not clear why one law should apply to contract performance and another to contract validity, or which rules were contract (e.g., breach of warranty) and which tort (e.g., negligence), or what distinguished a procedural rule drawn from the forum and a substantive rule subject to the vested rights system,[18] the courts could, and indeed had to, make their own ad hoc judgments.

Judicially crafted escape devices that enabled courts to reach desired results further hindered uniformity and thus the parties' ability to predict results. Most importantly, courts could refuse to apply a law of another state deemed contrary to the forum's "strong public policy,"[19] but courts were left on their own to determine which policies seemed strong. Adding to these difficulties, the parties were helpless to avoid the uncertainties of the traditional approach because it denied them an explicit right to contract for the law of their choice.[20]

Only a small minority of U.S. states still apply the traditional rules-based approach.[21] The courts have abandoned this approach for some version of the vague, standard-based, interest analysis approach discussed next. This wholesale abandonment of conflicts rules in favor of standards was unwise. While the traditional system was flawed, many of the individual rules generated under it were sensible. Moreover, by throwing out the traditional approach, courts may have been committing the Nirvana Fallacy of comparing flawed rules with an idealized alternative. Because all choice-of-law systems have flaws, and multiple and irreconcilable goals, courts could never develop a perfect system for choosing the applicable law. The more complicated, less predictable approaches that replaced the traditional approach plausibly create more harm than good for interstate and international commerce.

Instead of dumping the traditional approach, the courts might have developed a logical and internally consistent way of filling the inevitable gaps in the traditional approach, and at least narrowed the "public policy" escape hatch that undermined certainty and predictability. But the states that led the movement away from the traditional approach were uninterested in predictability, and, as large states with large internal markets (New York and California in the 1950s and 1960s), they likely felt unthreatened by commercial pressures to provide predictability. Put differently, the movement away from the traditional approach reflected U.S. states' preference for conflicts rules that emphasized local political and regulatory interests over consistency, predictability, and party choice.

C. Interest Analysis

Modern conflict of laws has been shaped significantly by Brainerd Currie, who proposed his system of interest analysis in the early 1960s.[22] Interest analysis is now used in some form by a majority of U.S. courts as the basis for conflict of law decisions, and sadly has done much to reduce predictability and increase the cost of doing business.

Currie took issue with the traditional approach's strong emphasis on a single, potentially arbitrary connecting factor between the facts of a case and the state whose law applies. To justify the application of their law, said Currie, states need more than a mere connection with the case. Currie thought a state should regulate the parties and their activities only if its connection to the case triggered the policy rationales behind the state laws. If the facts of the case implicated only one state's policies, then that state's law should control the outcome of the case in order to effectuate that state's policies.[23] Suppose, for example, a contract is entered into between two individuals who live in state X involving subject matter and performance in state X. However, the contract is signed in state Y while the parties are vacationing there. State Y has a connection to the case that might be controlling under the traditional approach (as the place of contracting), but Y has little interest in the enforceability, duties, and performance of that contract.[24]

Currie's identification of state interests under his proposed approach was formulaic and limited. In general, he seemed to recognize three types of state interests: states with plaintiff-favoring laws were presumed to have an interest in compensating resident plaintiffs, those with defendant-favoring laws were presumed to have an interest in protecting resident defendants, and states with regulatory laws were presumed to have an interest in regulating conduct within their borders. Whether a state had an interest in having its substantive law applied to a disputed issue thus turned on where the parties resided and where the relevant conduct occurred.[25]

Currie recognized the possibility that more than one state might have an interest in regulating the matter. He proposed that courts resolve these "true" conflicts between multiple interested states by applying forum law and justified this conclusion by stating that legislatures and constituents expect courts to enforce local policies whenever they are implicated. Note that with this position on forum law, Currie effectively trumped the party choice principle.

Currie's formulaic and limited determination of state interests, if adopted by courts, would have enabled conflict of laws determinations to be relatively (although not completely) predictable. But courts were apparently uncomfortable with the artificiality of Currie's conclusions. Judges thought, for example, that states sometimes have an interest in compensating non-resident visiting plaintiffs, a defendant's state sometimes has an interest in regulating the defendant's conduct wherever it occurred, and some states have an interest in compensating or protecting third parties, such as family members or medical creditors. Other tricky issues arise under interest analysis, including the appropriate basis for determining actual legislative intent, especially when the legislature has not expressed it.[26] These issues made it more difficult for parties to know the applicable law at the time of their conduct.

Even worse from the standpoint of jurisdictional choice, interest analysis creates biases in favor of residents, forum law, and plaintiffs.[27] Currie assumed that states' policies protect only local residents and that the forum law should apply both in cases of "true conflicts" and in cases where no state had an interest in applying its law. The bias for forum law, in turn, favors plaintiffs because they are generally in the best position to choose the forum. Academics' attempts to improve on Currie's interest analysis have not solved these problems and would indeed shrink party choice further.[28]

D. The Second Restatement and the UCC

The Restatement (Second) of Conflict of Laws, promulgated in 1971, is the most widely used set of choice-of-law principles in U.S. courts.[29] Courts likely find the Restatement attractive because, by combining elements of rules, interest analysis, and other choice-of-law analyses, it only lightly constrains their determinations of the applicable law. Some argue that this flexibility better enables courts to allocate sovereign authority wisely,[30] though we question whether parochial judges are well situated to exhibit the impartiality that wisdom requires. More importantly for our purposes, judicial flexibility comes at the significant price of further preventing parties from predicting what law courts will apply to their conduct. In addition, party choice is not followed, and parties find it harder to exercise the exit option.

The Second Restatement starts with general default rules for particular types of disputes that can always be overcome by another set of general factors to guide court choices. For example, if contracting parties have not agreed to the applicable law, the Restatement provides a series of default rules for different types of contracts. The law where the land is situated determines the validity of and party obligations under contracts for the transfer of interests in land;[31] the law of the state where the seller is to deliver the chattel determines the validity of contracts to sell chattels;[32] the law of the state where the insured resided at the time the contract was formed determines the validity of a life insurance contract;[33] the law of the state where the insured risk is principally located during the policy term determines the validity of a contract for fire, surety, or casualty insurance;[34] and so on. Although these default rules seem relatively clear, courts can always displace them when they prefer to apply some other law.

Section 188 provides a list of "contacts to be taken account" of, and these other states' laws might displace the default law if one is considered to have the most significant relationship to the transaction or the parties.[35] Courts make that latter determination by referring to several general conflicts factors, including "the needs of the interstate and international systems," the policies of the forum, other interested states and the field of law involved, protection of justified expectations, certainty, predictability, uniformity, and ease of determining and applying the law.[36] The Second Restatement at least acknowledges the importance of predictability, but only as one of several relevant factors. Courts likely cannot achieve the goal of furthering a predictable system when predictability is just one of several relevant objectives. Not surprisingly, then, in practice this factor is largely ignored.

The basic problem with all of these judicial approaches to choice-of-law is that courts make the final decision without sufficient (or in some cases, any) restraint on the exercise of judicial discretion. Moreover, courts that tend to favor plaintiffs in fashioning substantive rules often have a similar incentive to use conflict of law rules that enable them to apply these plaintiff-friendly laws,[37] and plaintiffs are quite adept at finding those fora. In short, choice-of-law rules in the U.S. fail to exploit the potential of the U.S. federal system to enable parties to exit oppressive laws.

Perhaps the most important provision in the Second Restatement is Section 187(1), which explicitly authorizes the enforcement of choice-of-law clauses in contracts. The recognition of this provision in every U.S. state provides significant predictability and makes choice-of-law clauses a critical mechanism for jurisdictional choice in U.S. contractual settings. Party choice is, however, constrained by two exceptions in Section 187(2): (a) where the parties chose the law of a state that "has no substantial relationship to the parties or the transaction and there is no other reasonable basis for the parties' choice," and (b) where the chosen law is "contrary to a fundamental policy of a state which has a materially greater interest than the chosen state in the determination of the particular issue" and that state would be chosen in the absence of a choice-of-law clause.

Although Section 187(2) is vague enough to enable courts to deny enforcement of choice-of-law clauses, courts have routinely enforced such clauses under the Second Restatement. Moreover, some states have adopted their own statutes providing for unqualified enforcement of choice-of-law clauses in large commercial transactions.[38] A search within a large contract database indicates that many parties choose from among a few major commercial jurisdictions—Delaware, New York, California, Texas, and Illinois,[39] the very states that compete for business by passing statutes mandating enforcement of choice-of-law clauses. This indicates that there is a market for *law* separate from a jurisdictional competition to attract firms' investments or business establishments. That conclusion is strengthened by the popularity of choosing Delaware law for many different types of contracts despite the fact that relatively few firms have significant contacts with Delaware other than as a state of incorporation. Another study of choice-of-law clauses in merger and acquisition contracts confirms the existence of a national market for law dominated by Delaware and New York.[40]

The principle of party choice is recognized in contracts governed by the Uniform Commercial Code. The UCC has long provided for the enforcement of a clause specifying the law of any state, provided that it bear a "reasonable relation" to the transaction.[41]

States' broad enforcement of choice-of-law clauses provides some cause for hope regarding party choice in the U.S. However, enforcement is not guaranteed for situations involving potentially unsophisticated parties, such as consumers, employees, and franchisees, and fails to assist in the many cases in which contracts are impracticable. Thus, firms beleaguered by consumer and tort litigation must rely on states' vague default conflict of law rules as a basis for making jurisdictional choices. This, combined with the broad jurisdictional rules discussed above, enables state courts to apply oppressive local consumer and tort law to remote firms that operate nationally and have little practical ability to avoid the opportunistic states.

The question addressed next is whether federal and U.S. constitutional law offers more promising routes to party choice. This might have the appearance of a paradox. We favor party choice and jurisdictional competition among U.S. states. As such, we generally view with disfavor federal substantive laws that restrict interstate competition by mandating national standards. Here, however, we argue for federal laws that would promote competition among states by facilitating exit from a state.

Federal Law

The U.S. Constitution empowers Congress to enact laws controlling conflict of law under the Full Faith and Credit Clause, which gives Congress the power to determine the effect states must give to other states' public acts or laws,[42] and the Commerce Clause, which enables Congress to regulate interstate and international commerce.[43] However, Congress has little incentive to meddle in traditional areas of state law unless interest groups demand action on a particular issue. Choice-of-law is the sort of "meta" issue on which an interest group consensus is hard to find. Thus, for example, Congress has been stirred to action on choice-of-law very rarely and recently only by the high-profile same-sex marriage issue implicated in the Defense of Marriage Act (DOMA).[44] Even there, Congress merely confirmed states' power to apply local public policy rather than other states' marriage laws.

A rare example of Congress's acting to specify choice-of-law was the National Bank Act provision enabling a bank to charge any interest rate permitted in the state where that bank was located, regardless of the usury laws in the state where the borrower resided.[45] This rule addressed specific policy concerns in response to strong interest group pressure and high inflation rates that severely limited available mortgage funds in states with fixed interest rate caps. The more usual situation is represented by the Class Action Fairness Act of 2005 ("CAFA"),[46] which responded to the problem of proliferating and burdensome state class action suits by giving the federal courts jurisdiction over large multi-state class actions.[47] Prior to CAFA, plaintiffs could choose to file class actions in state courts that would apply liability-friendly laws or that were willing to manipulate conflict of law doctrine to arrive at a single governing law for all claims, or both, thereby making it easier to obtain class action certification. Congress could easily have gone further in resolving the problem of plaintiffs shopping for favorable substantive law or certification decisions by adopting a federal conflict of law rule in CAFA to govern complex litigation.[48] Instead, Congress remained silent, thereby subjecting federal courts handling complex litigation to the same conflict of law chaos present in state courts.

A. Federal Courts and Diversity Jurisdiction

U.S. federal courts can hear suits based on state law, other than those covered by CAFA, only if all plaintiffs and all defendants are citizens of different states and the amount in dispute exceeds $75,000.[49] Where "diversity" jurisdiction is present, defendants can remove cases to federal courts even if the plaintiff originally filed them in state court. Under the *Erie* doctrine,[50] federal courts must apply substantive state law in these cases. Federal courts sitting in diversity also must apply the conflict of law rules of the state in which the federal court is located.[51]

Federal courts, which are less subject to state courts' incentives to attract litigation, have been more likely than state courts to enforce choice-of-law clauses. But federal courts must apply state conflict of law rules, which can sometimes constrain federal enforcement of choice-of-law clauses. Even if federal courts could fashion their own conflict of law rules, however, it is not clear these rules would be much clearer or more predictable than those created by state courts.[52]

B. The Federal Constitution

Several constitutional provisions arguably enable courts to address the chaos of common-law conflict of law rules directly without federal statutes. These include the Full Faith and Credit Clause, which allows courts to decide the respect that each state must give to one another's laws even where Congress is silent;[53] the Due Process Clause,[54] which protects parties from unfair surprise regarding the applicable laws; the Equal Protection[55] and

Privileges and Immunities Clauses,[56] which might be applied to constrain conflict of law approaches that discriminate in favor of state residents; and the "dormant" form of the Commerce Clause,[57] which prevents states from excessively interfering with interstate commerce.

The application of these provisions potentially could go a long way toward promoting jurisdictional choice. Indeed, the Supreme Court did start down the road of constitutionalizing conflict of law in the late 19th and early 20th centuries by applying the Due Process and Full Faith and Credit Clauses. The Court used the Due Process Clause in insurance contract cases to mandate application of the law of the place of contracting in determining the parties' obligations.[58] This formalistic use of the place of contracting rule served to protect party expectations. However, the Court has since retreated from this analysis to permit the application of any law connected with the contract at the time the contract was formed.[59] Although this approach was more flexible than a place of contracting rule, it at least prevented the application of laws unconnected to the transaction at issue.

The Court's use of the Full Faith and Credit Clause similarly evolved from clear recognition of the parties' ex ante expectations to a looser standard. In a series of cases involving fraternal benefit associations, the Court held that members' rights must be determined according to the law of the place of formation of the organization.[60] While the Court stressed the need for uniform rights for owners of a common fund, it refused to apply the internal affairs doctrine (which would make the law of the state of incorporation or organization govern).[61]

After *Erie* brought greater federal court deference to state law, the Court turned to something approaching state interest analysis,[62] rejecting party choice principles. Moreover, in *Allstate Insurance Co. v. Hague*,[63] the Court signaled that it was unlikely to second-guess state conflicts laws. The Court held that Minnesota could apply its own law to an insurance contract even though the policy was issued in Wisconsin, the insured resided in Wisconsin, and the accident occurred in Wisconsin. This choice was justified because the decedent worked in Minnesota, his widow became a Minnesota resident after the accident, and the insurer was doing business in Minnesota. The Court reasoned that there was "no element of unfair surprise or frustration of legitimate expectations as a result of Minnesota's choice of its law."[64] This very broad acceptance of the use of forum law gives parties little ability to plan their activities based on applicable law.[65]

Because courts have never used the Equal Protection and Privileges and Immunities Clauses in the context of choice-of-law, the dormant Commerce Clause is the final potential constitutional basis for scrutinizing state choice-of-law decisions. This ground is promising because it potentially enables courts to strike down decisions even where the parties might have expected a similar result from past decisions. The Court has sometimes invalidated state regulation under the Commerce Clause when the regulation would enable a single state to impose burdens on national businesses everywhere. For example, a state could not require interstate trucks passing through it to have different mudguards than those most states permitted and at least one state required.[66] The Court has similarly prevented states from requiring national firms to revise their tender offers for their Illinois shareholders.[67] However, the latter result was based on Congress's enactment of national tender offer legislation. It is unlikely the Court would compel a state to apply another state's law under the dormant Commerce Clause solely because that state was designated in a choice-of-law clause.

The basic problem in all these cases is that neither the Court nor Congress cares enough about the allocation of authority across the states to give choice-of-law sustained attention. We now turn to the question of the extent to which parties can use choice-of-court and arbitration clauses to enhance their choices of governing law.

Choice-of-Court Clauses

So far we have seen that conflict of law rules leave state and federal courts quite free to apply local law to cases before them even if the case involves a contract with a clause choosing the law of another state. Yet states differ in the extent to which they are willing to apply the chosen state's law. Not surprisingly, the chosen state is almost always willing to apply local law. As a result, there is a close connection between contractual selection of the *court* and the choice of the *law* to govern.

Typically, the key problem for potential defendants is that plaintiffs generally choose the court unilaterally by deciding where to sue. Firms can counteract plaintiffs' ability to choose the forum ex post by inserting choice-of-court clauses in their contracts that designate the state or federal court where the parties' disputes will be litigated. These clauses also operate as agreements to submit to the personal jurisdiction of the chosen court. Not surprisingly, a study of merger and acquisition agreements found that contracts choosing a particular law to govern the transaction are also likely to provide for resolution of the disputes in the same state's courts.[68]

It might seem that parties would gain little from choice-of-court clauses that they do not get from choice-of-law clauses. If a party sues in a court other than the one the contract selects, the forum will likely recognize that if it enforces the choice-of-court clause, then the chosen court will agree to apply its forum law. Thus, courts that are hostile to choice-of-law clauses would be expected also not to like choice-of-court clauses. Indeed, some scholars have criticized choice-of-court clauses as a way to manipulate the governing law.[69] Courts and commentators once generally held that enforcing these clauses would amount to an illegal "ouster" of a court's jurisdiction.[70]

Courts, however, have greater incentives to enforce choice-of-court clauses than they do choice-of-law clauses despite the clauses' apparently similar effects. The former type of contract relieves the court from explicitly weighing the policies in local law against those of another state. It also enables a court with a crowded docket to lighten its case load.

Today states quite routinely do enforce choice-of-court clauses, at least in commercial cases.[71] The Supreme Court spurred this development in decisions applying federal law, particularly those involving the federal courts' exclusive admiralty jurisdiction. *M/S Bremen v. Zapata Off-Shore Co.*[72] enforced a choice-of-court clause in a commercial admiralty case, concluding that the clause "was a vital part of the agreement" and that the "consequences of the forum clause [figured] prominently in [the parties'] calculations."[73] The Court extended this reasoning into the consumer context in *Carnival*

Cruise Lines, Inc. v. Shute,[74] in which it enforced a choice-of-court clause buried in the fine print of a consumer passenger cruise line ticket.

Even if state courts refuse to enforce choice-of-court clauses, defendants can remove their cases to federal courts seeking federal diversity jurisdiction and use the court selection clause as a basis for having the case transferred to the selected federal court. The Supreme Court held in *Steward Org., Inc. v. Ricoh Corp.*[75] that federal law, which would include the U.S. Supreme Court's policy on forum selection clauses, applies in deciding whether to grant the transfer motion.

Court selection clauses have found greater traction in federal courts because these courts are more responsive to national interests than to local state legislatures. These national interests in international commerce, in turn, are affected by potential competition from foreign countries. Indeed, the *Bremen* Court reasoned: "In an era of expanding world trade and commerce, the absolute aspects of the doctrine of [non-enforcement of choice-of-court clauses] have little place and would be a heavy hand indeed on the future development of international commercial dealings by Americans. We cannot have trade and commerce in world markets and international waters exclusively on our terms, governed by our laws, and resolved in our courts."[76]

The national interest looms large in connection with potential ratification of the Hague Convention on Choice of Court Agreements. Article 5(1) of the Convention provides that "the court or courts of a Contracting State designated in an exclusive choice of court agreement shall have jurisdiction to decide a dispute to which the agreement applies, unless the agreement is null and void under the law of that State."[77] Ratification of this Convention might spur the U.S. to adopt a federal law requiring states to enforce choice-of-court clauses in order to compete with other countries that ratify the Convention.[78]

Despite the broad enforcement of choice-of-court clauses, the ability of plaintiffs to unilaterally choose where to sue importantly undermines party choice. Consider, for example, a study showing that even in corporate cases, where jurisdictional choice is firmly entrenched through the internal affairs doctrine,[79] non-Delaware courts are hearing a sharply increasing number of cases involving Delaware corporations.[80] The study suggests that ex post forum selection could threaten one of the few seemingly un-qualified successes of ex ante jurisdictional choice.

Arbitration

Enforcement of arbitration agreements has significantly influenced en-forcement of choice-of-law and choice-of-court clauses. Commercial arbi-tration has spread globally because of international competition for trade. England began the competition by making arbitration clauses enforceable by statute in 1886 and attracting business to the London Court of Arbitra-tion.[81] The New York Chamber of Commerce lobbied the New York legisla-ture to compete with London by adopting a similar statute.[82] In the early 1920s, New York and New Jersey adopted the first U.S. arbitration statutes.[83] In order to ensure nationwide enforcement of arbitration awards, in 1925 Congress passed the Federal Arbitration Act (FAA), which binds state and federal courts to enforce arbitration provisions in contracts.

The New York Convention on Arbitration, signed by the U.S. in 1958 and today by more than 140 other nations, helped further promote global enforcement of arbitration awards and thereby prevented parties from evad-ing arbitration by moving assets into non-enforcing countries.[84] The Con-vention requires its signatories to enforce written agreements to arbitrate disputes[85] and to refrain from imposing substantially more onerous condi-tions on the recognition or enforcement of foreign arbitral awards than they impose on the recognition or enforcement of domestic arbitral awards.[86] Within the U.S., states have competed to be venues for arbitration proceed-ings and to have their laws selected in commercial contracts, and lawyers have found they can earn fees as arbitrators and represent parties in arbi-tration.[87]

The popularity of arbitration in the U.S. has been helped by pro-arbitration U.S. Supreme Court decisions interpreting the Federal Arbitra-tion Act. The Court has held, for example, that the validity of the contract (though not of the arbitration provision) is a matter for the arbitrator,[88] and that states may not require administrative review of regulated contracts as a prerequisite to arbitration.[89] The Court also has held arbitrable disputes involving such public laws as the antitrust,[90] securities,[91] antiracketeering,[92] civil rights, and employment discrimination statutes.[93] The Court often stresses in these cases that arbitration helps the U.S. compete in a world economy.

Although arbitration has been a success so far in the U.S. and globally, the same interest groups that oppose enforcement of contractual choice-of-law and court also are threatening arbitration. Arbitration is already unenforceable in franchise contracts between automobile manufacturers and dealers.[94] Some courts have held that arbitration clauses cannot circumvent class-wide dispute mechanisms, applying arguably stricter unconscionability standards to arbitration than to other contract terms,[95] and some companies, more afraid of class-wide arbitration orders than they are of U.S. courts, have responded to this development by removing arbitration clauses from their contracts. The Supreme Court reaffirmed the enforceability of arbitration agreements by holding that the Federal Arbitration Act preempts state laws mandating class arbitration as inconsistent with "the overarching purpose of the FAA . . . to ensure the enforcement of arbitration agreements according to their terms so as to facilitate streamlined proceedings."[96] Nevertheless, the interest group battle over arbitration is likely to continue, as Congress can weaken arbitration merely by reducing the scope and effect of the FAA. Indeed, Congress is considering a law that would broadly invalidate arbitration clauses in consumer and employment contracts.[97]

Notwithstanding this potential threat, arbitration clauses remain more enforceable in the U.S. than in any other nation, and the widespread enforcement of arbitration clauses somewhat tempers the effects of the American Illness present in U.S. courts.

Conclusion

In sum, the U.S. federal system offers significant potential for jurisdictional choice as a partial solution to misguided or inappropriate law. However, this system is not only an imperfect solution, but can itself be a source of bad law and runaway litigiousness. Firms that do business nationally or internationally have no guarantee that they can avoid being hauled into the courts of any of the 50 U.S. states and subjected to its oppressive law. Federal law and enforcement of contractual choice-of-law, choice-of-court, and arbitration clauses provide some, but only partial, relief. As such, the U.S. is losing an opportunity to exploit the edge it might get from its federal system in international competition.[98]

Notes

1. See Albert O. Hirschman, Exit, Voice, and Loyalty: Responses to Decline in Firms, Organizations, and States (1970).

2. On jurisdictional competition, see Erin O'Hara and Larry Ribstein, The Law Market (2009).

3. We explore this topic elsewhere. O'Hara & Ribstein, id.

4. World-Wide Volkswagen Corp. v. Woodson, 444 U.S. 286, 297 (1980).

5. Asahi Metal Indus. Co. v. Superior Ct., 480 U.S. 102, 111–12 (1987).

6. 201 N.J. 48, 987 A.2d 575 (2010), rev'd J. McIntyre Machinery Ltd. v. Nicastro, 564 U.S. ___ (2011).

7. 201 N.J. at 79, 987 A.2d at 593.

8. 681, S.E.2d 383, rev'd Goodyear Luxembourg Tires, S.A. v. Brown, 564 U.S. ___ (2011).

9. Id. at 386.

10. Id. at 391.

11. 1 J. Beale, A Treatise on the Conflict of Laws 6 (1935).

12. For a history of the vested rights concept, see Lea Brilmayer, Conflict of Laws 16–17 (2d ed. 1985).

13. Restatement (First) of Conflict of Laws §§ 214–54.

14. Id. at 377, Reporter's Notes.

15. Id. at §§ 332–47.

16. Id. at § 358.

17. For influential criticisms of Beale's approach, see Walter Wheeler Cook, The Logical and Legal Bases of the Conflict of Laws (1942); Brainerd Currie, Selected Essays on the Conflict of Laws (1963).

18. See First Restatement § 585 (providing that "all matters of procedure are governed by the law of the forum").

19. See First Restatement § 612 (providing that "no action can be maintained upon a cause of action created in another state the enforcement of which is contrary to the strong public policy of the forum").

20. Lea Brilmayer, Conflict of Laws: Cases and Materials 312–13 (4th ed. 1995).

21. Symeon C. Symeonides, Choice-of-law in the American Courts in 2005: Nineteenth Annual Survey, 53 Am. J. Comp. L. 559, 595–96 (2005).

22. Brainerd Currie, Selected Essays on the Conflict of Laws (1963).

23. Id. at 183–84.

24. Currie applies a similar analysis to an example involving restrictions on married women's ability to contract. Brainerd Currie, Married Women's Contracts: A Study in Conflict-of-Laws Method, 25 U. Chi. L. Rev. 227 (1958).

25. See Lea Brilmayer, Conflict of Laws § 2.1 (2d ed. 1995) (discussing probable views of Currie based on his case analyses).

26. See Brilmayer, id. at § 2.5.

27. See Patrick J. Borchers, The Choice-of-Law Revolution: An Empirical Study, 49 Wash. & Lee L. Rev. 357 (1992); Michael E. Solimine, An Economic and Empirical Analysis of Choice-of-law, 24 Ga. L. Rev. 49 (1989); Stuart E. Thiel, Choice-of-law and the Home-Court Advantage: Evidence, 2 Am. Econ. L. Rev. 291 (2000).

28. William Baxter, Choice-of-law and the Federal System, 16 Stan. L. Rev. 1 (1963); David F. Cavers, A Critique of the Choice-of-law Problem, 47 Harv. L. Rev. 173 (1933); Robert A. Leflar, Choice-Influencing Considerations in Conflicts Law, 41 N.Y.U. L. Rev. 367 (1966) (advocating application of "better" law as one of five choice-influencing considerations); Elliott E. Cheatham & Willis L. M. Reese, Choice of the Applicable Law, 52 Colum. L. Rev. 959 (1952).

29. See Symeon C. Symeonides, Choice-of-law in the American Courts in 2010: Twenty-fourth Annual Survey, 59 Amer. J. Compar. L. _____ (2011).

30. See, e.g., Peter Hay, Patrick J. Borchers, & Symeon C. Symeonides, Conflict of Laws (5th ed. 2010) ("for a whole generation, much of the academic literature seems to have demoted predictability to the lowest possible rank in the pyramid of conflicts goals and to have placed flexibility at the very top").

31. Restatement (Second) of Conflict of Laws §§ 189–90.

32. Id. at § 191.

33. Id. at § 192.

34. Id. at § 193.

35. Id. at § 188.

36. Id. at § 6.

37. See Erin Ann O'Hara, Opting Out of Regulation: A Public Choice Analysis of Contractual Choice-of-law, 53 Vand. L. Rev. 1551, 1559 (2000).

38. See Larry E. Ribstein, From Efficiency to Politics in Contractual Choice-of-law, 37 Ga. L. Rev. 363 (2003).

39. Id. at 434–35.

40. See Theodore Eisenberg & Geoffrey P. Miller, Ex Ante Choices of Law and Forum: An Empirical Analysis of Corporate Merger Agreements, N.Y.U. L. Econ. Res. Paper No. 06–31, 20 n.10 (2006), available at http://ssrn.com/abstract=918735.

41. UCC § 1-105(1) (2001). UCC § 1-301(f). This reflects another potential problem in federal systems—the states' ability in some situations to form a cartel through uniform laws to inhibit jurisdictional competition.

42. U.S. Const. art. IV, § 1.

43. U.S. Const. art. I, § 8.

44. Defense of Marriage Act 28 USCA § 1738c (2007) provides that "no State . . . shall be required to give effect to any public act, record, or judicial proceeding of any

other State . . . respecting a relationship between persons of the same sex that is treated as a marriage under the laws of such other State."

45. National Bank Act, 12 USCA. § 85 (2007). In Marquette Nat'l Bank v. First Omaha Serv. Corp., 439 U.S. 299 (1978), the Supreme Court determined that a bank was located in the State where it was chartered for purposes of this section.

46. Class Action Fairness Act of 2005, Pub. L. No. 109-2, 119 Stat. 4 (2005).

47. Pub. L. No. 109-2, 119 Stat. 4 (2005), section 4 of the Act provides that federal courts may exercise diversity jurisdiction over any class action in which "any member of a class of plaintiffs is a citizen of a State different from any defendant" so long as the claims aggregated total more than five million dollars.

48. Stephen B. Burbank, The Class Action Fairness Act of 2005 in Historical Context: A Preliminary View, draft manuscript available at http://www.ssrn.com /abstract=1083785.

49. 28 USC § 1332.

50. See Erie R.R. v. Tompkins, 304 U.S. 64 (1938).

51. Klaxon Co. v. Stentor Elec. Mfg., 313 U.S. 487 (1941).

52. See Arthur Miller & David Crump, Jurisdiction and Choice-of-law in Multistate Class Actions after Phillips Petroleum v. Shutts, 96 Yale L. J. 1, 79 (1986) (proposing federal statute to govern mass litigation in federal courts but expressing skepticism that the federal courts would ultimately do a better job than the states).

53. See U.S. Const. art. IV, § 1 ("Full Faith and Credit shall be given in each State to the public Acts, Records, and judicial Proceedings of every other State. And the Congress may by general Laws prescribe the Manner in which such Acts, Records and Proceedings shall be proved, and the Effect thereof").

54. See U.S. Const. amend. XIV, § 1 ("No state shall . . . deprive any person of life, liberty, or property, without due process of law").

55. Section 1 of the Fourteenth Amendment also provides that states may not deny any person within their jurisdiction the equal protection of the laws.

56. Article 4, section 2, of the Constitution provides that "the citizens of each State shall be entitled to all Privileges and Immunities of Citizens in the several States."

57. See U.S. Const. art. I, § 8, cl. 3 (providing that Congress has the power "to regulate Commerce . . . among the several states"). The Clause has also been interpreted to prevent state regulation of interstate commerce. The negative aspect of the Commerce Clause is often referred to as the Dormant Commerce Clause. The Commerce Clause plays an important role in preventing discrimination against out-of-state businesses because the Privileges and Immunities Clause does not apply to corporations or other businesses; rather, it protects only individual citizens.

58. N.Y. Life Ins. v. Dodge, 246 U.S. 357 (1918).

59. John Hancock Mut. Life Ins. v. Yates, 299 U.S. 178 (1936); Home Ins. Co. v. Dick, 281 U.S. 397 (1930).

60. See, e.g., Order of United Commercial Travelers v. Wolfe, 331 U.S. 586 (1947); Sovereign Camp of Woodmen of the World v. Bolin, 305 U.S. 66 (1938); Modern

Woodmen of America v. Mixer, 267 U.S. 544 (1925); Supreme Council of the Royal Arcanum v. Green, 237 U.S. 531 (1915).

61. Modern Woodmen, supra note 60, at 551.

62. See Watson v. Employers Liab. Ins., 348 U.S. 66 (1954) (applying law of customer's residence state in permitting customer's direct action against the manufacturer's insurer); Clay v. Sun Ins. Office, Ltd., 377 U.S. 179 (1964) (applying insured's residence state in invalidating time limit on suit).

63. Allstate Ins. Co. v. Hague, 449 U.S. 302 (1981).

64. Id. at 318 n.24.

65. Following Hague, the only case in which the Court struck down a state choice-of-law decision on constitutional grounds was where a Kansas court applied its law to land leases with no connection at all to Kansas in order to enable the court to hear a class action involving the leases. Phillips Petroleum Co. v. Shutts, 472 U.S. 797 (1985).

66. See Bibb v. Navajo Freight Lines, Inc., 359 U.S. 520 (1959).

67. Edgar v. MITE, 457 U.S. 624 (1982).

68. See Eisenberg & Miller, supra note 40. However, only half of the contracts with choice of forum clauses have choice-of-law clauses.

69. See Lee Goldman, My Way and the Highway: The Law-and-economics of Choice of Forum Clauses in Consumer Form Contracts, 86 Nw. U. L. Rev. 700 (1992); Linda S. Mullenix, Another Choice of Forum, Another Choice-of-law: Consensual Adjudicatory Procedure in Federal Court, 57 Fordham L. Rev. 291 (1988).

70. See Eugene F. Scoles & Peter Hay, Conflict of Laws § 11.3 (2d ed. 1992).

71. See Leandra Lederman, Viva Zapata!: Toward a Rational System of Forum-Selection Clause Enforcement in Diversity Cases, 66 N.Y.U. L. Rev. 422, 449 n.172 (1991); Michael E. Solimine, The Quiet Revolution in Personal Jurisdiction, 73 Tul. L. Rev. 1, 17 & n.107 (1998).

72. M/S Bremen v. Zapata Off-Shore Co., 407 U.S. 1, 15 (1972).

73. Id. at 13–14.

74. Carnival Cruise Lines, Inc. v. Schute, 499 U.S. 585, 593–94 (1991).

75. Stewart Org. v. Ricoh Corp., 487 U.S. 22 (1988).

76. M/S Bremen v. Zapata Off-Shore Co., 407 U.S. 1, 15 (1972).

77. Convention on Choice of Court Agreements, June 30, 2005, Hague Conference on International Law, available at http://www.hcch.net/index_en.php?act=conventions.pdf&cid=9.

78. See William J. Woodward, Jr., Saving the Hague Choice of Court Convention, 29 U. Pa. Int'l L. 657 (2008).

79. See Larry E. Ribstein & Erin A. O'Hara, Corporations and the Market for Law, 2008 Ill. L. Rev. 661.

80. See John Armour, Bernard S. Black, & Brian R. Cheffins, Is Delaware Losing Its Cases? (March 25, 2010), Northwestern Law & Econ Research Paper No. 10-03, http://ssrn.com/abstract=1578404.

81. Geoffrey P. Miller & Theodore Eisenberg, The Market for Contracts, 30 Cardozo L. Rev. 2073, 2081 (2009).

82. Id. at 23 & n.64.

83. Bruce L. Benson, An Exploration of the Impact of Modern Arbitration Statutes on the Development of Arbitration in the United States, 11 J. L. Econ. & Org. 479, 481 (1995).

84. See http://www.uncitral.org/uncitral/en/uncitral_texts/arbitration/NYConvention_status.html.

85. Convention on the Recognition and Enforcement of Foreign Arbitral Awards, June 10, 1958, 21 UST. 2517, 330 U.N.T.S. 3, Art. II (hereinafter New York Arbitration Convention).

86. Id. at Art. III.

87. Benson, supra note 83, at 496 & n.23.

88. See Buckeye Check Cashing, Inc. v. Cardegna, 126 S. Ct. 1204 (2006).

89. Preston v. Ferrer, 552 U.S. 346 (2008).

90. Mitsubishi v. Soler Chrysler-Plymouth, Inc., 473 U.S. 614 (1985)

91. Scherk v. Alberto-Culver, Co., 417 U.S. 506 (1974).

92. Shearson/American Express, Inc. v. McMahon, 482 U.S. 220 (1987).

93. Gilmer v. Interstate/Johnson Lane Corp., 500 U.S. 20 (1991) (age discrimination claims arbitrable).

94. Sec. 11028(a)(2) of Pub. L. 107–273, 116 Stat. 1836 (2002).

95. See Discover Bank v. Sup. Ct., 36 Cal.4th 148, 30 Cal.Rptr.3d 76, 113 P.3d 1100 (2005).

96. AT&T Mobility LLC v. Concepcion, 2011 WL 1561956, *8 (April 27, 2011).

97. Sec. 1782, Arbitration Fairness Act, Cong. Rev. S. 9144 (July 12, 2007).

98. A full analysis of international competition calls for a comparison with other jurisdictions, and particularly other federal systems. Elsewhere we undertake such a comparison. Erin Ann O'Hara & Larry E. Ribstein, Rules and Institutions in Developing a Law Market: Views from the United States and Europe, 82 Tul. L. Rev. 2147 (2008).

The Dramatic Rise of Consumer Protection Law

JOSHUA D. WRIGHT AND ERIC HELLAND

T he past few decades have seen a dramatic rise in state consumer protection legislation. Beginning in the early 1960s, these laws arose from a perception that market forces, the Federal Trade Commission (FTC), and state common law did not protect consumers adequately. State legislatures responded by enacting a diverse collection of statutes, commonly referred to as Consumer Protection Acts (CPAs), most of which were originally intended to supplement the FTC's objectives of protecting consumers from "unfair or deceptive acts or practices."[1] By 1981, all states had their own version of a CPA.

The federal government has returned to the field with the Dodd-Frank Act,[2] which regulates nearly every aspect of the financial services industry and consolidates all federal consumer protection duties in a single agency: the Consumer Financial Protection Bureau (CFPB). The statute was the product of a perfect storm: the onset of the financial crisis, the rise of behavioral law-and-economics, and the broader interpretation of state CPAs—which had already expanded the scope of consumer protection. Combined, these forces have proved potent.

Yet despite the meteoric rise in consumer protection legislation, it is unclear that consumers are better off. On the one hand, consumer protection laws help solve such problems as the informational asymmetries between well-informed manufacturers and poorly informed consumers. On the other hand, expanded liability can also increase prices beyond what consumers would be willing to pay and deter pro-competitive conduct.

Empirical evidence suggests that consumer protection legislation often fails to account for two factors: (1) the significant costs of regulation, both intended and otherwise, that are passed on to consumers, and (2) the sound and rational reasons why consumers borrow. These omissions inevitably lead to unintended consequences in regulated markets—which may have results as severe as pricing consumers out of the relevant market altogether or reducing incentives to generate pro-consumer information or innovations.

The Rise of Consumer Protection

The first CPAs were passed in the 1960s; in 1962, only eight states had CPAs. Less than twenty years later, they had become fixtures of every state regulatory regime. When first enacted, most CPAs were intended to supplement the perceived gap in consumer protection by allowing for private causes of action that mimicked enforcement actions brought by the FTC.[3] Since then, state CPAs have generally increased in scope. For example, while suits under the FTC Act require the litigation to serve the public interest, many state CPAs have eliminated this public interest requirement. Many define "injury" to a party more loosely and provide liberal standing requirements.[4] Additionally, CPAs are becoming more favorable and generous to consumer plaintiffs. Such factors have fueled an increase of 119% in the number of CPA decisions reported in federal district and state appellate courts between 2000 and 2007.[5] This increase has naturally been especially great in states with CPAs most friendly to consumer litigants.

The rise of behavioral law-and-economics has also played a significant role in the creation and adoption of recent consumer protection legislation. Behavioral law-and-economics suggests that consumers often make irrational decisions, and has been thought to argue for restrictions on consumer choice.[6] Indeed, behaviorist arguments ground legislative proposals as monumental as the CFPB itself, a product of behaviorists such as Oren Bar-Gill and Elizabeth Warren.[7] Behaviorists contend that consumers systematically make choices that are both to their detriment and unrepresentative of their true preferences.[8] Agencies such as the CFPB might then improve consumer decision making by altering the basic design of consumer credit products, adding disclosure requirements, reducing consumers' choices, or instituting default rules favoring products approved by the given legislative agency.[9]

Legislators have warmed to the behaviorist philosophy—unsurprising, given its purported ability to identify and alleviate significant consumer error. In addition, general behaviorist arguments have the benefit of allowing for a myriad of regulatory responses to perceived irrational decisions. Indeed, much of the appeal of behaviorism would seem to be the permission slip it offers to regulators.

Despite its popularity, behaviorist theory suffers from serious infirmities that should caution legislators against employing it as a basis for sweeping legislation. Behavioral law-and-economics currently lacks any theory that can provide the sufficient and necessary conditions to predict any specific bias. In part, this problem stems from a deficit of empirical information establishing the set of circumstances under which irrational decision making is increased. Additionally, behaviorist arguments generally fail to take sufficient account of the comparative costs and benefits of other legal regimes, leading to a "Nirvana Fallacy."[10] This fallacy arises in several ways. In one variant, behaviorist advocates assume consistent irrationality from consumers while assuming consistent (and costless) rationality from regulators. In another, behaviorists underestimate—sometimes to zero—the costs of drafting and implementing behaviorist "nudges."

Problematically, the financial crisis has exacerbated the use of behavioral law-and-economics by would-be regulators. The intellectual basis of the CFPB wrongly assumes that the exploitation of irrational consumers caused the financial crisis. As such, critics argue that the failure of current consumer protection law was a meaningful cause of the financial crisis and, further, that a novel federal agency with enhanced powers is required.[11] Employing behavioral law-and-economics specifically, advocates of the CFPB argue that a "supernanny" should be established to prevent consumers from utilizing their flawed evaluations of their ability to repay loans to their own detriment.[12]

However, such proponents fail to offer evidence that consumer irrationality or ignorance was a significant cause of the crisis. While consumers may very well tend to reach incorrect valuations of future values, this tendency was not a substantial cause of the financial crisis. Rather, loan terms that made defaulting attractive and rational to buyers logically established a situation in which defaulting proliferated.

Changes in Consumer Protection Law

Along with the dramatic rise of consumer protection legislation have come significant alterations to both state and federal regulatory regimes.

A. State Law

Today, every state has its own CPA, each of which provides for private causes of action. The original impetus for these regulations derived from three forces present in the 1960s: dissatisfaction with FTC consumer protection enforcement, popular demand for an increase in consumer protection (and business regulation as a whole), and dismay over the perceived inadequacies of common-law causes of action. These three forces touch on each of the existing mechanisms of consumer protection: federal regulation, market forces, and state common law.[13]

In the 1960s, the FTC was criticized for various reasons: it had misallocated its already insufficient resources, it suffered from political favoritism and regulatory capture, and it protected producers in the name of consumer protection. Proponents of stronger regulation further argued that market forces could no longer offer consumers adequate protection, as the marketplace had become too impersonal and too favorable to producers to properly rein in producers. Similarly, they claimed that common-law causes of action were ousted by this new marketplace dynamic. Most common-law actions cost impractically high amounts to enforce efficiently. Others still were doctrinally poor fits for prospective consumer protection. For example, common-law injury requirements precluded prospective injunctions.

State legislatures responded by enacting a diverse collection of CPAs, each intended to supplement public enforcement and to improve consumer outcomes. Most early CPAs authorized state attorneys general to seek injunctions against specific practices. Some even allowed the attorney general to seek restitution for injured consumers.[14] Many modern CPA characteristics can be traced back to uniform and model statutes that appeared in the late 1960s.[15] The Uniform Deceptive Trade Practices Act (UDTPA), for example, granted consumers a private right of action and allowed injunctive relief absent proof of actual damages and demonstrated intent to deceive.[16]

Another important model statute that appeared at this time was the Model Unfair Trade Practices and Consumer Protection Law (UTPCPL). The FTC developed the UTPCPL as a comprehensive and appealing collection of prior elements of consumer protection legislation. The 1970 version of the UTPCPL provided a choice of three forms of unlawful practices.[17] First, unlawful practices could be defined using essentially the same language as Section 5 of the FTC Act.[18] Second, unlawful conduct could be defined as "false, misleading, or deceptive acts or practices in the conduct of any trade or commerce," though this second option did not include a generally "unfair practices" category.[19] Third, a "laundry list" approach prohibited twelve competition-focused activities and provided a thirteenth provision addressing consumers.[20] The UTCPL deliberately attempted to maintain its similarities to the relevant FTC standards, noting that "due consideration and great weight" should be given to the FTC's own interpretations.[21] Currently, twenty-eight states reference the FTC in their CPAs.[22]

Recent amendments and expansive judicial interpretations have broadened consumer rights under most CPAs. Such amendments have generally increased consumer incentives to sue—for example, by allowing for class actions and private claims. Other amendments repeal the "public interest" requirement to sue under the CPA. Some CPAs have truncated rigorous common-law burdens of proof to tilt adjudications toward consumers.[23] Proponents of these amendments, hearkening back to the arguments of the 1960s, contend that consumers must be willing to file suit for CPAs to have any deterrent effect. However, critics have noted that such a structure raises the potential for harassment of legitimate business conduct,[24] and that vague consumer fraud statutes create an environment ripe for abuse.[25]

Nonetheless, the trajectory of state consumer protection law is clear. Economic theory predicts that the level of litigation under a CPA should be influenced by the expected value of a claim to a generic, potential CPA plaintiff. From the time the CPAs were originally adopted within a state, there has been significant variation in the content of CPAs between states, but the direction is clear: state consumer protection law has changed in favor of plaintiffs.[26]

B. Federal Law

Federal consumer protection has historically been more conservative than state CPAs. Unlike state CPAs, the FTC does not provide a private right of action. Additionally, the FTC requires reasonable reliance as a component of its definitions of unfair and deceptive practices. The FTC further employs a cost-benefit standard in determining what constitutes legally actionable "unfair" practices under Section 3 of the FTC Act.[27] Given the comparative constraints the FTC retains, it has periodically come under fire for the same reasons that underlie the establishment of state CPAs.

The Dodd-Frank Act represents a radical pro-plaintiff shift in federal consumer protection legislation. The CFPB is slated to assume the consumer protection responsibilities of all other federal regulatory agencies[28] in the market for consumer financial products and services. Two broad aspects of the Dodd-Frank Act will drastically affect the consumer credit market.

First, the Dodd-Frank Act dramatically alters current consumer financial protection laws.[29] For example, the Act limits the federal preemption of consumer protection regulation of nationally chartered financial institutions, by allowing states and municipalities to enact more exacting regulations than those promulgated by the CFPB.[30] Essentially, the Act simultaneously creates a regulation "floor" while encouraging the adoption of more stringent standards.[31] By doing so, the Act exposes financial institutions to substantial increases in compliance costs.

Additionally, the Act alters consumer protection laws as applied to financial products. The CFPB is explicitly authorized to take action to prevent a person "from committing or engaging in an unfair, deceptive, or abusive act or practice under Federal law in connection with any transaction with a consumer for a consumer financial product or service."[32] Unfortunately, the CFPB is further authorized to define which practices are "unfair" or "deceptive" in a manner that may not comport with the long-standing jurisprudence guided by the FTC.[33]

The Dodd-Frank Act also creates in the CFPB an entirely new agency with the authority to become directly and significantly involved in determining crucial aspects of the terms and conditions under which covered businesses are permitted to offer credit to consumers.[34] Importantly, the CFPB may consider mandating that lenders offer consumers "plain vanilla" products of the CFPB's own design. This power was explicitly included in the original CFPB legislation,[35] and may still be achieved pursuant to the wide grant of power in the Dodd-Frank Act. In fact, the CFPB could even require that consumers explicitly reject the plain vanilla option before the lender is permitted to offer its own option. Even if consumers reject the plain vanilla product, the CFPB may require firms to provide warnings to consumers of the increased risks of alternative, non-CFPB-approved products. These and similar changes would raise barriers to entry in consumer financial product markets, reduce incentives to innovate, and decrease competition.

An Empirical Perspective on the New Era of Consumer Protection

A. Theoretical Discussion

The behavioral incentives created by state CPAs generate, at a minimum, an ambiguous theoretical prediction concerning their net consumer welfare effects, and serious concerns that state CPAs could make consumers worse off in some contexts.[36] CPAs generally reach what might be classified as two broad categories of conduct: selling practices and marketing communications (including advertising). In theory, CPA liability that forces sellers to internalize the social costs associated with deceptive selling practices or marketing practices could increase efficiency and consumer welfare.

However, CPA liability can lead to serious social harms that must be offset against any benefits.

These harms can also be usefully classified into two categories. First, CPA liability in the market for consumer goods and services amounts to what Butler and Johnston describe as "what is effectively a tax on every good or service sold to consumers."[37] Like other forms of excise taxes, CPA liability can raise the marginal costs of production for the firm, and result in reduced output and higher product prices. The second category of harm applies most directly to marketing communications. Because such communications can disseminate valuable information to consumers, liability that chills informative advertising can reduce consumer welfare. There is some danger that state CPAs, especially those that are interpreted in a broad fashion, may deter firms from making partial disclosures of information that are likely to trigger liability but provide valuable information to consumers.

While these basic tradeoffs involving CPAs are well known and recognized even by their proponents,[38] there is no hard evidence on the relative magnitudes of any of the relevant effects on consumers. When theories of consumer protection are in conflict, the proper question to ask is clear: whether the rise of consumer protection legislation will optimally prevent consumer abuse. Proponents of the rise in consumer protection legislation proffer numerous arguments as to why such increases are beneficial. Both "gaps" in FTC enforcement and behaviorally documented consumer biases are frequently presented as justifying the additions to the consumer protection landscape. Indeed, state CPAs encourage individuals to bring small but meritorious suits they would not otherwise have an incentive to bring, due to restrictions on remedies, and consumers are not subject to the same political pressures as the FTC. Additionally, consumer protection laws can be important in correcting problems of informational asymmetries and in solving market failures. However, such arguments, without more, are incomplete.

As always, the potential benefits of additional state consumer protection regulations must be evaluated while accounting for existing and alternative frameworks, as well as any costs in changing the relevant legal regime.

As Butler and Johnston note, part of this inquiry requires asking whether consumer protection legislation optimally supplements other enforcement mechanisms (e.g., market forces, federal regulation, and state common law).[39] In determining what level of protection is optimal, costs of overprotection and expanded liability are important considerations, as they might increase prices beyond what consumers would want to pay and deter procompetitive behavior.

B. Empirical Evidence on State CPAs

The dramatic growth in state CPAs' scope warrants further scrutiny concerning the differences between consumer protection under state and federal law. One experiment analyzing the decisions of a "Shadow Federal Trade Commission" provides empirical evidence of how CPAs operate in relation to the FTC standard.[40] In this study, an expert panel evaluating the facts of litigated state CPA claims found that state CPAs appear to condemn conduct that would not be illegal under the FTC standard.[41] Indeed, the Searle Study found that only 22 percent of CPA claims would constitute illegal conduct under the FTC standards.[42] Significantly fewer (12 percent) would lead to FTC enforcement.[43] While this particular finding might be consistent with the proposition that CPAs are intended to supplement FTC enforcement, the Searle Study found that almost 40 percent of CPA claims in which the consumer plaintiff prevailed at trial would not amount to illegal conduct under the relevant FTC standard.[44]

By permitting such different, broader claims, CPAs raise serious questions about whether their existence actually benefits consumers. Many CPAs employ vague definitions of illegal conduct, creating costly uncertainty. Businesses must expend resources attempting to predict how vague CPA standards will be enforced; judges must expend further resources defining illegal conduct and sorting between meritorious and frivolous claims. These added costs are directly and indirectly filtered back to consumers in the form of higher prices. Measurement of these direct impacts on consumer welfare is an important area for future research.

Consumer litigants appear rationally responsive to CPA incentives: statutory language providing more generous remedies and less stringent requirements encourages more lawsuits.[45] Vague CPA language will further increase litigation in these states. Such a result is problematic when the litigation is costly and of such questionable value as here.

C. Empirical Evidence on the CFPB's Predicted Effects

The CFPB has the potential to raise the cost of providing credit significantly. By dramatically altering the legal regime under which financial institutions now operate, the CFPB will increase exponentially both uncertainty and costs of compliance for covered businesses. In turn, these cost increases will affect consumers both by reducing overall consumer access to (and use of) credit and by preventing some consumers from obtaining credit products at all.

The CFPB will force lenders to bear significant legal costs for lawsuits arising from the vague language of its enabling legislation and from state variance arising from Dodd-Frank's "floor" regulations. The CFPB not only departs from the traditional FTC definitions of "unfair" and "deceptive," but grants powers sufficient to establish entirely new causes of action— established by ambiguous terms that will necessarily require serious court interpretation, with no clear indication currently offered for what definitions approximate the optimal result. Such costs will likely be passed on to consumers, at least in part.[46]

The legal uncertainty created by the CFPB will impose further costs on the credit market. While waiting for courts to coherently and precisely define the Act's relevant terms and the CFPB's regulations, lenders will proceed with excessive caution. Added paperwork, new mandatory review processes, and a potential plain vanilla requirement also add costs.

Most importantly, the Dodd-Frank Act's consumer protection provisions and the rules and regulations promulgated and enforced by the CFPB may price certain consumers entirely out of the lending market. This exclusion will likely result in the unluckiest of consumers becoming liquidity constrained from the loss of sound and rational opportunities to borrow. First, lenders will stop offering some beneficial products that will become unprofitable under the new regime. Second, given the behaviorist rationale underlying its creation, the CFPB will likely assert its authority to prevent consumers from obtaining access to products that consumers want but that the CFPB subjectively believes are in some way bad for them. This second reason is particularly troubling given that consumers are necessarily in a better position than regulators to determine which credit options are most beneficial to their particular needs.[47]

Evans and Wright estimate that the Dodd-Frank Act will increase interest rates consumers pay by 160 basis points (or by 1.6 percent) and reduce consumer borrowing by 2.1 percent.[48] Naturally, the Act will impose a significant cost shock to lenders. As the Act will result in significant variation in state-by-state regulation, transactions costs for lenders will increase. Of course, the greater the variation between states, the greater these costs will be.

In addition to paying more for credit, consumers will use less credit—with a resulting negative impact on consumer spending. With an estimated long-run debt elasticity of 1.3 in consumer credit markets,[49] a 160 basis point increase would result in a 2.1 percent reduction in the amount of long-term debt or credit borrowing. This estimate serves as a likely lower bound, in part because of the likelihood that the CFPB will ban certain lending products that represent the only credit options for some consumers. Such a reduction in credit availability will likely generate significant consumer losses, as evidenced by economic literature suggesting that harmful effects of such reductions are felt both by the consumers in distress personally and by the communities that are left with diminished capacity to rebound from community shocks.[50]

D. Other Evidence

Additional evidence gleaned from other lending regulations suggests that paternalistic consumer protection legislation harms consumers as a group. These regulations decrease the availability of credit and exclude some consumers from the credit market altogether.

Usury regulation has long been a target of behaviorists and their forerunners. Supporters of additional regulation claim that excessive interest rates necessarily exploit irrational, misinformed borrowers. Behaviorists typically argue that usury works a willing, if unjust, redistribution of wealth from buyers in need to lenders with liquid capital.[51] Accordingly, they find that legal interest rates should be capped at "reasonable" levels. Such arguments suffer from a shortsighted and narrow perspective.

Although usury rates may be high, they are necessarily so, and benefit consumers nonetheless. Usury represents far more than a mere wealth transfer. Consumers in need are in need for a reason; this necessity means they pose a significant risk of default to lenders. Lenders in turn must be compensated to make these high-risk loans at all.[52] This compensation is the driving force behind both high-interest loans and permissive usury laws. Accordingly, capping legal interest rates will not eliminate the need for such compensation—it will only eliminate the lender's presence in the market for consumer borrowing.

Economic literature suggests that paternalistic restrictions that destroy consumers' ability to access nontraditional sources of lending, such as payday and auto title loans, have two significant and unintended consequences: term re-pricing and product substitution.[53] Term re-pricing, where lenders alter other terms of the agreement, harms consumers by increasing the costs of other lending terms—for example, by requiring higher down payments. Product substitution, where some consumers are denied access to traditional lenders, represents the reality that consumers will turn to less favorable credit options (such as pawn shops or loan sharks) or find themselves priced out of the credit market altogether. Proponents of paternalistic regulations argue that such exclusion is warranted, as borrowers would only be made worse off by the exploitative lending terms inherent in nontraditional options. Such proponents further argue that because consumers utilize these credit options for reasons that are not obvious, they are unable to estimate accurately the actual costs of such loans and cannot compare the costs of these loans to the costs of traditional credit options.[54] The theoretical and empirical literature, however, suggests that consumers are well aware of the costs of payday lending.[55] Moreover, both evidence and economic theory suggest that consumers benefit from nontraditional lending options. For example, auto title loans seem to be most beneficial for three types of rational consumers: moderate income borrowers priced out of traditional credit markets by damaged credit history; lower income, unbanked borrowers who utilize these loans to meet unexpected expenses; and small businesses.[56]

Similar behavioral law-and-economics arguments are made in the context of the credit card market. The "seduction by plastic" argument presumes that consumers are irrationally induced into credit arrangements through short-term benefits such as low introductory rates. Consumers then accumulate more debt than originally anticipated, and are eventually subject to higher interest charges than subjectively assumed.[57] This irrationality leads to welfare losses, or so the argument proceeds. Yet in this area as well, paternalistic arguments fail to demonstrate a need for stringent consumer protection regulations.[58] For example, these models predict clear welfare losses, but fail to explain how this might happen when lenders compete by offering greater short-term benefits to consumers until all supra-competitive profits are dissipated.[59] This competition is consistent with both rational consumers and a robust market for credit products. As such, paternalistic interventions would likely inhibit competition among lenders, and it is unclear that any consumer benefit from this intervention would outweigh these competitive losses.

Conclusion

The dramatic rise of consumer protection legislation has been thought to be justified by consumer ignorance or judgment biases. However, such legislation appears to have underestimated its social costs. These costs arise from increases in compliance costs and from failures to acknowledge the benefits inherent in existing consumer protection mechanisms, such as market forces, state common-law actions, and the FTC.

These cost increases will have serious impacts on consumers as a class. Consumer protection legislation can indeed play an important role in correcting market failures and eliminating information asymmetries. However, the recent additions to (and renovations of) the consumer protection landscape threaten to create significant deadweight losses by reducing consumer choice, deterring efficient firm behavior, expanding liability for lenders, and encouraging rent-seeking behavior. Accordingly, there is significant reason to be skeptical of claims that the dramatic rise of consumer protection law in the United States over the past forty years, and especially recently, has generated net benefits for consumers.

State CPAs in particular raise federalism challenges familiar to many areas of concurrent federal regulation. While it appears that state CPAs impose serious costs on the civil justice system and consumers, jurisdictional competition can play an important role in disciplining consumer protection institutions. It is, at this point, too early in the evolution of state CPAs to surrender the potential benefits from such competition and conclude that consumer protection should be left to federal regulators. Indeed, any discussion concerning the relative merits of federal and state consumer protection regulation must be informed by the troubled history of the FTC in this area as well as the expansive authority recently granted to the CFPB.

Notes

1. 15 U.S.C. § 45(a)(1) (2006).

2. Dodd-Frank Wall Street Reform and Consumer Protection Act, 12 U.S.C. § 5301 (2010) [hereinafter Dodd-Frank Act].

3. Nat'l Ass'n of Att'ys Gen. Comm. on the Office of Att'y Gen., Report on the Office of Attorney General 395 (1971).

4. Searle Civil Justice Institute, State Consumer Protection Acts, An Empirical Investigation of Private Litigation (2009), available at http://www.law.northwestern .edu/searlecenter/issues/index.cfm?ID=86 [hereinafter Searle Study]; Henry N. Butler and Jason S. Johnston, Reforming State Consumer Protection Liability: An Economic Approach, 2010 Colum. Bus. L. Rev. 1, 9 (2010).

5. Searle Study, supra note 4, at 20.

6. See Oren Bar-Gill and Elizabeth Warren, Making Credit Safer, 157 U. Pa. L. Rev. 1 (2008).

7. Id.

8. Id.

9. David S. Evans and Joshua D. Wright, The Effect of the Consumer Financial Protection Agency Act of 2009, 22 Loy. Consumer L. Rev. 277 (2010).

10. See Harold Demsetz, Information and Efficiency: Another Viewpoint, 12 J. L. Econ. 1, 1–3 (1969) ("The view that now pervades much public policy economics implicitly presents the relevant choice as between an ideal norm and an existing 'imperfect' institutional arrangement. This nirvana approach differs considerably from a comparative institution approach in which the relevant choice is between alternative real institutional arrangements").

11. United States Department of the Treasury, Financial Regulatory Reform: A New Foundation 55–75 (2009) [hereinafter New Foundation], available at

http://www.financialstability.gov/docs/regs/FinalReport_web.pdf (outlining proposals for various governmental regulations of financial services and credit products).

12. See, e.g., Michael S. Barr, Sendhil Mullainathan, and Eldar Shafir, Behaviorally Informed Financial Regulation (New American Foundation, Working Paper,
October 2008) (arguing that the CFPB is necessary to "nudge" consumers toward
better decision making in lending markets).

13. See Timothy J. Muris, The Federal Trade Commission and the Future Development of U.S. Consumer Protection Policy (George Mason Univ. Sch. of Law, Law &
Econ. Working Paper Series No. 04–19, 2004), available at http://ssrn.com/abstract
_id=545182 (describing the institutions of consumer protection yet neglecting the
role of state consumer protection laws).

14. See, e.g., 1960 New Jersey Laws, ch. 39, at § 5.

15. See Nat'l Ass'n of Att'ys Gen. Comm. on the Office of Att'y Gen., supra note 3,
at 400.

16. Comm'rs on Unif. State Laws, Handbook of the National Conference of Commissioners on Uniform State Laws and Proceedings of the Annual Conference
Meeting in Its Seventy-third Year 253, 262 (1964).

17. 29 Council of State Gov'ts, 1970 Suggested State Legislation 142 (1969).

18. Unfair Trade Practices and Consumer Protection Law (Council of State Gov'ts
1970).

19. 1 Mary Dee Pridgen and Richard M. Alderman, Consumer Protection and the
Law, § 2:10 (2009).

20. See 29 Council of State Gov'ts, supra note 17, at 142, 146–47; see also 1 Pridgen and Alderman, supra note 19, at § 210.

21. 29 Council of State Gov'ts, supra note 17, at 147.

22. 1 Pridgen and Alderman, supra note 19, at § 210, app. at 3B.

23. David A. Rice, Exemplary Damages in Private Consumer Actions, 55 Iowa
L. Rev. 307, 307 (1969).

24. William A. Lovett, Louisiana Civil Code of 1808: State Deceptive Trade Practice Legislation, 46 Tul. L. Rev. 724, 744 (1972).

25. See, e.g., David A. Rice, Exemplary Damages in Private Consumer Actions,
55 Iowa L. Rev. 307, 340 (1969).

26. See Searle Study, supra note 4. The Searle Study generated an index (the
"Expected Value Index" or EVI) to capture the overall "plaintiff friendliness" of the
state CPA. For each 2008 statute, 27 variables were coded as either "benefits" or
"restrictions." Id. The study found that that the EVI is positively correlated with the
log of reported CPA decisions. Id.

27. See Federal Trade Commission Act Amendments of 2006, Pub. L. 109-455,
§ 3, 120 Stat. 3372 (codified at 15 U.S.C. § 45(n)) (defining an unfair act as one that
"causes or is likely to cause substantial injury to consumers which is not reasonably
avoidable by consumers themselves and not outweighed by countervailing benefits
to consumers or competition"); J. Howard Beales III, The FTC's Use of Unfairness

Authority, Its Rise, Fall, and Resurrection (May 30, 2003), http://www.ftc.gov
/speeches/beales/unfair0603.shtm.

28. These include the Federal Reserve Board of Governors, Office of the Comp-
troller of the Currency, Office of Thrift Supervision, Federal Deposit Insurance
Corporation, National Credit Union Administration, and the Federal Trade Commission. See Dodd-Frank Act, supra note 2, at § 1061.

29. The following examples listed here arise either from provisions of the Dodd-
Frank Act as passed or from proposals once contained by the CFPA Act. As the
Dodd-Frank Act grants the CFPB virtually plenary regulatory authority to promulgate rules in the public interest, virtually all of these requirements—even those not
encapsulated by the final bill—could easily be implemented by procedures authorized under the Administrative Procedure Act and Dodd-Frank.

30. Dodd-Frank Act, supra note 2, at §§ 1041(a)(1), (b).

31. New Foundation, supra note 11, at 50–51.

32. Dodd-Frank Act, supra note 2, at § 1031(a).

33. Id. at § 1031(c).

34. Id. at § 1031.

35. United States Department of the Treasury, Consumer Financial Protection
Agency Act of 2009 § 1036(b) (2009), available at http://www.financialstability.gov
/docs/CFPA-Act.pdf (proposing 2009 Consumer Financial Protection Agency legislation for passage by Congress).

36. Butler and Johnston, supra note 4, at 44–53.

37. Id. at 44.

38. See, e.g., Jeff Sovern, Toward a New Model of Consumer Protection Statutes:
The Problem of Increased Transaction Costs, 47 Wm. & Mary L. Rev. 1365, 1705–09
(2006) (recognizing that state CPAs can increase transaction costs and arguing for
regulation that would prevent firms from passing these costs on to consumers).

39. Butler and Johnston, supra note 4, at 4–5.

40. Searle Study, supra note 4.

41. Id. at 49–50.

42. Id. at 39.

43. Id.

44. Id. at 49.

45. Id.

46. Other industries have had to pass on to consumers costs imposed on them by
exposure to state litigation. See, e.g., Professor Michael J. Saks's letter to Sen. Ernest
Hollings, S. 687. The Product Liability Fairness Act: Hearing before the Subcommittee on Consumer of the Committee on Commerce, Science, and Transportation,
United States Senate, One Hundred Third Congress, First Session, September 23,
1993, 126.

47. Creditors face serious problems of information asymmetry in deciding to
whom to lend. Consumers are aware of specific factors affecting their likelihood of
default that creditors cannot hope to know, including their individual incentive to

pay back a loan given possibly generous debt relief laws. For a comprehensive discussion of the risks and benefits of consumer borrowing, see Evans and Wright, supra note 9.

48. Evans and Wright, supra note 9.

49. Financial economists have used changes in nominal credit card interest rates to arrive at this estimate. David Gross and Nicholas Souleles, Consumer Response to Changes in Credit Supply: Evidence from Credit Card Data (Wharton Bus. Sch., Working Paper, Feb. 4, 2000), available at http://knowledge.wharton.upenn.edu/papers/1161.pdf. These estimates are based on credit cards and could be different for other debt products.

50. See Adair Morse, Payday Lenders: Heroes or Villains? (Booth Sch. of Bus., Working Paper, Jan. 2009) (finding that restrictions on financial products can result in 1.2 more foreclosures and 2.67 more larcenies per 1,000 homes).

51. See, e.g., Brian M. McCall, Learning from Our History: Evaluating the Modern Housing Finance Market in Light of Ancient Principles of Justice, 60 S.C. L. Rev. 707, 713 (2009), available at http://ssrn.com/abstract=1462280.

52. See, e.g., Wendy Edelberg, Risk Based-Pricing of Interest Rates in Household Lending Markets 2–5 (FEDS Working Paper No. 2003-62, Dec. 2003), available at http://ssrn.com/abstract=484522 (noting the increase in risk-based pricing of interest rates in consumer lending markets).

53. Todd J. Zywicki, Consumer Use and Government Regulation of Title Pledge Lending, 22 Loy. Consumer L. Rev. 425, 428–33 (2010).

54. Nathalie Martin, 1,000% Interest—Good While Supplies Last: A Study of Payday Loan Practices and Solutions 52 Ariz. L. Rev. 563 (2010), 35 (Univ. N.M. Sch. of Law Research Paper No. 2010-05), available at http://ssrn.com/abstract=1664616.

55. Gregory Elliehausen, An Analysis of Consumers' Use of Payday Loans, 36–37 (Div. of Research & Statistics, Bd. of Governors of the Fed. Reserve Sys. & Fin. Servs. Research Program, The George Washington Univ. Sch. of Bus.).

56. Zywicki, supra note 53, at 426.

57. Oren Bar-Gill, Seduction by Plastic, 98 Nw. U. L. Rev. 1373, 1399–1400 (2004).

58. See Joshua D. Wright, Behavioral Law-and-economics, Paternalism, and Consumer Contracts: An Empirical Perspective, 2 N.Y.U. J. L. Liberty 470–511 (2007).

59. Id.

PART 7:

CORPORATE AND SECURITIES LAW

How American Corporate and Securities Law Drives Business Offshore

STEPHEN M. BAINBRIDGE

The first decade of the new century was a tumultuous one in many areas of life, not least the business and financial world. The decade opened with the bursting of the dot-com bubble and confidence-shaking frauds at Enron and WorldCom, among all too many others. In conjunction with the economic fallout from the 9/11 attacks, these shocks brought to a halt the 10-year expansion that had begun in 1991.

As the decade wound down, an even larger crisis was sparked when the housing bubble burst in 2007. The financial crisis that followed triggered the so-called Great Recession, which was one of the longest and deepest downturns since the Great Depression of the 1930s.

The United States' capital markets naturally suffered throughout much of the decade. In the wake of the dot-com bubble's bursting as the decade opened, the secondary equity trading markets suffered the first three-year consecutive stock market decline since the 1930s. In turn, the financial crisis at the end of the decade triggered an extended bear market that ran from October 2007 to March 2009.

The primary equity markets also suffered for much of the decade. A decline in primary market transactions such as initial public offerings (IPOs) was to be expected given the adverse economic climate, of course. The data, however, reveal a far more troubling trend. U.S. capital markets steadily became less competitive globally throughout the decade.

The U.S. share of the global IPO market declined, for example, as foreign firms no longer treated the American stock markets as their first choice for raising capital. Similarly, foreign companies long present in the U.S. delisted from U.S. stock markets, while U.S. firms went dark or private at an unusually high rate. At around the same time, the Eurobond market surpassed the U.S. bond markets in the global share of debt issuances.

The growing concern surrounding these developments prompted three major studies, each of which reached broadly similar conclusions and offered comparable policy prescriptions: the Bloomberg-Schumer Report,[1] the Paulson Committee Interim Report,[2] and the U.S. Chamber of Commerce Report.[3] Taken together, and evaluated in light of subsequent developments, the evidence they gathered confirms that the U.S. capital markets became less competitive vis-à-vis other markets in the past decade.

There are many factors contributing to this decline. While it is generally agreed that the growing maturity and liquidity of European and Asian markets is a very important factor, there is less agreement as to the role that corporate governance played. On the one hand, the U.S. political establishment blamed the various economic crises of the decade in part on perceived corporate governance flaws. Faced with an anti-market, anticorporate populist backlash among the polity, Congress responded to the decade's first crisis by passing the Sarbanes-Oxley Act (SOX) in 2002. At the end of the decade, yet another populist backlash led to passage of the Dodd-Frank Act in 2010. Proponents of both SOX and Dodd-Frank identified alleged corporate governance deficiencies as causal factors in the respective crises to which they responded. Accordingly, both acts created important new corporate governance regulations at the federal level.

On the other hand, a number of commentators identified not flawed corporate governance but rather flawed corporate governance regulation as being an important causal factor in the declining competitiveness of U.S. capital markets. In this view, U.S. corporate governance was not at fault in the economic crises, but rather generally worked well throughout the period. Instead, it was "quack corporate governance" regulation that was at fault.[4]

It is this debate to which this essay is addressed. So as not to hide the ball, the essay comes down squarely on the latter side of the question.

The Decline in U.S. Capital Market Competitiveness

In the 1990s, the number of foreign issuers listed on the New York Stock Exchange (NYSE) roughly quadrupled, with NASDAQ experiencing similar growth, while London and the other major European exchanges lost market share. Since 2000, however, the situation appears to have reversed. Using global IPOs as an indicator of the relative competitiveness of capital markets, for example, there was a dramatic decline in the U.S. market share from 48 to 8 percent between 2000 and 2006.[5]

Although the Paulson Committee reported slight improvement in 2008 and 2009, by the first quarter of 2010 the Committee was again reporting continued "deterioration in the competitiveness of U.S. public equity markets."[6] As a result, by nearly all measures, the U.S. capital market today remains "much less competitive than it was historically."[7]

Was Corporate Governance the Problem?

There is little evidence that poor corporate governance practices contributed to either the economic turmoil of the past decade in general or the declining competitiveness of U.S. capital markets. In the wake of the tech stock bubble, Bengt Holmstrom and Steven Kaplan published a comprehensive review of U.S. corporate governance that concluded the U.S. corporate governance regime was "well above average" in the global picture.[8] Even when the fallout from the bubble was taken into account, returns on the U.S. stock market equaled or exceeded those of its global competitors during five time periods going back as far as 1982. Likewise, U.S. productivity exceeded that of its major Western competitors. In general, the trend with respect to major corporate governance practices had been toward enhanced management efficiency and accountability. Pay-for-performance compensation schemes, takeovers, restructurings, increased reliance on independent directors, and improved board of director processes all tended to more effectively align management and shareholder interests. As for the bursting of the housing bubble, "[a] striking aspect of the stock market meltdown of 2008 is that it occurred despite the strengthening of U.S. corporate governance over the past few decades and a reorientation toward the promotion of shareholder value."[9] A recent report commissioned by the New York Stock Exchange reached the same conclusion, finding that "the current corporate governance system generally works well."[10]

If corporate governance was not the problem, what drove the decline in U.S. capital market competitiveness? According to the Paulson Commission, "one important factor contributing to this trend is the growth of U.S. regulatory compliance costs and liability risks compared to other developed and respected market centers."[11] This essay therefore focuses on two questions: First, has the risk of anti-fraud liability affected the competitiveness of U.S. capital markets? Second, did the federalization of key aspects of corporate governance during the past decade generate net regulatory costs adversely affecting those markets?[12]

The Impact of Anti-Fraud Liability Risk

In 2008, the Supreme Court handed down one of the most consequential securities cases to come before it in many years, *Stoneridge Investment Partners v. Scientific-Atlanta.*[13] What makes *Stoneridge* instructive for our purposes is not the specific legal issues or the holding, but rather the Supreme Court majority's concern for the loss of U.S. competitiveness.

> The practical consequences of an expansion [of Rule 10b-5 liability] . . . provide a further reason to reject petitioner's approach. In *Blue Chip*, the Court noted that extensive discovery and the potential for uncertainty and disruption in a lawsuit allow plaintiffs with weak claims to extort settlements from innocent companies. Adoption of petitioner's approach would expose a new class of defendants to these risks. As noted in *Central Bank*, contracting parties might find it necessary to protect against these threats, raising the costs of doing business. Overseas firms with no other exposure to our securities laws could be deterred from doing business here. This, in turn, may raise the cost of being a publicly traded company under our law and shift securities offerings away from domestic capital markets.[14]

The point is not that we should live in a world of caveat emptor. An effective anti-fraud regime has obvious benefits. It serves to compensate defrauded investors. It deters fraud. It makes a bond making issuer's disclosures more credible and thereby lowers the cost of capital. The question remains, however, whether the current U.S. anti-fraud regime imposes costs that exceed these benefits.

An affirmative answer to that question is suggested by a survey of global financial services executives, which found that the litigious nature of U.S. society and capital markets has a negative impact on the competitiveness of those markets.[15] The key problem appears to be the prevalence of private party securities fraud class actions, which do not exist in most other major capital market jurisdictions.

Between 1997 and 2005 there was a steady increase in both the number of securities class action filings and the average settlement value of those suits.[16] The total amount paid in securities class actions peaked in 2006 at over $10 billion, even excluding the massive $7 billion Enron settlement.[17] The vast majority of such settlement payments have historically been made either by issuers or by their insurers, rather than by individual defendants.[18] As a result, the vast bulk of securities settlement payments come out of the corporate treasury, either directly or indirectly in the form of higher insurance premiums. In either case, settlement payments reduce the value of the residual claim on the corporation's assets and earnings. In effect, the company's current shareholders pay the settlement, not the directors or officers who actually committed the alleged wrongdoing.

The effect of securities class actions thus is a wealth transfer from the company's current shareholders to those who held the shares at the time of the alleged wrongdoing. In the case of a diversified investor, such transfers are likely to be a net wash, as the investor is unlikely to be systematically on one side of the transfer rather than the other. Because there are substantial transaction costs associated with such transfers, moreover, the diversified investor is likely to experience an overall loss of wealth as a result of the private securities class actions. Legal fees to plaintiff counsel typically take 25 to 35 percent of any monetary class action settlement, for example, and the corporation's defense costs are likely comparable in magnitude.[19]

The circularity inherent in the securities class action process reduces the effectiveness of private anti-fraud litigation as both a deterrent and a means of compensation. As to deterrence, because it is the company and not the individual wrongdoers that pays in the vast majority of cases, the system fails to directly punish those individuals. As to compensation, the transaction costs associated with securities litigation ensure that investors are unlikely to recover the full amount of their claims. Indeed, there is evidence that investors recover only 2 to 3 percent of their economic losses through class actions.

The analysis to this point has implicitly assumed that all securities fraud class actions are meritorious. When one considers the potential for frivolous or nuisance litigation, the potential impact of litigation on the capital markets is compounded. To be sure, the Private Securities Litigation Reform Act of 1995 and the Securities Litigation Uniform Standards Act of 1998 heightened the pleading standards for securities fraud claims, allowed an automatic stay of discovery while a motion to dismiss is pending, created a uniform federal cause of action, and otherwise tried to reduce frivolous securities class action. While there is some empirical evidence that the PSLRA and SLUSA have reduced—but not eliminated— the number of frivolous suits, there is also evidence that they have had the unintended effect of reducing meritorious suits in which pre-filing indicia of fraud are more difficult to identify and plead with particularity as required by the new pleading standard.[20]

It is generally known that exposure to the U.S. capital markets significantly increases an issuer's litigation risk, and this has a measurable impact on the attractiveness of those markets. A study of domestic issuers found that issuers with prior experience with securities fraud class actions and those in standard industry classifications having a high incidence of such litigation tended to resort to offshore financing more often than other issuers.[21] As for foreign issuers, they are "deeply" concerned by the "cost of litigation" associated with securities class actions and "risk of huge enforcement actions."[22]

When asked which aspect of the legal system most significantly affected the business environment, senior executives surveyed indicated that propensity toward legal action was the predominant problem. Worryingly for

New York, the city fares far worse than London in this regard: 63 percent of respondents thought the U.K. (and by extension London) had a less litigious culture than the United States, while only 17 percent felt the U.S. (and by extension New York) was a less litigious place than the United Kingdom.[23] Because "the only way foreign companies can protect themselves" from litigation risk "is to move out of the United States altogether . . . a lot of companies are doing" precisely that.[24]

The litigation risk problem is not limited to securities class actions. We see essentially identical concerns in areas such as state corporate law derivative litigation. In a seminal empirical study of derivative litigation, Professor Roberta Romano found that derivative litigation is relatively rare.[25] Of those cases that go to trial, shareholder-plaintiffs almost always lose. As is generally true of all litigation, however, most derivative suits settle. Only half of the settled derivative suits in the study resulted in monetary recoveries, with an average recovery of about $6 million. In almost all cases, the legal fees collected by plaintiff counsel exceeded the monetary payments to shareholders. Romano further concluded that nonmonetary relief was typically inconsequential in nature.

Like securities class actions, derivative litigation serves mainly as a means of transferring wealth from investors to lawyers. At best, derivative suits take money out of the corporate treasury and return it to shareholders minus substantial legal fees. In many cases, moreover, little if any money is returned to the shareholders, but legal fees are almost always paid.

As for deterrence, there is no compelling evidence that derivative litigation deters a substantial amount of managerial shirking and self-dealing. To the contrary, there is evidence that derivative suits do not have significant effects on the stock price of the subject corporations, which suggests that investors do not believe derivative suits deter misconduct.[26] There is also substantial evidence that adoption of a charter amendment limiting director liability has no significant effect on the price of the adopting corporation's stock, which suggests that investors do not believe that duty of care liability has beneficial deterrent effects.[27]

A radical solution to these problems would be to limit state and federal private rights of action. We might bar corporate liability in private class actions except for cases in which the issuer was a party to the fraudulent transaction as seller or buyer of its securities. This would eliminate the circularity problem inherent in such suits to the benefit of diversified investors. At the same time, it would allow the continued use of criminal and civil enforcement by the Justice Department and the Securities and Exchange Commission (SEC), as well as private party class actions against culpable officers and directors. Because these tools are likely much more effective deterrents, the costs of such a reform would probably not exceed the benefits to investors.

Similarly, we might eliminate state law derivative litigation. As we have seen, derivative litigation appears to have little if any useful deterrent effects. Further, eliminating derivative litigation would not eliminate director accountability. Directors would remain subject to various forms of market discipline, including the important markets for corporate control and employment, proxy contests, and shareholder litigation where the challenged misconduct gives rise to a direct cause of action. The same is true with respect to eliminating corporate liability in securities class actions, of course.

If eliminating securities class actions or derivative litigation seems too extreme, why not allow firms to opt out of the derivative suit process by charter amendment? Virtually all states now allow corporations to adopt charter provisions limiting director and officer liability. Since corporate law properly consists of a set of default rules the parties generally should be free to amend, there seems little reason not to expand the liability limitation statutes to allow corporations to opt out of derivative litigation or securities class actions.

Regulatory Compliance Costs

Issuers seeking access to the U.S. capital markets face a daunting array of complex and costly regulatory requirements. In contrast to the U.K., where the Financial Services Authority (FSA) is the sole regulator, U.S. capital market participants are slotted into multiple regulatory silos, each with one or more government regulatory agencies. Dealing with multiple bodies of regulation and multiple regulators inevitably adds complexity, redundancy, and cost to transactions. Accordingly, as the Chamber of Commerce concluded, "this patchwork structure is not keeping up with the extraordinary growth and internationalization of our markets."[28]

In the U.K., the FSA has adopted a principles-based approach to regulation, in contrast to the rules-based approach of U.S. securities regulation.[29] While principles are broad and abstract, rules are detailed and complex. Principles confer a substantial amount of discretion upon regulators on a case-by-case basis. While rules are defined ex ante with little scope for ex post discretion, principles are set out broadly ex ante and are developed ex post in a highly contextual way.

Proponents of principles-based regulatory schemes argue that they allow firms to adapt their individual compliance procedures to their own unique business needs and practices. In contrast, rule-based systems assume that one size fits all. In addition, principles-based regulatory schemes are less adversarial and litigious than rules-based ones because regulators in the former tend to focus on guidance rather than litigation. The Bloomberg-Schumer Report argued that these differences put U.S. capital markets at a significant disadvantage:

> Without the benefit of accepted principles to guide them, U.S. regulators default to imposing regulations required by various legislative mandates, many of which date back several decades. These mandates are not subject to major reviews or revisions and therefore tend to fall behind day-to-day practice. This failure to keep pace with the times has made it hard for business leaders to understand how the missions of different regulators relate to their business, and this in turn means that regulators have come to be viewed as unpredictable in their actions toward business.

The Report also noted that the cost of compliance with U.S. regulations has risen dramatically in recent years.

> Securities firms reported on average almost one regulatory inquiry per trading day, and large firms experienced more than three times that level. The cost of compliance estimated in a Securities Industry Association report had reached $25 billion in the securities industry alone in 2005 (up from $13 billion in 2002). This increase is equivalent to almost 5 percent of the industry's annual net revenues. Although there are benefits from an increase in compliance-related expenditures, the report found that "a

substantial portion of these increased costs were avoidable, reflecting, among other things: duplication of examinations, regulations and supervisory actions; inconsistencies/lack of harmonization in rules and regulations; ambiguity; and delays in obtaining clear guidance."[30]

The problem is not simply the rules-based nature of the U.S. system, but also the sheer volume of regulations with which issuers must comply:

> A recent study by the Federal Financial Institutions Examination Council, the coordinating group of U.S. banking and thrift regulators, revealed that more than 800 different regulations have been imposed on banks and other deposit-gathering institutions since 1989. Regulations to implement the legislative requirements of the Sarbanes-Oxley Act of 2002 (SOX) are a good example. They are universally viewed by CEOs and other executives surveyed as being too expensive for the benefits of good governance they confer. Consequently, SOX is viewed both domestically and internationally as stifling innovation. "The Sarbanes-Oxley Act and the litigious environment are creating a more risk-averse culture in the United States," one former senior investment banker stated. "We are simply pushing people to do more business overseas rather than addressing the real issues head on."[31]

The Sarbanes-Oxley Debacle

Over the past decade, the Sarbanes-Oxley Act has emerged as the poster child for burdensome compliance costs. Four key SOX provisions were criticized from the outset for preempting state corporate law and for lacking justification in the empirical literature.[32] These were:

- Section 301 required public corporations to have an audit committee composed exclusively of independent directors;
- Section 201 prohibited accounting firms from providing a wide range of non-audit services to the public corporations they audit;
- Section 402(a) prohibited most loans by corporations to their executives, even though many such loans were effected to facilitate managerial acquisitions of their employer's stock, which would have the desirable effect of aligning managers' and shareholders' interests; and
- Sections 302 and 906 required the chief executive officer (CEO) and chief financial officer (CFO) to certify their firm's SEC filings.

These provisions have proven to be extremely burdensome and costly. The additional audit committee responsibilities imposed under § 301 have been a prime factor in the increased workload of corporate directors and, as a result, in the increase in director compensation.[33] In addition, there are important conflicts between § 301's mandate that the audit committee establish and oversee a corporate whistle-blowing program and European Union directives with respect to data protection. As a result, for example, the French data protection authority struck down whistle-blowing systems proposed by two subsidiaries of U.S. corporations subject to both § 301 and French data protection law.[34]

A study of Mexican corporations listing on and delisting from U.S. capital markets found that SOX sections 302 and 906 contributed significantly to delisting decisions.[35] SOX § 302 provides that when a reporting corporation files either an annual or quarterly report, both the CEO and CFO must individually certify that they have reviewed the report and, to their knowledge, the report does not contain any material misrepresentation or omission of material fact. Both officers must also certify that, to their knowledge, the financial statements and other financial information contained in the report fairly present in all material respects the corporation's financial condition and results of operations for the period covered by the report. Section 302 also requires that the CEO and CFO individually certify in writing that they have disclosed to the outside auditors and the audit committee "all significant deficiencies in the design or operation of internal controls which could adversely affect the issuer's ability to record, process, summarize, and report financial data and have identified for the issuer's auditors any material weaknesses in internal controls." They must also certify to having told the auditors and audit committee about "any fraud, whether or not material, that involves management or other employees who have a significant role in the issuer's internal controls." Finally, they must identify any significant changes in internal controls subsequent to the date of their evaluation, including any actions taken to correct any significant deficiencies and material weaknesses in those controls.

Congress liked the certification idea so much that Congress put it into SOX in two different places. In addition to the various certification requirements of § 302, § 906 amended the federal criminal code to add a new provision requiring that each "periodic report" filed with the SEC be accompanied by a written certification from the CEO and CFO that the "periodic report . . . fully complies with" the relevant statutes and that the "information contained in the periodic report fairly presents, in all material respects, the financial condition and results of operations of the issuer."

Taken together, sections 302 and 906 significantly increase the regulatory burden on the CEO and CFO. In turn, because best practice requires the assistance of other key corporate executives, much of the top management team's time will now be devoted to preparing these certifications instead of conducting business. In addition, of course, the heightened liability exposure created by these sections increases the risks to which these executives are subject, for which they will demand compensation. The monetary and opportunity costs associated with compliance are not insignificant.

Section 404

As it turned out, however, none of the provisions discussed above proved to be SOX's most contentious mandate. Instead, that dubious honor fell to § 404's requirement that management and the firm's outside auditor certify the effectiveness of the company's internal controls over financial reporting. SOX § 404(a) ordered the SEC to adopt rules requiring reporting companies to include in their annual reports a statement of management's responsibility for "establishing and maintaining an adequate internal control structure and procedures for financial reporting" and "an assessment, as of the end of the most recent fiscal year of the issuer, of the effectiveness of the internal control structure and procedures of the issuer for financial reporting." Section 404(b) required that the company's independent auditors attest to the effectiveness of the company's internal controls.

Section 404 looks at first like a mere disclosure requirement. It requires inclusion of internal control disclosures in each public corporation's annual report. This disclosure statement must include: (1) a written confirmation by which firm management acknowledges its responsibility for establishing and maintaining a system of internal controls and procedures for financial reporting; (2) an assessment, as of the end of the most recent fiscal year, of the effectiveness of the firm's internal controls; and (3) a written attestation by the firm's outside auditor confirming the adequacy and accuracy of those controls and procedures. It is not the disclosure itself that makes § 404 significant, of course; instead, it is the need to assess and test the company's internal controls in order to be able to make the required disclosures. These costs have two major components. First, there are the internal costs incurred by the corporation in conducting the requisite management assessment. Second, there are the fees the corporation must pay the auditor for carrying out its assessment.

When SOX was adopted, neither Congress nor the SEC appreciated just how costly these compliance processes would prove. The SEC estimated that the average cost of complying with § 404 would be approximately $91,000.[36] In fact, however, a 2005 survey put the direct cost of complying with § 404 in its first year at $7.3 million for large accelerated filers and $1.5 million for smaller accelerated filers.[37] "First-year implementation costs for larger companies were thus eighty times greater than the SEC had estimated, and sixteen times greater than estimated for smaller companies."[38]

These costs include average expenditures of 35,000 staff hours on § 404 compliance alone, which proved to be almost 100 times the SEC's estimate. In addition, firms spent an average of $1.3 million on external consultants and software. Finally, on average, they incurred an extra $1.5 million (a jump of 35 percent) in audit fees.[39]

To be sure, some of these costs were one-time expenses incurred to bring firms' internal controls up to snuff. Yet many other SOX compliance costs recur year after year. For example, the internal control process required by § 404 relies heavily on ongoing documentation. As a result, firms must constantly ensure that they are creating the requisite paper trail. Accordingly, while second-year compliance costs dropped, those costs remained many times greater than the SEC's estimate of first-year costs.[40]

In addition to the direct costs of complying with § 404, firms incurred a number of indirect costs. Director workload increased, for example, forcing firms to increase director compensation. Audit committees have been especially impacted, on average meeting more than twice as often post SOX as they did pre SOX. Director liability exposure also increased due to the harsh criminal and civil sanctions associated with violations of § 404 and other SOX requirements. As a result, not only did director compensation rise, but directors and officers (D&O) insurance premiums more than doubled post SOX.

These costs are disproportionately borne by smaller public firms. Director compensation at small firms increased from $5.91 paid to non-employee directors on every $1,000 in sales in the pre-SOX period to $9.76 on every $1,000 in sales in the post-SOX period. In contrast, large firms incurred 13 cents in director cash compensation per $1,000 in sales in the pre-SOX period, which increased only to 15 cents in the post-SOX period. Likewise, companies with annual sales less than $250 million incurred $1.56 million in external resource costs to comply with § 404. In contrast, firms with annual sales of $1 billion to $2 billion incurred an average of $2.4 million in such costs. Accordingly, while SOX compliance costs do scale, they do so only to a rather limited extent. At many smaller firms, the disproportionately heavy additional costs imposed by § 404 are a significant percentage of their annual revenues. For those firms operating on thin margins, SOX compliance costs can actually make the difference between profitability and losing money.

Both the recurring nature and disproportionate impact of these costs is confirmed by a recent study of the impact SOX had on the operating profitability of a sample of 1,428 firms. Average cash flows declined by 1.3 percent post SOX. Costs ranged from $6 million for small firms to $39 million for large firms. These costs were not limited to one-time first-year implementation expenses. Instead, substantial costs and reduced profits recurred throughout the four-year study period. In the aggregate, the sample firms lost about $75 billion over that period.[41]

Section 404 admittedly had laudatory goals. Faulty internal controls, after all, contributed to many corporate scandals during the dot-com era. Section 404 has also had some beneficial effects. Some of the fall in securities filings mid-decade may have resulted from companies having adopted better internal controls and disclosure procedures in response to § 404, for example. Some companies may have benefited from greater intra-firm transparency.

While regulators and Congress have sought to alleviate some of the costs associated with § 404 compliance,[42] there is no doubt that § 404—along with the rest of SOX and the broader U.S. regulatory regime—has had and continues to have a deleterious effect on the U.S. capital markets. As the Financial Economists Roundtable observed, there is "little reason to believe that . . . the benefits of § 404 will exceed the costs."[43]

These costs have substantially distorted corporate financing decisions. First, SOX discouraged privately held corporations from going public. Startup companies opted for "financing from private-equity firms" rather than using an IPO to raise money from the capital markets. Because "going public is an important venture capital exit strategy, partially closing the exit could impede start-up financing, and therefore make it harder to get ideas off the ground."[44] In addition to the decline in domestic IPOs, there was a decrease in new foreign listings on U.S. secondary markets.[45] The net effect was the declining market share of U.S. markets in such transactions as global IPOs. "Martin Graham, director of the London Stock Exchange's (LSE's) market services, said that Sarbanes-Oxley has 'undoubtedly assisted our efforts' and emphasized the LSE's ability to draw new listings from foreign companies."[46]

Second, there has been a trend toward public companies exiting the public capital markets. A Foley & Lardner survey, for example, found that after SOX some 21 percent of responding publicly held corporations were considering going private.[47] A study by William Carney of 114 companies going private in 2004 found that 44 specifically cited SOX compliance costs as one of the reasons they were doing so.[48]

In light of this evidence, it is hardly surprising that all of the major reports on capital market competitiveness viewed SOX and, especially, § 404 as a significant drag on the competitiveness of those markets. The Bloomberg-Schumer Report cited the "concerns of small companies and non-US issuers regarding the Section 404 compliance costs involved in a U.S. listing."[49] The Paulson Committee noted that § 404 compliance "costs can be especially significant for smaller companies and foreign companies contemplating entry into the U.S. market."[50] The Chamber of Commerce argued: "European, Chinese, and Indian companies that do not list their shares on U.S. markets are not required to comply with Section 404. They can save that money—this year and for every year hereafter—and direct it toward R&D, customer discounts, or a host of other uses that serve to improve their long-term competitiveness and make it that much harder for U.S. companies to compete."[51] Citing the probability that the costs of compliance would continue to outweigh any benefits thereof, the Financial Economists Roundtable recommended that issuers be allowed to opt out of § 404.[52]

The Recurrent Problem

Egregious as it was, the failure of Congress and the SEC to accurately forecast the impact of § 404 in particular and SOX in general was not especially surprising. In a remarkably brief period, with minimal legislative processing, Congress slapped together a number of reform proposals that had been kicking around Washington for a long time and sent the mix to President Bush for signing.

Simply put, the corporate governance provisions were not a focus of careful deliberation by Congress. SOX was emergency legislation, enacted under conditions of limited legislative debate, during a media frenzy involving several high-profile corporate fraud and insolvency cases. These occurred in conjunction with an economic downturn, what appeared to be a free-falling stock market, and a looming election campaign in which corporate scandals would be an issue. The healthy ventilation of issues that occurs in the usual give-and-take negotiations over competing policy positions, which works to improve the quality of decision-making, did not occur in the case of SOX.[53] It's hardly surprising that legislation crafted in such a haphazard fashion turned out to be far more costly than anyone expected.

Unfortunately, SOX is merely one instance of the larger, ongoing problem with the way corporate governance is regulated in the United States. Since the founding of the U.S., states have had primary responsibility for regulating corporate governance. "It . . . is an accepted part of the business landscape in this country for states to create corporations, to prescribe their powers, and to define the rights that are acquired by purchasing their shares."[54] Hence, the Supreme Court opines that "no principle of corporation law and practice is more firmly established than a State's authority to regulate domestic corporations."[55] Although the claim is contested, the better view is that the states—by which I mean Delaware—have done a good job in this area.[56]

Around the beginning of the twentieth century, however, economic progressives began arguing for federal preemption. After the Great Crash of 1929, serious consideration in fact was given to creating a federal law of corporations. Instead, of course, Congress chose to adopt the now familiar federal securities laws. Although these laws federalized some aspects of corporate governance, they left the primary regulatory responsibility to the states.

In the interim, Congress has normally had far more important things on its agenda than corporate governance. It is only in the aftermath of the sort of crises that took place in the past decade that corporate governance becomes a matter of national political concern. Because Congress acts on corporate governance in response to a crisis, it tends to act hurriedly, as in the case of SOX.[57] The pressure of time tends to give advantages to interest groups and other policy entrepreneurs who have prepackaged purported solutions that can be readily adapted into legislative form. Hence, for example, many of SOX's provisions were "recycled ideas" that had been "advocated for quite some time by corporate governance entrepreneurs."[58] Unfortunately, because these policy entrepreneurs tend to be critics of markets and corporations, the resulting new laws often "impose regulation that penalizes or outlaws potentially useful devices and practices and more generally discourages risk-taking by punishing negative results and reducing the rewards for success."[59]

Both Roberta Romano and the late Larry Ribstein independently demonstrated that this pattern is a reoccurring phenomenon in American law, going back even before the New Deal.[60] Indeed, according to Stuart Banner, the same pattern of boom, bust, and regulation can be seen far back into the nineteenth century: "Banner contends that the reason for the association is that deep-seated popular suspicion of speculation comes in bad financial times to dominate otherwise popular support for markets, resulting in the expansion of regulation. That is to say, financial exigencies embolden critics of markets to push their regulatory agenda. They are able to play on the strand of popular opinion that is hostile to speculation and markets because the general public is more amenable to regulation after experiencing financial losses."[61] At that time, SOX was merely the latest iteration of this process.

When the economy suffered through an even worse patch at the end of the decade, it was thus perfectly predictable that another round of regulation would be forthcoming. The story of the housing bubble's burst, the subprime mortgage crisis, and the Great Recession is far too complex to recount herein. Suffice it to say that, as was the case with SOX, populist outrage motivated Congress to pass the Dodd-Frank Act, which I have elsewhere characterized as "Quack Federal Corporate Governance Round II."[62]

Can Anything Be Done?

There are three major reasons why federal intervention in corporate governance tends to be ill conceived. First, federal "bubble laws" tend to be enacted in a climate of political pressure that does not facilitate careful analysis of costs and benefits. Second, they tend to be driven by populist anti-corporate emotions. Finally, the content of federal bubble laws is often derived from prepackaged proposals advocated by policy entrepreneurs skeptical of corporations and markets.

In her critique of SOX, Roberta Romano proposed that these problems could be addressed in several ways:

> The straightforward policy implication of this chasm between Congress's action and the learning bearing on it is that the mandates should be rescinded. The easiest mechanism for operationalizing such a policy change would be to make the SOX mandates optional, i.e., statutory default rules that firms could choose whether to adopt. An alternative and more far-reaching approach, which has the advantage of a greater likelihood of producing the default rules preferred by a majority of investors and issuers, would be to remove corporate governance provisions completely from federal law and remit those matters to the states. Finally, a more general implication concerns emergency legislation. It would be prudent for Congress, when legislating in crisis situations, to include statu-

tory safeguards that would facilitate the correction of mismatched proposals by requiring, as in a sunset provision, revisiting the issue when more considered deliberation would be possible.[63]

In adopting Dodd-Frank, Congress ignored that advice. As a result, Dodd-Frank suffers from the same three flaws as its predecessors.

The federal role in corporate governance thus appears to be a case of what Robert Higgs identified as the ratchet effect.[64] Higgs demonstrated that wars and other major crises typically trigger a dramatic growth in the size of government, accompanied by higher taxes, greater regulation, and loss of civil liberties. Once the crisis ends, government may shrink somewhat in size and power, but rarely back to pre-crisis levels. Just as a ratchet wrench works in only one direction, the size and scope of government tends to move in only one direction—upward—because the interest groups that favored the changes now have an incentive to preserve the new status quo, as do the bureaucrats who gained new powers and prestige. Hence, each crisis has the effect of ratcheting up the long-term size and scope of government.

We now observe the same pattern in corporate governance. As we have seen, the federal government rarely intrudes in this sphere except when there is a crisis. At that point, policy entrepreneurs favoring federalization of corporate governance spring into action, hijacking the legislative response to the crisis to advance their agenda. Although there may be some subsequent retreat, the overall trend has been for each major financial crisis of the past century to result in an expansion of the federal role. The unfortunate conclusion thus seems to be that there is no cure in sight for the corporate governance aspects of the American Illness.

Notes

1. Michael R. Bloomberg and Charles E. Schumer, Sustaining New York's and the U.S.'s Global Financial Services Leadership (2007) [hereinafter the Bloomberg-Schumer Report].

2. Comm. on Capital Mkts. Reg., Interim Report of the Committee on Capital Markets Regulation (2006). The Committee on Capital Markets Regulation—or, as it is better known, the Paulson Committee—subsequently issued a follow-up report identifying thirteen competitive measures that the Committee tracks on a quarterly

basis. Comm. on Capital Mkts. Regulation, The Competitive Position of the U.S. Public Equity Market (2007) [hereinafter the Paulson Committee Report].

3. U.S. Chamber of Comm., Capital Markets, Corporate Governance, and the Future of the U.S. Economy (2006) [hereinafter the Chamber Report].

4. I here borrow Roberta Romano's description of SOX. See Roberta Romano, The Sarbanes-Oxley Act and the Making of Quack Corporate Governance, 114 Yale L. J. 1521 (2005).

5. Luigi Zingales, Is the U.S. Capital Market Losing Its Competitive Edge 2 (ECGI Fin. Working Paper 192/2007). Global IPOs are those in which the issuer sells shares outside of its domestic market.

6. Press Release, Comm. on Capital Mkts. Reg., Q1 2010 Sees Fresh Deterioration in Competitiveness of U.S. Public Equity Markets, Reversing Mild Improvements (June 2, 2010).

7. Press Release, Comm. on Capital Mkts. Reg., Third Quarter 2009 Demonstrates First Signs of Mild Improvement in Competitiveness of U.S. Public Equity Markets, Reversing Mild Improvements (Dec. 1, 2009).

8. Bengt Holmstrom and Steven N. Kaplan, The State of U.S. Corporate Governance: What's Right and What's Wrong? 1 (ECGI Finance Working Paper No. 23/2003, Sept. 2003).

9. Brian R. Cheffins, Did Corporate Governance "Fail" during the 2008 Stock Market Meltdown? The Case of the S&P 500, 65 Bus. Law. 1, 2 (2009).

10. Report of the New York Stock Exchange Commission on Corporate Governance 2 (Sept. 23, 2010).

11. Paulson Committee Report, supra note 2.

12. In addition to the factors discussed herein, the Paulson Committee also argued that state corporate law inadequately protects shareholder rights in such areas as takeover defenses, shareholder voting, shareholder access to the proxy statement, and executive compensation. For analysis and defense of state law in these areas, see Stephen M. Bainbridge, Reshaping the Playing Field, Reg., Winter 2008, at 28; Stephen M. Bainbridge, Unocal at 20: Director Primacy in Corporate Takeovers, 31 Del. J. Corp. L. 769 (2006); Stephen M. Bainbridge, Executive Compensation: Who Decides?, 83 Tex. L. Rev. 1615 (2005).

13. Stoneridge Investment Partners, LLC v. Scientific-Atlanta, Inc., 552 U.S. 148 (2008).

14. Id. at 163–64 (citations omitted).

15. Bloomberg-Schumer Report, supra note 1, at 73.

16. See Paulson Committee Report, supra note 2, at 75. A mid-decade dip in filings was probably caused by the lack of volatility in U.S. stock markets during the period and the fading of the substantial litigation generated by the bursting of the dot-com bubble. Bloomberg-Schumer Report, supra note 1, at 74.

17. Statement of the Financial Economists Roundtable on the International Competitiveness of U.S. Capital Markets, 19 J. Applied Corp. Fin. 54, 55 (2007) [hereinafter FER].

18. Id.

19. Id.

20. Stephen J. Choi, The Evidence on Securities Class Actions, 57 Vand. L. Rev. 1465 (2004).

21. Stephen J. Choi, Assessing the Cost of Regulatory Protections: Evidence on the Decision to Sell Securities outside the United States (Yale Law & Economics Research Paper No. 253, March 21, 2001), available at SSRN: http://ssrn.com/abstract =267506.

22. Howell E. Jackson, Summary of Research Findings on Extra-territorial Application of Federal Securities Law, 1743 PLI/Corp 1243, 1253 (May 20, 2009).

23. Bloomberg-Schumer Report, supra note 1, at 75, 77.

24. Jackson, supra note 22, at 1254.

25. Roberta Romano, The Shareholder Suit: Litigation without Foundation?, 7 J. L. Econ. & Org. 55 (1991).

26. See Daniel R. Fischel and Michael Bradley, The Role of Liability Rules and the Derivative Suit in Corporate Law: A Theoretical and Empirical Analysis, 71 Cornell L. Rev. 261 (1986).

27. See, e.g., Michael Bradley and Cindy A. Schipani, The Relevance of the Duty of Care Standard in Corporate Governance, 75 Iowa L. Rev. 1 (1989); Roberta Romano, Corporate Governance in the Aftermath of the Insurance Crisis, 39 Emory L. J. 1155 (1990).

28. Chamber Report, supra note 3, at 5.

29. See generally Lawrence A. Cunningham, A Prescription to Retire the Rhetoric of "Principles-based Systems" in Corporate Law, Securities Regulation, and Accounting, 60 Vand. L. Rev. 1411 (2007), which nevertheless criticizes the principles versus rules dichotomy as imprecise and inexact.

30. Bloomberg-Schumer Report, supra note 1, at 83.

31. Id.

32. See generally Romano, supra note 4, at 1529–42, on which the following discussion draws.

33. Judith Burns, Corporate Governance (A Special Report)—Everything You Wanted to Know about Corporate Governance but Didn't Know to Ask, Wall St. J., Oct. 27, 2003, at R6.

34. Michael Delikat, Developments under Sarbanes-Oxley Whistleblower Law, in Internal Investigations 2007: Legal, Ethical & Strategic Issues (June 2007), available on Westlaw at 1609 PLI/Corp 19.

35. Eugenio J. Cardenas, Mexican Corporations Entering and Leaving U.S. Markets: An Impact of the Sarbanes-Oxley Act of 2002?, 23 Conn. J. Int'l L. 281 (2008).

36. Joseph A. Grundfest and Steven E. Bochner, Fixing 404, 105 Mich. L Rev. 1643, 1646 (2007) (footnotes omitted).

37. Id.

38. Id. at 1645–46.

39. Stephen M. Bainbridge, The Complete Guide to Sarbanes-Oxley 4 (2007).

40. Grundfest and Bochner, supra note 36, at 1646.

41. Anwer S. Ahmed et al., How Costly Is the Sarbanes Oxley Act? Evidence on the Effects of the Act on Corporate Profitability (Sept. 2009), available at http://ssrn .com/abstract=1480395.

42. The Wall Street Reform and Consumer Protection Act of 2010, Pub. L. No. 111-203, 124 Stat. 1376 (2010) (hereinafter cited as "The Dodd-Frank Act") permanently exempted non-accelerated filers from compliance with § 404(b). Meredith P. Burbank, Dodd-Frank Act Permanently Exempts Non-Accelerated Filers from SOX Auditor Attestation Requirement, http://www.lexology.com/library/detail.aspx ?g=8ee7ed34–1fe6–40a7-b31c-655070fd9f1d. The Act further "directs the SEC to conduct a study within the next nine months to determine how the burden of compliance with Section 404(b) could be reduced for companies with market capitalizations between $75 million and $250 million." Id.

43. FER, supra note 17, at 57.

44. Bainbridge, supra note 39, at 6 (quoting Larry Ribstein). The undesirability of becoming subject to the SOX regime is further confirmed by evidence of a trend for startups to follow an exit strategy of selling to private rather than public companies. Ehud Kamar et al., Going-Private Decisions and the Sarbanes-Oxley Act of 2002: A Cross-Country Analysis (Rand Working Paper No. WR-300-2-EMKF, 2008).

45. See Joseph D. Piotroski and Suraj Srinivasan, Regulation and Bonding: The Sarbanes-Oxley Act and the Flow of International Listings, 46 J. Acct. Res. 383 (2008).

46. Chamber Report, supra note 3, at 7.

47. Bainbridge, supra note 39, at 6.

48. William J. Carney, The Costs of Being Public after Sarbanes-Oxley: The Irony of "Going Private," 55 Emory L. J. 141 (2006).

49. Bloomberg-Schumer Report, supra note 1, at 20.

50. Paulson Committee Report, supra note 2, at 5. The Committee downgraded the importance of § 404 relative to the other concerns it identified, which Romano suggests may have been the result of political calculations about the feasibility of obtaining legislative approval for the Committee's various recommendations and the Committee's focus on the problems faced by the stock markets rather than those of small companies. Roberta Romano, Does the Sarbanes-Oxley Act Have a Future?, 26 Yale J. on Reg. 229, 246 (2009).

51. Chamber Report, supra note 3, at 14.

52. FER, supra note 17, at 57.

53. Romano, supra note 4, at 1528.

54. CTS Corp. v. Dynamics Corp., 481 U.S. 69, 91 (1987).

55. Id. at 89.

56. See Stephen M. Bainbridge, Corporation Law-and-economics 15 (2002) (citing authorities).

57. Romano, supra note 4, at 1523 ("SOX was enacted in a flurry of congressional activity").

58. Romano, supra note 4, at 1523.

59. Larry E. Ribstein, Bubble Laws, 40 Hou. L. Rev. 77, 83 (2003).

60. Ribstein, id. at 83–94; Romano, supra note 4, at 1590–94.

61. Romano, supra note 4, at 1593.

62. Stephen M. Bainbridge, Dodd-Frank: Quack Federal Corporate Governance Round II, 95 Minn. L. Rev. 1779 (2011).

63. Romano, supra note 4, at 1594–95.

64. See Robert Higgs, Crisis and Leviathan: Critical Episodes in the Growth of American Government 150–56 (1987) (describing the "ratchet effect" by which Congress increases not only the scale but also the scope of the federal government on a permanent basis).

PART 8:

CRIMINAL LAW

Corporate Crime, Overcriminalization, and the Failure of American Public Morality

JEFFREY S. PARKER

C orporate crime presents an unusual case of American legal exceptionalism. In terms of substantive legal doctrine, it is neither recent nor completely exceptional: the practice of holding corporate entities criminally liable goes back at least 150 years, in both the United States and other systems based on English common law, and has occasionally appeared elsewhere.[1] Where America is exceptional is in its enforcement efforts, and in the social and political context in which the idea of "corporate crime" was invented and promoted.

Outside of the United States, corporate criminal liability as a legal doctrine appears to be gaining ground, especially within some of the European Union countries.[2] However, it is unlikely that such changes have or ever will produce the incidence or rigor of criminal law enforcement against corporations observed in the United States,[3] because of profound differences in the legal and political systems.

Within the United States, there have been dramatic changes since 1991 in the manner in which the criminal law is brought to bear on corporate enterprises, and these changes are not attributable to changes in liability doctrines. Instead, there has been a shift in enforcement structures. As late as 1990, legal limitations on the enforcement options available against corporations held in check many of the potentially destructive effects of corporate criminal liability. However, since the advent of new federal guidelines on corporate criminal sentencing in 1991,[4] the constraints have been removed, and enforcement policy has begun to spin out of control.

The expansion of corporate criminal enforcement has not taken place in a vacuum, but is accompanied by an even more dramatic case of American legal exceptionalism: America is overcriminalized in general. The comparative data are breathtaking. Contrary to popular belief, American crime rates today are, in most instances, comparable to those in other developed Western nations.[5] However, in its per capita rates of incarceration for crime—which provide a rough measure of a country's relative reliance on criminal law enforcement—America is a dramatic outlier. The United States has the highest incarceration rate on earth.[6] Excluding Russia and Eastern Europe, our incarceration rate of about 750 per 100,000 in population is five times higher than the highest European country (the U.K., at about 150, which is also the approximate world average), nearly six times higher than Canada (116), and about ten times higher than such countries as Sweden, Switzerland, and Denmark, all of which have crime rates similar to that of the U.S., or higher. The United States simply punishes its own people more severely than our peer nations. Nor is this severity limited to individual imprisonment: all forms of criminal punishment, including those applied to corporate offenders, are on a rising trend.

This condition is especially ironic within a legal culture that contains robust administrative and regulatory enforcement procedures against corporations, and also permits a comparatively high incidence of private civil enforcement, which itself is often criticized as excessive. The interplay of these conditions produces a potentially toxic mix: every move toward "tort reform" or the like in turn can produce still more strident calls for more severe criminal law enforcement, which under prevailing political conditions is likely to produce still more criminalization.[7] At the same time, criminal law enforcement is becoming increasingly concentrated at the federal level.

Much of the new criminalization and federalization is directed toward business enterprise, both corporate and non-corporate. When relatively routine business regulation becomes increasingly criminalized, on ever more dilute concepts of both "harm" and "fault," the cost of compliance can become prohibitive.

Given the severe consequences associated with criminal law enforcement in America, no business person can afford to run a substantial risk of criminal liability. Therefore, the incentive is to devote more resources to law compliance, which leaves less for production and innovation. Excessive burdens of compliance can undermine global competitiveness, and ultimately destroy firms and even entire industries.

There has been little recognition in the public debates of the potentially disproportionate and destructive effects of criminal liability, over and above the usual regulatory burden. The "crime" label has become a trump card that paralyzes thinking about the costs and benefits of more law and more punishment. That paralysis extends into the enforcement function: at the federal level, the Department of Justice exclusively decides whether to institute and how to conduct criminal law enforcement; there is no general institutional check provided by the civil regulatory authorities or by laws that provide meaningful limitations on prosecutorial designs.[8] We thus get increasingly more criminal prohibitions, more attenuated standards of liability, higher penalties, and more prosecution.

While some of these problems are shared by our peer nations, what makes America different is that we take our criminal law enforcement very seriously—many would say too seriously—as measured by the overall rate of punishment we impose on our own citizens. In contrast, most Western societies treat criminal law enforcement primarily as a morality play, a supplement to other enforcement institutions and not a primary means of ensuring legal compliance. Their punishment practices—much lower sentences and liberal paroles as compared with practices in the U.S.—indicate that their systems recognize, though perhaps only implicitly, the potentially destructive effects of over-reliance on the criminal sanction. In this respect, the American system has lost its compass.

Corporate Crime: Definitions and History

Though commonly used, the phrase "corporate crime" is ambiguous, and may refer to three different but partially overlapping phenomena:

1. "entity criminal liability," under which a corporate entity (as distinct from its owners or agents) might be criminally liable for an event that may or may not be a "crime" when committed by agents of the corporation;

2. the criminal liability of an individual agent for an action taken (or omitted) in relation to the operations of a corporation or other business enterprise, which may or may not be a "crime" if committed outside the corporate or business context; and

3. a popular synonym for "white-collar crime," or misbehavior by a corporation or its officers, which may or may not be a crime at law.

However defined, corporate crime bears only a tangential relationship—if any at all—to the core definition of crime as it has traditionally been understood in Western legal systems. In the past, the hallmark of criminal liability was the guilty mind or *mens rea* of the accused, and in abandoning this safeguard of individual liberty, corporate criminal liability tends to corrupt the ethical premises of criminal responsibility. Further, this corruption tends to spread into the body of criminal law more generally, as the need to show personal fault is abandoned. It is thus the third sense of "corporate crime"—the non-legal sense—that ultimately dominates public debates and leads to the self-reinforcing tendency toward overcriminalization, through a degradation of the ethical foundations of criminal liability.

A. Entity Criminal Liability

Entity criminal liability is "corporate crime" *strictu sensu,* and is the most obvious departure from the general premises of criminal law. At the same time, it is criminal law at its most primitive, in the manner in which it resembles the forms of proto-corporate and collective liability of pre-Modern societies. The Enlightenment's rejection of such liability, and the rise of mens rea and personal responsibility, was a crucial advance in individual liberty. By the time of Blackstone's Commentaries, neither English nor American law recognized entity criminal liability, even though corporate forms were by then well established. Because corporations, as abstract instrumentalities, could neither act in their proper person nor form a mens rea, they were not subject to criminal liability.[9]

However, beginning in the mid-19th century, English and American courts began to recognize entity corporate liability, at first for public nuisance cases of omission and later as a matter of vicarious liability for the act of agents. The corporate entity was treated as a person and endowed with a corporate "mind" that could be found guilty. The culmination of these developments at the federal level came with the 1909 decision of the U.S. Supreme Court in *New York Central and Hudson River Railroad Company v. U.S.*,[10] which upheld the validity of a federal statute expressly providing for entity criminal liability and brushed aside concerns about the lack of mens rea at the corporate level. While limited in scope to a particular (and unusual) statute,[11] the *New York Central* decision has been taken to establish a rule in federal law of vicarious entity criminal liability that is "strict" liability in the sense that it requires no mens rea.

Vicarious entity criminal liability violates two of the fundamental premises of criminal law. The first is the idea that vicarious liability might ground liability in tort but not in criminal law. The second is the idea that criminal liability should not be imposed in the absence of personal fault of a sufficient degree to produce moral condemnation of the offender.[12] More recent developments in entity liability present a third departure from the classical conception of criminal law: the "collective knowledge" doctrine, which imposes entity criminal liability where no individual is actually guilty of a crime, by the imaginary conflation of knowledge separately held by several different corporate agents, but never communicated to one another or to corporate management.[13] This is a case of purely imaginary crime.

At the state level, entity liability is less expansive, though still troubling. One restraining influence was the American Law Institute's Model Penal Code, developed in the 1950s, which would limit strict entity liability to minor offenses and recognize an affirmative defense of entity due diligence. More serious offenses were governed by something similar to the English "alter ego" rule, which attributes to the entity the knowledge and acts of its board of directors or "high managerial agents" when these have performed, directed, or "recklessly tolerated" the commission of the underlying offense.[14] In any event, there appear to be very few criminal prosecutions of corporations under state laws.

The American developments, while similar to those in the other English-speaking legal systems, were not paralleled in Continental European law, which in most countries continued to reject criminal entity liability on principle until relatively recently, and still do in some important European systems, such as Germany.

B. Corporate Agent Criminal Liability

At first blush, the practice of holding individual corporate agents liable for crimes committed in the course of their agency seems not to depart from traditional criminal law principles. However, corporate agency liability represents a move to a more vicarious and strict form of liability, as a consequence of the rise of what Francis Sayre dubbed the "public welfare offense."[15] These are criminal prohibitions that enforce regulatory standards, usually in the name of public health or safety, and tend to reduce or dispense with a mens rea requirement.

Public welfare offenses also employed vicarious liability, imposing liability on agents for action or inaction by the firm. The paradigmatic example is known as the "responsible corporate officer" doctrine, or the Dotterweich-Park doctrine, after the names of the leading U.S. Supreme Court cases.[16]

Under this doctrine, a corporate manager might be held criminally responsible, without a showing of personal fault or personal action, merely by virtue of his or her position within the firm's management. Thus the responsible officer doctrine introduces yet another type of vicarious criminal liability, which might be called respondeat inferior. This is a form of reverse vicarious liability, as it makes the agent vicariously liable for the action of the firm.

These doctrines were said to be justified by the "circumstances of modern industrialism" and by the nature of the liability, since "penalties commonly are relatively small, and conviction does no grave damage to an offender's reputation."[17] However, some of the early cases plainly did not meet that description. The 1922 case of U.S. v. Balint[18]—routinely cited by the Court as an early example—involved a felony prosecution under the Harrison Narcotic Act of 1914, carrying a penalty of five years' imprisonment, in which the Court held that ignorance that the drugs were of the type prohibited was not a defense. While some subsequent Supreme Court cases sought to restrict the scope of strict liability offenses,[19] the omission of mens rea require-ments for some or all elements of an offense has become commonplace.[20]

C. White-Collar Crime

"White-collar" crime is more of a popular epithet than a legal doctrine. The term was coined by the sociologist Edwin Sutherland,[21] whose unease about industrialization and the rise of the corporation can be traced to ear-lier Populist and Progressive attacks on big business. Sutherland believed that corporate business structures were corrupting and criminogenic and sought to push the envelope on what constitutes a crime.

The vast majority—84 percent—of the cases Sutherland studied were civil and not criminal matters. However, he argued that these cases should have been treated as crimes, as they were wrongs against the state or the public. A similar pattern is found in subsequent sociological studies by fol-lowers of Sutherland, into the late 1970s and early 1980s.[22] In sum, white-collar crime blurs the legal distinction between crime and non-crime.

As an exercise in political rhetoric, this movement has been enormously successful in shifting the terms of legislative debates (and enactments), criminalizing behavior that no one would have thought criminal in the past. As such, white-collar crime tends to result in overcriminalization and a politicization of justice that is inconsistent with the rule of law.

Ever since Sutherland, the ideological roots of white-collar crime have lurked just beneath the surface of public debates about corporate and individ-ual criminal liability. What animates the discussion are tendentious economic theories and class warfare sentiments.[23] Proponents of white-collar crime tend to feel a deep ambivalence about the institutions of free markets and pri-vate enterprise that have brought America its extraordinary prosperity, and are apt to attribute any market misfortune to corporate wrongdoing or "greed," for which someone should have to pay through a criminal prosecution.

The Recent Expansion of Corporate Crime and Enforcement

As late as 1990, criminal prosecutions against corporations were relatively infrequent, the penalties were modest, and nearly all of the prosecutions were against small, closely held firms.[24] Criminal enforcement against corporations was a minor supplement to a robust civil and administrative enforcement structure and was generally not invoked in response to the diffusion of responsibility within complex corporate structures. The giant, immoral institutions of the sociologists' imaginations were simply not there.

Over the ensuing two decades, however, enforcement conditions changed dramatically, and entity criminal liability has been transformed from a minor anomaly into a serious threat to our economic well-being. Ironically, this transformation has come during a period in which there has been growing scholarly opinion in America that the entire "corporate crime" exercise is economically destructive.

The seemingly unlikely catalyst for the expansion of entity criminal liability was the federal Sentencing Reform Act of 1984,[25] which authorized the creation of a regime of mandatory criminal sentencing guidelines for the federal courts. As it pertains to corporate crime, the significant changes wrought by that Act were: (1) raising and restructuring statutory maximum penalty levels, and (2) authorizing the imposition of an independent non-monetary sanction of corporate "probation."[26] Ultimately, these new authorities were used by the Sentencing Commission's guidelines to force corporations into adopting a governmentally specified compliance regime to prevent and detect violations of law.[27] The resulting guidelines set the penalty levels many times higher than prior law,[28] and the discretion accorded prosecutors gives them in most cases what amounts to an unlimited threat point.[29]

At the same time, the Sentencing Reform Act focused scholarly attention on the problem in the law-and-economics literature. Fischel and Sykes[30] and Khanna[31] showed that entity criminal liability had no benefits to enforcement and potential costs to both enforcement and business efficiency. The basic logic of the economic critique is straightforward: while a good case can be made for entity-level monetary penalties, based upon vicarious and strict liability, this does not justify criminal as opposed to civil penalties.

A further literature examines the reputational effects of criminal prosecutions. Apart from the criminal sanction itself, the firm bears a real cost when its customers and the public react to news of a conviction or even a prosecution. In general, reputational considerations argue for civil and not criminal enforcement.[32] Related to this, a theory of "expressive retribution"[33] has been advanced to argue for a social value in blaming the blameless. What this might accomplish is not clear, and it certainly undermines whatever moral authority there might be in a criminal conviction.[34]

The problems of corporate criminal liability have been exacerbated by the enforcement approach taken by the Department of Justice. In contrast with civil regulators, who are constrained by administrative law to openly articulate implementing policy, subject to judicial review, criminal prosecutors operate behind closed doors and are neither legally nor politically accountable. Criminal prosecutors can decide to prosecute or not prosecute; they can decide what charges to bring and what evidence and legal arguments to present, all without any scrutiny by any other authority. They can demand concessions from their targets in exchange for deferring or declining prosecution. At the federal level, prosecutors operate largely in secret, with virtually unlimited and unreviewed powers to compel citizens' cooperation through the secret grand jury process. Through a combination of vague criminal prohibitions with minimal proof requirements, plus the astronomical penalties authorized under the federal sentencing guidelines, they can credibly threaten virtually any target with destruction, and therefore in the end dictate the terms on which the threat is withdrawn. Most importantly, they are accountable to no one for the welfare consequences of their decisions. The institutional structure actually discourages criminal prosecutors from considering those consequences; to an official whose only incentive is enforcement, more enforcement is always better, no matter how much it costs the economy and the society.

In the case of corporate criminal enforcement under the 1991 sentencing guidelines, the Justice Department used its prosecutorial powers to extend the "compliance" emphasis of the guidelines into a "compliance and cooperation" policy to guide enforcement decisions. Under a series of policy memos issued in the 1990s and bearing the names of successive deputy attorneys general—the best known being the "Thompson" memorandum, after Larry Thompson—the department encouraged prosecutors to base their prosecutorial decisions on the degree to which the target firm embraced the "compliance" philosophy and "cooperated" with the department's investigation.[35] This included assisting the department in obtaining convictions of the firm's own agents, through such means as extracting a waiver of the firm's attorney-client privilege or work product protection, conducting an internal investigation on behalf of the department, or breaching its contractual duty to indemnify agents for their defense costs. In sum, corporate officers and (more often) mid-level employees were hung out to dry by their firms, who succumbed to the threat of economically devastating criminal charges against them.

As these tactics usually involved either deferred or non-prosecution agreements with the firm, in which it agrees to adopt specific compliance requirements in exchange for a decision not to prosecute, the Justice Department's policies generally evaded judicial review. However, they were eventually pushed so far as to come to the attention of the Second Circuit, which threw out charges against employees of the accounting firm KPMG, based upon unwarranted pressure brought to bear on the firm itself, which had been coerced into agreeing to dishonor its obligation to indemnify the employees' defense costs.[36] In the wake of the decision, the department issued a revised policy statement, withdrawing the most offensive parts, but nevertheless did not back off of its basic compliance-and-cooperation model.[37]

The Justice Department has thus begun to see itself as a general superintendent of American corporate behavior, the ultimate manager of firm management. Moreover, the use of non-prosecution or deferred prosecution agreements usually insulates the practice from judicial review.[38] Because a criminal prosecution, whether or not successful, might amount to a death sentence to a firm, the Justice Department now has an unprecedented degree of control over the economy.

Unlike a civil regulatory agency, the Justice Department has neither the expertise, nor the appropriate institutional incentives, nor the legal framework to operate as an economic regulator that can balance costs and benefits. It can be expected to err systematically in the direction of overestimating the benefit, and underestimating the cost, of its compliance-and-cooperation regime. Forms of regulation that would be considered intolerable if proposed in Congress or in the regulations of the Securities and Exchange

Commission (SEC) or Federal Trade Commission (FTC) are now being imposed, behind closed doors, on an ad hoc basis, by criminal prosecutors who may never have studied corporation law, and all without any review by the judiciary or even, in many cases, by more senior Justice Department officials.

Even slight errors in the specification of compliance effort can have profoundly destructive effects on the American economy, especially in a globally competitive world.[39] And the irresistible incentives for the firm to "cooperate" by seeing to the conviction of its own agents can undermine the accuracy and fairness of the criminal justice process, which was the Second Circuit's rationale in the *KPMG* case.

Moreover, what underlies this entire problem is the major departure from rule of law values embodied in the secrecy and unfettered discretion now granted to American criminal prosecutors.[40] What was once a relatively small pocket of official unaccountability has now been expanded into a major threat to Americans' prosperity and personal freedoms, through the growth of "corporate crime" enforcement to its current role as an ultimate regulator of corporate management, on virtually any topic. But even so, the "corporate crime" problem is only one part of the still larger problem of overcriminalization.

Overcriminalization

"Corporate crime" is synergistic with overcriminalization, because admitting the deviant case of "corporate crime" into the criminal justice system tends to corrupt the standards of criminal responsibility more generally.

"Overcriminalization" refers to the excessive use of criminal sanctions, and embraces at least five different factors:

1. the sheer proliferation of criminal prohibitions, especially at the federal level;
2. the vague, arcane, or trivial nature of such prohibitions, which undermine citizens' ability to conform and debase the moral moment of the criminal sanction;
3. the lack of adequate mens rea standards in criminal prohibitions;

4. the politicization of crime, especially at the federal level, which produces a "one-way ratchet" always leading to more criminalization, because elected politicians all want to be "tough on crime" for the benefit of their constituents, and prosecutors want to become elected officials; and

5. overpunishment, in the sense of both excessive sentences and the proliferation of forfeiture provisions, both civil and criminal, which in turn leads to "policing for profit."[41]

At least the first four, and perhaps all five, factors help explain the rise of "corporate crime." Our system has permitted too much "artificial" crime to enter the system, with too much leeway for both legislators and enforcers, which is an unjustified abuse of the extraordinary power of the criminal sanction. More concisely, power corrupts.[42]

One measure of the problem is the number of Americans now incarcerated (over two million) or otherwise subject to deprivations of physical liberty under what is euphemistically termed "criminal justice supervision"—that is, probation, parole, or supervised release (another five million).[43] America has long been something of an outlier among its peer group in terms of incarceration rates. However, we are now in unprecedented territory. As a result of an enormous run-up during the 1980s and 1990s, our current incarceration rates per capita are now four times higher than the traditional U.S. average, which had been stable for several decades before.[44] Moreover, most of this growth in per capita U.S. incarcerations began *after* U.S. crime rates began to decline, a trend that in most categories has now been continuing for 30 years.[45] The cumulative decline in U.S. crime rates is quite dramatic: homicide rates have declined by nearly 50 percent, rape by 82 percent, and burglary by 76 percent, and these rates began dropping in the 1974–81 time period.[46] But while these traditional crimes have continued to fall, the rate of prosecutions continues to rise, especially at the federal level.[47] Apart from the direct criminal sanction, convictions impose spillover losses, including the social stigma and collateral disabilities such as the loss of professional or occupational licenses, debarment from certain business opportunities, and potentially disproportionate forfeiture of property. The impact is not limited to the convicted individual alone, but extends to family members, social and business networks, and the like. Some of these consequences are under the direct control of criminal justice procedures, but others are not. Their cumulative effect may be disproportionate to either or both the nature of the harm done—if any—and the culpability of the offender—if any.

The general overcriminalization problem is interrelated with the expansion of corporate criminal liability, by attenuating the moral responsibility of both the punished and the punisher, and thus reducing the criterion of criminalization to mere political convenience or expediency. It has proved impossible to limit this idea only to entity liability. It first spreads to condemn not only the corporation but also an individual corporate officer without fault because it is convenient, and it eventually becomes the rationale for condemning an individual non-corporate officer without fault, if deemed convenient. The reasoning ultimately consumes the entire rationale for distinguishing criminal from non-criminal liability.

The criminal sanction has an inherent tendency toward destructive effects on human welfare, and those effects are difficult to control even by the well-intentioned and well-informed policy makers and functionaries.[48] In moral terms, criminal punishment (from the Latin root *poena,* meaning "pain") is inherently evil, and it should never be deployed without recognition of that property. However, punishment, like government, may sometimes be a necessary evil, in the sense of being the lesser of two evils. That is the basic rationale for the traditional limitation of criminal punishment solely to those who are sufficiently morally blameworthy to be justly condemned by the community, which is the traditional office of the fundamental criminal law doctrines of mens rea and legality. Criminal condemnation makes the convict a social pariah of sorts, with predictably severe consequences of unpredictable magnitude. To apply that treatment to the non-blameworthy is itself immoral.

Implications

Corporate crime is both a symptom and a cause of the more systemic illness of overcriminalization in America. There is no good reason why the land of the free should also be the land of the largest incarcerated population on earth, both per capita and, with the possible exception of China,[49] in absolute terms. With 5 percent of the world's population, we hold nearly 25 percent of its prisoners. That is embarrassing.

All legal systems at all times can be tempted by expediency. Once expediency is allowed into the discussion as a decision point, it tends to dominate. But why has America proved so vulnerable?

While there is evidence of erosion in the institutional and constitutional structures that have helped to restrain overcriminalization in the past, I believe that the more fundamental cause is a failure of American public morality. What I mean by that is a shared sense—by both officials and private citizens—of the responsibility entailed in the deployment of the criminal sanction. The criminal sanction is an inherently destructive and evil thing, which should never be used for mere convenience, but only in cases of strict necessity, which are few and far between, and then only to the degree necessary. It is society's sanction of last resort, difficult to control in its ultimate consequences, and unjustified whenever another form of sanctioning— of which there are many—would do as well, or possibly better. Moreover, even when thought necessary, it is not to be applied in the absence of blameworthiness in the offender, because it is such a profound attack on its target. Because the criminal sanction is society's sanction, every member of the polity has a personal moral responsibility for its imposition, a responsibility we have shirked.

Along with the attenuation of personal moral responsibility comes a certain degree of denial, or reluctance to give up a false pride. We Americans remain proud of our rule of law tradition and wish to consider our criminal justice system the gold standard of the world. But many of the realities of that system are uncomfortable and therefore tend to be ignored or discounted as aberrational. Non-specialists claim ignorance of the facts, and some specialists seek to rationalize our deviations from the rule of law. In other words, the mythology of the American rule of law may dominate over its reality. While prosecutors are an obvious focus of concern because prosecutorial discretion is a long-recognized pocket of lawlessness within a rule-of-law society, I do not wish to suggest that prosecutors as a group are any worse or better than anyone else. And yet, our current system of essentially no scrutiny of a vast range of prosecutorial behavior seems to be based on the counterfactual assumption that prosecutors are either idealized philosopher-kings or constrained by some unseen hand. We know better than that.

Although there is some variance across systems, political accountability is weak to nonexistent, and legal accountability is virtually nil. Here we need to distinguish political accountability from political visibility. At both state and federal levels, political visibility might induce a prosecutor to choose "high profile" cases against prominent defendants or based on well-known current events in order to enhance the prosecutor's political career. These types of cases invite their own forms of abuse, which are matters of concern,[50] but not the most fundamental problem. Even in those systems where some political accountability is possible—as where prosecutors are locally elected—it is rare for a prosecutor to be turned out of office for prosecuting too much, partly because the public is generally not allowed to compare the prosecutor's decisions to charge with her or his decisions not to charge. It is equally rare for a prosecutor to be re-elected for declining to prosecute. This is another place where the institutional incentives are askew to the rationale for prosecutorial discretion: prosecutors are expected to prosecute, whereas prosecutorial discretion doctrine assumes that they are equally likely to decline.

At the federal level, there is no direct political accountability, and very little supervision even from the main Justice Department. The 93 local United States attorneys are appointed by the president, and theoretically are subject to his oversight, but the last time a president sought to exercise his power, it created an uproar about "politicizing" the federal prosecutorial function.[51] In any case, most decisions are made by one of the thousands of assistant United States attorneys, with little or no supervision by anyone. Thus, the federal system involves a theoretically professionalized system, largely insulated from political pressures, but exercising a political function, with political visibility, but without external constraint. Nor does professional or internal discipline have a very good track record. The Department of Justice's internal disciplinary arm, the Office of Professional Responsibility, is not independent of the department's management, and has a notoriously weak record of discipline, to the limited extent that such data are publicly available. [52] Nor does the department seem very serious about actually enforcing its "Principles of Federal Prosecution," published as part of the *United States Attorneys' Manual*.[53] The Principles themselves are fairly porous, but, even so, they cannot be legally enforced, and do not appear to be enforced through either managerial direction or disciplinary action.

There is one time when the prosecutor in all systems must justify his or her legal case, which is when the case is presented for a jury's consideration and the court rules upon requested instructions and considers motions to acquit. However, criminal procedure is lax in comparison with the procedures available for early legal and factual tests in civil cases. By the time that stage is reached in a criminal case, the defendant may be bankrupted by defense costs (and pre-indictment forfeitures), intimidated into a guilty plea, or both.[54]

Even the minimal legal check at trial has lost much of its vigor due to overcriminalization. When the substance of criminal law consisted of a relatively short list of crimes known by everyone to be criminal—such as murder, rape, robbery, burglary, arson, assault, and theft—the lax procedure may have been sufficient, and a small pocket of unfettered prosecutorial discretion tolerable. However, the proliferation of a multitude of vague and overlapping criminal prohibitions, covering matters both trivial and serious, and embodying a logic well beyond the ordinary citizens' ken, has rendered legal control of this type largely ineffective. The prosecutors themselves are continually pushing the envelope of criminalization, and usually have multiple redundant theories expressed in numerous counts.[55] In many sentencing systems, such as that prevailing in the federal courts, there is essentially no difference in sentencing outcome between conviction on one count or many. In such systems, the stakes are asymmetrical: the prosecutor need win only one, while the defense needs to win them all.[56] Even if one assumes a very low rate of erroneous conviction, at some point the numbers overwhelm even the innocent, and prosecutions embodying 50 to 100 charged counts, or more, are commonplace in the federal system today.

Of course, the litigating resources available to the two sides also are radically asymmetrical: on the prosecution side are all of the resources of the government, and on the defense side, a single individual or firm. In the federal system, as a practical matter, the resources available to the prosecution are unlimited, and resources matter. That is the point made by the *KPMG* case: the government's overreaching was induced by the federal prosecutors' desire to deny the individual defendants access to the wherewithal necessary to mount a defense. The asymmetry extends beyond money and personnel alone: the government also possesses extraordinary investigative powers. In the federal system, the grand jury has morphed over time from a screening process to protect defendants against unwarranted charges into an enormously powerful tool of the prosecution. Federal grand jury investigations operate in secret and can go on for years, prosecutors have access to the subpoena power to compel the assistance of anyone, and no aspect of the process—either its predicate or the fairness or reasonableness of its procedures—is scrutinized by the courts, notwithstanding that the grand jury operates under the aegis of the judiciary.[57] In the course of such investigations and subsequent prosecutions, the prosecutors have the power to buy favorable testimony, and effectively preclude defense testimony, by casting suspicion on witnesses and then selectively granting or denying immunity from prosecution. The exercise of this power is also not subject to judicial control.

Thus, the extraordinary powers of the prosecution are matched by an extraordinary reticence on the part of the judiciary to exercise any control over those powers. The legislature, while not as quiescent as the courts, is also complicit. On rare occasions, the federal Congress has sought to constrain prosecutorial abuse. However, its few efforts in this regard have been met with a hostile reception in the courts.[58]

More commonly, Congress is the main contributor to the overcriminalization problem, both directly and indirectly. As no legislator wishes to be seen as "soft on crime," Congress continually votes for more prohibitions and more punishment, often without regard to the traditional legal limits on criminal liability.[59] With rare exceptions, legislators benefit politically from broad prosecutorial discretion coupled with broad and vague criminal statutes: should a particular case be seen as overcriminalization, the legislators have the political cover that they relied on the common sense of prosecutors; at the same time, they escape the opposite problem of being criticized as "soft on crime" by failing to provide prosecutors with the tools needed to deal with the issue du jour. The delegation of the power to criminalize to administrative agencies, and the power to set penalty levels to the Sentencing Commission, performs the same function.

In this respect, the failure of Congress reflects the more general failure of American public morality. Members of Congress simply do not accept their responsibility for the negative consequences of overcriminalization: they have delegated that responsibility away from themselves and can shift the blame to other branches, which lack political and legal accountability. These branches, in turn, maintain that their actions were authorized by Congress and thus reflect the vox populi. Whether the electorate will continue to accept this cynical ploy is an open question. But the electorate itself also needs to reexamine its acquiescence in criminalization for convenience.

Sooner or later, the costs—both economic and moral—of overcriminalization will become too obvious to ignore. In the meantime, "corporate crime" provides an instructive example of the problem: having unregulated criminal prosecutors dictate private corporate management procedures cannot be good for our economy, and it may be one of the causes of the downward spiral of boom-and-bust cycles observed over the past two decades. As overcriminalization spreads into small business, the professions, and individual entrepreneurs, the welfare costs will mount. But the more fundamental cost is to our shared morality, because it leads us into a state where the basic concept of criminality no longer has a special moral meaning. At that point, we will have abandoned our Enlightenment heritage and fallen back into medievalism. We will have sacrificed the most valuable thing a polity can have: a commitment to the rule of law, not only in myth but also in fact.

Notes

1. For a historical and analytical treatment, current through about 1990, see Parker, Doctrine for Destruction: The Case of Corporate Criminal Liability, 17 J. Managerial and Decision Econ. 381 (1996) [hereinafter Parker, Doctrine]. Traditional European exceptions include selective corporate liability in Denmark beginning in 1926, and more expansive corporate liability in The Netherlands beginning in 1976. Elsewhere in Europe, the recognition of corporate criminal liability dates from the mid-1990s onward.

2. For a survey of the developments in Europe, see Beale and Safwat, What Developments in Western Europe Tell Us about American Critiques of Corporate Criminal Liability, 8 Buffalo Crim. L. Rev. 89 (2004).

3. While it is generally believed that the United States is far and away the foremost practitioner of corporate criminal prosecution, my research has located no country, including the United States, that regularly publishes official data on the incidence of corporate prosecutions. The closest approximation is the United States Sentencing Commission's reports on corporate sentencings (not prosecutions) in the federal courts, in its annual Sourcebook of Federal Sentencing Statistics (Tables 51–54), available at www.ussc.gov, which is believed to reflect relatively complete data. Otherwise, empirical study in this area relies upon unofficial sources, such as media reports of cases or episodic access to official data for special studies, such as the study of federal prosecutions conducted by this author in the late 1980s while a member of the Sentencing Commission's staff. See Parker, Criminal Sentencing Policy for Organizations: The Unifying Approach of Optimal Penalties, 26 Am. Crim. L. Rev. 513 (1989) [hereinafter cited as Parker, Criminal Sentencing Policy]. This dearth of official data has made empirical research in the field extremely difficult, and it has been suggested that the relative lack of empirical data and analysis of actual enforcement places all policy decisions in doubt. See Geis and DiMento, Empirical Evidence and the Legal Doctrine of Corporate Criminal Liability, 29 Am. J. Crim. L. 341 (2002). Instead, most "empirical" research in this field consists of anecdotal "case studies," which tell us nothing about systemic effects.

4. United States Sentencing Guidelines, Chapter 8 (initially effective on November 1, 1991).

5. International crime statistics must be used with care, given the vast differences among definitions of crime, police-reporting and survey methods, the rigor of data collection, and incentives for under- or over-reporting. One broad-based measure from the UN's International Crime Victimization Survey of the cumulative incidence of 10 "common crimes" indicates that the U.S. has a lower crime rate than such countries as the U.K., The Netherlands, Belgium, Denmark, New Zealand, Iceland, and Switzerland, and is roughly comparable to Canada, Australia, and Sweden. Dijk, van Kesteren, and Smit, Criminal Victimization in International Perspective, Chapter 2, Tables 3 and 5 (UNODC/UNICRI: 2007). Another recent UN report, based upon police reporting of crimes, provides a similar picture, though with variations on specific offenses. Harendorf, Heiskanen, and Malby, International Statistics on Crime and Justice, Chapters 1 and 2 (UNODC/HEUNI: 2010). In that report, while the U.S. still ranks relatively higher on homicide than most Western European countries, it has lower rates of rape than Sweden, Canada, Australia, and New Zealand, lower rates of burglaries than the U.K., Denmark, Sweden, Switzerland, and New Zealand, and so on.

6. International data on incarcerated populations tend to be more comparable and consistent among multiple sources. The figures given here are based upon Walmsley, World Prison Population List, 8th edition (data as of 2008) (King's College

London: International Centre for Prison Studies), available at www.prisonstudies .org. See also Pew Center on the States, One in 100: Behind Bars in America 2008, table A-7; U.S. Department of Justice, Bureau of Justice Statistics, Correctional Populations in the United States, 2009 (giving official U.S. data). As indicated in the U.S. Department of Justice report, the U.S. total of about 2.3 million prisoners is only part of the story: an additional five million people in the U.S. are under "criminal justice supervision"—that is, parole, probation, or supervised release. The combined total of 7.2 million people (excluding most juvenile detentions) represents "about 3.1% of adults in the U.S. resident population." Id. at 2.

7. The Sarbanes-Oxley Act of 2002, which introduced newly diluted standards of individual criminal liability for corporate officers, see 18 U.S.C. § 1350, may be one example of this effect. That Act followed upon the corporate accounting scandals associated with Enron and Broadcom, but the failure of earlier detection and enforcement against accounting irregularities may itself have been attributable to the weakening of private civil enforcement through a previous "reform" measure, the Private Securities Litigation Reform Act of 1995, Pub. L. No. 104-67. See Choi, The Evidence on Securities Class Actions, 57 Vand. L. Rev. 1465 (2004).

8. For a recent survey of the breadth of prosecutorial discretion in the United States, see Krug, Prosecutorial Discretion and Its Limits, 50 Am. J. Comp. L. Supp. 643 (2002). Over time, the courts' willingness to review prosecutorial conduct has actually weakened. See Holderman and Redfern, Preindictment Prosecutorial Conduct in the Federal System Revisited, 96 J. Crim. L. & Criminology 527, 576–77 (2006).

9. These points, and those in the following paragraph, are developed more fully in Parker, Doctrine, supra note 1.

10. 212 U.S. 481 (1909). In 2009, the American Criminal Law Review published a symposium commemorating the 100th anniversary of this decision, including several papers raising contemporary issues concerning its authority. Symposium, 46 Am. Crim. L. Rev. 1433–1534 (2009).

11. That statute, the Elkins Act, compelled cartel pricing by shippers, and New York Central was punished for giving a discount from the cartel price. See Fischel and Sykes, Corporate Crime, 25 J. Leg. Studies 319, 334 (1996).

12. See 2 LaFave, Substantive Criminal Law at 13.5(b) (2d ed. 2003).

13. United States v. Bank of New England, 821 F.2d 844 (1st Cir. 1987). See also Parker, Criminal Sentencing Policy, supra note 3.

14. Model Penal Code at 2.07. The classic critique of the Model Penal Code's approach is Meuller, Mens Rea and the Corporation, 19 U. Pitt. L. Rev. 21 (1957).

15. Sayre, Public Welfare Offenses, 33 Col. L. Rev. 55 (1933). Jerome Hall, in his extensive and disapproving treatment of strict liability in crime, suggests that "public welfare offenses" can be traced back to 19th-century French positivists. Hall, General Principles of Criminal Law 333 (2d ed. 1960).

16. United States v. Dotterweich, 320 U.S. 277 (1943); United States v. Park, 421 U.S. 658 (1975).

17. Morissette v. United States, 342 U.S. 250 (1952).

18. 258 U.S. 250 (1922); see also United States v. Behrman, 258 U.S. 280 (1922).

19. Morissette, supra note 17, distinguished "public welfare offense" from codified "common law" offenses. Staples v. United States, 511 U.S. 600 (1994), turned back an effort to classify a prohibition on the possession of automatic weapons as a public welfare offense, based in part on the "potentially harsh" statutory maximum sentence of 10 years. See also United States v. X-Citement Video, Inc., 513 U.S. 64 (1994).

20. Partial mens rea, as to some but not all material elements of an offense, is discussed in Parker, The Economics of Mens Rea, 79 Va. L. Rev. 741 (1993).

21. Sutherland, The White Collar Criminal, 5 Am. Soc. Rev. 1 (1940). The locus classicus of the movement to criminalize corporate behavior is Sutherland's White Collar Crime (1949).

22. See Marshall Clinard, Illegal Corporate Behavior (1979: US DOJ); Clinard and Yeager, Corporate Crime (1980). In Clinard's data, 97.5 percent of these "corporate crime" cases were actually civil matters.

23. See Baker, "The Sociological Origins of 'White-Collar Crime,'" in Rosenzweig and Walsh, One Nation under Arrest ch. 14 (2010).

24. See Parker, Criminal Sentencing Policy, supra note 3. More detailed examinations of the same data set can be found in Cohen, Corporation Crime and Punishment: A Study of Social Harm and Sentencing Practice in the Federal Courts, 1984–87, 26 Am. Crim. L. Rev. 605 (1989), and Cohen, Ho, Jones, and Schleich, Organizations as Defendants in Federal Court: A Preliminary Analysis of Prosecutions, Convictions, and Sanctions, 1984–87, 10 Whittier L. Rev. 103 (1988).

25. Pub. L. 98-473, tit. II, ch. 2. For a more complete discussion of the Act's provisions affecting corporate sentencing, see Parker, Criminal Sentencing Policy, supra note 3.

26. Prior to the Reform Act, a probationary sentencing could be imposed only as an alternative, and so the permissible burden was limited functionally by the maximum penalty otherwise imposable, which in the case of corporations was the maximum fine, then set at more modest levels.

27. The final federal corporate guidelines in 1991 took the compliance model to an extreme, characterizing its theory (or lack thereof) as a "carrot and stick" approach. See Parker, The Current Corporate Sentencing Proposals: History and Critique, 3 Fed. Sent. Rep. 133 (1990); Parker, Rules Without . . . : Some Critical Reflections on the Federal Corporate Sentencing Guidelines, 71 Wash. U. L. Q. 397 (1993).

28. According to the most recent four years of data (2006–2009) from the federal Sentencing Commission's Sourcebook, supra note 3, Table 52, the average corporate fine ranged from $5.7 million (2008) to $17.3 million (2009). The four-year offender-weighted average in 2006–09 was $8.85 million, as compared with the 1984–87 average of $57,000. See Parker, Criminal Sentencing Policy, supra note 3. Even at the low end of the recent range, average corporate fines are now 100 times higher than in the mid-1980s, an increase of 10,000 percent.

29. Given the functionally unlimited threat point available to the federal prosecutors, it may not be necessary even to issue an indictment. As illustrated by the famous (or infamous) prosecution of the Arthur Andersen accounting firm, the mere issuance of an indictment—even if unfounded—can impair or destroy a firm's value. Though ultimately vindicated in the Supreme Court, Arthur Andersen LLP v. United States, 544 U.S. 696 (2005), the firm did not survive the litigation.

30. Fischel and Sykes, Corporate Crime, 25 J. Legal Stud. 319 (1996).

31. Khanna, Corporate Criminal Liability: What Purpose Does It Serve?, 109 Harv. L. Rev. 1477 (1996). See also Parker, Doctrine, supra note 1.

32. Empirical research shows a large but disparate effect for different types of offenses. Karpoff and Lott, The Reputation Penalties Firms Bear from Committing Fraud, 36 J. L. & Econ. 757 (1993); Karpoff, Lott, and Wehrly, The Reputational Penalties for Environmental Violations: Empirical Evidence, 48 J. L. & Econ. 653 (2005). However, a limited empirical test failed to find any significant difference in the reputational effects of criminal versus civil sanctions against firms. Block, Optimal Penalties, Criminal Law and the Control of Corporate Behavior, 71 B.U.L. Rev. 395 (1991).

33. See Friedman, In Defense of Corporate Criminal Liability, 23 Harv. J. L. & Pub. Policy 833 (2000).

34. Albert Alschuler has aptly characterized this theory as a revival of the primitive practice of "deodand"—destroying an inanimate object that was an instrument of harm. Alschuler, Two Ways to Think about the Punishment of Corporations, 46 Am. Crim. L. Rev. 1359 (2009).

35. The current version of this policy, now called the "Filip" memo, is codified in the United States Attorneys' Manual (USAM), at 9–28. Although the "Thompson" memorandum is the best known, the basic policy goes back at least to the Clinton administration, in which Eric Holder (the current attorney general) served as the deputy, and perhaps even earlier, as the basic policy was embraced in the previous administration and was followed by every subsequent administration of both political parties. Thus, this policy is not dependent on the political party in power; it reflects the institutional interests of the Justice Department.

36. United States v. Stein, 541 F.3d 130 (2d Cir. 2008).

37. In May 2010, the Justice Department issued a new document on "Additional Guidance on the Use of Monitors in Deferred Prosecution Agreements and Non-Prosecution Agreements with Corporations," Guidance 166, USAM Part 9, to supplement its previous statement (Guidance 163, id.).

38. The use of such agreements plausibly explains why actual indictments against corporations appear to have fallen in recent years, below their levels of the 1980s. See USSC Sourcebook, supra note 3, at Table 51. Much of the Department's "corporate crime" work is obscured from view. See Garrett, Structural Reform Prosecution, 93 Va. L. Rev. 853 (2007), for a description of some of the practices leading up to the KPMG case. In 2009, a congressional bill was introduced to create an entirely new system of regulation of deferred and non-prosecution agreements in

corporate cases. H.R. 1947, 111th Cong. (2009), but there has been no enactment to date.

39. See Block, supra note 32.

40. Even apologists for the rule of law in America, such as Ron Cass, concede that criminal prosecutors' broad discretion "pulls our practice away from the rule of law." Cass, The Rule of Law in America 29 (2001).

41. See Williams, Holcomb, Kovandzic, and Bullock, Policing for Profit: The Abuse of Civil Asset Forfeiture (2010), available at www.ij.org.

42. As a measure of the seriousness of the problem, the objection to overcriminalization transcends political ideologies. See Adam Liptak, Right and Left Join Forces on Criminal Justice, New York Times, November 23, 2009, at A1. See further Davis, Arbitrary Justice: The Power of the American Prosecutor (2007); Husak, Overcriminalization (2008); Lynch, In the Name of Justice (2009); Silverglate, Three Felonies a Day (2009); Rosenzweig and Walsh, One Nation under Arrest: How Crazy Laws, Rogue Prosecutors, and Activist Judges Threaten Your Liberty (2010). The critics also include several former attorneys general of the United States. See, e.g., Thornburgh, The Dangers of Over-criminalization and the Need for Real Reform: The Dilemma of Artificial Entities and Artificial Crimes, 44 Am. Crim. L. Rev. 1279 (2007); Meese, "Introduction," in One Nation under Arrest, supra.

43. Supra note 6.

44. According to Justice Department data, imprisonment rates trebled from 1982 to 2007, see "Key Facts" at www.ojp.usdoj.gov/bjs/. A longer-term series is given in United States Sentencing Commission, Fifteen Years of Guideline Sentencing 39, at Figure 2.1 (2004), which comments that "both federal and national imprisonment rates—the number of prisoners per 100,000 adult residents—remained fairly steady for fifty years before climbing to over four times their historic levels by 2002." Id. at 40. Consistent with other trends, the per capita growth in federal prisoners has been higher—a more than fivefold increase from 1980 through 2002. US DOJ, Sourcebook of Criminal Justice Statistics—2002, Table 6.23. As a result, the federal government has roughly doubled its share of the overall national total of prisoners.

45. The trend is shown by reference to underlying rates as estimated by the National Crime Victimization Survey (set out in note 46 infra), as opposed to the separate series of "Crimes Reported to the Police," which lags the underlying rates because of changes over time in reporting rates.

46. Here are the summary data, as of 2008, taken from the Justice Department's survey estimates (except homicide, which is taken from the Federal Bureau of Investigation's Uniform Crime Reports):

Violent crimes are offenses per 1,000 population; property crime rates are per 1,000 households. The underlying data can be found at www.ojp.usdoj.gov/bjs/.

47. Though not as dramatic as the rise in incarcerated populations (thus reflecting the parallel growth in sentence severity), annual federal prosecutions (excluding misdemeanor offenses prosecuted before federal magistrates) rose from 55,000

Table 8.1   Survey Crime Estimates

Offense	Peak Year	Peak Rate	2008 Rate	Cumulative Decline
Total Violent Crime	1981	52.3	19.0	−64%
Homicide	1980	0.102	0.054	−47%
Rape	1979	2.8	0.5	−82%
Robbery	1981	7.4	2.2	−70%
Aggravated Assault	1974	12.9	3.3	−74%
Simple Assault	1994	31.5	12.9	−59%
Total Property Crime	1975	553.6	134.7	−76%
Burglary	1974	111.8	26.3	−76%
Theft	1975	424.1	101.8	−76%
Vehicle Theft	1991	22.2	6.6	−70%

defendants in the mid-1980s (a figure largely unchanged since the 1950s) to 99,000 defendants in 2010, which is an increase of about 40 percent per capita. Administrative Office of the U.S. Courts, Annual Report of the Director, 2010 Table D (defendants); Economic Report of the President, Table B-34 (on population) (February 2011).

48. See Parker, "The Blunt Instrument," in Debating Corporate Crime (Lofquist, Cohen and Rabe, eds., 1997).

49. According to the data compiled by Walmsley, supra note 6, in absolute terms China could exceed the U.S. if one counts some 850,000 people held in "administrative detention" as opposed to criminal imprisonment. But even so, China's total of 2.4 million (in a population of 1.3 billion) would exceed the U.S. total of 2.3 million by only 100,000, and the necessity of making that comparison is embarrassing to American values.

50. See Barkow and George, Prosecuting Political Defendants, 44 Ga. L. Rev. 953 (2010).

51. I refer here to the controversy surrounding the dismissal of nine U.S. attorneys in late 2006, by President George W. Bush, with produced congressional hearings and other investigations. See USDOJ, An Investigation into the Removal of Nine U.S. Attorneys in 2006 (September 2008), available at www.usdoj.gov.

52. For a development of these points, see Davis (cited in note 42 supra).

53. USAM, § 9-27.

54. In recent years, more than 90 percent of the convictions obtained in federal courts were by guilty plea. Administrative Office Annual Report, supra note 47, Table D-4. Virtually all of these pleas are the result of "plea bargains"—which is

another aspect of discretionary prosecutorial practices that the courts will not scrutinize. Under Rule 11 of the Federal Rules of Criminal Procedure, the courts may accept or reject a plea, but they generally will not evaluate the bargain.

55. For a useful discussion of how redundant criminalization exacerbates the problem of prosecutorial discretion, see Brown, Prosecutors and Overcriminalization: Thoughts on Political Dynamics and a Doctrinal Response, 6 Ohio St. J. Crim. L. 454 (2009).

56. In the federal system, this result is accomplished by an amorphous concept of "relevant conduct" to be considered at sentencing (see USSG § 1B1.3) and facilitated by Supreme Court decisions allowing the consideration of both uncharged conduct and conduct for which the defendant actually was acquitted. See United States v. Watts, 519 U.S. 148 (1997); Witte v. United States, 515 U.S. 389 (1995).

57. Milestones in this line of cases include United States v. R. Enterprises, 498 U.S. 292 (1991), in which the Supreme Court declined to review the basis for an ongoing grand jury investigation, and held that grand jury subpoenas need not even be shown to seek relevant material; and United States v. Williams, 504 U.S. 36 (1992), where the Court struck down a lower court's effort to scrutinize a prosecutor's alleged suppression from the grand jury of evidence exonerating the target—conceded by all to be unethical—on the view that the grand jury had an "operational separateness from its constituting court." Id. at 49.

58. The only two notable examples in recent years are the Hyde Amendment, 18 U.S.C. § 3006A, which provides a fee-shifting remedy for acquitted federal defendants who can show that their prosecution was "vexatious, frivolous, or in bad faith," and the McDade Amendment, 28 U.S.C. § 530B, which purports to make state ethical rules binding on federal prosecutors. Neither has produced any substantial result. According to a recent series published by USA Today, federal courts have expressly found prosecutorial misconduct in 201 cases since the Hyde Amendment was enacted in 1997, but only 13 fee awards have been made. USA Today, "Misconduct at the Justice Department" (September 2010–January 2011), at www.usatoday.com. Even the few awards given are sometimes reversed on appeal, under an extremely grudging interpretation of the statute. See, e.g., United States v. Capener, 608 F.3d 392 (9th Cir. 2010), cert. denied, 131 S.Ct. 997 (2011); United States v. Knott, 256 F.3d 20 (1st Cir. 2001), cert. denied, 534 U.S. 1127 (2002). The Supreme Court has yet to grant review of a Hyde Amendment case.

59. See Walsh and Joslyn, Without Intent: How Congress Is Eroding the Criminal Intent Requirement in Federal Law (Heritage/NACDL: 2010), available at www.nacdl.org and www.heritage.org.

PART 9:

HOW NATIONS GROW (OR DON'T)

The Legacy of Progressive Thought

DECLINE, NOT DEATH, BY A THOUSAND CUTS

RICHARD A. EPSTEIN

y task in this essay is to sum up the causes of the American Illness, which by all accounts seems to engulf our nation today.[1] Exactly when this illness began is a matter of genuine controversy. It seems clear that American power and prestige peaked at the end of World War II, only to follow an erratic downward course since that time. It is difficult to identify any single cause that accounts for that long-term trend in either domestic or foreign affairs. It is equally difficult to identify any one person who bears unique responsibility for the current condition. But if I had to name one constellation of ideas that has exerted disproportionate influence, it would be the stunning persistence in the United States of Progressive thought, which more than any other intellectual movement has driven the overall expansion in the size of government for the past 100 years.

Progressive ideals have been embraced at both the state and national levels, not only through taxation, but (equally critically) through direct regulation, which in turn has spawned a huge growth in follow-on litigation that has multiplied a thousand-fold in recent years. Even in the early Reagan years, no enduring reversal of that trend took place: The major government achievement of the period was to slow the rate of growth, not to shrink the size of government at the federal level. Changing the sign on the second derivative does not a political transformation make.

Whatever the precise path, all pretense of current optimism has faded: The answer to the question, "do you think your children will have a better life than you have today?" generally receives a negative answer,[2] and for good reason. No longer is it just a matter of slower rates of growth, which has marked the United States since the official end of the recession in the summer of 2009, and which continues unabated through the "jobless recovery" in the winter of 2011. The feeble increases in GDP during this last recovery have been insufficient to offset normal population growth, leading inexorably to the recent two-year decline in average family income.[3] The explanation for this negative trend does not rest in technological changes, for that pool of knowledge continues to grow. Rather, the explanation has to lie in some cross between our failed political philosophy and our broken political institutions. The decline is not only at the national level, either, for the expression "failed states" is routinely applied to California, Illinois, and New York, along with other states that are now overrun by public debt. The financial position of the federal government has declined as well, with higher taxation, greater public expenditure, larger deficits, and chronic high levels of unemployment, which just dipped below 10 percent, in part because of all the discouraged workers who have, at least in the short run, exited the market.

The stark economic system has exacted a steep political toll. In particular, the Congress of the United States is widely held in low repute, with approval rates at under 20 percent. The recent midterm elections of 2010 marked a clear electoral repudiation of the current Democratic policies in Congress. The Republicans made major gains in governorships and state legislatures as well. Ironically, however, it would be a mistake to read into these electoral changes any stunning endorsement of the Republican Party, which when in power showed a rare ability to increase deficits and expand the size of government policy for its favored clientele. Out of office, the Republican Party's performance has been better, especially in resisting health care and financial reform. Still, the verdict is out for the time being. The current uncertainty and want of confidence in public institutions may itself count as one of the obstacles to a vigorous economic recovery. It is that much more difficult to hire and invest if the government position on such key matters as taxation, regulation, and liability are left unclarified. The two questions are: What has brought this impasse about, and what should be done to reverse course before it is too late?

In dealing with these questions, I do not think that any single variable explains the ever more rapid decline in American institutions and practices, which is why the title of this Jeremiad is decline—not death—by a thousand cuts. It appears that the decline has taken place on several fronts simultaneously. To make matters worse, I do not think that there is any novel philosophical movement that has driven this decline. It is not as though Marxism or socialism is all the rage, even in the outer precincts of the Democratic Party. Rather, as noted earlier, the most likely culprit of the immediate dislocations is the striking return in the Obama administration to the Progressive ideals of the New Deal, which did so much harm at the moment of its initial triumph. In some sense, the President has not taken the lead on this issue, for he has been pummeled by the left wing of the Democratic Party, which would prefer to nationalize health care through a single-payer plan, and might possibly also wish to nationalize the banks. In and of itself, a Progressive cast on matters is not alone sufficient to push the nation backward. But it is more than the label that matters. The older philosophy is now being pressed into the service of newer and ever more ambitious programs, whose combined impact can only be to deaden the economy in a thousand ways both large and small.

In this essay, I shall examine several arenas in which I think that these Progressive forces are at work in order to explain why the long-term national prognosis continues to be negative. In sorting out these causes, I do not think that the driving force has come through private litigation, although the expansion of tort liability and class actions is surely an important part of the overall story that needs a proper interpretation. Rather, I think that the chief source of difficulty in the United States lies in the expansion of direct regulation through the administrative state at the national, state, and local levels.

In commenting on these issues, some features of the American experience are distinctive; others we share with the European Union, which has its own serious economic difficulties. This article is not, however, a study of comparative institutional failures, so my purpose is not to show that we do something better or worse than it is done in Europe—or, for that matter, Asia. It is enough simply to show that the United States has done badly in many critical areas relative to any sensible standard of political prudence.

In Part I of this essay, I identify the key features of the Progressive cast of mind—strong faith in the combination of public deliberation and administrative expertise—that has driven the recent government policies. In Part II, I argue that Progressive policies have led to an unwise increase in taxes and stimulus spending when the appropriate response is a consistent and stable regime of low taxes with no special stimulus program at all. In Part III, I extend the analysis to cover free trade in the international arena. Part IV then turns to examine the affliction of permititis that affects so much of our regulatory culture at the federal and state levels. Part V takes a look at the recent developments with the Obama health care legislation. Part VI turns to the looming crisis in the entitlement world. Part VII examines employment relations in both the public and private sectors. Part VIII then rounds out the discussion by showing how the Progressive spirit has taken tort litigation far beyond its justifiable configuration. A brief conclusion follows.

The clear message is that not one of these major systems works well today, and there is little likelihood of any immediate fix tomorrow. The normative critique thus leads to a pessimistic overall assessment.

I. The Progressive Mindset

The most distinctive feature of the successful Obama 2008 presidential campaign was his uncommon ability to reignite the nation's connection to older Progressive and New Deal traditions. Obama did not run, for example, on the civil rights and abortion issues that dominated American politics during the 1960s. Rather, he returned to the themes of economic security and social justice that defined the Progressive and New Deal eras. The legislative and administrative actions of these earlier periods worked on well-articulated political philosophies that mounted a frontal assault on the once regnant classical liberal philosophy, which rested on a tradition of strong property rights, open markets, and divided and limited government powers at both the state and national levels. To the Progressives, any effort to bring America into the twentieth century started with their painful recognition that the classical liberal principles of the founding period, which might have worked in a nation of farmers and shopkeepers, could not keep up with the dynamic expansion of the industrialized age—an age in which isolated workers and consumers were pitted against large corporate interests.

This distrust of private ordering led to an intellectual program that lauded the rise of the administrative state, backed by an expanded set of private actions, as the only effective means to curtail the operation of unfettered market forces. The grubby self-interest of the marketplace was to be displaced by a new regime that depended, for its first line of defense, on high-level public deliberation coupled with disinterested administrative expertise. Uncontroversially, the expanded set of duties created a new set of tort actions against parties whose violation of their duties created harms to others. The truly innovative rule, however, was the decision that compliance with regulatory standards was not a defense against private rights of actions. Rather, the dominant view became one in which regulation set minimum standards, which juries could reject or accept as they saw fit with little or no judicial oversight. Two bites of the apple thus became standard operating procedure.

Consistent with the Progressive mindset, this vast expansion of regulatory and private remedies was undertaken on the view that the more legal sanctions the better. This rush to greater government control over the economy downplayed the risks of faction and confiscation, and belittled the role of the traditional institutional safeguards—separation of powers, checks and balances, constitutional protection of economic interests—that had been put in place to blunt their force.

In advancing their agenda of expanded administrative and judicial oversight, the Progressives never thought to distinguish between the size of firms and the structure of the market in which they operated. The classical liberal positions that were displaced did accept the case for the regulation of natural monopolies in such key industries as communications, electricity, and power, and strove mightily to devise a sensible set of rules, of no little sophistication, to implement that program in practice. In contrast, the Progressive critique of big business did not limit regulation to natural monopolies, but extended it to all large firms, even those that operated in a competitive market.

The Progressives were often upset about the decline in dickered transactions that led both parties to a contract price, but they were never able to grasp that the low transaction costs from standardized transactions worked for the benefit of consumers and producers alike by increasing the flow of voluntary transactions. Similarly, they looked askance at explicit contractual provisions that limited consequential damages, thinking that these were a way to escape responsibility for defective products; when, properly understood, their role was to provide incentives for downstream care to avoid serious product losses.

Taken as a whole the contrast could not have been more vivid. The traditional view of markets was aimed at increasing the number of transactions for any given level of transaction costs. The Progressive view took comfort in the high level of transaction costs, which slowed down the volume of market transactions, as if there were some patriotic duty to wait in supermarket check-out lines.

This Progressive philosophy of intervention expressed itself in a wide range of markets, many of which are under siege today. Here are some of the most notable examples: free trade, drug regulation, land use regulation, mortgage and payment markets, health care, labor markets, and of course private rights of action under various tort or consumer protection theories. In addition, the Progressive's aversion to competitive markets led to their insistence on a broad class of positive rights against the state, which led to the adoption of the capstone programs of Social Security and, a long generation later, Medicare and Medicaid. These social demands pushed Progressives to champion the progressive tax first as a means to pay for the positive rights that they have championed, and next to ensure the redistribution of wealth thought desirable on egalitarian grounds. Their implicit assumption was that high tax rates would have at most a modest effect on productivity, so that the achievement of their distributional goals would generate little collateral damage. The extended "Socialist Calculation" debate of the late 1930s and 1940s is the most conspicuous manifestation of this trend, as many prominent economists thought they could craft a system of taxes and subsidies that combined optimal social production with an ideal social distribution of wealth. All problems of information and incentives were regarded as soluble.[4]

Finally, as night follows day, the effort to create powerful government monopolies at home could not take place in an environment in which free competition from overseas was encouraged or even tolerated. Hence the Progressive program featured an acceptance of the need to restrict trade and immigration from foreign nations, both of which compromised the ability of organized labor to maintain its monopoly position in domestic labor markets. At all stages of this program, a larger administrative state was needed to implement every aspect of this new political structure, which in turn could not function well if the perceived limitations on government authority crimped the administrative state.

The thesis of this article is, quite simply, that these various elements supply abundant grist to be ground into an ever-insistent expansion of government power over all aspects of the economy. Put otherwise, the key constitutional and institutional elements for a major level of government expansion were all in place as early as 1940. Most of these elements survived (relatively well) the short-term reaction to the New Deal in the immediate aftermath of World War II—which featured the passage of both the Administrative Procedure Act[5] and the Taft-Hartley Act[6]—before the Democrats reasserted control of the Congress in the 1948 elections. The Progressive philosophy then reasserted itself during the 1960s, leading to an additional set of reforms with long-term consequences.

The first of such lasting reforms was the entrenchment of public unions, dating to the early 1960s, at both national and state levels. This entrenchment was started by an executive order[7] of President John F. Kennedy that authorized collective bargaining for federal employees through an unenacted expansion of the reach of labor laws, including multiple extensions of the Fair Labor Standard Act[8] and the adoption of an extensive body of employment discrimination laws, which the unions of an earlier age, with their unenviable record of racial discrimination, had stoutly resisted.[9] The second was the rise of the environmental movement, which marks, among other things, an expansion of the systems of land use regulation used for

zoning purposes. The third was the creation of the large entitlement programs of Medicare and Medicaid to complement Social Security. In addition, the Nixon years featured the adoption of extensive programs for
environmental protection,[10] endangered species,[11] health and safety,[12] and
pensions and retirement.[13] To be sure, there were pockets of deregulation
in the airline[14] and banking industries, but on balance the persistent trend
has been toward more, rather than less, regulation.

I do not regard any of these major innovations as a philosophical departure from the earlier Progressive agenda. They are better understood as
a delayed implementation of business-left-unfinished when the political
tides turned sharply against the Democrats in 1938. These issues quickly
came back to life after the 1964 Democratic rout of the Republicans under
Barry Goldwater. In the end, the complete Progressive agenda has these key
features: high levels of marginal taxation, major restrictions on international
trade, extensive administrative regulation of private banks and businesses,
a large menu of positive rights, strong labor laws, and vigorous use of private rights of action to backstop this wide range of regulatory programs.

What is the best way to understand the periodic resurgence of the
Progressive agenda? My take on this critical issue is relatively simple. The
New Deal settlement was marked by two related elements. The first of
these was the constitutional blessing afforded in the post-1937 period to
virtually all of these legislative arenas. The second was the extent to which
the Congress and the states have, over time, taken advantage of the blank
check that was signed over to them by the judiciary.

There were three key elements to the constitutional permission slip
granted to legislators. The first was the decision of the Supreme Court to
solidify the place of independent administrative agencies.[15]

The second was the decision of the post-1937 Supreme Court to give a
broad reading to the Commerce Clause, which essentially allowed the federal government constitutional free rein to introduce whatever program
of general economic regulation that it found appropriate.[16] The federal
government could, by virtue of its dominant position, block any state law
program that was inconsistent with the federal government's objectives.
Indeed, with the expansion of the federal commerce power, the question of

federal preemption assumed greater urgency: Did the federal government mean to block state efforts, or was it quite happy to have a dual set of controls at both levels, including private lawsuits, which became a staple of the Supreme Court with the expansion of both tort law and the scope of federal power in the years after the Great Society? The recognition of a "presumption against preemption" pointed the way to the exercise of concurrent spheres of regulation over a wide range of activities,[17] where the more stringent was likely to prevail unless Congress clearly stated the opposite. The issue was of especial importance in connection with the possible federal preemption of suits involving state laws, which have been read narrowly except in those cases where the federal law contains explicit prohibitions on private rights of action. Although I shall not explore this development here, the bottom line is this: A deep fear that industry has captured regulatory authorities has unleashed a torrent of private lawsuits in industries like the Food and Drug Administration (FDA). But the interventions work in precisely the wrong direction. The paramount need is to find ways to prod the FDA to move forward on new drugs and new medical devices, lest innovation and development move overseas.[18] Tort litigation only reduces the incentive to innovate further, a point that is missed in the recent implied preemption cases.[19]

The third piece of this constitutional settlement was that claims of property rights[20] and economic liberties had relatively little traction outside the area of rate regulation, which was subject to more stringent rules.[21] In the case of property rates, strong property protection was offered only to the right to possess land and exclude others—clearly not a trivial safeguard. But the ability to use, develop, or alienate property was subject to extensive restrictions, blocking easy access to courts and forcing the adoption of a narrow vision of property rights. The result was that it took longer to get to court than ever before, and once the landowner got there the prospects of relief were in general slim.[22] With respect to economic liberties, an aggressive version of the rational basis test (which imposed a burden on those objecting to a regulation to show that it lacked a rational basis) made it difficult to attack on constitutional grounds widespread government regulation of all manner of voluntary transactions.

In one sense, therefore, all the necessary pieces for an expanded state were in place by the end of the New Deal. But however necessary constitutional approval is to the expansion of state power, it is surely not a sufficient condition to presage some persistent level of economic decline.

Of greater importance is the extent to which the Congress and the states have, over time, taken advantage of the powers given to them by the judiciary. On that score, it is possible to see where the generational shifts have taken place. There is no question that the interventions of the latter New Deal have exerted, and continue to exert, a powerful influence on the current state of affairs in this country. Even if the various spending and public works of the New Deal withered and died with the onset of World War II, the legislative agenda dealing with key matters of labor, agriculture, banking, securities, and social security are still very much with the U.S. today, in the form of the National Labor Relations Act, the Fair Labor Standards Act, and the Agricultural Adjustment Acts.[23] These trends jumped into high gear, with the aggressive promotion of a legislative agenda that seeks in many ways to exploit the full range of constitutional powers, many of which had not been pushed to their extremes in earlier times. The election of a Republican House of Representatives in 2010 reverses this calculation to a degree, and the current legislative expansion might perhaps proceed at a slower rate or even be cut back, if only through a slowdown in the appropriations needed to secure the timely implementation of the two centerpieces of the first two years of the Obama administration: the Dodd-Frank Wall Street Reform and Consumer Protection Act of 2010[24] on financial reform and the Patient Protection and Affordable Health Care Act,[25] or ObamaCare. But, in and of itself, this will not be sufficient to undo the status quo, which has in it the potential for many further general dislocations.

In evaluating the burden of the excessive regulation, liability, or taxation—I treat all three as close substitutes for one another[26]—the relevant comparison is with the outcomes that would be dictated by a pure competitive system. In making this claim, I am well aware that there are many complex industries in which competitive solutions are just not possible. With respect to these, the test of legislative error has to be modified in order to measure the more elusive gap between the current and ideal

forms of regulation—which became enormous under the 1996 Telecommunications Act,[27] as construed by the Federal Communications Commission (FCC). But in this grand project the details do not matter. What
matters is the extent of the deviation from competitive solutions. In dealing with these issues, moreover, I think that it is important to consider not
only the initiatives that have been enacted into law, but also those that have
been high on the agenda, for even though these initiatives may have failed,
the mere fact that they have been proposed skews the universe of legislative opportunities in ways that lead to the prospect of more regulation.

Let us now look at particular cases to see how matters are moving.

II. Taxation and Stimulation

One of the key questions every society has to face is how to allocate
scarce resources between public and private expenditures. On that question, the presumption should be set in favor of the private control of investment capital, on the ground that owners of the capital will have the strongest
incentives to seek the highest rate of return commensurate with the risk
they bear. Capital markets can thus segment in a variety of ways into risky
ventures and stable firms. For both types of groups, specialists can emerge
on both the equity and debt side of the market, and into equity and debt on
the other, with ever higher degrees of specialization. With the proper pricing of these various instruments, investors can then assemble portfolios
that fit their own personal circumstances. The decentralized system of
control ensures that competitive markets can operate at every stage of the
process.

Of course, this system is not self-sustaining. We would all agree that
governments have some claim on scarce resources. The tasks of ensuring
social order to protect against violence, to secure property rights, and to
enforce contracts require a monopoly of force that ideally should be in the
hands of a government subject to constitutional constraints on the way in
which it uses its power. In addition, the creation of infrastructure, which
often requires the use of an eminent domain power to overcome hold-
out problems, also requires a measure of government control, which in
part may be contracted out to private operators under various business

arrangements. For certain essential facilities—that is, those with monopoly power—one might need some negotiated limitation on rates. Yet even here, the strong preference should be for private ownership of regulated firms, not for government operation of these facilities.

The underlying issue remains what it has always been, in both good times and bad: What is the sensible role for major government involvement? The ideal mix of public and private roles should in general incline toward low (and broad) taxation coupled with high levels of private investment. One key question is whether this formula works only in times of relative prosperity, or whether it works in bad times as well. In my view, the clear answer to that question is: Stick to your guns. Keep this formula in place regardless of the state of the macroeconomic world. The appropriate way to even out the ups and downs is for private individuals to equalize their wealth across different periods by some combination of two strategies: If cash-poor, borrow in bad times and repay debts in good times; if cash-rich, save during good times in order to cover losses in bad times. Most people and most firms adopt some combination of both strategies, individually and in families.[28] It is yet another version of Milton Friedman's permanent income hypothesis, by which ordinary individuals, ever-cognizant of their personal diminishing marginal utility of wealth, seek to equalize their income across all time periods and all states of the world.

So long as these private devices of income equalization are in place, the worst possible strategy is one that combines high taxation with public investments that are not directly tied to the maintenance of social order and the creation of needed public infrastructure. The decision to keep taxes high necessarily takes money out of private hands, thereby forcing the government to make its own investment choices so that capital constriction does not destroy the economy. The benefits of decentralized decision-making are lost, and the dangers of perverse political intervention become rife, with the government subsidizing just about every silly investment under the sun as "needed infrastructure improvements" or "green friendly" investment. As the huge influx of cash reduces the level of needed quality control on projects that can be exerted from the center, the line between essential facilities and political pork becomes ever harder to police.

The net effect is that job creation will suffer as capital is diverted from sensible to wasteful projects. It is therefore no surprise that the constant succession of stimulus programs done at a grand level has done nothing to improve overall social output on the one hand, or to increase employment levels on the other hand. The constant delusion that the stimulus program will spark consumption that will then create jobs overestimates the ability of central planners to predict how ordinary individuals will respond to infusions of cash. The result is an overall decline in the return from these investments, which is one big reason why the economy is in its current rut and is likely to remain there for the foreseeable future.

The low tax/high private investment strategy thus dominates any stimulus program. The emphasis on higher levels of taxation, of course, is tied not only to the stimulus but also to questions of income distribution. As noted in connection with the permanent income hypothesis, the diminishing marginal utility of wealth surely applies to the way in which people allocate their wealth over time. It also could be used as a basis to allocate wealth across individuals at any given time, which is the heart of the case for the progressive income tax, under which marginal dollars are taxed at ever higher rates. The real hardships at the bottom of the income distribution are hard to gainsay, especially in hard times with jobless recoveries. But it hardly follows that the direct remedy of progressive taxation is the appropriate way to respond to the problem.

The problems with progressive taxation are manifold, starting with how to determine the optimal level of progressivity. Even if we assumed (which is decidedly not the case today) that all tax expenditures were directed toward the creation and maintenance of public goods—social order and infrastructure—the following question still remains: How progressive ought the tax to be in order to achieve the optimal rate of income distribution?

On the one side, low levels of progression generate relatively little income shifting, so that they are not worth the administrative costs that are needed to put them into place. On the other side, high levels of progressivity run the real risk of dulling incentives to produce, which in turn will shrink the overall size of the social pie. However, just because we can identify the two extremes does not mean that it is possible to identify abstractly, or implement politically, some ideal progressive tax that falls between these two extremes. On this issue, the public choice dynamics—"tax the rich!"—run the real risk that the largest burdens will fall on the most productive members of society. The result is a heavily skewed system where a tiny fraction of the population pays the lion's share of the income tax, which it then seeks to minimize by a set of socially counterproductive ways to shield its wealth from taxation. Right now the approximate numbers are that about 20 percent of the income is concentrated in the top 1 percent of the population, which in turn pays 40 percent of the total tax burden. The skewed nature of that distribution indicates that the wealthy are not able to resist the popular pressures for massive income redistribution, which in turn promises a reduction in the overall level of wealth creation going forward.

The sober lesson here is that no form of income redistribution can off-set the unambiguous gains from growth. The miracles of compound interest are much with us, and a 1 percent increase in growth rates would in the course of a generation lead to nearly a doubling of income.

The pressures in favor of government redistribution would soften no-ticeably if people paid more attention to the vast gulf between patterns of income and consumption. What happens to the 20 percent of the wealth that 1 percent of the population earns? Expanding—some would say gorg-ing—on self-indulgent individual consumption is one part of the picture, but it is by no means the only part that matters. First, the highest earners also tend to be the highest savers, and hence the highest investors in new firms and businesses that can create jobs for others. Regimes of high taxa-tion leave less to invest at the outset, and promise a lower rate of return on investment down the road. The net effect is to encourage a shift toward the conspicuous consumption that it is so easy to decry. Second, high income earners do more than just consume or invest. They also engage in major efforts of redistribution of their own, both to their families and through various charitable activities. The reduced rate of return also dampens these activities, which can easily sap the support that major cultural insti-tutions receive from the largest of donors.

In light of these general considerations, the ideal system would feature a flat tax imposed on a broad base of taxpayers. That system produces a level of rate stabilization that can eliminate the constant class struggles. It simplifies the overall administration of the tax system by removing all incentive to shift income over time and across individuals in order to reduce the tax burden. It makes it easier to calculate the return on investments, which are calculated to increase the size of the social pie. It could be used to replace the more regressive sales tax. It places no artificial dollar limitation on the amount of cash that can be allocated to the public sphere. It cannot limit the level of subsidies that can be funneled through public transfer programs. But it does place one important constraint on the perils of factional politics: So long as everyone knows that they cannot escape their share of those payments, it reduces the temptation of people with low incomes to petition adamantly for high levels of taxation that could increase, in one form or another, the transfer payments to themselves. Thus, if this requirement were put in place in the health care program, the desire to subsidize those with preexisting conditions would have to be funded through general payroll or income taxes and not the individual mandate to purchase health care, which lies at the heart of the constitutional challenges to the Affordable Care Act.[29] The solution will necessarily be imperfect unless independent constraints can be imposed on the spending side, a major challenge of institutional change that I cannot address here.

In light of these considerations, the current unstable system of taxation has to count as a serious cause of the American Illness. Far from creating a stable economic basis over time, the tendency to change short-term tax policies produces an unhappy succession of peaks and valleys that only increase overall levels of social insecurity. Just that result was all too evident from the cash-for-clunkers program that produced an orgy of new car purchases (and old car destruction) followed by a real trough in the industry. The government subsidies for new home purchases had the same result: a short-term burst followed by a long-term decline in the sales of new and existing homes that persists to this day. Stability of expectations is the chief task of any sound tax or regulatory regime, which these programs violated.

The same can be said of the constant tax pressures to impose heavy estate taxes and high levels of progressivity on income tax, which now are determined by short-term political compromises with a two-year time fuse.[30] Whatever income is raised by the estate tax is likely dissipated by the constant efforts to arrange private transactions in ways that minimize its impact—even at the cost of the overall efficiency in the operation of small businesses. The strong effort to impose tax increases on the most productive citizens will just replicate the pattern of short bursts of public revenues coupled with long-term decline, which reduces state revenues even if taxation rates are increased.

One of the key tasks of any sound system of taxation is to develop a stable platform that eases the uncertainty in the general marketplace. The stimulus and tax programs that have luxuriated in the past several years, and which can be laid at the feet of the Progressive mindset, count as a major cause of the American Illness. It remains to be seen whether steps will be taken—and if so which ones—to remove the gimmicks, flatten the tax rates, and cut out the stimulus. Such changes are long overdue.

III. International Free Trade

One of the low points of the Great Depression was the passage of the Smoot-Hawley Tariff, which placed a major dent in international trade relationships and hampered economic recovery worldwide during the 1930s. It is, of course, difficult to calculate the exact economic losses of this legislation, but there is no mistake about the negative social consequences it produced, as all tariff regulation adds high administrative costs while simultaneously reducing the gains from trade.

International markets should be informed by the ideal of fostering competition across national borders, just as domestic markets should seek to foster competition within borders. Moreover, the argument for free trade is stronger now than it was during the Great Depression. The effectiveness of competitive markets depends in large measure upon their geographical reach. As communications and transportation become more inexpensive, it makes ever more sense for firms to mount global campaigns to find the most efficient trading partners in order to exploit new possibilities for gains from trade.

In these circumstances, government should seek to facilitate seamless connections between domestic and foreign firms. This objective does not require that all foreign firms be exempt from domestic regulation, a practice that would give them an unfair trading advantage over domestic firms producing the same product. Thus labeling and purity requirements for foreign goods imported into the United States should be the same as the restrictions that are imposed on domestic firms, and it is perfectly appropriate for the FDA to exercise powers to stop adulterated or misbranded goods at the border. The goal, then, is a nondiscrimination rule that does not distinguish between foreign and domestic firms, and that allows firms that are incorporated in different jurisdictions to compete on equal terms.

The nondiscrimination rule applies only to the regulation of the products and services themselves, not to the inputs used to make them. Thus, if the host nation has a minimum wage law for its workers, it should not restrict imports from nations that do not follow the same policy. (Which, of course, is not to say that one should be indifferent to egregious rights abuses, such as the use of slave labor.) Similarly, the decision of poorer nations to accept less attractive environmental conditions is generally a matter of local concern only. Those conditions will improve without foreign intervention, once the income levels rise, which they will do more rapidly when trade barriers are removed. The simple proposition is that, in any well-governed society, people desire at the margin to achieve the highest possible living standard by a correct apportionment of wealth between public and private amenities, so that the last dollar spent on each yields the same social return as the last spent on the other.

To be sure, many nations do not follow nondiscrimination policies consistently—including the United States. But it is a mug's game to apply unilateral trade sanctions in the fruitless effort to improve the domestic policies of foreign nations, who will most likely ignore our entreaties and shift their business elsewhere. Once these collateral matters are put to one side, what matters in the end is only the condition of the goods and services rendered, not the mode of their production. Indeed, the entire purpose of the free trade regime is to use a constant and nonselective external check to limit the ability of any group, be it management or labor, to gain a monopoly footing in its own land.

Once this logic of free trade is accepted, then the loss of jobs or customers through foreign competition in any particular instance does not justify any form of legal protection any more than it does when all domestic competition displaces other domestic workers. It is therefore a large mistake to adopt worker retraining programs that drain public resources by subsidizing skills that may well not be marketable in their own right. The better approach by far is to husband the human and physical resources from failed firms, so that they can be recombined into new packages that could prove more successful in domestic and foreign competition. Any effort to forestall this mechanism, whether by trade barriers or currency manipulation, is therefore counterproductive. It is, for example, not feasible to enter into international trade negotiations on the static assumption that any gain in jobs overseas translates into a loss of jobs in the United States. To do so, as President Obama did in his failed negotiations with South Korea in late 2010, is to engage in false advertising by making it appear as though all international negotiations should be treated as zero-sum games in which the successes of the United States in creating jobs is exactly offset by the loss of jobs in other nations. "Exporting Our Way to Stability"[31] sends exactly the wrong message because it diverts everyone's attention from the main focus, mutual gains through trade, which necessarily depends on a willingness to import as well as export. The eventual approval of the South Korea trade pact in October 2011 was a welcome, if tardy, step in the right direction.[32]

By the same token, it is unwise to seek to weaken one's own currency in order to spur exports abroad. The strategy can never have any long-term success, even if other nations do nothing to counter the trend. The ability to create competitive exports depends on the ability to secure inputs from firms located all around the world. Let those inputs become more expensive because of a cheap monetary policy and the price of domestic goods will increase in both the domestic and the export markets, reflecting the high component prices. And if the decision is made to shift to a cheaper source for American components, the social loss will manifest itself in a decline in product quality, not in increased price.

Against this backdrop, it is possible to see why the failure in recent trade policy has done much to contribute to the current national malaise. One of the more misguided initiatives in the early Obama years was the Buy American initiative,[33] which was imposed in early 2009 and had the nasty effect of adding paperwork at home in order to achieve a less efficient product mix for domestic and foreign markets. That initial mistake has been compounded by the general reluctance of the Obama administration to expand its bilateral trade agreements with Panama and South Korea, in response to opposition from environmental and labor groups. It is surely aggravated by the step-up in efforts to use antidumping laws to keep out subsidized goods from other nations. The revival of American protectionism stands in sharp contrast to the way in which America's competitors embrace free trade agreements and illustrates how, in this respect, our economic malaise is fairly labeled the American Illness.

The real losers from American protectionism are the American taxpayers who have to bear the brunt of these efforts. The dislocation in the position of some domestic U.S. firms is real, but equally real are the gains the American importers can reap from cheaper imports under free trade. In the end, the case for free trade shows once again the wisdom of the late Robert Nozick in his insistence that "patterned principles"—whereby individuals seek to find the justice in certain institutional arrangements by making some assessment of the end-state distribution of goods, services, and income—are always a delusion.[34]

In sum, the economic logic of voluntary exchange is not limited to national borders. The purpose of international agreements is to allow the same principle of comparative advantage that works at home to work in a larger arena. Any efforts to turn the clock back on free trade, in the name of a Progressive ideology, will, in the aggregate, have negative consequences on the efficiency of domestic markets in a way that will contribute to overall domestic decline.

IV. Permititis

Turning to more national-level issues, one feature of the American decline that bears notice is the rise of the permit culture. I coined the term "permititis" in connection with the actions of the Food and Drug Administration, which has institutionalized an exceedingly risk-averse attitude about allowing new drugs and medical devices onto the market.[35] Alas, that regulatory disease is by no means confined to this one federal agency, but has become a staple feature of federal regulation with respect to all dangerous substances—fungicides and toxins—and a wide range of land regulation programs dealing with both environmental and urban growth issues. Although the application varies across subject areas, the consistent pattern represents a misunderstanding as to the proper way of dealing with uncertainty in both public and private disputes.

In all legal settings, the law has to make key decisions on the incidence and sweep of regulation. First, it has to decide whether to stop actions that might cause harm before they begin, or to allow the harm to take place, after which it punishes the activities. Second, it has to decide whether these control functions are best administered by public or private actors.

In dealing with these questions, the first issue is what counts as a harm against which government action should be applied. That question received a relatively narrow definition in traditional legal analysis. The harms that were redressible in the tort system were confined to physical injuries to person and property, and to interference with advantageous relationships by the use of force or fraud. Outside this calculation lie various kinds of social harms, such as the want of green space in the middle of a community or the public offense that one group of individuals takes against the activities undertaken by others. The narrower definition of harms thus limited the potential scope of government action to activities in which the private harm of the plaintiff corresponded with some overall social loss.

Side by side with this definition was the realization that any determination on when and how to use force had to contend with two forms of error. The first involves intervention that is too late, so that the harm actually occurs. The second involves the intervention that is too soon, so that gainful activities that would have otherwise taken place were not allowed to go forward. The traditional private law solution was to call for a mix of injunctive remedies before the fact and damages after the fact, with the balance tilted against early intervention by injunction.

The principle behind this rule is that major financial actors would take appropriate steps to avoid harm, making it appropriate to let them seek independent gain without premature legal interference. These parties would still be pinioned in place by the realization that an injunction before harm could be imposed when harm became imminent, and that damages would follow if the harm itself materialized.

That rule tended to work well for many years for such key issues as drug development and land development. With regard to the former, the downstream protection afforded by physicians and hospitals made rapid deployment the preferred strategy with drugs, which allowed for the seizure of impure or misbranded products before they reached the market. And with land use, the absence of an extensive permit process allowed the construction of major landmarks, which are far more difficult to build under the current approval process.

No one claimed that this presumption against public permits or licensing was or should be universal. Driver's licenses for new drivers issued after the routine tests is a perfectly sensible form of public regulation that gains salience precisely because no individual driver could ever have the knowledge or incentive to keep anonymous bad drivers off the road. In similar fashion, the condition of public roads and rivers matters as well. Where these are threatened by activities that amount to traditional public nuisances—blocking a right of way, or polluting a river—public administrative action is the best way to attack the issue, up front, leaving injured persons with "special damages" the right to bring individual law suits—a solution that in its modern essentials has been in place since the early sixteenth century.[36]

The rise of the Progressive era challenged all parts of this synthesis. First, the definition of harm became far more expansive, which in turn led to greater scrutiny of medicines for their adverse side effects, land use regulation for its effect on the character of a community, and indeed of new businesses for their effects on established firms all across the industrial spectrum. In the land use area, the judicial decisions meant that federal and state governments could prevent most of these newly defined harms without paying compensation to the persons injured therein, which only stoked the demand for further regulation and the political intrigue that went with it. The situation was made even worse as liberalized standing requirements allowed all citizens to move to block various kinds of action with which they had no connection.

That kind of broad-based standing is, I believe, appropriate in those cases where there is a serious question of whether certain government action is ultra vires of its various administrative agencies. But when the activity in question is clearly within the power of the government branch—issuing permits or taking the initiative on public projects—then it is wholly inappropriate. At the same time, the relative balance between the remedies ex ante and the remedies ex post shifted, so that the errors of commission loomed large, while those of keeping new products off the market and new projects off the ground were treated as far less serious.

The explosion in regulation has led to a massive slow-down in the introduction and approval of new drugs. The permit culture with respect to real estate has grown by leaps and bounds at both the federal[37] and the state levels,[38] which in turn mobilizes political opposition, delays new development, cuts down on the local tax base, and generally reduces the level of economic activity in ways that contribute to the overall decline of economic efficiency. Reversing this strong trend is hard to do, to say the least, but undoing the preference for early legal intervention is critical to any program that seeks to reverse the worst effects of the American Illness.

V. Health Care

ObamaCare also represents an expression—but not the only expression—of Progressive sentiments on health care issues. My few brief remarks about this legislation touch on several key features of the legislation, some of which represent a marked extension of government power.

The first of these features, and the one that has attracted the most attention, is the so-called individual mandate, which requires all individuals to acquire private health care insurance or pay the government $750 per year for the privilege of remaining uninsured. The ostensible justification for this program is to offset a free-rider problem that is created when certain individuals decide to forgo health care coverage, by relying instead on free emergency room coverage in their time of need. In this instance, however, the free-rider question does not follow from the public goods character of health care, but from the peculiar set of government regulations that operates on an embedded system of cross-subsidies.

A public good represents a type of service, like police power or public amenities of all sorts, which can be supplied to one individual only if it is supplied on equal terms, with equal benefits, to all others.[39] The non-excludable nature of the good leaves people with an incentive to sit back and pay nothing toward an amenity that they can enjoy just as much as someone else who pays for it. The problem with this strategy is that virtually everyone can opt for the passive approach, at which point the amenity does not get constructed at all. A set of taxes that matches benefits with burdens is one way to deal with this version of the Prisoner's Dilemma game, by securing the needed funds for projects, which leaves all members of the public better off with the tax-plus-improvement than without either.

Health care does not meet the definition of a public good because it is possible, indeed inevitable, to supply the care to some without supplying it to all. The free-rider problem in question arises only because of the insistence that the cost of health care to some, including elderly patients and those with preexisting conditions, be cross-subsidized by others—a provision enjoying virtually unanimous support on both sides of the aisle. The reason, therefore, that many people decline health care is to avoid the cross-subsidy.

The individual mandate to purchase health care insurance is just a mandate to participate in the program of cross-subsidies. The supposed free-riding is in part an effort to resist transfer payments to others. It is also part of an effort to get the subsidized care from other means, at least in some cases. Given this pattern, the way to avoid both the subsidy and free-riding problem is to do away with both the individual mandate and the expanded cross-subsidy program that lies at the heart of ObamaCare.

The constitutional challenge that is based on the proposition that Congress has no power to force people to engage in any activity, even if it has plenary power to regulate all economic activities in which people engage, is an odd but effective way to make the point. There is a difference between requiring people to become insured if they drive and requiring people to get insurance irrespective of whether they actually drive. But the real claim here is one of individual autonomy, which has nothing to do with enumerated powers. The police powers of the state would not extend that far either. The case is really a substantive due process case ingeniously packaged as a Commerce Clause challenge when brought against the federal government.

Beside the points expressed above, the current unpopularity of the health care measure could well lead to acceptance of this argument, which gained traction in the Florida litigation of *McCollum v. HHS*[40] and the subsequent Virginia suit in *X v. Y*.[41] But what happens if the mandate is struck down? It is, in short, a crisis of major proportions. Under current constitutional law, the costs now attributable to the individual mandate could be collected as general taxes from all individuals. The object of the coercion shifts, but the level of coercion remains high. Alternatively, Congress could refuse to find new taxes for the mandate, which is sure to leave the program in limbo. Stay tuned.

As this battle goes on, the larger administrative fight is over the implicit price control system that applies to all private plans that seek to gain access to the health care exchanges. These institutions are not involved in the usual kind of exchange, where parties are allowed to list their wares for sale so long as they can make good on their contractual obligations. Instead, these health care plans impose by statute, but fleshed out by regulation, a rich set of obligations that are beyond the means of the people of limited income for whom they are intended. The government thus has to pick up the slack, although (with shades of Hayek)[42] the government cannot figure out how to set the prices for these services when its own contribution is so large in individual cases, while the private market to which it might otherwise make reference is overheated by excessive government regulation of every element of the pricing system.

How this will play out is an open question, but the one government feature that seems wholly dubious is the requirement of the so-called medical loss ratio, which requires individual health care plans to cap their administrative expenses at 20 percent and group plans at 15 percent—figures that are well below current market rates, even before their compliance costs rise sharply under ObamaCare. A huge set of government regulations is now in the process of review as to how this is best to be achieved, but no variation can hit the fundamental point that the price controls cannot bleed out waste in health care, any more than rent control can bleed out waste in rental housing markets.

It is therefore no surprise that the government has been inundated with requests for waivers by hard-hit plans, most of which have been granted.[43] But government by waiver is a precarious business because it is never clear who gets these waivers, why they are awarded, or whether they will be renewed. The clear message is that additional employees create additional uncertainties, which in turn puts greater pressure on entitlement programs, an area to which I shall now turn.

VI. Entitlements

The difficulties with the health care system offer a nice bridge to the entitlement question. On this point, the basic structural flaw of Medicare and Medicaid is built-in on the ground floor. The founders of the system have never explained how the consumption of medical services could be constrained when they were offered at a marginal cost of close to zero. The low marginal costs lead to all sorts of overconsumption by people acting in good faith. Whatever the moral case for some "positive" right to health care is, the descriptive consequences are clear. The positive right at zero (or some nominal price) generates an acute over-demand. But at the same time, the want of cash into the system from its customers leads to budget shortfalls, which require an increase in fixed fees (a small part of the current solution) and most critically a massive expansion in taxation to fund the shortfall.

All of this was apparent in principle in 1966, but the politics of denial have pushed the U.S. to the point where the budget sleights-of-hand in the initial ObamaCare regulation cannot paper over the systematic shortfalls in the fund. The issue has become so bad that Richard Foster, the fund's actuary, issued a personal disclaimer to the report he had signed in his institutional role. Foster could not ignore the simple fact that the harsh reductions in government reimbursements to physicians would have to be lifted for Medicare to continue in operation. It is yet another instance of how disguised price controls necessarily fail.

The entitlement difficulties extend to Medicaid, which in fact becomes a more expensive program under ObamaCare. But here, too, the entire structure is coming apart at the seams. The current proposals require the states to fund much of these costs as of 2014, without supplying the revenue to allow the states to do this. The only way to meet these mandates is to cut other programs that are under stress, given the difficulty of dealing with pensions of unionized public workers, on which more in a moment. Opting out is, however, hard to do because it comes with two strings attached. First, the opt-out requires that the state assume the cost—using its own revenues—of Medicaid payments for the large and costly group of individuals in the 100–133 percent of poverty range. Second, the opt-out does nothing to allow the state citizens to hold back their Medicaid dollars from the federal program, where they can then be funneled to other states. The whole scheme has the whiff of federal commandeering of state activities, which since *New York v. U.S.*[44] raises a credible claim that state sovereignty has been curtailed by overzealous federal oversight—an argument that may have some constitutional legs.

VII. Labor Markets

The next piece of the puzzle involves employment markets. Left to their own devices, employment markets are competitive, so that direct regulation is hardly needed. But by the same token, there are powerful institutional pressures that could easily make these markets a hotbed for government regulation, to be enforced by some combination of direct control and private litigation. One clear reform is to undo this whole regulatory structure, which is more easily said than done. But any analysis of the American Illness requires at least some consideration of these issues, both for public and private unions.

A. Public Unions

It is quite clear that President Obama and many of the Democratic members of Congress owe their political lives to the strong intervention of American labor unions, which are active in both the public and the private spheres. It is equally clear that the same level of political dependence is found at the state level as well. At present, the most conspicuous feature of most state budgets is that their balance sheets are in desperate shape because of the tens, if not hundreds, of billions of dollars in deferred pension obligations that cannot be met from current sources of public revenue. The situation has boiled over as of late as governors of many Republican states are pushing hard not only for union concessions but for a more fundamental reorganization of bargaining in the public sector that puts a hold on union monopoly power—a proposal that is fiercely resisted by Democratic legislative walkouts, in states like Wisconsin and Ohio (as this is written). It is too early to determine whether the tide on this matter has turned, but the ability of Wisconsin governor Scott Walker to survive a recall election in June 2012 may well be an early signal that popular sentiment on the question of teacher's unions is beginning to change.

The short-term impasse is so acute that the absolute priority of these pension obligations over other state budget items has led to a sharp contraction in funding for education at all levels—from K–12 on the one hand to university support on the other. Moreover, other social welfare services have been cut back as well. Until recently, the dominant strategy has been to try to negotiate some givebacks with respect to future pension obligations, both for current workers and for those who have yet to be hired. These two-tier systems (which are also invoked in private labor negotiations with unions in declining markets) offer powerful testimony to the enduring monopoly power of labor unions in many key service industries. No such price discrimination is possible in competitive markets.

The overall disparities between public and private wages have been often noted and much deplored. Yet now that these wages are entrenched, it will take a powerful antiunion coalition to undo these vested rights. By the same token, however, it often takes only the signature of the governor to extend certain key privileges—the card check is one—to government employees, with a consequent increase in union power.

One specific approach, which has gone from the improbable to the highly possible in a matter of months, is to engage in massive decertification of public unions at all levels, coupled with a major revision of union wages and especially pension benefits until these budgets are brought into balance. The current law treats union contracts as vested constitutional rights that cannot be reversed by legislative action. I believe that this conclusion is premature, at least before it is attacked in concerted litigation. The level of political influence that led to the expansion of pensions for union members shows a degree of political self-dealing. There is little doubt that any corporate officers who sought to create these sweetheart deals for their employees (in exchange for political support) would be set aside as a breach of fiduciary duty. It is hard to achieve that result in the public context. Indeed, at the federal level there is some question about whether taxpayers or citizens even have standing. But it is surely worth the effort to mount those challenges in light of the evident size of the stakes. In addition, any ability to subcontract work to nongovernment employees should be strongly supported as yet another way to undo union power in this area.

In dealing with these issues, it is probably a mistake to think that only unionized systems are vulnerable to expropriation. The problems go deeper because other nonunion parties can obtain similar benefits. One sensible way to deal with the system is to monetize all future pension obligations by simply switching, as private firms have done, from a defined benefit plan (where the shortfall lies with the state) to a defined contribution plan that liquidates all future liabilities at the moment of payment, and forces workers to decide the best pattern for asset allocation with their portfolios. For these purposes, the key point is that the dollar figure allows for prudent cash management at the state level, and for greater public oversight of the entire process. That system is compatible, moreover, with any independent rules that limit the amount of money that recipients can allocate to equities or other risky ventures. What is desperately needed is a way to stop the excesses.

B. Private Unions

The situation with private unions is more complex. As noted earlier, union membership has been in steep decline, and it seems clear that the best union strategy for organization under current laws is likely to fall short when confronted with the best management defense. That result does not occur because management has received some hidden bonus from a change in the substantive law in recent years; labor law has been very steady for at least the past fifty years.

It is far more likely that the result derives from the ability of most employers to avoid the silly mistakes in employee relationships that could easily turn their workers against them. Unions have constantly attacked employers for their all-out resistance to organization campaigns. But while unions have been quick to denounce the effectiveness of such resistance, they have been much more hard-pressed to prove that labor's organizational setbacks are attributable to employer unfair labor practices that have either gone undetected or been punished with only a mild slap on the wrist. The signs of unionized failure in major industries—automobiles, steel, and construction, for starters—are known everywhere. The expected gains to workers from staying out of unions are greater than those of joining unions, once the risks of lost wages and benefits to layoffs, strikes, and bankruptcy are taken into account. Employers may not be allowed to make threats of what they will do to respond to unions, but they are surely allowed to make predictions, usually painfully accurate, as to the likely outcome of union membership. The drive from within is just not there.

In response to this decline, unions have resorted to a variety of other tactics that do not require their success at the bargaining table, and on these unions have been far more successful. They have pressed the Obama administration and state governments to make unilateral changes through executive order whenever this is possible. The Obama administration has put through recess appointment Craig Becker on the National Labor Relations Board, knowing full well that he was not confirmable by an up-or-down Senate vote. More recently, the White House's Middle Class Task Force, headed by Vice President Biden, has announced an initiative whereby the American Bar Association and the Department of Labor will pair up to bolster the enforcement of the Fair Labor Standards Act (FLSA).[45] The "Middle Class Task Force" should be understood as a term of art for organized labor's drive to secure the passage of labor reform, including the Employee Free Choice Act,[46] of which more below. At present, there are about 6,000 class action lawsuits under FLSA, each of which can be initiated by a complaint from a single employee.[47]

Unions have also been active in opposing free trade by filing antidumping cases under current law and pushing hard to slow down the rate of bilateral trade agreements with places like Colombia and South Korea. At the local level, unions have pushed hard to use zoning ordinances as a way to keep big-box stores out of urban areas where they stand a good chance of underselling their more established unionized rivals, which have, on average, expanded at a far lower rate than the nonunionized firms. Unions have also fought for increases in the minimum wage law, an effort that has had more bite than anyone expected given the collapse in demand for labor after the market meltdown in September 2008.

For the moment, at least, unions have failed to gain traction for their most powerful reform, the Employee Free Choice Act (EFCA), which goes far beyond the National Labor Relations Act of 1935. The earlier statute had two features that, with time, have become bulwarks for the employer. The first was the requirement of the secret ballot at the close of any organization campaign, which does much to eliminate the risks of coercion from either side. The second was the ability of the employer to bargain to impasse, on the ground that the requirement of bargaining in good faith did not require either side to make any particular concession. The good faith requirements impose powerful restraints on the pattern of collective bargaining that make it ever more convoluted. It is typically unlawful for an employer to take a "take-it-or-leave-it" approach. But it is nonetheless perfectly proper to draw out negotiations that lead to that final position, but only after an increase of delay, uncertainty, animosity, and expense.

The EFCA promised to work a transformation in both of these key features. The card check of eligible workers allows a union to force the election if 50 percent of the members of a relevant bargaining union sign up. Once that is done, a form of binding interest arbitration awaits the firm that cannot enter into a binding first contract with a union within 130 days of the official recognition of the union. The arbitrations are chosen by unspecified processes by a political employee in the Department of Labor, the most politicized of the cabinet positions. These provisions have rightly provoked a fierce and unified managerial opposition, and their defeat will surely help to loosen labor markets in the short run. But the adverse effect that the provision had on job formation during the first year or so of the Obama administration is hard to calculate.

VIII. Tort Liability

The last portion of the Progressive synthesis that I want to touch upon has to do with the radical expansion of tort liability through the common law system. Anyone who took a snapshot of tort law in 1850 would have seen a field that was dominated by private liability of landowners and others for harms committed against the person or property or strangers. At this point, a tough legal system that deals with these "boundary crossings" has a strong libertarian feel to it, given that the law's major function is to reinforce the separation between neighbors. The rules in these cases tend, imperfectly, to gravitate to a strict liability system that does not allow parties to escape liability by showing that they exercise due care or had no intention to harm. Indeed the most conspicuous expansion of liability in this period was through the doctrine of vicarious liability under which employers, including the newly minted corporations, could be held responsible to strangers for harms that arose in the course of their employment. Meshing limited with vicarious liability was a great achievement, insofar as it expanded the pool of assets available to protect strangers, by encouraging unconnected strangers to contribute fixed and bounded sums to a common venture.

The changes in the twentieth century, which are now seeping into the twenty-first century, require a more subtle analysis. The vaunted expansion of product liability law through the first sixty years of the twentieth century was largely sound and fury signifying nothing. On the medical malpractice front, tort liability was universally limited to cases of physicians who deviated from the customary standard of care, where the notion of custom gave the physician the benefit of choosing what school of practice to join. In effect, non-contractual standards were not superimposed on private behavior. The newly minted system of strict liability for defective products was likewise hedged with sensible limitations that prevented its undue expansion. Thus, after a prolonged oration of how it was "to the public interest" to run a risk-sharing program through the tort system, Judge Roger Traynor concluded his remarks with the observation that the new strict liability system (which was in any event not very different from the system that put the burden of disproving negligence on the defendant) applied only when the product was still in its original condition when the defect manifested itself, and that, even then, recovery was permissible only when it was used in the normal and proper way.[48]

In effect, the better production techniques meant that tort liability rules were but a ripple on the pond until one key development: the inability to vary the rules of the game by voluntary contract, which arose in 1960 in the first product liability cases[49] and shortly thereafter in medical malpractice cases.[50] The hostility toward freedom of contract that had worked itself through so many other parts of the legal system finally crept into the tort law. The key feature of this new approach was that it made it impossible for private parties to correct allocation mistakes made by judges in setting out what they thought were the correct rules of the system.

It was only a matter of time until the expansionist tendencies that were part of Progressive thought worked themselves into the fabric of the law. On the malpractice side, the standards of care became more exacting, the proof of causation more pliable, and the level of damages more expansive. Similarly, on the product side, the definition of defects expanded, and the normal and proper use defense quickly eroded until the presumption became that upstream providers had to take care of downstream users even against conditions that were fully disclosed and thus remediable by a user, or (in workplace situations) a user's employer. All of these changes were multiplicative, at which point it is easy to see how the overall system can start to overload, with the usual negative effects on innovation.

Conclusion

The basic thesis of this article is that the combined impact of bad government policies has taken its toll on the fabric of American institutions. We speak now of the American Illness, and the once familiar talk of American Exceptionalism becomes an ever more distant memory, invoked today only with a sense of irony that it does not remotely describe our current situation.

The implications of this great transformation in the American economy and psyche are not easy to predict. As a general matter, the weaknesses at home will lead to systematic weaknesses abroad. God favors the big battalions in international affairs. The decline in American production leads to constant calls to weaken the military presence overseas, which in turn allows nations like China (who have thus far avoided some of our structural mistakes in their youthful capitalist phase) greater sway in international affairs, which in turn will make it more difficult to succeed in a variety of international commercial ventures.

Domestically, the want of one single national cause is what makes it so difficult to reverse a pattern of behaviors and laws that have become so entrenched in the American psyche. But the effort has to be made. The fact that major declines come from multiple causes does not mean that they do not have long-term corrosive effects. Unless and until we embrace the classical liberal provisions that allowed for innovation and growth, we can expect more of the same: a grim stagflation in which technological improvements cannot quite offset the major dislocations in the regulatory state, for which we have the Progressive movement to thank.[51]

The final inquiry is what lesson we should learn from this set of disparate elements. The major lesson is that it is not so disparate at all. The changes all come with distinct doctrinal labels in what appear to be unrelated substantive areas of law. Each of these changes is made on the implicit assumption that the rest of the system remains constant, so that the interactive effects of different maneuvers are never made part of the law. The inability to trace long-term adverse consequences to earlier political maneuvers lends the entire operation political cover. Since we are no longer dealing with push-pull relationships, it is easier to argue that there is always something, indeed anything, else that accounts for the brake that is seen on development. But the dangers here lie in the compounding of these errors over long periods of time. No one can say that any of these changes itself is that "big," but assume modestly that all these errors are put in the right position for a period of many years, and lo, one comes up with the conclusion that Robert Cooter develops in his excellent essay in this book. Think growth over the long run, and you will not do too badly in the short run. As a general matter, the gains from long-term overall improvements will swamp the supposed gains from short-term ameliorative programs. This leads to the final irony. The Progressive movement is an intellectual failure because it stifles the long-term systematic growth and social welfare that its supposedly "scientific" foundation was intended to promote.

Notes

I benefited from comments on this article made by the participants of a faculty workshop at Ohio State University. My thanks to Frank Buckley for his organization of the topic, and to Brett Davenport, Maxine Sharavsky, and Christopher Tan, NYU Law School class of 2012, for their usual prompt and careful research assistance.

1. For two recent expressions of the point, see Thomas L. Friedman, Got to Get This Right, N.Y. Times, Nov. 28, 2010; Frank Rich, Still the Best Congress That Money Can Buy, N.Y. Times, Nov. 28, 2010. For Friedman, the solution lies in lower corporate and payroll taxes, and cuts in entitlement programs—all welcome changes. Deregulation is not on his list. Frank Rich rails against Citizens United v. Federal Election Commission, and corporate money in politics, a clear nonstarter for structural reform.

2. See, e.g., Peter Wallsten & Eliza Gray, Confidence Waning in Obama, U.S. Outlook, Wall St. Journal, June 23, 2010, available at http://online.wsj.com/article/SB10001424052748703900004575325263274951230.html.

3. See, e.g., Amanda Noss, Household Income for States: 2008 and 2009, U.S. Census Bureau (2010), available at http://www.census.gov/prod/2010pubs/acsbr09 -2.pdf. The decline continued in 2010. See also Carmen DeNavas-Walt et al., Income, Poverty, and Health Insurance Coverage in the United States: 2010, U.S. Census Bureau (2011), available at http://www.census.gov/prod/2011pubs/p60-239 .pdf ("real median household income was $49,445 in 2010, a 2.3 percent decline from 2009").

4. Ludwig von Mises, Economic Calculation in the Socialist Commonwealth (1920), available at http://mises.org/econcalc.asp; see generally F. A. Hayek, The Road to Serfdom (1944) (remarking on the Socialist Calculation debate).

5. Pub. L. No. 79-404, 60 Stat. 237, codified at 5 U.S.C.A. §§ 501 et seq.

6. The Labor–Management Relations Act, Pub. L. No. 80-101, 61 Stat. 136, enacted June 23, 1947.

7. Executive Order No. 10,988 (Jan. 17, 1962), available at http://www.presidency .ucsb.edu/ws/index.php?pid=58926.

8. See Nat'l League of Cities v. Usery, 426 U.S. 833 (1976), overruled by Garcia v. San Antonio Metro. Transit Auth., 469 U.S. 528 (1985); see also Fair Labor Standards Act, 28 U.S.C. §§ 201–212 (1938).

9. Title VII of Civil Rights Act of 1964, 42 U.S.C. 2000e et seq. (2011).

10. See, e.g., Clean Water Act of 1972, Pub. L. No. 92-500, 86 Stat. 816 (codified as amended in 33 U.S.C. §§ 1251–1387 (2002)); Nat'l Environmental Policy Act of 1969, Pub. L. No. 91-190, 83 Stat. 852 (codified as amended in 42 U.S.C. §§ 4321–4370); Clean Air Act of 1963, Pub. L. No. 88-206, 77 Stat. 392 (codified as amended in 42 U.S.C. §§ 7401–7671 (2011)).

11. Endangered Species Act of 1973, Pub. L. No. 93-205, 87 Stat. 884 (codified as amended in 16 U.S.C. §§ 1531–1599 (2011)).

12. Occupational Safety and Health Act of 1970, Pub. L. No. 91-596, 84 Stat. 1590 (codified as amended at 29 U.S.C. §§ 651–78) (2010).

13. Employee Retirement Income Security Act of 1974, Pub. L. No. 93-406, 88 Stat. 829 (codified as amended at 29 U.S.C. §§ 1001 et seq. (2010)).

14. See Airline Deregulation Act of 1978, Pub. L. No. 95-504, 92 Stat. 1705 (codified as amended in various sections of 49 U.S.C.).

15. Humphrey's Executor v. United States, 295 U.S. 602 (1935).

16. See NLRB v. Jones & Laughlin, 301 U.S. 1 (1937); Wickard v. Filburn, 317 U.S. 111 (1942).

17. See Rice v. Santa Fe Elevator, 331 U.S. 218, 230–31 (1947).

18. See, for one manifestation, Andrew Pollack, Medical Device Makers Shun U.S., N.Y. Times, Feb. 9, 2011, available at http://www.nytimes.com/2011/02/10/business /10device.html.

19. Contrast Wyeth Co. v. Levine, 552 U.S. 312 (2008) (virtually no implied preemption), with Riegel v. Medtronic, Inc., 129 S. Ct. 1187 (2009); see also Richard A. Epstein, What Tort Theory Tells U.S. about Federal Preemption: The Tragic Saga of Wyeth v. Levine, 65 N.Y.U. Ann. Surv. Am. L. 485 (2010); David A. Kessler & David C. Vladeck, A Critical Examination of the FDA's Failure to Preempt Failure-to-Warn Claims, 96 Geo. L. J. 461 (2008).

20. The truncation began earlier. See Block v. Hirsh, 256 U.S. 135 (1921); Euclid v. Ambler Realty, 272 U.S. 365 (1926).

21. Hope Nat'l Gas Co. v. Fed. Power Comm'n, 320 U.S. 591 (1944); Duquesne Light Co. v. Barasch, 488 U.S. 299 (1989).

22. See Williamson County Reg'l Planning Comm'n v. Hamilton Bank, 473 U.S. 172 (1985).

23. With time, the ability of an economy to adapt to these shocks improves. The most conspicuous illustration of this transformation is the decline of non-public employee union membership, which grew rapidly after the passage of the National Labor Relations Act of 1935, only to shrink from a peak of about 35 percent of the private labor force in 1954 to a little more than 7 percent of the work force by 2009. The relatively stable body of labor law has allowed most employers to develop coherent strategies to control the level of union penetration.

24. Pub. L. No. 111-203 (2010) (codified at 7 U.S.C. § 1 et seq.).

25. Patient Protection and Affordable Care Act ("ObamaCare"), Pub. L. No. 111–148, 124 Stat. 119 (2010).

26. See generally Richard A. Epstein, Takings: Private Property and the Power of Eminent Domain (1985).

27. Telecommunications Act of 1996, Pub. L. No. 104-104, 110 Stat. 56.

28. And it is not without biblical support. Genesis 41:29-37.

29. Virginia v. Sebelius, 702 F.Supp.2d 598 (E.D. Va. 2010); Florida v. U.S. Dep't Health & Human Serv., Case No. 3:10-cv-00091-RV/EMT (2010).

30. Nicholas Johnston, Obama Wants Upper Income Tax Cuts Ended in 2012, Business Week, Jan. 6, 2011, available at http://www.businessweek.com/news/-2011-01-06/obama-wants-upper-income-tax-cuts-ended-in-2012-jarrett-says.html.

31. Barack Obama, Exporting Our Way to Stability, N.Y. Times, Nov. 6, 2010, available at http://www.nytimes.com/2010/11/06/opinion/06obama.html.

32. See Elizabeth Wilson & Tom Barkley, Congress Approves Trade Pacts, Wall St. J., Oct. 13, 2011, available at http://online.wsj.com/article/SB1000142405297020400230457662709124472676.html.

33. American Recovery and Reinvestment Act, Pub. L. 111-5 (2009). Its key provision states that, subject to exceptions, "no Recovery Act funds may be used for a project for the construction, alteration, maintenance or repair of a public building or public work unless all of the iron, steel, and manufactured goods used in the project are produced or manufactured in the United States." Dep't of Energy, Frequently Asked Questions about the Buy American Provisions, http://www1.eere.energy.gov/recovery/buy_american_faq.html#q1 (last visited Feb. 28, 2011). The Steelworkers are perhaps the most insistent protectionist union in the United States.

34. Robert Nozick, Anarchy, State, and Utopia (1974).

35. Richard A. Epstein, Against Permititis: Why Voluntary Organizations Should Regulate the Use of Cancer Drugs, 94 Minn. L. Rev. 1 (2009).

36. Anon., Y.B. Mich. 27 Hen. 8, f. 27, pl. 10 (1535).

37. See, for federal intervention, the inconclusive decision in Rapanos v. United States, 547 U.S. 715 (2006).

38. On which, see the elaborate procedures for land use approval in New York City, under its Uniform Land Use Review Process, or ULURP, http://www.nyc.gov/html/dcp/html/luproc/ulpro.shtml, whose multiple layers of approval have little to do with prevention of abuse.

39. For the classic account, see Mancur Olson, The Logic of Collective Action (1965).

40. Florida v. U.S. Dep't Health & Human Serv., Case No. 3:10-cv-00091-RV/EMT (2010).

41. Virginia v. Sebelius, 702 F.Supp.2d 598 (E.D. Va. 2010).

42. F.A. Hayek, The Use of Knowledge in Society, 35 Am. Econ. Rev. 519 (1945).

43. For a more extensive discussion, see Richard A. Epstein, Government by Waiver, National Affairs, Spring 2011, at 39.

44. 505 U.S. 144 (1992).

45. WhiteHouse.gov, Helping Middle-Class Families Pursue Justice (Nov. 19, 2010), http://www.whitehouse.gov/blog/2010/11/19/helping-middle-class-families-pursue -justice.

46. See, e.g., the Congressional Hearings that have used that title. Strengthening America's Middle Class through the Employee Free Choice Act: Hearing on H.R. 800 before the H. Subcomm. Health, Employment, Labor, and Pensions, 110th Cong. 4 (2007).

47. See 1-800-Trial Bar, Wall St. J., Nov. 27, 2010, available at http://online.wsj .com/article/SB10001424052748704369304575633482885808438.html.

48. See, e.g., Escola v. Coca-Cola, 150 P.2d 436 (1944).

49. Henningsen v. Bloomfield Motors, 161 A.2d 69 (N.J. 1960).

50. Tunkl v. Regents of Univ. of California, 60 Cal. 2d 92 (Cal. 1963).

51. For a general discussion of these themes, see Tyler Cowen, The Great Stagnation (2011).

Overtaking

ROBERT COOTER AND AARON EDLIN

T he other articles in this book deal with economic pathologies in the American legal system. None of these essays discusses what economic goals the legal system should pursue. This article discusses what we consider to be the first economic goal of the legal system: sustained growth. We will explain why sustained growth should be the first economic goal of the legal system. We will also discuss pathologies in conventional legal reasoning about the economic goals of two areas of law—intellectual property and technology policy. Other articles in this book, such as those by Ramseyer-Rasmusen and Bainbridge on securities laws, contain concrete discussions of particular laws that slow U.S. economic growth compared with that of other countries.

Compounded over a century, 2 percent annual growth (roughly the recent growth rate of the U.S. economy) increases wealth more than seven times, and 10 percent annual growth (roughly the recent growth rate of the Chinese economy) increases wealth by almost 14,000 times.[1] Differences in sustained growth cause one country's wealth to overtake that of another country faster than the mind can grasp.

Like individuals, nations are highly competitive. Poor nations hope to overtake rich nations, and rich nations fear being overtaken. Besides relative income, individuals and nations care about absolute income. Most people want to live a long time and educate their children in absolute terms. Life expectancy at birth is 83 years in Japan and 66 years in Bangladesh.[2] Enrollment in secondary school is 98 percent among Japanese children of the appropriate age and 42 percent in Bangladesh.[3] Almost everyone would prefer to live at the level of Japan rather than Bangladesh.

Much contemporary policy discussion concerns redistribution of income, but growth has more powerful effects on human welfare. The lowest wage earners in the U.S. or any country would benefit far more in the long run from a faster growth rate in national income than from redistributing existing national wealth in their favor. Even people who depend on transfer payments would benefit more from faster growth than income redistribution. A faster growth rate increases wages and tax revenues available for transfer payments, and this increase overtakes gains in welfare from redistributing income.[4] Returning to our previous comparison, 1 percent of an increase of 14,000 is 20 times more than 100 percent of an increase of seven times.

To appreciate the mathematics of overtaking, consider two sequences of utility in an infinite number of generations. In the first sequence, income per capita grows at a faster rate. In the second sequence, growth is slower and initial utility is higher. The sum of utilities in the first sequence overtakes the sum of utilities in the second sequence whenever policy makers give weight to future generations that is similar to the weight given to the present generation.[5] Although this proposition concerns infinite time, in practice overtaking occurs quicker than people imagine, because they fail to appreciate fully the effects of compound growth. Given overtaking, anyone who values human welfare should recognize growth's importance as a policy goal.

In the preceding propositions, "growth" has two attributes lacking in standard measures of national income such as gross domestic product (GDP). The first attribute is sustainability. Growth overtakes other welfare considerations when it is sustainable and continues into the future. Sustainable growth uses natural resources in fixed supply at a decreasing rate, whereas unsustainable growth uses them at a constant or increasing rate (or a rate that does not decrease fast enough). The second attribute is comprehensiveness. A comprehensive measure of wealth encompasses *all* valuable goods, including non-market goods such as public goods and the environment. By contrast, a partial measure of wealth such as GDP excludes goods that are not sold in markets. When comparing welfare, partial measures may make little sense because a loss in unmeasured wealth may offset a gain in measured wealth. Thus, burning more coal to power air conditioners increases the simplest measure of market income, but it does not necessarily increase a full measure of wealth if pollution increases significantly.

The case for increasing the rate of sustainable, comprehensive growth is compelling, but how is it to be done? Innovation proximately causes sustained growth in income per capita. In fact, innovation is the only way to have sustainable growth in a world of finite resources. Education, communication, transportation, immigration, organization, taxation, and many other factors affect innovation. From a legal perspective, the normative question of growth economics is, "Which laws increase the pace of economic innovation?"

An innovator has a temporary advantage over competitors until they catch up. While the temporary advantage lasts, the innovator enjoys extraordinary profits, which we call "venture profits." When venture profits increase, so do the incentives for innovation. To increase the pace of innovation, laws should increase venture profits so that entrepreneurs invest more in innovation. The question of this essay is, "Which laws increase venture profits?"

We will characterize two errors in the foundations of laws and policies that impede growth in the United States. The first error especially concerns intellectual property law, although it is found more widely. Strengthening patents or copyright increases venture profits sometimes (but not always). Consumers will probably face higher prices. What should the state do? According to the standard economic analysis, the state should balance the gain from faster innovation and the loss from higher consumer prices. According to overtaking theory, however, the state should maximize innovation and ignore consumer prices. The state should not sacrifice sustained growth for another objective, including lower consumer prices, because growth will overtake temporary losses to consumers from higher prices. Overtaking theory favors maximizing a comprehensive measure of sustained growth, whereas standard analysis advocates balancing growth and lower consumer prices.

The second error in laws and policies for growth concerns the rationale for subsidizing firms and industries to promote growth. Every state subsidizes some firms and industries, either directly through cash grants or indirectly through tax preferences. Promoting growth is often part of the rationale for subsidizing firms and industries. Thus the U.S. government currently subsidizes solar power on the theory that this infant industry needs nourishment in order to grow into a strong adolescent. The infant-industries argument is the same one used to justify cross-subsidies in developing countries that had remarkably little success.[6]

The error in the rationale for growth subsidies concerns the very concept of innovative ventures. State subsidies go to preferred firms and industries, but, unfortunately, the state seldom knows which ventures are most promising. It seldom knows because it cannot find out. Innovators with promising ideas have strong reasons for secrecy. Combining new ideas and capital must overcome the "double-trust dilemma of innovation": Innovators fear that others will steal their ideas, and investors fear that others will steal their money. Innovators with very promising ideas do not want to share them with the state, and the state is not very good at preventing special interests from stealing the taxpayers' money. The double-trust dilemma mostly precludes the state from accelerating the rate of innovation by subsidizing preferred industries or firms. In contrast, venture capitalists have found ways to mitigate the double-trust problem that put them far ahead of the state.

Innovation

The development of an innovation often goes through stages illustrated by the following example: An engineer in Silicon Valley has an idea for a new computer technology. Developing it requires more money than the engineer can risk personally. He drafts a business plan and meets with a small group of investors. They accept his invitation to form a corporation with the innovator as chief executive and the investors as board members. Having financed the firm, the innovator hires collaborators to build an organization and develop the new idea. Perhaps the firm keeps the innovation secret, or perhaps the firm applies for a patent. Next the firm markets the innovation and proves its economic value. Finally, the founder and the investors sell the firm to an established company.

Innovations in Silicon Valley usually have a technological basis, such as new computer chips or programs that were previously unknown to the world. In other times and places, innovation has a different basis. Instead of improving technology, many innovations improve organizations and markets.[7] Philip Knight, co-founder of the Nike Corporation, began by making running shoes with soles formed on the family waffle iron and selling them out of his car's trunk in 1972. In 2006 the company reported $15 billion in worldwide sales of sports equipment and clothing. Knight obviously discovered something new, but what was it? Nike does not manufacture anything. The business of Nike is research and marketing. It thinks up new products, contracts with foreign firms to make them, and then markets them through extensive advertising. This new organizational form has spread dramatically in the U.S. as more and more companies "outsource" manufacturing and focus on research and marketing. Other examples of recent innovations in markets and organizations in the U.S. include debit cards, hostile takeovers, networks of innovators, and team production (imported from Japan).

Innovations in technology, organization, or markets often go through the four phases described in the Silicon Valley engineer's story. First, someone discovers a new idea, which might occur after years of research or simply over coffee one morning. Second, the idea is developed into something with economic value, which requires combining it with capital and labor. Once the idea is developed, it is an *economic innovation*. Third, the idea is marketed. Unlike discovering and developing ideas, marketing innovations can be profitable. Fourth, if the previous steps occur in a small, independent firm, the final step is for the innovators to sell the startup to an established firm or to sell stock to the public.

Growth quickens by increasing the pace of innovation, and the pace of innovation quickens when it is more profitable. Law has everything to do with innovations' profitability. Intellectual property law affects how much an innovator earns by developing a new idea. Contract law and corporate law affect the cost of developing ideas by combining them with capital and labor. Financial law affects the ease of entering or exiting from a startup business. Beyond property, contracts, corporations, and finance, the list of laws that affect innovation is open-ended. Laws that affect the flow of ideas include regulations on immigration, trade, and communications. Instead of surveying all of the legal obstacles to sustained growth in the U.S., we will discuss some examples.

Intellectual Property Law

Legal ownership sometimes goes to the first person to invent a machine, create a molecule, extract a vaccine, compose a song, write a book, or record a performance. The first person to embody a new idea in an innovation may acquire private ownership of it through patent or copyright law. Intellectual property rights differ in duration—U.S. patent lasts for 20 years and a U.S. copyright lasts for the creator's life plus 70 years. Patents also differ in breadth. Thus, a patent on all umbrellas is broader than a patent on umbrellas that open automatically (spring-loaded). "Stronger" intellectual property rights are wider in breadth or longer in duration.

To be profitable, the development costs of an innovation must be less than the profits from its future sales. Stronger intellectual property rights can make an unprofitable innovation profitable, or they can make a profitable innovation more profitable. Either way, higher profits increase the incentive to innovate.

Which ownership rules will maximize investment in innovation? Perhaps you think the answer is, "The ownership rules that give innovators the strongest property rights." You might reason that stronger intellectual property rights always increase the profitability of innovating, which causes more of it. If that is what you think, you are half right. Increased profitability of innovating causes more of it, but stronger intellectual property rights do not always increase the profitability of innovating.

Assume that computer firm B invents and patents an improved computer chip. A stronger patent increases the market power of firm B. According to standard economics, an increase in market power causes a firm to increase profits by raising prices and lowering production. If firm B could foresee that it would receive a stronger patent, it might have invested more to develop the computer chip sooner. In general, stronger patents on the innovative outputs of a firm increase its profitability and its incentive to innovate, holding all else equal.

To illustrate concretely, assume that consumers buy all of an industry's innovations and innovators buy none of them.[8] By definition, these innovations are "final goods" that households consume. Strengthening property rights for final innovations increases the market power of innovators against consumers. The innovators can raise prices and reduce production, thus transferring wealth from consumers to themselves. This increase in the profitability of innovation increases its pace.

There is, however, another side of the story. Steve Jobs once complained to Bill Gates, "It's like you broke into my house and stole my TV set!" "That's not true, Steve," replied Gates. "We had a rich neighbor named Xerox, and we both took Xerox's TV set—you just took it first."[9] This anecdote illustrates that innovators often borrow (or steal) from each other, which can accelerate the process of innovation. Today's new idea usually comes from, or uses, yesterday's new idea. Innovations cascade with prior innovations propelling subsequent innovations. Today's new molecule is discovered by using yesterday's new molecule, today's new search algorithm is discovered by using yesterday's new search algorithm, and so forth. In general, the science and technology of today develop from the science and technology of yesterday. If someone owns yesterday's innovation, then researchers will have to pay to use it to develop today's innovation. Stronger intellectual property rights for innovations in a cascade increase the revenues from and the costs of creating.

To illustrate a pure case, assume that innovators buy all of an industry's innovations and consumers buy none of them. By assumption, these innovations are "intermediate innovations" that other firms use as inputs in innovating. Strengthening intellectual property rights for intermediate innovations causes the profitability of innovating to go up or down depending on whether the cost of developing innovations increases more of less than the revenues from marketing them.

Which effect is stronger? In the standard economic analysis, when a firm acquires a monopoly in producing an intermediate good, the monopolist's profits increase by less than the decrease in profits of firms that buy from the monopolists. The shortfall between the monopolist's increase in profits and the buyers' decrease in profits is monopoly's "dead weight" loss.[10] Consequently, profitability among firms will go down overall.

Recall the pure case where all of the customers of a patent holder are innovators. A strong intellectual property right increases the profits of the patent holder, who is a temporary monopolist. Assume that the patent holder sells its product to other firms for use in innovation ("intermediate innovation"). Stronger intellectual property rights increase the profits of its owner by less than the decrease in the profits of other innovators. Consequently, when this patent's strength increases, the overall profitability of innovating falls,[11] and the pace of innovation slows.

A different line of reasoning reaches the same conclusion. Stronger intellectual property rights require firms to negotiate more contracts for the inputs that they need to use to innovate. Thus, stronger intellectual property rights can increase the transaction costs of developing complementary innovations (but not always).[12] Conversely, if intellectual property rights were weaker, fewer negotiations would be necessary to develop innovations.

We have explained that stronger intellectual property rights often increase the pace of final innovations and decrease the pace of intermediate innovations. Baldly stated, the general principle is "strong rights for a final innovation and weak rights for an intermediate innovation." Many innovations are not purely one or the other. The same innovations are enjoyed by consumers and used by firms to innovate. The degree of their mixture depends on technical characteristics of the innovating industry.

Figure 8 represents the optimal strength of patents for maximizing innovation in three technologies. Curve A depicts a technology with final innovations where strengthening patents always increases the rate of innovation, so the optimal patent is strong. Curve C represents a technology with intermediate innovations where strengthening patents always decreases the rate of innovation, so the optimal patent is weak. Curve B represents a technology used in final and intermediate innovation, where strengthening patents increases the rate of innovation up to a point, after which further strengthening decreases the rate of innovation. The optimal patent law is moderately strong for technology B.

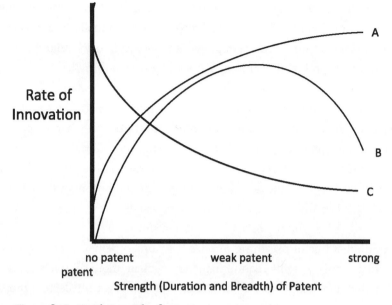

Figure 8. Optimal strength of patent

Figure 8 reveals a basic confusion in the standard normative analysis of innovation. According to the standard analysis, strong patents increase the profitability of an innovation as in curve A, but they do so at a cost of higher consumer prices. In the standard analysis these two effects should be balanced. According to overtaking theory, the standard analysis frames the problem of law wrongly, because growth overtakes the welfare effects of other objectives. Consequently, law and policy for intellectual property should maximize the rate of sustained growth, not balance growth against other values. By relying on the standard analysis, law and policy for intellectual property have built on the wrong foundation. In general, patents should in the first instance have the strength that maximizes the rate of innovation. This is the correct measure of whether patents are currently too strong or too weak. As a secondary matter, one turns to a static analysis of efficiency only if two patent policies cannot be ranked according to growth. For intellectual property, officials should worry little about static losses and much about incentives for foundational and follow-on innovations.

To maximize sustained growth, how strong should patents be? Since strengthening a patent raises revenues and costs of innovating, the strength of patent that maximizes the profitability of innovation is uncertain in theory. The answer depends on facts. Some observers think that the answer for some technologies is less restrictive copyrights and patent rights, and more common ownership.[13] Many academics feel that curtailment of copyrights in academic publications would speed the dissemination of new ideas. In any case, much empirical research needed for policy conclusions remains to be done, and research will progress faster by switching from the standard analysis to maximizing growth.

State Subsidies

Law provides a framework for the economy, rather like FIFA provides a framework for soccer.[14] Given background conditions and the right laws, entrepreneurs will innovate. Similarly, given background conditions and the right rules for soccer, the best teams will reach the World Cup. We can adjust the rules to improve the competition among entrepreneurs and soccer teams, even though we cannot predict the firm that will innovate or the team that will win the World Cup. Growth requires an effective legal framework that releases the energies of entrepreneurs and allows innovation to take its creative, unpredictable path.

The innovator who comes up with a new idea seldom has sufficient resources to develop it. As a result, economic innovation usually requires uniting someone's new ideas with someone else's capital. To combine new ideas with capital, the innovator must trust the financier with his idea, and the financier must trust the innovator with her capital. Startup firms and the research subsidiaries of international corporations face this problem. To put the matter starkly, if the innovator tells his idea to the financier, what will stop her from developing the idea herself or selling it to others? And, if they get past this issue, what will stop the innovator from stealing the money that the financier contributes?

Somehow, they must trust each other. We call this problem the "double-trust dilemma."[15] Their trust will not be blind, but rather a trust supported by laws—contracts, corporate, bankruptcy, securities, trade secrets, and intellectual property laws, among others.

Besides capital, developing an idea requires labor. The person who has an idea needs help from others to develop it. Developing an idea usually requires collaboration among people with different talents and training. Combining ideas and labor creates some of the same problems as combining ideas with capital. Once the idea is explained to a collaborator, what will stop her from developing the idea herself or selling it to others? Effort and productivity are hard to observe. What will prevent a collaborator from slacking? Combining the expertise of different people requires them to keep secrets and supply effort—the "collaborators' dilemma."[16] Formal contracts will not do the job completely because unobservable events are not provable in court. Incomplete contracts require supplementing with trust. As with capital, trust will not be blind, but a trust supported by law.

Each of these stark problems has milder counterparts. Instead of stealing the money, the innovator may waste it. Financiers gave billions of dollars to innovators with no management experience during the dot-com boom in the late 1990s in Silicon Valley. One person with no management experience often hired others with no experience, who in turn hired still others, and meanwhile, money burned. These problems have legal solutions, and each solution has more problems. In the end, law can reduce the transaction costs of combining new ideas with capital and labor, but not eliminate all of the problems.

This essay suggests that the state should take the *indirect* approach to promoting growth by developing laws that help entrepreneurs solve the double-trust dilemma. The state should not attempt the *direct* approach of promoting growth by subsidizing selected industries or granting them special privileges. Here's why. In making economic policy, the state should rely mostly on public information. When officials decide by using public information, they can explain and justify their policies to the citizens. Public discussion, debate, and criticism create a basis for accountability that dampens nepotism, favoritism, and corruption. Conversely, state officials can easily divert secret investments to their cronies. Politicians direct public money mostly to their supporters in order to build loyalty, however much they may talk about high-minded purposes. So the citizens in most democracies are right to demand that officials base economic policies on public information.

Soccer teams often surprise the opposing team and the fans in the stands. Similarly, innovative businesses often surprise competitors and outside observers, including economists and government officials. People who invest in innovative ideas keep many secrets in order to earn extraordinary profits. This is an aspect of the problem of trust at innovation's core. Thus, economists and government officials did not predict the invention of the "personal computer,"[17] or the explosive growth of the computer industry. Similarly, Japanese planners did not predict the surge of automobile manufacturers after 1960, and Indian planners did not predict the surge of computer firms in Bangalore after 1990.

When using public information, state officials can seldom predict the surge of a particular firm or industry. In this respect, state officials are in much the same situation as most investors. Most private investors cannot profit by trading on public information except by chance.[18] Similarly, most state officials cannot accelerate growth by investing public funds in particular firms or industries except by chance. Industrial policies that allegedly redirect capital to growth industries mostly waste resources without increasing growth rates.[19] Unlike state officials, private investors can appropriately invest on the basis of private information obtained by establishing trust with innovators.

Conclusion

An old disagreement between left and right animates debate about the economy's legal framework: To what extent should the state regulate markets? There is, however, a more fundamental question: What kind of law will promote growth? To maximize growth, law and policy should maximize the profitability of innovation. Developing an innovative idea requires combining it with capital (the double-trust dilemma) and labor (the collaborators' dilemma), which is what business ventures do. To solve these dilemmas, business ventures especially need the legal framework of property, contracts, and corporate law.

Law and policy for dynamic industries in the United States currently fails to maximize growth because it fails to maximize the profitability of innovation. Intellectual property law balances growth and the loss to consumers from higher prices. Instead, to maximize innovation, intellectual property law should balance higher revenues from monopoly power and higher costs from buying past innovations to develop future innovations. In industrial policy, the state should not attempt to promote growth by subsidizing selected industries or granting them special privileges. Rather, the state should subsidize infrastructure, education, basic research, and other goods where public decisions can rely exclusively on public information.

Notes

This article is based on Chapter 2 of a book manuscript on law and growth economics currently being written by Cooter and Edlin with support from the Ewing Marion Kauffman Foundation.

1. 1.02 to the power 100 equals 7.2; 1.10 to the power 100 equals 13,781. Growth in national income per capita is a better indicator of welfare than growth in national income. According to the Central Intelligence Agency's World Factbook, U.S. population growth rate is roughly 1 percent (among the highest among developed countries), and China's population growth rate is 0.5 percent.

2. Life expectancy at birth, total (years) in 2008, World Bank. http://data.world bank.org/indicator/SP.DYN.LE00.IN. Note that life expectancy is in the 40s in many African countries.

3. Data & Statistics on Education for 2007 and 2008, World Bank, http://web .worldbank.org/WBSITE/EXTERNAL/TOPICS/EXTEDUCATION/0,,contentMDK: 20573961~menuPK:282404~pagePK:148956~piPK:216618~theSitePK:282386,00 .html.

4. The largest effect of income redistribution on human welfare is through growth. Sometimes more inequality causes more growth by improving incentives for innovation, as in China after 1980. Redistributive expenditures sometimes promote growth by improving the education and health of workers, as with free primary schools and prenatal clinics.

5. Robert Cooter and Aaron Edlin, Maximizing Growth vs. Static Efficiency or Redistribution, Berkeley Law and Economics Working Paper (2010), prove formally that overtaking always occurs, provided the social planner's preferences for equality are not too strong.

6. See Robert Cooter and Hans-Bernd Schaefer, Solomon's Knot: How Law Can End the Poverty of Nations ch. 13 (forthcoming).

7. We distinguish innovations into technology, organization, and markets. Joseph Schumpeter distinguished a new good, a new method of production, a new organization, and a new market. Since technological innovations yield new goods and methods, his categories resemble ours. However, he adds a fifth type: new sources of raw materials. We omit his fifth type because, unlike ideas, resources are exhaustible. In general, our theory of innovation draws heavily on Schumpeter, especially his idea of entrepreneurs creatively disrupting equilibria. See Joseph A. Schumpeter, The Theory of Economic Development: An Inquiry into Profits, Capital, Credit, Interest, and the Business Cycle (transl. Redvers Opie, 1936).

8. Complete vertical integration would produce this result. If all innovating firms vertically integrated, then no innovating firm would buy innovations from any other firm. Instead, all innovating firms would sell exclusively to consumers. Stronger patents, consequently, would always increase the profitability and rate of innovation in an economy of complete vertical integration. However, vertical integration has various costs that preclude complete vertical integration.

9. Stephen S. Cohen and J. Bradford DeLong, The End of Influence 125 (2010).

10. Deadweight loss is the pure waste of resources due to the fact that the cost to the monopolist of making the good is less than its value to buyers.

11. This is true in the short run. The analysis is somewhat different in the long run, where all competitive firms earn the ordinary rate of return.

12. Intellectual property rights reduce the need for secrecy, which can decrease transaction costs among buyers and sellers.

13. Mark Lemley argues that growth in computer technology industries would benefit from less restrictive copyright and patent rights, and more common ownership. See Mark Lemley and Julie E. Cohen, Patent Scope and Innovation in the Software Industry, California Law Review 89 (2001); Mark Lemley and Dan L. Burk, The Patent Crisis and How the Courts Can Solve It (2009), especially chapter 12.

14. This section applies and develops themes about information and planning found in F. A. Hayek, notably in The Road to Serfdom (1944) and Law, Legislation, and Liberty (1973).

15. See Cooter and Schaefer, supra note 6, at ch. 3.

16. See Robert Cooter and Aaron Edlin, Law and Growth Economics: A Framework for Research, Berkeley Law and Economics Working Paper (2010).

17. IBM coined the name "personal computer" to market its first desktop computer in 1981.

18. The technical name for this proposition is the "efficient market hypothesis." According to the efficient market hypothesis, market prices incorporate all public information, so no investor can do better than chance when relying on public information. This is the "semi-strong" form of the efficient market hypothesis. If private investors cannot profit by trading on public information except by chance, then public officials are unlikely to do better. You don't have to accept the semi-strong form of the efficient market hypothesis in order to conclude that much business innovation is unpredictable from public information.

19. To illustrate, inflation-adjusted oil prices increased sharply from the mid-1970s until 1980, and then fell back to the previous low levels, where they remained until turning up again in 2002. Whereas public officials mistakenly predicted a sharp rise in oil prices, they remained stable for 20 years. U.S. politicians, however, used the prediction of rising oil prices to justify subsidies for private companies to construct and operate plants to extract oil from shale. The plants were uneconomic at current prices, but politicians and state officials predicted that prices would rise enough to justify the investment. In fact, these plants never became economic, and they closed down after the subsidies expired. U.S. taxpayers lost a massive amount of money, and some very large energy companies profited handsomely.

The Rule of Law and China

FRANCIS FUKUYAMA

The historical pattern of institutional development between the West and China differs significantly with regard to the rule of law. In the West, the rule of law was one of the first major institutions to emerge, preceding both the rise of the modern state and democracy by several centuries. In China, by contrast, a strong state coalesced early on, a state that did not feel normatively bound by any prior set of legal rules. As a result, law plays a very different role in contemporary China: While there are legal institutions, they are much weaker and less autonomous than their Western counterparts, and there is no rule of law as such. This has not prevented China from growing rapidly over the past three decades, which should force Westerners to re-examine the current orthodoxy that a strong rule of law is critical to economic growth.

The China model, encompassing a strong centralized state unconstrained by either rule of law or democratic elections, has been remarkably successful in managing the country's economic modernization and emergence as the world's second largest economy over the past 30 years. Whether such a system devoid of checks and balances can continue to perform at this level into the future is one of the central questions of contemporary political economy.

Unhelpful Economists

The first problem that arises in thinking about the rule of law is how to define it. As with the term "democracy," there is a wide variety of meanings given to the rule of law that makes theorizing difficult. There has been a huge amount of attention paid to what is labeled the "rule of law" in the past couple of decades as a practical issue in democracy and governance promotion. Much of this interest has been driven by economists, who have their own peculiar understanding of the rule of law and who have, as a result, distorted thinking about what it is and how it comes about.[1]

When economists speak about the rule of law, they are usually referring to modern property rights and contract enforcement. Modern property rights are held by individuals, who are free to alienate their property without restrictions imposed by kin groups, religious authorities, or the state. The theory by which property rights and contract enforcement are related to economic growth is straightforward. No one will make long-term investments unless they know that their property rights are secure. Similarly, trade requires contracts and a legal machinery to enforce contracts and to adjudicate the disputes that inevitably arise among contracting parties. The more transparent the contracting rules, and the more evenhanded their enforcement, the more trade will be encouraged. This is why many economists emphasize the importance of "credible commitments" as a hallmark of a state's institutional development. There is at this point a substantial empirical literature that correlates strong property rights to long-term economic growth.[2]

The problem with the close identification of rule of law with property rights is that it excessively narrows the definition of law, and is inconsistent with the understanding of the term traditionally held by lawyers. By this older definition, the law is a body of rules of justice that bind a community together. In premodern societies, the law was believed to be fixed by an authority higher than any human legislator, either by a divine authority or by nature. Kings, barons, presidents, legislatures, and warlords could issue new positive legislation. But if they are to function within the rule of law, they must legislate according to the rules set by the pre-existing law, and not according to their own volition.

This earlier understanding of the law as something fixed either by divine authority or by nature implied that the law could not be changed by human agency, though it could be interpreted to fit novel circumstances. With the decline of religious authority and belief in natural law in modern times, we have come to understand the law as something created by human beings—that is, as a species of positive law—but only under a strict set of procedural rules that guarantee that they correspond to a broad social consensus over basic values. The distinction between law and legislation now corresponds to the distinction between constitutional and ordinary law, where the former has more stringent requirements for enactment, such as supermajority voting. In the contemporary United States, this means that any new law passed by Congress must be consistent with a prior and superior body of law, the U.S. Constitution, as interpreted by the Supreme Court.

There is obviously some relationship between the traditional legal understanding of the rule of law and the economists' identification of law with property rights. If a government does not feel bound by a pre-existing rule of law, but considers itself fully sovereign in all respects, there will be nothing preventing it from taking the property of its citizens, or of foreigners who happen to be doing business in its territory. If general legal rules are not enforced in the cases of powerful elites, or against the most powerful actor of all, the government, then there can be no ultimate certainty about the security of either private property or trade.[3]

If we define the rule of law not as credible property rights and contract enforcement but as the government's acceptance of the sovereignty of a pre-existing body of law representing a social consensus on rules of justice, then we can proceed to ask the question, where has the rule of law come from historically, and how might we expect it to emerge in the future?

Religion and the Rule of Law

If one wants to look for a source of social rules that is invariant and reflects the shared moral values of a community, the obvious place to go is religion—not religion as practiced in modern, pluralistic societies, but the religions that defined premodern societies like ancient Israel, medieval

Europe, or the early Islamic world. Religious rules are held by their believers to be the products not of human agency but of divine authority, and are therefore binding on all human agents, including the political sovereign. Indeed, most rulers in such societies never claimed they were sovereign; God was sovereign, and the ruler merely acted as God's deputy or vicar on earth.

It is therefore not surprising that the rule of law first originated in societies that were dominated by a transcendental religion, and that the first laws that rulers had to respect were religious ones. The Hebrew Bible and Talmud, the Roman Twelve Tables, the early Church decretals and canons, the sunna and hadith, the vedas and sastras were all recognized in their respective societies as shared rules of justice, and in each society—Israelite, Roman, Christian, Muslim, and Hindu—rulers explicitly recognized a duty to live under the religiously defined law.

The rulers of many societies outside of East Asia thus recognized that they lived under a law that they themselves did not create. And yet, the degree to which this would impose real restrictions on their behavior depended not just on this theoretical acknowledgment, but on the institutional conditions surrounding the formulation and enforcement of law. The law would become a more binding constraint on rulers under certain specific conditions: if it was codified into an authoritative text; if the content of the law was determined by specialists in law, and not by political authorities; if the law was protected by an institutional order separate from the political hierarchy, with its own resources and power of appointment; and finally, if the law actually corresponded to the lived social norms and values of the community to which it was applied, including the ruling elites who presided over the political system.

In contrast to other law-governed societies, western Europe was exceptional insofar as law was institutionalized early on and to a higher degree than elsewhere. This was probably less a function of the underlying religious ideas than of historically contingent circumstances of European development, since the Eastern Orthodox Church never went through a comparable development. It led to an unusual situation in which rule of law became embedded in European society even before the advent not just of democracy and accountable government, but the modern state-

building process itself. This is evident in all the dimensions of institutionalized law.[4]

Codification. In contrast to India, where the vedas were transmitted
orally and written down only at a relatively late point, the three monothe-
istic religions of Judaism, Christianity, and Islam were all based from a
very early point on authoritative scriptures. In the eastern and western
Christian churches, the Bible was supplemented by a confusing welter
of Church canons, decrees, and interpretations. This changed in the late
11th century with the rediscovery of the *Corpus Iuris Civilis*, the great sixth-
century compilation of Roman law under the emperor Justinian. The
sprawling body of canon law was systematized in the following century in
the *Decretum* of Gratian. No similar rationalization of law ever occurred in
the Eastern Church, or in the Hindu or Muslim traditions until the codifi-
cations that were carried out under western influence in the 19th century.

Legal specialization. The new system based on Roman law was spread
throughout the whole of Europe from the great law school at the University
of Bologna. Whereas kings, emperors, and other temporal rulers had made
ecclesiastical law before the 11th century Gregorian reform, law became the
province first of the Church, and then of a legal profession trained in
canon and civil law. In this respect Christianity does not differ substantially
from Islam, which also put law under the custody of a hierarchy of legal
specialists, the ulama, or Hinduism, where the priestly Brahmin class had
a monopoly as specialists in law.

Institutional autonomy. Caesaropapism is a term coined by Max Weber
to denote a regime in which temporal authorities have power to appoint
and dismiss religious ones. Both the eastern and western Christian churches
were caesaropapist until the Investiture Conflict of the 11th century, in
which a strong-willed pope, Gregory VII, challenged the Holy Roman Emperor's right to appoint popes and bishops. The prolonged struggle between pope and emperor resulted in the Concordat of Worms in 1122, in
which the Catholic Church won the right to name its own cadres. Together
with the practice of celibacy for the priesthood, the Church was able to free
itself from temporal politics, and created what legal scholar Harold Berman
labels the first modern bureaucracy on which later state bureaucracies

would be modeled.[5] No religious establishment in any other cultural tradition ever succeeded in institutionalizing itself to this extent.

Correspondence between law and social norms. The normative dimension of law—that is, the shared belief that the law is fundamentally just and the subsequent willingness of people to abide by its rules—is key to the rule of law. The most secure form of law should depend not on draconian punishments but rather on voluntary compliance on the part of most citizens. It is not clear that Europe had a particular advantage over India or the Middle East in this regard, since the religiously based law of all three civilizations shaped and reflected broad social norms. However, one of the great problems with trying to import modern western legal systems into societies where they did not exist previously is the lack of correspondence between the imported law and the society's existing social norms. The importation of legal rules can sometimes speed up a process of social change, as when laws mandating equal rights for women are imposed in a society dominated by males. But if the gap between law and lived values is too large, the rule of law itself will not take hold.

European political development was unusual insofar as a strong, dominant legal culture emerged in western Europe during the Middle Ages before there were modern states. There was in fact a kind of trans-national legal culture, underpinned by the ecclesiastical law of the Catholic Church, which shaped and constrained the ability of early modern state-builders in France, England, Spain, and other western countries to accumulate unchecked power. Few absolutist monarchs were willing to openly violate the property and personal rights of their elite subjects without something approaching due process, unlike state-builders in China or Russia who could act with much more arbitrariness and brutality. The emergence of a uniform common law in England, which was originally an extension of the law of the king's court and enforced by centralized royal authority, did much to legitimize property rights at a very early point in the country's history.

Europe was no different from other societies insofar as a rule of law protecting citizens against arbitrary actions of the state itself was initially applied only to a minority of privileged subjects. Take, for example, a letter quoted by Alexis de Tocqueville in *Democracy in America* by Mme. de Sévigné, one of the greatest salon patrons of 17th-century France. This witty and sensitive woman describes how soldiers in Brittany were enforcing a new tax, turning old men and children out of their houses in search of assets to seize. Some 60 townspeople were to be hanged the following day for non-payment. She goes on: "The fiddler who had begun the dance and the stealing of stamped paper was broken on the wheel; he was quartered [i.e., cut into four pieces] and his four quarters exposed in the four corners of the town."[6]

Obviously, the French state would not enforce such drastic penalties on Mme. de Sévigné and her circle. It is therefore not true that there was no rule of law in 17th-century France, but the law did not regard commoners as legal persons entitled to the same rights as the aristocracy. The same was true of the United States at its founding, as it excluded blacks, women, and white men without property from the right to vote. The process of democratization is one in which a rule of law applying only to elites is gradually expanded to include all adult persons. This pattern continues to the present day, where the elite rule of law of apartheid South Africa was expanded to apply to non-whites after that country's transition to democracy in 1992. It is much easier to expand an existing elite rule of law than to create one from scratch.

Law in China

The only major world civilization in which a religiously derived rule of law did not emerge is China, and the East Asian countries influenced by Chinese culture. The reason is that China never developed a transcendental religion higher than ancestor worship that was broadly accepted by its elites as authoritative. Ancestor worship is not a good source of law since no one has an obligation to worship anyone else's ancestors; it therefore cannot impose generally binding obligations on a large society. Hence, while the Chinese developed extensive legal codes in the Qin, Han, Tang, and Ming dynasties, these were all positive law—that is, enactments by the emperor who did not recognize any authority higher than himself.[7] The religions introduced into China, such as Daoism, Buddhism, and Christianity, were mostly protest religions not reflecting a larger social consensus.

The rule of law in the sense defined here continues up through the present day. The Chinese Communist Party does not accept the authority of any other institution in China as superior to it, such as an institution like a Supreme Court that is able to overturn its decisions. While the People's Republic of China (PRC) has a constitution, the party makes the constitution rather than the reverse. If the current Chinese government wanted to nationalize all existing foreign investments in China, or re-nationalize the holdings of private individuals and return the country to Maoism, there is no legal framework preventing it from doing so.

Dynastic China was one of the world's greatest and longest-enduring civilizations. It did not, however, create the institutions necessary to generate or sustain the increases in productivity necessary for long-term per capita economic growth.[8] Today, by contrast, China possesses the world's second-largest economy in absolute output and has achieved an extraordinary rate of growth over the past three decades. It would not appear, however, that the change in economic performance was due to modern China's development of a rule of law and modern property rights in the sense understood in the West. This suggests that the theory placing rule of law front and center as the explanation for modern economic growth is somehow wrong.

The absence of rule of law or other procedural checks on a Chinese emperor's power meant that China was periodically subject to a type of despotism unknown in most of western European history. Chinese history is littered with cases of "bad emperors," like Qin Shi Huangdi, the monarch who created the first unified Qin state, or the "evil Empress Wu" of the Tang dynasty, who succeeded in killing off much of the Tang aristocracy, or the Wanli emperor in the Ming dynasty who refused to come out of his quarters for nearly a decade and let state affairs languish in the face of a growing foreign threat from the Manchus. Chinese rulers, unlike their European counterparts, did not have to seek permission from sovereign courts or parliaments in order to raise taxes. Not only could they arbitrarily set tax rates through simple executive order, but they could also confiscate property at will. Unlike the absolutist monarchs of early modern France and Spain who had to proceed very gingerly when confronting powerful elites, the first Ming emperor, Taizu, simply confiscated the lands of the largest landowners in the realm. He was said to have liquidated "count-less" affluent households, particularly in the Yangtze delta, where he be-lieved he faced particularly strong opposition.[9]

Nevertheless, the majority of Chinese emperors did not abuse their powers to the degree theoretically possible, both in matters of routine taxa-tion and in their willingness to violate the personal integrity of their elite subjects. The real constraints on Chinese power were different, and were of three basic sorts.

First, some Chinese emperors were not concerned to maximize their revenues. Mancur Olson's assumption that any ruler would want to do so reflects the common assumption of modern economics that maximi-zation is a universal characteristic of human behavior.[10] But this is an anachronistic projection of modern values backward into societies that didn't necessarily share them. The first Ming emperor Taizu was an austere autocrat who cut the size of the central government and avoided foreign wars; his granaries actually ran surpluses. Chinese monarchs, no less than rulers of other premodern societies, often exhibited what economist Herbert Simon has labeled "satisficing" rather than maximizing behav-ior.[11] That is, in the absence of an urgent need for revenue like a war, they were often content to let sleeping dogs lie and collect only the amount of revenues required for their regular needs. A truly determined emperor could decide to behave like a maximizer, and some did so, but the idea that all autocratic political leaders automatically maximize is manifestly not true.

Second, there was a simple lack of administrative capacity to carry out orders and in particular to extract a high level of taxes. China was already a huge country at the beginning of the Ming dynasty, with a population of over 60 million in 1368 that grew to 138 million by the 17th century.[12] The challenges of collecting taxes over so vast a territory were daunting. The draconian powers of taxation and confiscation held by emperors also tended to be a wasting commodity. It could be used early on in a dynasty when the emperor was consolidating power and settling scores with for-mer opponents. But as time went on, the palace found it often needed the cooperation of those same elites and dramatically reduced tax rates in the same areas it had earlier confiscated property.

A third limitation, related to the second, was the need for delegation. All large organizations, whether governments or private corporations, have to delegate authority, and when they do, the "sovereign" sitting at the top of the administrative hierarchy loses an important degree of control over the organization. The delegation can be to functional specialists, such as budgeting officers or military logisticians, or it can be regional, to a hierarchy of provincial, prefectural, municipal, and local authorities. These delegations are necessary because no ruler can ever have enough time or knowledge to actually make all of the important decisions in his or her realm.

With the delegation of authority, however, goes power. The agents to whom power has been delegated have authority over the delegator in the form of knowledge. This can be either the technical knowledge that goes with the running of a specialized ministry or agency, or the local knowledge of particular conditions existing in a certain region. It is for this reason that organizational specialists like Herbert Simon have argued that authority in any large bureaucracy flows not only from the top of the hierarchy to the bottom, but often in a reverse direction as well.[13]

Indeed, it is clear that the greatest threat to the property and liberties of ordinary Chinese in traditional China was not a despotic central government, but rather a combination of local aristocratic oligarchs who used their first-mover advantages to accumulate large latifundia at the expense of peasants, together with precisely those local government agents designated to carry out the emperor's orders, but who were not effectively controlled by him. Chinese history is replete with often unsuccessful attempts by emperors to engage in land reform or otherwise protect the interests of non-elite subjects.

Although its basis of legitimation is very different, the contemporary government of the PRC bears many structural similarities to that of dynastic China. Then as now, what the Chinese are good at is centralized, impersonal bureaucratic administration. The Chinese Communist Party, while not formally accountable through democratic elections or bound by a rule of law, nonetheless tries to respond to popular demands and serve what it construes as public interest. Unlike certain African dictatorships, Chinese authoritarians are not predatory rulers trying to extract the maximum possible rents out of their society for their own personal benefit.

In many ways, property rights today are not terribly different from what they were in dynastic China. Deng Xiaoping's 1978 reforms that de-collectivized agriculture did not lead to the creation of modern property rights. The state continues to own most land in China; private individuals hold usufructuary rights to its use under long-term leases. Then as now there is no Chinese equivalent of the 14th Amendment and its guarantees of "due process"; illegal "takings" occur all the time throughout China.

Indeed, property rights are disregarded in modern China to the same degree as in historical times. Most often, a private developer in league with a local government arbitrarily takes land from hapless peasants or other non-elites. The worst forms of corruption are said to occur at a local rather than at a national level, and the central government is often called upon to correct these abuses. Accountability goes upward only to the higher levels of the party, as it once did to the emperor; justice is served only when the abuse is egregious or word leaks out and the party feels compelled to discipline its own cadres. One advantage that contemporary Chinese rulers have is the availability of modern information technology through which they can track local developments: though they control political dissent closely, they also try to respond to citizen complaints on the Internet and other forms of social protest that come to their attention.

It is clear that contemporary China does not possess either the rule of law or property rights in anything close to the form that Westerners associate with those institutions. There are no formal legal constraints on the discretion of the Chinese state; the courts are not powerful, autonomous institutions capable of disciplining Chinese political leaders; most property is held in usufruct and not owned absolutely; and property rights are often violated in an arbitrary way. Nonetheless, China has a controlled market economy and has grown extraordinarily rapidly in the past generation. This suggests that any theory that associates economic growth with the procedural forms of the rule of law that exist in the West need to be seriously rethought. China obviously has property rights that are "good

enough" to sustain rapid economic development. Both the Chinese themselves and foreigners make large investments in confidence that they will
be able to earn a return over relatively long periods of time. But this has
much more to do with the informal character of these rights than their
formal or procedural nature.

The China Model

The China model is a form of authoritarian capitalism with very specific
Chinese characteristics that distinguishes it from other varieties found in
Russia, Iran, Singapore, or other countries with which it is often compared. The economic part of the model is unpinned by a heavy export emphasis driven by pervasive state intervention in an otherwise competitive
market economy. This intervention takes several forms: management of
the currency to keep it below market-clearing levels through careful control
of currency reserves and heavy financial repression; a modified industrial
policy, such as the South Korean version, that seeks not so much to promote winners as to create generally favorable conditions for employment-
generating exporters; and continuing use of state-owned enterprises and
banks as a means of managing the economy. The political side of the model
consists of a monopoly of political power by the Chinese Communist Party
and its replication of government functions in its own bureaucracy; relatively high-quality economic decision-making at the higher levels of the
party; collective leadership that, within the party, is fairly well institutionalized; and a degree of development-mindedness and willingness to respond
to popular demands that sets it apart from more predatory authoritarian
regimes.

The legal part of the China model is harder to describe because many
of the institutions are informal. There is of course a formal legal system,
as well as a relatively large arbitration system (as in other Asian countries)
that performs dispute-resolution functions for ordinary people.[14] These
courts, however, are not institutionally autonomous from executive power
in China, and in matters deemed important to the Party they can be overridden. There is a high level of perceived corruption in China, particularly

at lower levels of government. The reason that domestic and foreign investors are still willing to take long-term risks in China has to do with their perception that the Chinese government in its own self-interest will not harm their property rights, which makes them "good enough" to underpin growth. Most of the unjust and illegal "takings" that the Chinese government engages in are against relatively powerless peasants and non-elites, and are done in the name of rapid economic development. Unlike the situation in Russia, there have been relatively few cases of the government confiscating or otherwise strong-arming large foreign investors (something that has nonetheless not deterred substantial foreign investment in Russia either). China thus remains an example of what North and Weingast label a "limited access order," in which the government decides who will and will not be able to compete in the economic system.[15]

The Future of the Model

The Chinese model has been remarkably successful in promoting economic growth in a very large country up to now, but what are its long-term prospects when compared with a liberal democracy like those in North America, Europe, or Asia? China has some clear advantages with regard to the speed with which it can make large, complicated decisions over a typical democracy with lobbies, interest groups, and need for political consensus. However, the Chinese system has at least three long-term liabilities that are likely to impact its performance in the future.

The first has to do with the ability of a centralized bureaucratic system to continue to manage a large, complex, and rapidly changing society. As noted above, the system is much more responsive to popular pressures than many other authoritarian regimes; the party monitors public protest and encourages competition among local government units in meeting public goals. But the system ultimately faces immense information problems in actually knowing what is going on in the society, in the absence of institutions like elections and a free media.

The second problem is what the Chinese have traditionally labeled the "bad emperor" problem, which is most directly related to the absence of a rule of law. An authoritarian government run by competent and publicly minded technocrats can often outperform a democracy precisely because it can cut through the procedural niceties imposed by elections and a rule of law. But what guarantees that it will always have good leaders? Chinese history, as we have seen, is littered with periodic "bad emperors" who wreaked enormous havoc on the society. The last bad emperor generally acknowledged as such by many Chinese was Mao Zedong, who unleashed the Cultural Revolution, the trauma of which still haunts the memories of many living Chinese. While the rule of law may lead law-bound societies to underperform in certain circumstances, they provide a floor protecting society from the worst rulers.

The final problem with the Chinese model is the lack of legitimacy. The basis of the legitimacy of the Chinese Communist Party's continued rule is not clear, since its Marxist ideological self-justification has been under-cut by its own policies. It has sought alternative forms of legitimacy on the basis of its management of economic growth and through the cultivation of Chinese nationalism. Both of these paths are fraught with danger, how-ever. Double-digit growth and employment expansion will not continue forever, and nationalism is a two-edged sword that eludes the Party's con-trol. The egalitarian pretensions of the Party are contradicted by the sharply rising degree of economic inequality in Chinese society and a broad per-ception of corruption among China's new elites. A society with a strong rule of law, by contrast, finds legitimacy and social consensus in the law itself, which is superior to and more stable than the performance of a given government.

The western European pattern of development was one in which the rule of law existed before anyone tried to construct a strong, modern state. As a result, law prevented the most tyrannical forms of government from ever appearing in the first place. In China, the reverse happened: a strong state arose early in its history, and the state has never seen itself bound by pre-existing law. Both of these systems appear to be capable of generating rapid economic growth. We should admit to ourselves that we have very little historical experience with how a rule of law might evolve in a country like China that has not experienced institutional constraints on executive power.

And we also do not know how sustainable such an unbalanced, unchecked system will be under the external conditions it will face in the future.

Notes

Portions of this article were drawn from the author's The Origins of Political Order: From Prehuman Times to the French Revolution (2011).

1. See Stephan Haggard and Andrew MacIntyre, The Rule of Law and Economic Development, 11 Annual Review of Political Science 205 (2008).

2. See, e.g., Daniel Kaufmann and Aart Kraay, Governance Matters IV: Governance Indicators for 1996–2004 (Washington, DC: World Bank Institute, 2005). There was also a prolonged debate over the dubious assertion that common-law systems were friendly to growth than civil law ones. Rafael La Porta, Florencio Lopez-de-Silanes, Andrei Shleifer, and Robert W. Vishny, Law and Finance, 106 J. Pol. Econ. 1113 (1998).

3. This was the theme in Douglass C. North and Barry R. Weingast, Constitutions and Commitment: The Evolution of Institutions Governing Public Choice in Seventeenth-Century England, 49 J. Econ. Hist. 803 (1989).

4. On this point, see Joseph R. Strayer, On the Medieval Origins of the Modern State (1970).

5. Harold J. Berman, Law and Revolution: The Formation of the Western Legal Tradition (1983).

6. Alexis de Tocqueville, II Democracy in America, 3.1, at 537 (trans. Mansfield and Winthrop) (2000).

7. In theory, the Chinese developed an amorphous concept of "Heaven" after the Shang dynasty whose mandate emperors bore; this hardly amounted to law, however, and was mostly invoked ex post to legitimize a dynastic transition.

8. Some have speculated that the country was caught in a high-level equilibrium trap in which there were no incentives to invest in the technology necessary to move beyond a pre-industrial economy. See, for example, Joseph Needham, Science and Civilization in China, 25 vols. (1954–); Mark Elvin, The Pattern of the Chinese Past: A Social and Economic Interpretation (1973).

9. Denis Twitchett and Frederick W. Mote (eds.), The Cambridge History of China, Vol. 8, The Ming Dynasty, 1368–1644, Part 2, 110 (1978); Ray Huang, "Fiscal Administration during the Ming Dynasty," in Charles O. Hucker and Tilemann Grimm (eds.), Chinese Government in Ming Times; Seven Studies 105 (1969).

10. Mancur Olson, Dictatorship, Democracy, and Development, 87 Am. Pol. Sc. Rev. 567 (1993).

11. Herbert Simon, Theories of Decision-making in Economics and Behavioral Science, 49 Am. Econ. Rev. 253 (1959); Herbert Simon, A Behavioral Model of Rational Choice, 59 Q. J. Econ. 98 (1955).

12. Angus Maddison, Chinese Economic Performance in the Long Run, 960–2030 24 (2d. ed. 2007).

13. Herbert Simon, Administrative Behavior: A Study of Decision-making Processes in Administrative Organization 180 (1957).

14. Martin M. Shapiro, Courts: A Comparative and Political Analysis (1981).

15. Douglass C. North and Barry R. Weingast, Violence and Social Orders: A Conceptual Framework for Interpreting Recorded Human History (2009).

PART 10:

CHANGING COURSE

Reversing

F.H. BUCKLEY

If I tell you how things are, I have told you why things cannot change.
—EDWARD BANFIELD

W hat can be done to slow the pathology I have described? That was Lucky Jim's question. The essays in this book have found fault with and sought changes to American private and criminal law, and these changes, if they are to come, must come from either judges or legislators. Legislative reform would seem to hold the most promise, since courts, particularly courts with a conservative agenda that would be inclined to reverse pro-plaintiff rules, generally defer to legislators. Yet when one turns to the federal legislative arena there are little grounds for optimism. I explain why here.

Federal Legislation

Two nations emerged from the American Revolution. The first, populist and Republican, was the United States. The second, Tory and monarchical, was Canada. The descendants of the American Loyalists who fled to Canada and gave the country one-half of its founding myths saw it accede to self-government not through revolution but through a gradual and peaceful transfer of power to elected representatives.

There is another, less obvious, difference between the manner in which America and Canada achieved independence, and this was a consequence of contemporaneous ideas about government. Both countries took their inspiration from the freest country then in existence: Great Britain. But Great Britain in 1867, at the time of the British North America Act that unified Canada and gave it a constitution, was a different country than it was in 1787 when the Framers gathered in Philadelphia to draft a Constitution.

What the Framers of the American Constitution saw, when they looked to Great Britain, was a divided government, a constitution where sovereignty resided in the King-in-Parliament, composed of the King, the House of Lords, and the House of Commons. That wasn't quite the tripartite division identified by the "celebrated Montesquieu," with his executive, legislative, and judicial branches, but it nevertheless was seen as an example of the separation of powers, and that was the kind of government that the Framers gave their country, after the rise of Democracy made presidents popularly elected.

When Canada acceded to self-government in 1867, the Fathers of Confederation also looked to Great Britain as a model. However, something had happened during the interim. The British Constitution in the time of Disraeli and Gladstone was not the same as that of Blackstone and Chatham. The crucial change came in 1832 with the Reform Act, passed over the initial objections of the King and the House of Lords. From that time onward, the British Constitution abandoned the separation of powers, as this was understood by Americans. Instead, it gave Britain a unitary government, with virtually all power residing in the House of Commons. When Walter Bagehot published *The English Constitution*, in the same year as the British North America Act, it seemed clear to him that the "efficient secret of the English Constitution may be described as the close union, the nearly complete fusion, of the executive and legislative powers."

When Canada achieved independence, then, it was taken for granted that both federal and provincial governments should be modeled on the British lines of the day. What Britain offered Canada was a system of responsible, parliamentary government, and what Canada offered the remaining British colonies was a method of achieving independence without a revolution or break with the British connection. The British North America Act was a Canadian creation, drafted in Canada and passed by a British parliament preoccupied with the Second Reform Act and only too happy to let go of a burdensome colony.[1] This was not a model calculated to inflame the passions or result in television mini-series, but it was followed by more than 50 countries with a combined population of over two billion people, and that is no small thing.

A. Constitutional Infirmities

Americans take justified pride in their political institutions and method of achieving independence, but was the Anglo-Canadian model a superior one in the end? American theorists, particularly conservatives, tend to assume without question the superiority of divided government and the separation of powers. The alternative, it seems to be thought, is one-party governance and a quick slide into dictatorship. "The American system of government separates power," observes Tom Campbell. "It thereby achieves protection for its citizens against the potential of tyranny."[2] In *Federalist* 47, Madison was even more emphatic. "The accumulation of all powers legislative, executive and judiciary in the same hands, whether of one, a few or many, and whether hereditary, selfappointed, or elective, may justly be pronounced the very definition of tyranny."

That's not been our historical experience, however. There are a good many more presidents-for-life than prime ministers-for-life.[3] Nearly every country from the former Soviet Union that adopted a presidential system has become an autocracy. Only the parliamentary systems remain democracies. The U.S. Constitution seemingly was not made for export. It has served America well, but was that because it was American, and not because of the constitutional machinery?

Madison's fears about majoritarian tyranny seem therefore to have been excessive. In addition, the American system of separation of powers suffers from various defects not found in the Anglo-Canadian parliamentary model of government. By making prime ministers accountable to the House, parliamentary systems reduce the agency costs of presidential misbehavior or incompetence.[4] In recent years we have seen not a few examples of administrations that would have fallen in votes of non-confidence in a House of Commons. Second, laws are enacted in excessive detail in presidential systems, as a consequence of the competition between the executive and legislative branches, where the latter seeks to bind the hands of present and future executives.[5] Third, bad laws such as Sarbanes-Oxley are more likely to be enacted when individual congressional leaders, and not the administration, can put their names on bills and take ownership of them. Grandstanding of this kind gives us the bubble laws decried by Stephen Bainbridge. Fourth, the separation of powers promotes wasteful spending at the initiative of individual congressional leaders. Divided government empowers holdouts (especially in the U.S. Senate) who can extract major concessions in return for their support. This is the "commons" problem to which Steven Magee alludes.

While all of these are troubling, our concern is with a further defect: the *reversibility* problem of presidential government. Bad laws get enacted in both systems, but they can more easily be reversed in a parliamentary system.

B. Reversibility

It is generally conceded that America's immigration system is broken. As noted in Part 2, it sends valuable immigrants to other countries and weakens our economy. Admitting a greater number of economic immigrants would assist both them and native-born Americans. As I write there is talk of an immigration reform package in Congress, which may provide a path to citizenship for "illegals." What is less likely is a reform that would provide a suitable gateway for economic migrants.

Immigration is one example of the reversibility problem. Part 2 suggests other examples, notably the burden of America's debt crisis.[6] As a percentage of GDP, total government expenditures (federal, state, and local) in the past few years exceed spending during the First World War and amount to three-quarters of our spending on the Second World War. The difference is that today we won't see much of a peace dividend that comes when a war is over. What we will see are the enormous additional demands placed on Social Security and Medicare as the boomers retire. The question, then, is whether America can reverse course, as Canada did.

In 1994 the Canadian economy was in crisis. The country had a federal debt-to-GDP ratio of 67 percent (about where America is today), and the *Wall Street Journal* labeled it an honorary member of the third world. Over the next 16 years, Canada's federal debt fell to 29 percent of GDP, almost entirely from spending cuts. Economist David Henderson explains why it would be difficult for America to duplicate the Canadian experience.

> There is . . . one important political factor that would make reform more difficult in the United States than in Canada: the structure of the U.S. political system. In Canada, once the Prime Minister has decided on the budget, the members of his or her Party almost always vote for it. Moreover, under Canada's Constitution, the government, meaning the ruling party, has sole power to initiate expenditure proposals. Parliament's only power on spending is to approve the government's proposals in full, approve them at a reduced level, or reject them. In the United States, by contrast, there are three important players or sets of players: the president, the House of Representatives, and the Senate.[7]

It will similarly prove difficult to reverse the federal legislation that contributes to the decline in the rule of law. The Sarbanes-Oxley legislation described in Part 7, the luxurious growth of federal criminal laws seen in Part 8, and the costly entitlement programs deprecated by Richard Epstein in Part 9 all seem likely to remain features of our political landscape.

Reversing course is always harder than starting afresh. It's easier to start a new program than to close an existing one; it's easier to hire a public servant than to fire one. Every time a new program is begun, interest groups coalesce around it. Businesses and groups that profit from it will fight tooth and nail to prevent its repeal. This will happen in both presidential and parliamentary systems, but there are special reasons why reversibility is particularly difficult in the former case.

Getting legislation passed or repealed in America is like waiting for three cherries to line up in a Las Vegas slot machine. Absent a supermajority in Congress to override a presidential veto, one needs the simultaneous concurrence of the president, Senate, and House. In a parliamentary system, by contrast, one needs only one cherry.[8] In Canada, neither the Governor-General nor the senate has a veto power. All that matters is the House of Commons, dominated by the prime minister's party. While his party commands a majority in the House and he enjoys his party's support, the prime minister, like Hobbes' Leviathan, is immune from the infirmities of divided sovereignty.[9]

The difference between the two systems is magnified by the greater power enjoyed by political parties in parliamentary systems. In the United States, politicians, especially in the Senate, enjoy far greater independence from their parties than M.P.'s do in a parliamentary system. In Canada, Prime Minister Trudeau famously described his backbenchers as "no-bodies," and their lack of power was recently underlined by another Liberal prime minister: "Over the last forty years or so, Canadians have seen the influence of individual members of parliament eroded as the power of the prime minister and the executive branch of government grew.... They vote according to the dictates of their party, and too often, when their party is in power, no one in the government cares particularly what they have to say."[10]

Canada and the United States are both eminently democratic countries. However, the centralization of power in the modern prime minister's office exceeds that in American politics. That's a particular problem in modern politics, since decentralization of power in a presidential system makes it easier for concentrated interest groups, such as trial lawyer groups and the K Street lobbyists of Washington, to shape our laws at the expense of the general welfare. Decentralization increases lobbying costs, which a concentrated group can bear relatively more easily than a dispersed group. One would therefore expect to see more interest groups bargains, which redistribute wealth from everyone in society to a small, concentrated, and powerful group within society, in the United States.

To reverse this, what is needed is a grand coalition, a coalition of the whole of the voters, who will vote for the general welfare rather than the narrow interest of their congressional district. Mancur Olson called this a "superencompassing majority,"[11] one that treats minorities as well as it treats itself and stands in proxy for the nation as a whole. Discovering and empowering such a majority might then be thought the very goal of constitution-making. It was the idea behind Bolingbroke's idealized Patriot King, who governs "like the common father of his people . . . where the head and all the members are united by one common interest."[12]

Not everyone will endorse a constitutional regime that empowers a super-encompassing majority. Some Americans identify less with the nation as a whole and more with the interests of a particular group within the nation.

For them, questions of social justice turn primarily on how members of a particular class, defined by race, sex, or sexual preference, might fare. They might not be willing to sacrifice the interests of their identity group, or might take the national interest to be nothing more than the sum of the interests of similar progressive groups. Further, those who take a broader view of the national interest might fear that majoritarian coalitions will not be superencompassing, that they will treat minorities unfairly; and that was precisely the problem that separationism's checks and balances was meant to address. Even if one takes the national interest as the primary good, then, one might see the threat of majoritarian misbehavior as a greater evil than the minoritarian misbehavior of interest groups that prey off the public purse.

If it's a tradeoff between the two kinds of oppression, however, minoritarian misbehavior seems the greater concern. If majoritarian misbehavior were to be feared in America, we might expect to find that minorities have fared poorly in similar parliamentary countries, such as Britain and Canada, which lack America's separation of powers. But without putting too fine a point on it, there is simply no evidence of this.

As for the minoritarian misbehavior of wasteful rules adopted at the behest of narrow interest groups, these seem less of a problem in a parliamentary regime. In a presidential system, where national partiers are weaker, one votes for the representative who brings home the bacon to one's district. That doesn't happen to the same extent in parliamentary systems, where national parties are stronger. With a two-party system and a diverse electorate a party requires broad, national support to be elected, a parliamentary party will have a greater incentive to acquire a reputation that puts what it understands as the common good ahead of wasteful local projects. For their part, voters will have compelling reasons to believe that the party will behave in ways consistent with its reputation. In this way, the party's interests will be more closely aligned with those of the country, and members of the party will be personally motivated to pursue the country's collective interests.

Similarly, a prime minister's interests will be aligned with those of his party and through it to the country as a whole. A prime minister needs the day-to-day support of M.P.'s to remain in office. Though he may dominate his party he is ultimately responsible to it, and if he is seen to be a drag on its fortunes can be removed when the party turns against him , as happened to Margaret Thatcher in 1990 and (in Canada) Jean Chrétien in 2003.[13] A prime minister who has adopted unpopular measures (e.g., the Iraq War in 2006, Obamacare in 2010) is more likely to reverse course than a president who is elected for a fixed term and who cannot run for a third term. As such, prime ministers internalize their party's interests, and the party internalizes the country's interests. One is thus more likely to find Olson's superencompassing majority in a parliamentary system than in the United States.[14]

C. Parliamentary Moments in Presidential Systems

The concern about separationism might nevertheless be thought to be overstated, given the way in which the shape of American politics might reduce the problem. While the separation of powers tends to produce gridlock, this does not happen when one party scores a hat trick and takes the presidency and both branches of Congress. This has happened more often than one might think (40 percent of the time since the Second World War), and this helps to explain how, for example, President Clinton passed his tax reform in 1993 with no Republican votes.

That's not to say that bipartisanship is unknown in Congress. American political parties are not cohesive, and the 1964 Civil Rights bill and the North American Free Trade Agreement in 1993 were passed with mainly Republican support. In the past, as many bills were passed in periods of divided government, as when one party controlled all three branches of government.[15] However, politics have recently become much more ideological. The smoke-filled backrooms of American politics are no more, their place taken by the energized grass-roots of democratized parties, and divided government is more likely to result in gridlock today.

This also understates the gridlock problem, in failing to account for the filibuster in the U.S. Senate, which since 1975 has permitted 41 senators to limit debate. Since 1979, no party has controlled all three branches and enjoyed a 60-person majority in the Senate, but for a nine-month period in 2009. Obviously, the filibuster is strongly anti-democratic. Sadly, it has been defended on the grounds that it enhances the doctrine of separation of powers at the core of the U.S. Constitution.[16]

D. Pre-enactment Screening versus Reversibility

There is a downside to the dominance of the prime minister's office in a parliamentary system. Since bills require the concurrence of different branches of government, they might be thought to be vetted more closely in a presidential system. If so, the greater degree of pre-enactment screening under the separation of powers would make it less likely that a truly horrible bill would be enacted. However, it's harder to repeal a bad law in a presidential system, which raises the question whether pre-enactment screening is more desirable than reversibility.

Which is preferable is an empirical or historical question. If the separation of powers really served the purpose of filtering out bad laws and bad ideas, then America should have fewer of them than parliamentary systems. Yet if one compares American policies with those of the parliamentary system it most closely resembles, what stands out are strong similarities, not differences: a broad franchise, federal incursion into provincial responsibilities via the spending power, social security, Medicare, and so on. Where there are differences, some relate to particular cross-country differences (e.g., bilingualism in Canada, affirmative action in the U.S.). And other differences (the litigation regimes of the two countries, for example) are ones where, this book has argued, the Canadian system seems preferable. If America had been helped by separation of powers, one might have expected that it would score higher than parliamentary systems on measures of freedom—in which case the Heritage rankings discussed in Part 2 might seem an embarrassment.

The question whether reversibility matters more than pre-enactment screening will always give rise to partisan feelings. In the past, conservatives thought that ex ante screening was more important.[17] Progressives, in contrast, lamented the brake that the separation of powers placed on new legislation. They looked back fondly to the first 100 days of the Roosevelt administration in 1933, when the executive drafted bills that Congress rubber-stamped without debate. That was the closest that America ever came to a parliamentary system, and Progressives thought that that was how government should work.[18] However, in 2011, when much of their agenda has been adopted, it is the Progressives who might prefer separationism and conservatives who will see a value in parliamentary government. The federal government is maxed out on its credit card, and we're not likely to see many costly new initiatives from Washington.

There are nevertheless four reasons, generally free from the partisanship of the moment, why reversibility trumps pre-enactment screening. First, and most obviously, the bad laws passed without separationist screening can more easily be reversed in a parliamentary system. Easier passed, easier mended.

Second, it is easier to identify bad laws with the benefit of hindsight. Bad laws, based on bad ideas, with what are conceded to have bad consequences, are enacted everywhere. In dictatorships, bad laws are often bad from the start. In democratic regimes, bad ideas are typically recognized only after the fact. When one parliament reverses a prior parliament, it does so with more information than the prior enacting parliament. It will know better what works and what doesn't. In America, by contrast, the benefit of hindsight is greatly diminished. To take but one example, no one seemed to expect how the 1965 immigration act would work out. Ted Kennedy clearly did not anticipate that he would have to sponsor an immigration lottery to bring Irish immigrants to Boston.[19] But that is the law we are stuck with. What separationism has given us is a one-way ratchet in which bad ideas are adopted and then turned into the laws of the Medes and the Persians.[20]

Third, such pre-enactment screening as might occur does not seem greater in the U.S. than in parliamentary systems. Major amendments are quietly inserted at the last moment, escaping the scrutiny of regulators charged with overseeing the bill.[21] Bills passed in the U.S. are significantly longer than their counterparts in a parliamentary system. At the extreme, a statute might be so lengthy as to greatly reduce any possibility of meaningful pre-enactment screening. One might have expected the chair of the House Judiciary Committee to have had something to say about Obamacare, whose constitutionality raised vexed questions. John Conyers' difficulty was that it's a little hard to have an opinion about a bill one has not read. One can't be unsympathetic, however. "What good is reading the bill if it's a thousand pages," said Conyers, "and you don't have two days and two lawyers to find out what it means after you've read the bill?"[22]

Finally, reversibility matters more than pre-enactment screening in the current economic crisis. Had one to choose between a presidential and a parliamentary system without knowing what year or country one was in, the choice might be not be so easy. For example, there is empirical evidence that, between 1960 and 1998, presidential systems with their separation of powers were associated with smaller governments and smaller deficits.[23] That period, however, was the high tide of Keynesianism, an illness to which parliamentary systems succumbed more quickly than presidential ones. Prior to that point, there wasn't much difference between the two systems, as may be seen in Table 2.5. In recent years, the United States has caught the same disease, and parliamentary systems are in recovery. The question today, then, is whether things can be turned around.

In sum, the greatest challenge for Western countries is to step back from economically harmful redistributionist policies adopted in happier financial times, and this will prove harder to do in America than in countries with a parliamentary system of government. At the moment, American decline is masked by a free-falling Eurozone. It remains to be seen whether it and other countries will pull out before the U.S.

The Courts

While the differences between parliamentary and presidential systems are significant, one must be careful not to exaggerate them. Democratic countries, peopled by voters with similar values, tend to end up, if not in a similar place, at least not too far apart. In particular, the Supreme Court has in recent years moved to reduce the burden of excessive litigation. As Kip Viscusi notes, the Court's *State Farm* decision has been taken to place an upward bound on punitive damages of no more than 10 times the amount of compensatory damages,[24] and a subsequent maritime law decision suggested the Court might be even more comfortable with a 1:1 ratio.[25] The Court has also toughened the standards for what counts as expert evidence[26] and limited standing to sue where the plaintiff does not suffer a direct harm.[27] In June 2011, the Court tightened the rules for class action certification in a sex discrimination suit where the plaintiffs were unable to show that the claims of all the members of the class rested on a common contention.[28] In another June 2011 case discussed by Viscusi, the Court rejected an action brought by several states and private groups to enforce Environmental Protection Agency regulations.

In both presidential or parliamentary systems, federalism provides an important safety value. As O'Connor and Ribstein explain, states that ship business to other states because of inefficient laws have an incentive to cure them, and most states have in fact enacted some kind of tort reform legislation. That explains why interest groups prefer to promote legislation at the national level, since one cannot exit a national law by moving to another state. Even then, not all federal legislation is plaintiff-friendly, and several recent federal statutes have sought to address the problem of excessive litigation, notably the Class Action Fairness Act of 2005, which expanded federal jurisdiction over class actions to reduce forum-shopping for favorable state courts.[29]

The opposite mistake is to assume that first-world legal systems do converge. As the essays by Jutras, Trebilcock, and Bridge have shown, the differences between the private law rules of the U.S. and those of similar countries are substantial. While foreign countries have adopted American-style procedural and substantive rules, they have done so in the context of a very different legal culture, and the gap between America and the rest of the world never seems to narrow. Moreover, while tort reform statutes have been passed by most states, these have often been struck down by state supreme courts, as Michael Trebilcock notes.

A. Are State Courts the Problem?

If a legal rule should be reversed, one might not think to look to state courts for help. The difficulties described in this book are, in many cases, judge-made in state courts, and even if a rule is recognized as inefficient the doctrine of stare decisis restrains a court that seeks to depart from established precedent. In addition, state courts may lack an incentive to adopt the benign rules proposed in this book. State judges, particularly ones who are elected by the voters, might be expected to favor local plaintiffs as against out-of-state defendants, as this amounts to a wealth transfer from outside the state to their home state. Got to keep the base happy.

All state officials have an incentive to effect wealth transfers of this kind.[30] Left unchecked, such policies may result in the wasteful beggar-thy-neighbor competition decried by Hamilton in *Federalist* 22. For this reason, the Constitution's dormant Commerce Clause, discussed by O'Connor and Ribstein, prohibits states from erecting trade barriers against out-of-state firms. Similarly, federal environmental protection legislation prevents an in-state firm from polluting a neighboring state. The same kind of interstate exploitation might arise through an abuse of the litigation system. Where a state court imposes massive punitive damages on an out-of-state firm, as described by Trebilcock and Viscusi (on product liability), what it does is the economic equivalent of dumping pollution onto another state.

Ten years ago, I might have concluded that interstate exploitation by state courts is endemic in the United States. Now I am less than sure, for the departures from the rule of law discussed in this book are increasingly addressed by many of the same state courts that were the source of the problem. The excessively plaintiff-friendly decisions of which George Priest complained came from judges who were elected by the voters rather than appointed by governors or legislatures. Within the past 10 years, however, these problems have increasingly been resolved by these same courts.

First a word about how states choose their judges. In 12 states (mostly in the east), judges are appointed by politicians. Another 12 states elect judges in partisan elections. The remaining states have modified electoral systems. In some of them, elections are non-partisan and judges run without a party label. In other states, judges are appointed by a "merit" panel and thereafter run for retention.

In the past, the role played by judicial elections in the shaping of private law rules did not attract much notice. Some scholars regretted that judges elected in partisan elections were tougher on criminal sentencing, but there was little discussion about their views on private law issues. Partisan elections were sleepy, low-key affairs, with judges nominated by trial lawyers, from among their members, who contributed most of the moneys it took to run a campaign. This blissful pre-lapsarian world came to an end over the past 20 years, especially after 2002 when the U.S. Chamber of Commerce began spending money—big time—on an election for a Mississippi Supreme Court judge.[31]

What preceded this was the great increase in tort liability described by George Priest, beginning in the 1960s, and the discovery by plaintiffs' lawyers of favorable jurisdictions that welcomed forum-shopping. The Chamber called these "judicial hellholes," and one of them was Mississippi, a state with an anti-business judiciary that favored trial lawyers. "Hellhole" has a pejorative ring to it. As Ramseyer and Rasmusen note, Dickie Scruggs preferred to call Mississippi a "magic jurisdiction." It was one of those states where, according to Scruggs, it was almost impossible for defendants to get a fair trial. In particular, Jefferson County, Mississippi, pop. 7,726, one of the poorest counties in the nation, was especially welcoming for plaintiffs. Indeed, there were almost as many plaintiffs as there were residents in the county.[32] But all that is gone with the wind. In the past 10 years Mississippi has enacted tort reform legislation and (after the Chamber stepped in) the voters turfed out a former president of the Mississippi Trial Lawyers Association from the state supreme court.

Since then the costs of judicial campaigns have greatly increased. Both sides have campaigned furiously, with all of the vulgarities of modern electioneering. If anything, it's worse in judicial elections. A friend of mine, a law-and-economics academic at the University of Alabama, ran for his state's supreme court and was opposed by trial lawyers. Their television ads told viewers, in a shocked tone, "Did you know that Harold See never even passed the state bar!" Actually, Harold didn't have to write the state bar exams; as a law professor in the state, he was waived in. Harold won, as it turned out, but not before learning that the trial lawyers' ad had backfired on one voter. An old farmer told him, "I want you to know that I'm going to vote for you because I hate lawyers."

B. Are Judicial Elections the Problem?

In recent years, business groups have outspent the competition, and judicial elections, which formerly favored trial lawyers, now give conservatives the advantage. This trend received an assist from the Supreme Court, which in 2002 held that judicial candidates could not be barred from discussing issues that might come before them if elected.[33] Unsurprisingly, the change is unpopular with judges, who now must spend more time campaigning and raising money. The change has also upset the legal ethics community (which had not been conspicuous in objecting to the *ancien régime*).

Various reform measures have been passed to remove the taint of money and politics from judicial elections. In North Carolina, for example, elections are non-partisan, and judicial candidates are not identified by party.[34] The result is that voters go to the polls with essentially no information about who the candidates are or what they believe. Party-line voting for judges might seem a little déclassé, but party membership does tell voters something about judicial candidates. Brand-name advertising offers the same kinds of informational benefits in judicial elections as it does in consumer markets. As Joshua Wright and Eric Helland note, consumer advertisers have an incentive to acquire a reputation that buyers trust, and the same is true of political parties in partisan judicial elections. A party will screen candidates and select those who can competently contribute to its reputation and its views on civil justice. Voters will know better for whom they are voting, and the judges they elect will better reflect their views. Such a system would seem considerably more faithful to the constitutional value of free speech than one that banned party affiliations. As Chief Justice Roberts has noted, "In a democracy, campaigning for office is not a game. It is a critically important form of speech."[35]

Of course, the disfavored brand would like nothing better than to ban brand advertising. For Number 2, it beats trying harder.

The most widely copied model for election reform is the "Missouri Plan," in which judges are first appointed by a merit commission composed of lawyers, judges, and political nominees. After sitting for a year, the newly appointed judge must run in a retention election, in which voters can decide to either retain or dump him. Sometimes judges do get dumped, but the Missouri Plan does tend to promote stability and (its proponents argue) integrity and competence on the bench.

Three criticisms of the Missouri Plan and other efforts to weaken voter rights in judicial elections have nevertheless been made. First, it is said that such efforts are politically motivated, and that, as a matter of fact, lawyer-run merit commissions are biased in favor of liberal judges and the plaintiffs' bar.[36] Missouri itself provided an instructive example of this in 2004, when Republican Governor Matt Blunt tried to appoint a conservative to the state supreme court. Blunt had run on a pledge to rein in a liberal bench, but the merit commission presented him with a stacked choice: two qualified liberals and one less than qualified conservative. If Blunt had rejected all three, the choice would have been left to the commission.[37] For conservatives, games of this sort breed cynicism about merit commissions and the ethical watchdogs who complain about judicial elections. Things were fine when the plaintiff's lawyers dominated the process, but it's a scandal when the Chamber takes a round or two. At times one is reminded of Citizen Kane. When it becomes clear that Kane will lose an election, editors at his newspaper sadly abandon the "Kane Elected" headline for "Fraud at Polls!"

Second, judges elected in partisan elections do not appear to be of inferior quality. As a proxy for intellectual ability, scholars today look to cite counts, which for judges would be the number of times their opinions are cited by other judges. Individual opinions by appointed judges are cited more frequently than those for elected judges. Nevertheless, elected judges are cited more frequently in total, since they write more opinions, and judges elected in partisan elections are cited most of all.

Another measure of the quality of a judge is his independence. We would want our judges to be free of political bias and to judge each case on its merits. Once again, however, there is not much difference between the two kinds of judges on measures of independence, such as the willingness to write opinions in which one disagrees with ostensible political allies.[38]

An elected judge's independence might be in question if he or she is seen to favor contributors to his or her campaign. In exceptional cases, this might indeed be a problem. In Caperton v. Massey, for example, the Supreme Court held that a judge's failure to recuse himself violated the plaintiff's right to a fair trial, when the defendant's CEO had spent over $3 million in support of the judge in the previous election.[39] One must nevertheless distinguish between such cases and that of the judge who, elected with corporate support, is subsequently found to adopt pro-business views in his decisions. That is not enough to impeach a judge's independence. Absent the special facts of a case such as *Caperton,* one should assume that judges act in good faith and that they receive donor support because of their prior beliefs, and not that they have tailored their beliefs to their donors' wishes.

Corporations, trial lawyers, and individuals support candidates with whom they agree (and water flows downhill). We would therefore expect judges elected with corporate support to be less plaintiff-friendly than merit-appointed judges.[40] However, that's not evidence of improper bias unless one assumes that merit-appointed judges are free from bias, and that's just what conservatives deny, since they assert that merit-appointed judges elected by lawyers are excessively plaintiff-friendly.

Third, partisan elections for judges will appeal to those who see the law as political in nature. For Formalists such as Williston, law was a separate discipline, with its own integrity, and clearly distinguishable from the practice of politics. With the decline of Formalist conceptions of the law, and the expansion of the role of courts into matters once thought political, the distinction between law and politics is harder to make. Today, judges manage school boards and prisons; they enforce broad social policies about race and gender; they decide who wins a close election. If these aren't political decisions, then what is? Formerly this was a point made by Critical Legal Scholars on the left, but now some conservatives say much the same thing. If the bench has become politicized, then why not elect judges directly and cut out the middleman?

C. Judicial Elections and the Rule of Law

We end, therefore, where we began, in search of a definition of the rule of law. I have argued that the rule of law must have a substantive component, that it must embrace private law rules that promote the security of property and of contract rights, that what Ramseyer and Rasmusen call "judicially sanctioned theft" is inconsistent with the rule of law. But I have also suggested that judicial elections might usefully promote the rule of law, so understood.

Have I been inconsistent? One thing that the rule of law requires is a border between law and politics. Does that mean that Mississippi, where judicial candidates are identified by party label, has a rule of law problem and that North Carolina does not? This sort of reasoning is apt to be thought persuasive by one who thinks that federal judges, appointed by the president with the advice and consent of the senate, are sterilized from politics because they are not elected. If it's voting that politicizes an office, then what must one say of the voters who compose the Senate Judiciary Committee? They are, if anything, more politicized and more ideological than most voters, and yet, if anyone upholds the rule of law, it is federal judges. Political inputs don't necessarily mean politicized outputs.

When given the kind of informed choice that only campaign spending provides, voters tend to elect judges who favor the more conservative civil justice principles of Britain and Canada, as seen in the essays of Michael Bridge and Michael Trebilcock. Members of the judicial ethics establishment who object to this must be thought to regard Anglo-Canadian law as retrograde. They defend a kind of American Exceptionalism that plausibly weakens the substantive rule of law and contributes to American decline.

In sum, I have argued that America's retreat from the rule of law contributes to its decline. What I have not done is examine the weaknesses of other countries. As I write this, there is increasing unrest in China and a fiscal crisis in southern Europe that threatens European economic integration. America and its competitors all have their own infirmities. As these become apparent, what matters is reversibility, through the courts, through the legislature.

Notes

1. This was a free trade era, when the burdens of colonial possessions were thought to exceed any benefits Britain might derive from them. The idea of imperialism, which we associate with preferential tariffs and Joseph Chamberlain, with the white man's burden and Kipling, was a subsequent British invention.

2. Tom Campbell, Separation of Powers in Practice 1 (2004).

3. The evidence is reviewed in Pippa Norris, Driving Democracy: Do Power-Sharing Institutions Work? ch. 6 (2008). See also Adam Przeworski et al., Democracy and Development: Political Institutions and Well-being in the World, 1950–1990 128–36 (2000). For evidence that presidential regimes are associated with higher levels of political corruption, see Jana Kunicova and Susan Rose-Ackerman, Electoral Rules and Constitutional Structures as Constraints on Corruption, 35 British J. Political Science 573 (2005).

4. See Bruce Ackerman, The New Separation of Powers, 113 Harv. L. Rev. 633 (2000).

5. See Terry M. Moe, "The Politics of Structural Choice: Toward a Theory of Public Bureaucracy," in Organization Theory 116, 136 (Oliver Williamson, ed., 1990).

6. For a popular account of America's failure to fix its runaway budgetary problems, see Jonathan Rauch, Government's End: Why Washington Stopped Working (1999).

7. David R. Henderson, Canada's Budget Triumph, Mercatus Working Paper 10-52 (2010).

8. For a simple model explaining why it is harder to enact legislation in a separation of powers presidential system than in a parliamentary system, see Robert D. Cooter, The Strategic Constitution 213–15 (2000). For a more elaborate model, see George Tsebelis, Veto Players: How Political Institutions Work ch. 1 (2002).

9. "There is a sixth doctrine, plainly and directly against the essence of a Commonwealth, and it is this: that the sovereign power may be divided. For what is it to divide the power of a Commonwealth, but to dissolve it; for powers divided mutually destroy each other." Leviathan, ch. 29 (1660).

10. Paul Martin, Hell or High Water: My Life in and out of Politics 244–45 (2008).

11. Mancur Olson, Power and Prosperity: Outgrowing Communist and Capitalist Dictatorships 19–23 (2000).

12. Bolingbroke Political Writings 257–58 (David Armitage ed., 1997).

13. Which happens more frequently than one might think. David J. Samuels and Matthew S. Shugart, Presidents, Parties, and Prime Ministers: How the Separation of Powers Affects Party Organization and Behavior 96–97 (2010), reports that, of the 374 changes of prime ministers in parliamentary systems, 13 percent resulted from intraparty pressure.

14. See Gary W. Cox and Mathew D. McCubbins, Legislative Leviathan: Party Government in the House 121–22 (2d ed., 20007). The distinction between presidential and parliamentary systems is sharpest when the latter is effectively unicameral (Britain and Canada) and the upper house cannot veto a bill. There are intermediate systems: a bicameral parliamentary system (Australia) or a multiparty parliamentary system, either with proportionate representation (New Zealand) or without (Canada, at times). See George Tsebelis, Veto Players: How Political Institutions Work (2002).

15. See David R. Mayhew, Divided We Govern: Party Control, Lawmaking, and Investigations, 1946–2002 (2005).

16. Bruce Ackerman, The Good Filibuster, Balkinization, Jan. 4, 2011, at http://balkin.blogspot.com/2011/01/good-filibuster.html; John O. McGinnis and Michael B. Rappaport, In Praise of Supreme Court Filibusters, 33 Harv. J. Law & Pub. Policy 39 (2010) (defending filibusters of judicial nominees); George F. Will, Why Filibusters Should Be Allowed, Wash. Post, March 20, 2005.

17. See, e.g., James Q. Wilson, Does the Separation of Powers Still Work?, 86 The Public Interest 49 (1987).

18. See E. E. Schattschneider, Party Government (1942); James MacGregor Burns, Deadlock of Democracy (1963). An earlier progressive, Woodrow Wilson, had argued for the superiority of parliamentary systems in Congressional Government (1889). See generally James L. Sundquist, Constitutional Reform and Effective Government ch. 1 (1992).

19. See Anna Law, The Diversity Visa Lottery—A Cycle of Unintended Consequences in United States Immigration Policy, 21 J. Am. Ethnic Hist. 3 (2002).

20. Reversibility might introduce a credible commitment problem. To attract investment, whether from natives or foreigners, a state must make an implicit promise not to change the rules of the game. Douglass C. North and Barry R. Weingast, Constitutions and Commitment: The Evolution of Institutional Governing Public Choice in Seventeenth-Century England, 49 J. Econ. Hist. 803 (1989). By making it difficult to amend laws, then, the separation of powers might be thought to solve the credible commitment problem and attract investment. However, the sharp decline in America's share of global foreign direct investment, seen in Part 2, suggests that investors do not see the U.S. as uniquely able to offer credible commitments. A parliamentary system in countries with a long tradition of political and economic liberty where economic stakeholders are well represented in parliament and where a government is more readily held responsible for economic decline, and with, moreover, a federal system of government, a strong auditor-general, an independent judiciary, and central bank independence, might seem as easily able to bond itself to protect the expectations of investors. For an empirical study of credible commitments and economic growth rates, see Irfan Nooruddin, Coalition Politics and Economic Development: Credibility and the Strength of Weak Governments (2011).

21. For example, the cost that the housing crash imposed on the federal government was greatly increased by an obscure amendment inserted by Senator Dodd (D. Ct.) that made FDIC emergency financing available to insurance companies, most of whom were located in the senator's state. Gretchen Morgenson and Joshua Rosner, Reckles$ Endangerment: How Outsized Ambition, Greed, and Corruption Led to Economic Armageddon 40–41 (2011).

22. Abby Schachter, Quick Fix for Congress: Speak English, N.Y. Post, Dec. 15, 2010.

23. Torsten Persson and Guido Tabellini, The Economic Effects of Constitutions 107 (2005).

24. State Farm Mutual Automobile Insurance Co. v. Campbell, 538 U.S. 408 (2003).

25. Exxon Shipping Co. et al. v. Baker, 554 U.S. 471 (2008).

26. Daubert v. Merrell Dow Pharmaceuticals, 509 U.S. 579 (1993); Kumho Tire Co. v. Carmichael, 526 U.S. 137 (1999).

27. Lujan v. Defenders of Wildlife, 504 U.S. 555 (1992).

28. Wal-Mart Stores, Inc. v. Dukes, 564 U.S. ___ (2011).

29. Pub. L. No. 109-2, 119 Stat. 4, 28 U.S.C. §§ 1332(d), 1453, and 1711–1715. Just how much the statute cures the forum-shopping problem remains controversial.

See Cato Handbook for Policymakers (7th ed.), at http://www.cato.org/pubs/hand book/hb111/hb111–11.pdf.

30. Saul Levmore, Interstate Exploitation and Judicial Intervention, 69 Va. L. Rev. 563 (1983).

31. Prior to then, judicial elections appeared to favor the plaintiffs' bar. See Alexander Tabarrok and Eric Helland, Court Politics: The Political Economy of Tort Awards, 42 J. Law & Econ. 157 (1999).

32. See Robert Pear, Mississippi Gaining as Lawsuit Mecca, N.Y. Times, Aug. 20, 2001, at A1; Betty Liu, The Poor Southern County That's Big on Lawsuits, Fin. Times, Aug. 20, 2001, at 5.

33. Republican Party of Minnesota v. White, 536 U.S. 765 (2002).

34. North Carolina's election law, which permitted publicly financed candidates to receive matching public funds if they were outspent by a privately financed opponent, must now be thought unconstitutional. McComish v. Bennett, 546 U.S. ___ (2011).

35. Id.

36. See Brian T. Fitzpatrick, The Fallacies and Fixables of Merit Selection and the Constituencies That Support Missouri Plan Reform: The Politics of Merit Selection, 74 Mo. L. Rev. 675 (2009).

37. Editorial, Without Judicial Merit, Wall Street Journal, Aug. 23, 2008; Matthew Schneider, Why Merit Selection of State Court Judges Lacks Merit, 56 Wayne L. Rev. 649–50 (2010).

38. Steven J. Choi, Mitu G. Gulati, and Eric A. Posner, Professionals or Politicians: The Uncertain Empirical Case for an Elected Rather than an Appointed Judiciary, 26 J. Law, Econ. & Org. 290 (2010). See also Chris W. Bonneau and Melinda Gann Hall, In Defense of Judicial Elections (2009).

39. Caperton v. A. T. Massey Coal Co., 556 U.S. ___ , 129 S. Ct. 2252 (2009).

40. Michael S. Kang and Joanna M. Shepherd, The Partisan Price of Justice: An Empirical Analysis of Campaign Contributions and Judicial Decisions, 86 N.Y.U.L. Rev. 69 (2011).

CONTRIBUTORS

STEPHEN M. BAINBRIDGE is the William D. Warren Distinguished Professor of Law, UCLA School of Law.

MICHAEL BRIDGE is the Cassel Professor of Commercial Law, London School of Economics.

F.H. BUCKLEY is a Foundation Professor, George Mason University School of Law.

ROBERT COOTER is the Hernam F. Selvin Professor of Law, University of California, Berkeley, and Co-Director of the Berkeley Program in Law and Economics.

AARON EDLIN is the Richard Jennings Professor of Economics and a Professor of Law at the University of California, Berkeley.

RICHARD A. EPSTEIN is the Laurence A. Tisch Professor of Law, New York University School of Law; the Peter and Bedford Senior Fellow, The Hoover Institution; and the James Parker Hall Distinguished Service Professor of Law, The University of Chicago.

FRANCIS FUKUYAMA is the Olivier Nomellini Senior Fellow at Stanford University's Freeman Spogli Institute for International Studies.

ERIC HELLAND is a Professor of Economics, Claremont-McKenna College, and a senior economist at RAND.

DANIEL JUTRAS is the Wainwright Professor of Civil Law and Dean of the Faculty of Law, McGill University.

JEREMY KIDD is an assistant professor at Walter F. George School of Law, Mercer University.

JONATHAN KLICK is a professor at the University of Pennsylvania Law School and holds the Erasmus Chair of Empirical Legal Studies at Erasmus University, Rotterdam.

STEPHEN P. MAGEE holds the Bayless/Enstar Chair and is a professor of in the Department of Finance, Economics and Business at the University of Texas, Austin.

ERIN O'HARA O'CONNOR is the FedEx Professor of Law at Vanderbilt Law School.

JEFFREY S. PARKER is a professor at George Mason University School of Law.

GEORGE L. PRIEST is the Edward J. Phelps Professor of Law and Economics and Kauffman Distinguished Research Scholar in Law, Economics, and Entrepreneurship, Yale Law School.

J. MARK RAMSEYER is the Mitsubishi Professor of Japanese Legal Studies, Harvard Law School.

ERIC B. RASMUSEN is the Dan R. and Catherine M. Dalton Professor, Kelley School of Business, Indiana University.

MARTIN H. REDISH is the Louis and Harriet Ancel Professor of Law and Public Policy, Northwestern University School of Law.

LARRY E. RIBSTEIN held the Mildred Van Voorhis Jones Chair, University of Illinois College of Law.

PETER B. RUTLEDGE is a Professor of Law, University of Georgia School of Law. He wrote his chapter while a Fulbright Visiting Professor of Law, Universitaet Wien, Institut fuer Zivilverfahrensrecht.

ROBERT E. SCOTT is the Alfred McCormack Professor of Law and Director, Center for Contract and Economic Organization, Columbia University.

MICHAEL TREBILCOCK is a Professor of Law and Economics, University of Toronto Faculty of Law.

PAUL-ERIK VEEL is an adjunct professor at the University of Toronto and an associate at Lenczner Slaght Royce Smith Griffin LLP, Toronto.

W. KIP VISCUSI is the University Distinguished Professor of Law, Economics, and Management, Vanderbilt University.

JOSHUA D. WRIGHT is an associate professor at George Mason University School of Law and Department of Economics.

TODD J. ZYWICKI is a Foundation Professor at George Mason University School of Law and a Senior Scholar, Mercatus Center.

INDEX

Allstate Ins. Co. v. Hague, 350–51
American Electric Power Co. v.
    Connecticut, 286
American Exceptionalism, 12–13,
    43–63, 102
American litigiousness, 69–95,
    100–115, 230–31
Arbitration, 354–55
Asbestos litigation, 89–93

Baird Textile v. Marks & Spencer,
    301–2
Bar-Gill, Oren, 362
Barro, Robert, 110
Bates v. State Bar, 218
Behavioral law-and-economics, 151, 153,
    362–64, 371–73
"Beijing Consensus," 33
BMW v. Gore, 147, 234
Bolingbroke, Lord, 510
Brown v. Meyer, 359–60
"Bubble" laws, 27, 396–98
Burke, Edmund, 3–4
Burton, Steven, 303

Campbell Soup Co. v. Wentz, 295
Caperton v. Massey, 520
Carnival Cruise Lines v. Shute, 352–53
Champerty, 216–17
China, 7–8, 11, 32–35, 61, 467,
    487–501
Choice-of-court clauses, 26, 351–54
Choice-of-law clauses, 26, 337–51
Civil juries, 236–37
Civil procedure: American, 19–21,
    175–94, 201–9; Canadian, 18, 159–71,
    185, 236–41
Class Action Fairness Act, 348–49
Class action litigation, 84–94, 128–31,
    168–71, 238–39, 259–62
Coase, Ronald, 22, 250, 253, 255–58
Comparative law, 11–12
Conflicts of law, 26, 336–56
Consumer Financial Protection Bureau,
    361–63, 366–67, 370–71
Consumer protection, 130, 132–34,
    361–74
Contract, interpretation of terms,
    312–30

Contract law: American, 24–25,
    291–307, 312–30; English, 24,
    291–307
"Contract with America," 107
Conyers, John, 514–15
Cooper, Edward, 185
Corbin, Arthur, 319
Corruption, 6–7
Costs, 237–38
Credible commitments, 488
Criminal law, 27–30, 407–24; entity
    criminal liability, 410–12; public
    welfare offences, 412; white collar
    crime, 410, 412–13
Currie, Brainerd, 343–45

Decline, absolute and relative, 47–48
Denning, Lord, 294, 296–97
Discovery, 162–63, 175–94, 201–9,
    239–40
Dodd-Frank Act, 361–63, 366–67,
    370–71
"Double-trust" problem, 475, 481–83

Economic mobility, 44–45
Eisenberg, Ted, 323–24
Endogenous legal rules, 20–21,
    213–15
Engle v. R. J. Reynolds, 147–48
Entrepreneurship, laws favoring, 31
Epstein, Richard, 259, 296
Escola v. Coca-Cola Bottling Co.,
    251–52
Exxon Shipping Co. v. Baker, 149, 234

Federalism, 350–51, 442–43, 516–17
Federalist, 22, 517
Feldstein, Martin, 54–55
Ford Pinto cases, 152
Free trade, 48–50, 451–53
Friedman, Milton, 4–5, 446
Fuller, Lon, 8–10, 177, 301
Future generations, 31, 473

Galanter, Marc, 167–68
Gilmore, Grant, 301
Good faith in contract law, 298–307
Greenman v. Yuba Power, 255

Hamilton, Alexander, 517
Higgs, Robert, 399
Hindsight bias, 151
Hirschman, A. O., 336
Human capital, 58–63

Immigration, 50–53
Inferior goods, 101
Innovation: laws disfavoring, 144–53,
    262–63; laws favoring, 31, 474–81
Intellectual property law, 477–81
Interest groups, 113–14

Judges, appointment and election of,
    25–26, 241, 515–22

Katrina litigation, 93–94
Kauffman, Daniel, 5
Kennedy, Robert, 114–15
KPMG case, 416–17

Labor markets, 460–65
Langbein, John, 160, 162, 175–76
Lawyer advertising, 217–22
Lawyers, number of, cross-country,
    80–82, 100–115
Lawyers and economic growth,
    107–13
Lawyers in congress, 102–13
Legislative Reform, 505–15
Leval, Pierre, 299–300
Litigation crisis, 13–17, 100–15, 143–44,
    166–67, 181–82, 265–66
Litigation rates, cross-country, 73–79,
    161–62, 164, 166–67
Llewellyn, Karl, 293–94, 319,
    321
Lloyds Bank v. Bundy, 296–97

Macneil, Ian, 301

Madison, James, 100, 114

Maine, Henry, 21

Master Settlement Agreement, 276–87

Miller, Geoffrey, 323–24

M/S Bremen v. Zapata Off-shore Co.,
    352–53

New York Central v. U.S., 411

Nicastro v. McIntyre Machinery,
    359–60

Normal goods, 101

Notice pleading, 162–63, 178–79,
    239–40

"Obamacare," 449, 456–60, 514–15

Olson, Mancur, 495, 510, 512

Olson, Walter, 107

Overcriminalization, 417–19

Permanent income hypothesis, 446

"Permititis," 453–56

Posner, Richard, 22–23, 256–58,
    304–5

Pound, Roscoe, 179

Pre-enactment screening of legislation,
    513

Private Securities Litigation Reform
    Act, 87, 182, 386

Product liability law, 137–54, 231–33,
    466

Progressivism, 30–31, 435–68; and
    regulation, 442–45

Property rights, 443, 488

Prosecutorial misbehavior, 415–17,
    420–24

Public debt, 56–58, 508–9

Public investment, 481–83

Punitive damages, 146–50, 154,
    233–37

Regulation, 442–50, 456–59; and
    capture by industry, 120–21; and

litigation, 17, 118–34, 270–87, 271;
    and tort law, 23–24

Regulatory compliance defense,
    273–87

Religion and the rule of law, 489–93

Rent-seeking and size of law schools,
    81

Reversibility, 509–15

Romano, Roberta, 387, 397, 398–99

Rule of law, 3–35, 489–93, 521–22; in
    China, 493–501

Sarbanes-Oxley Act, 26–27, 382,
    390–99

Sayre, Francis, 412

Scruggs, Richard F., 89–94, 518

Second-best, Theory of, 20–21,
    211–22

Securities litigation, 86–89, 120,
    384–88

Securities Litigation Uniform Stan-
    dards Act, 386

Sentencing Commission, 414

Sentencing Reform Act, 414

Separation of Powers, 507–15

Shavell, Steve, 122–23

State Farm v. Campbell, 149, 515

State Subsidies, 446, 481–84

State tobacco litigation, 275–87

Steward Org. v. Ricoh Corp., 353

Steyn, Lord, 291–92

Stigler, George, 120

Stoneridge Investment v. Scientific-
    Atlanta, 384

Strict liability in tort, 141–42, 255

Summers, Robert, 303

Sunstein, Cass, 149

Tax policies, 53–56, 445–50

Third-party financing of litigation,
    216–17

"Thompson Memorandum,"
    415–16

TIAA v. Tribune, 299–300
Time-consistency, 32
Traynor, Roger, 251–52, 264–65
Tort law: American, 21–24, 249–66,
    465–66; Canadian, 21, 229–42
Towers-Perrin-Tillinghast Study,
    83

Uncertainty in the law, 150–51, 153–54
Unconscionability, 294–98

Usury legislation, 371–72
U.S. v. Balint, 412

Wade, John, 254–55
Wallford v. Miles, 300
Warren, Elizabeth, 362
Washington Consensus, 5
Williston, Samuel, 24, 318–20

Y2K Act, 182